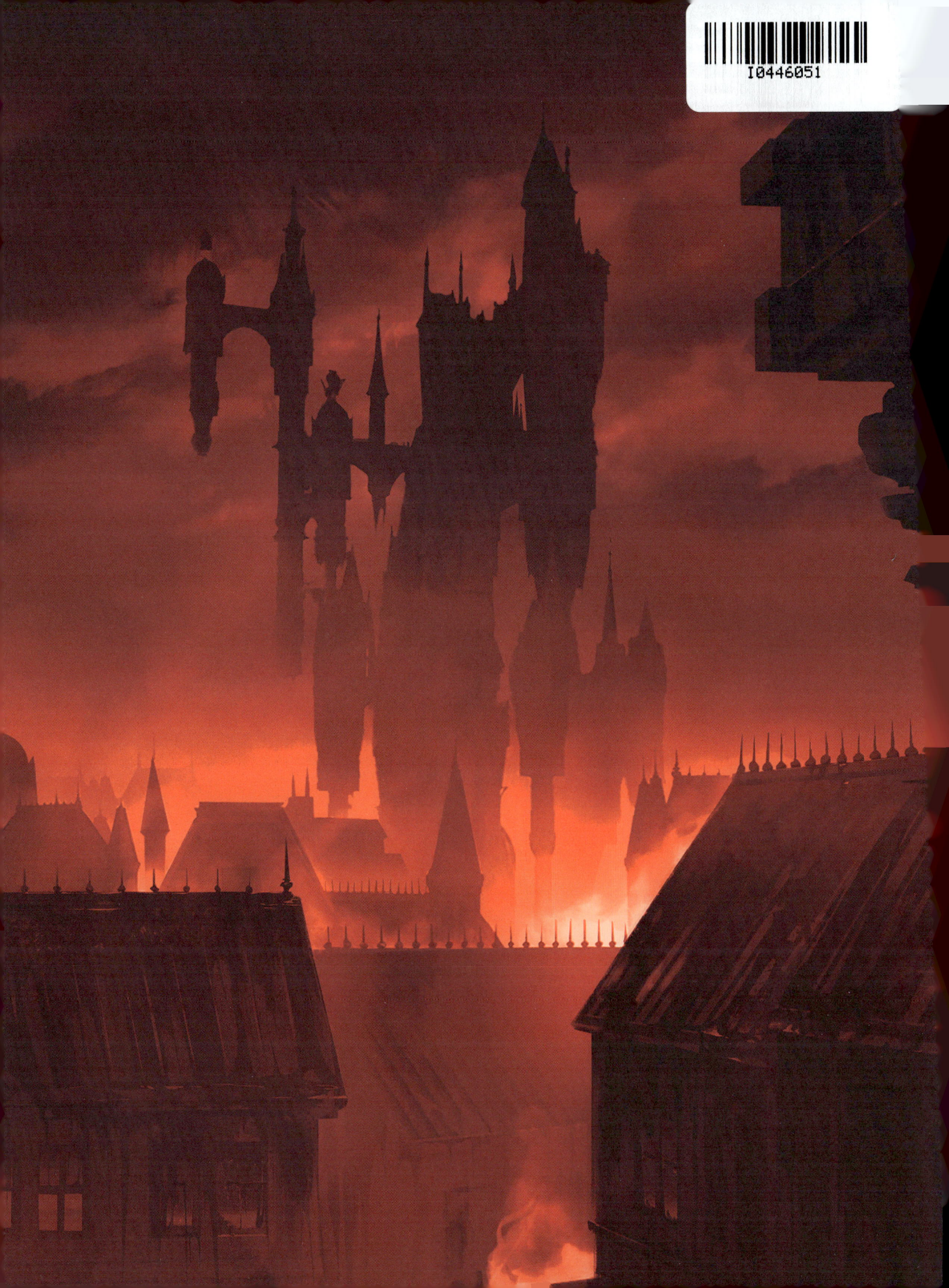

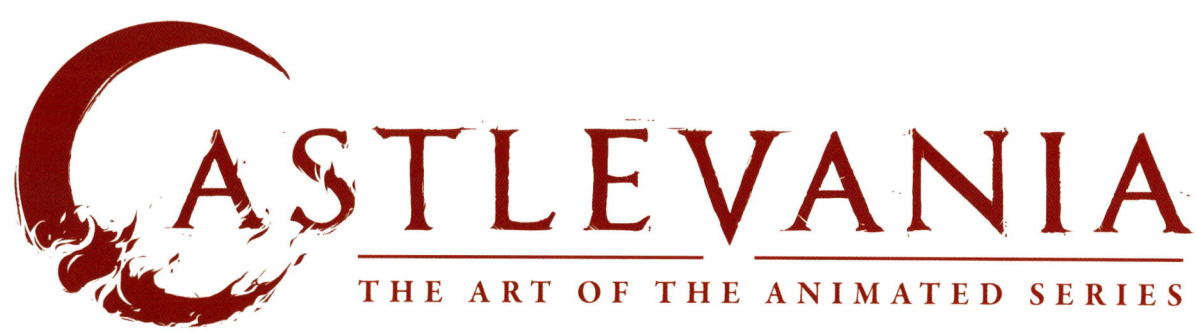

CASTLEVANIA

THE ART OF THE ANIMATED SERIES

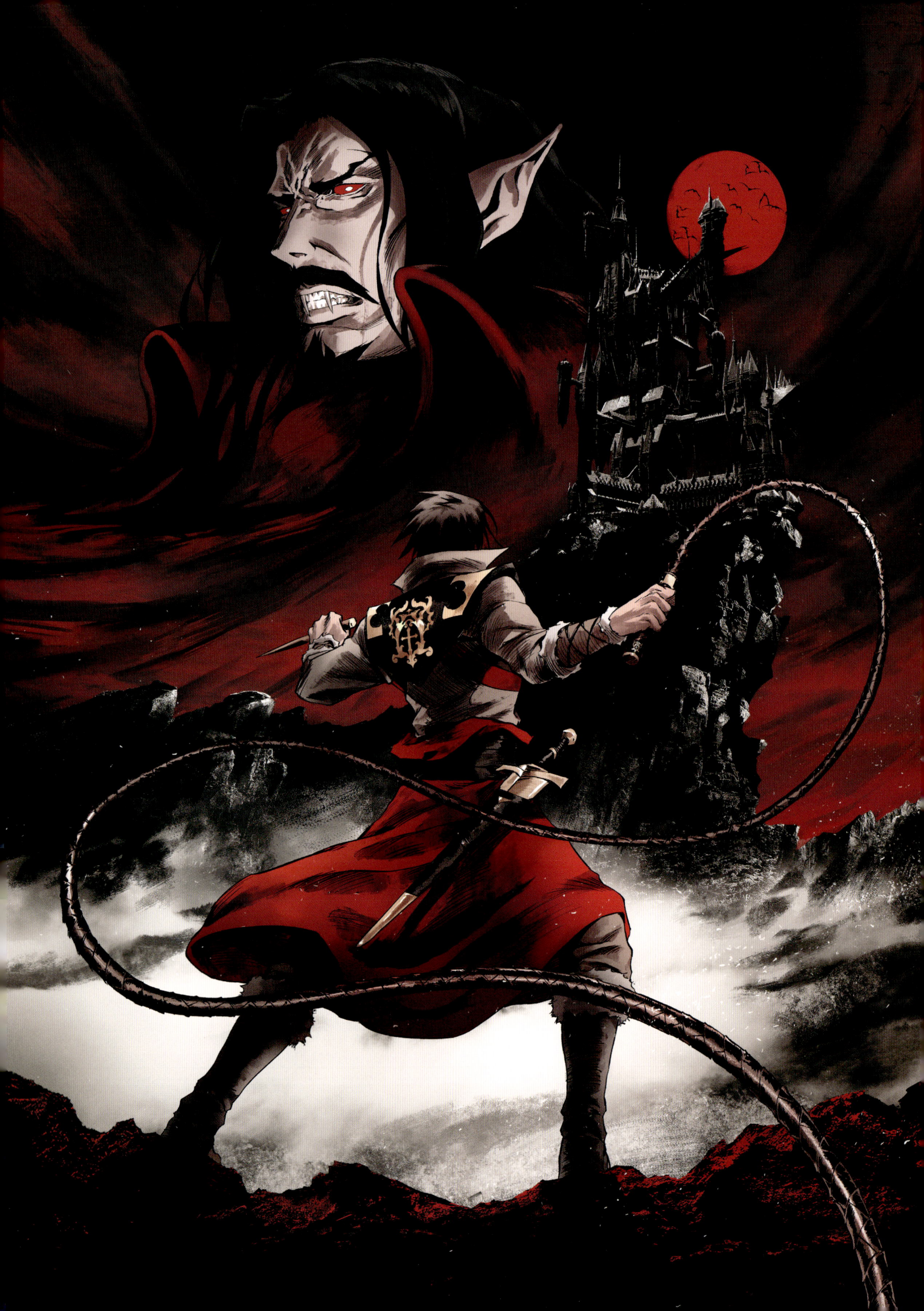

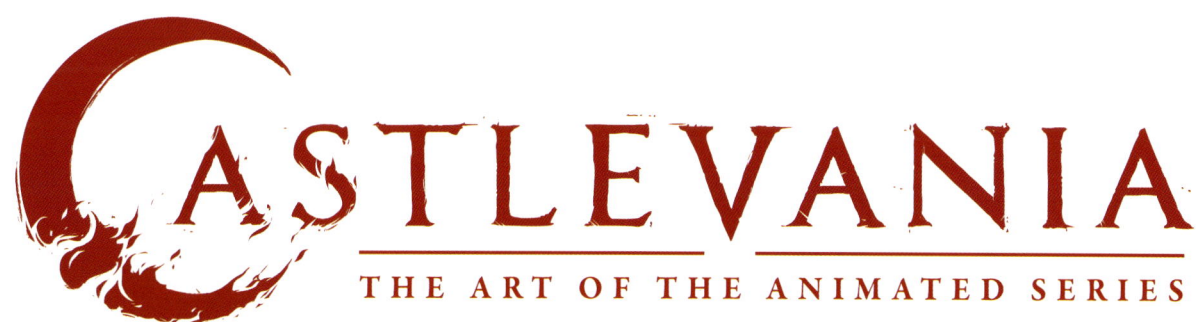

CASTLEVANIA

THE ART OF THE ANIMATED SERIES

DARK HORSE BOOKS

President and Publisher
Mike Richardson

Editor
Ian Tucker

Designers
Stephen Reichert and **Keith Wood**

Digital Art Technician
Allyson Haller

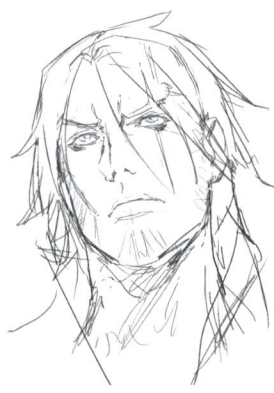

Page 2 artwork by Sam Deats. Page 5 artwork by Katie Silva.

CASTLEVANIA: THE ART OF THE ANIMATED SERIES

Published by Dark Horse Books
A division of Dark Horse Comics LLC
10956 SE Main Street, Milwaukie, OR 97222

DarkHorse.com

Represented in the EU by Authorised Rep Compliance Ltd.
Ground Floor, 71 Lower Baggot Street
Dublin, D02 P593, Ireland
ARCCompliance.com

First edition: August 2021
Ebook ISBN 978-1-50671-559-9 | Hardcover ISBN 978-1-50671-570-4

7 9 10 8 6
Printed in China

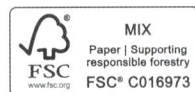

Library of Congress Cataloging-in-Publication Data

Names: Tucker, Ian (Editor), editor. | Frederator Studios.
Title: Castlevania : the art of the animated series / editor, Ian Tucker.
Other titles: Castlevania (Dark Horse Books)
Description: Milwaukie, OR : Dark Horse Books, [2021] | Summary: "Explore
  the artistry behind the gorgeous animated series, Castlevania! This art
  book contains stunning, never-before-seen concept art for the wildly
  popular series. Fans will covet this opportunity to learn all there is
  to know about the development of the show with this beautiful hardcover
  tome!"-- Provided by publisher.
Identifiers: LCCN 2020039000 | ISBN 9781506715704 (hardcover) | ISBN
  9781506715599 (epub)
Subjects: LCSH: Castlevania (Television program)
Classification: LCC NC1766.U53 C393 2021 | DDC 741.5/8--dc23
LC record available at https://lccn.loc.gov/2020039000

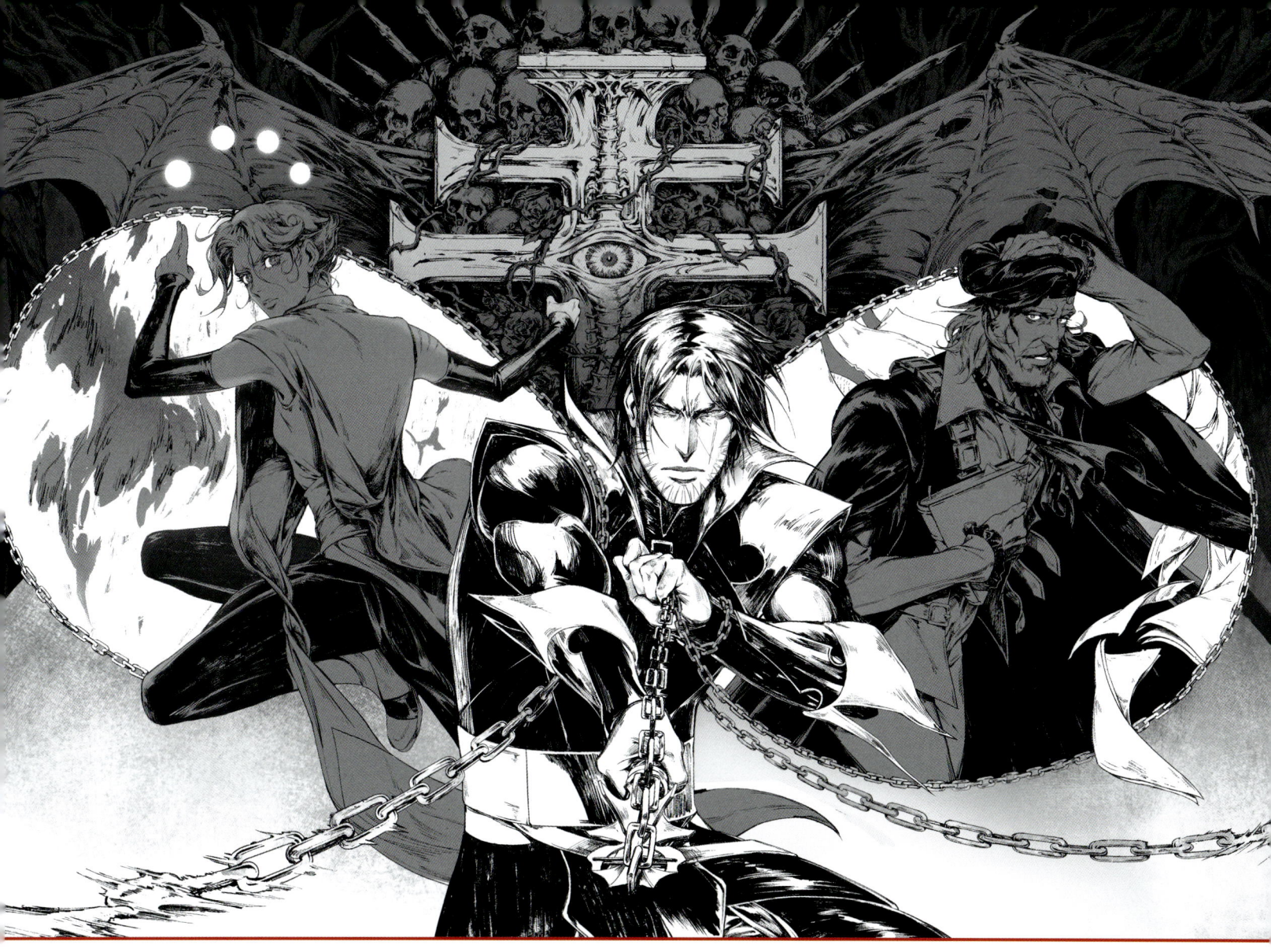

Table of Contents

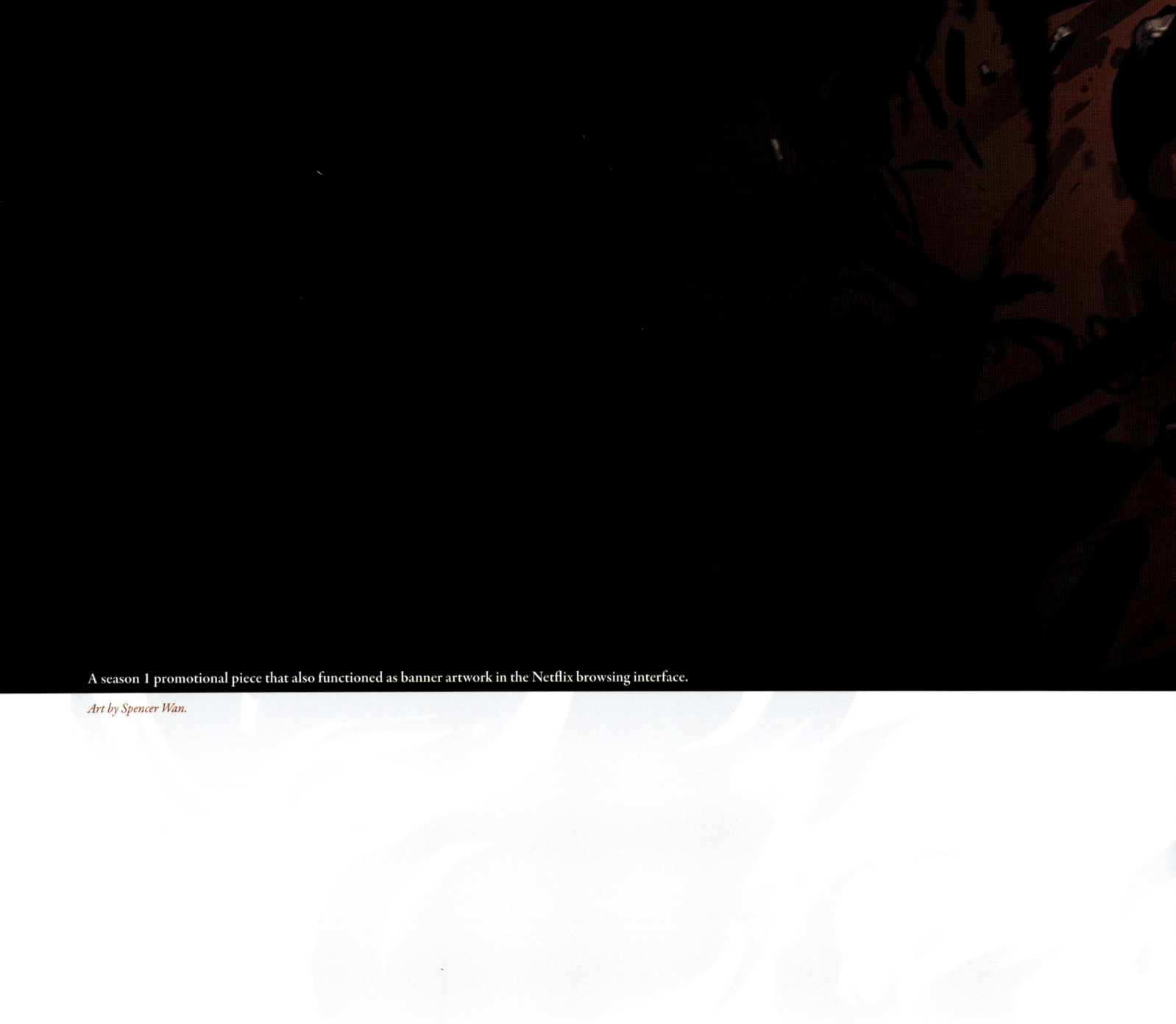

A season 1 promotional piece that also functioned as banner artwork in the Netflix browsing interface.

Art by Spencer Wan.

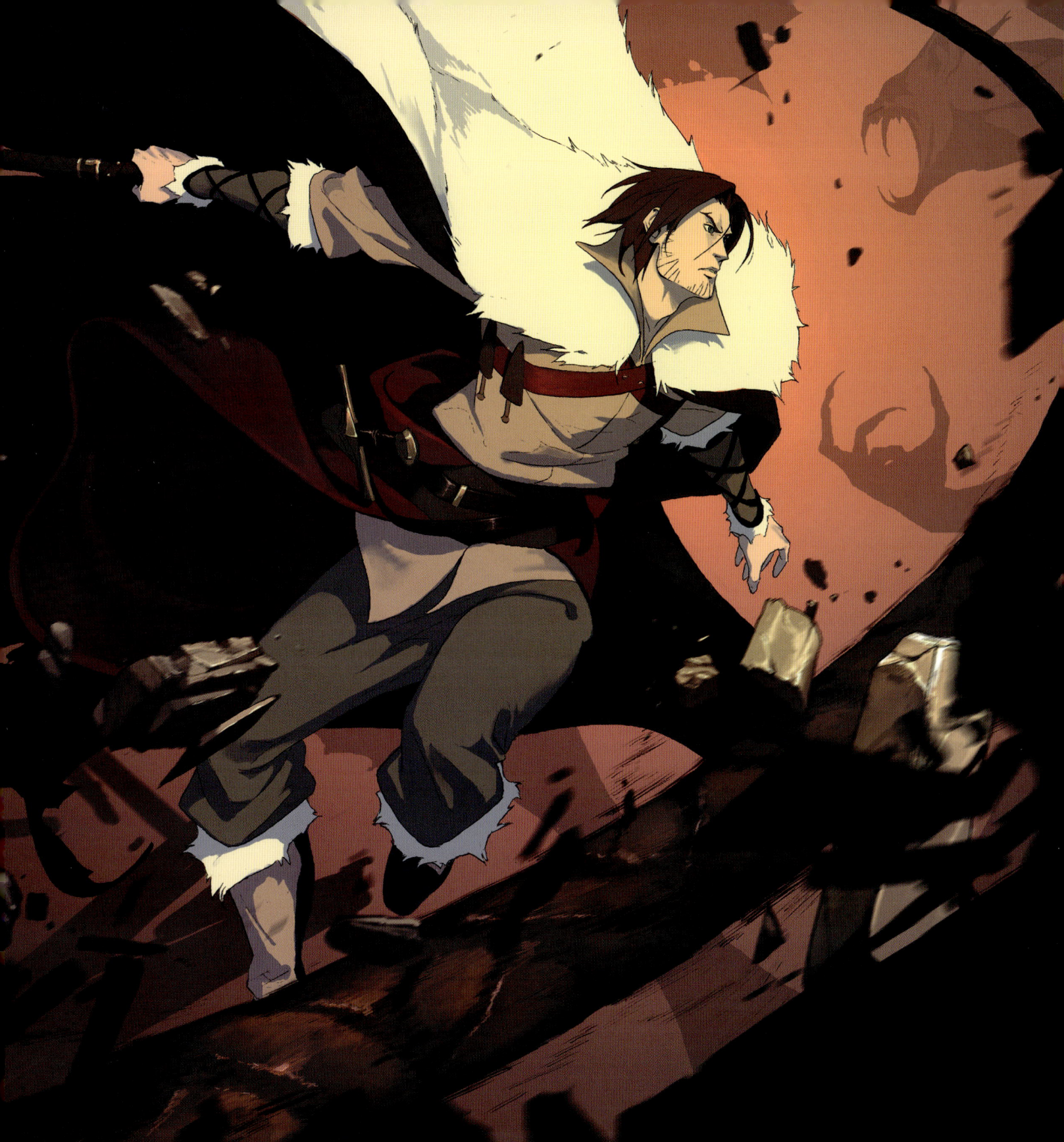

CHAPTER I

Saviors and the Innocent

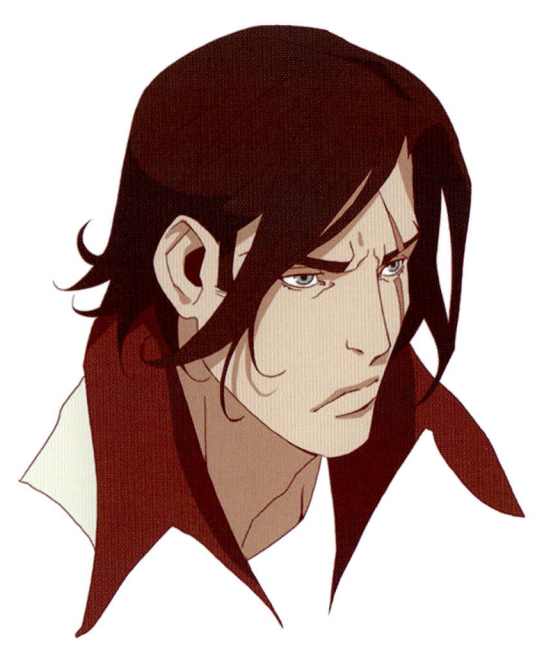

Trevor Belmont

Trevor Belmont, the last surviving member of the monster-hunting Belmont family, makes his series debut in episode 1 as an inebriated loner stumbling into an unwanted confrontation.

This page: Early art explored Trevor's design. *Opposite:* In a pitch to producers to sell Powerhouse Animation as the studio of choice for the series, Sam Deats created an initial deck of concept art including a moody monochrome portrait.

All art on these pages by Sam Deats.

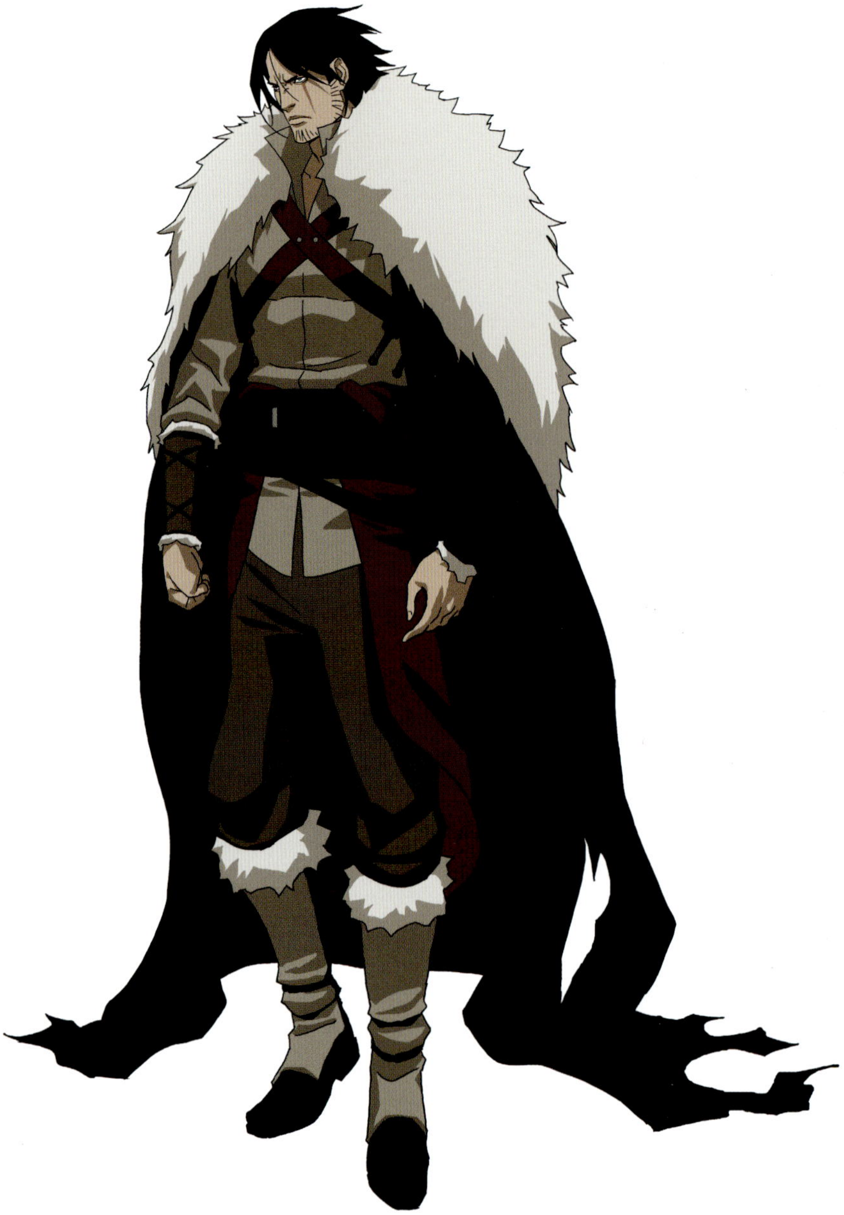

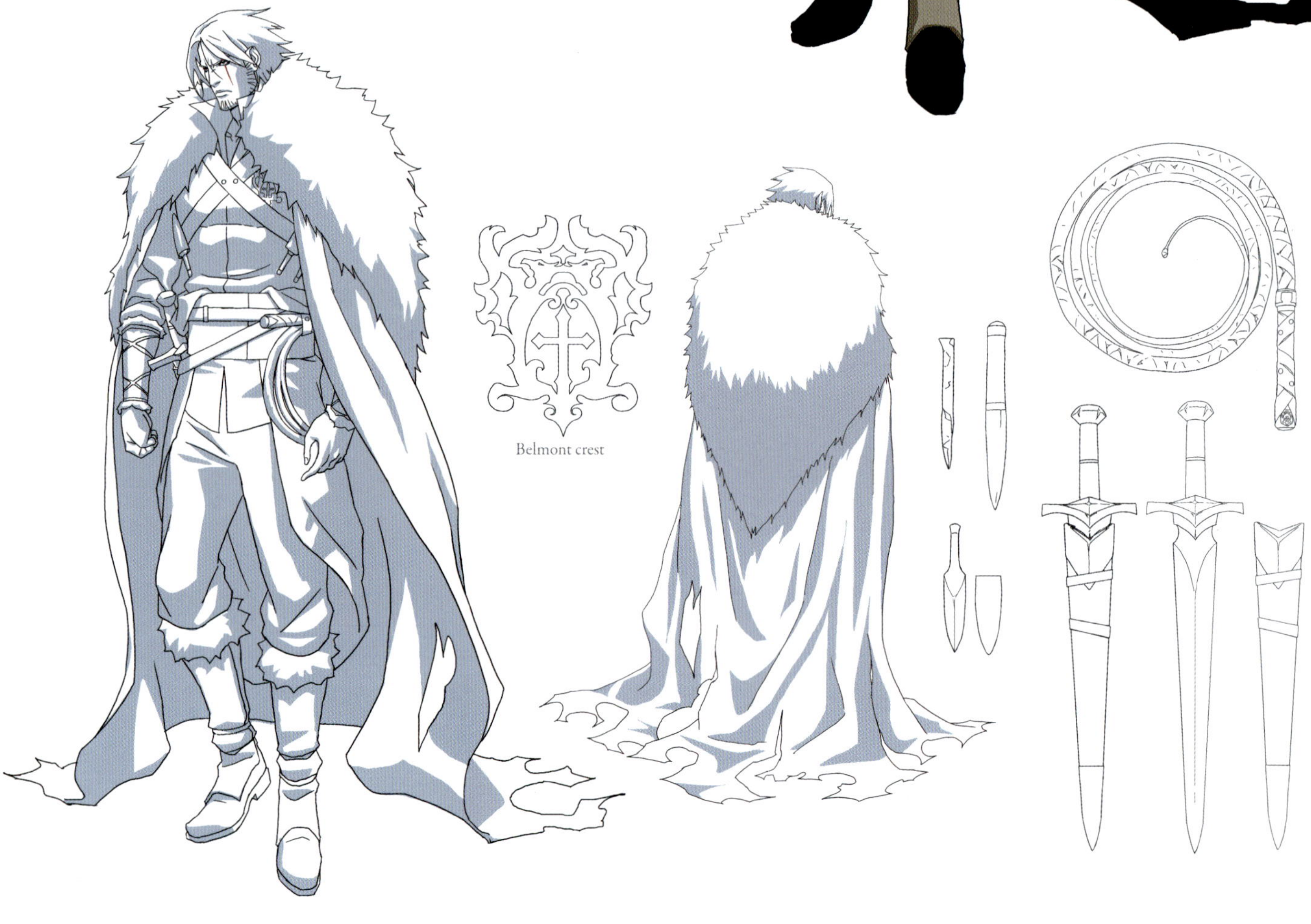

Belmont crest

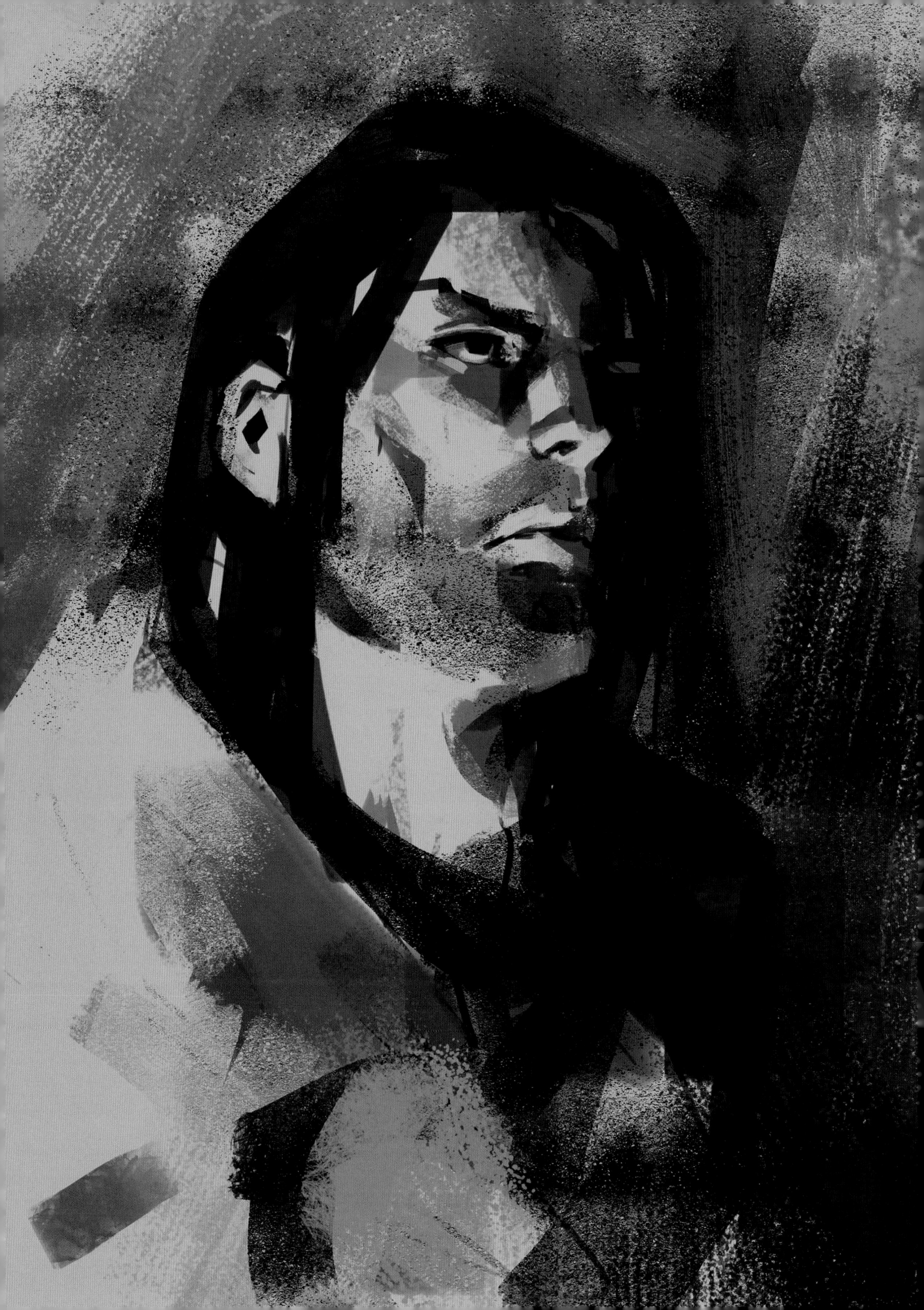

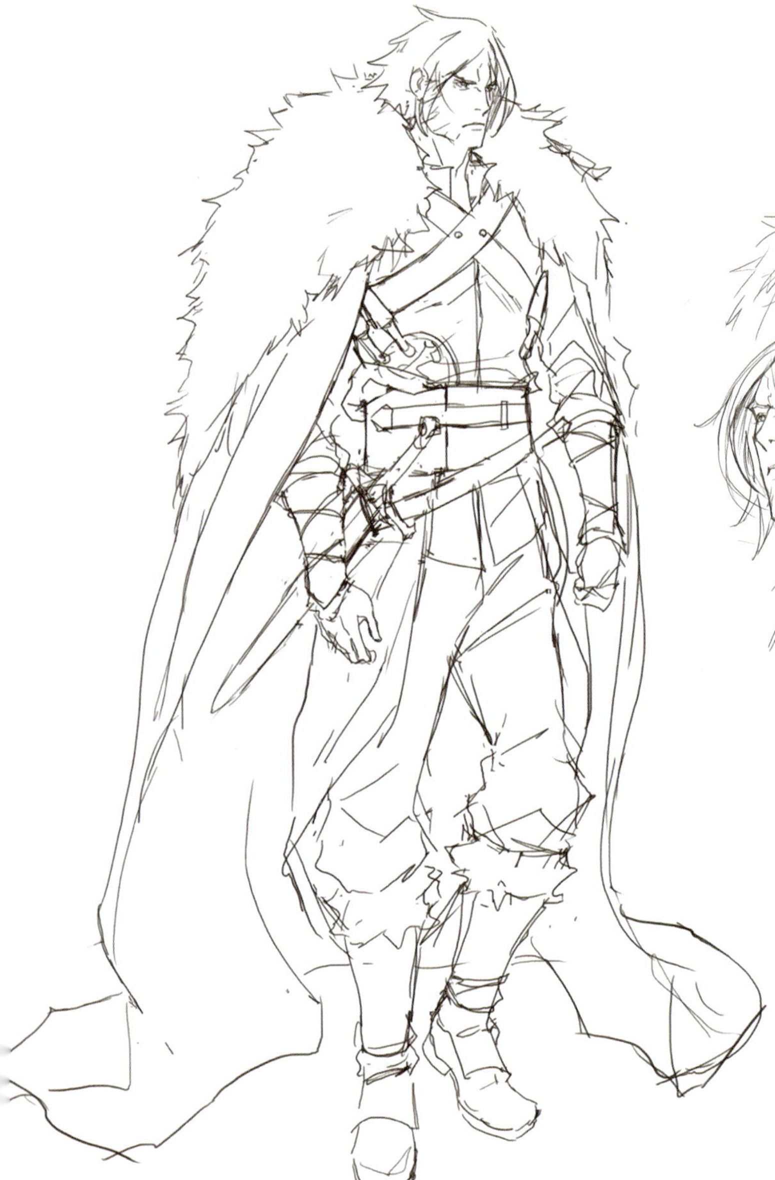

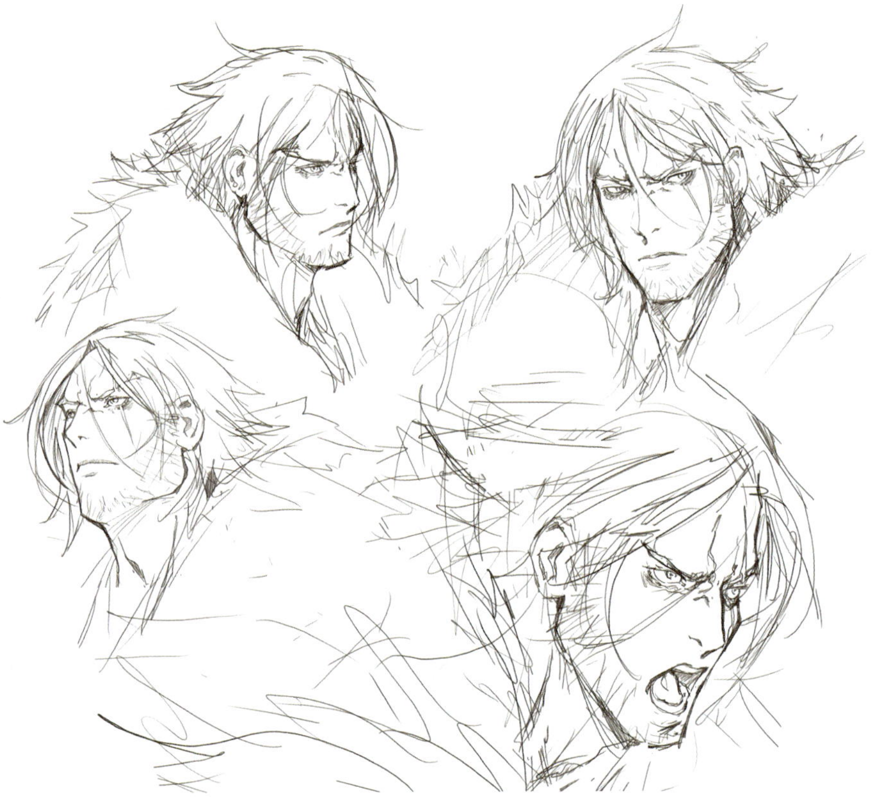

FINDING TREVOR

"I had initially drawn Trevor to look older, but the voice actor we had been talking to sounded a lot younger, so I started playing around with younger-looking versions [*bottom of opposite page*]. Then, as more voice actors auditioned and some fell through and so on, I started drawing older versions again. It was a struggle. I remember one night I sat down to draw and it all came together. I drew a sketch of Trevor holding his whip up with the snow falling and I had an epiphany with that sketch. He was this surly, pissed-off, much more grim take on him, rather than the young, less-beat-up version that was in these other sketches. From there it fell into place, I just had to draw that one sketch before the rest came flooding out." —Sam Deats

All art on these pages by Sam Deats.

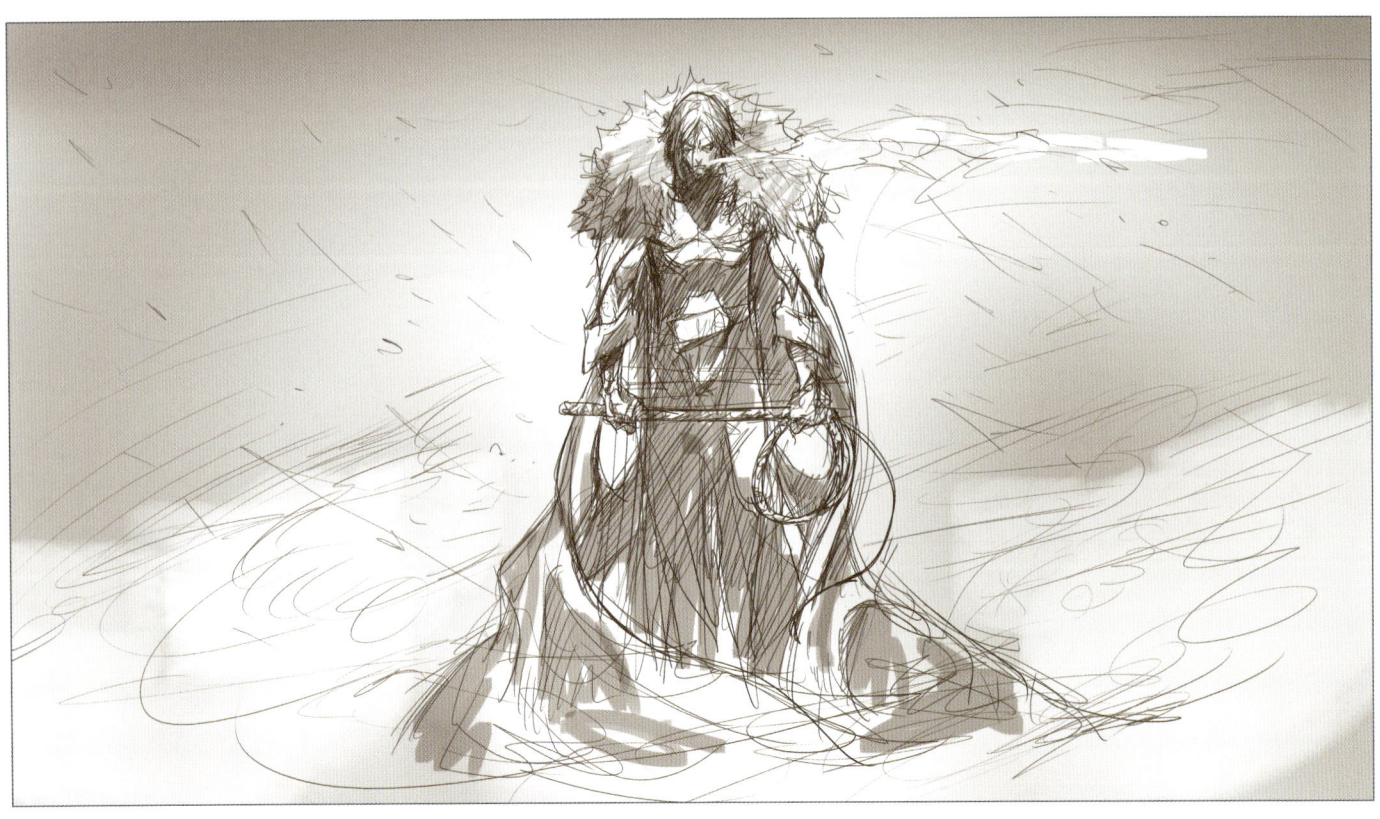

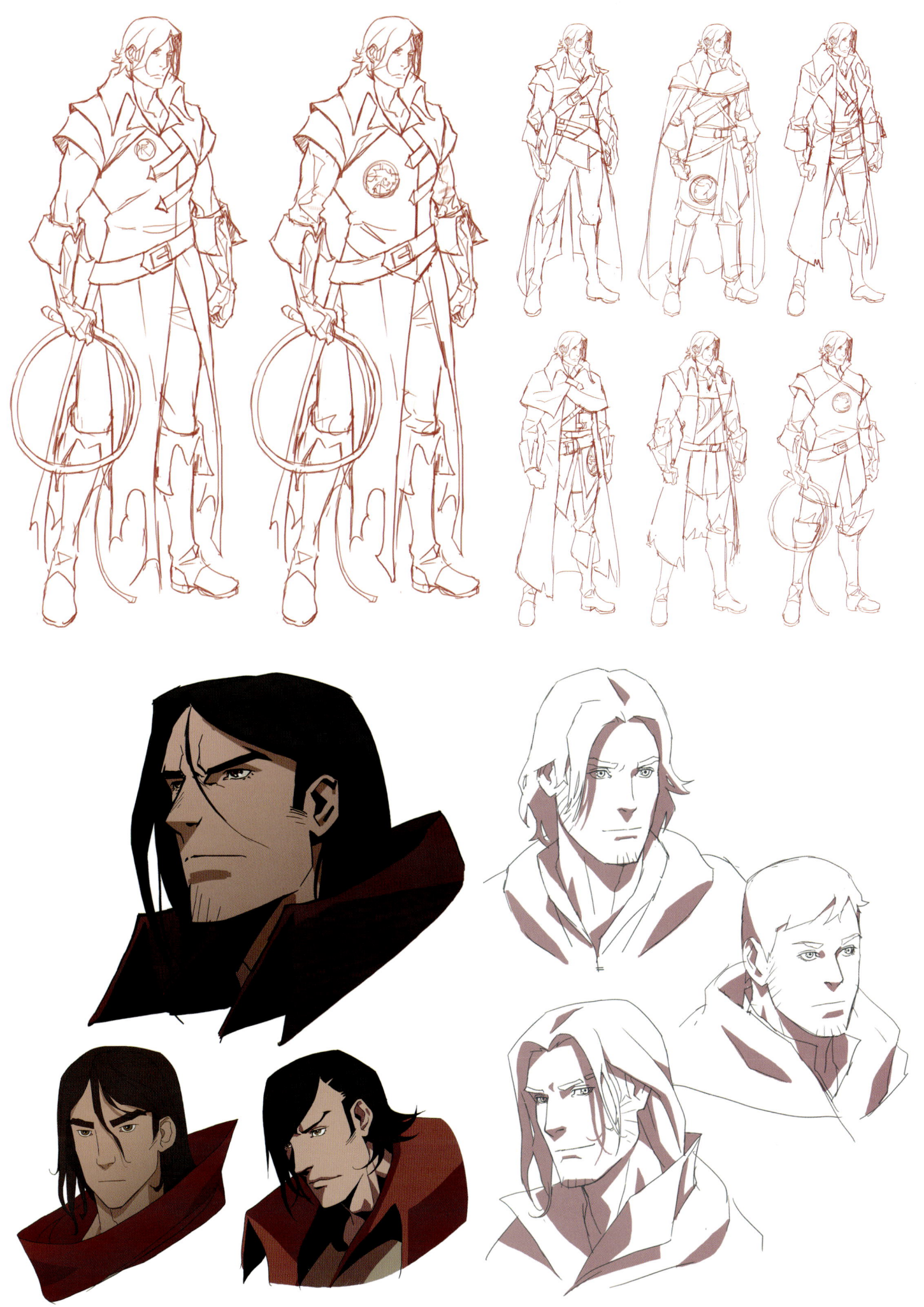

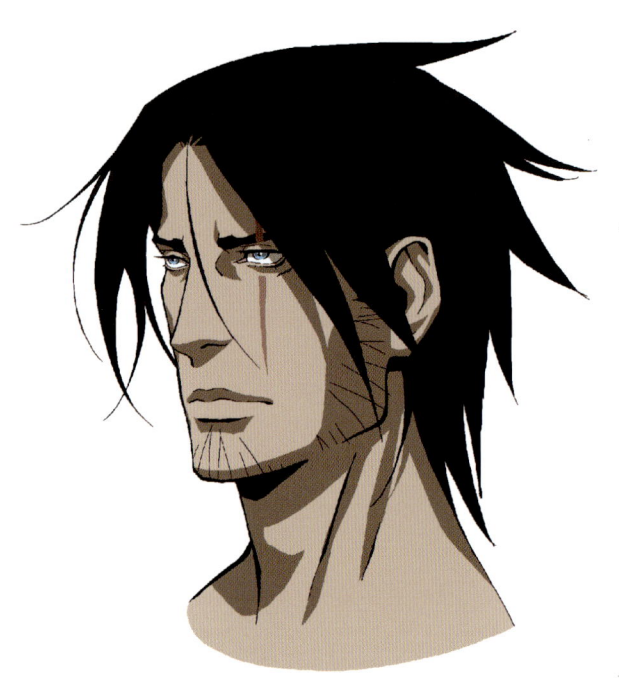

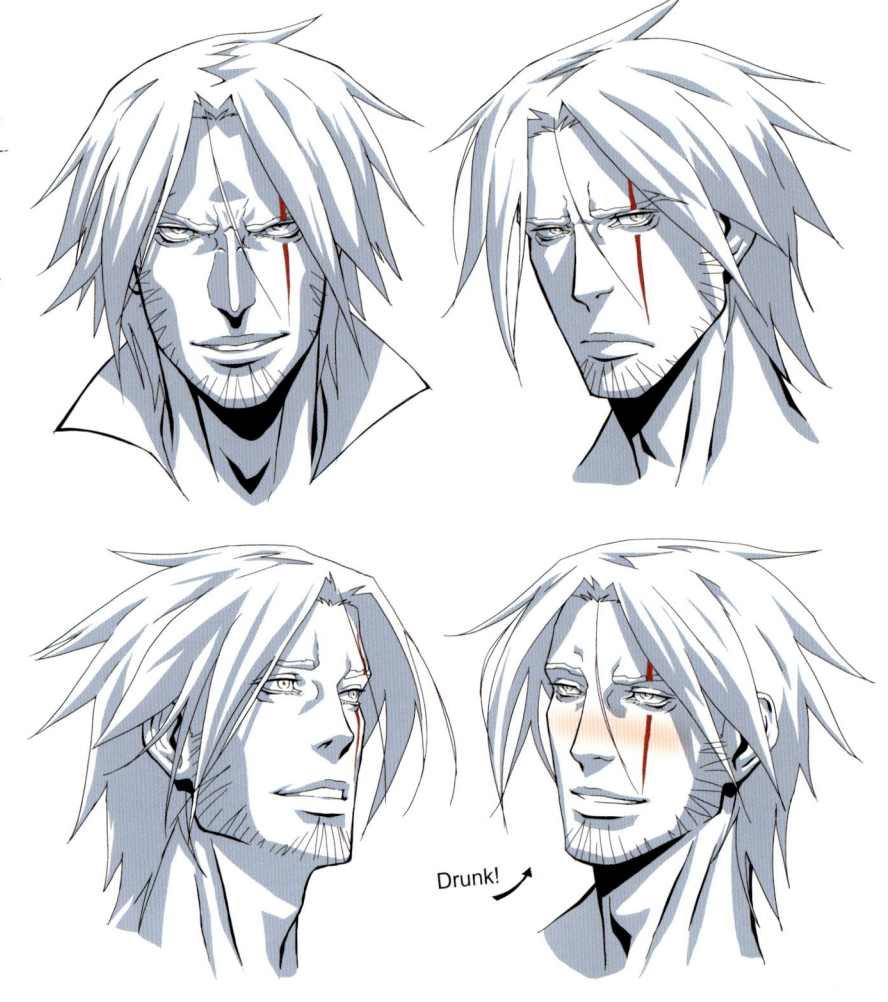

Drunk!

TREVOR EXPRESSIONS

"Trevor resembling his voice actor, Richard Armitage, was a happy accident! His design was completed when a different actor was up for the role, but happily Richard took it and he was perfect!" —Sam Deats

An expression model sheet serves as a guide for animators.

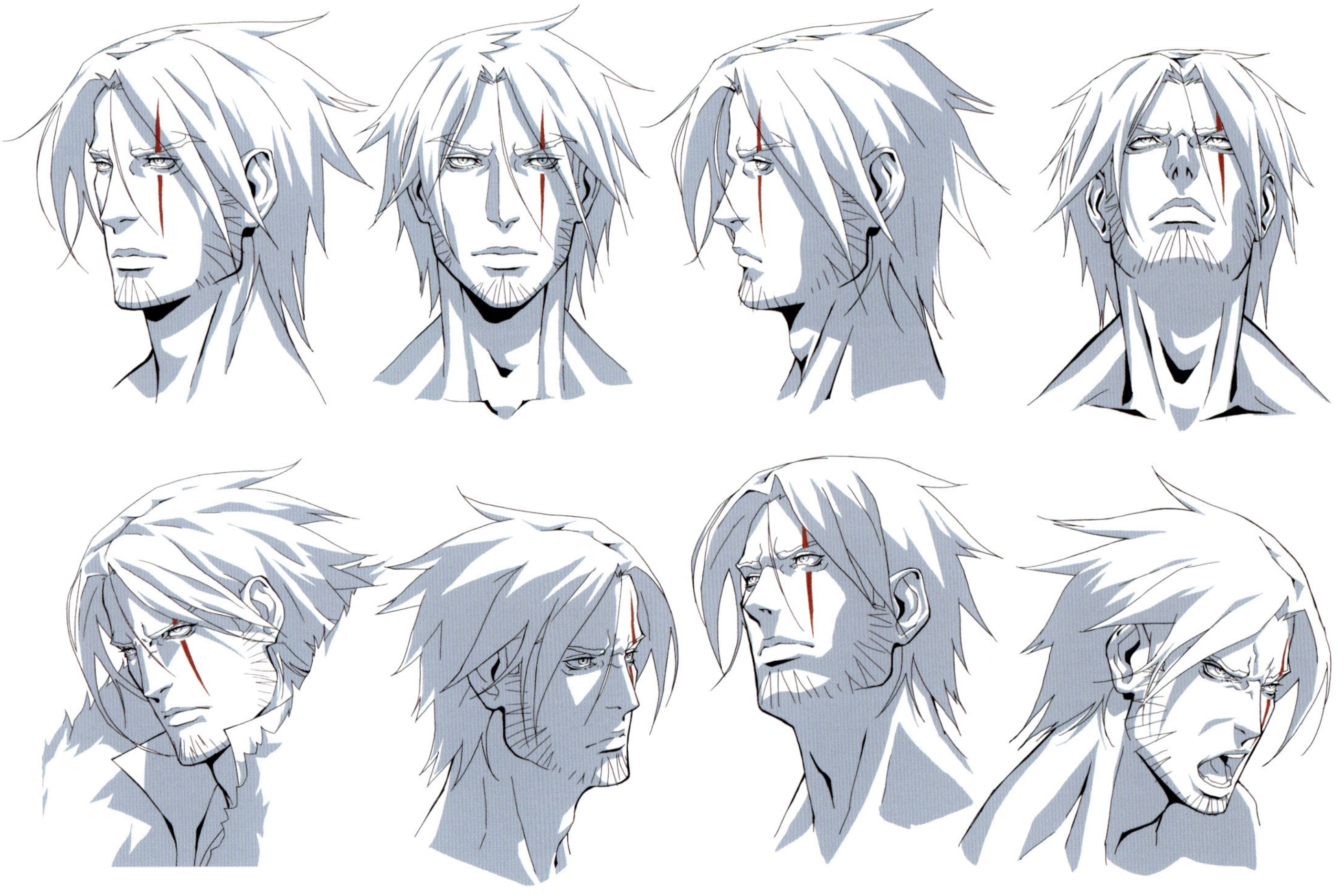

Left page: Trevor expressions by Sam Deats. Right page: Early style tests. Character art by Sam Deats, background by Robby Johnson.

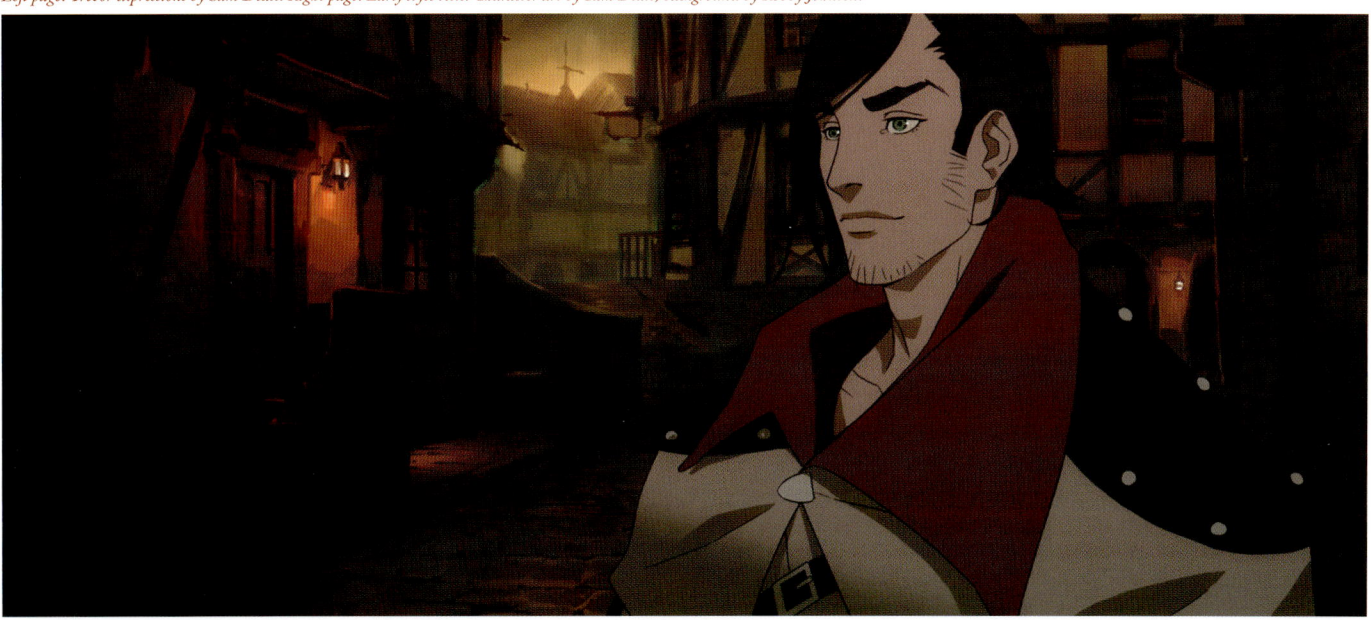

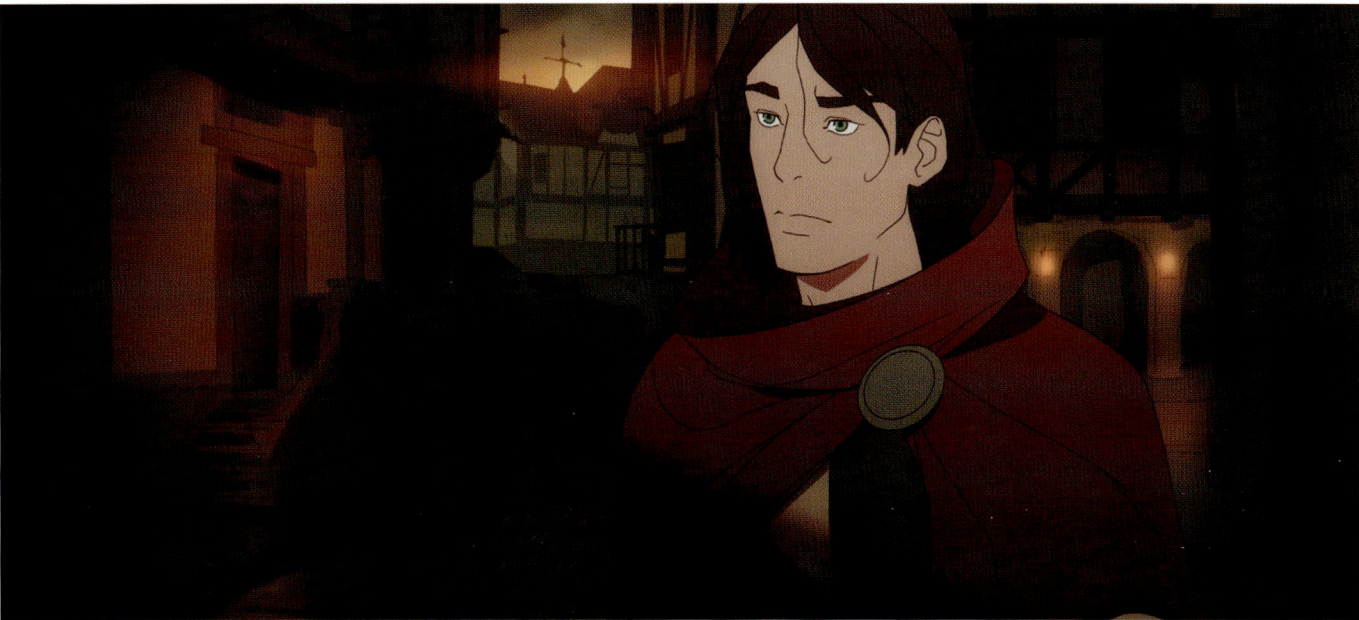

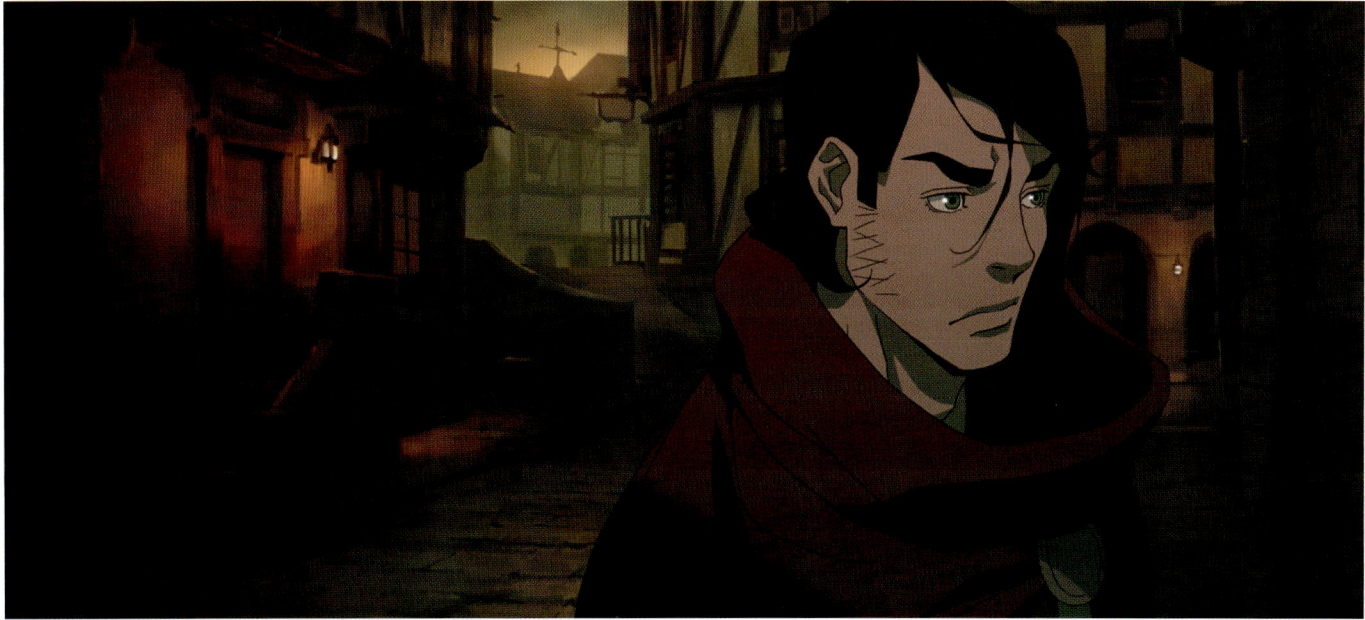

"The only note that I ever had for Sam on the designs was that I wanted the main characters to each have a color scheme that felt close to their old game sprites. Trevor has that same kind of tan-brown palette with some red flourishes, Sypha has the blues, and Alucard has the yellow and black." —Adam Deats

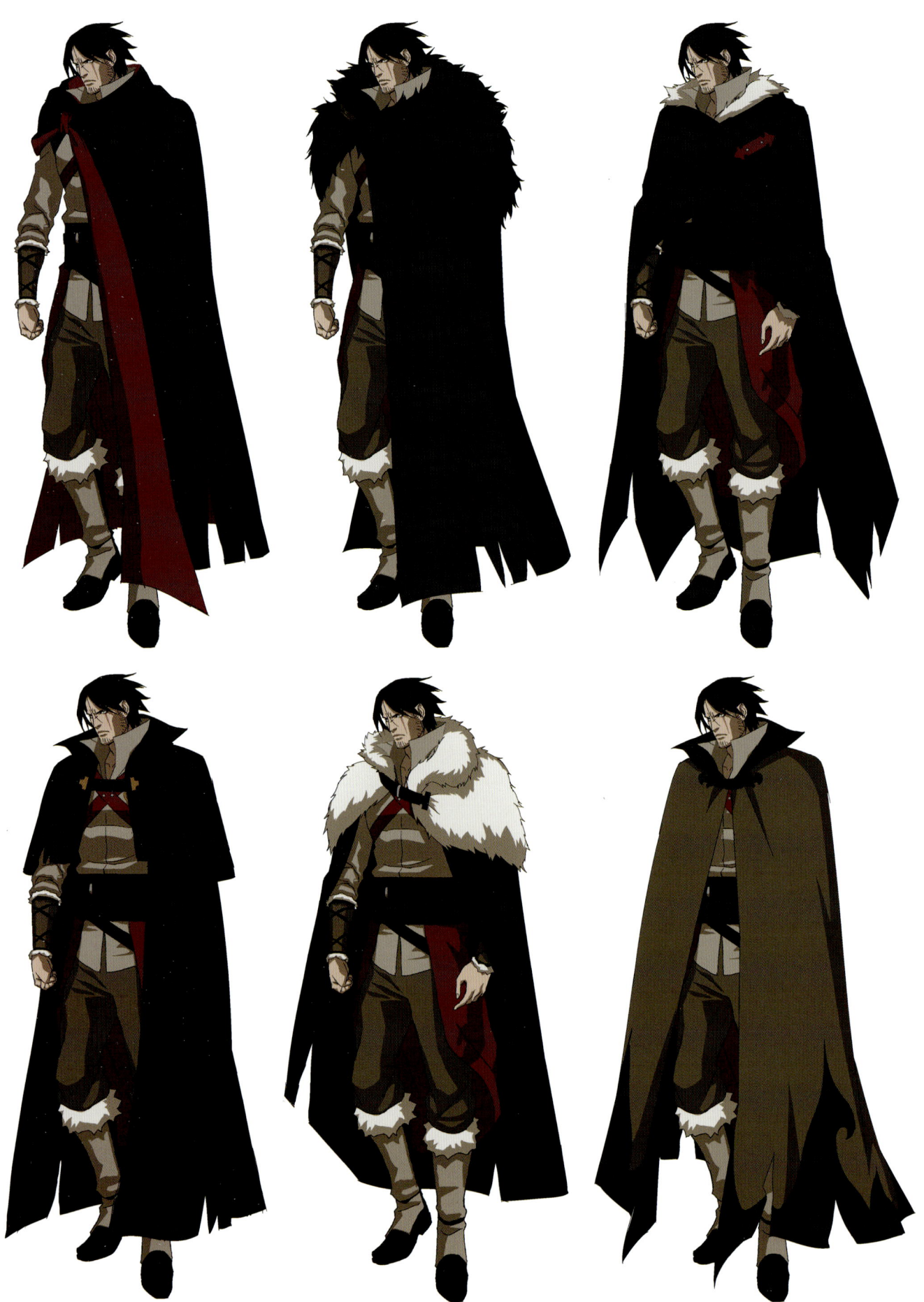

"For costume research, artwork from the games is important obviously, and fashion shows, oddly enough, can be really inspirational. They have a lot of interesting shapes. There's historical looks too, which are often kind of dull, however, so you end up wanting to take advantage of the fantasy setting and add some anime flair to a lot of things." —Sam Deats

"We looked up costuming from this time period and they all would have been wearing those puffy short pants. [*laughs*]" —Kevin Kolde

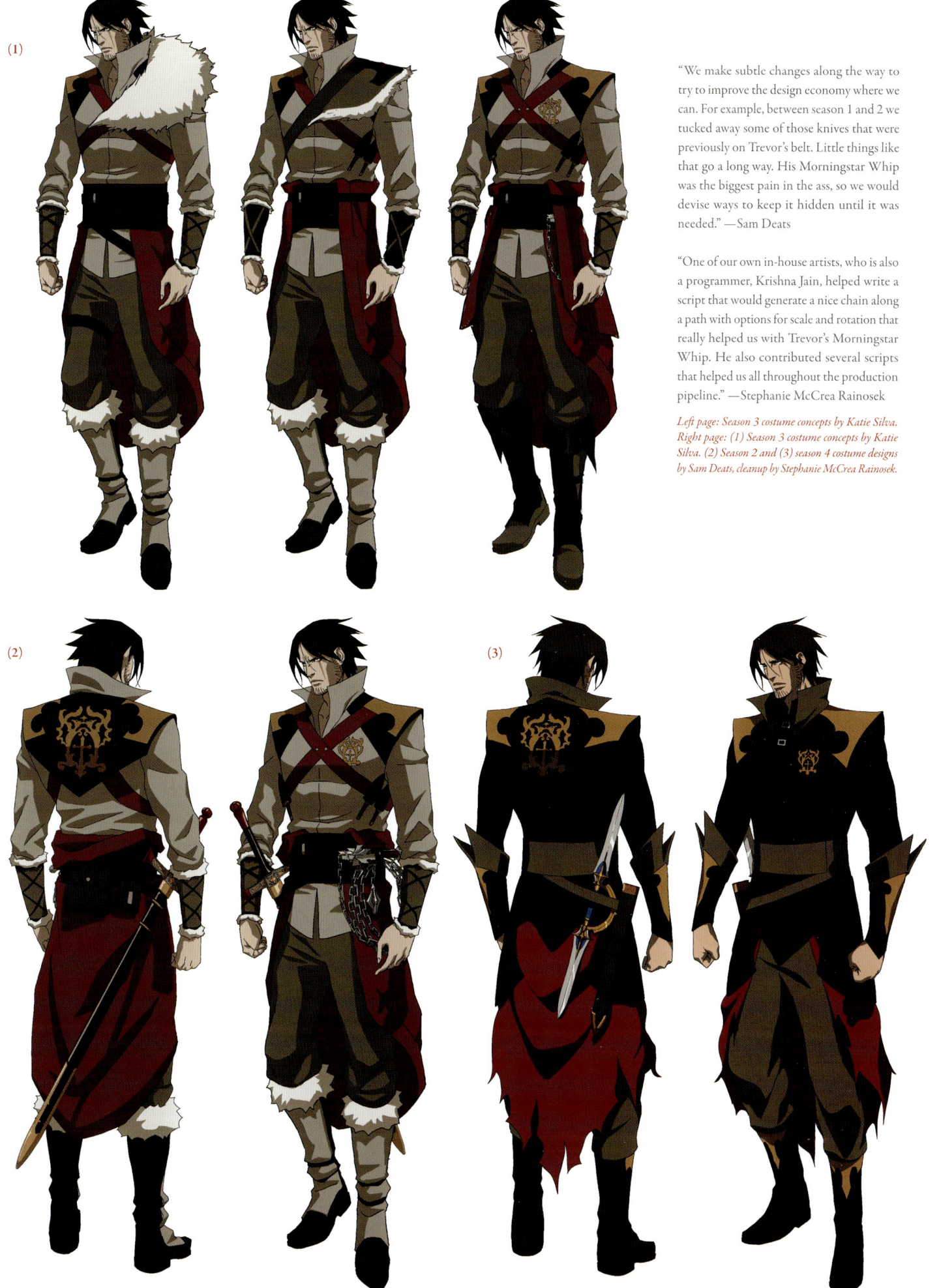

(1)

"We make subtle changes along the way to try to improve the design economy where we can. For example, between season 1 and 2 we tucked away some of those knives that were previously on Trevor's belt. Little things like that go a long way. His Morningstar Whip was the biggest pain in the ass, so we would devise ways to keep it hidden until it was needed." —Sam Deats

"One of our own in-house artists, who is also a programmer, Krishna Jain, helped write a script that would generate a nice chain along a path with options for scale and rotation that really helped us with Trevor's Morningstar Whip. He also contributed several scripts that helped us all throughout the production pipeline." —Stephanie McCrea Rainosek

Left page: Season 3 costume concepts by Katie Silva. Right page: (1) Season 3 costume concepts by Katie Silva. (2) Season 2 and (3) season 4 costume designs by Sam Deats, cleanup by Stephanie McCrea Rainosek.

(2)

(3)

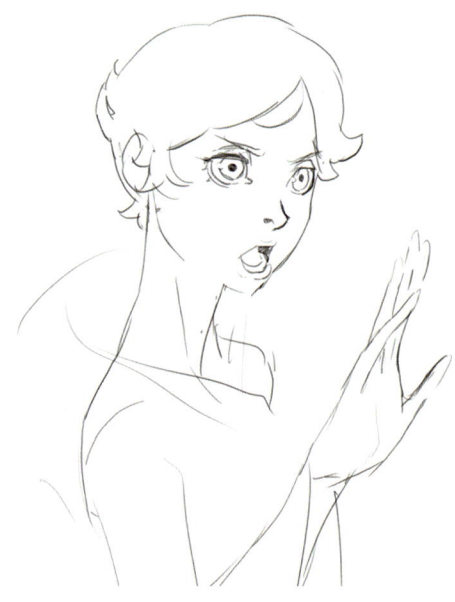

Sypha Belnades

Using only an oral tradition, Speakers commit their knowledge to memory and pass it on through generations, gathered from all corners of the Earth. Sypha, the granddaughter of the Elder Speaker, has formidable magic powers and a cheerful exuberance that make her an excellent partner for Trevor's mission and foil for his melancholy.

Left page: Early concepts by Sam Deats. Right page: Character designs by Sam Deats, backgrounds by Robby Johnson.

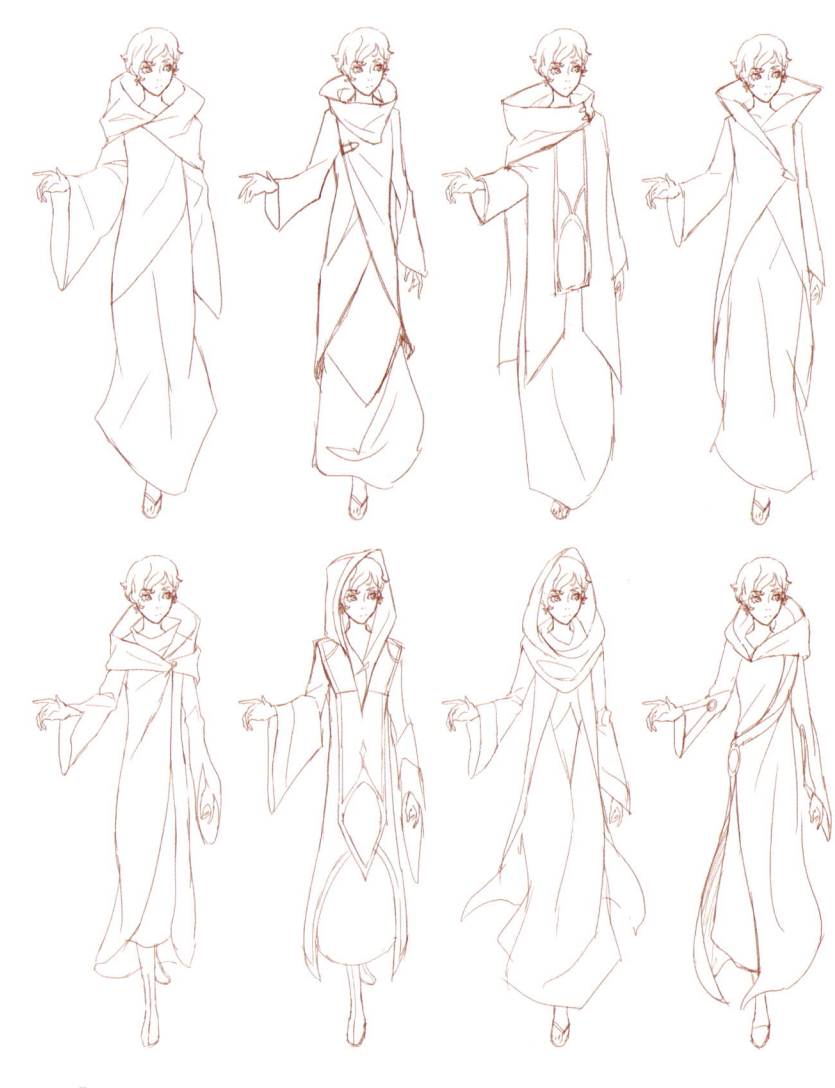

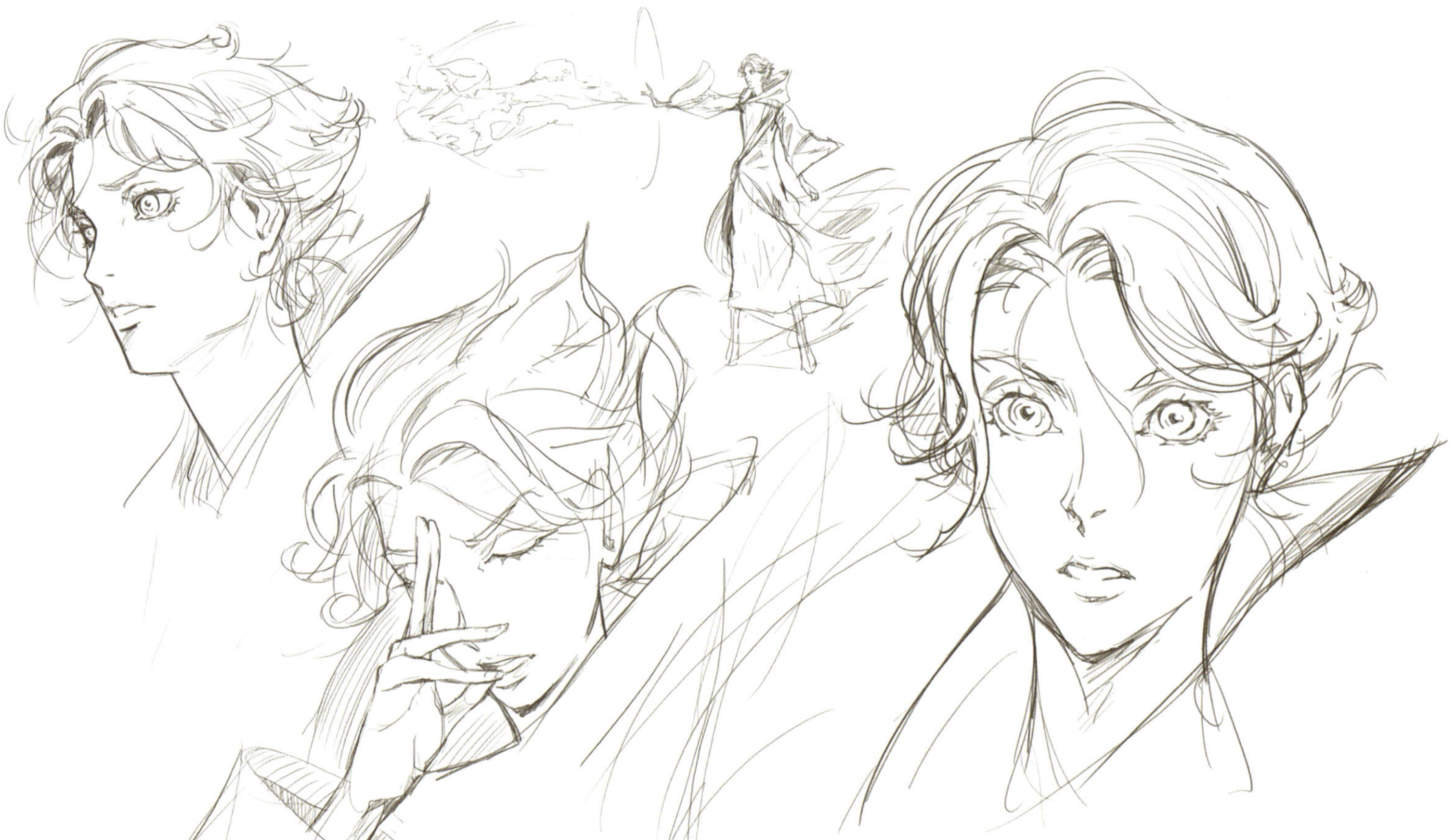

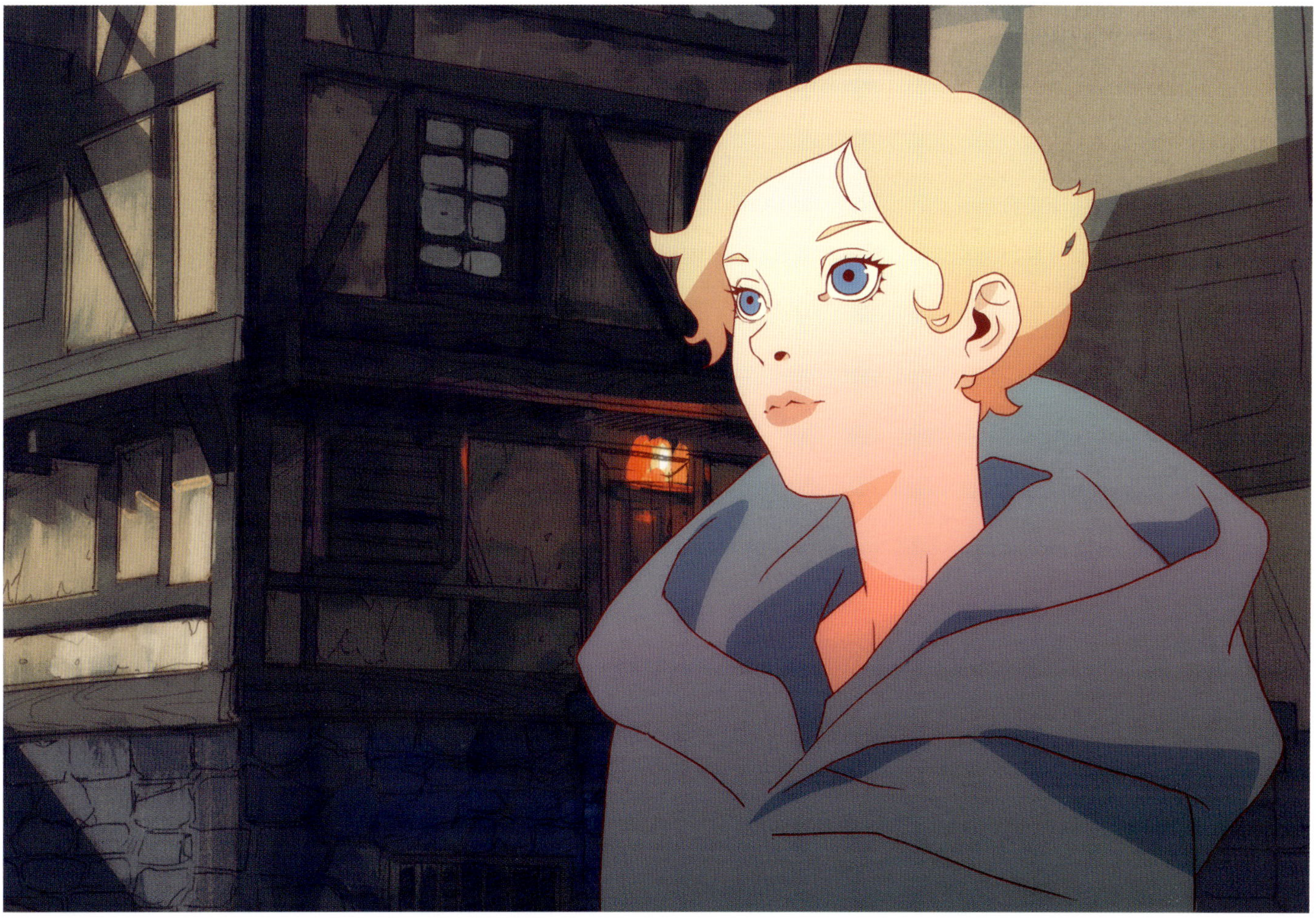

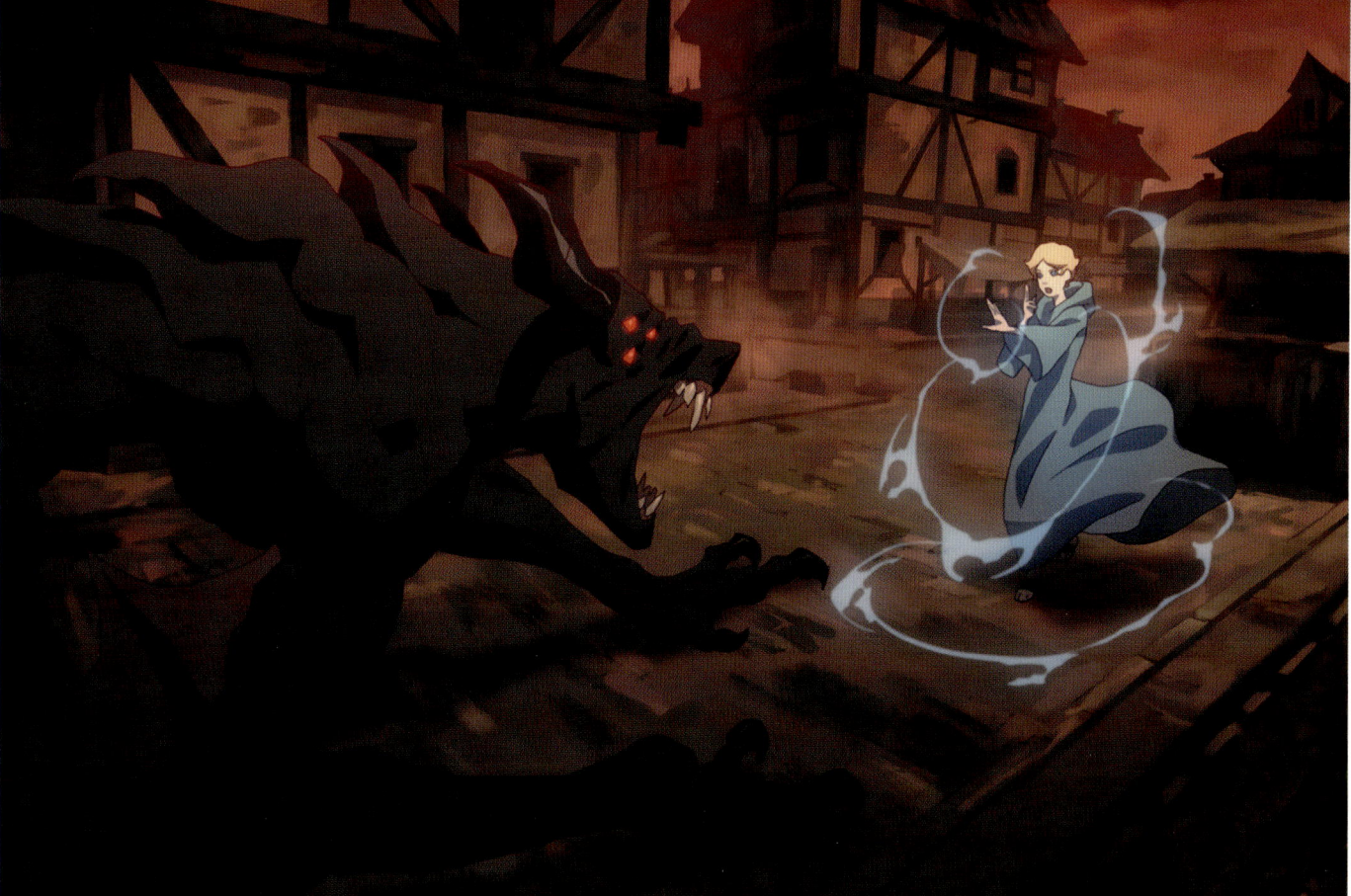

Opposite: Early concepts of Sypha at the top pictured a youthful direction that wasn't quite right. After Sam found the direction for Trevor, the Sypha designs on the bottom flowed out immediately as an extension of that direction. *Above:* Early style tests and character art.

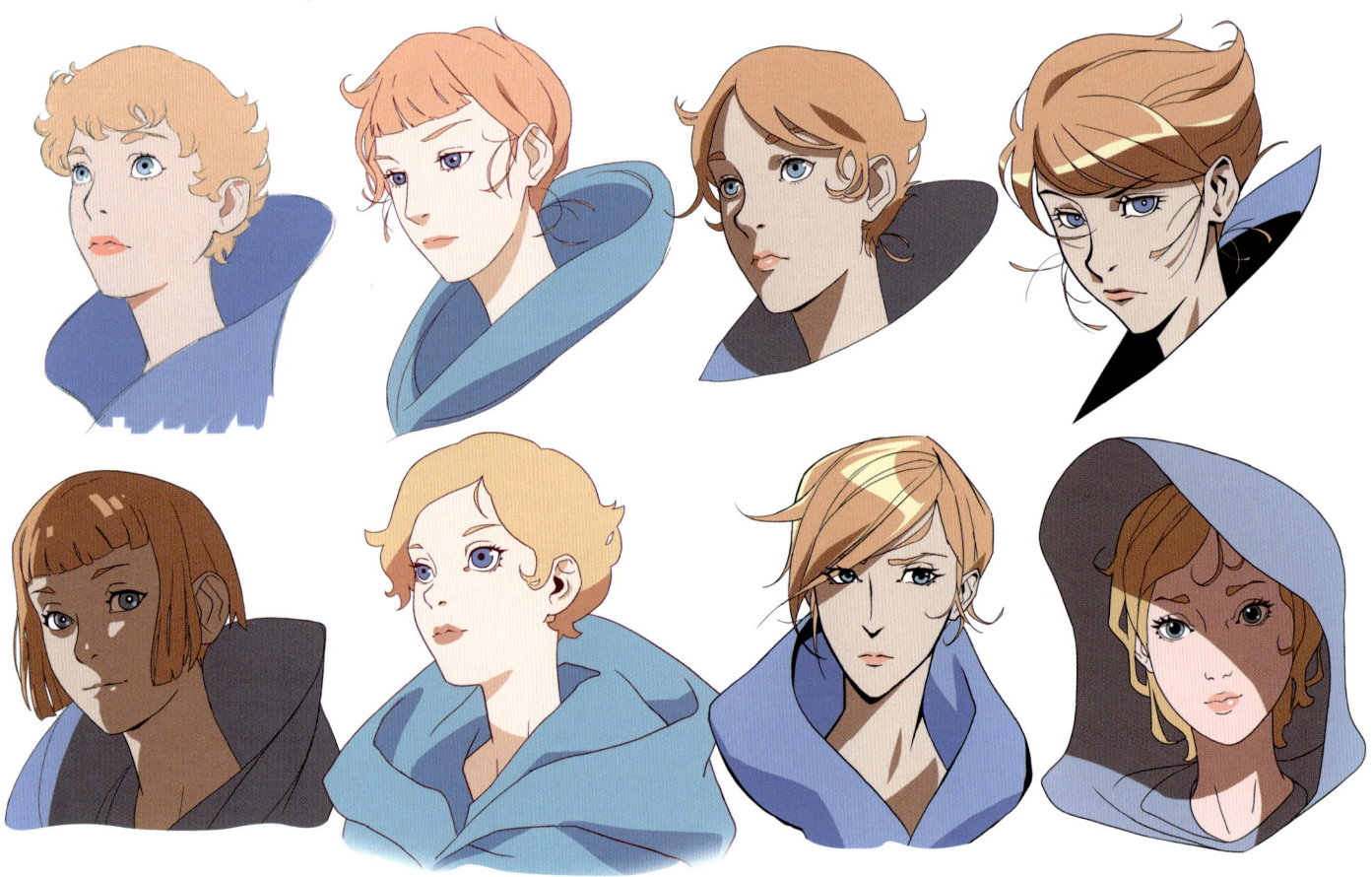

In the games, Sypha was originally written as a magician for the church. This was no longer the case for the series, and so any shape language in the designs that might recall the church was avoided. Sam felt that his explorations of hairstyles for Sypha included a subconscious '70s and '80s anime influence that felt appropriate.

Left page: Early concepts and expressions by Sam Deats.
Right page: (1) Sypha season 3 costume concepts by Katie Silva. (2) Sypha season 1 design by Sam Deats.

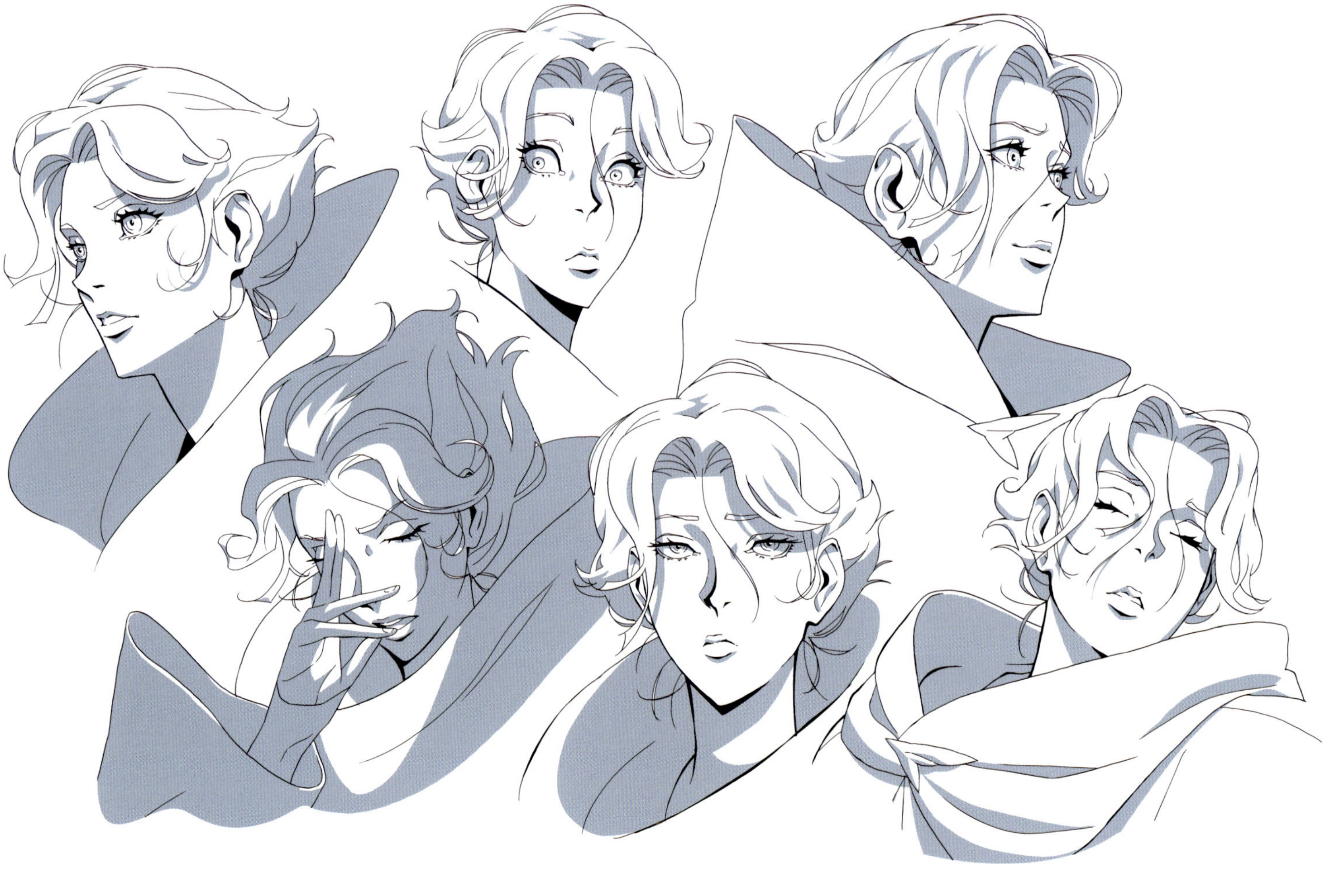

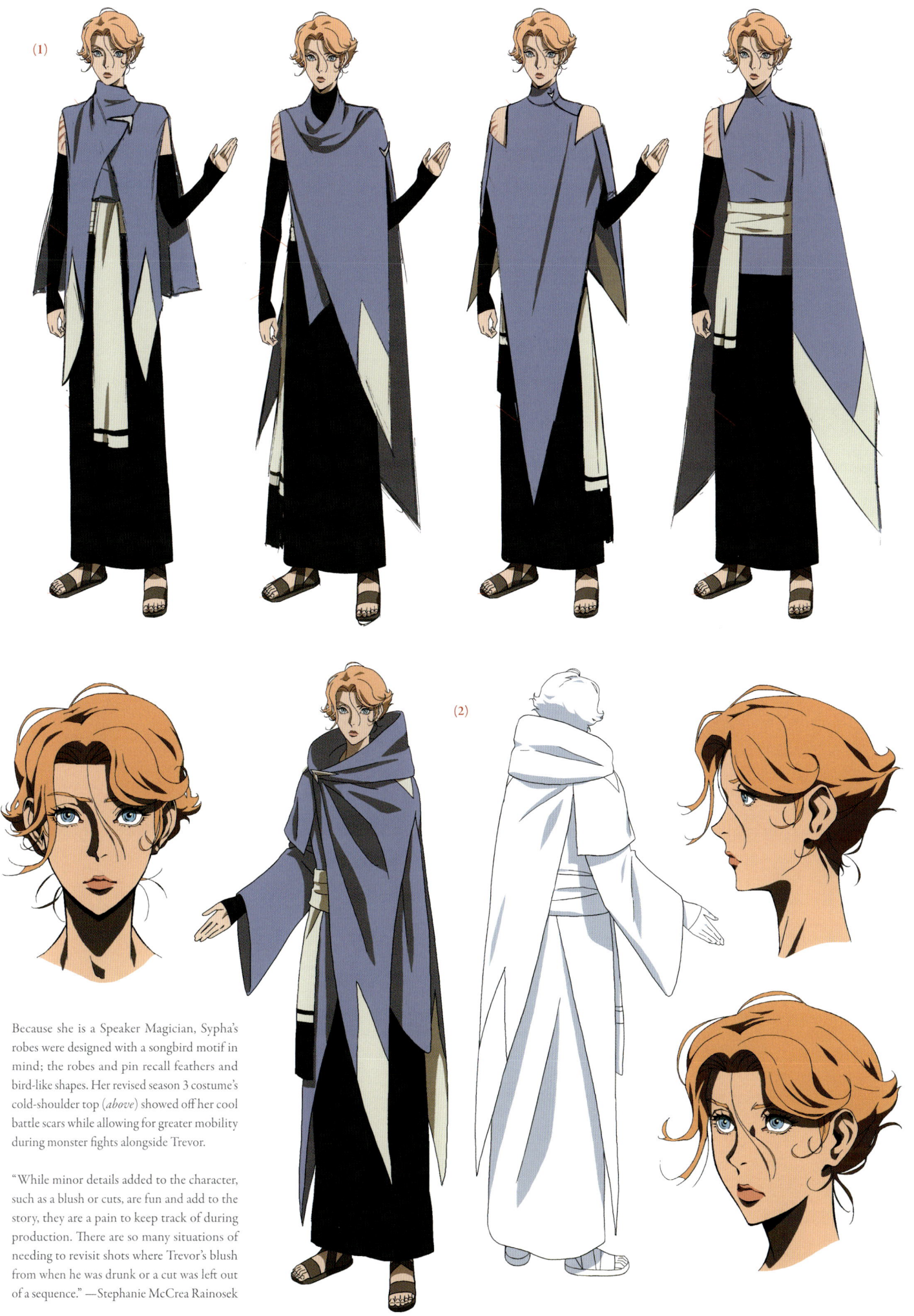

(1)

(2)

Because she is a Speaker Magician, Sypha's robes were designed with a songbird motif in mind; the robes and pin recall feathers and bird-like shapes. Her revised season 3 costume's cold-shoulder top (*above*) showed off her cool battle scars while allowing for greater mobility during monster fights alongside Trevor.

"While minor details added to the character, such as a blush or cuts, are fun and add to the story, they are a pain to keep track of during production. There are so many situations of needing to revisit shots where Trevor's blush from when he was drunk or a cut was left out of a sequence." —Stephanie McCrea Rainosek

Adrian Alucard Tepes

The son of Dracula and the human Lisa Tepes, Alucard awakens from his self-induced slumber to resist his father's vengeful mission to destroy humanity. Below you see early style variations and the more heavily Ayami Kojima–influenced direction that the series followed. On the opposite page is a preliminary piece included in the Powerhouse Animation deck proposed to producers.

All art on these pages by Sam Deats.

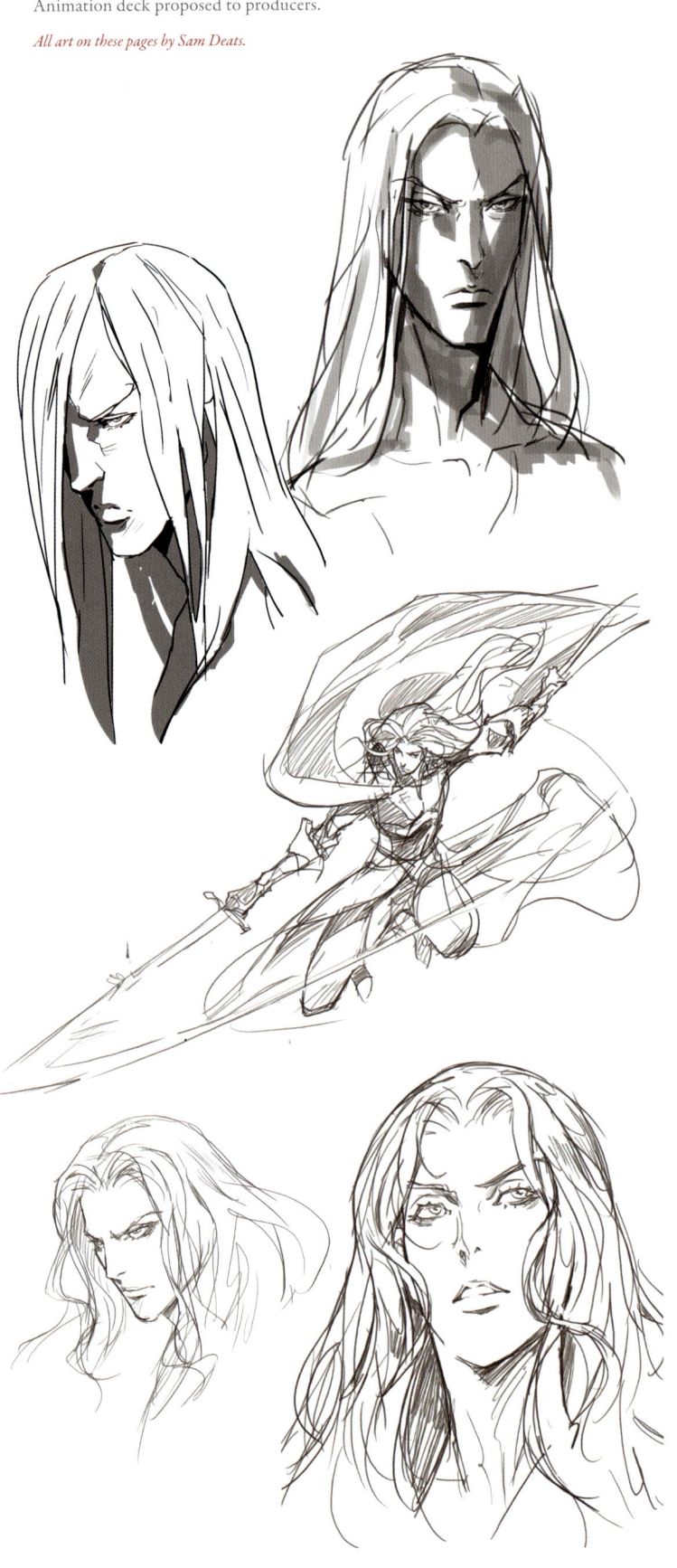

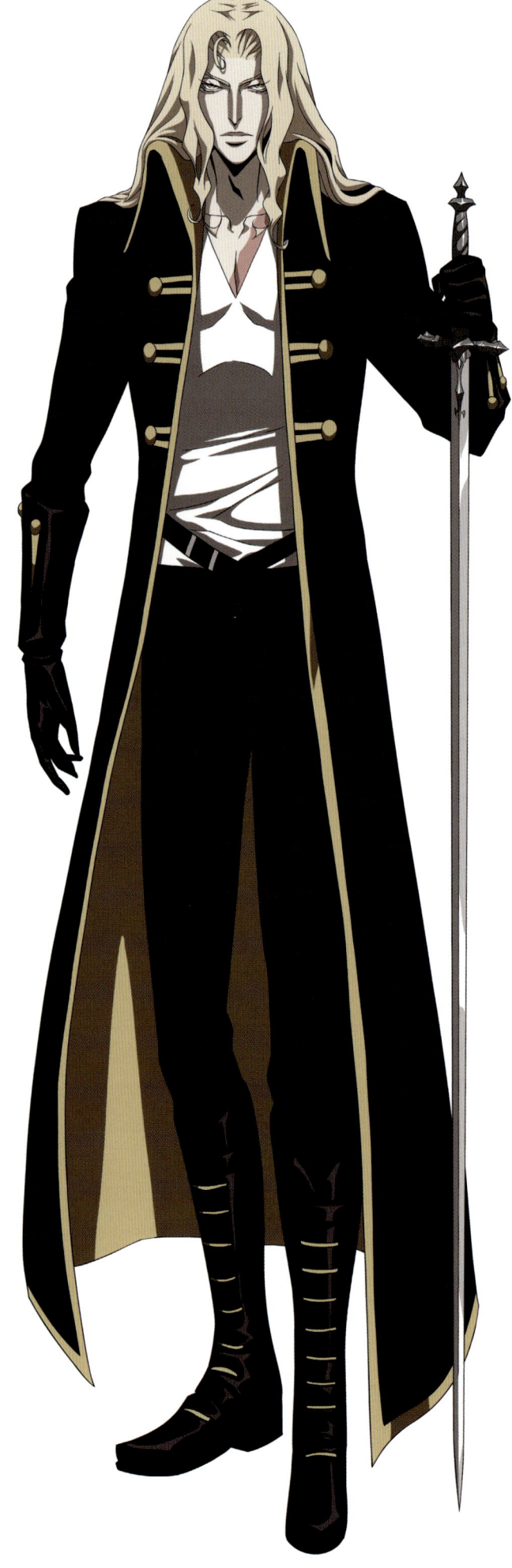

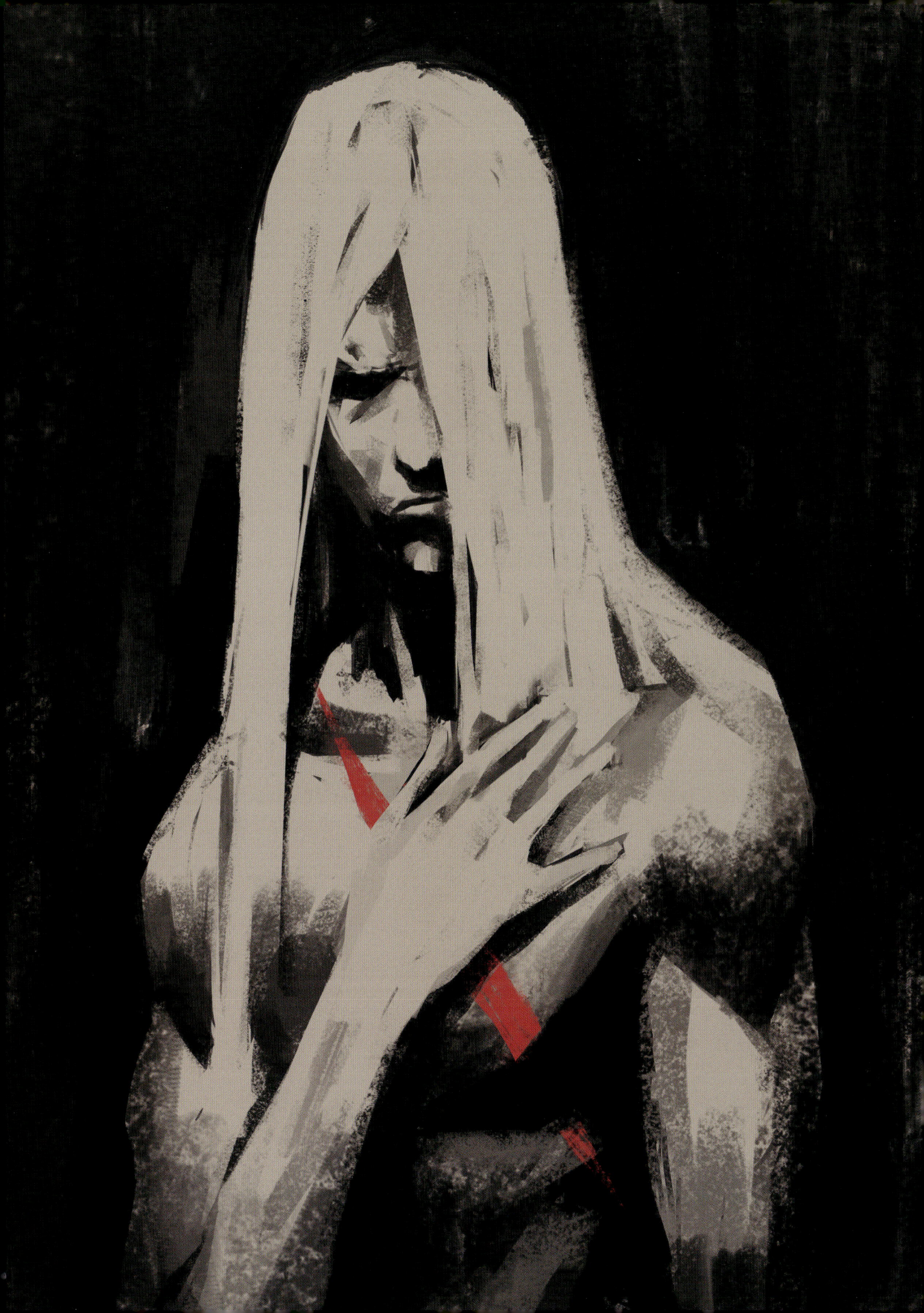

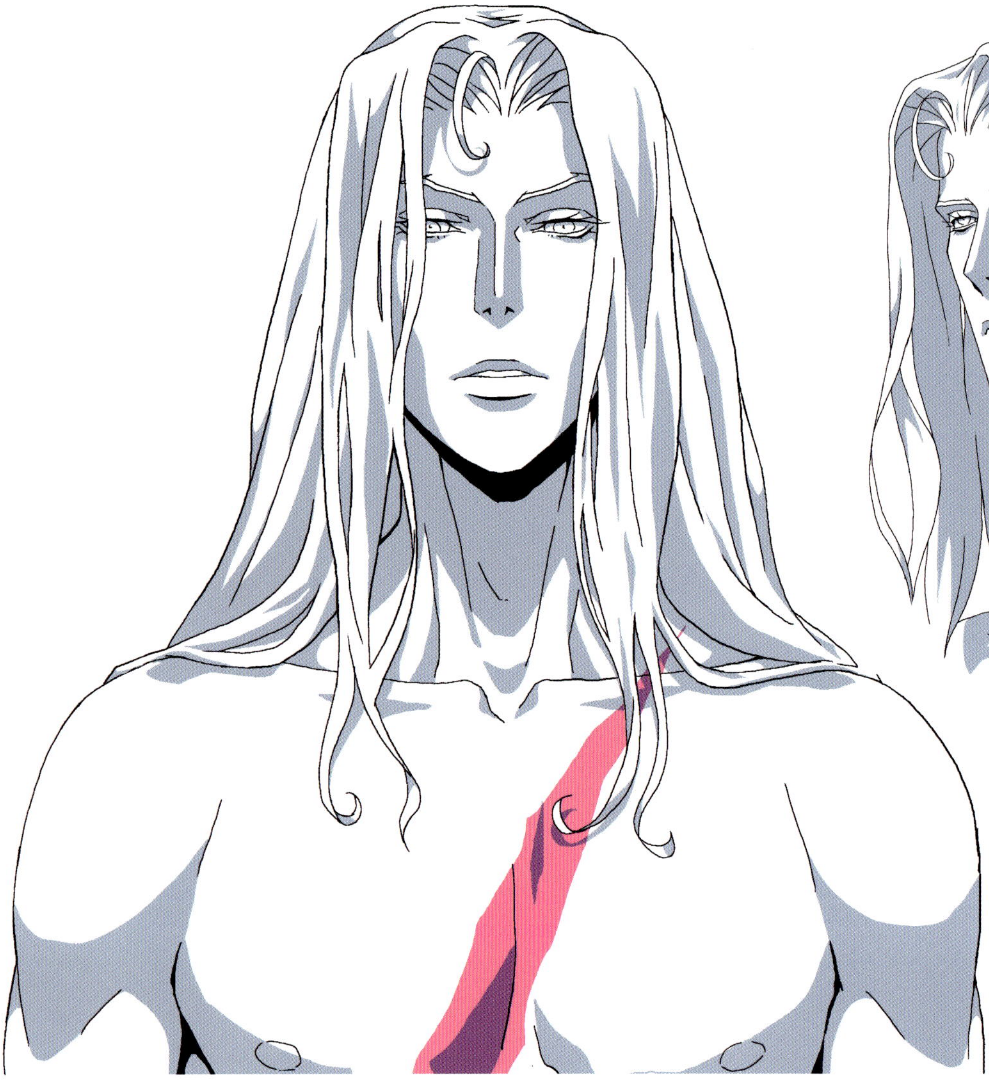

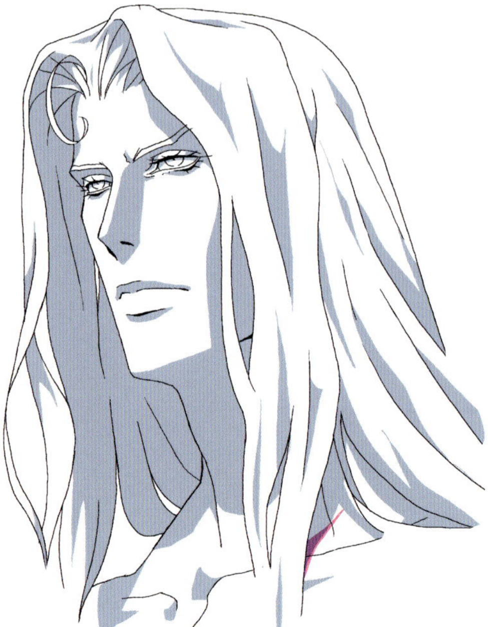

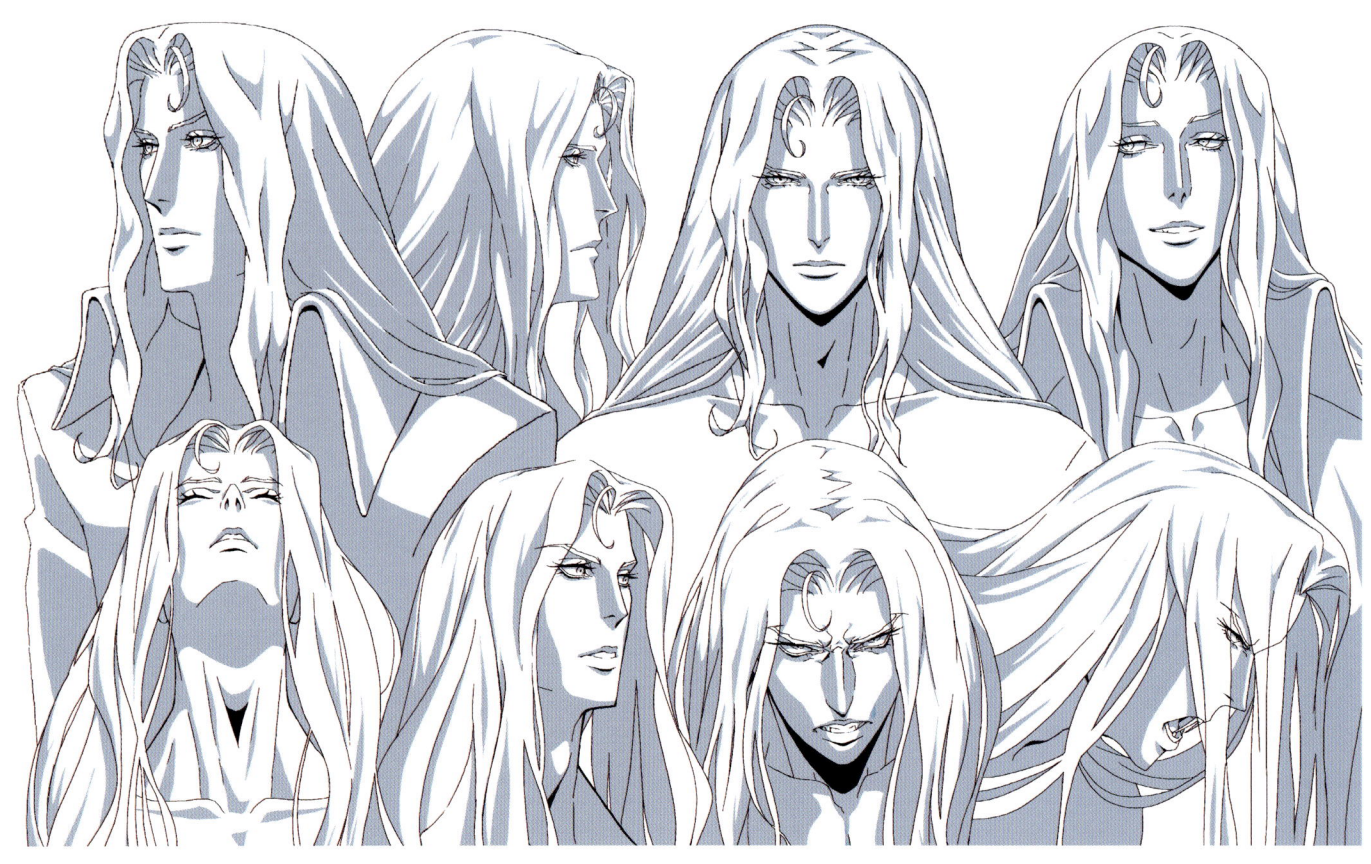

MODELS

Above: Two key animation drawings.
Below: An expression sheet showing Alucard's moods from different angles, and lots of hair.

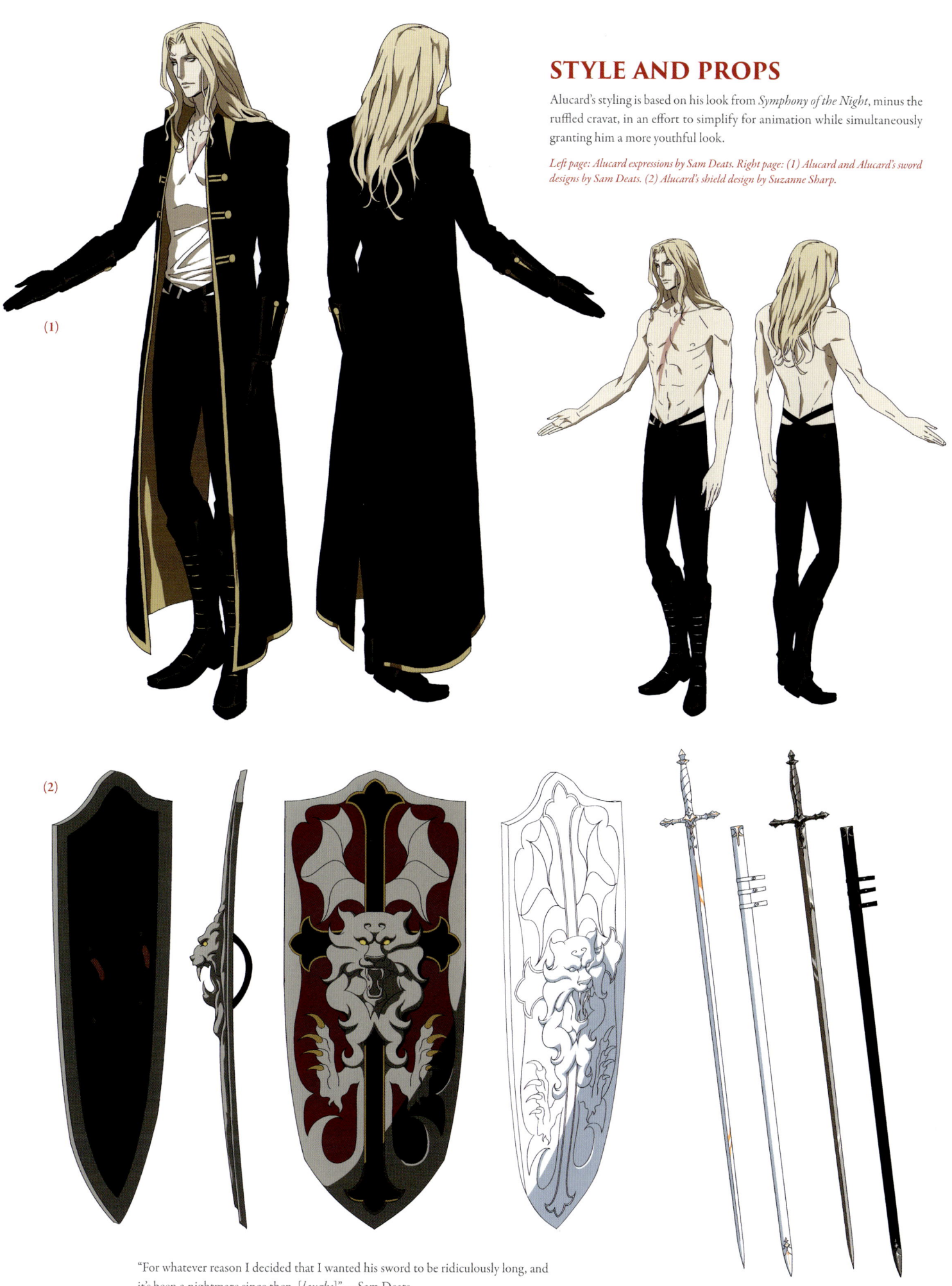

STYLE AND PROPS

Alucard's styling is based on his look from *Symphony of the Night*, minus the ruffled cravat, in an effort to simplify for animation while simultaneously granting him a more youthful look.

Left page: Alucard expressions by Sam Deats. Right page: (1) Alucard and Alucard's sword designs by Sam Deats. (2) Alucard's shield design by Suzanne Sharp.

(1)

(2)

"For whatever reason I decided that I wanted his sword to be ridiculously long, and it's been a nightmare since then. [*laughs*]" —Sam Deats

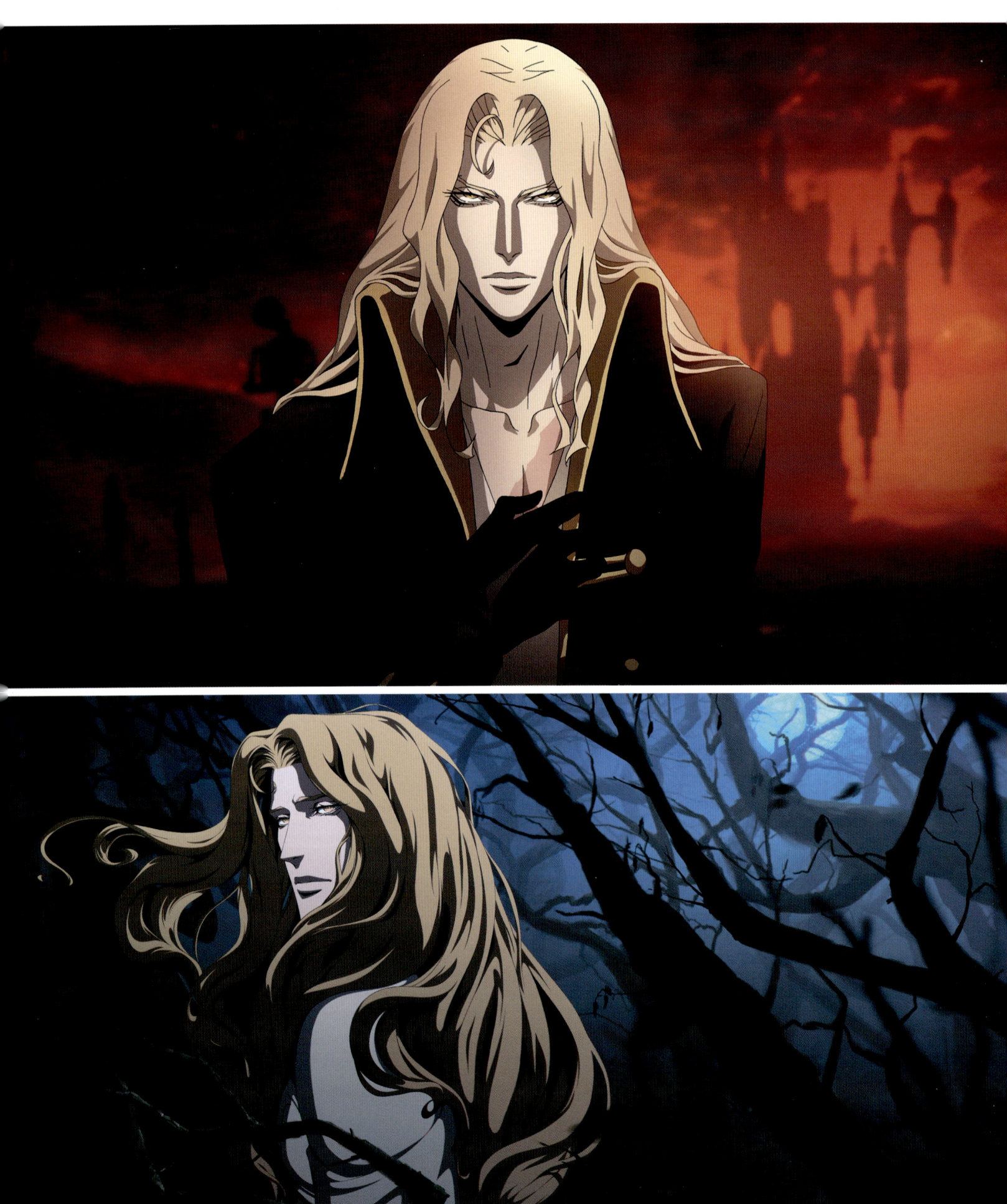

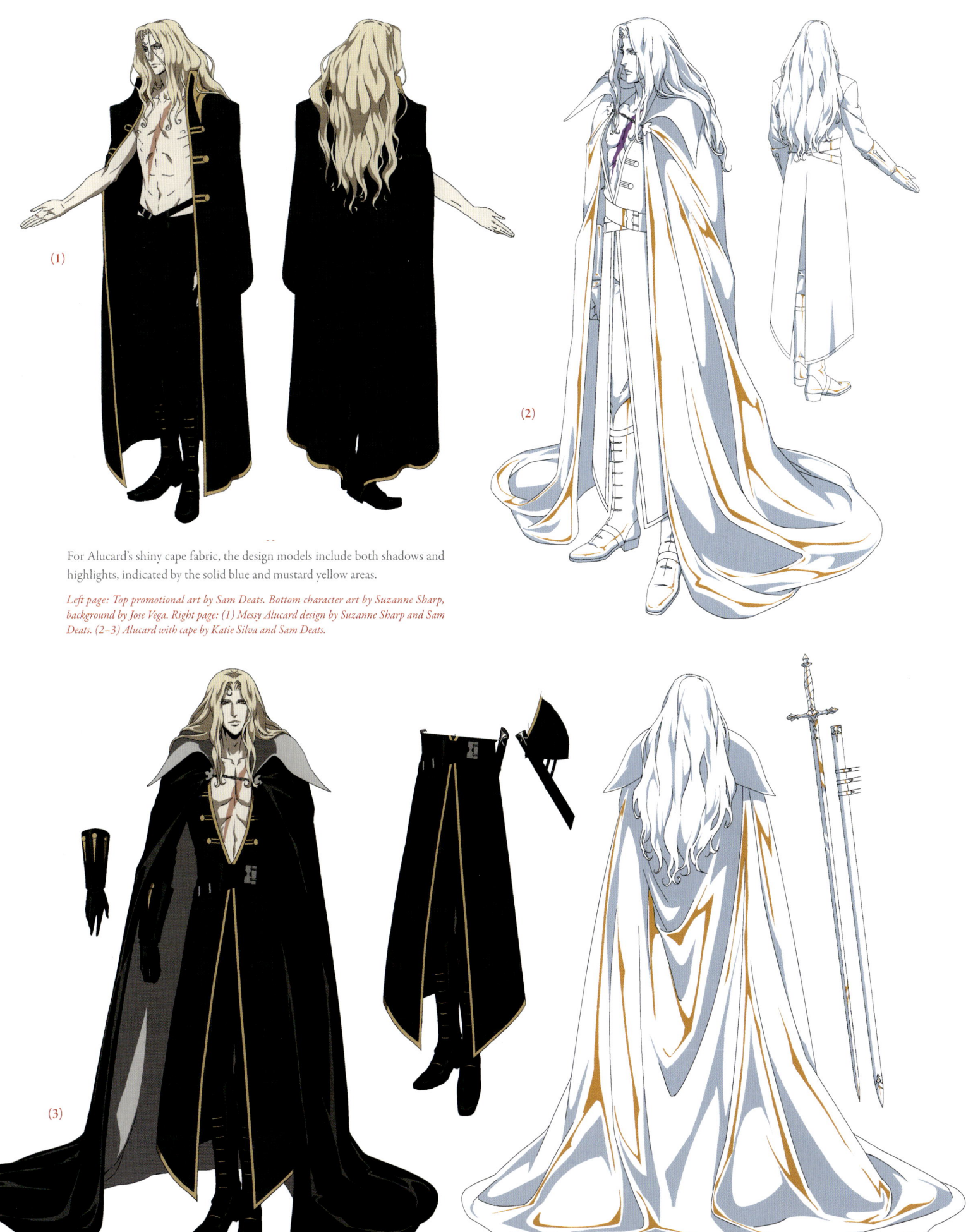

For Alucard's shiny cape fabric, the design models include both shadows and highlights, indicated by the solid blue and mustard yellow areas.

Left page: Top promotional art by Sam Deats. Bottom character art by Suzanne Sharp, background by Jose Vega. Right page: (1) Messy Alucard design by Suzanne Sharp and Sam Deats. (2–3) Alucard with cape by Katie Silva and Sam Deats.

(1)

(2)

(3)

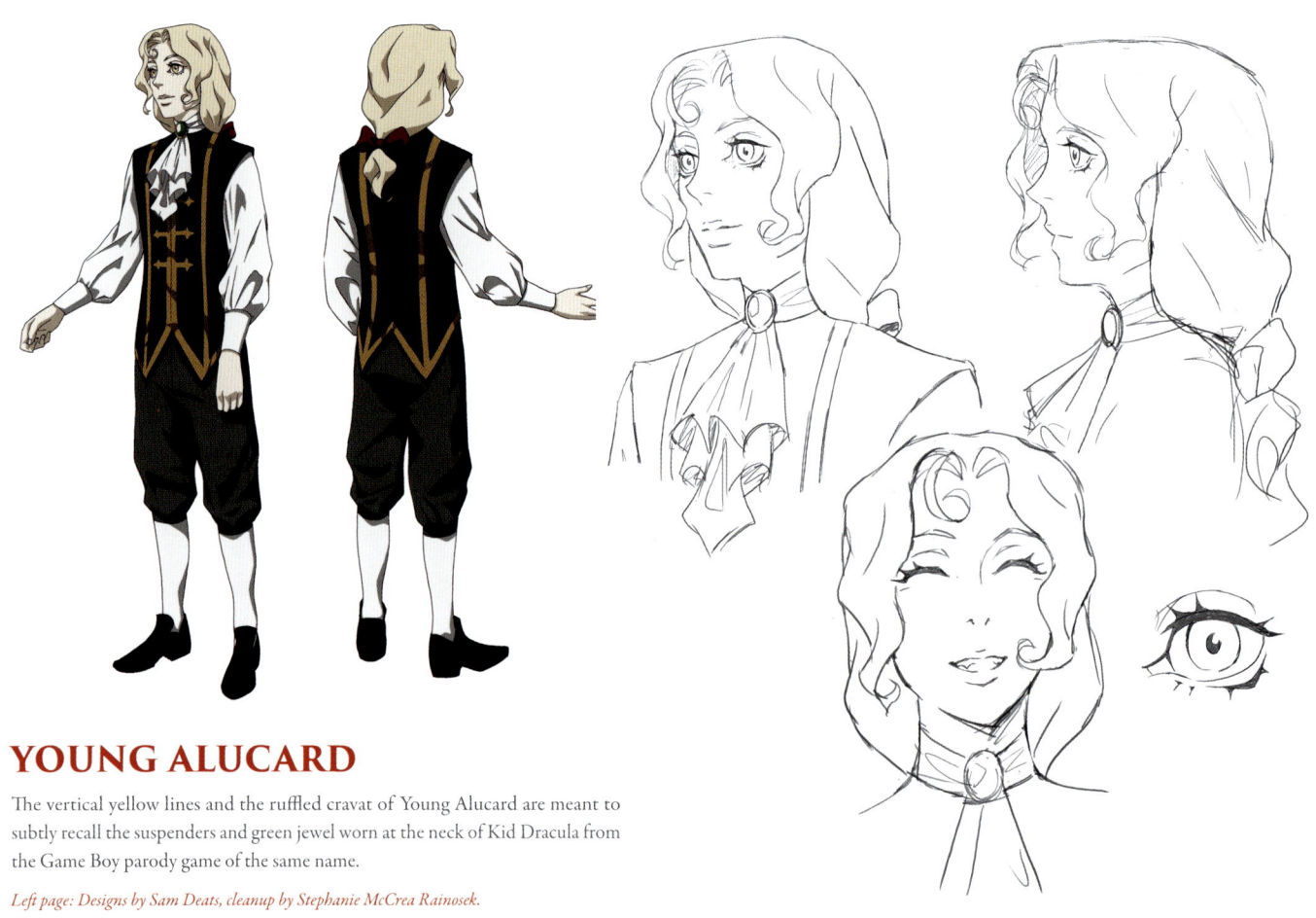

YOUNG ALUCARD

The vertical yellow lines and the ruffled cravat of Young Alucard are meant to subtly recall the suspenders and green jewel worn at the neck of Kid Dracula from the Game Boy parody game of the same name.

Left page: Designs by Sam Deats, cleanup by Stephanie McCrea Rainosek.

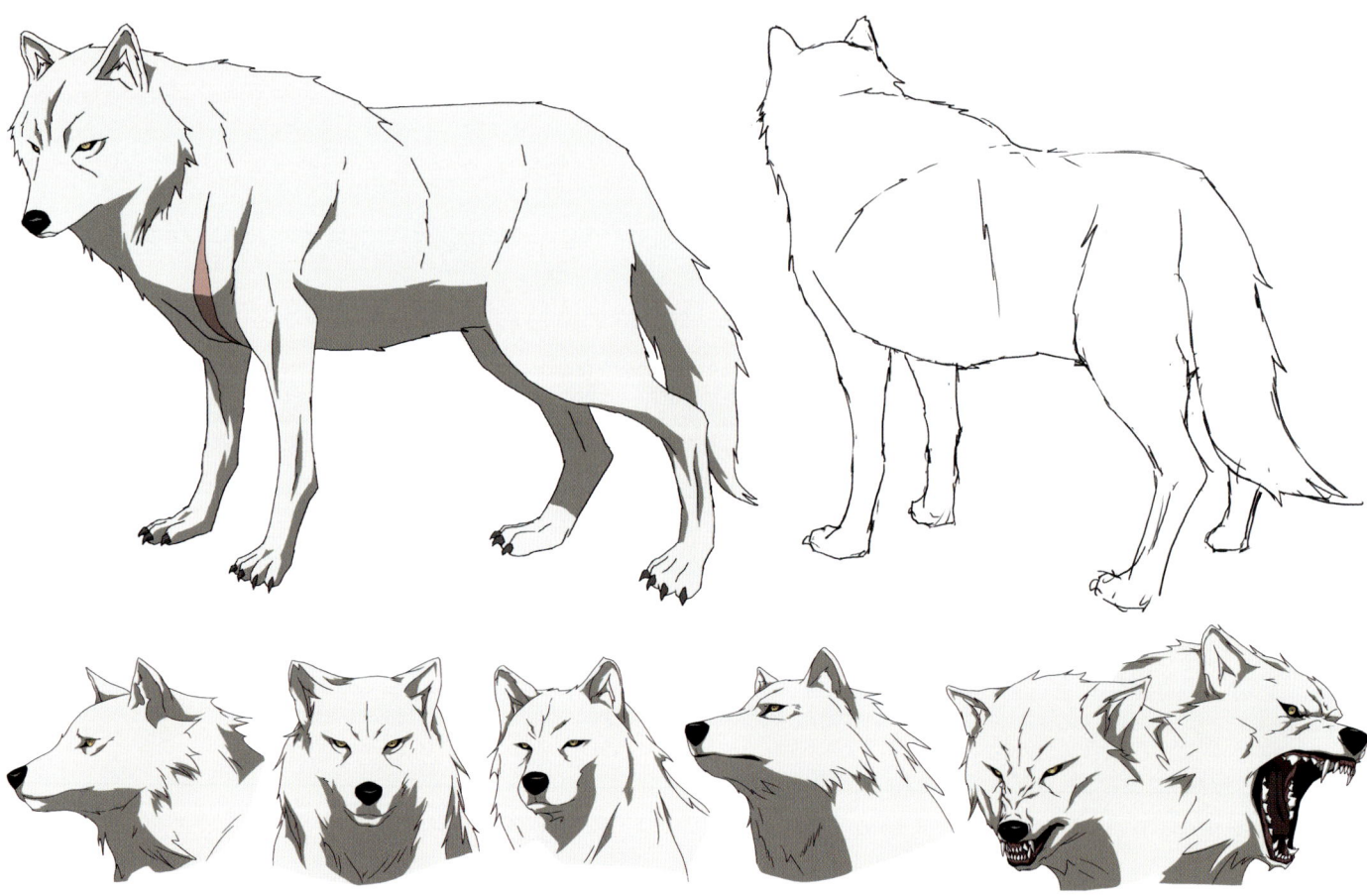

ALUCARD'S WOLF FORM

An internal debate was waged in the studio over whether Alucard's wolf form should also share the color of his golden locks. In reference to the wolf form depicted in *Castlevania: Lords of Shadow*, the white wolf option won out, but it retained his body scars.

Lisa

Lisa, a learned practitioner of medicine and science, as well as Dracula's beloved wife, was accused of witchcraft and burned at the stake. "The eyelashes and eye designs were a big focus for us when we were looking for the touchstone that we could grab and use from the Kojima designs, and we had lots of debates on the amount of eyelash to use and how to draw them." —Kevin Kolde

(1) Season 1 Lisa by Sam Deats. (2) Season 2 Lisa designs by Sam Deats, cleanup by Stephanie McCrea Rainosek.

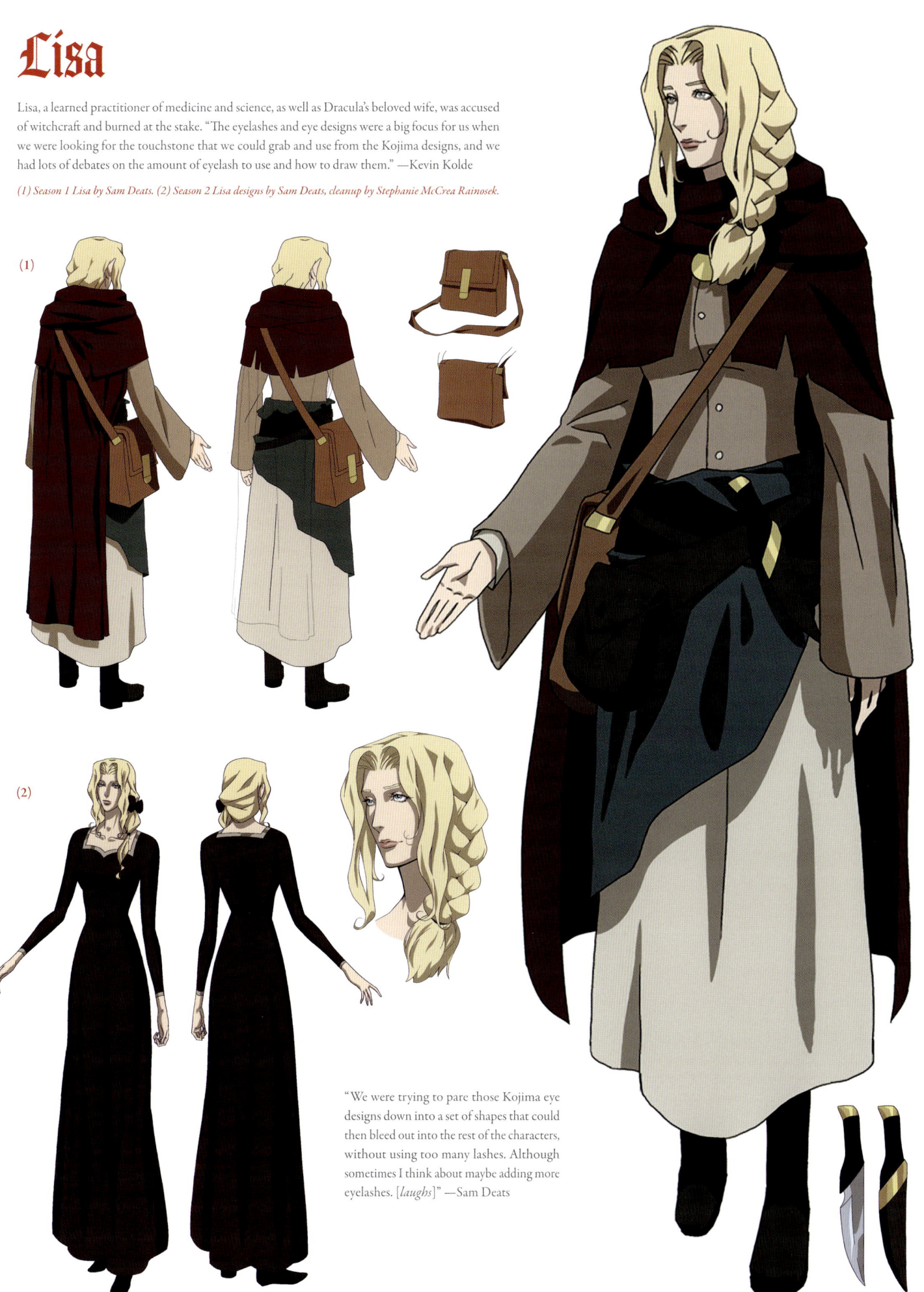

(1)

(2)

"We were trying to pare those Kojima eye designs down into a set of shapes that could then bleed out into the rest of the characters, without using too many lashes. Although sometimes I think about maybe adding more eyelashes. [*laughs*]" —Sam Deats

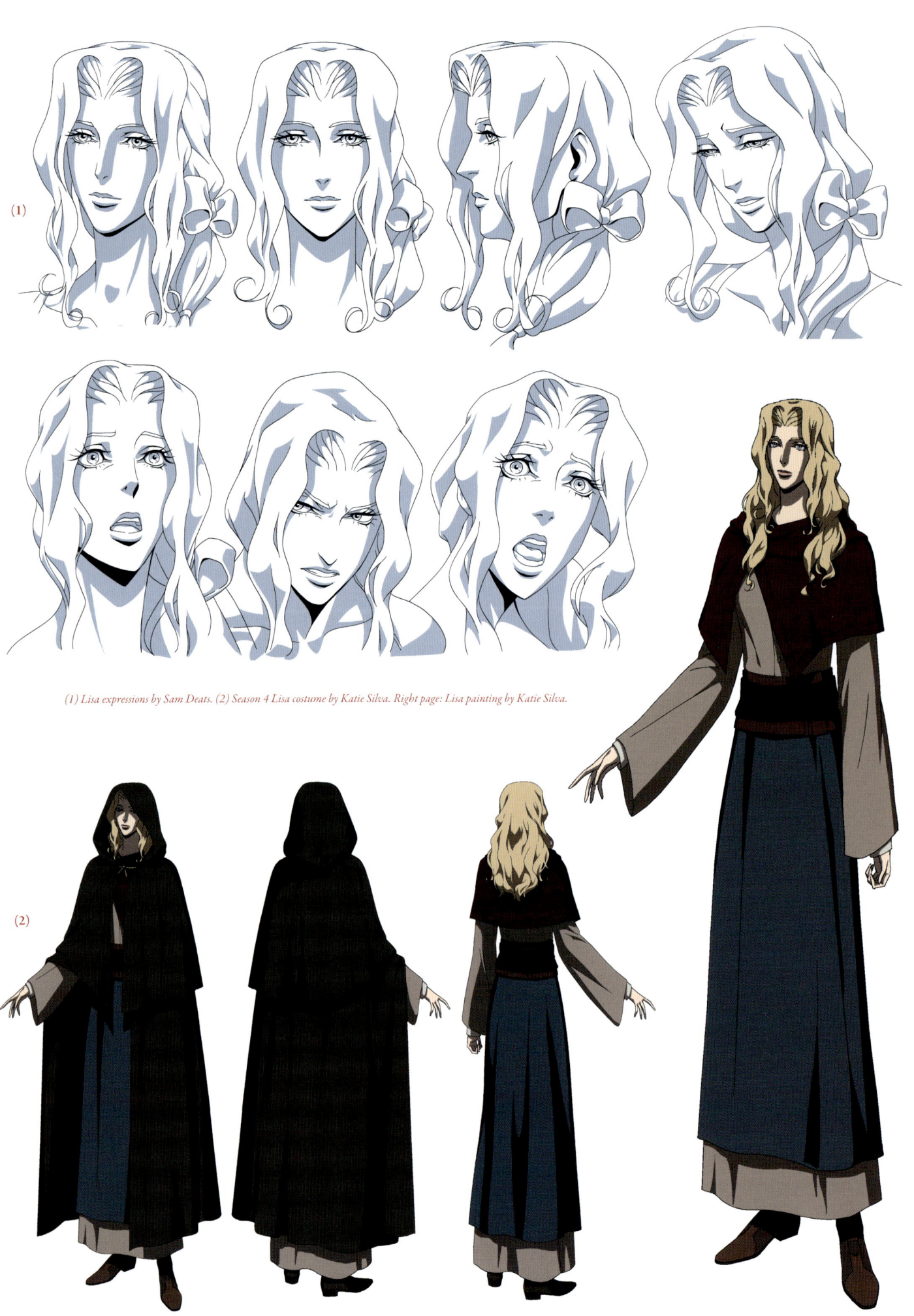

(1) Lisa expressions by Sam Deats. (2) Season 4 Lisa costume by Katie Silva. Right page: Lisa painting by Katie Silva.

(1)

(2)

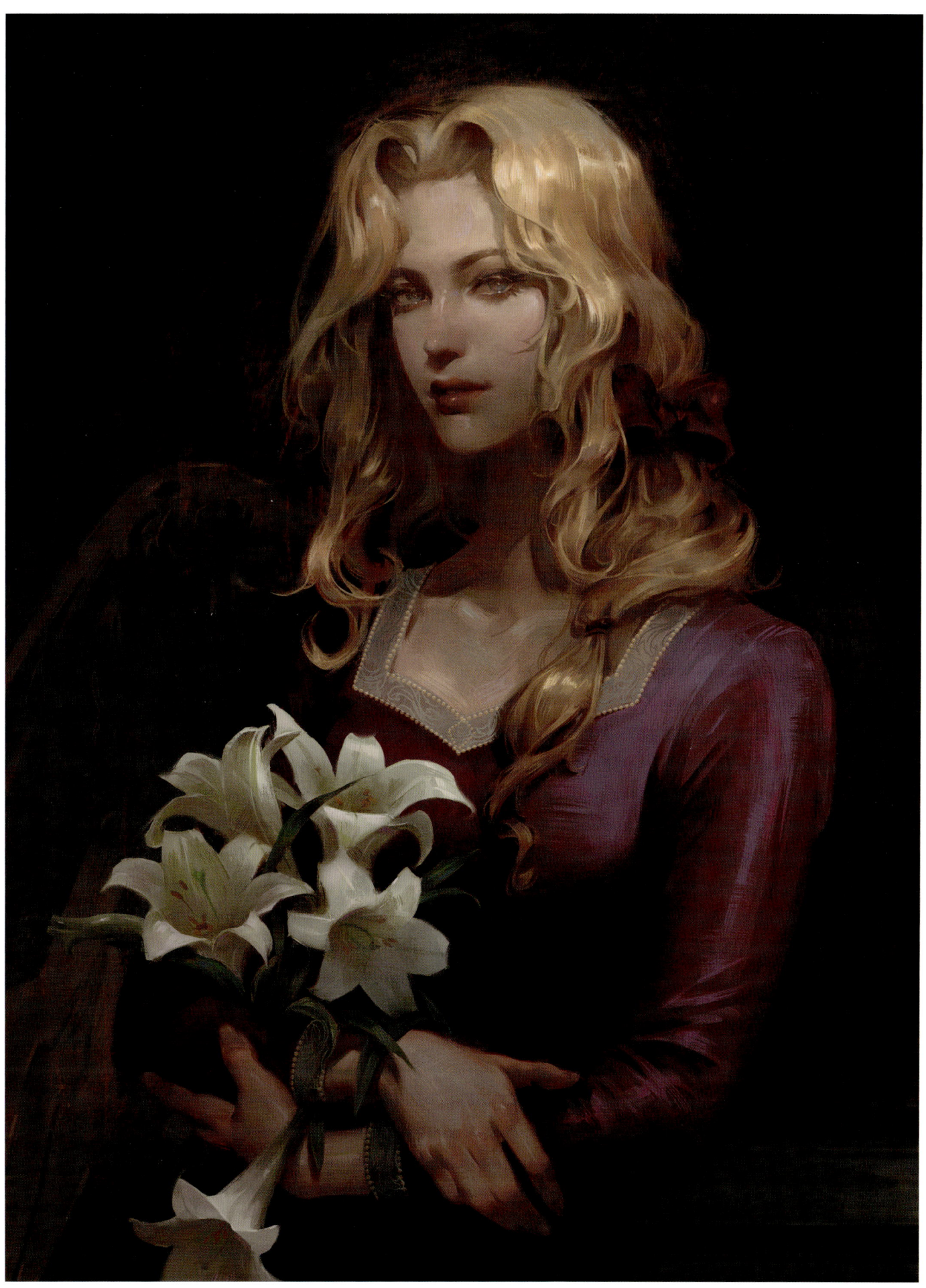

Completed by Katie Silva as a freelance gig while she was still studying charcoal and oil painting at art school, this digital oil painting of Lisa prompted the Powerhouse team to ask her to come work full time as a designer for the series. This initial batch of paintings included Lisa, the Dracula family portrait (page 135), and the portrait of Leon Belmont (page 149).

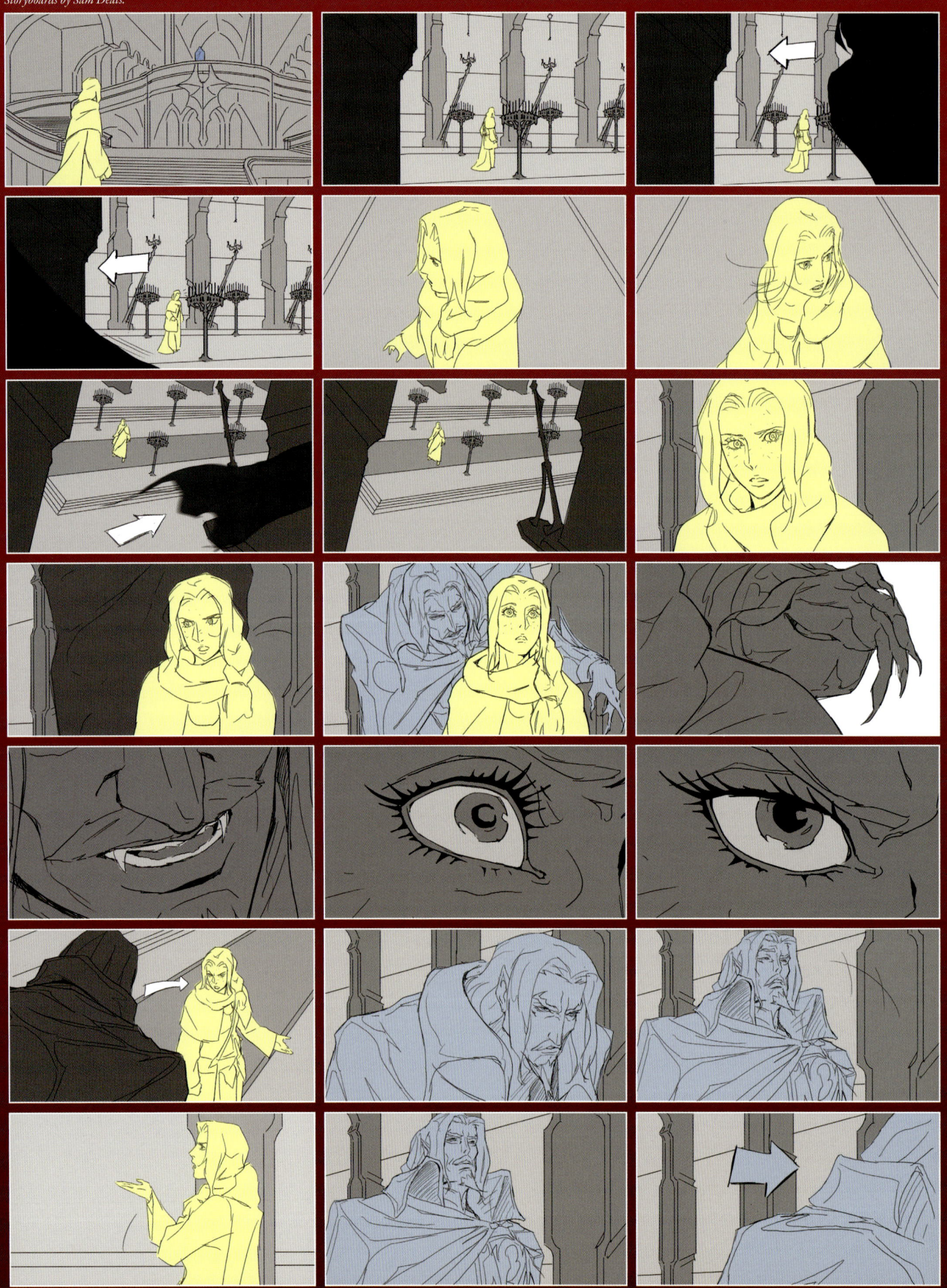

Final storyboards from the first episode on the show include some background layouts placed in from the background crew, depicting Lisa's initial visit to Dracula's castle. The color coding of the characters is to make them visible and differentiate them, which is especially useful when and where boards may become looser than these relatively refined drawings.

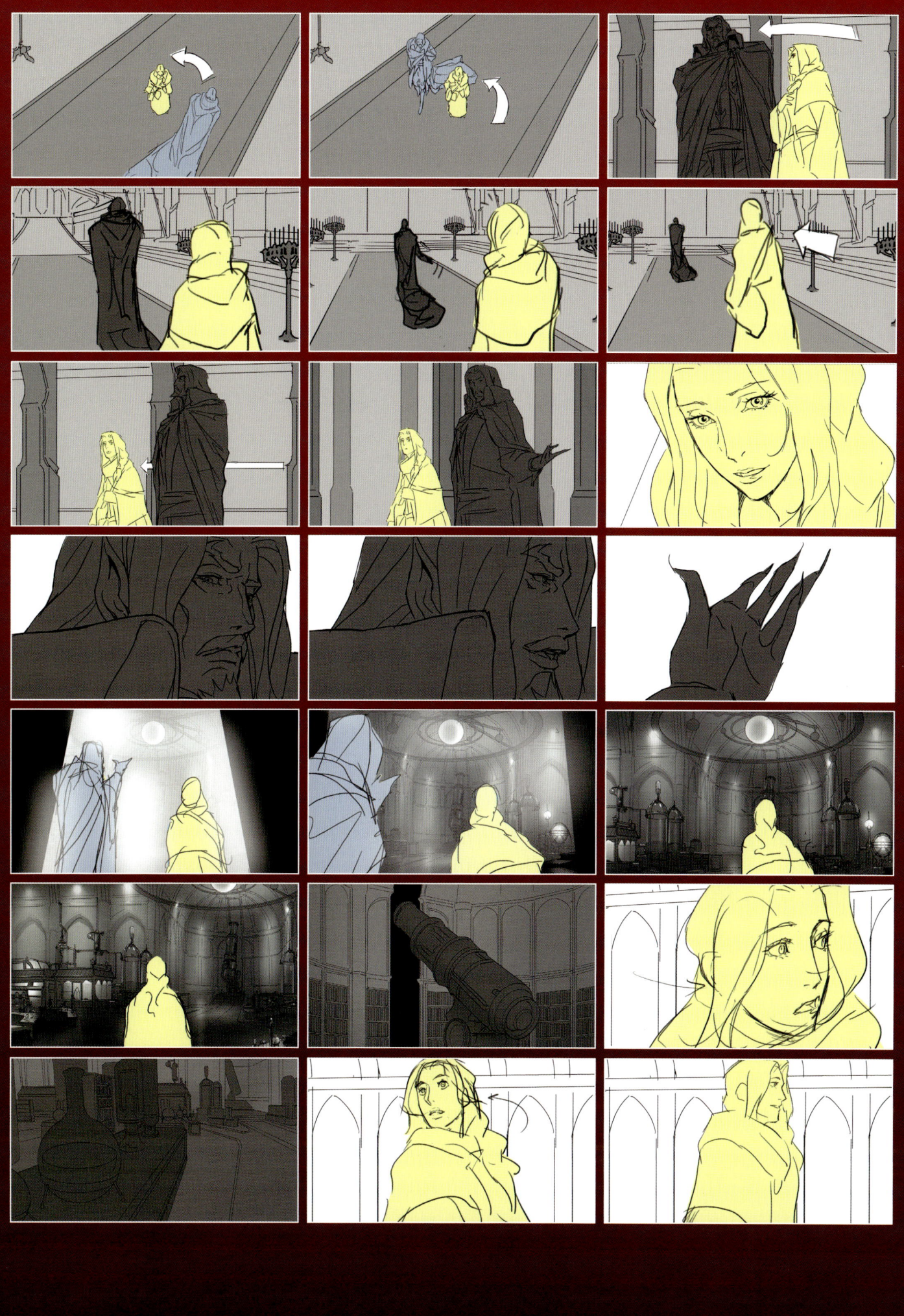

Background Characters

No matter how small their part, each character onscreen needs to be thoughtfully designed with model and expression sheets for the animation team to reference.

Left page: Designs by Sam Deats.

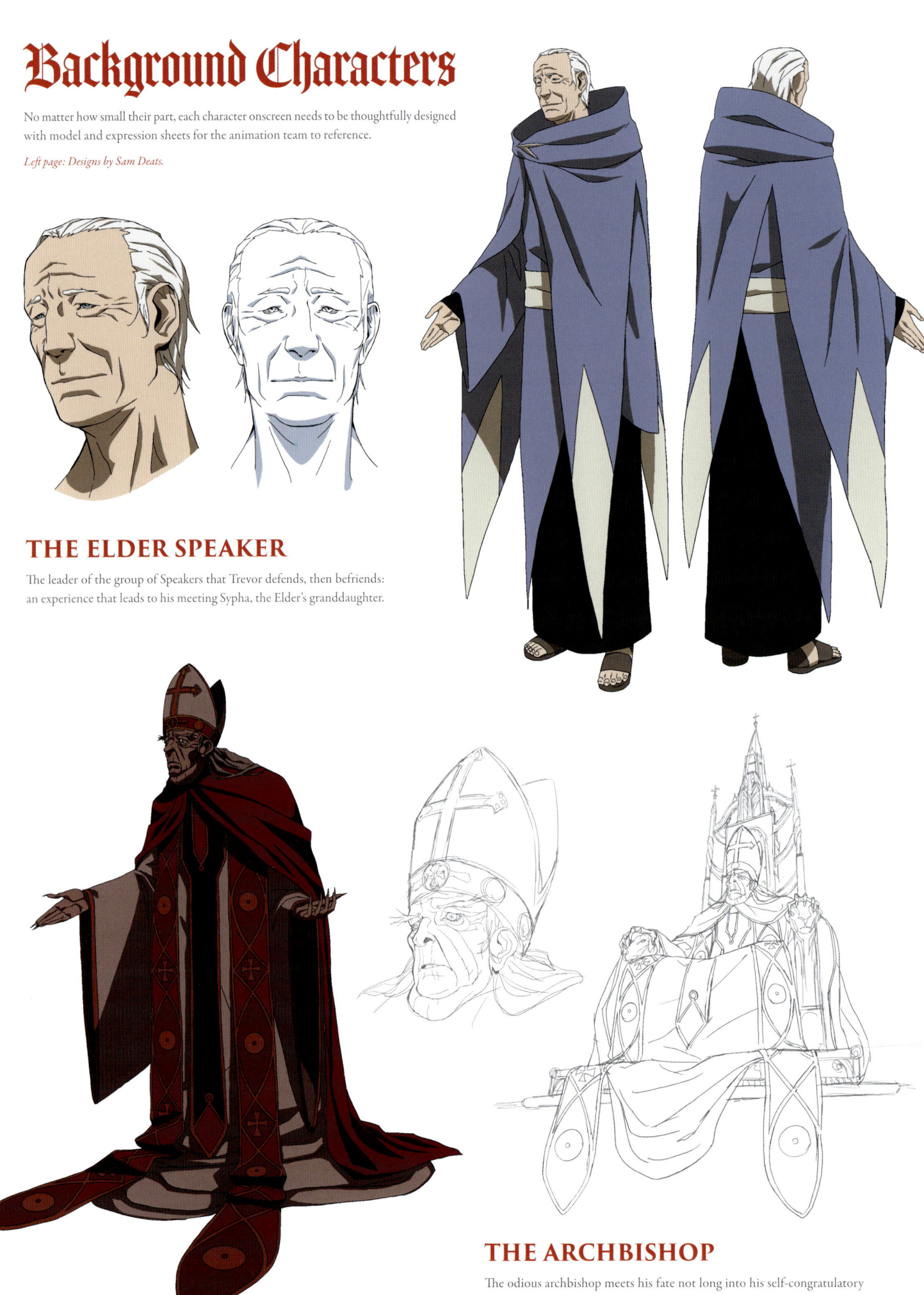

THE ELDER SPEAKER

The leader of the group of Speakers that Trevor defends, then befriends: an experience that leads to his meeting Sypha, the Elder's granddaughter.

THE ARCHBISHOP

The odious archbishop meets his fate not long into his self-congratulatory speech in episode 1 when Dracula destroys Targoviste.

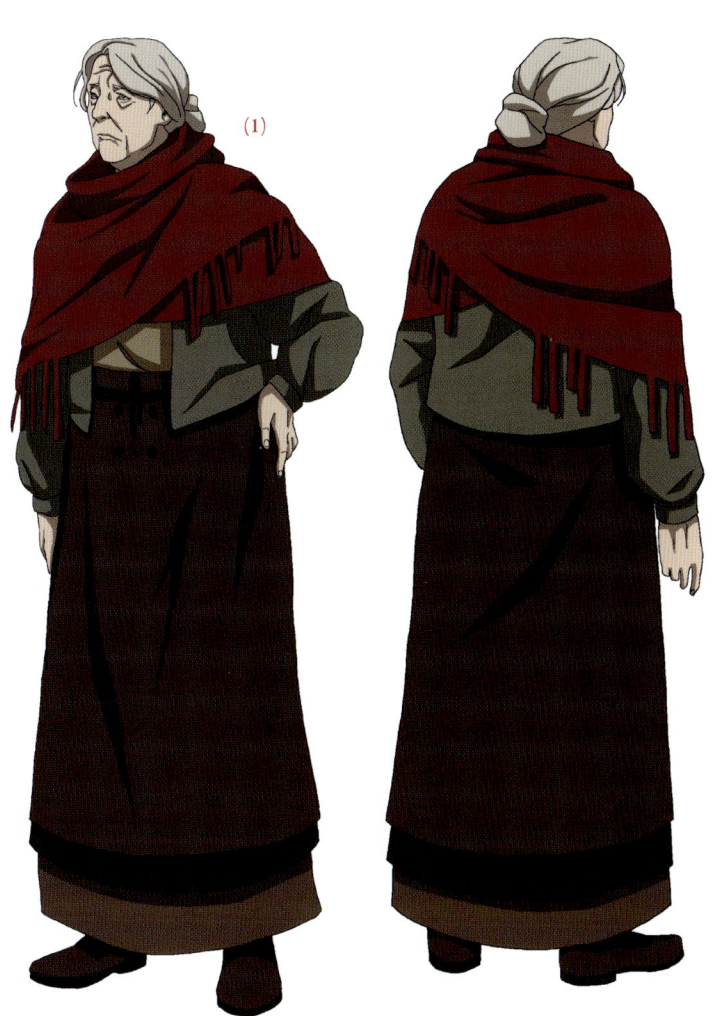

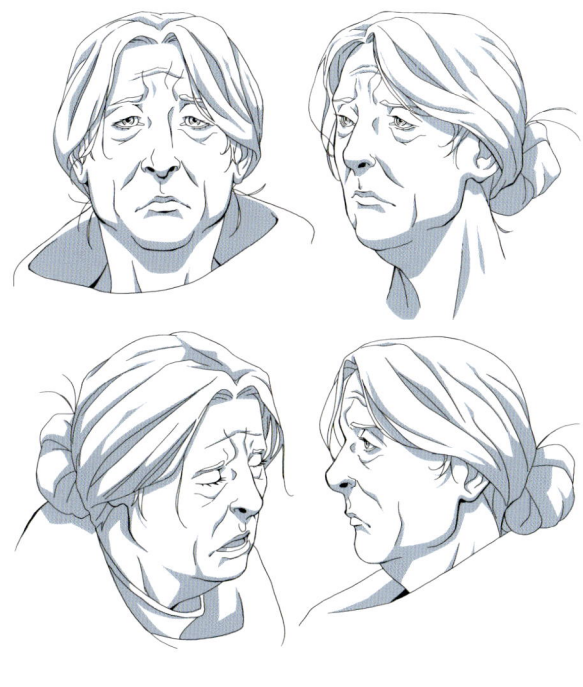

MRS. DJUVARA

Lisa's last patient before the bishop's priest goon squad destroyed her cottage and her life's work, and took her away for execution, was the simple villager Mrs. Djuvara.

(1) Mrs. Djuvara design by Sam Deats. (2) Merchant design by Joanne Wong, cleanup by Ed Booth. (3) Sleazy merchant design by Julia Shi, cleanup by Evgeny Lubaev.

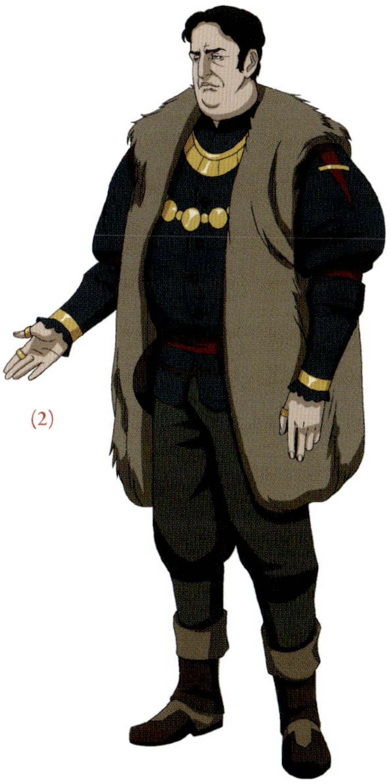

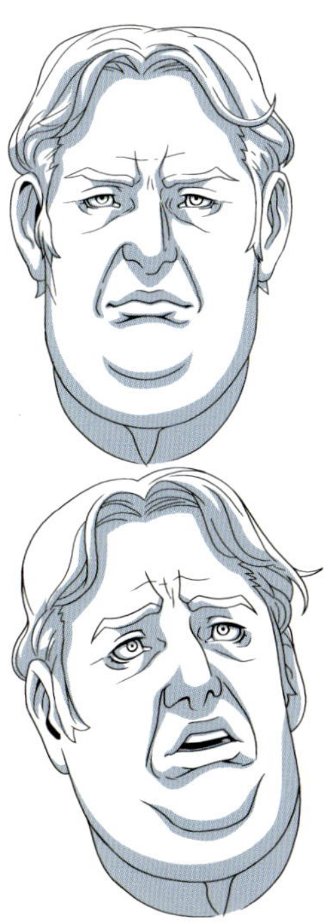

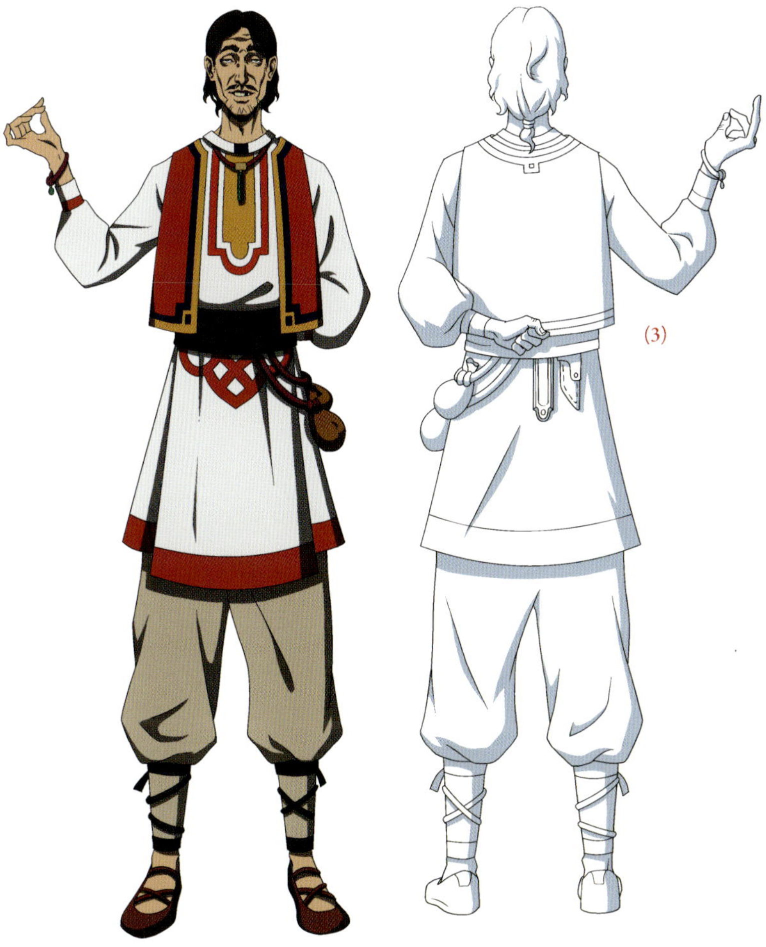

MERCHANTS OF THE LAND

Left: A season 2 merchant design. *Right:* A season 3 sleazy merchant (who extracts the teeth of the dead Wolfman).

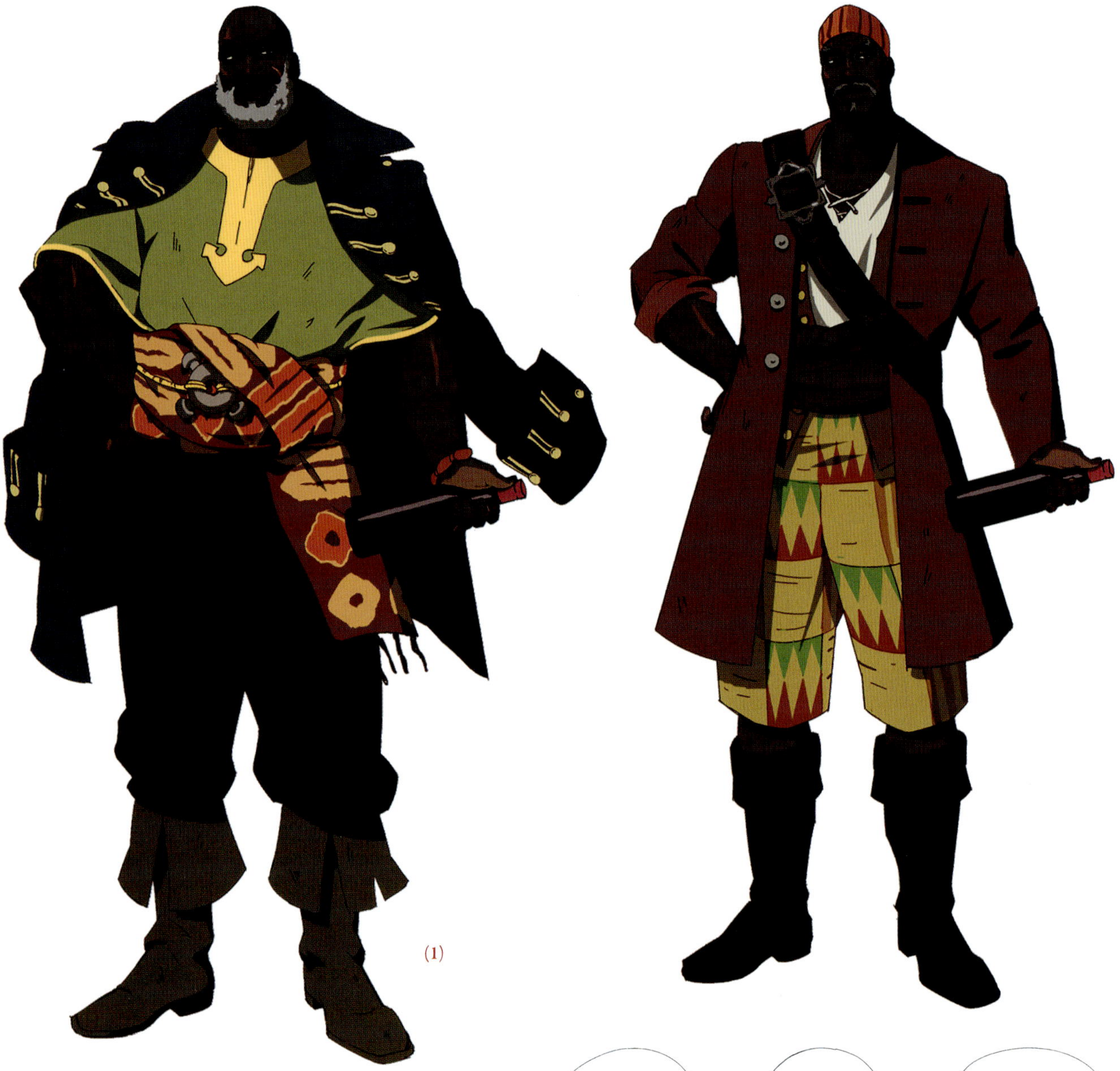

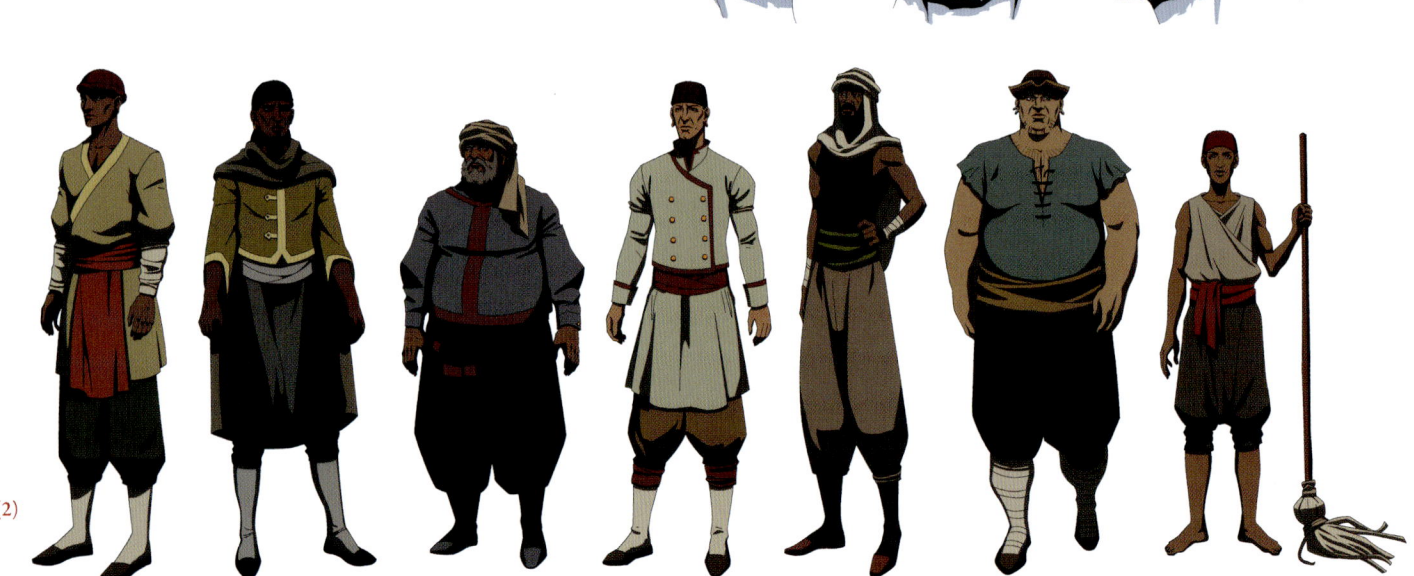

SHIP CAPTAIN

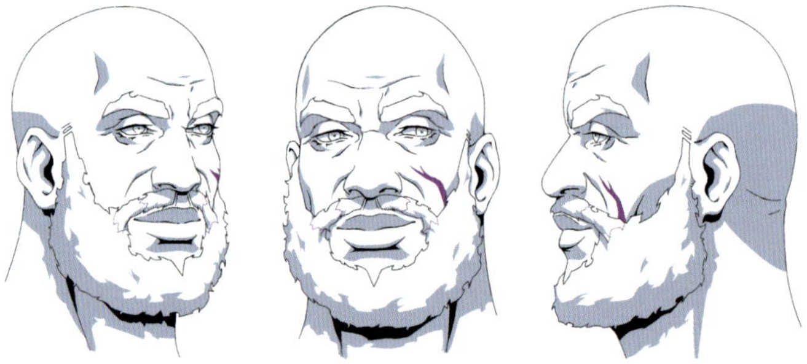

"For reference, I looked at fabrics from the Kru people of Liberia because they have such a strong maritime history. The design on the top right was just another option, but they chose the better captain, on the left!" —Katie Silva

(1) Captain designs and early concept by Katie Silva. (2) Crewmen designs by Evgeny Lubaev, cleanup by Bo Li.

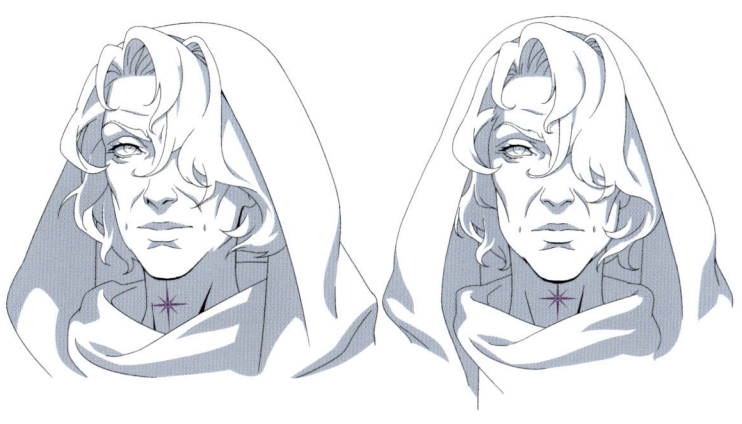

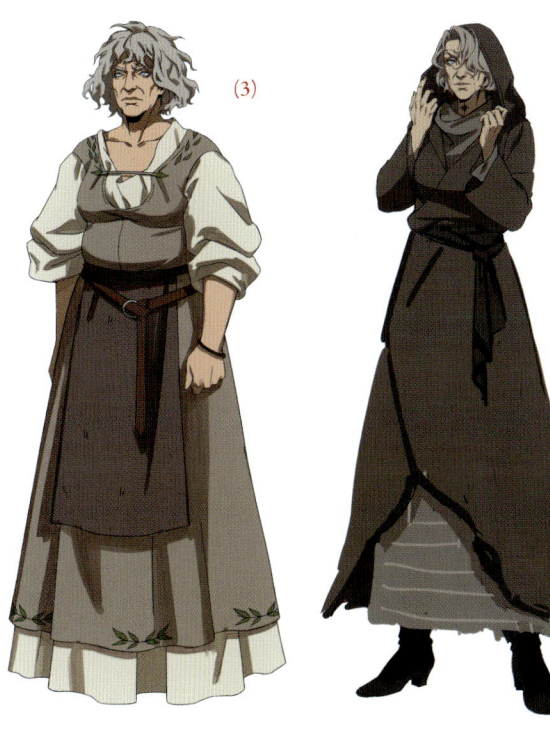

MIRANDA

While most designs were typically completed before casting, the reverse was true for the magician Miranda, and so a request was made for her face to resemble Barbara Steele, her voice actor.

(3) Miranda and shopkeeper designs by Katie Silva. (4) Tunis overseers designs by Evgeny Lubaev, cleanup by Bo Li.

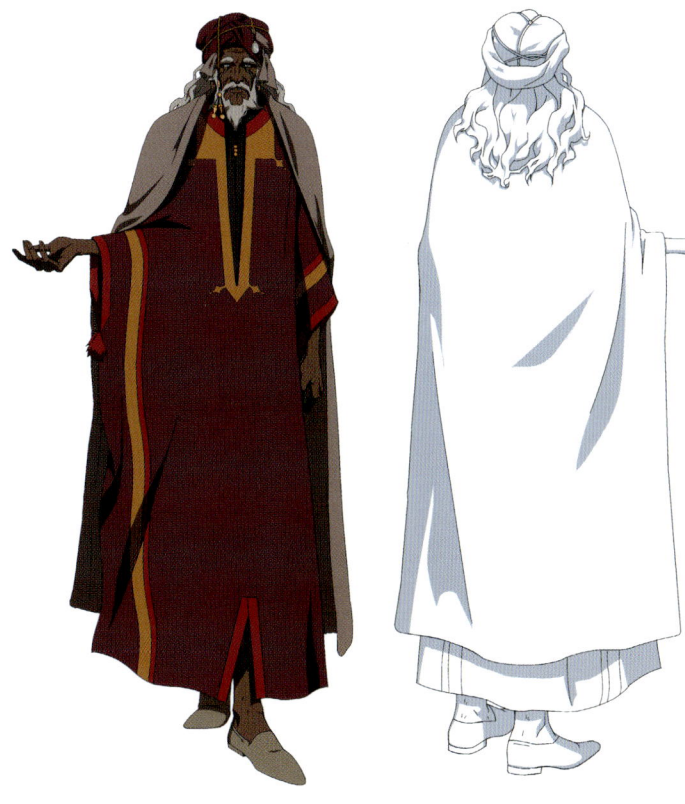

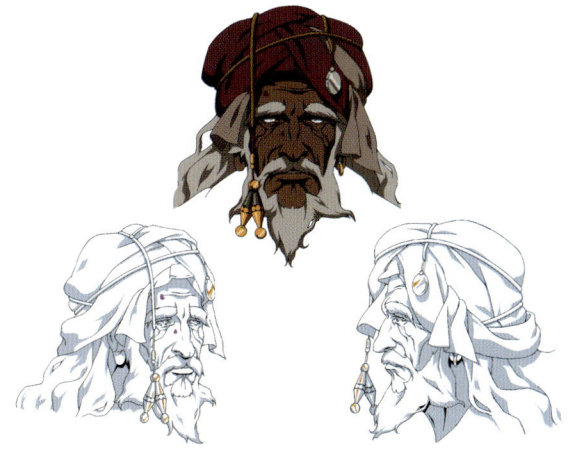

SHOPKEEPER

Blind, but with such a keen sense of smell that he can identify a forgemaster by scent alone, the Tunis shopkeeper, a purveyor of occult items and weapons, wisely aids Isaac by giving him a magic mirror that reveals Hector's whereabouts: Carmilla's castle in Styria. Isaac uses this important information on his quest to avenge Dracula's murder, and the shopkeeper remains alive and uneaten by Isaac's horde of night creatures, who are patiently waiting just outside.

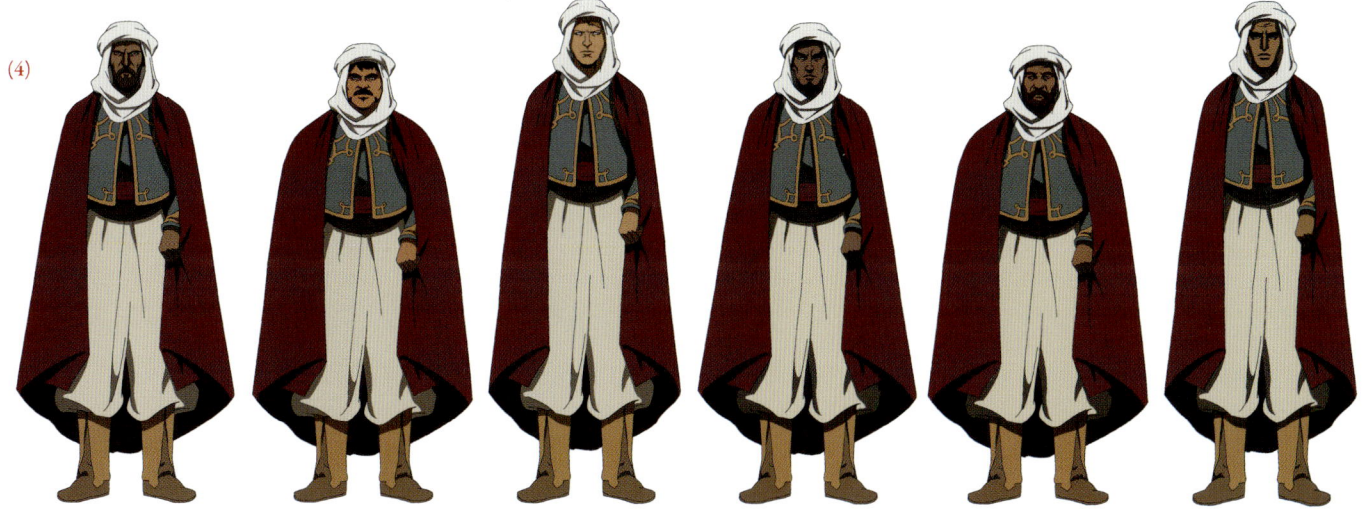

SAINT GERMAIN

A curious, secretly magical man whose mission to find his lost love through the Infinite Corridor intertwines with Trevor and Sypha's demon-hunting prerogative. "His outfit has a combination of Shakespearean and Tudor references, and his cloak has the drab green color of an old black garment that's been washed and worn for a long time. His hair is the color that it was in the games, but he's got more facial hair now to show that this is an older version of him. He's not put himself together neatly; he's not really trying too hard!" —Katie Silva

All art on these pages by Katie Silva.

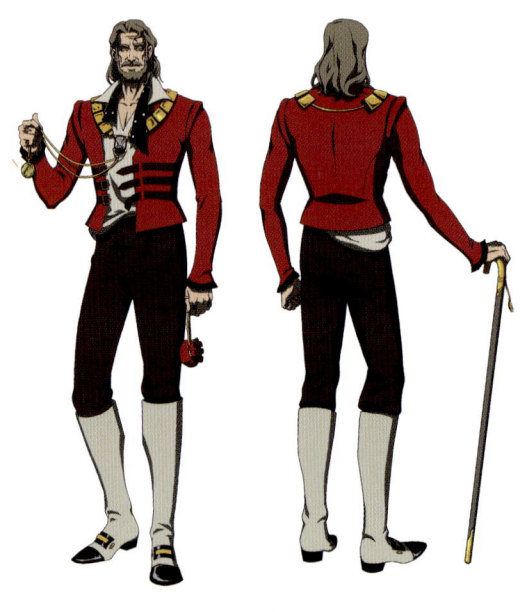

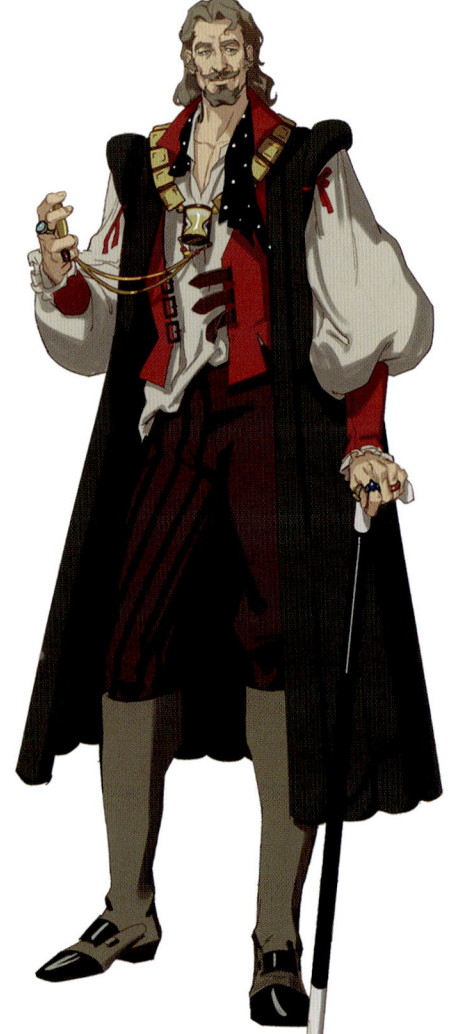

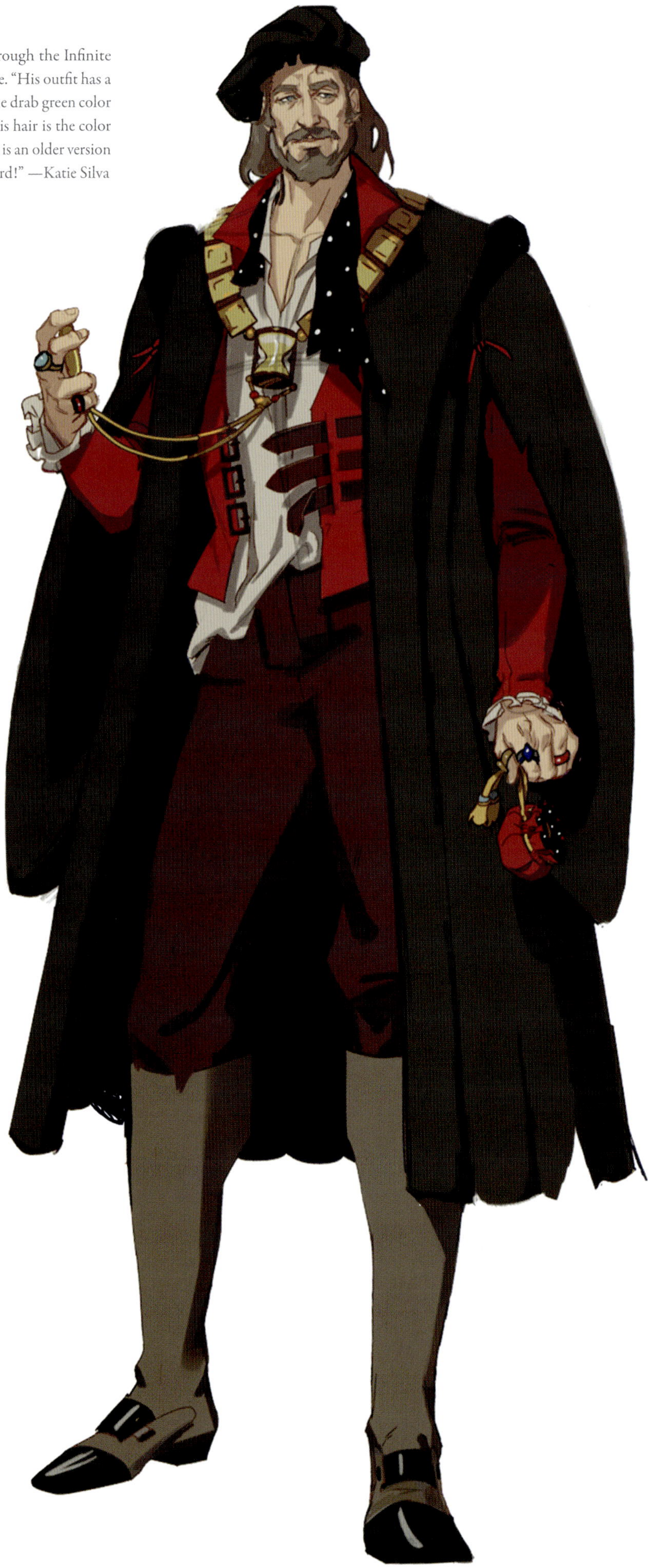

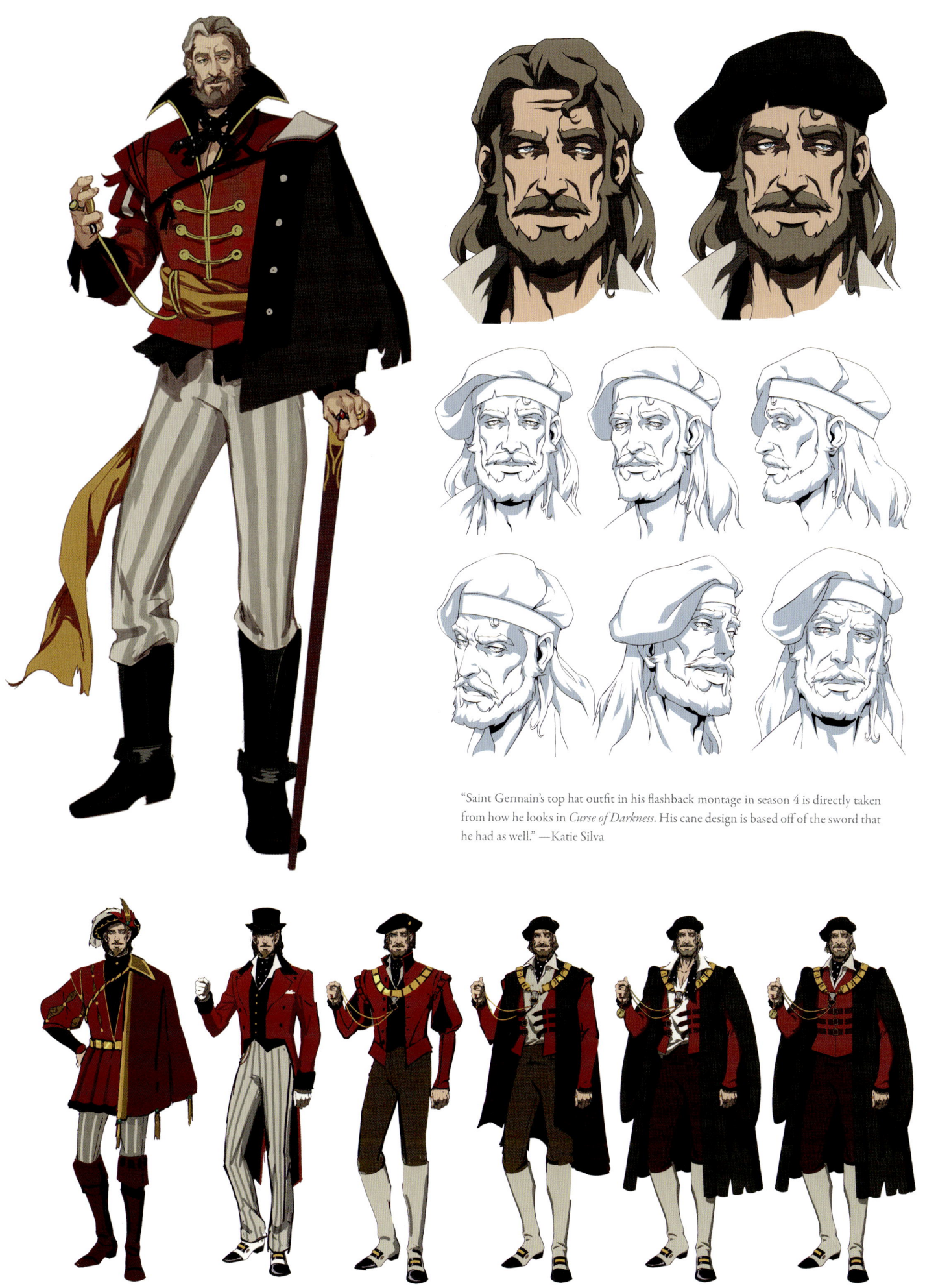

"Saint Germain's top hat outfit in his flashback montage in season 4 is directly taken from how he looks in *Curse of Darkness*. His cane design is based off of the sword that he had as well." —Katie Silva

SUMI

The designs here are based on research of the Sengoku period in Japanese history. Sumi wears a straw rain cape. The bottom row of this spread includes imperial court guard outfits with an original symbol created for Cho's court.

All art on these pages by Katie Silva.

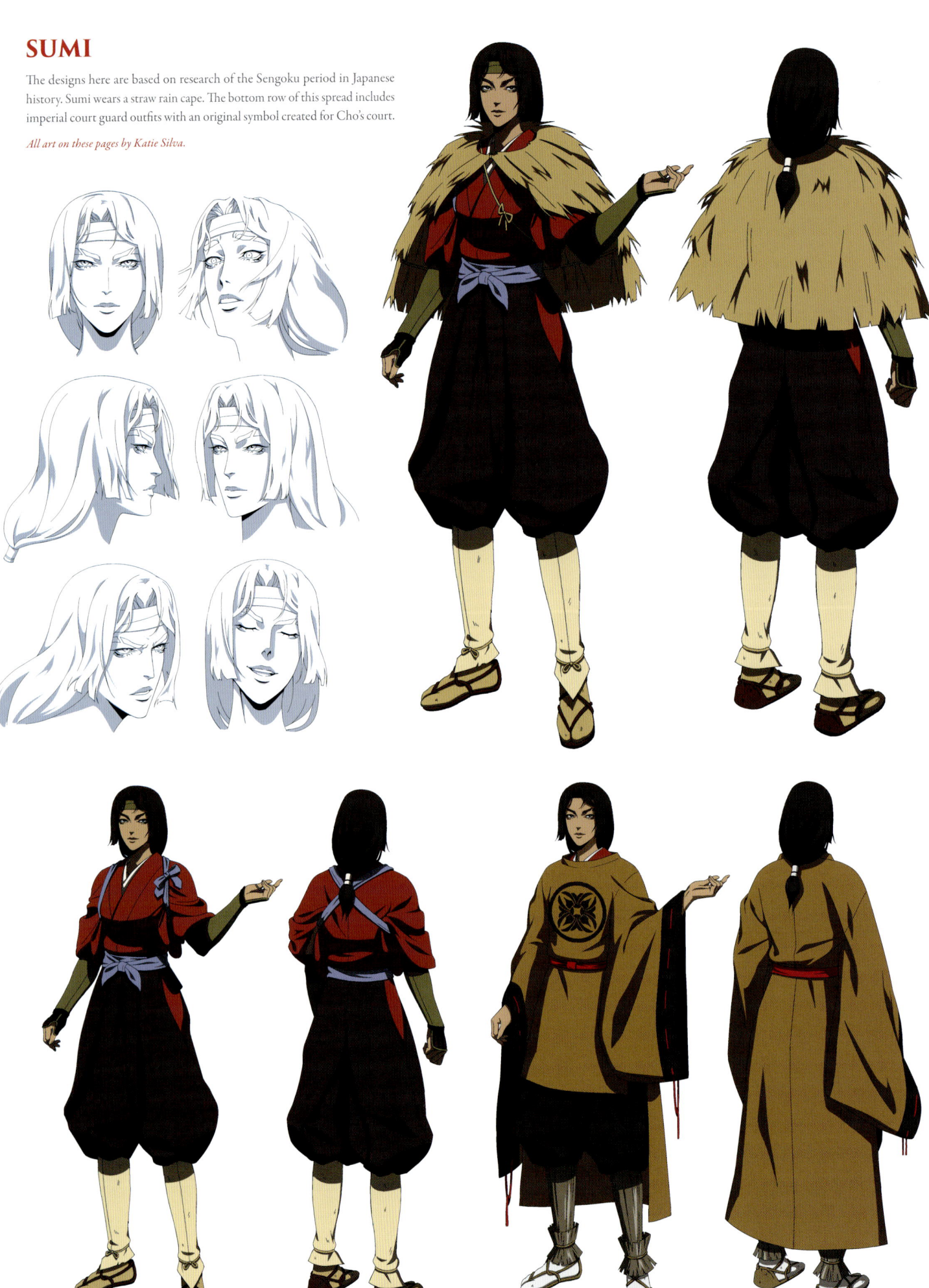

TAKA

Taka sports a deer hide worn for horseback archery. Perhaps because of their youthful naiveté, Sumi and Taka both meet an unfortunate end after their attempt to trick the immortal Alucard. "Taka and Sumi were very, very vaguely supposed to mirror Trevor and Sypha thematically. Katie designed Sumi's sash with Sypha blue and made Taka's hair messy as a visual touch in this direction." —Adam Deats

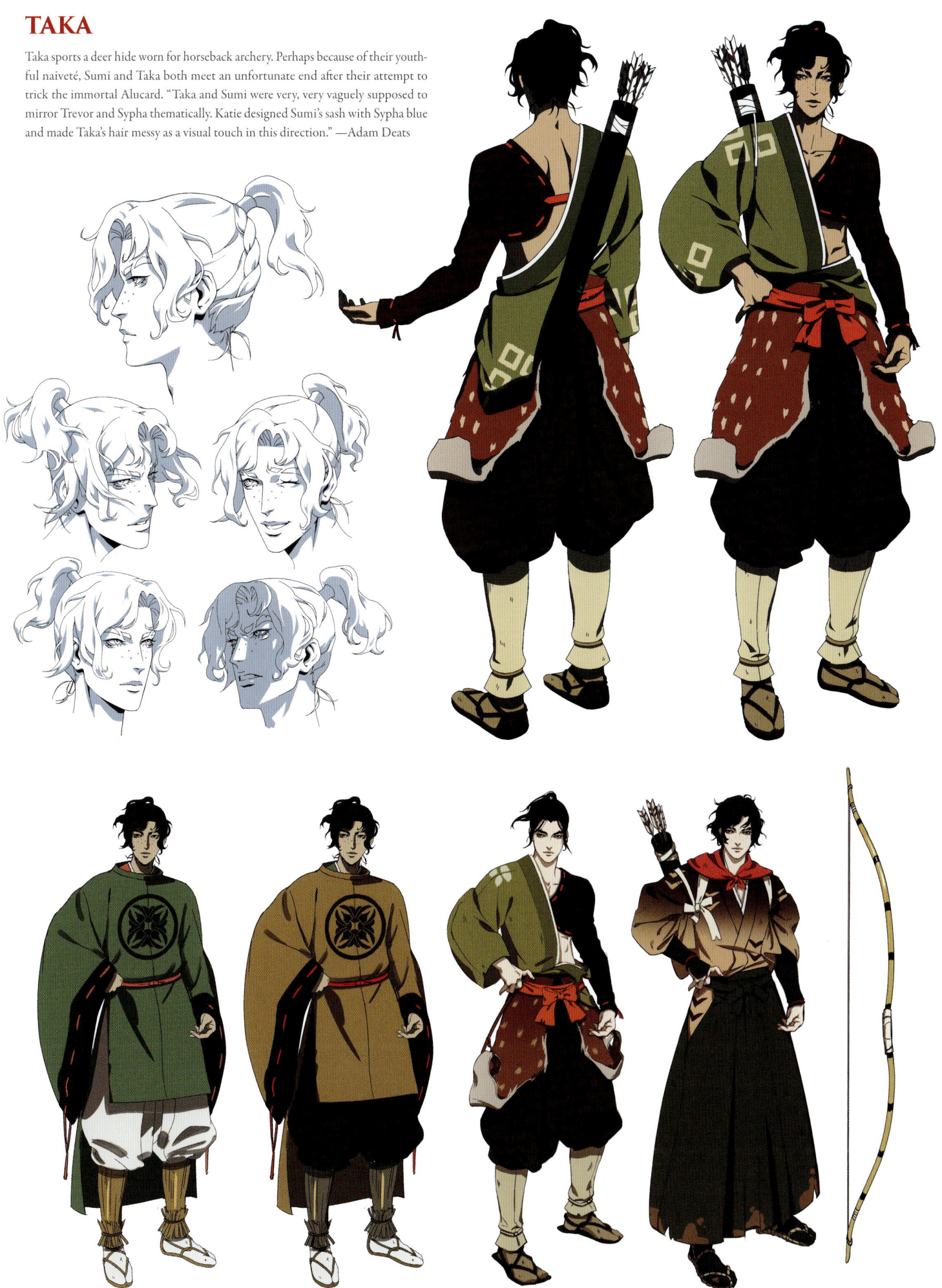

GRETA

"Sometimes I'll get stuck in my head on a design, and it's one of the reasons that it's really great to work alongside a team. My two Greta designs on the top left played with layering of fabrics and details. Lina Ngo's version, which ended up being the design picked, went with an outfit more geared toward Greta's combat animation in season 4's battle scenes. By having multiple artists involved in the early design process we're able to bring a few options to the producers and discuss from there." —Katie Silva

(1) Greta early concepts by Katie Silva. (2) Greta final design and expressions by Lina Ngo, cleanup by Katie Silva and Lina Ngo.

(1)

(2)

ZAMFIR

"Zamfir is the leader of the warriors of Targoviste who have been fighting against the night creatures that Dracula unleashed in season 1. She was designed by Lina Ngo, and her belt pattern is inspired by a Romanian embroidery symbol called the Eye, which means protection." —Katie Silva

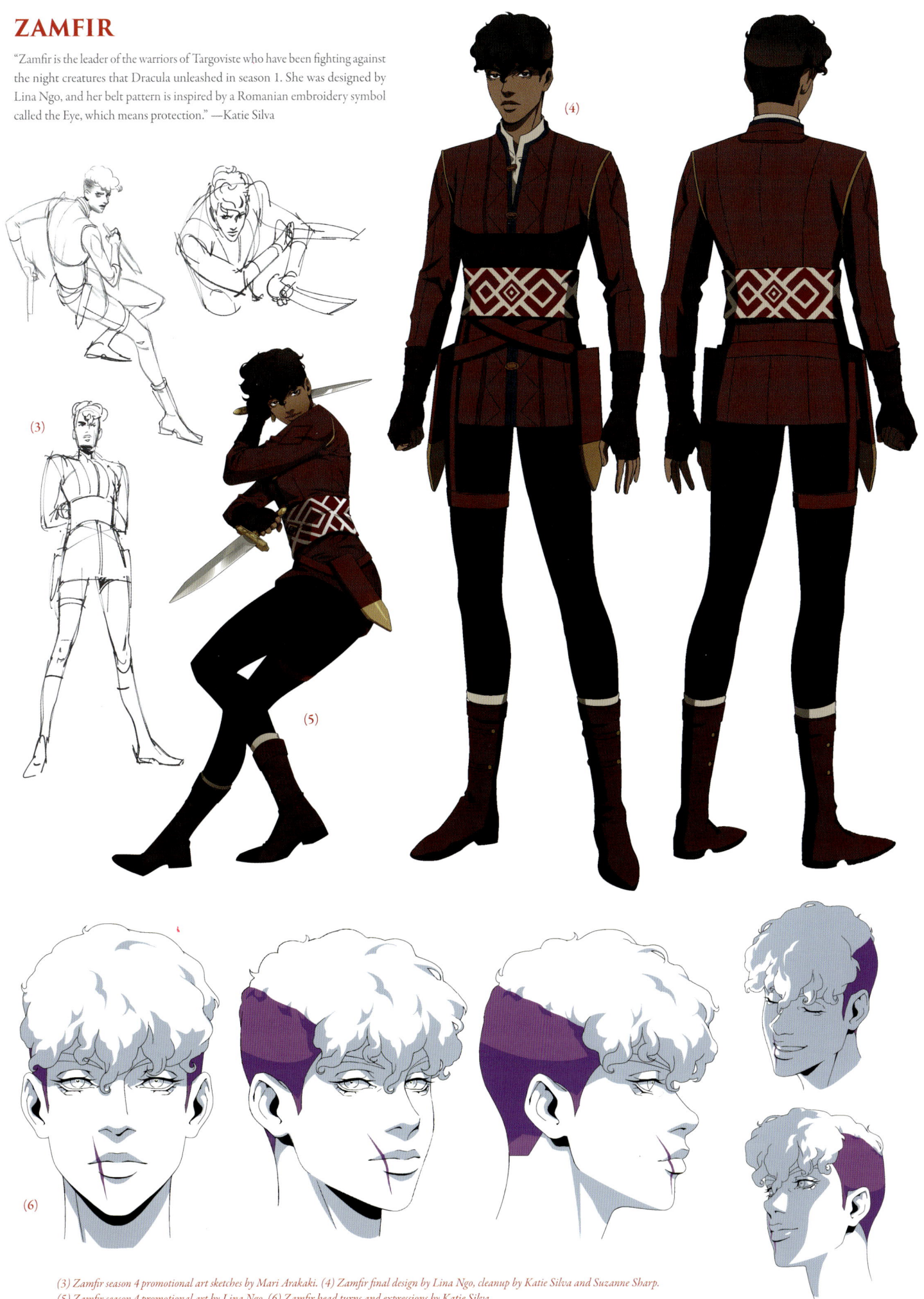

(3) Zamfir season 4 promotional art sketches by Mari Arakaki. (4) Zamfir final design by Lina Ngo, cleanup by Katie Silva and Suzanne Sharp.
(5) Zamfir season 4 promotional art by Lina Ngo. (6) Zamfir head turns and expressions by Katie Silva.

THE WIZARD

The wizard's coat of many coats was meant to give him the appearance of a poser king, with the trappings and symbols of royalty gained only through magical treachery.

"The wizard was specifically described in the design brief as having an ermine cape—but what we ended up with looks like a big strawberry candy to me." —Lina Ngo

(1) Wizard design by Lina Ngo.

(1)

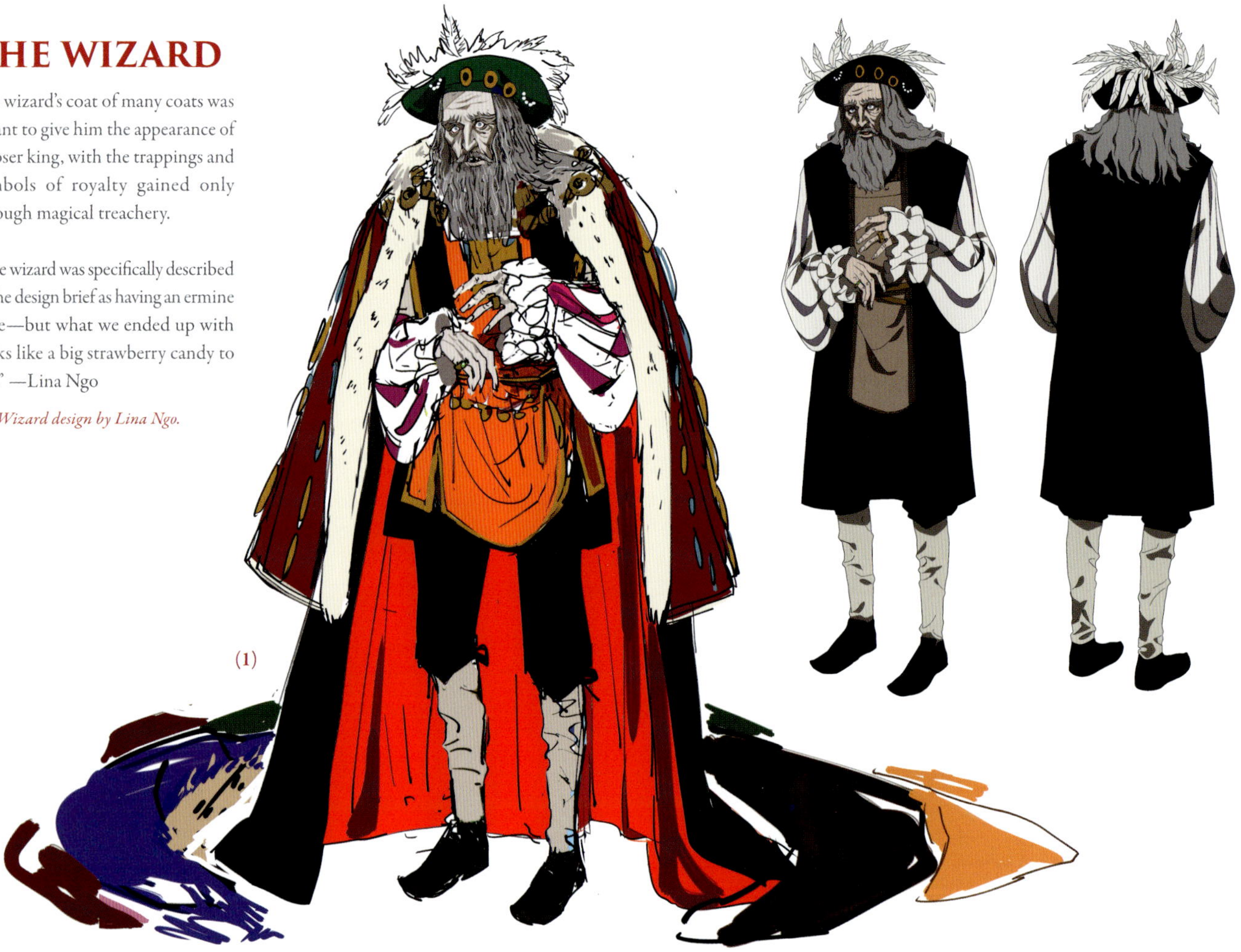

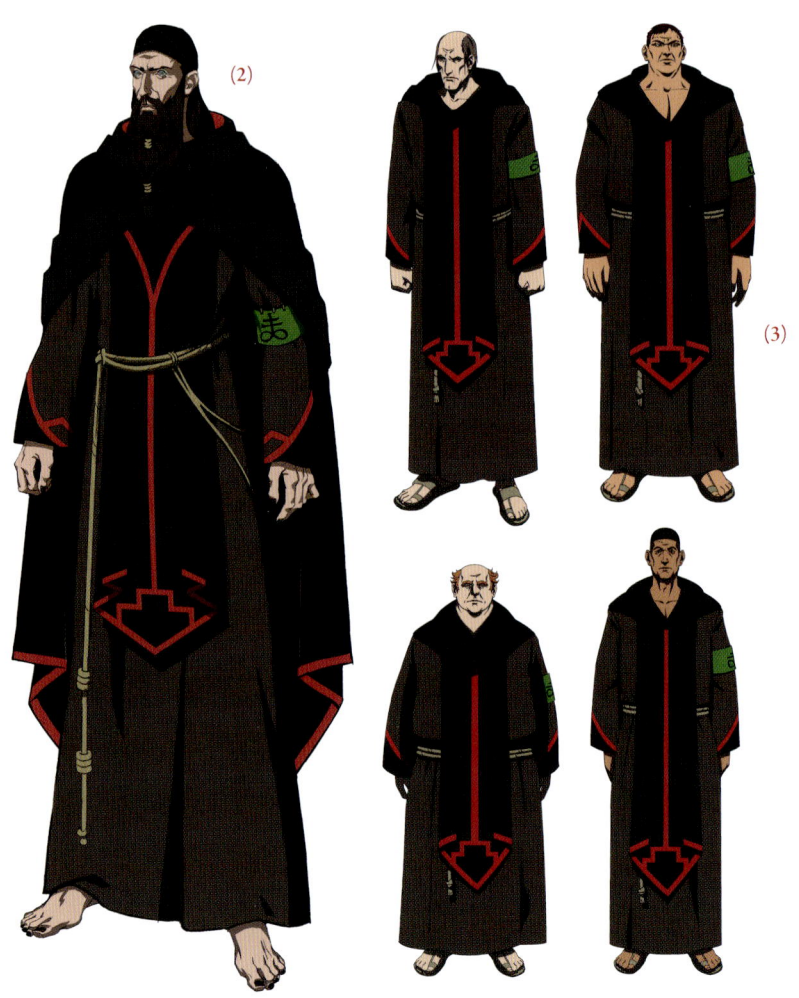

(2)

(3)

SALA & THE CULTISTS

"Sala's huge anime eyes were there to give him the look of that kind of old Byzantine painting that stares into your soul. His design also has a bunch of intentional tangents in the clothing to get that old medieval icon painting feel. You don't want this guy looking at you. He's my absolute favorite to draw!" —Katie Silva

(2) Sala design by Katie Silva. (3) Sala's monks designs by Evgeny Lubaev, cleanup by Bo Li.

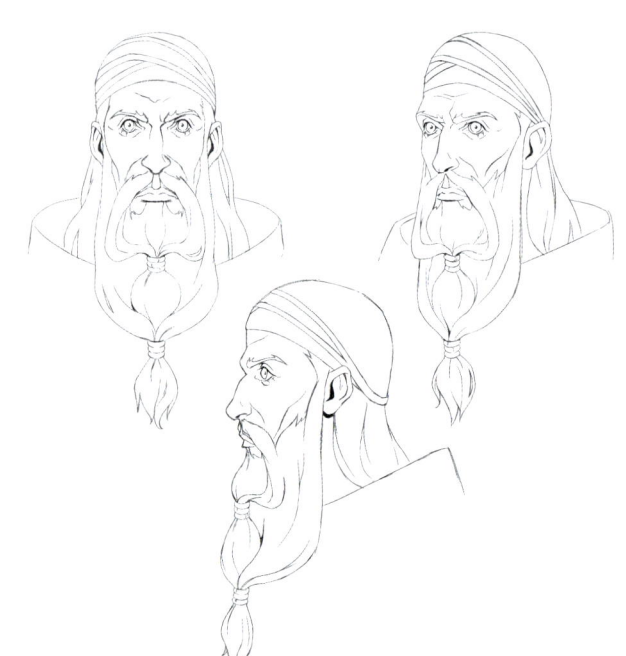

ADVENTURER LADY

Design briefs for the adventurer lady requested that she have a Katharine Hepburn / Indiana Jones–type aura, in a Tudor-era costume with anachronistic flourishes.

(4) Adventurer Lady design and (5) early concepts by Katie Silva.

(4)

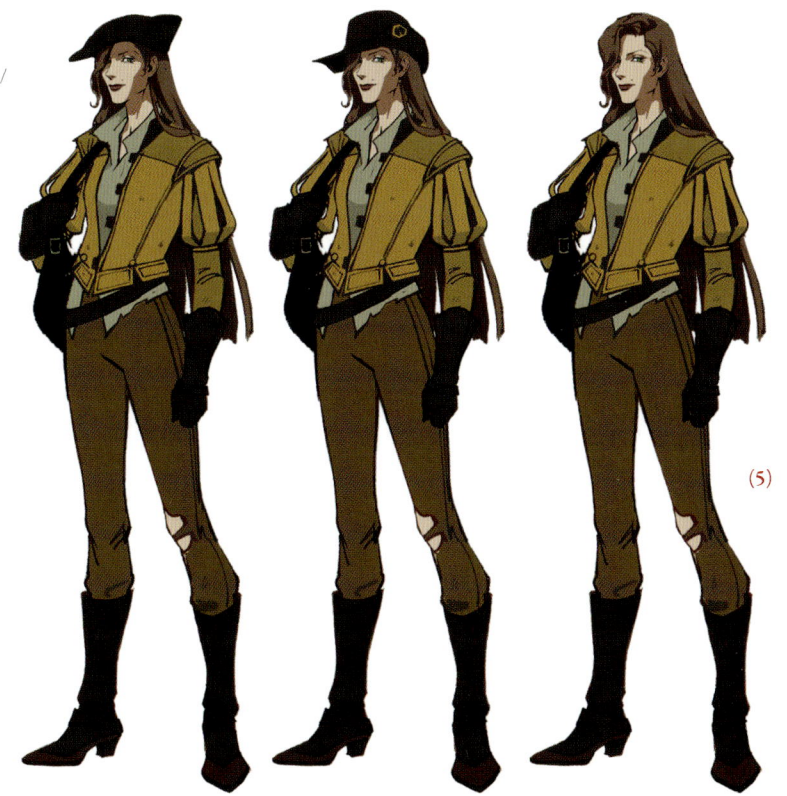

(5)

THE ALCHEMIST

The key necklace, used to open a portal to the Infinite Corridor, includes symbols that are a visual nod to the portal device in *Symphony of the Night* that opens a portal with a visual flavor similar to the Infinite Corridor.

(6) Alchemist early concepts and (7) final design by Lina Ngo.

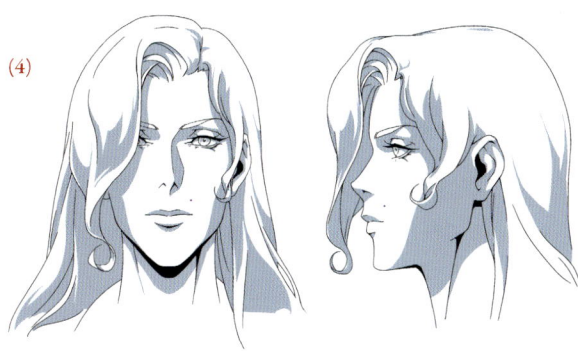

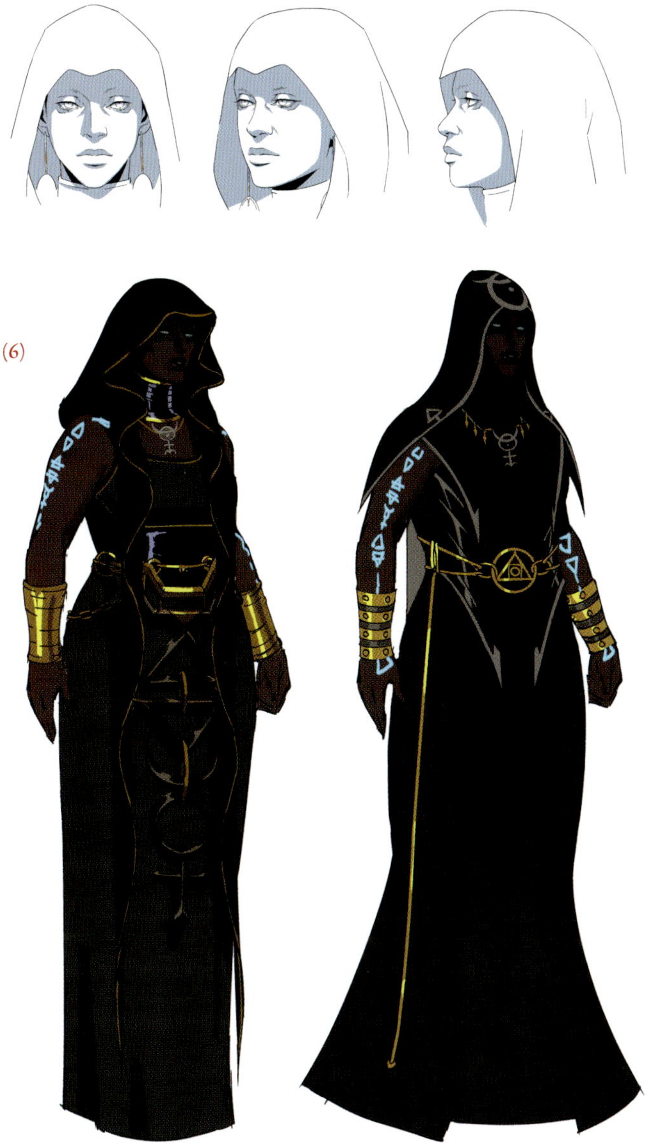

(7)

(6)

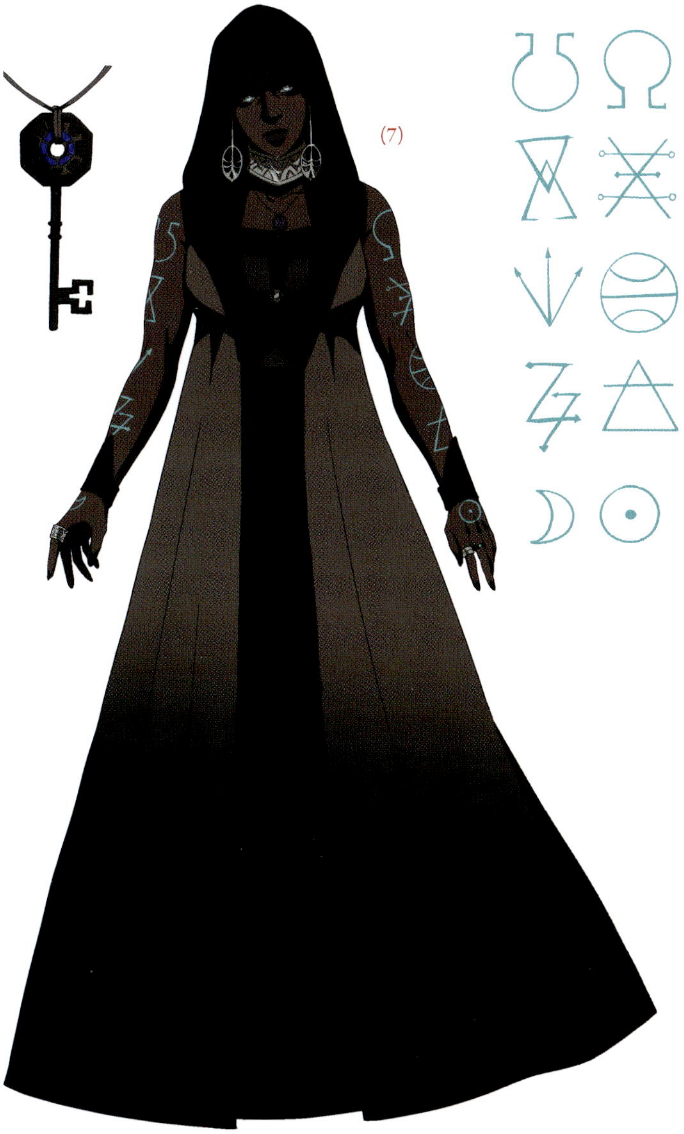

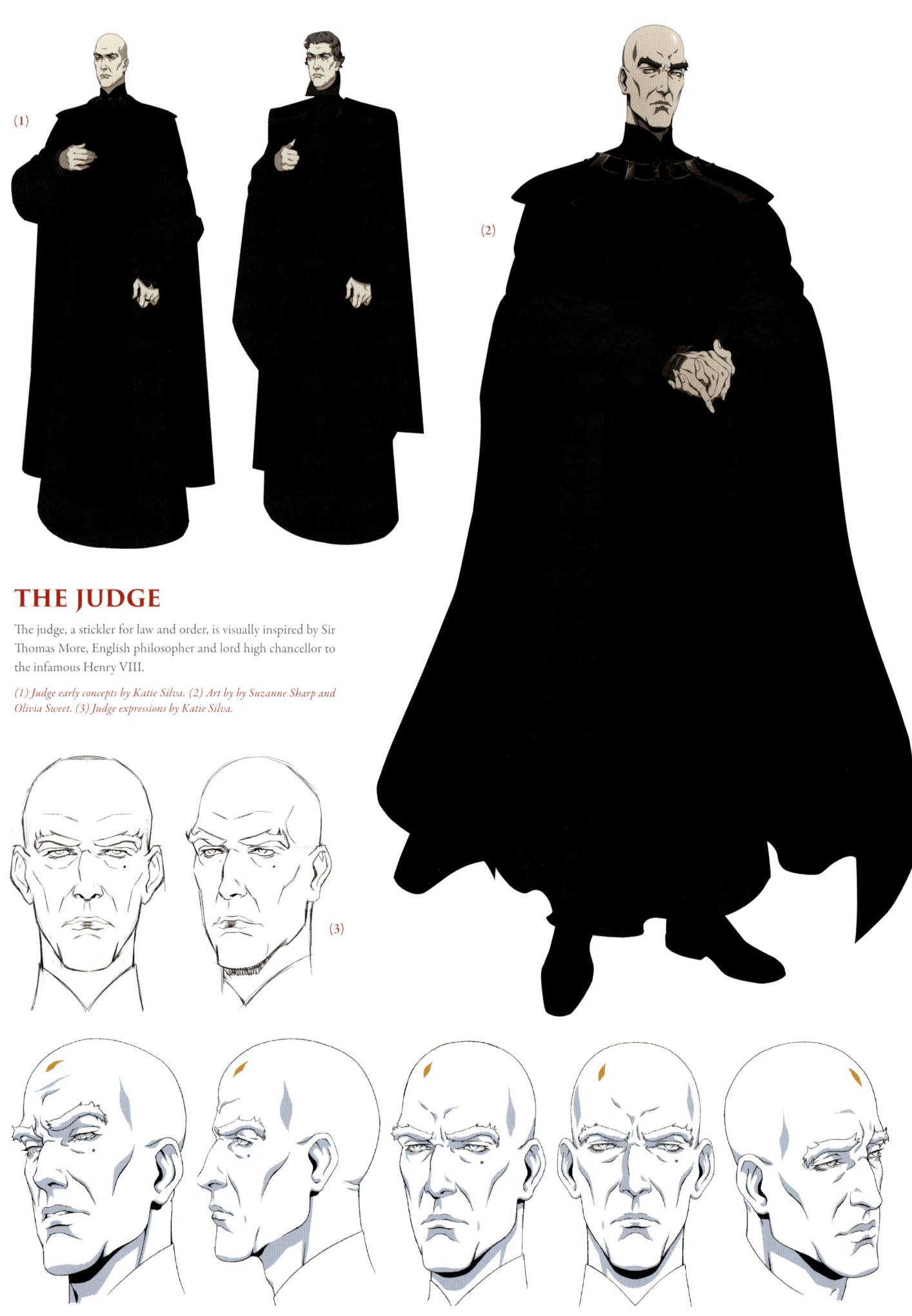

THE JUDGE

The judge, a stickler for law and order, is visually inspired by Sir Thomas More, English philosopher and lord high chancellor to the infamous Henry VIII.

(1) Judge early concepts by Katie Silva. (2) Art by by Suzanne Sharp and Olivia Sweet. (3) Judge expressions by Katie Silva.

LINDENFELD VILLAGERS

The villagers in general are more historically and regionally based than the vampires, but none are necessarily historically accurate.

(4) Bartender by Evgeny Lubaev. (5) Lindenfeld women designs by Evgeny Lubaev, cleanup by Julia Shi. (6) Young farmer design by Katie Silva, cleanup by Evgeny Lubaev. (7) Lindenfeld family designs by Evgeny Lubaev.

(4)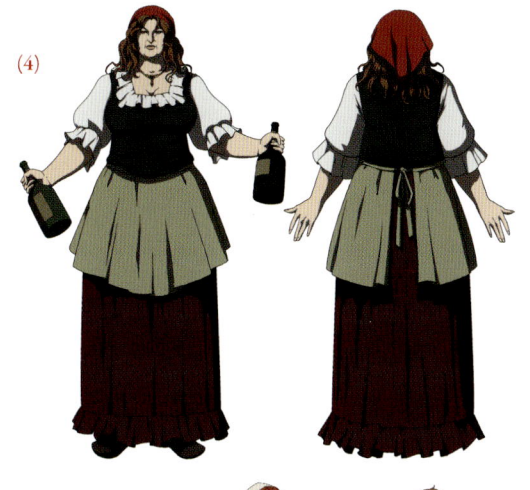

(5)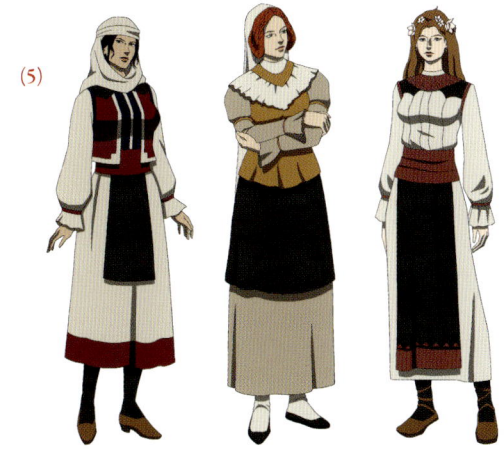

(6)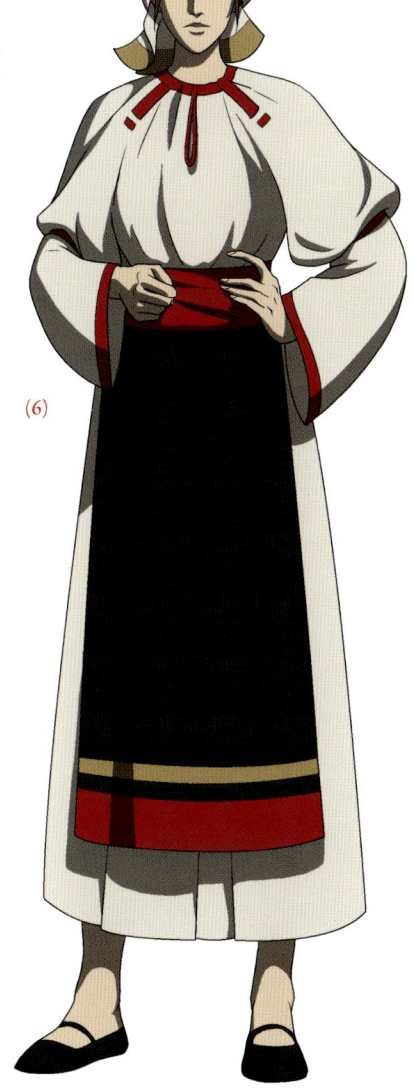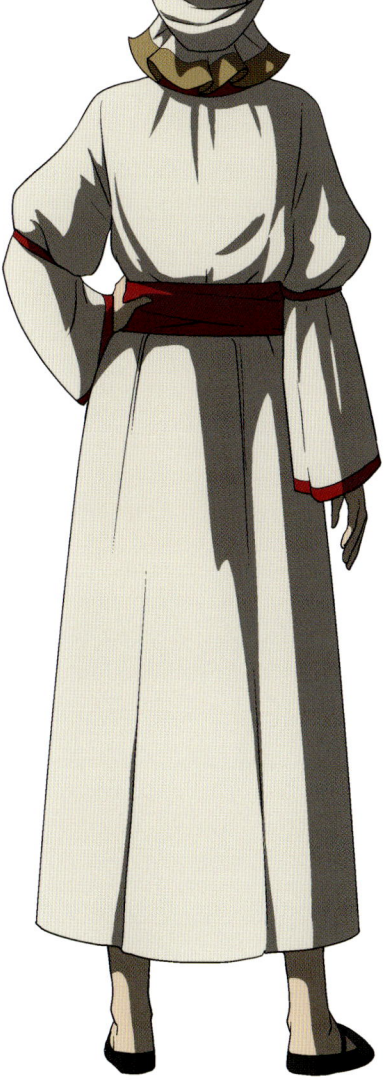

(7)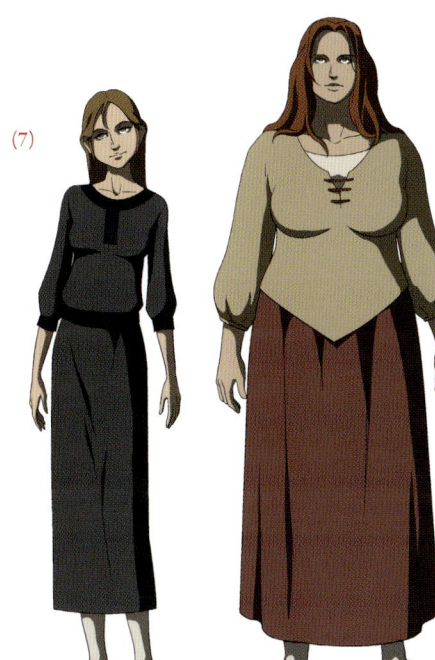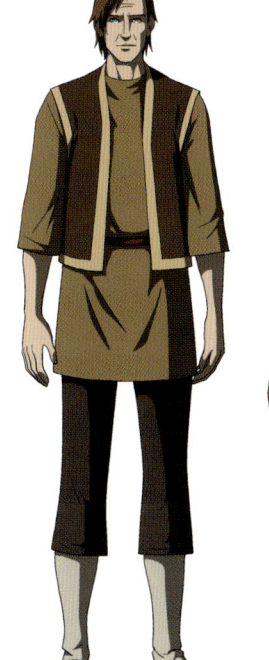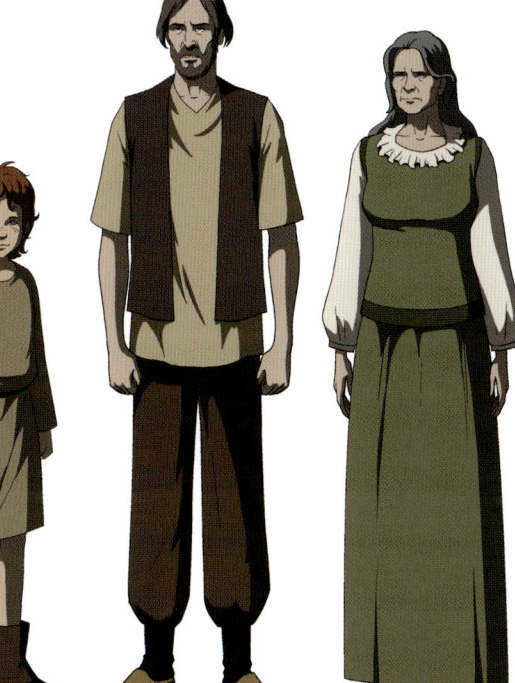

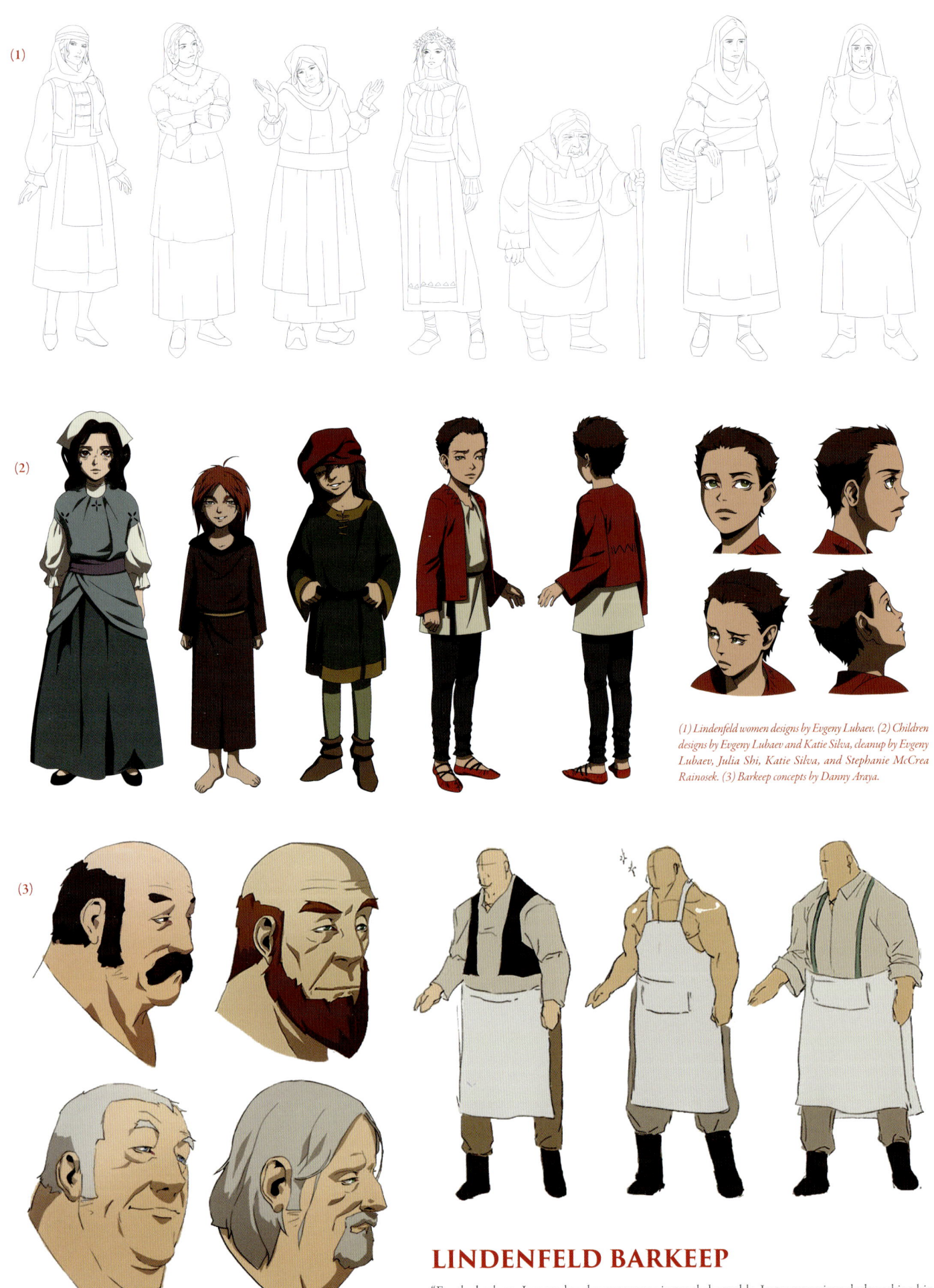

(1) *Lindenfeld women designs by Evgeny Lubaev.* (2) *Children designs by Evgeny Lubaev and Katie Silva, cleanup by Evgeny Lubaev, Julia Shi, Katie Silva, and Stephanie McCrea Rainosek.* (3) *Barkeep concepts by Danny Araya.*

LINDENFELD BARKEEP

"For the barkeep, I wanted to draw someone instantly huggable. Just a gregarious dude making his living who probably knows the personal problems of half the village. He only had the one line about giving Trevor a free beer but it kinda says a lot about him." —Danny Araya

TARGOVISTE PEOPLE

(4) Targoviste adults by Suzanne Sharp. (5) Targoviste children by Evgeny Lubaev and Katie Silva. (6) Design by Evgeny Lubaev.

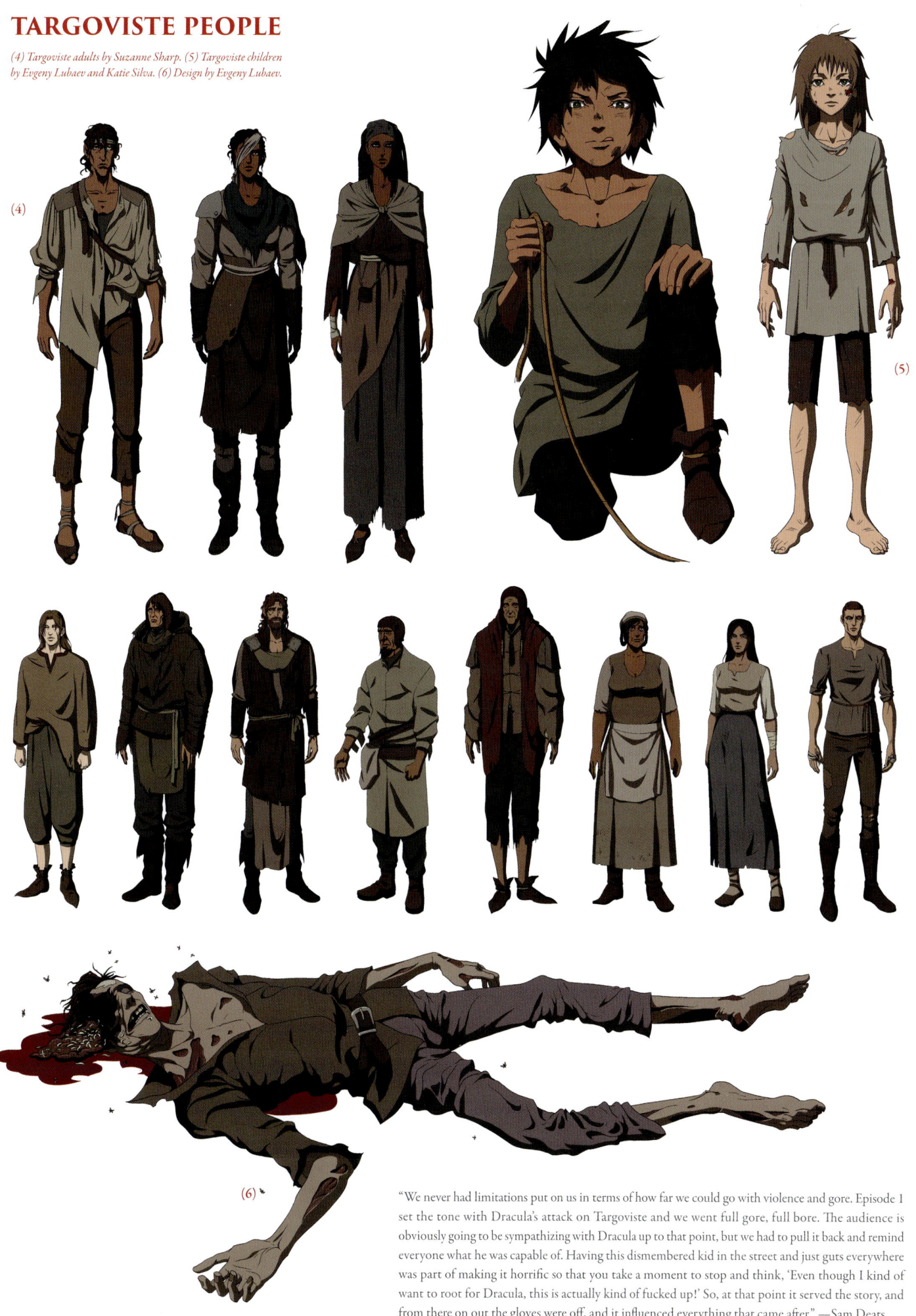

(4)

(5)

(6)

"We never had limitations put on us in terms of how far we could go with violence and gore. Episode 1 set the tone with Dracula's attack on Targoviste and we went full gore, full bore. The audience is obviously going to be sympathizing with Dracula up to that point, but we had to pull it back and remind everyone what he was capable of. Having this dismembered kid in the street and just guts everywhere was part of making it horrific so that you take a moment to stop and think, 'Even though I kind of want to root for Dracula, this is actually kind of fucked up!' So, at that point it served the story, and from there on out the gloves were off, and it influenced everything that came after." —Sam Deats

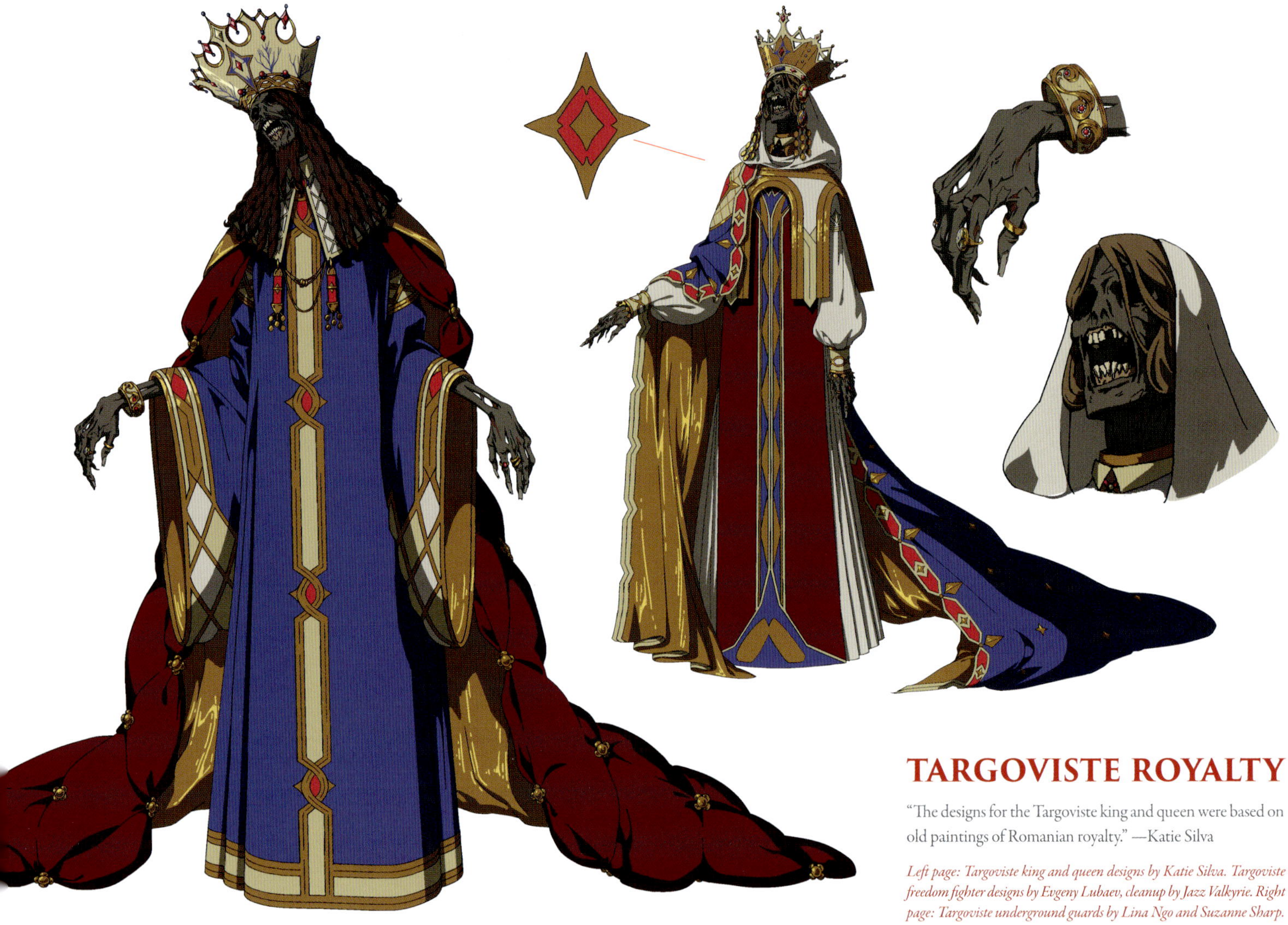

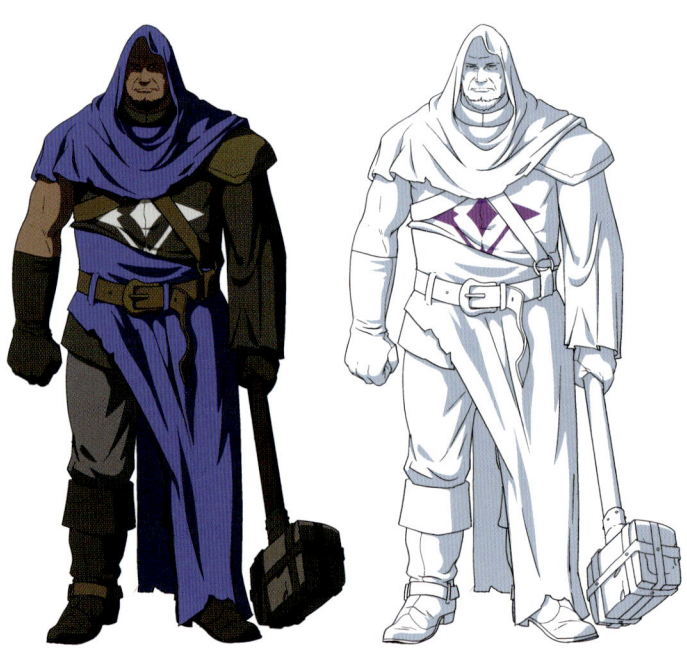

TARGOVISTE ROYALTY

"The designs for the Targoviste king and queen were based on old paintings of Romanian royalty." —Katie Silva

Left page: Targoviste king and queen designs by Katie Silva. Targoviste freedom fighter designs by Evgeny Lubaev, cleanup by Jazz Valkyrie. Right page: Targoviste underground guards by Lina Ngo and Suzanne Sharp.

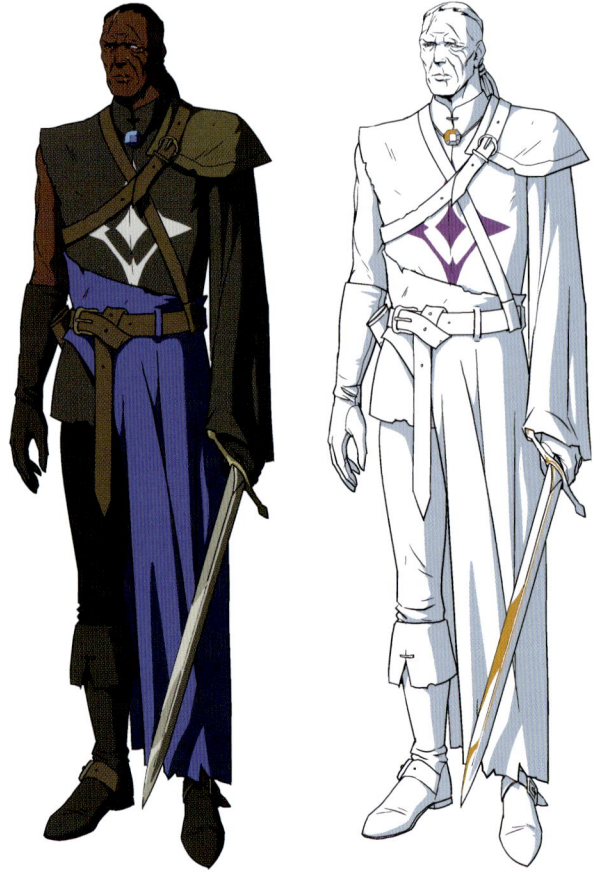

TARGOVISTE UNDERGROUND

"We wanted the soldiers to look worn, but not beaten, and willing to fight for the precious last of their city. The Targoviste insignia on their uniforms draws from the intensely Gothic city typology with its soaring, angular architecture. I modeled the soldier with the cool face scar off of my sister—I thought she'd love a part as a giant fighter lady." —Suzanne Sharp

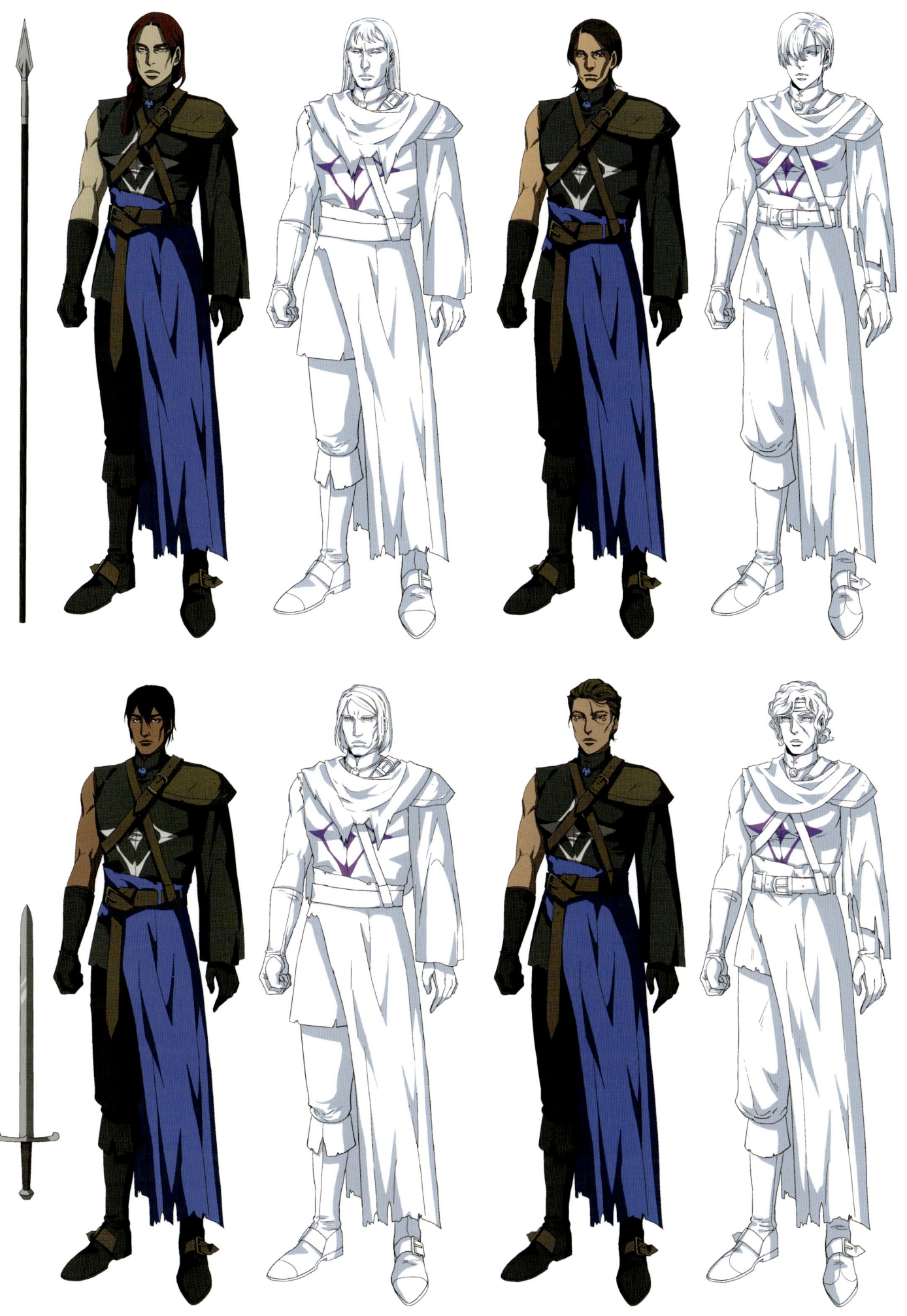

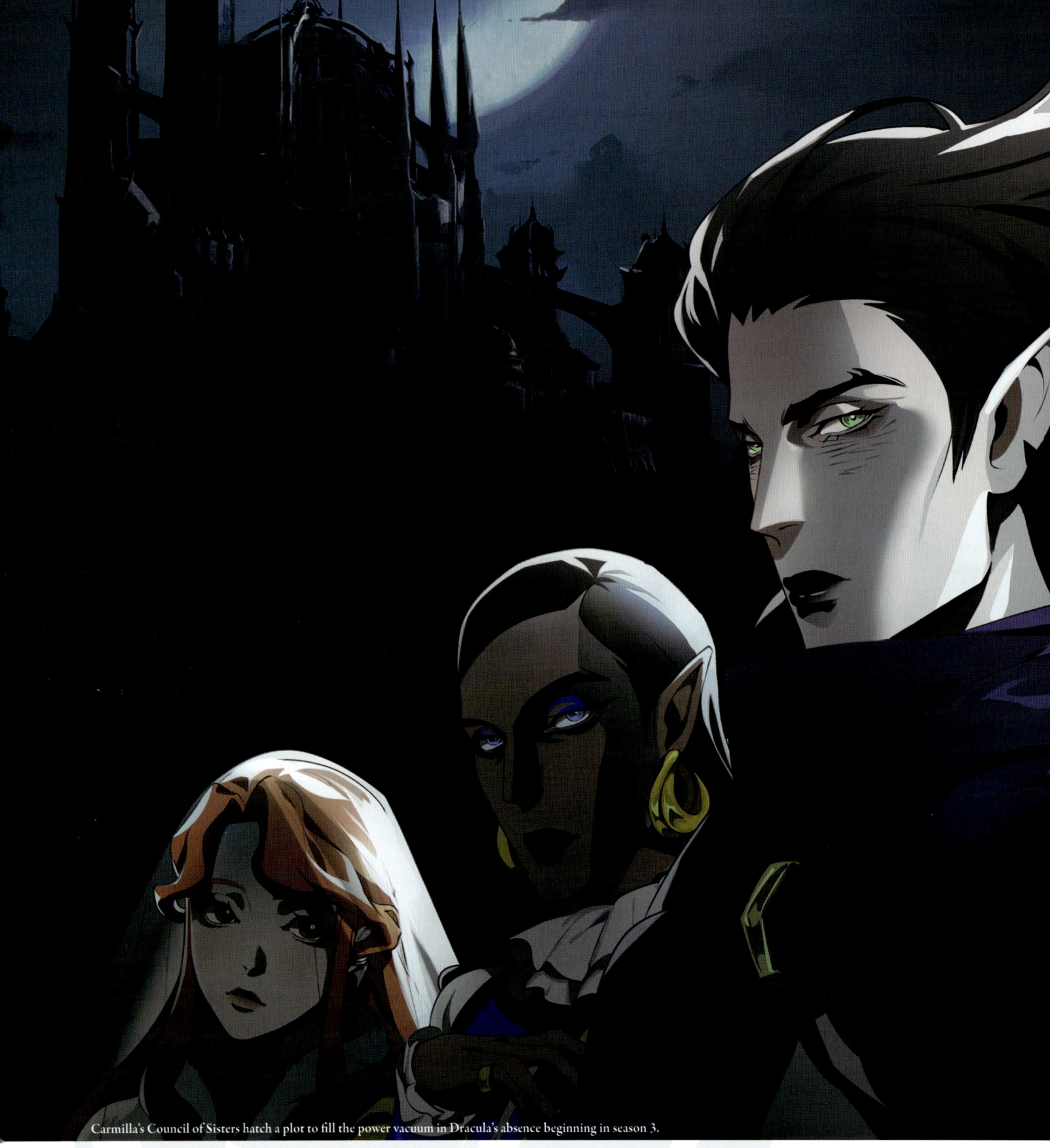

Carmilla's Council of Sisters hatch a plot to fill the power vacuum in Dracula's absence beginning in season 3.

Character art by Lina Ngo, background by Jose Vega.

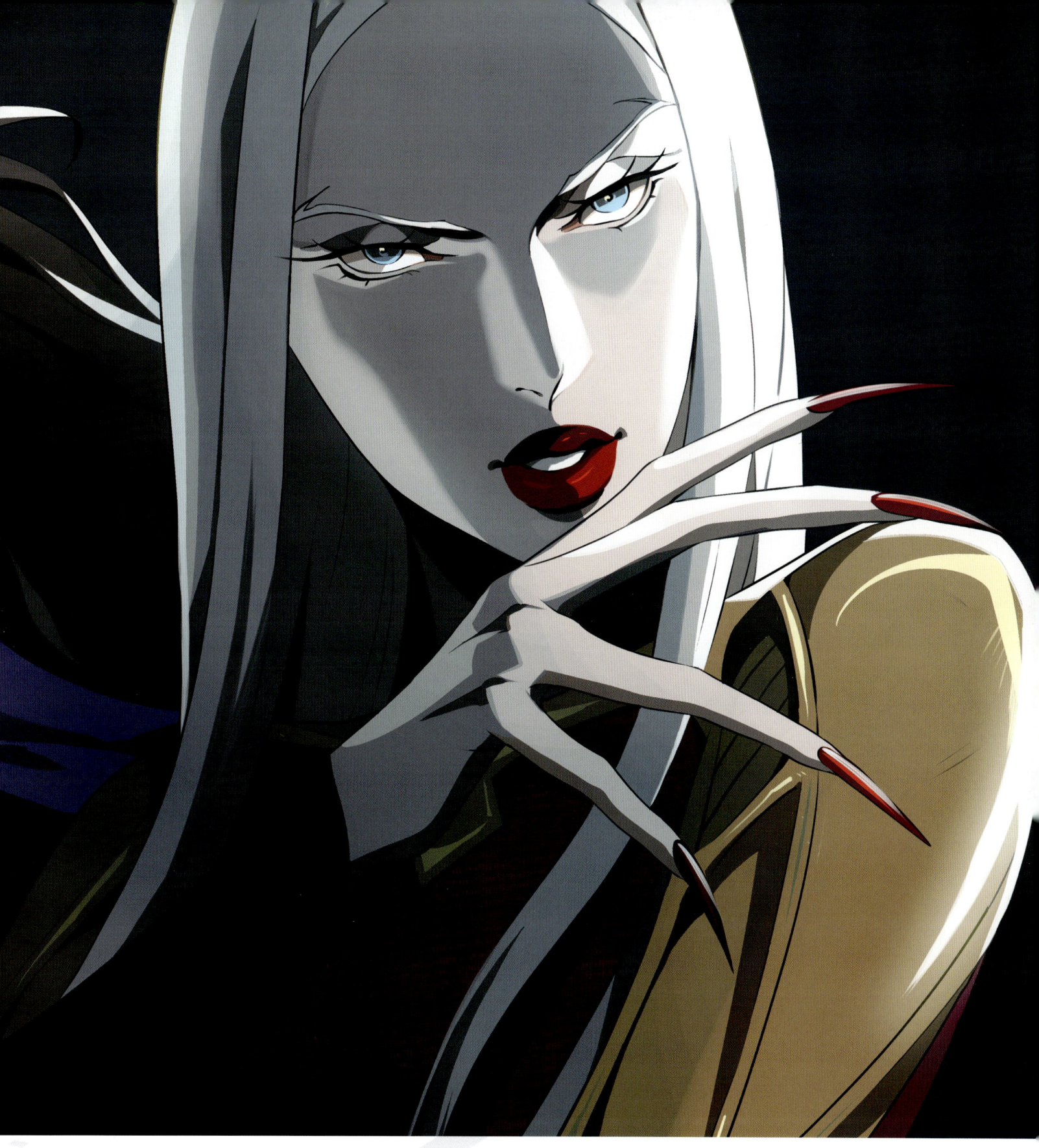

CHAPTER II

Demons and the Damned

Vlad Dracula Tepes

The classic Dracula shapes and silhouette are based directly on the designs by Ayami Kojima. A towering presence projecting power and strength wherever he goes, Dracula is about eight feet tall, which was also a nod to the games, in which a tiny Belmont sprite had to jump to hit the head of Dracula during battle.

All art on these pages by Sam Deats.

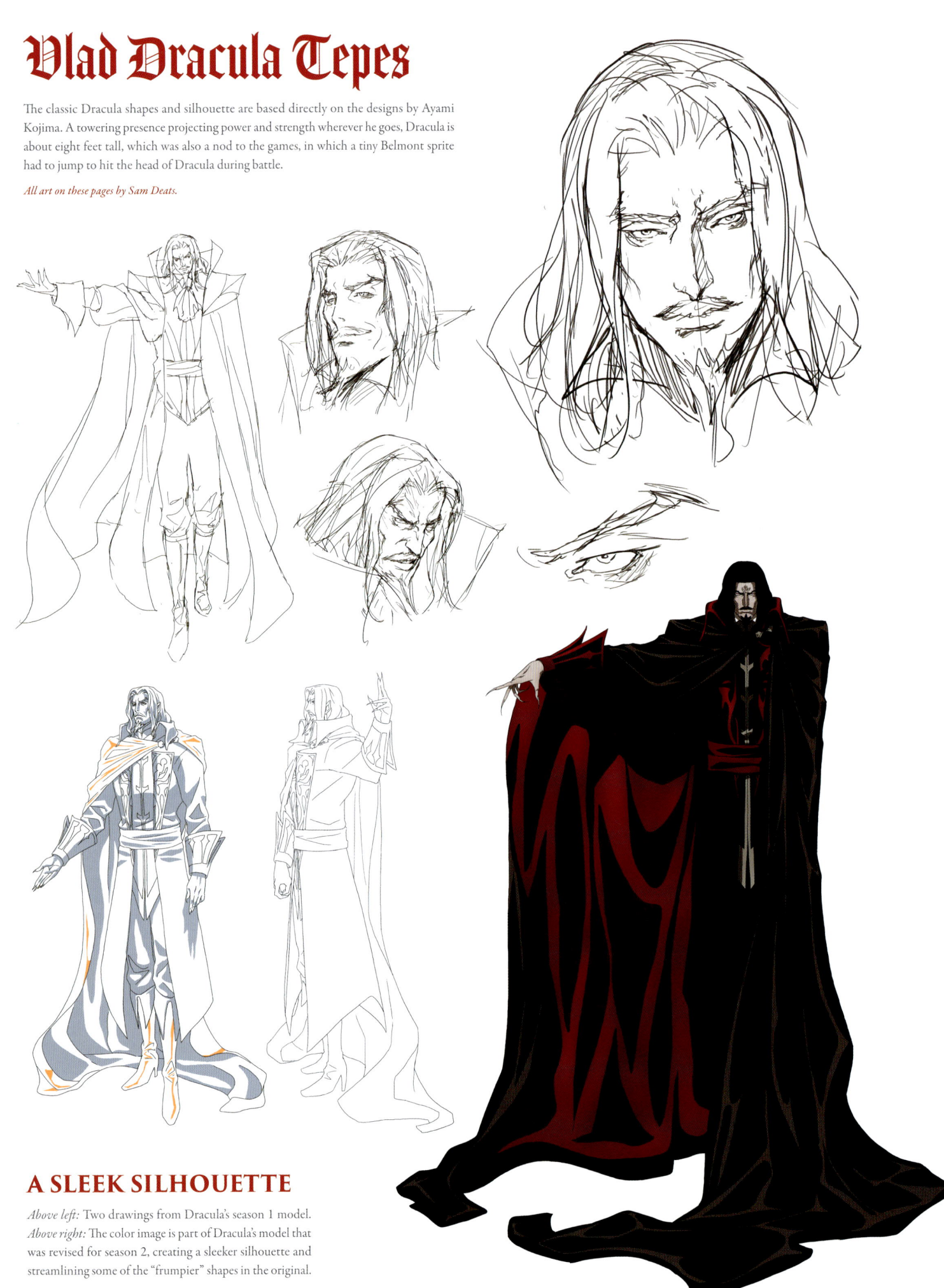

A SLEEK SILHOUETTE

Above left: Two drawings from Dracula's season 1 model.
Above right: The color image is part of Dracula's model that was revised for season 2, creating a sleeker silhouette and streamlining some of the "frumpier" shapes in the original.

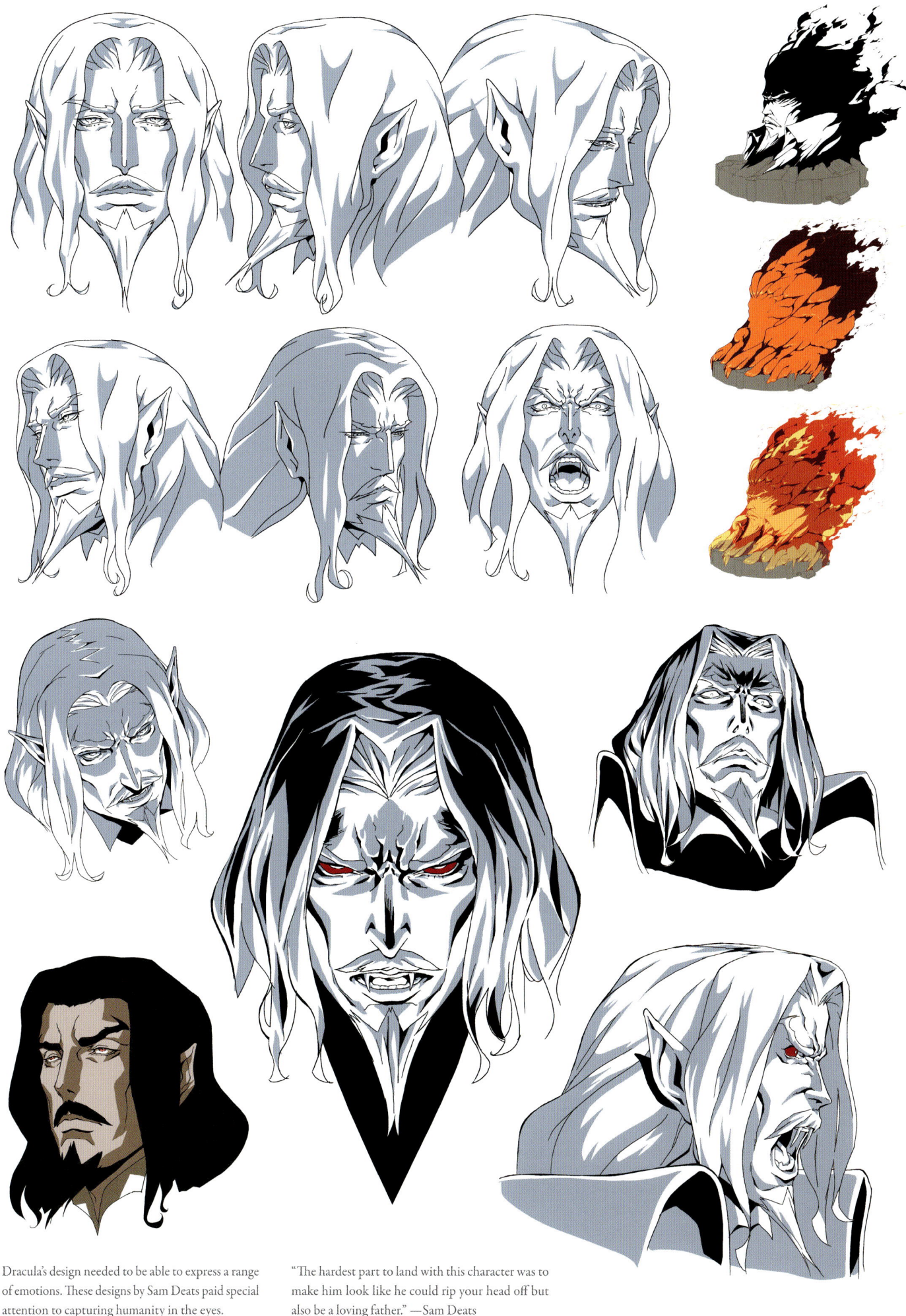

Dracula's design needed to be able to express a range of emotions. These designs by Sam Deats paid special attention to capturing humanity in the eyes.

"The hardest part to land with this character was to make him look like he could rip your head off but also be a loving father." —Sam Deats

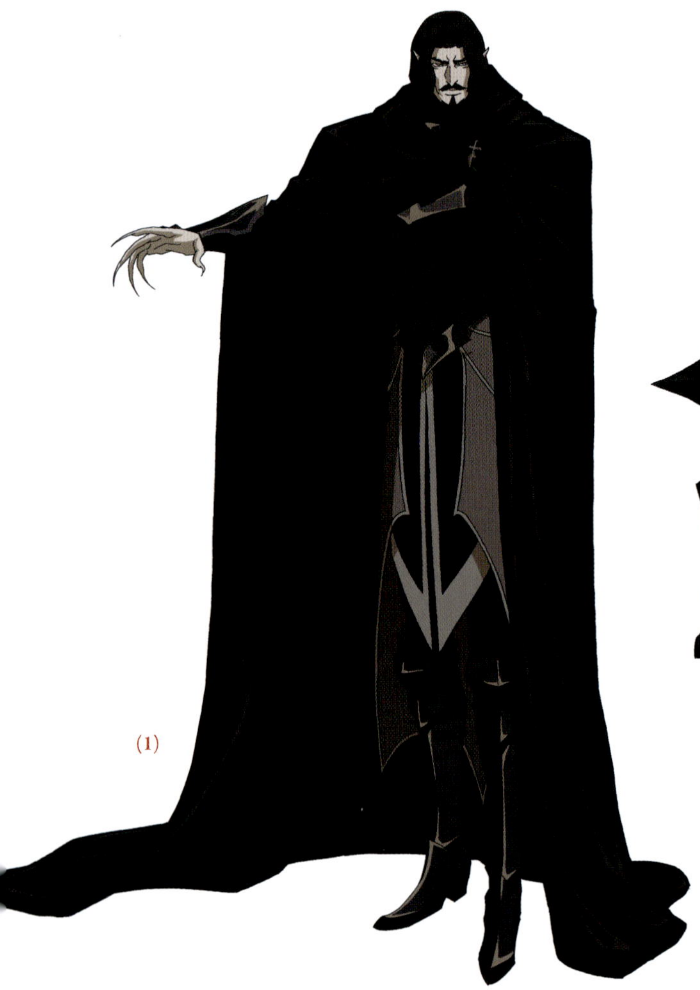

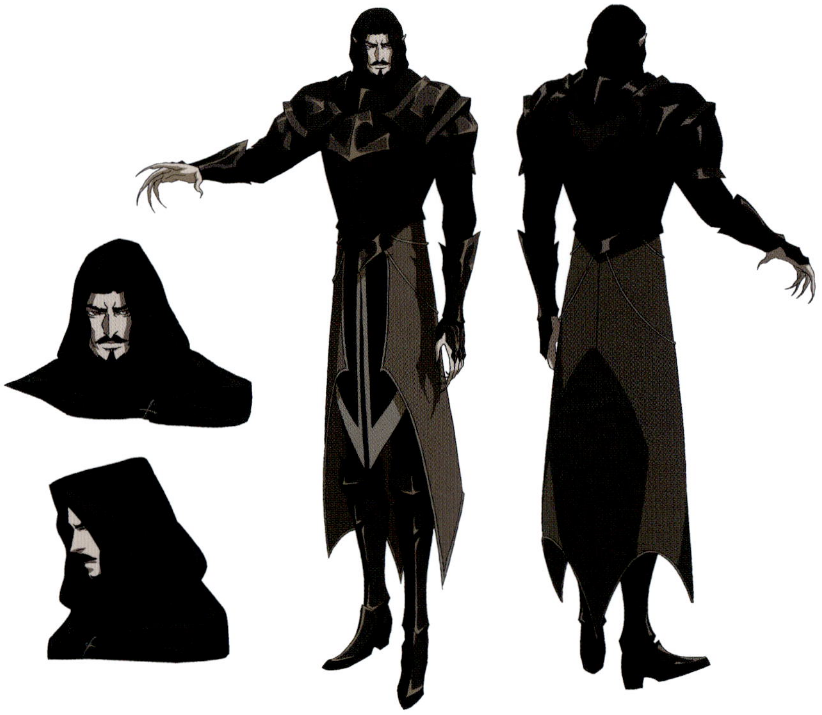

(1)

DRACULA'S ARMOR

In a flashback during the episode "Last Spell," Dracula dons armor designed with the "rule of cool" in mind—no historical research needed. It was, however, designed with Dracula's established shape language, and created to feel real, substantial, and functional.

(1) Armored Dracula design by Sam Deats, cleanup by Stephanie McCrea Rainosek. (2) Season 1 Dracula by Sam Deats. Right page: Season 4 Dracula effigy portrait by Katie Silva.

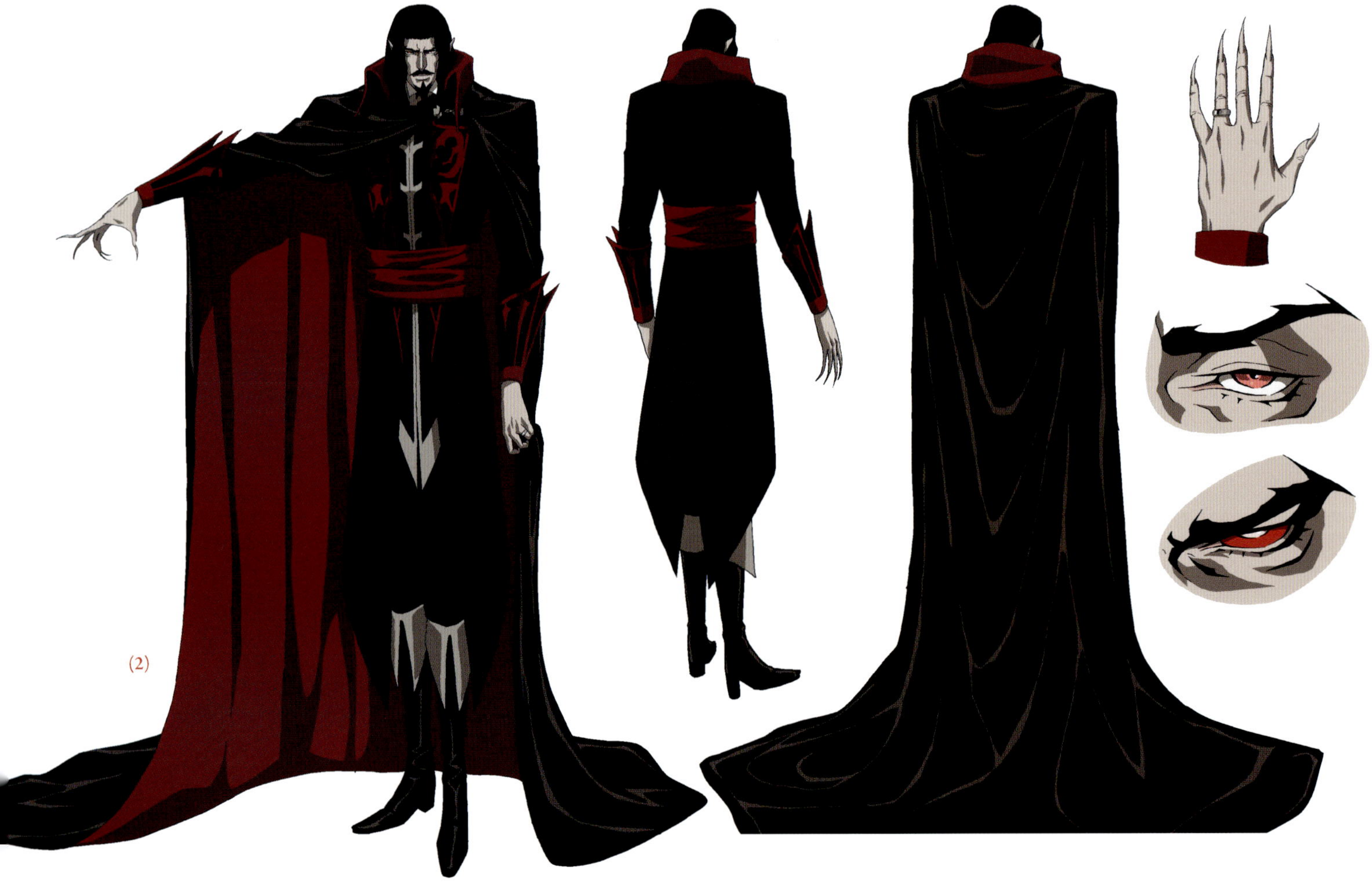

(2)

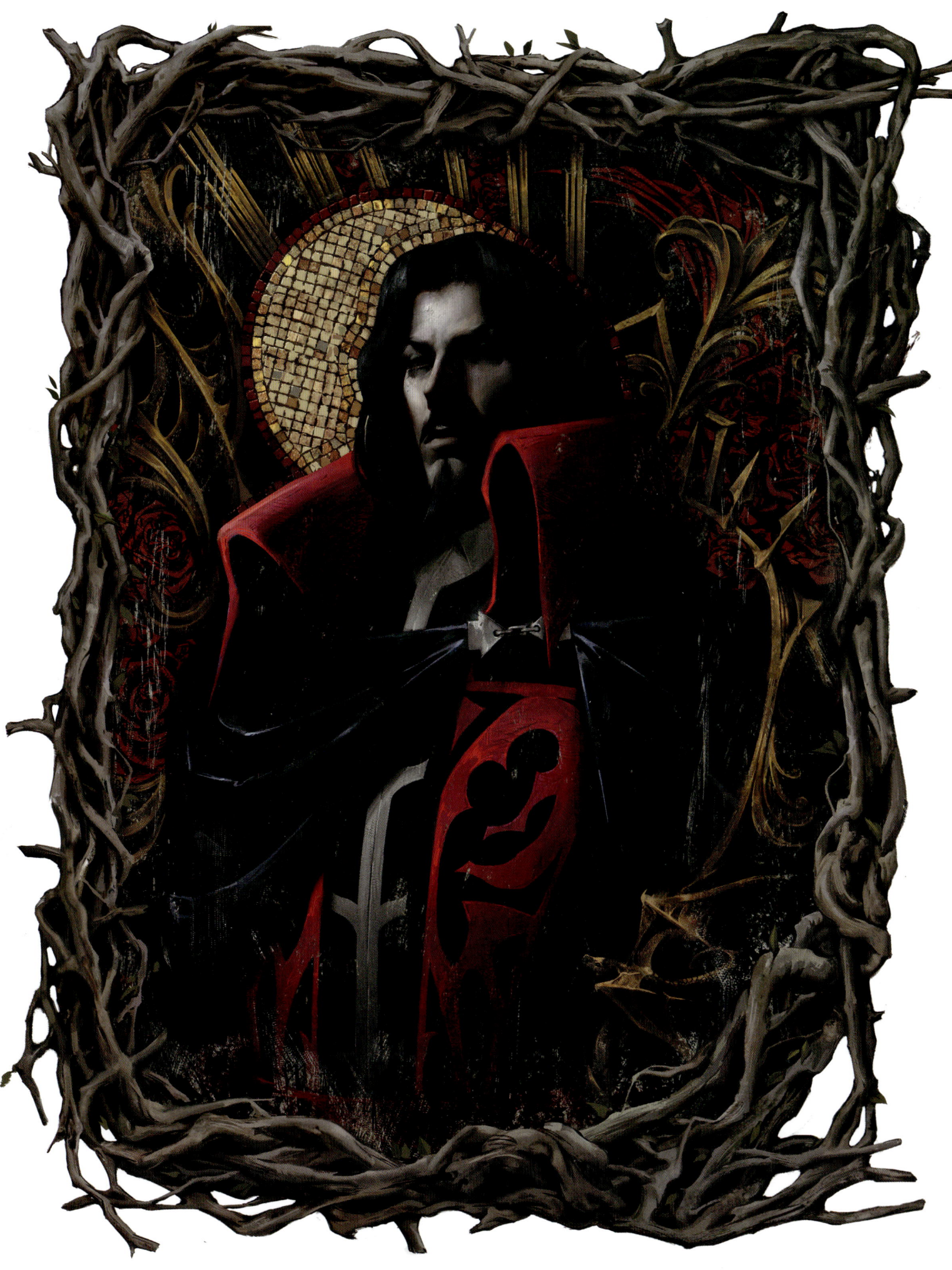

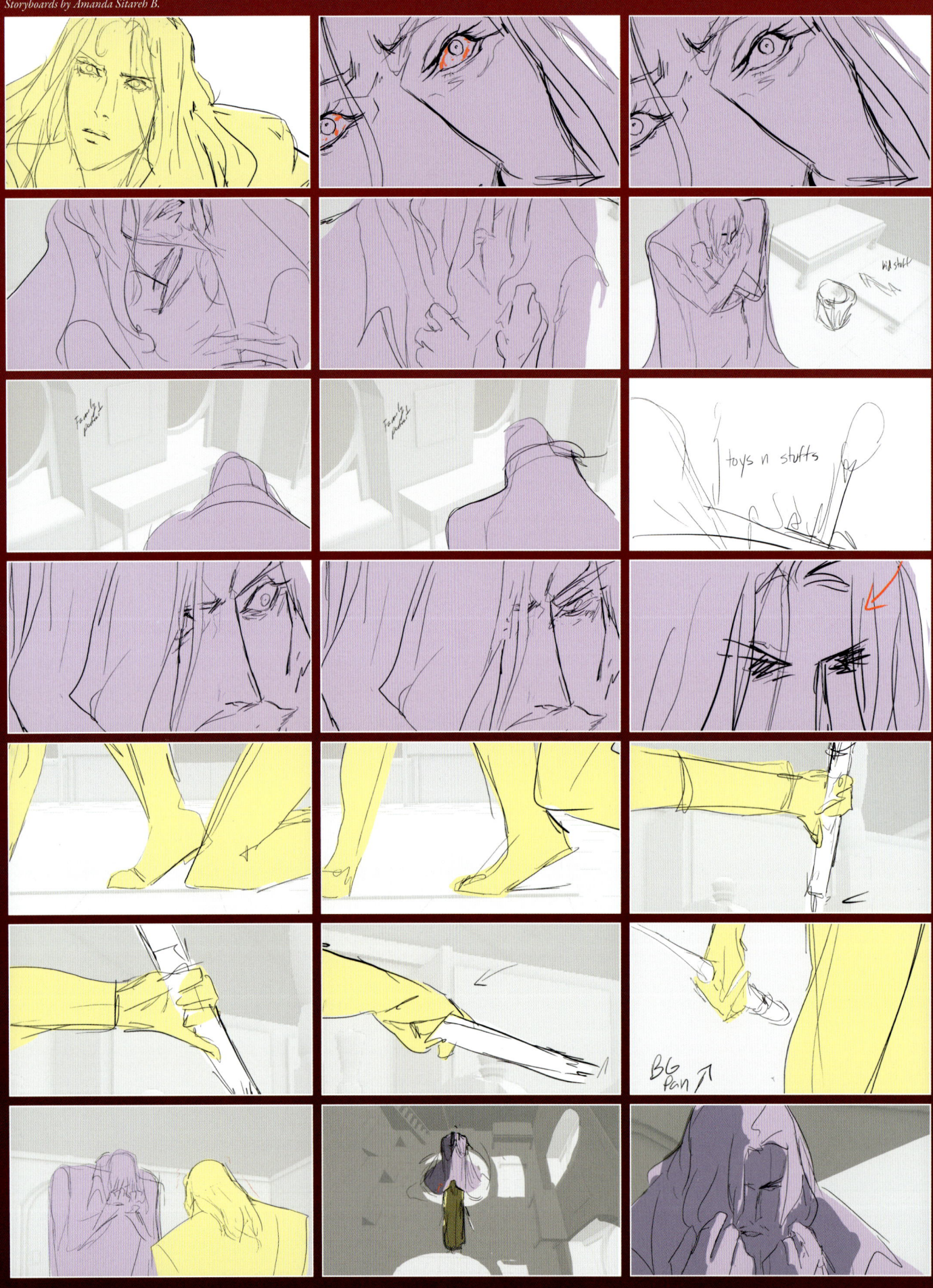

After a prolonged battle, Alucard stakes Dracula.

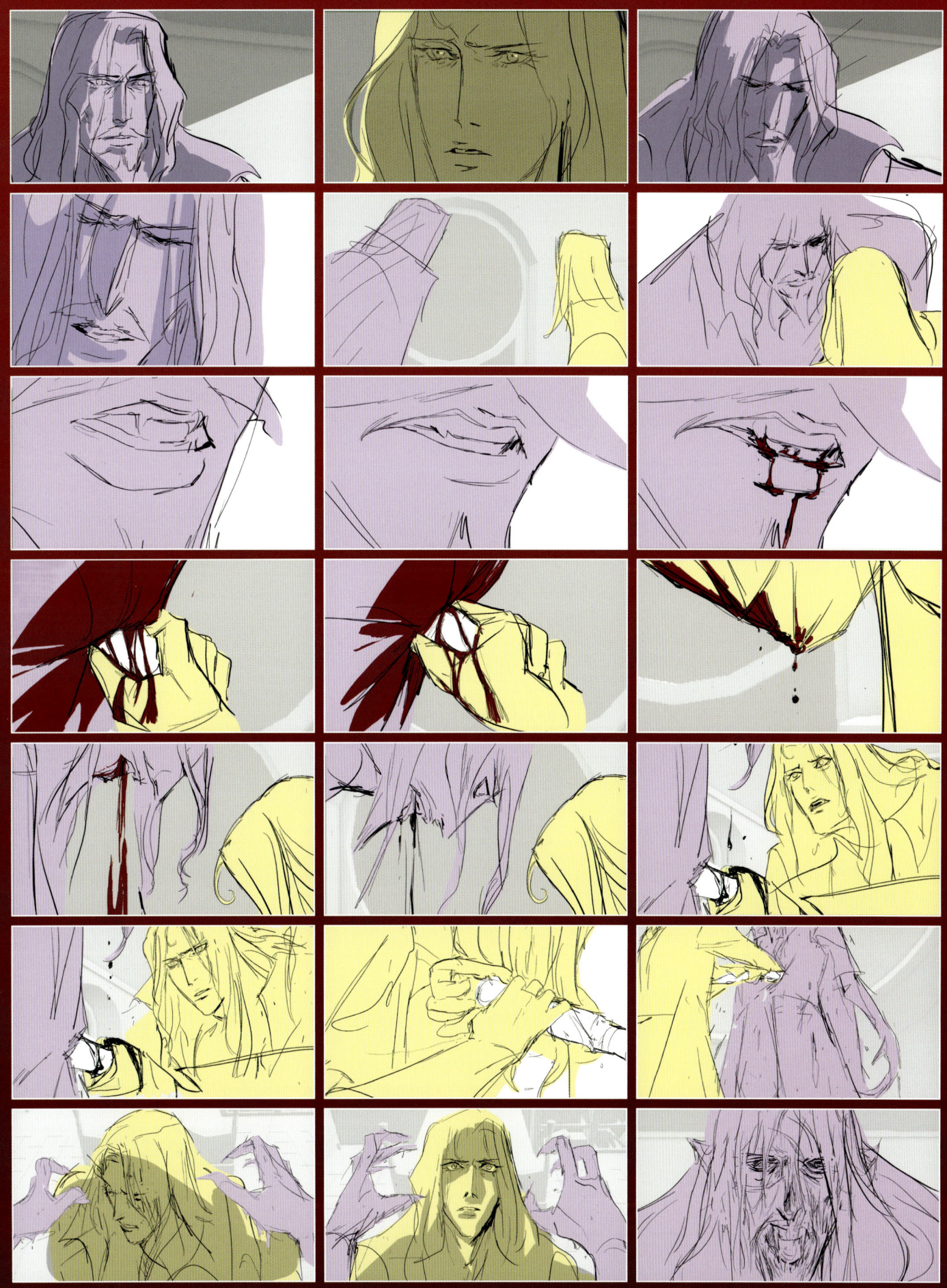

"I don't know if we'll ever get anything this emotionally stark and powerful again. This was an emotional peak for the series." —Adam Deats

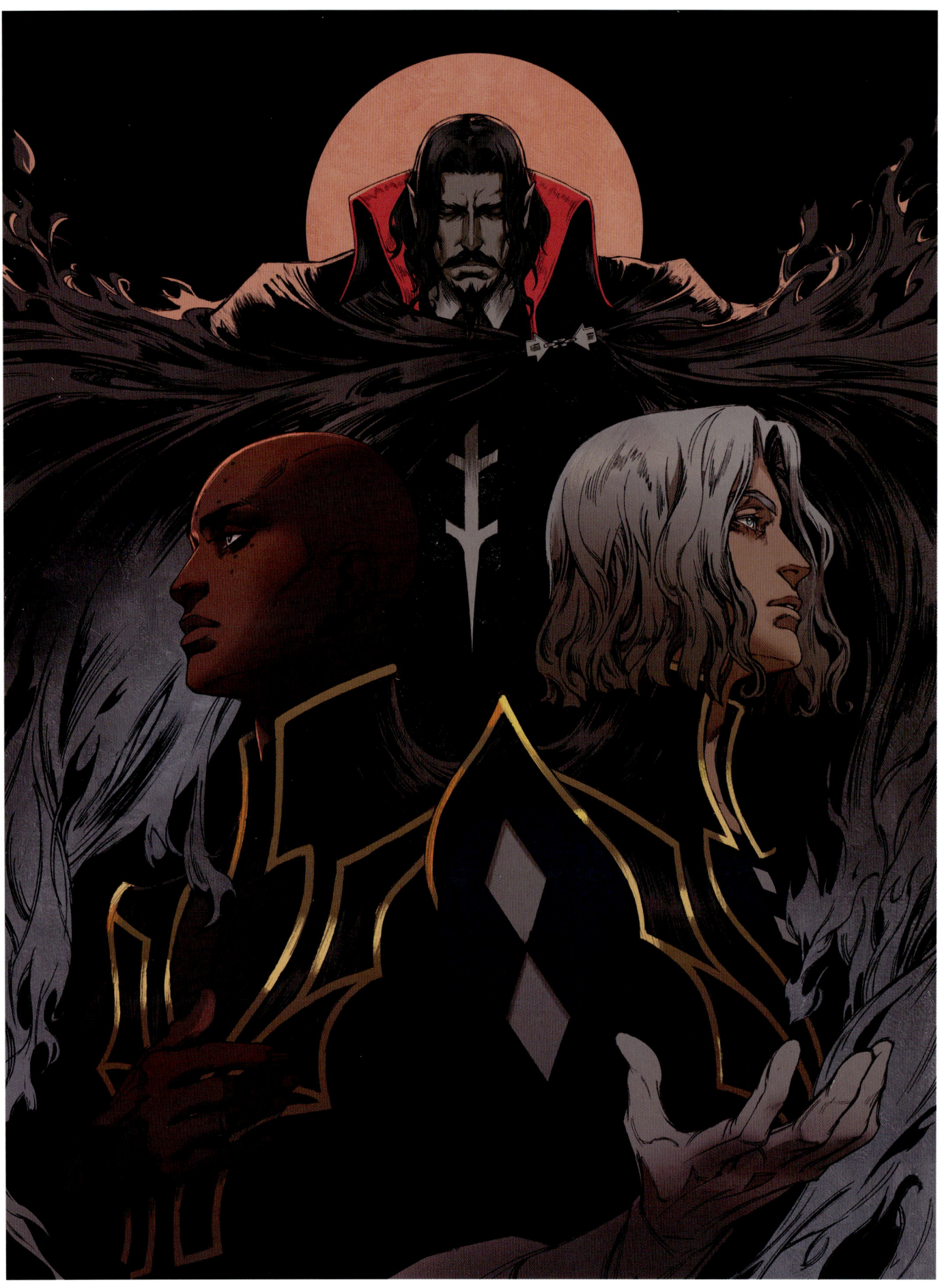

Inspired by Ayami Kojima's line art, Katie Silva created this promotional illustration of the forgemasters Isaac and Hector for season 2. The piece was used on the back of the Blu-ray case, for press releases, and in additional user interface elements on the Netflix application.

"I wanted Isaac to look more like he knew what he was doing, and Hector to appear more like he had his head in the clouds." —Katie Silva

The Bishop

The bishop meets his fate early on in the series as the instigator of the primary chain of events. "Luckily" for him, he makes a reanimated return appearance later in the series.

Left page: Art by Katie Silva. Right page: (1) Bishop design by Sam Deats.
(2) Reanimated bishop design by Isaak Ramos.

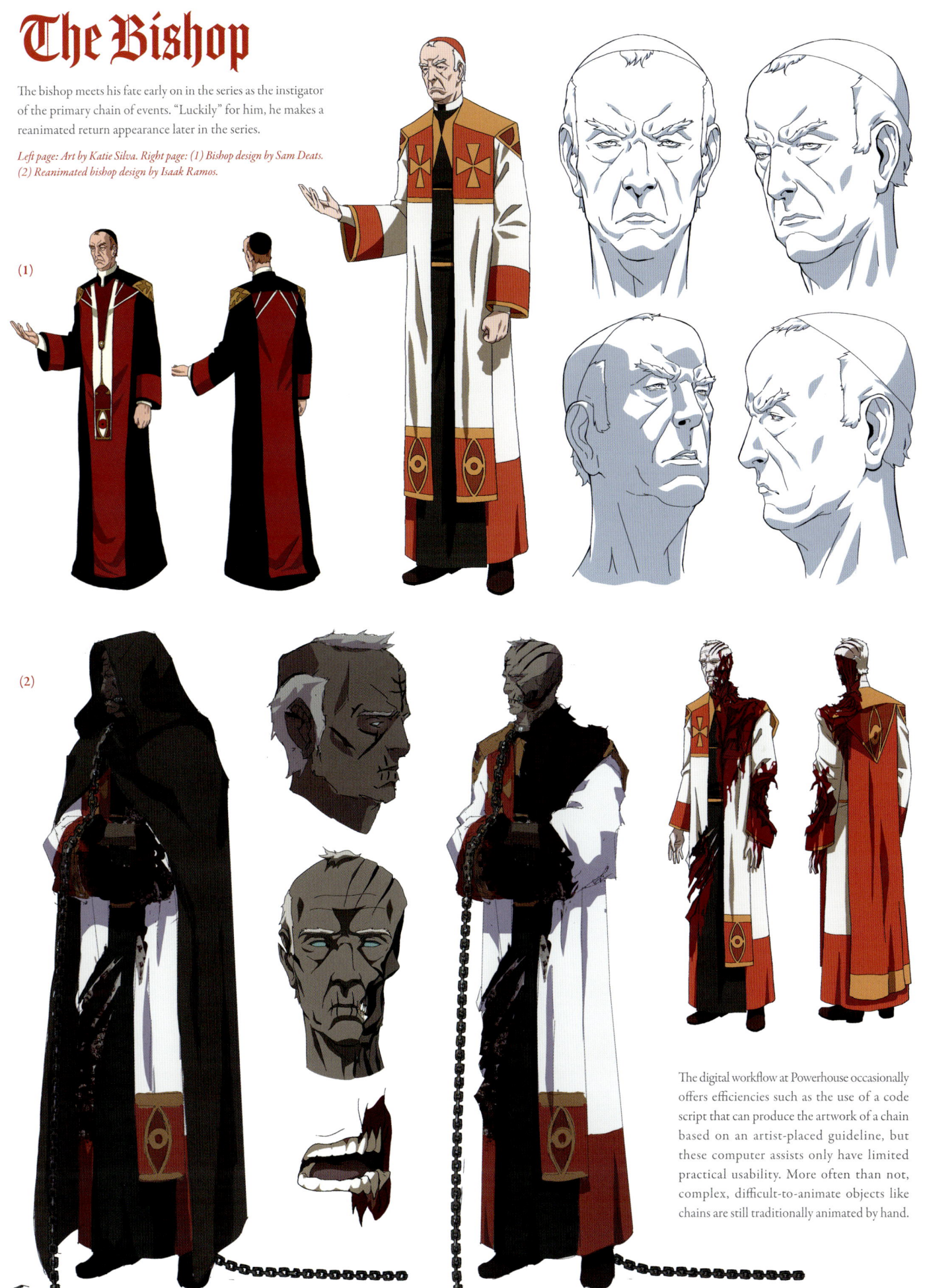

(1)

(2)

The digital workflow at Powerhouse occasionally offers efficiencies such as the use of a code script that can produce the artwork of a chain based on an artist-placed guideline, but these computer assists only have limited practical usability. More often than not, complex, difficult-to-animate objects like chains are still traditionally animated by hand.

Hector

One of two human forgemasters in Dracula's court, Hector has the ability to reanimate the dead. "Because he's Greek, we explored some Greek-influenced designs and shapes for his outfit, but it never felt quite right so we ended up with his game design outfit and his silver hair as well." —Sam Deats

All art on these pages by Sam Deats.

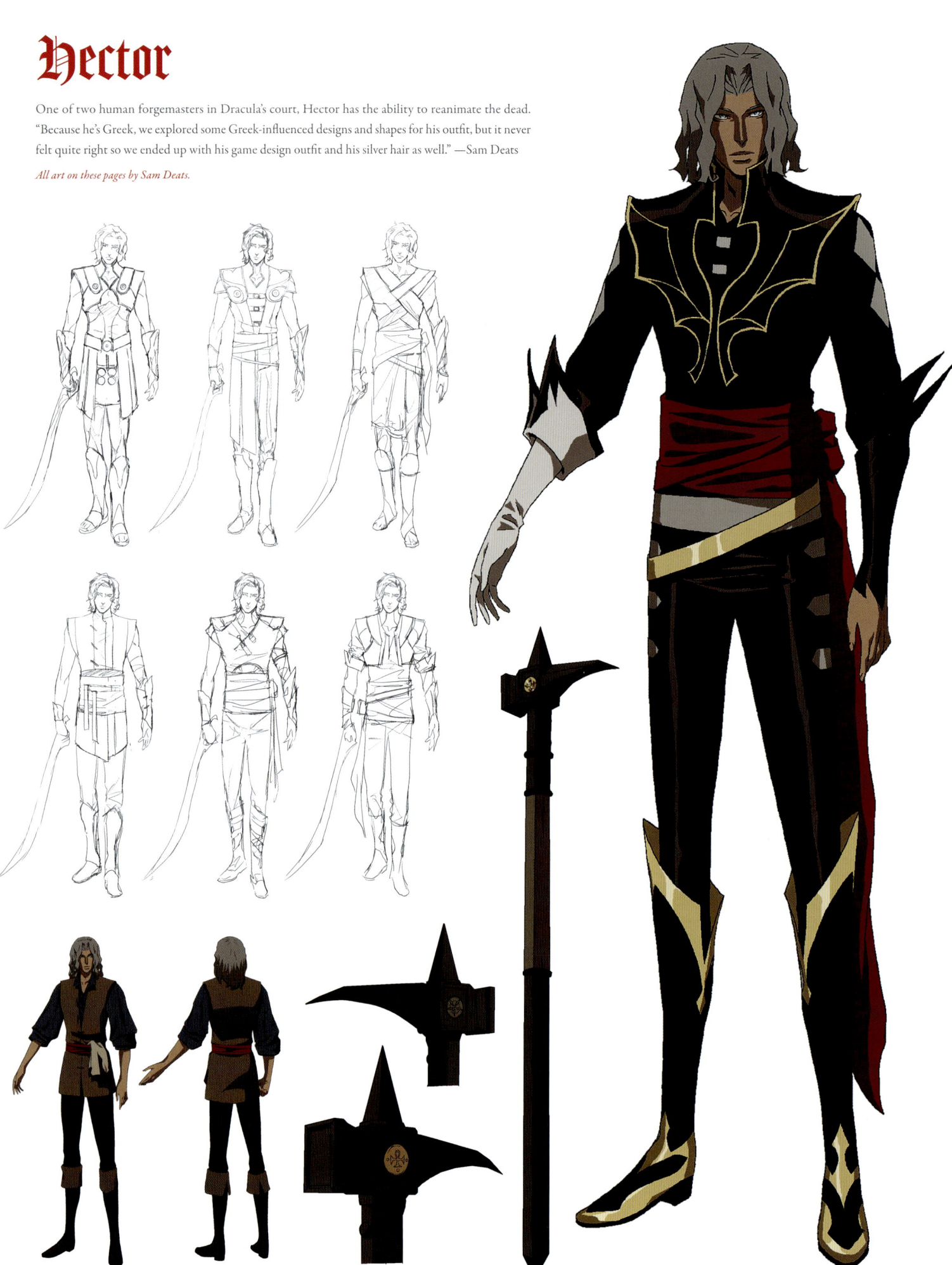

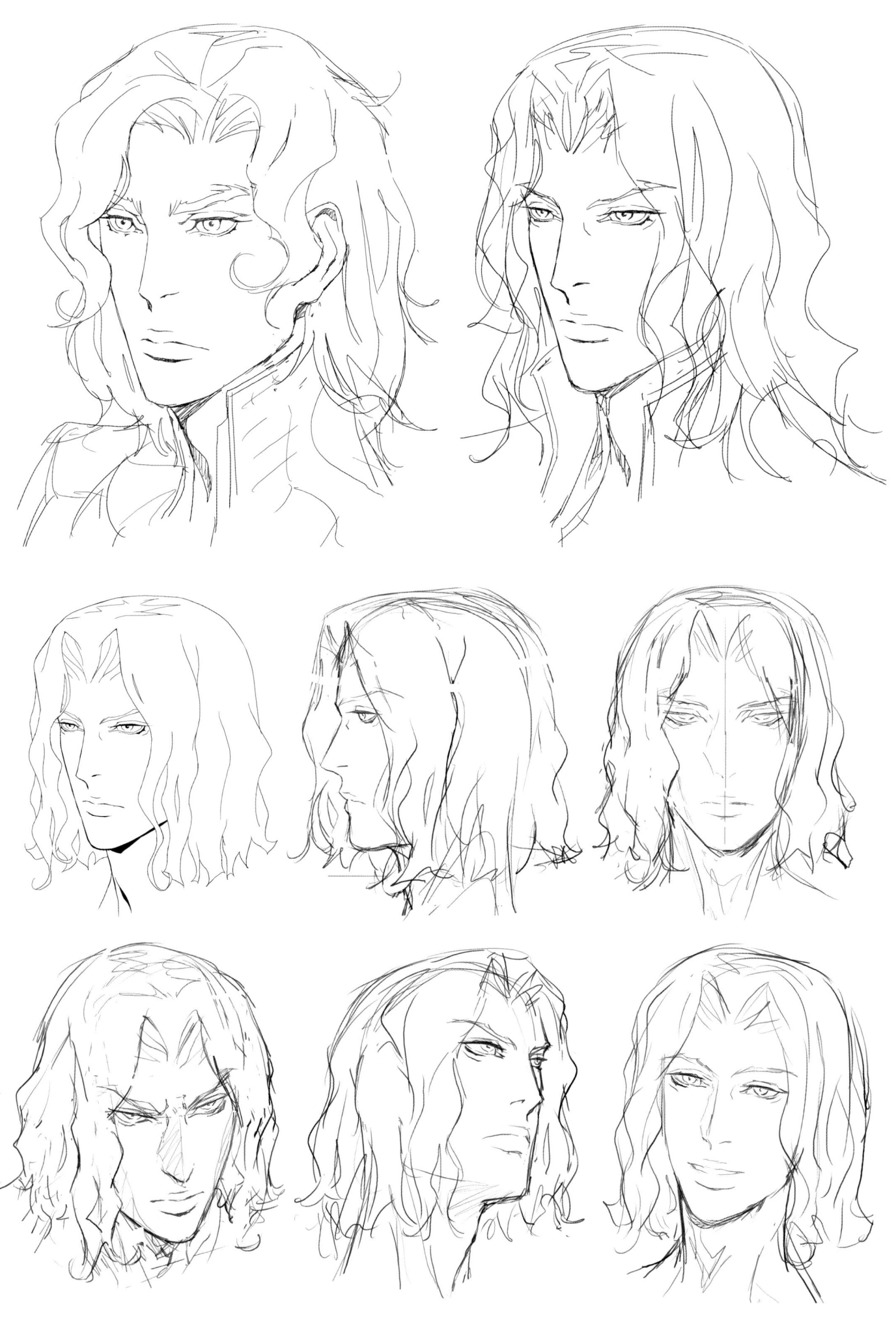

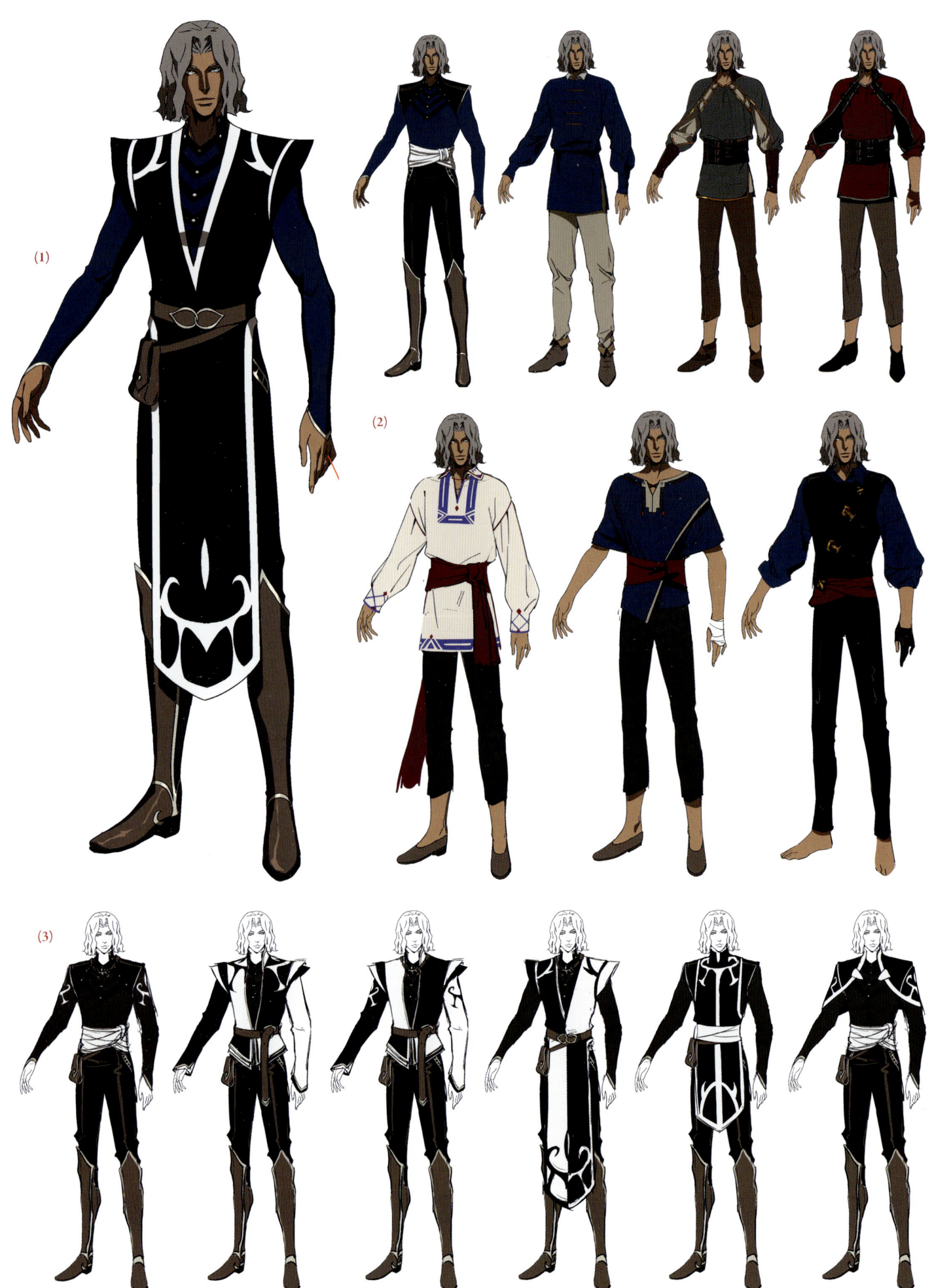

(1) Hector Styrian livery design by Suzanne Sharp. (2) Season 4 casual Hector costume concepts by Katie Silva. (3) Styrian livery early concepts by Suzanne Sharp.

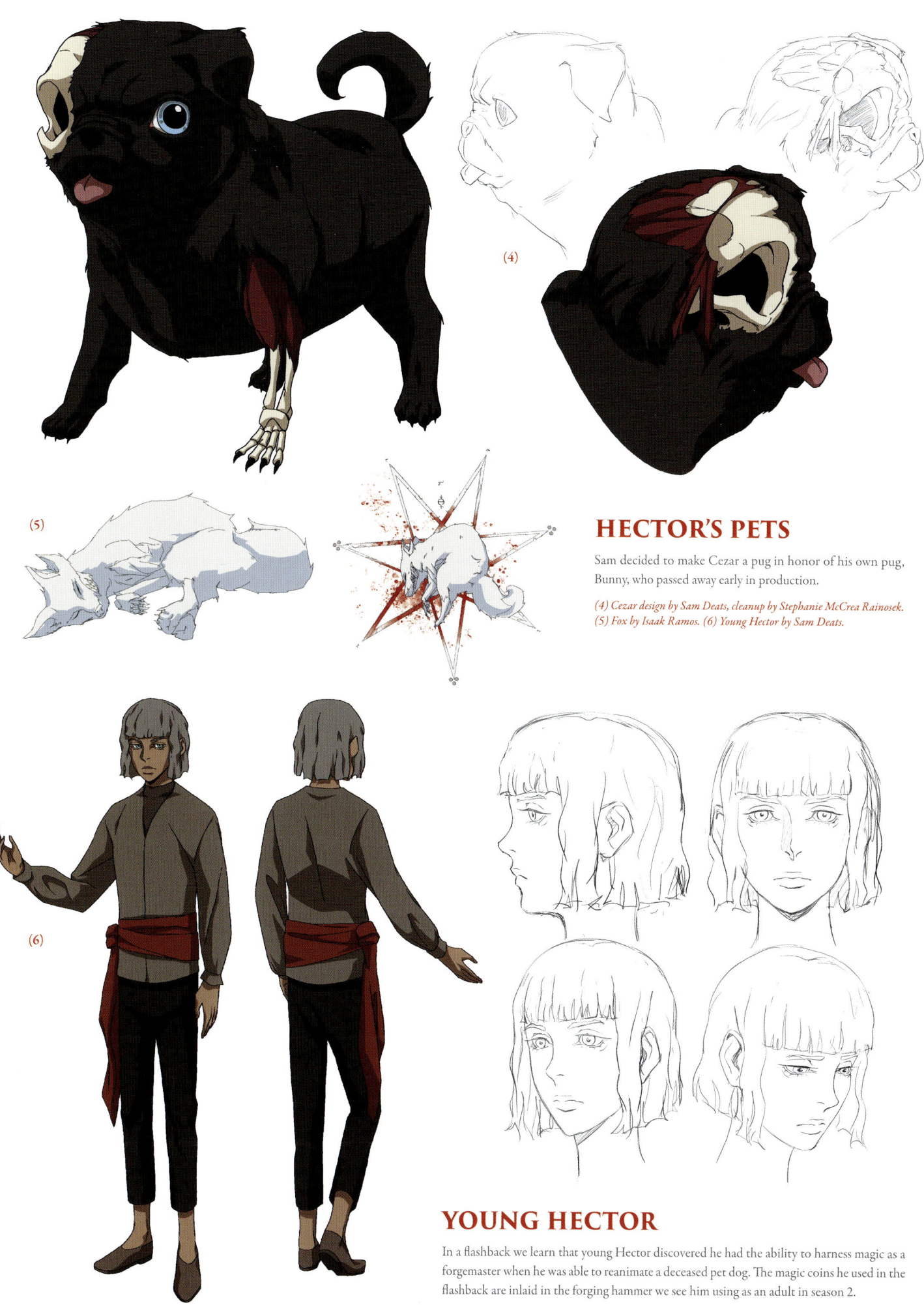

HECTOR'S PETS

Sam decided to make Cezar a pug in honor of his own pug, Bunny, who passed away early in production.

(4) Cezar design by Sam Deats, cleanup by Stephanie McCrea Rainosek.
(5) Fox by Isaak Ramos. (6) Young Hector by Sam Deats.

(4)

(5)

(6)

YOUNG HECTOR

In a flashback we learn that young Hector discovered he had the ability to harness magic as a forgemaster when he was able to reanimate a deceased pet dog. The magic coins he used in the flashback are inlaid in the forging hammer we see him using as an adult in season 2.

Isaac

After being teleported by Dracula to the north African desert against his will, Isaac sets off to seek vengeance against Hector, and to ultimately complete Dracula's mission to destroy humanity. Isaac is accompanied on his mission by his growing army of night creatures, reanimated and transformed from enemies defeated along the way.

(1) Isaac season 2 design by Sam Deats. (2) Isaac promotional art by Katie Silva. (3) Flog and Isaac's knife prop designs by Isaak Ramos. (4) Isaac expressions by Sam Deats. (5) Isaac early costume concepts by Sam Deats. (6) Young Isaac character design by Sam Deats, model sheet cleanup by Stephanie McCrea Rainosek.

(1)

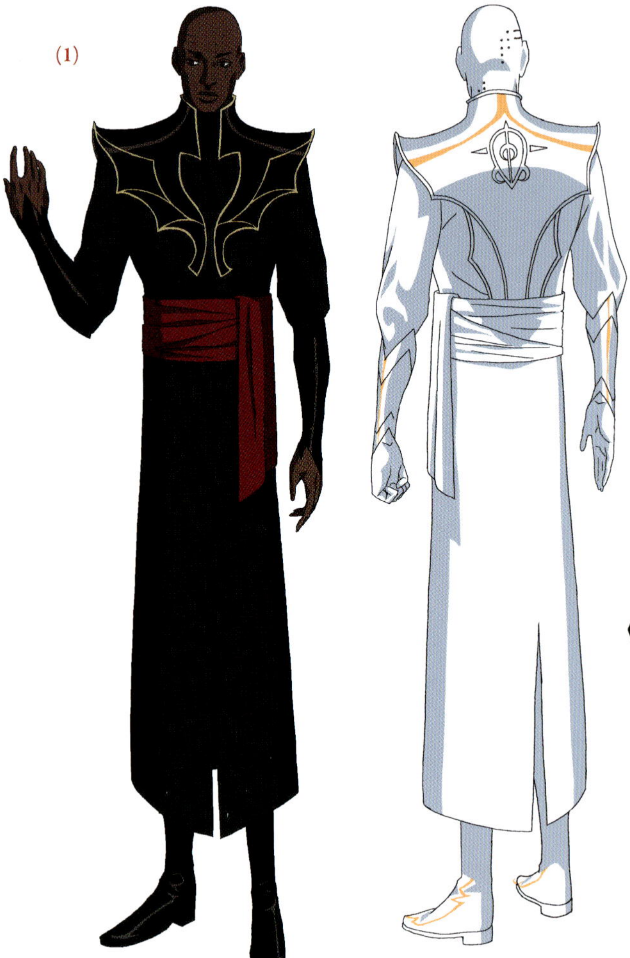

(2)

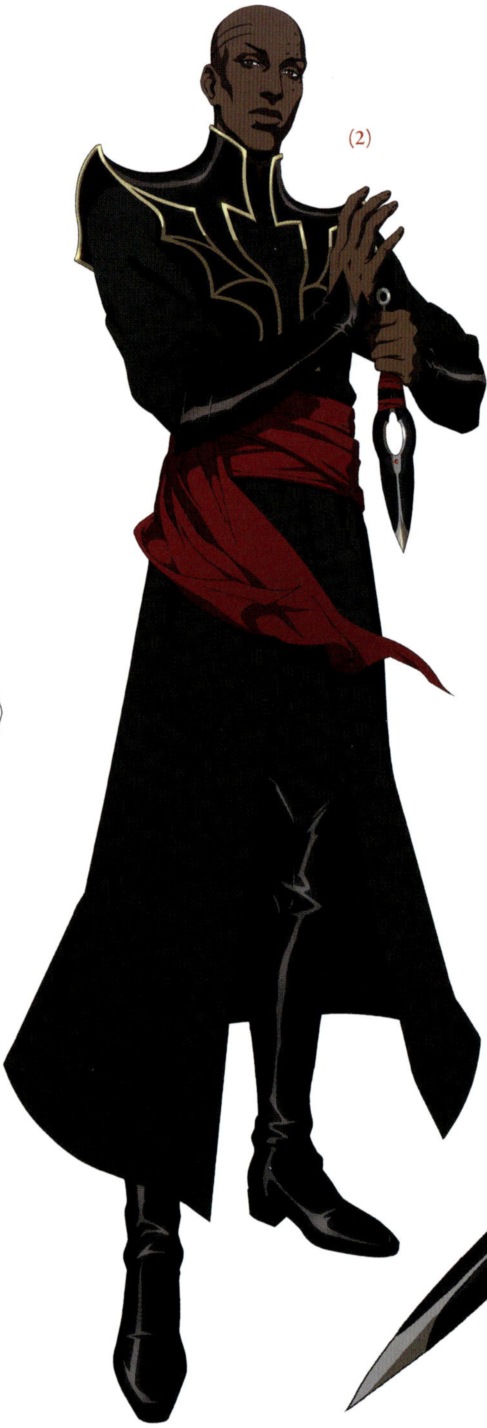

(3)

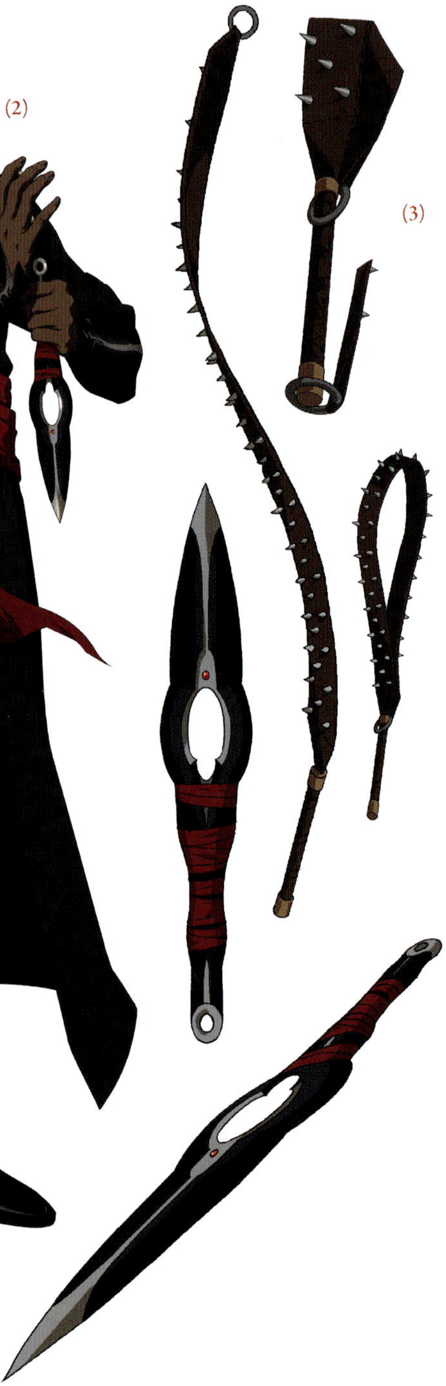

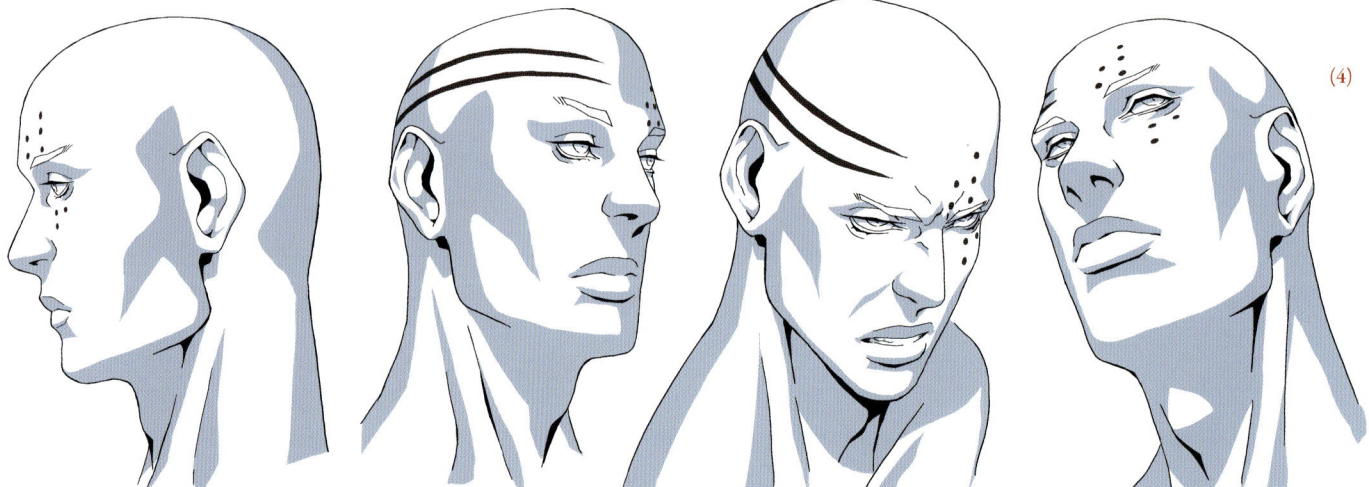

(4)

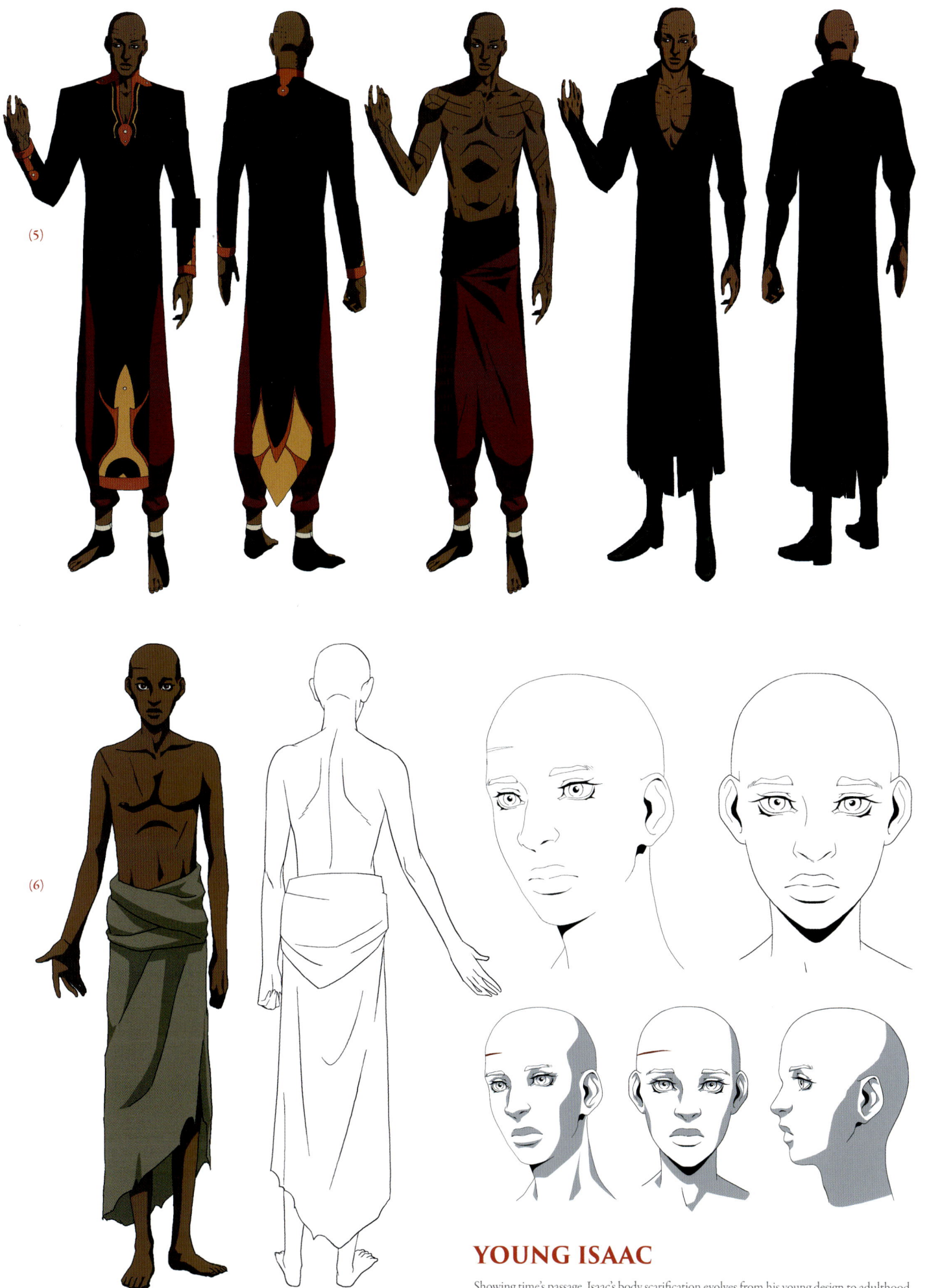

(5)

(6)

YOUNG ISAAC

Showing time's passage, Isaac's body scarification evolves from his young design to adulthood.

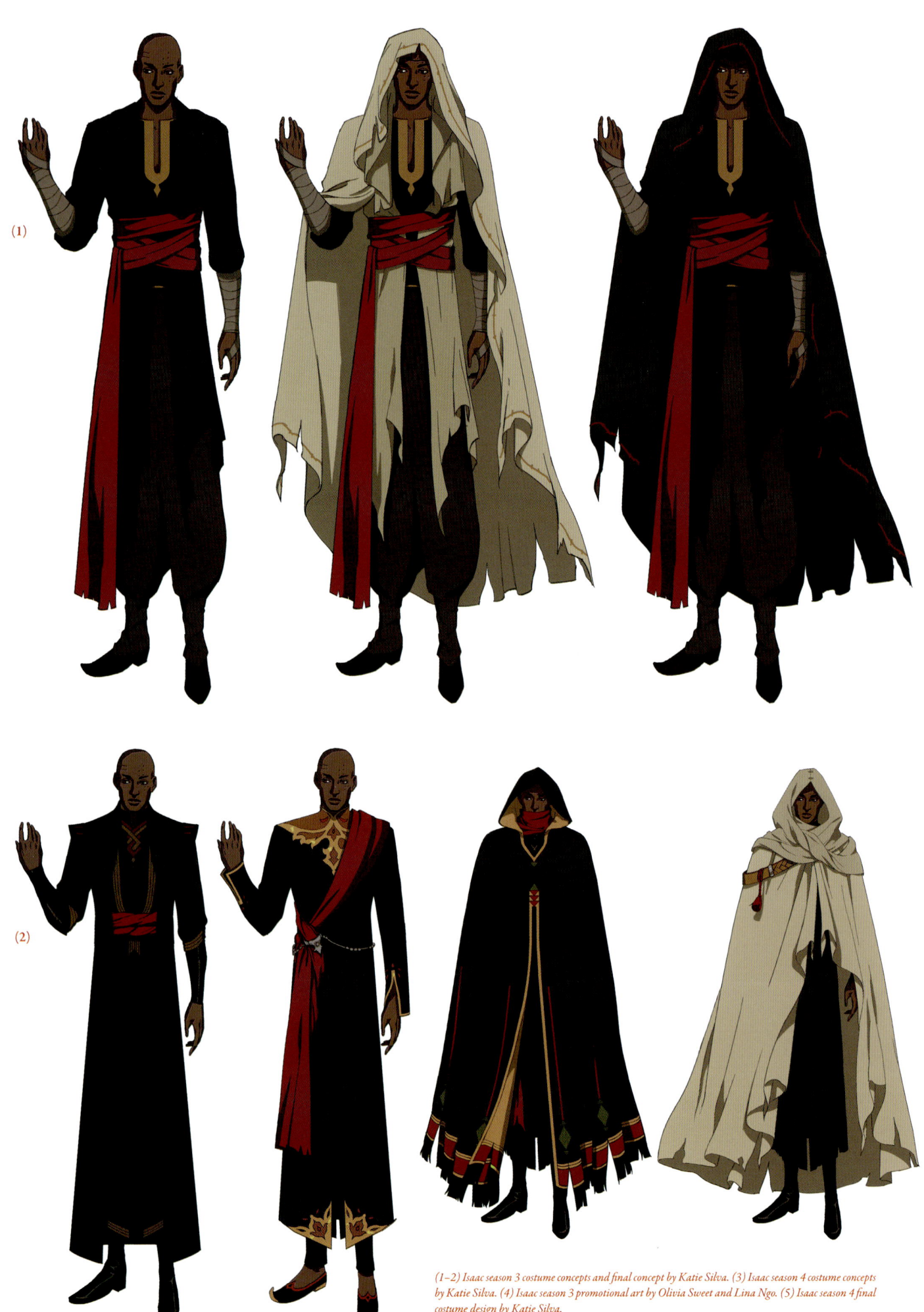

(1)

(2)

(1–2) Isaac season 3 costume concepts and final concept by Katie Silva. (3) Isaac season 4 costume concepts by Katie Silva. (4) Isaac season 3 promotional art by Olivia Sweet and Lina Ngo. (5) Isaac season 4 final costume design by Katie Silva.

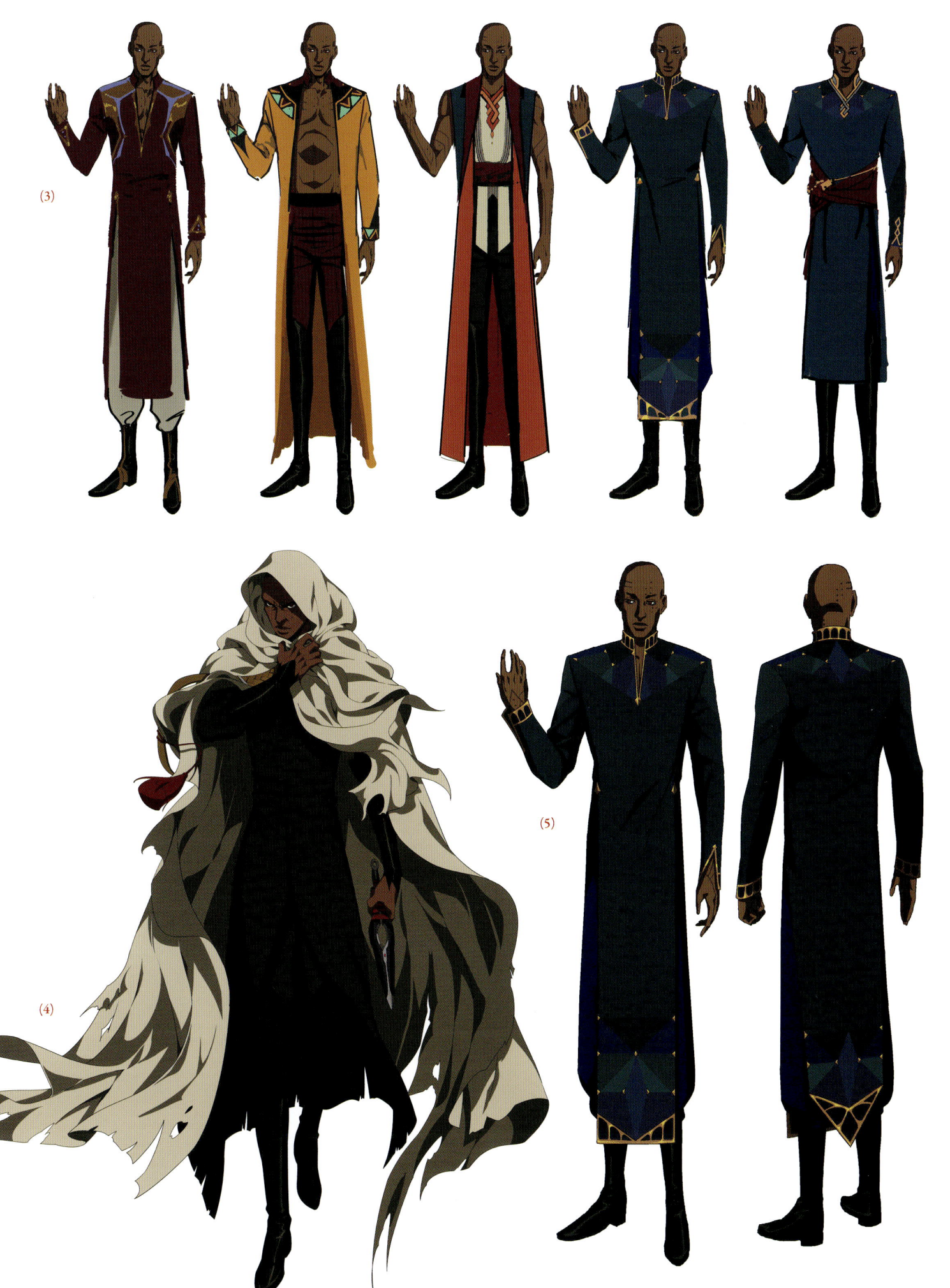

(3)

(4)

(5)

Godbrand

Early Godbrand concepts, including the first, chubbier, design (*bottom left*) described by Sam Deats as too "generic Viking" to do the job. The vocal performance by Peter Stormare, the asymmetrical, vaguely Viking-influenced armor, and a design reference of a gaunt Iggy Pop pushed Godbrand's direction toward the "sloppy rock star" version used in the series.

Left page: Godbrand early concepts by Sam Deats. Right page: (1) Godbrand final design by Sam Deats. (2) Viking crew members by Joanne Wong and Sam Deats.

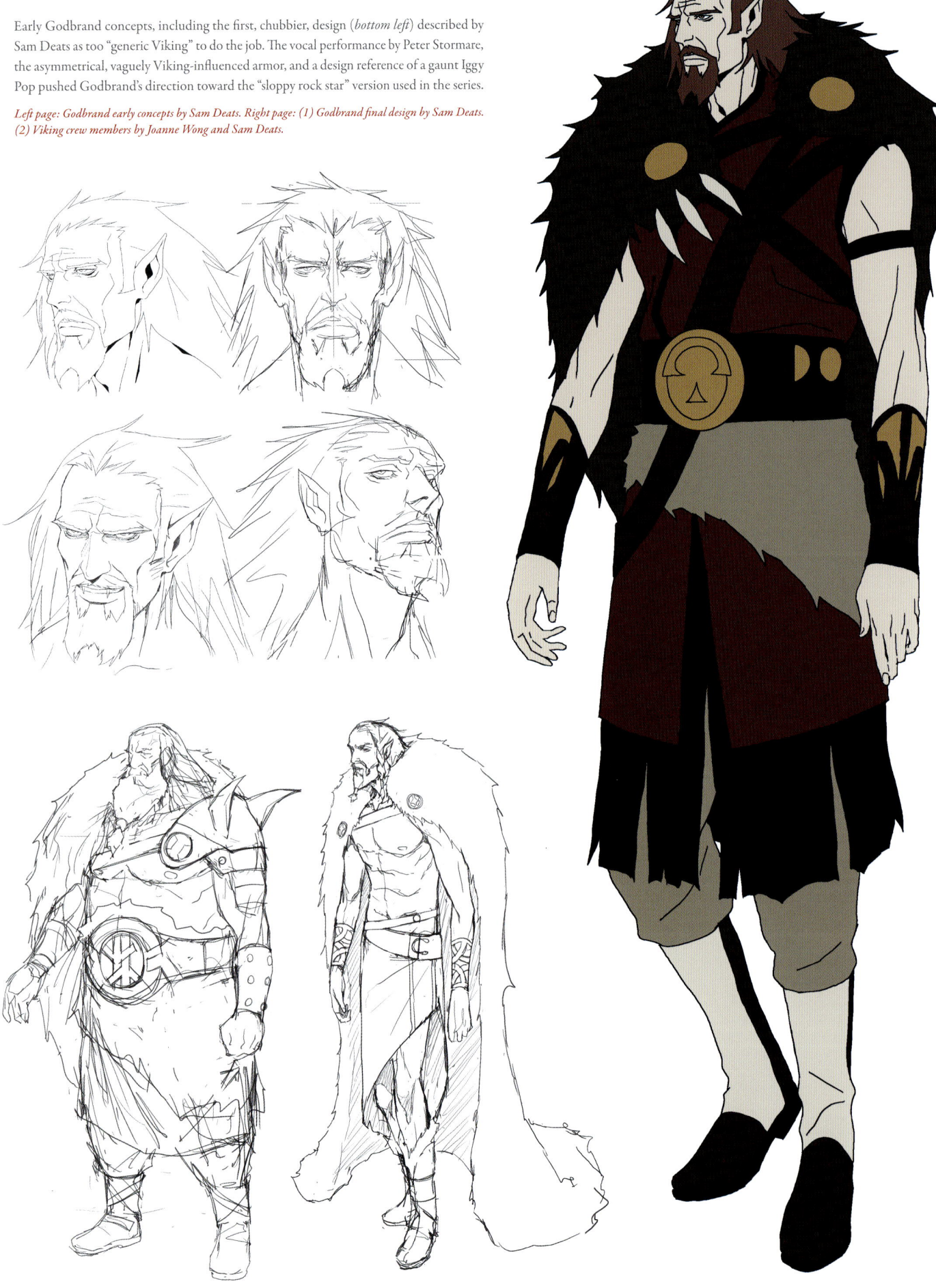

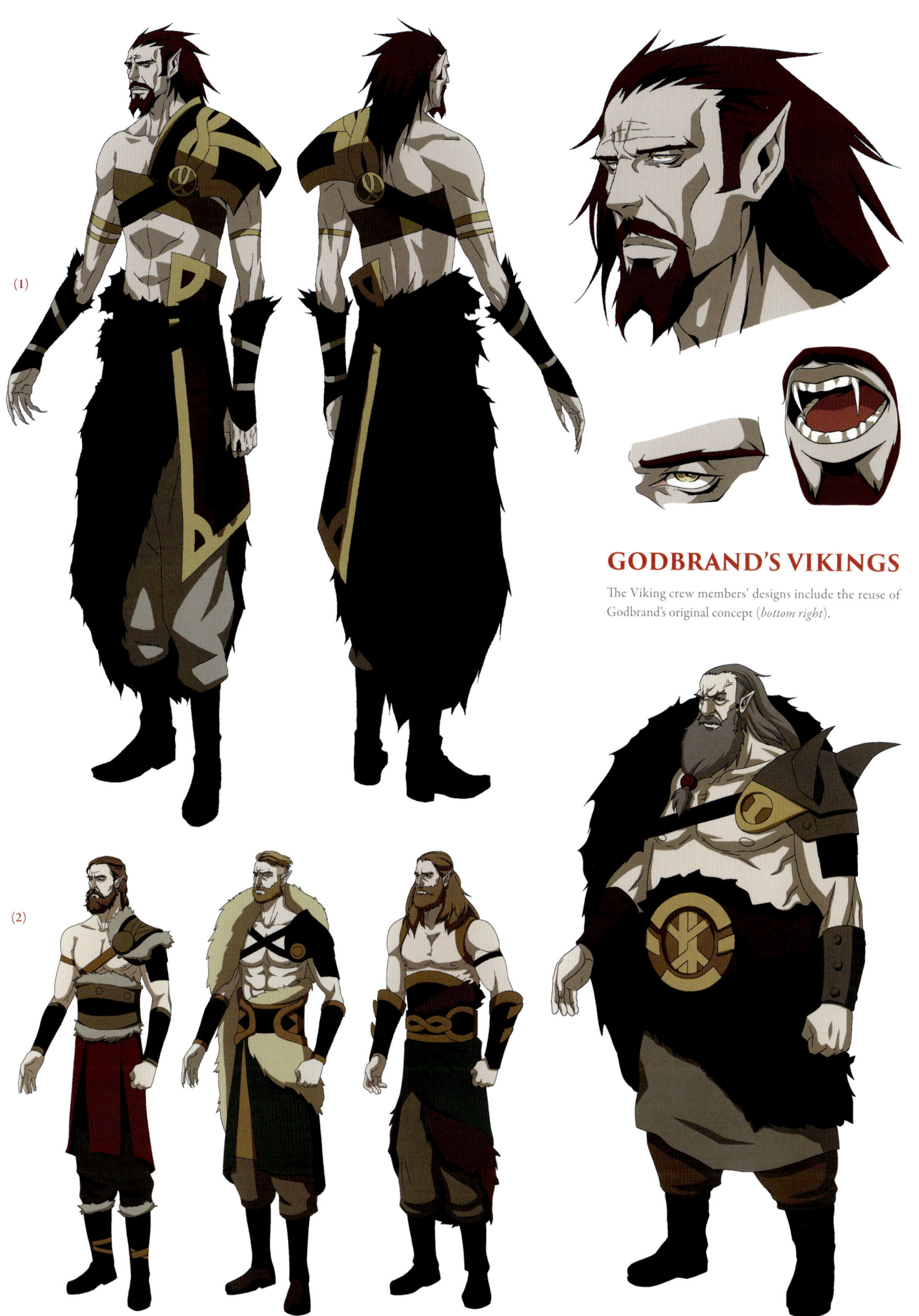

(1)

GODBRAND'S VIKINGS

The Viking crew members' designs include the reuse of Godbrand's original concept (*bottom right*).

(2)

Carmilla

The leader of the Council of Sisters, Carmilla swooped in with a plan to fill the power vacuum left by Dracula's demise. *Left:* This early Carmilla concept references her Lords of Shadow design, but the gratuitously featured bosom from the game ultimately didn't fit the character as she appears in the series. *Center:* Carmilla's flashback costume design.

(1) Carmilla early concept by Sam Deats. (2) Carmilla flashback costume design by Joanne Wong. (3) Art by Olivia Sweet, cleanup by Lina Ngo. (4) Carmilla early concepts and designs by Sam Deats.

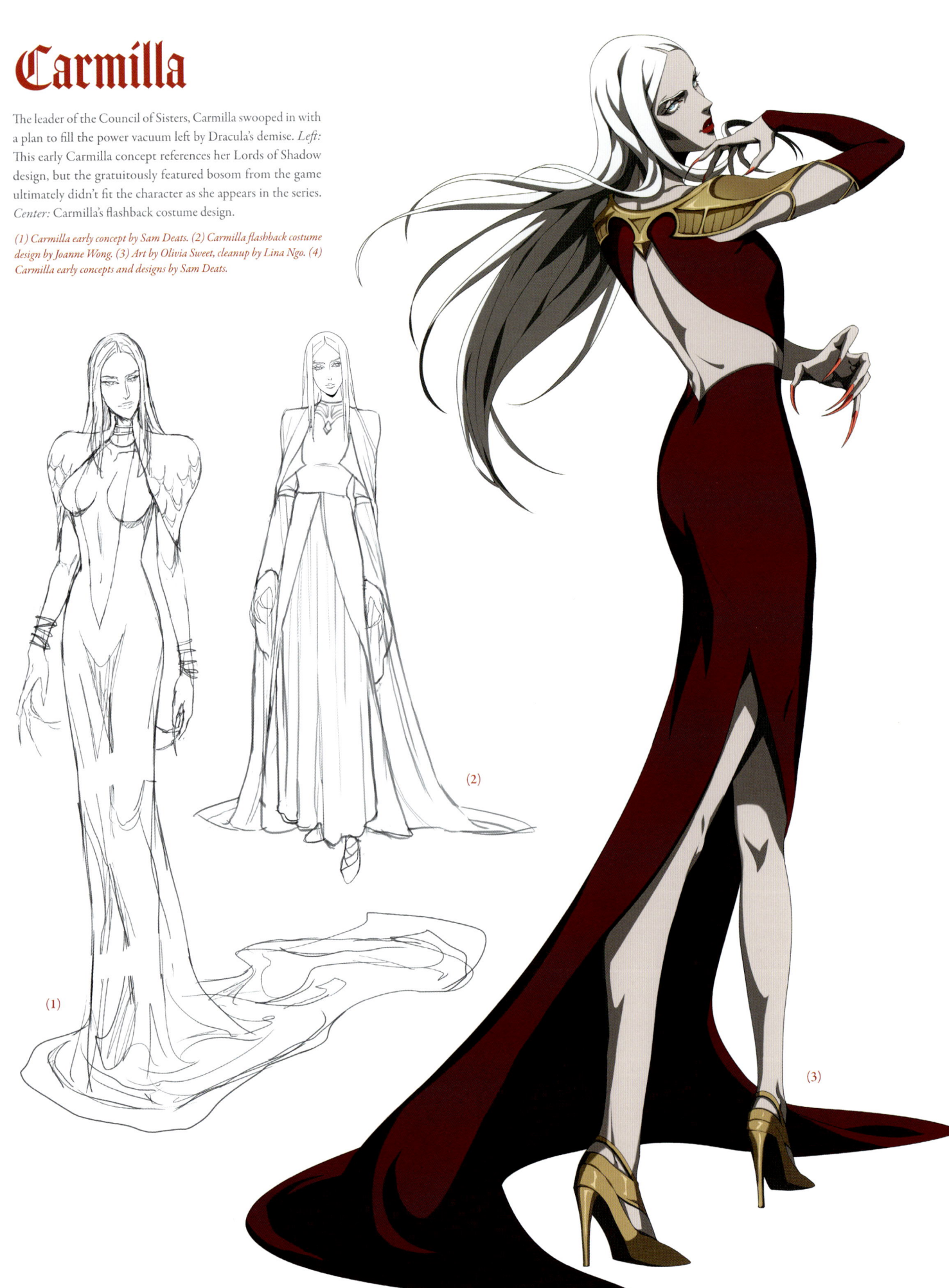

(1)

(2)

(3)

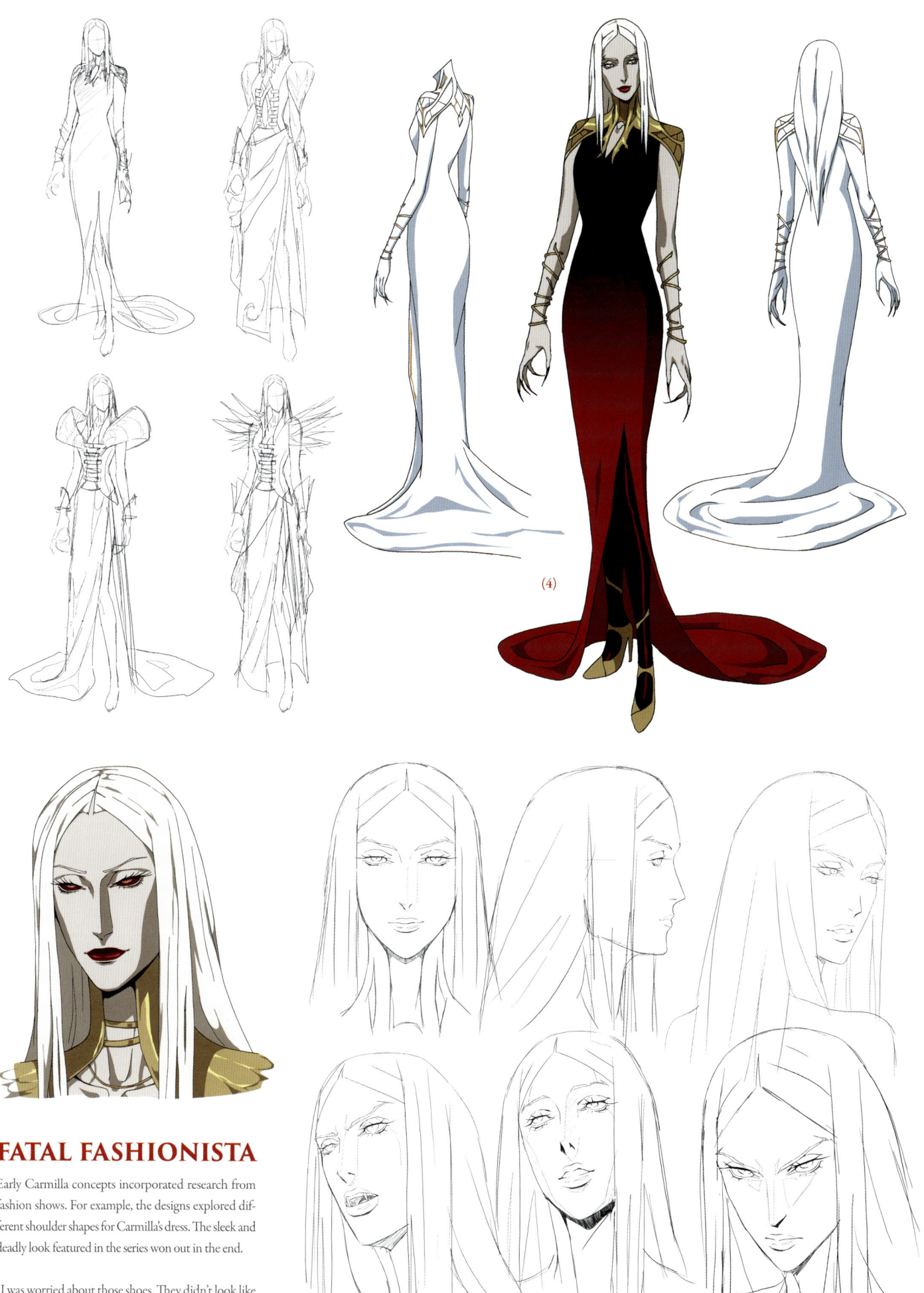

(4)

FATAL FASHIONISTA

Early Carmilla concepts incorporated research from fashion shows. For example, the designs explored different shoulder shapes for Carmilla's dress. The sleek and deadly look featured in the series won out in the end.

"I was worried about those shoes. They didn't look like sensible fighting shoes to me. [*laughs*]" —Kevin Kolde

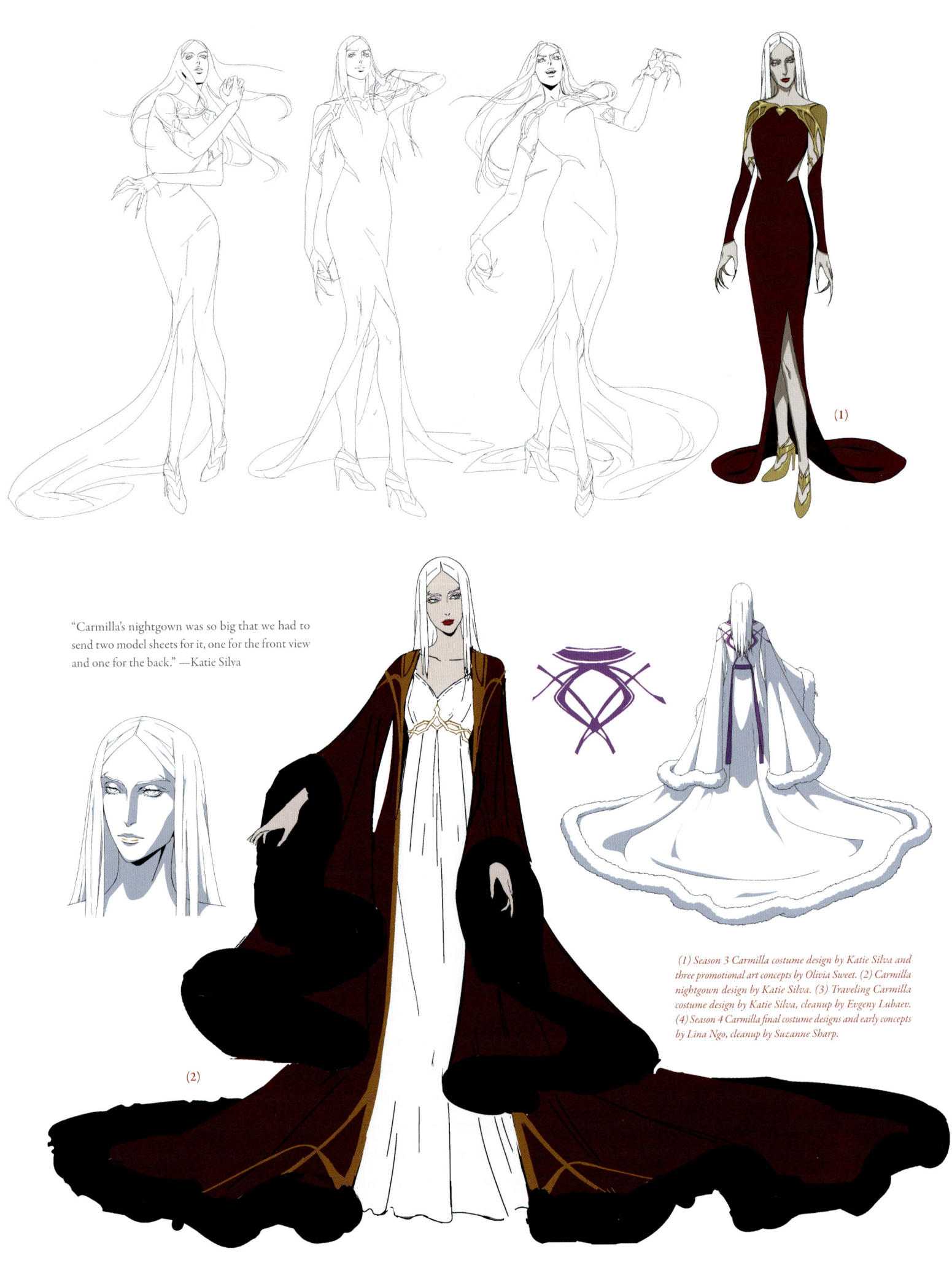

"Carmilla's nightgown was so big that we had to send two model sheets for it, one for the front view and one for the back." —Katie Silva

(1)

(2)

(1) Season 3 Carmilla costume design by Katie Silva and three promotional art concepts by Olivia Sweet. (2) Carmilla nightgown design by Katie Silva. (3) Traveling Carmilla costume design by Katie Silva, cleanup by Evgeny Lubaev. (4) Season 4 Carmilla final costume designs and early concepts by Lina Ngo, cleanup by Suzanne Sharp.

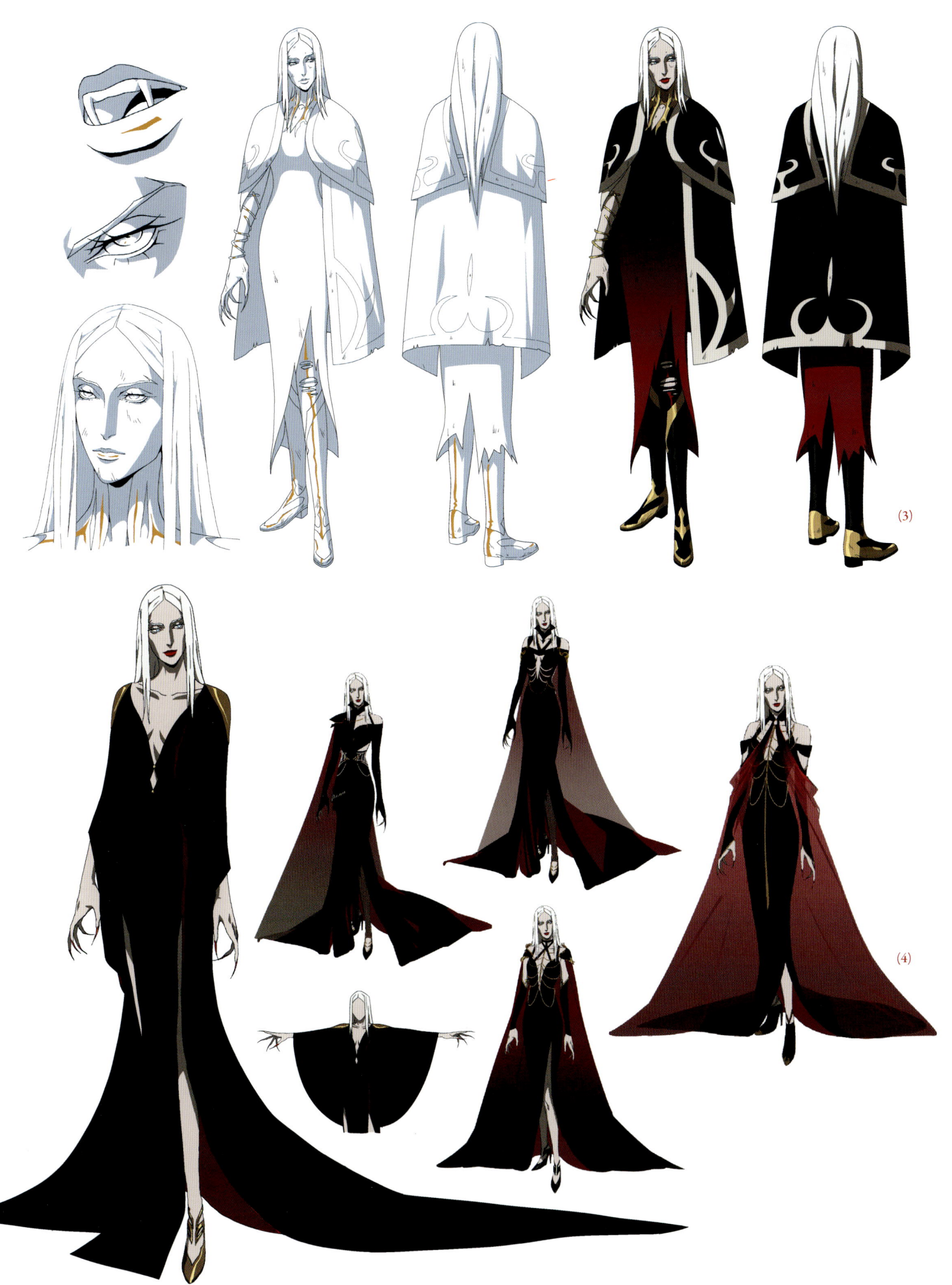

Striga

"Striga was originally supposed to be more of a sneaky rogue–type character who would stab you in the back or take you out with poison, but no one was really feeling those designs, so we kept drawing her bigger and bigger with each pass until she became a seven-foot-tall warrior with a huge sword." —Katie Silva

(1)

(1) Striga design by Katie Silva.
(2) Season 3 promotional art by Jazz Valkyrie, cleanup by Lina Ngo. (3) Striga early concepts by Katie Silva. (4) Striga uncloaked casual design, early design concepts, and (5) day armor and sword designs by Katie Silva.

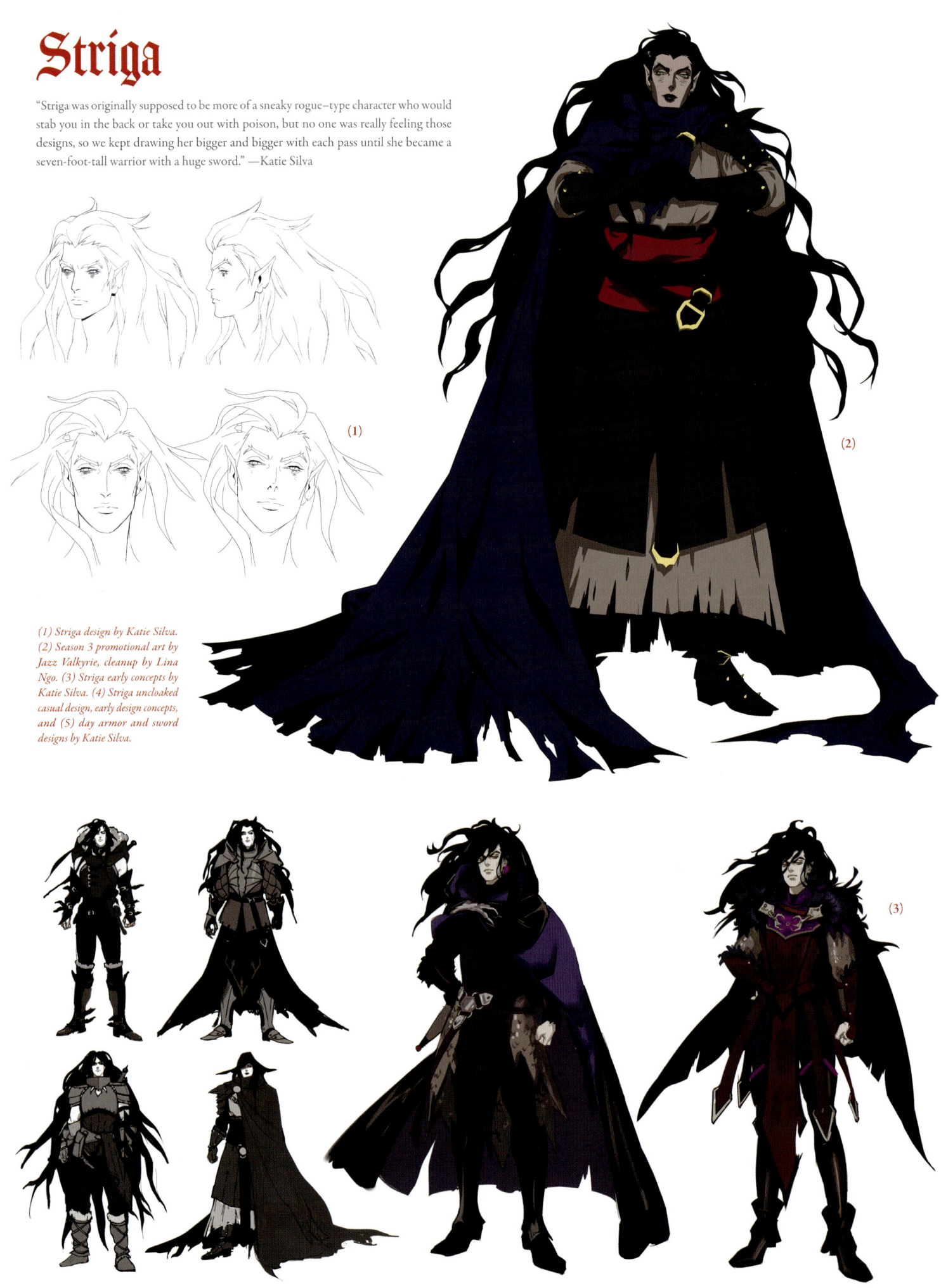

(2)

(3)

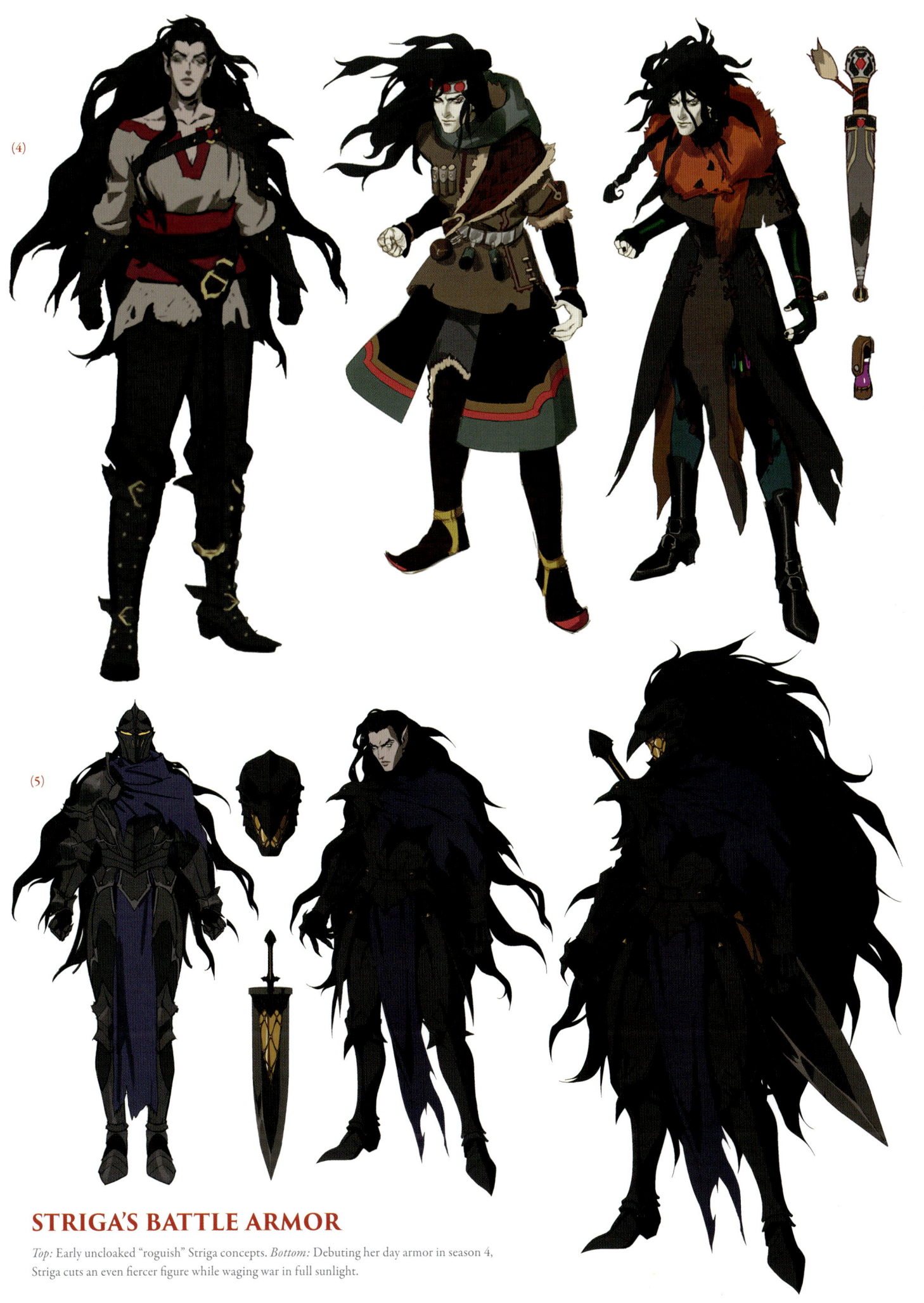

STRIGA'S BATTLE ARMOR

Top: Early uncloaked "roguish" Striga concepts. *Bottom:* Debuting her day armor in season 4, Striga cuts an even fiercer figure while waging war in full sunlight.

Morana

With origins in ancient Sumeria or Mesopotamia, Morana is the oldest of the Council of Sisters. Morana's name was inspired by the Slavic pagan goddess who is connected to seasonal rites about the cyclical death and rebirth of nature. Designer Katie Silva incorporated Elizabethan silhouettes with accessories inspired by more ancient times.

"Her earrings reference ancient Sumerian designs that might be worn by a queen. Her shawl is based off of something called a *kaumake*, which is only depicted in ancient stone carvings, so we don't actually know whether it was made of leaves, or feathers, or fabric, but it is supposed to be something that she's had for a very long time. She's got modern cut-crease eyeliner!" —Katie Silva

All art on these pages by Katie Silva.

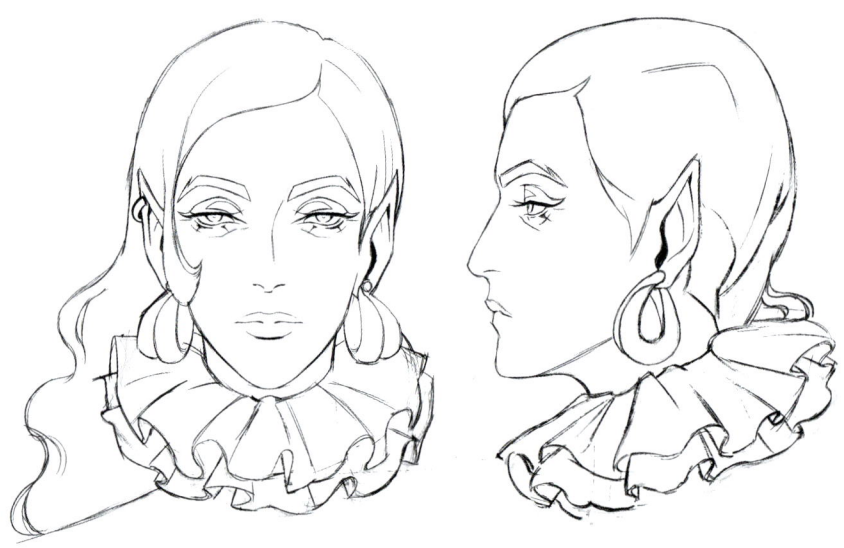

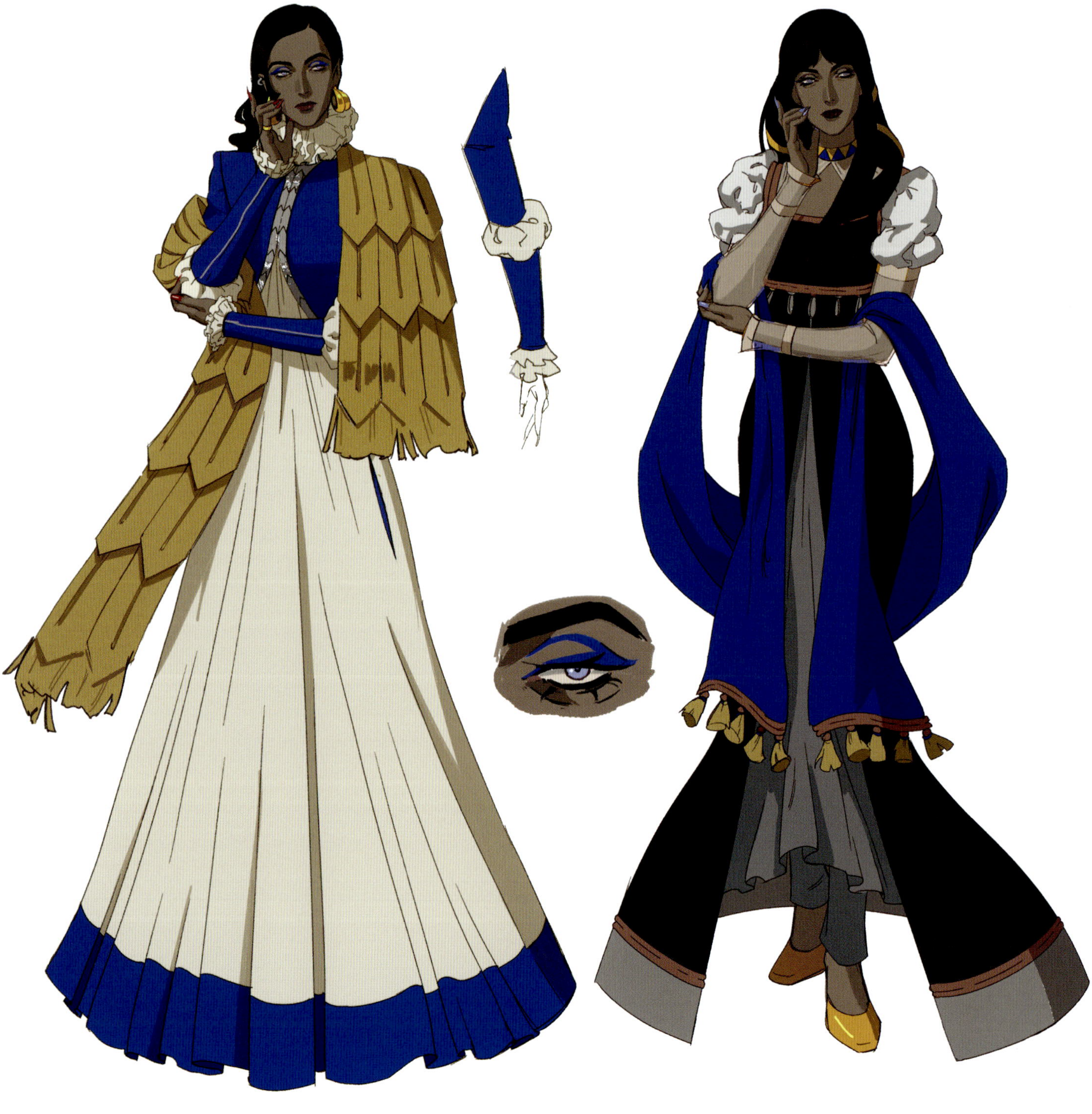

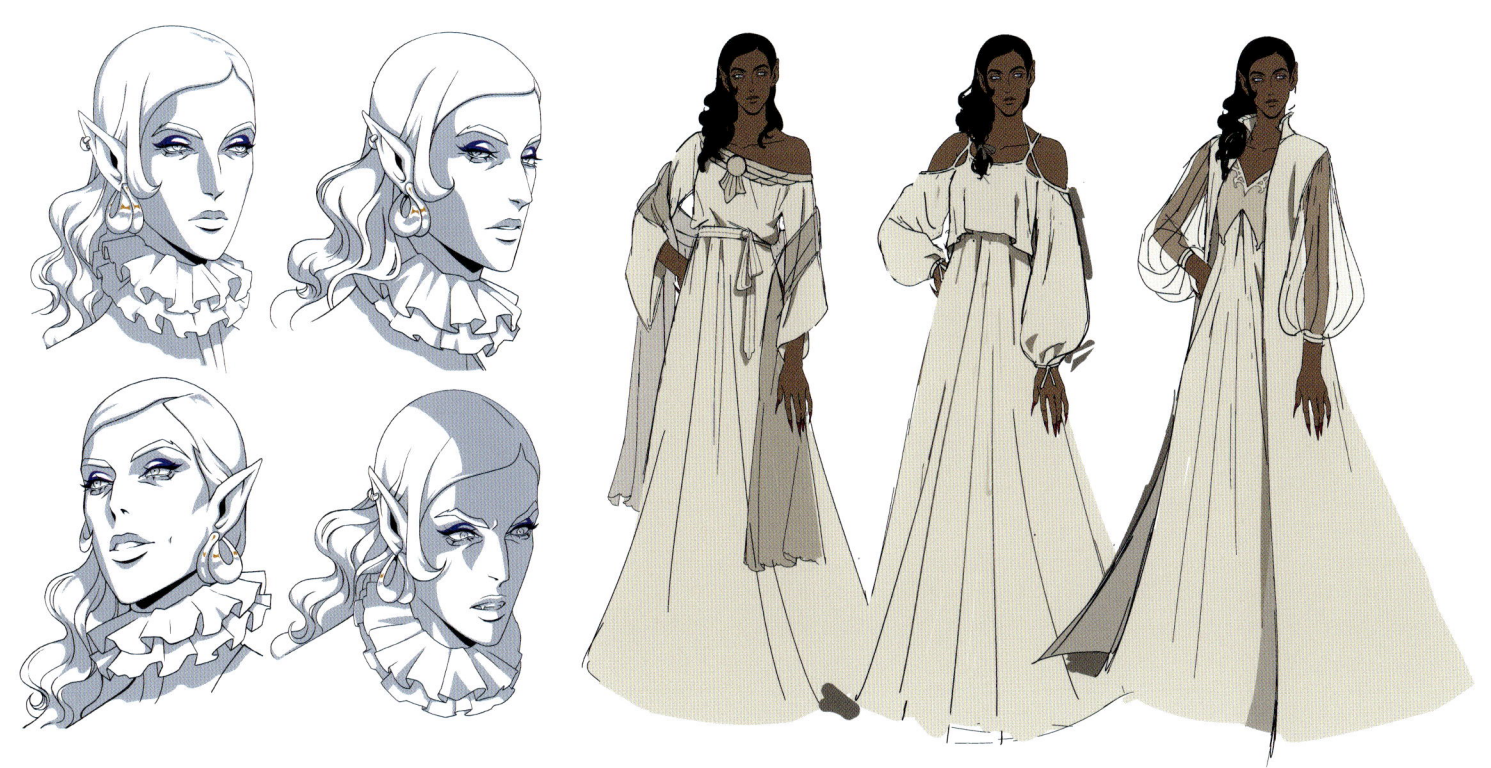

"In our show, vampire clothing in general is more anachronistic than human clothing, so we can draw from a lot more time periods and places for their outfits instead of sticking to the Middle Ages. Sam always says to just ask ourselves if the outfit we are designing is any more modern than Alucard's V-neck, and if the answer is no, then we're probably okay." —Katie Silva

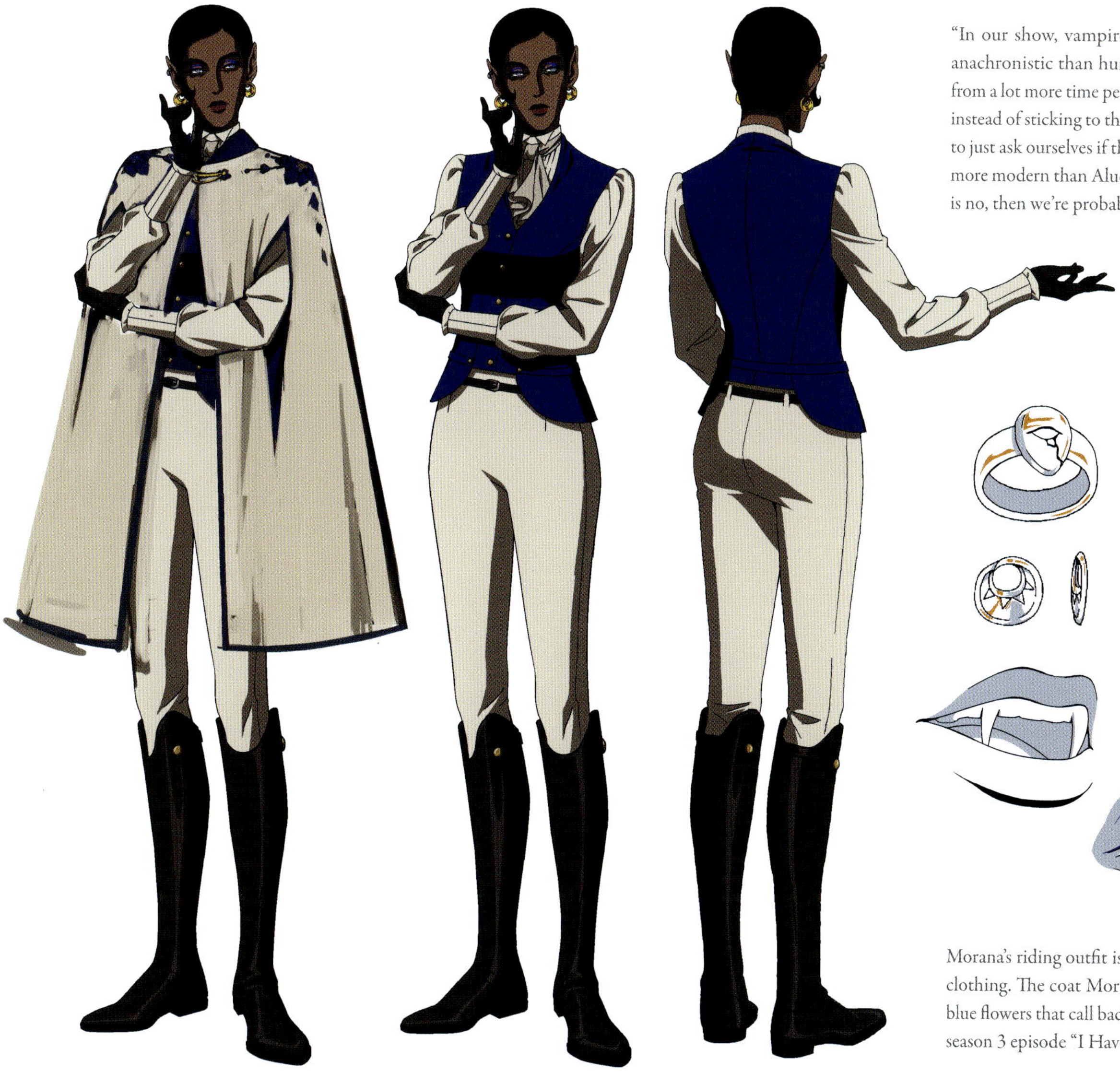

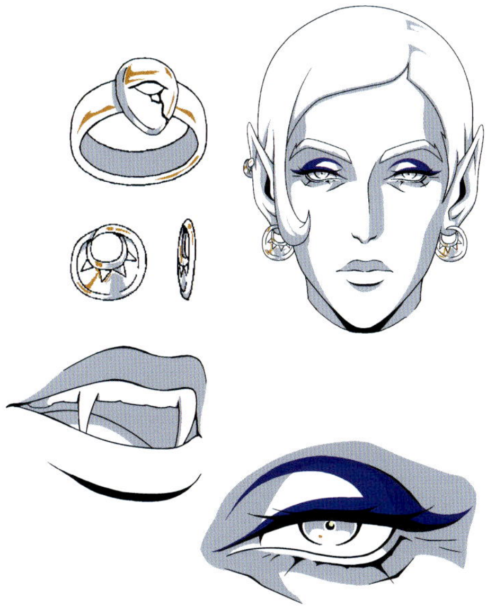

Morana's riding outfit is essentially a modern piece of clothing. The coat Morana wears in season 4 features blue flowers that call back to her date with Striga in the season 3 episode "I Have a Scheme."

Lenore

The diplomatic vampire among the Council of Sisters, Lenore uses her skills to manipulate Hector into doing their bidding until he is molded into their own resident forgemaster. Lenore was Katie Silva's first design on the series after joining the Powerhouse crew.

All art on these pages by Katie Silva.

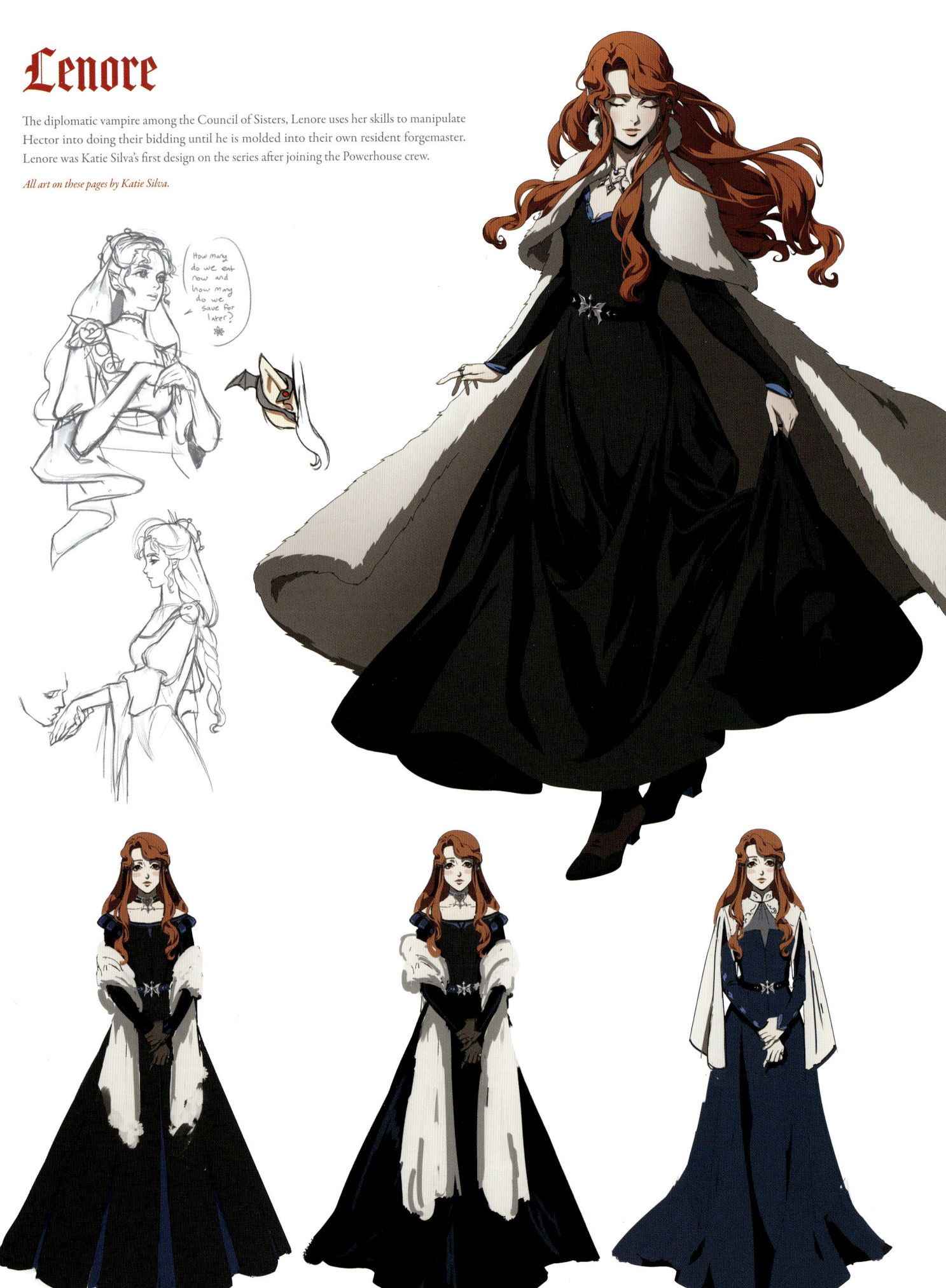

How many do we eat now and how many do we save for later?

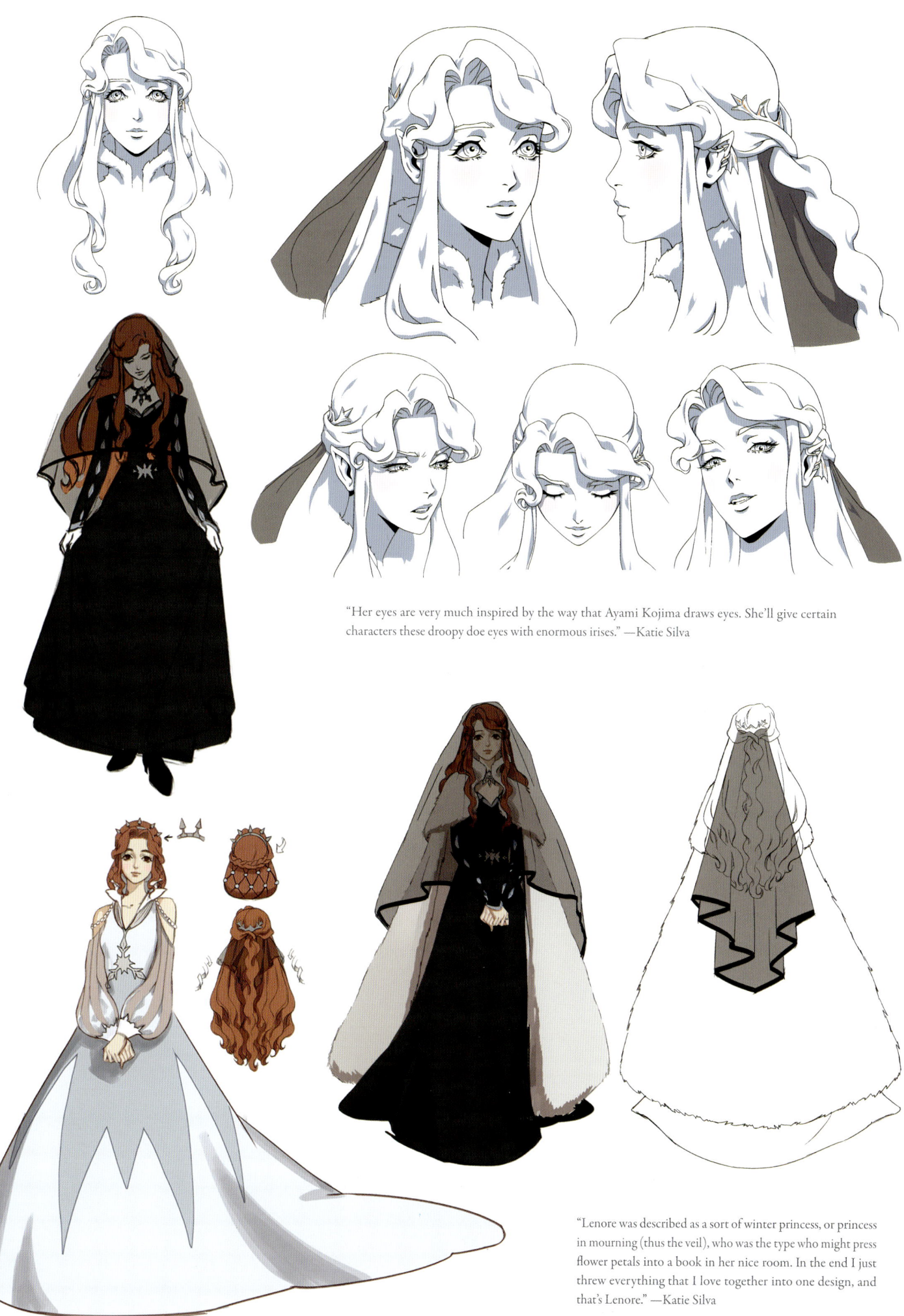

"Her eyes are very much inspired by the way that Ayami Kojima draws eyes. She'll give certain characters these droopy doe eyes with enormous irises." —Katie Silva

"Lenore was described as a sort of winter princess, or princess in mourning (thus the veil), who was the type who might press flower petals into a book in her nice room. In the end I just threw everything that I love together into one design, and that's Lenore." —Katie Silva

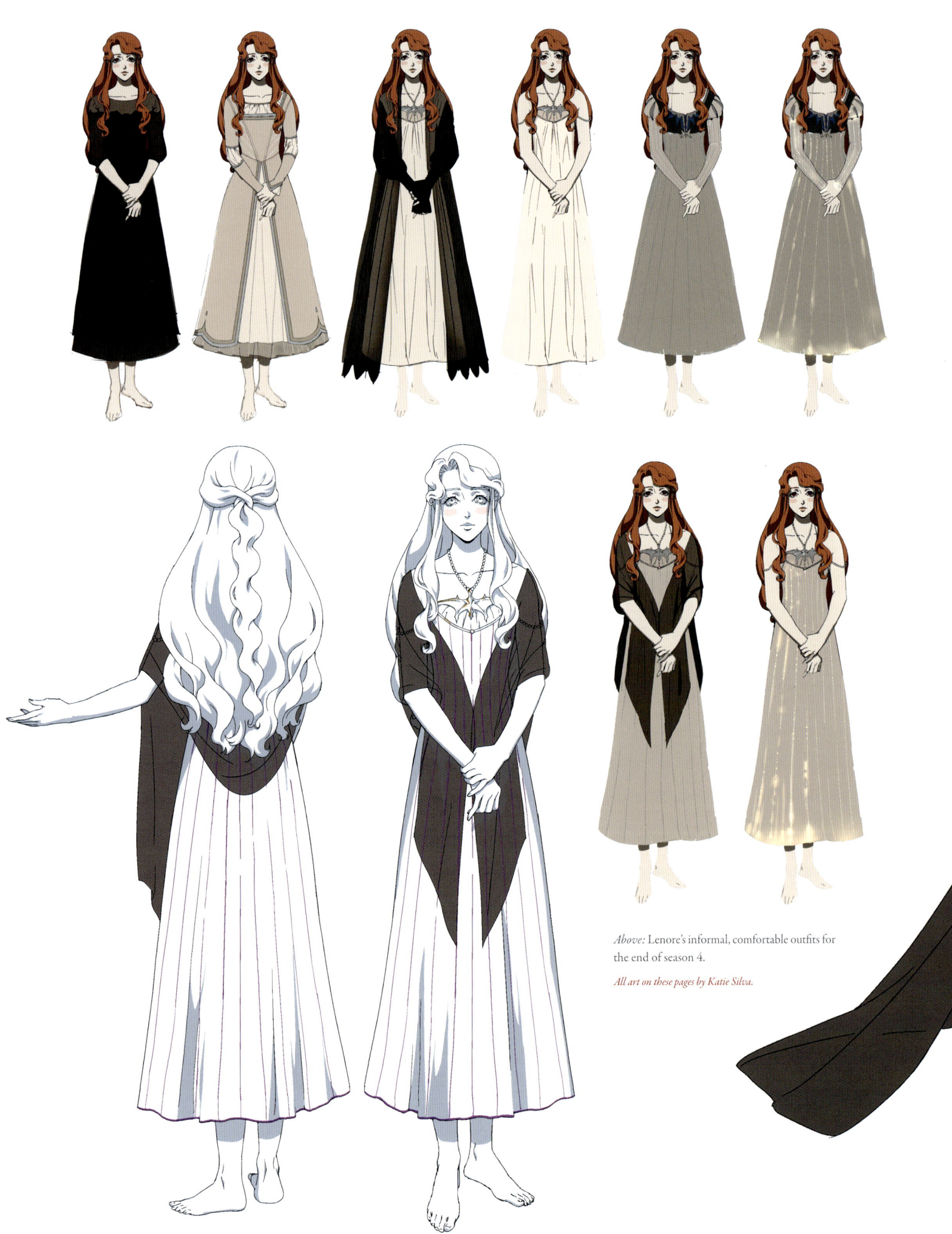

Above: Lenore's informal, comfortable outfits for the end of season 4.

All art on these pages by Katie Silva.

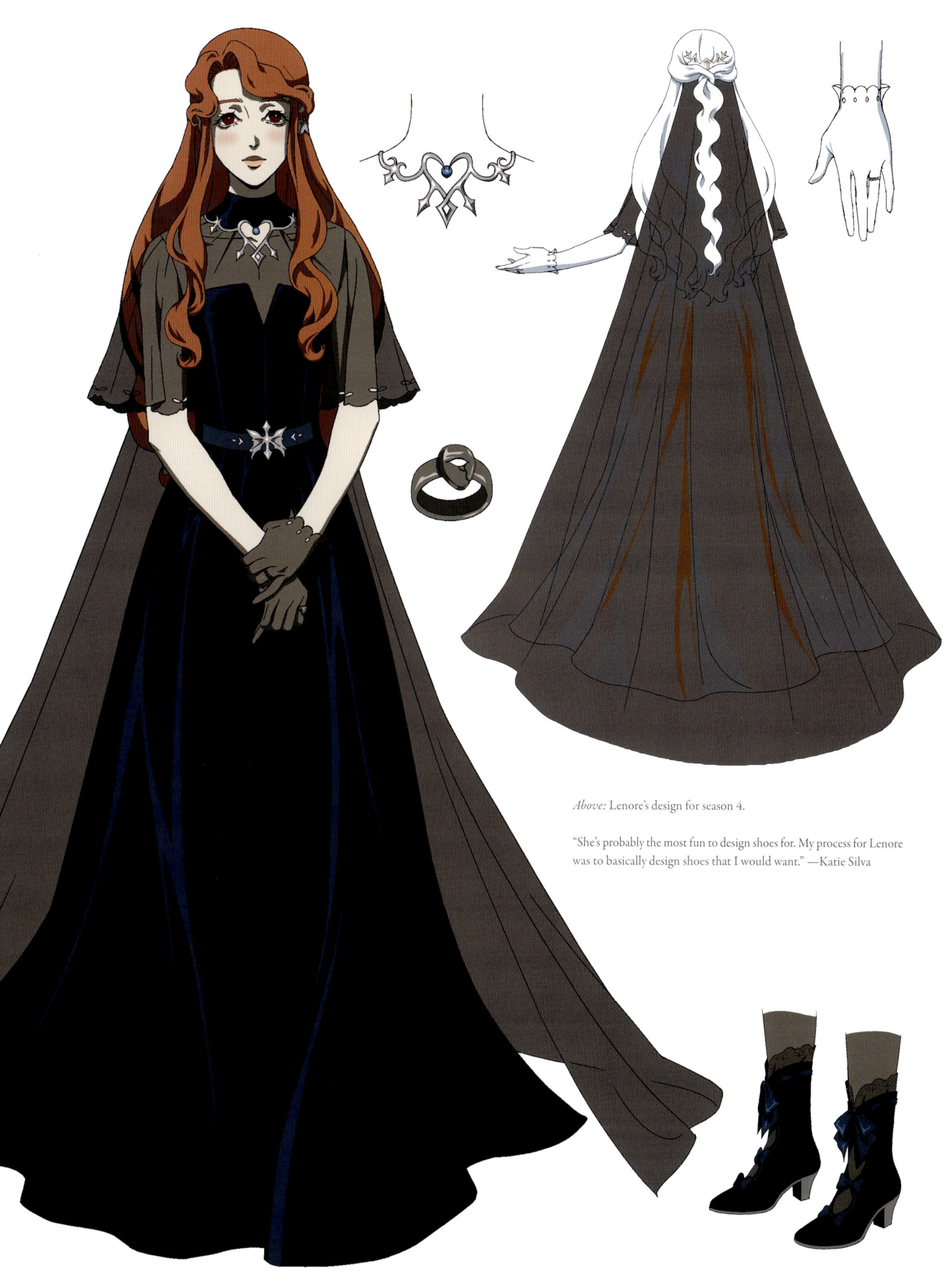

Above: Lenore's design for season 4.

"She's probably the most fun to design shoes for. My process for Lenore was to basically design shoes that I would want." —Katie Silva

Vampire Generals

Originally scripted to perish in the flood of holy water along with their vampire troops in season 2, Dracula's vampire generals were spared by a special request from Sam Deats.

"We wanted to have them stick around a bit longer so that Trevor, Sypha, and Alucard could have some good minibosses to fight in the upcoming opening battle." —Sam Deats

Character designs by Sam Deats, cleanup by Stephanie McCrea Rainosek and Robby Cook.

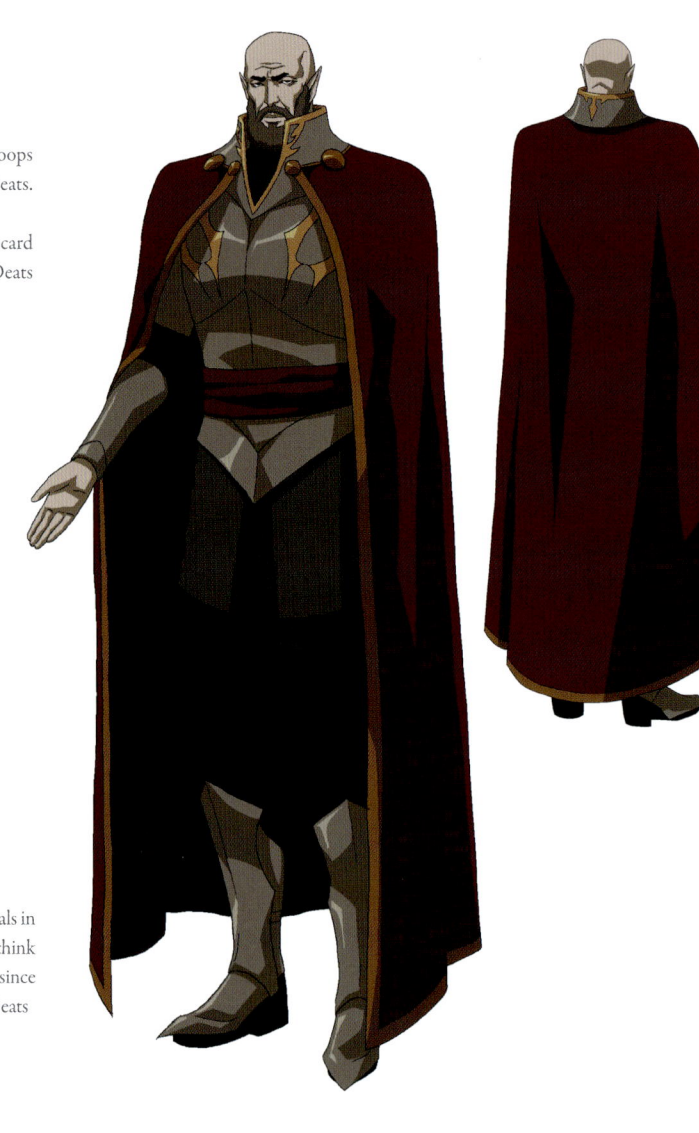

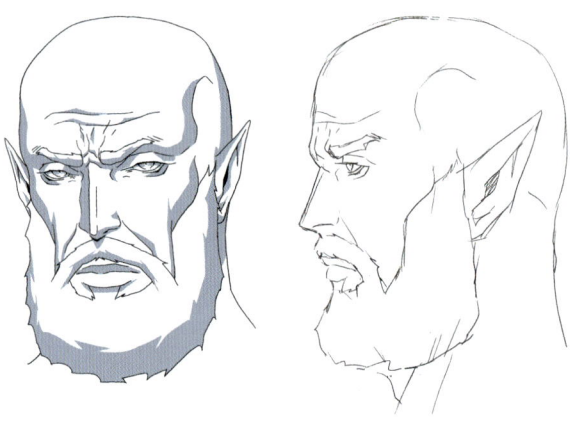

DRAGOSLAV AND ZUFALL

Dragoslav and Zufall were designed to be intimidating if somewhat understated generals in Dracula's army—especially when compared to some of the more eccentric members. "I think Dragoslav is Slavic and Zufall is German. That was basically their whole description, since they weren't originally scripted and were just written as 'Dracula's generals.'" —Sam Deats

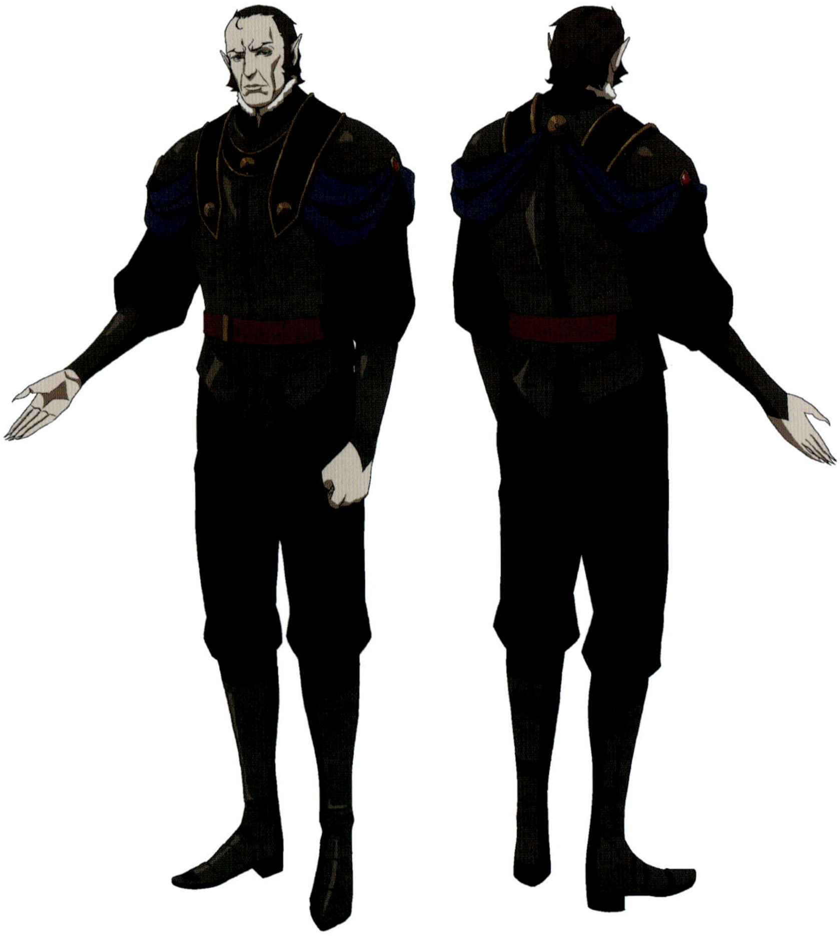

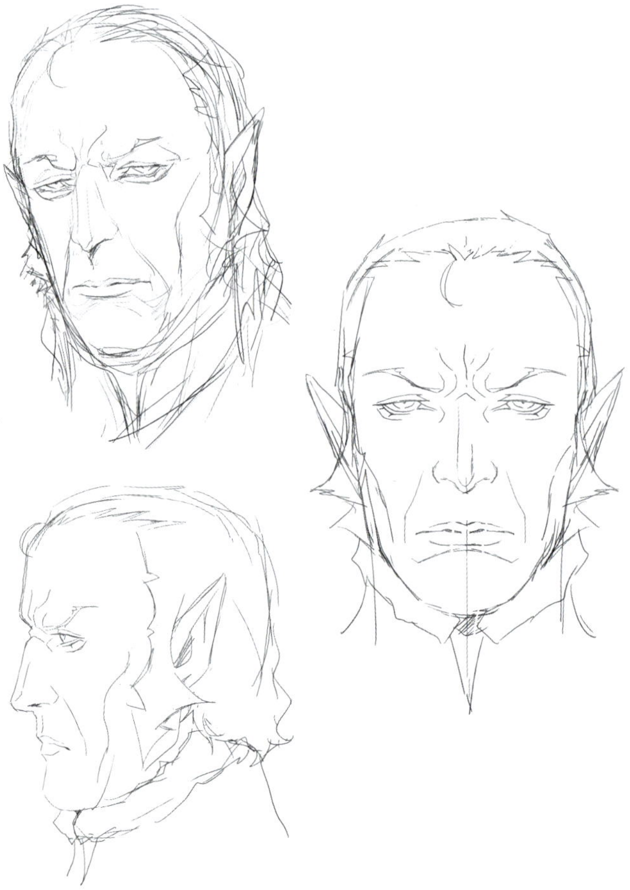

RAMAN

Raman is a vampire general from India inspired by some of India's own vampiric lore.

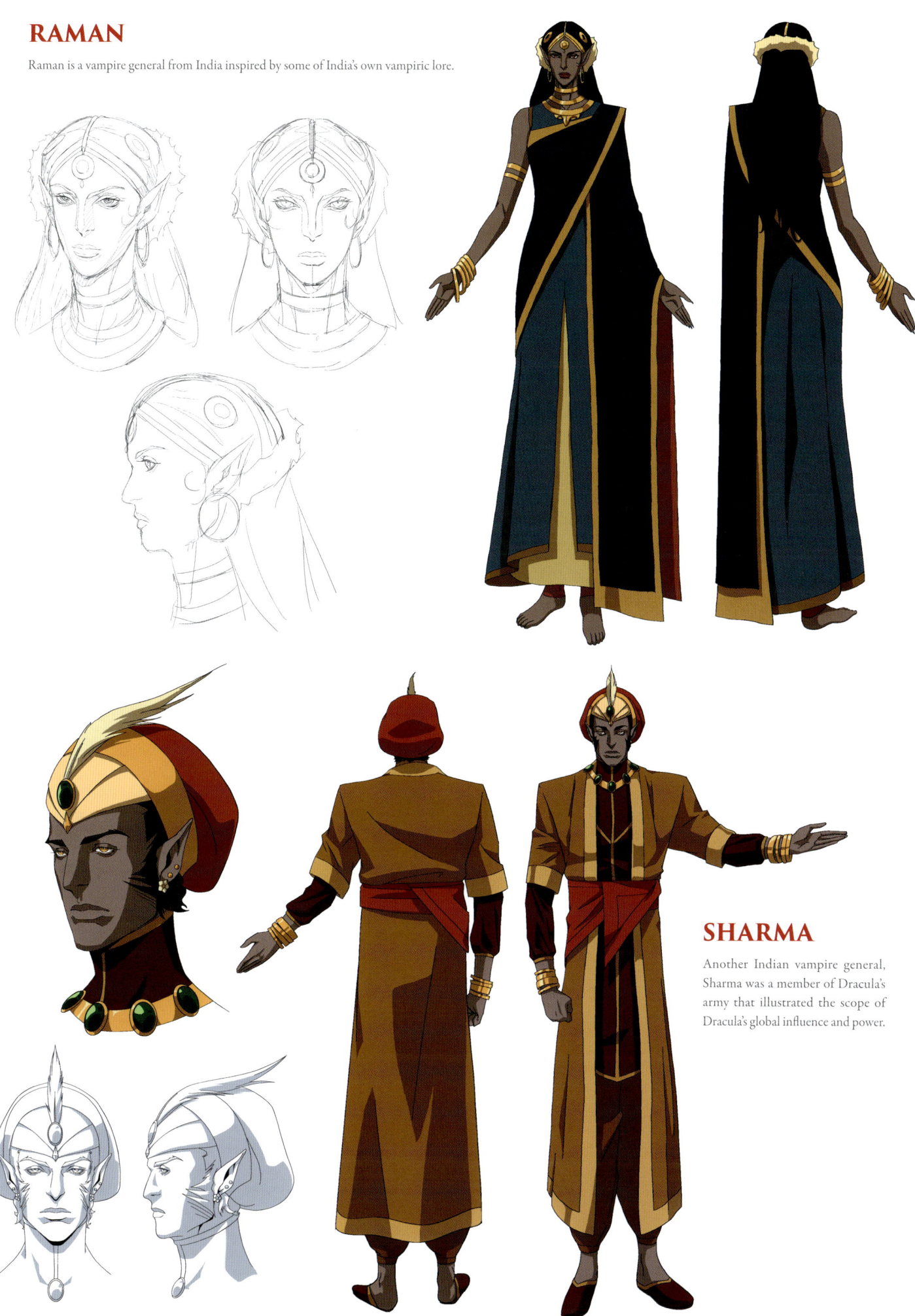

SHARMA

Another Indian vampire general, Sharma was a member of Dracula's army that illustrated the scope of Dracula's global influence and power.

CHO

A vampire general from Japan, Cho first appeared in season 2. Later, in Sumi and Taka's flashback, we learn of her cruel imperial court stocked with human slaves who are forced to watch as she battles oncoming challengers before drinking their blood.

(1) Cho design by Sam Deats, model sheet cleanup by Stephanie McCrea Rainosek. (2) Cho's court guards design by Katie Silva. Mon design by Sean Randolph. (3) Human slave designs by Evgeny Lubaev, cleanup by Stephanie McCrea Rainosek and Katie Silva.

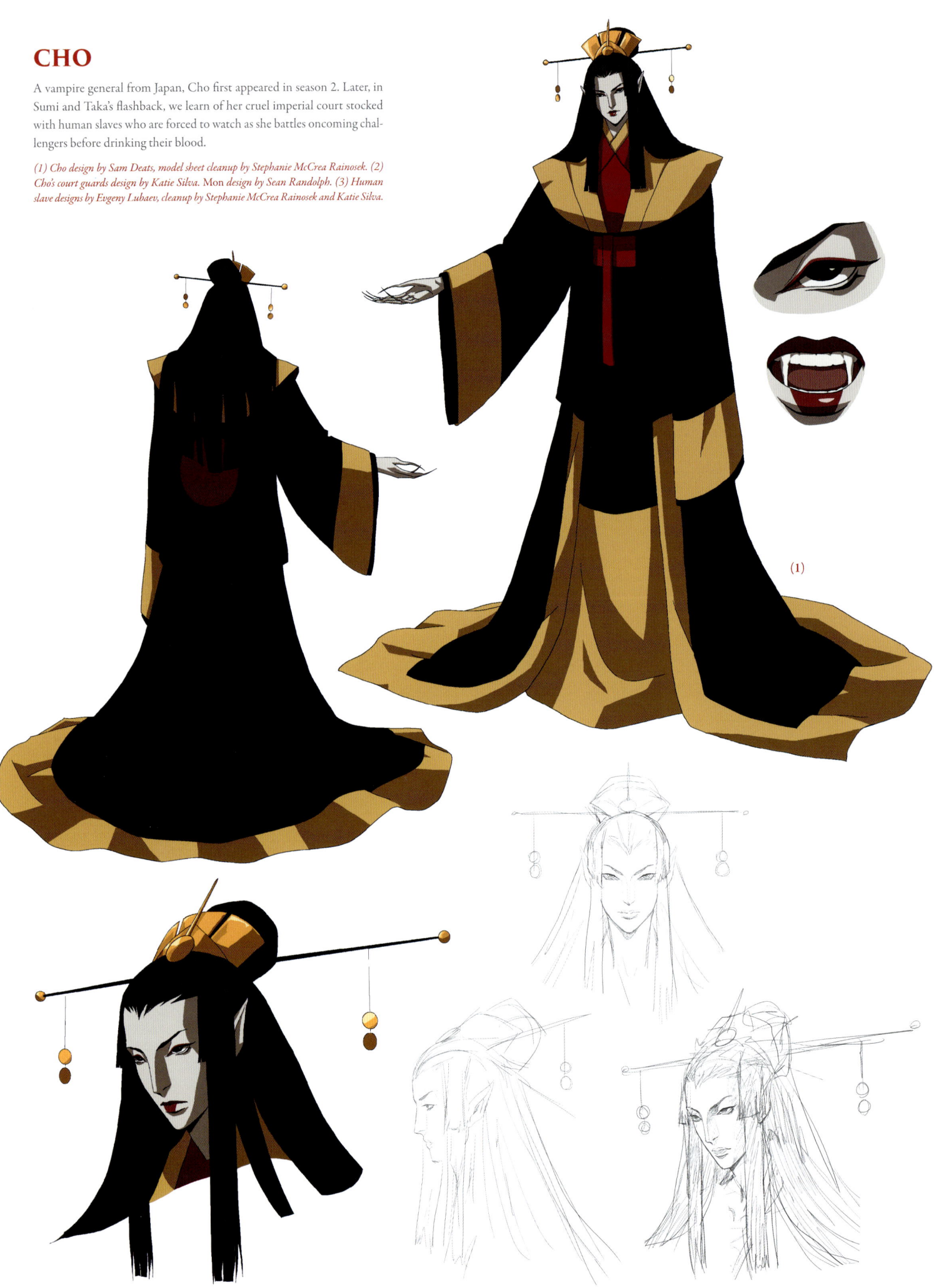

(1)

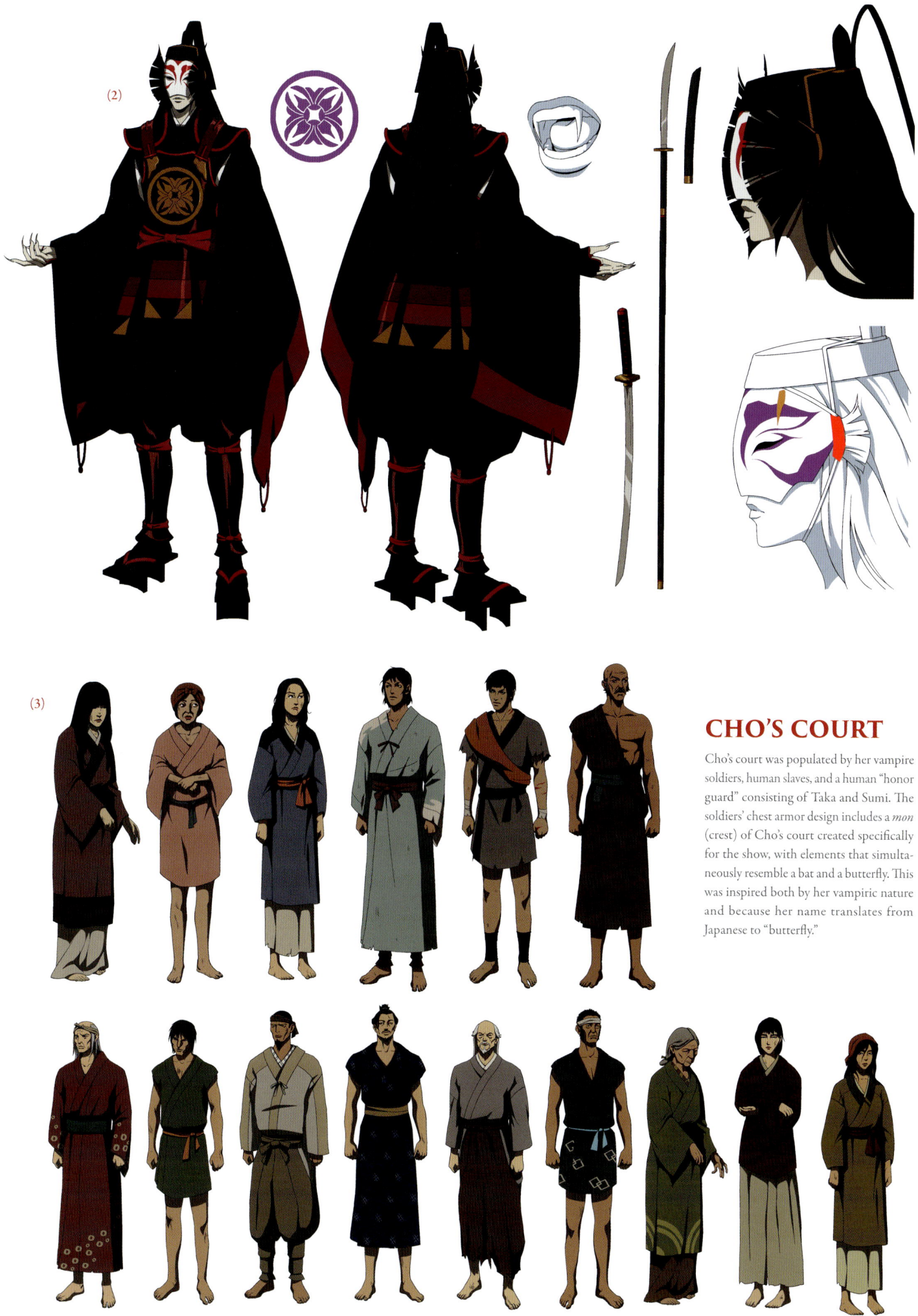

(2)

(3)

CHO'S COURT

Cho's court was populated by her vampire soldiers, human slaves, and a human "honor guard" consisting of Taka and Sumi. The soldiers' chest armor design includes a *mon* (crest) of Cho's court created specifically for the show, with elements that simultaneously resemble a bat and a butterfly. This was inspired both by her vampiric nature and because her name translates from Japanese to "butterfly."

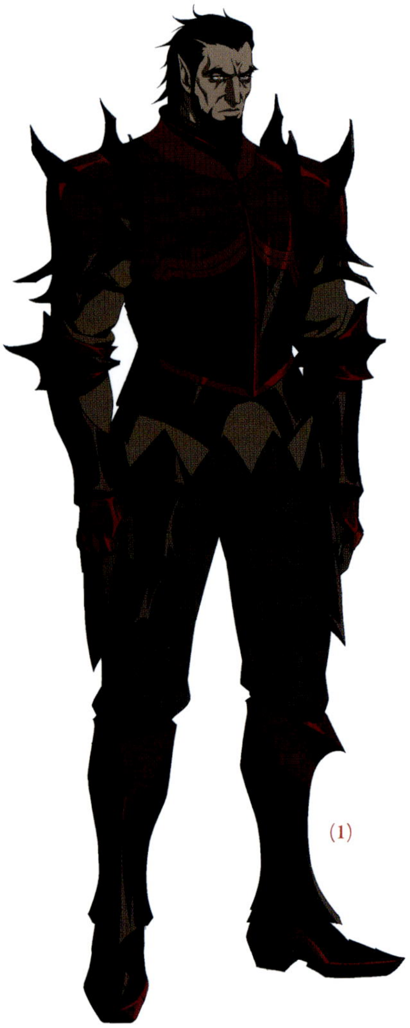

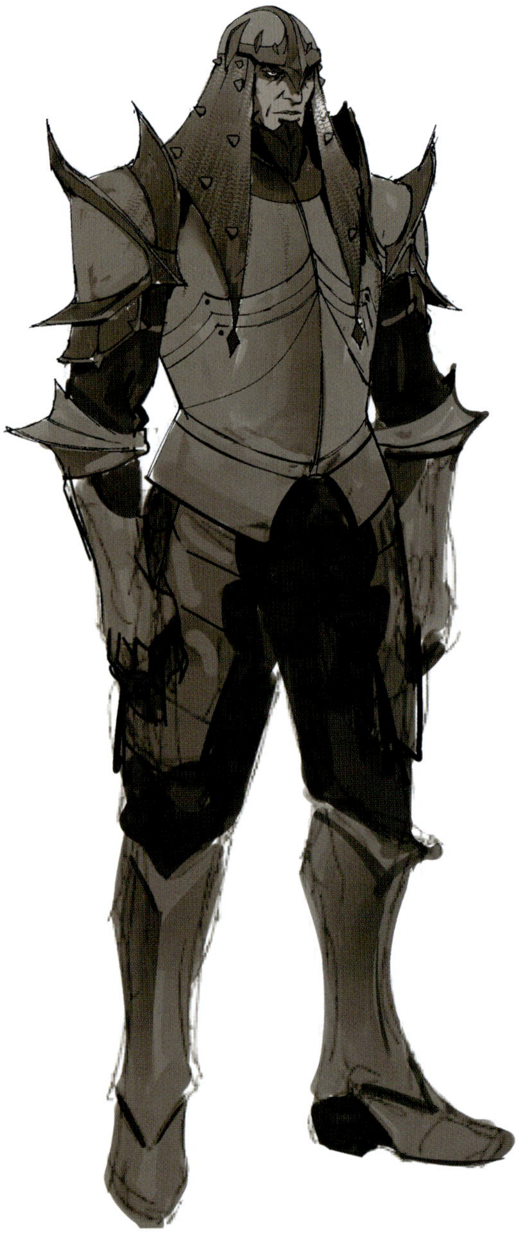

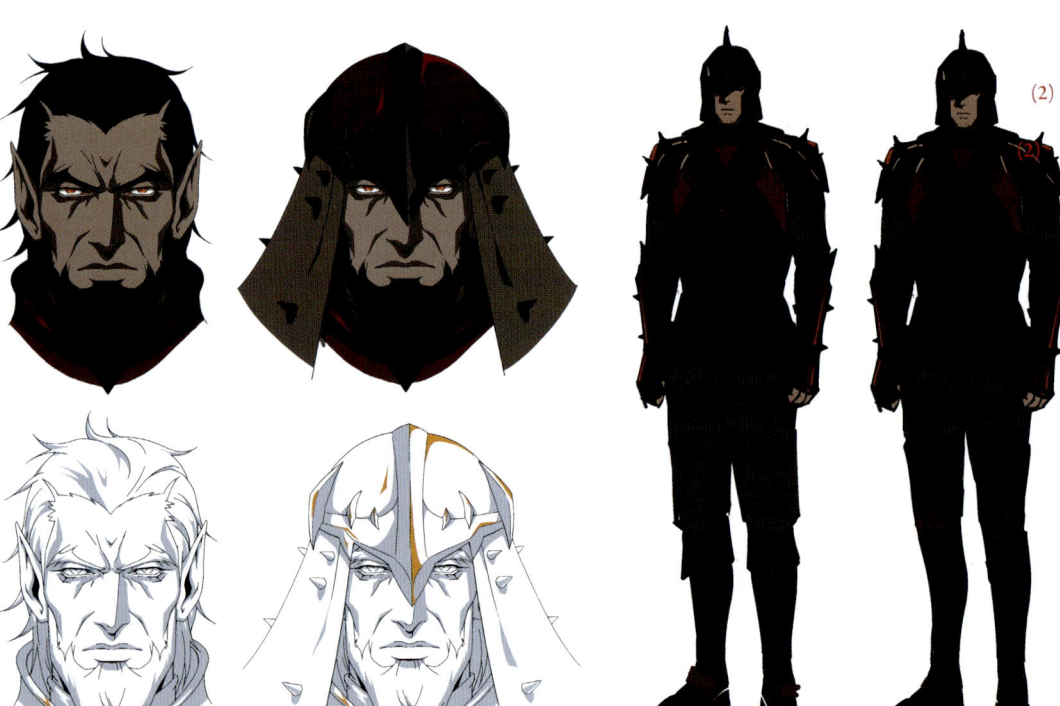

DRAGAN

"Dragan's design was intended to be big, masculine, and spiky, with lots of red and black. I wanted him to look like the vampire general equivalent of an expensive gaming chair. The feedback on his design was that he looked like 'a proper nun-eating bastard.'" —Katie Silva

(1) Dragan designs by Katie Silva. (2) Dragan soldier designs by Lina Ngo. (3) Ivan design by Katie Silva, cleanup by Suzanne Sharp. (4) Sladek design by Katie Silva.

IVAN AND SLADEK

Ivan and Sladek are some of the more rough-and-tumble vampires in season 4.

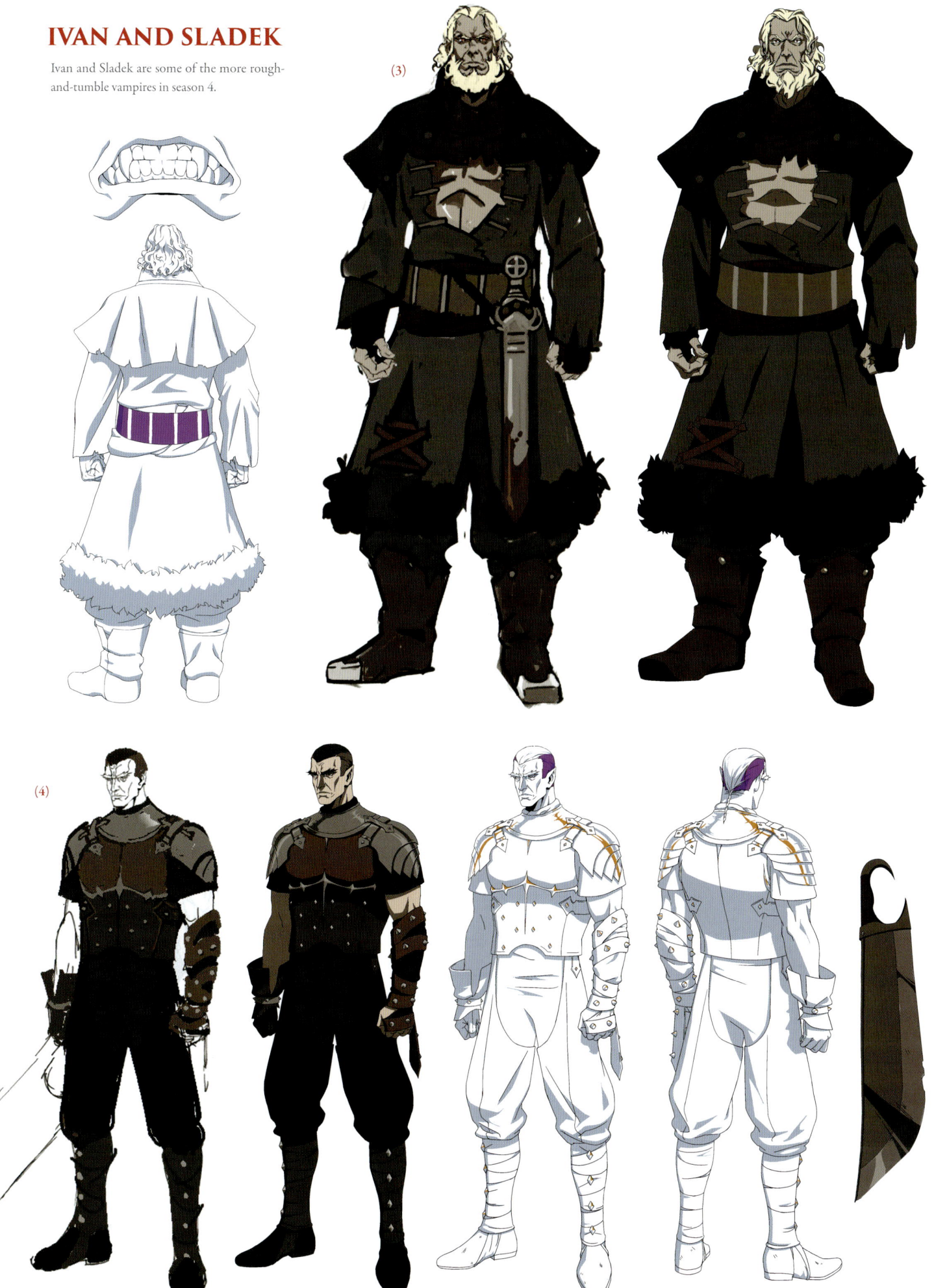

(3)

(4)

RATKO

Ratko is a "big, buff warrior-type vampire" who uses a stabbing sword as his weapon of choice. Ratko and Varney are both Targoviste vampires.

Ratko and Varney designs by Katie Silva.

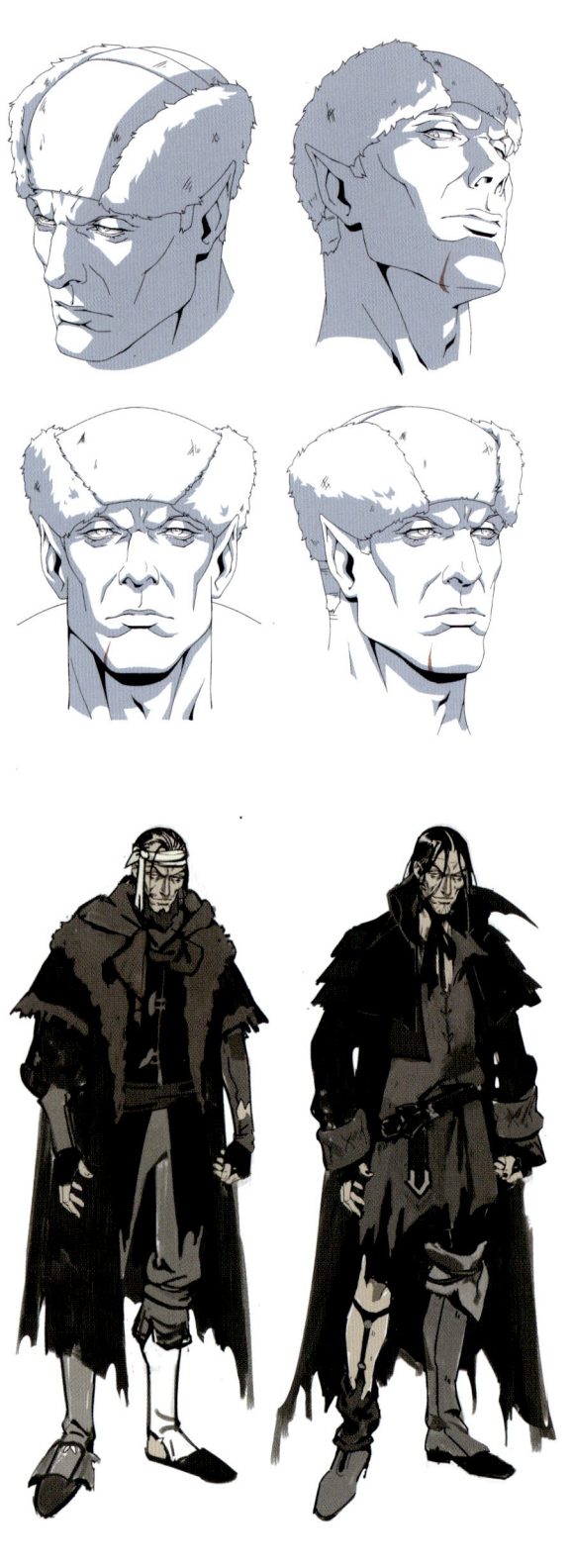

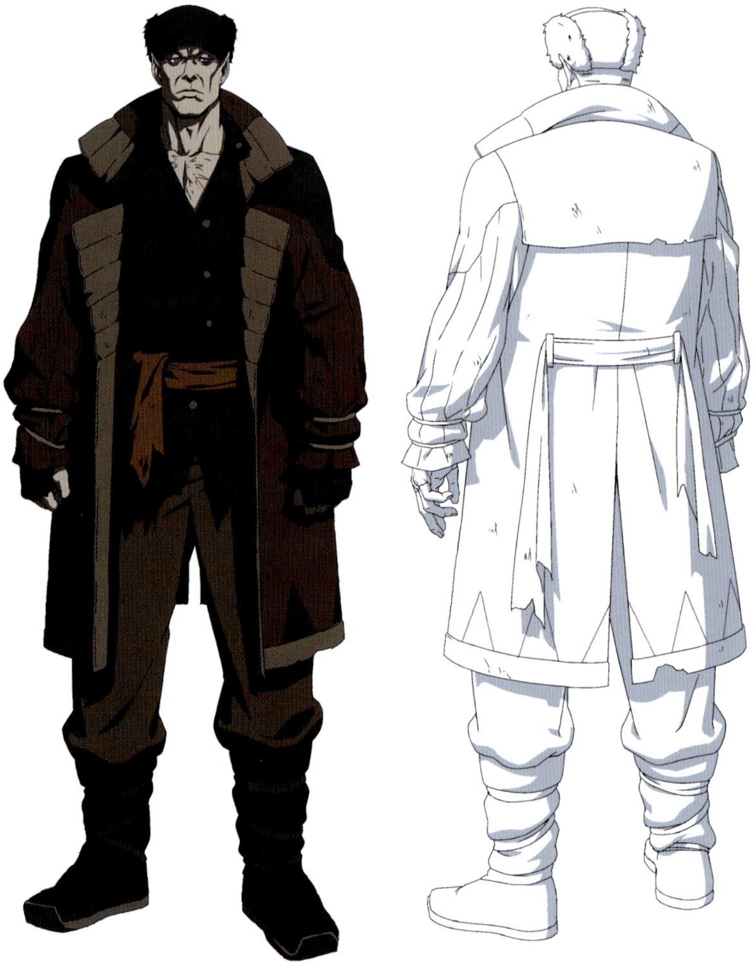

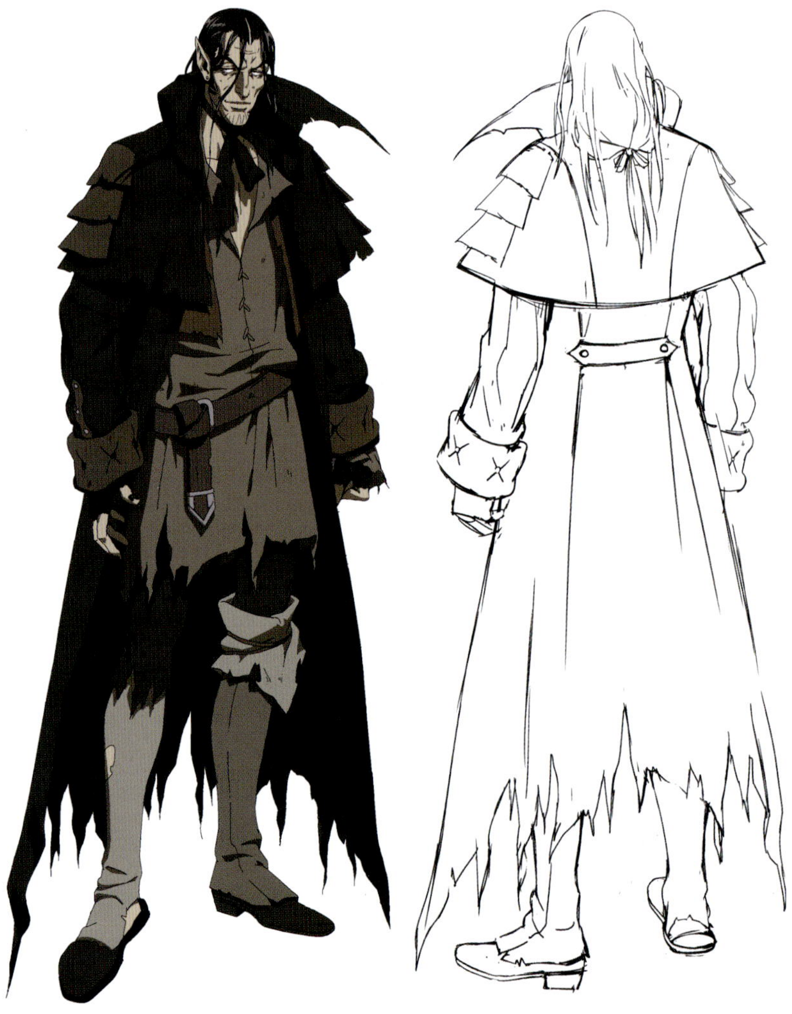

VARNEY

Viewed from certain angles, Varney's collar visually recalls the scythe of Death, and for good reason. "Varney is my favorite character to draw. He is the only character drawn with hair highlights, to emphasize his greasiness. I remember when designing him, we only sent two rough designs, and the only feedback was 'Take the fucked-up sock off of design A and put it on design B.'" —Katie Silva

Death

Sam Deats wanted the Death design to extend beyond the typical Death imagery.

"I wanted to do something that felt a little more organic, because Trevor describes Death as 'a creature,' as he would the other monsters in the show. I wanted him to feel more like an ethereal spirit than a skeleton in a robe." —Sam Deats

Death design by Sam Deats and Katie Silva.

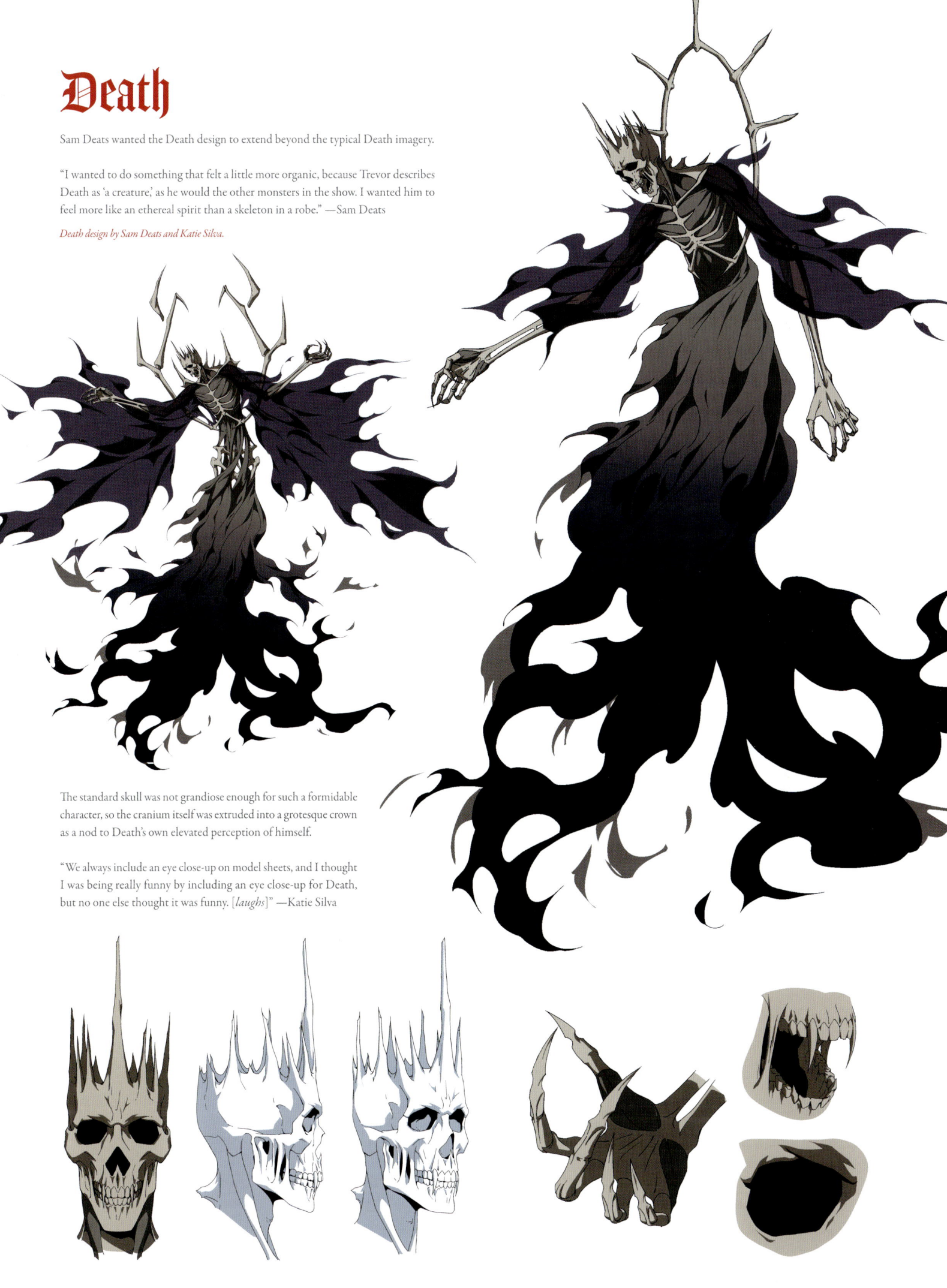

The standard skull was not grandiose enough for such a formidable character, so the cranium itself was extruded into a grotesque crown as a nod to Death's own elevated perception of himself.

"We always include an eye close-up on model sheets, and I thought I was being really funny by including an eye close-up for Death, but no one else thought it was funny. [*laughs*]" —Katie Silva

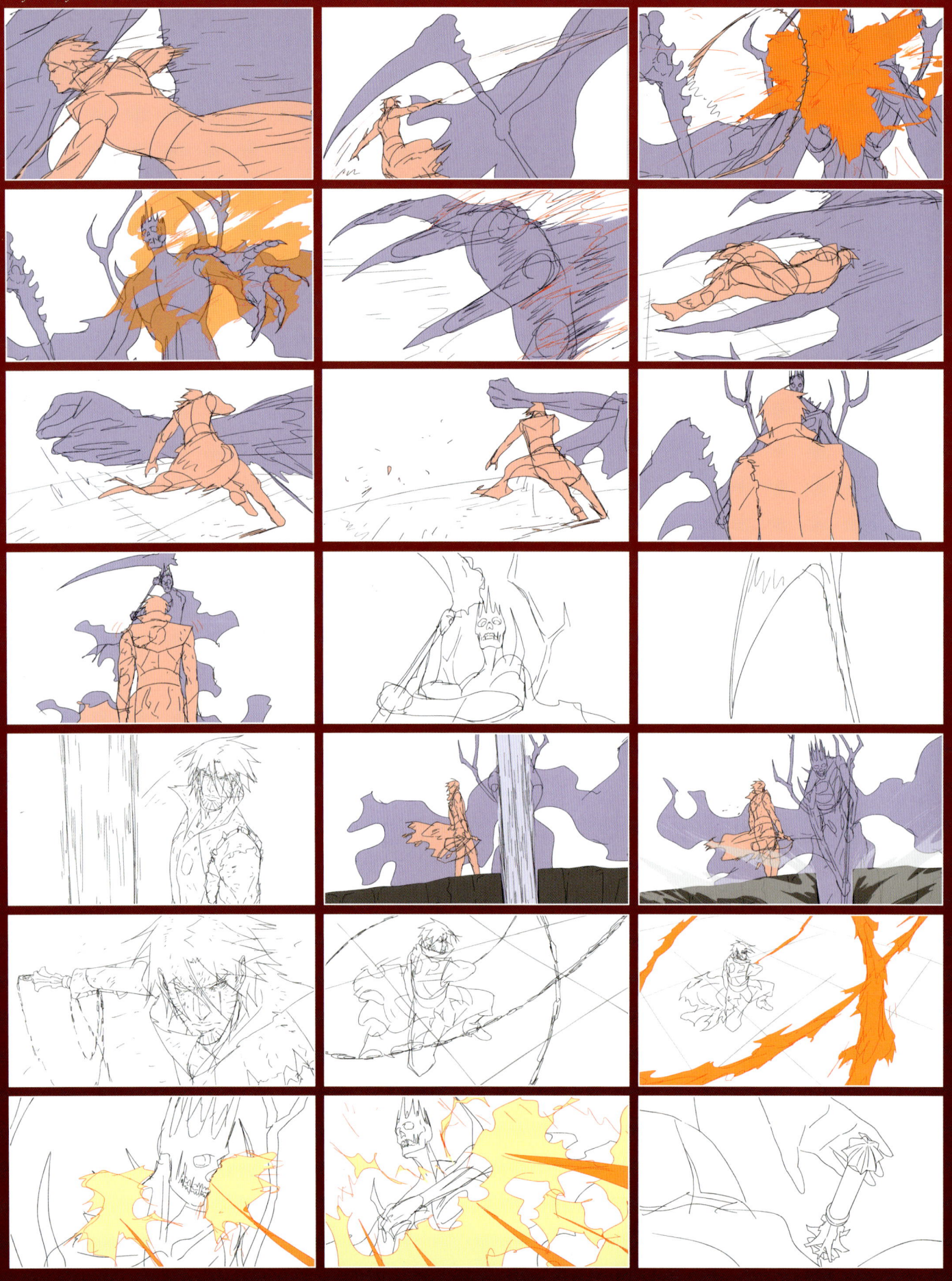

Storyboards featuring Trevor's fight with Death in [E9S4]. A battle sequence played for cool action with less formidable foes precedes this, but the stakes continue to elevate for Trevor after his companions are lost and he is left alone. Trevor is grievously wounded, fighting through evident pain and in mortal danger.

"The script would say things like, 'Trevor hits Death ten times,' and so I had the freedom to just figure out how all that plays out onscreen. Death grows into this huge form, so you see Trevor leaping through his fingers here. Working with this level of scale difference was a fun challenge." —Sam Deats

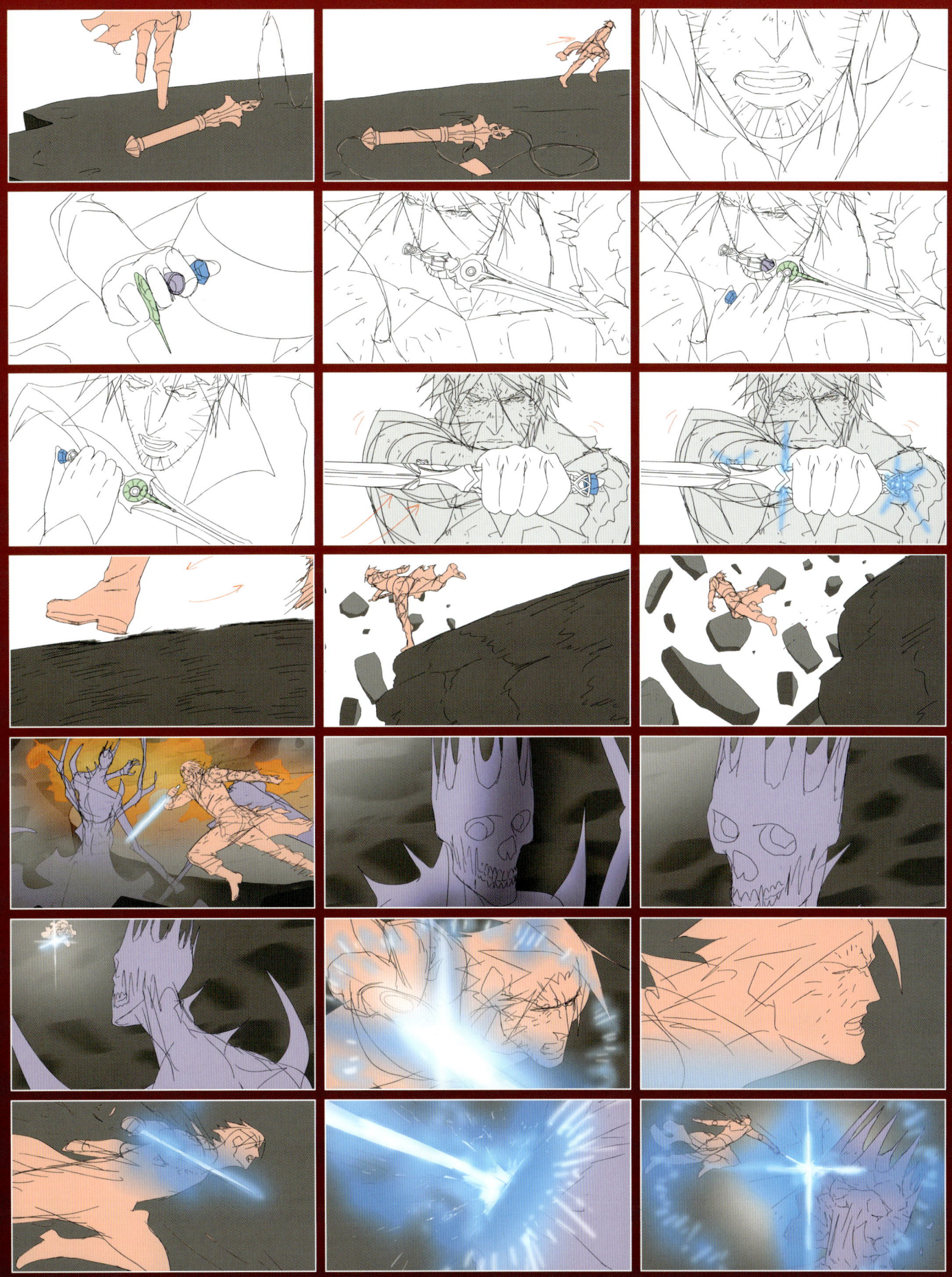

"The final line in the script is 'Trevor Belmont just died,' but episode 9 isn't the final episode in the season. I actually had the scripts for episode 9 and 10 at the same time but deliberately only sent episode 9 to Sam because I wanted him to cry. But he was really busy so he didn't get around to reading it until he also had 10 later, thwarting my evil plan." —Kevin Kolde

Dracula's Soldiers

Dracula's vampire soldiers don long dark capes with hoods that obscure most facial elements beyond glowing red eyes, a relatively generic look that made it easier to duplicate character animation to fill out big crowds or battle scenes in postproduction.

(1) Dracula's soldiers design by Sam Deats, cleanup by Stephanie McCrea Rainosek.

(1)

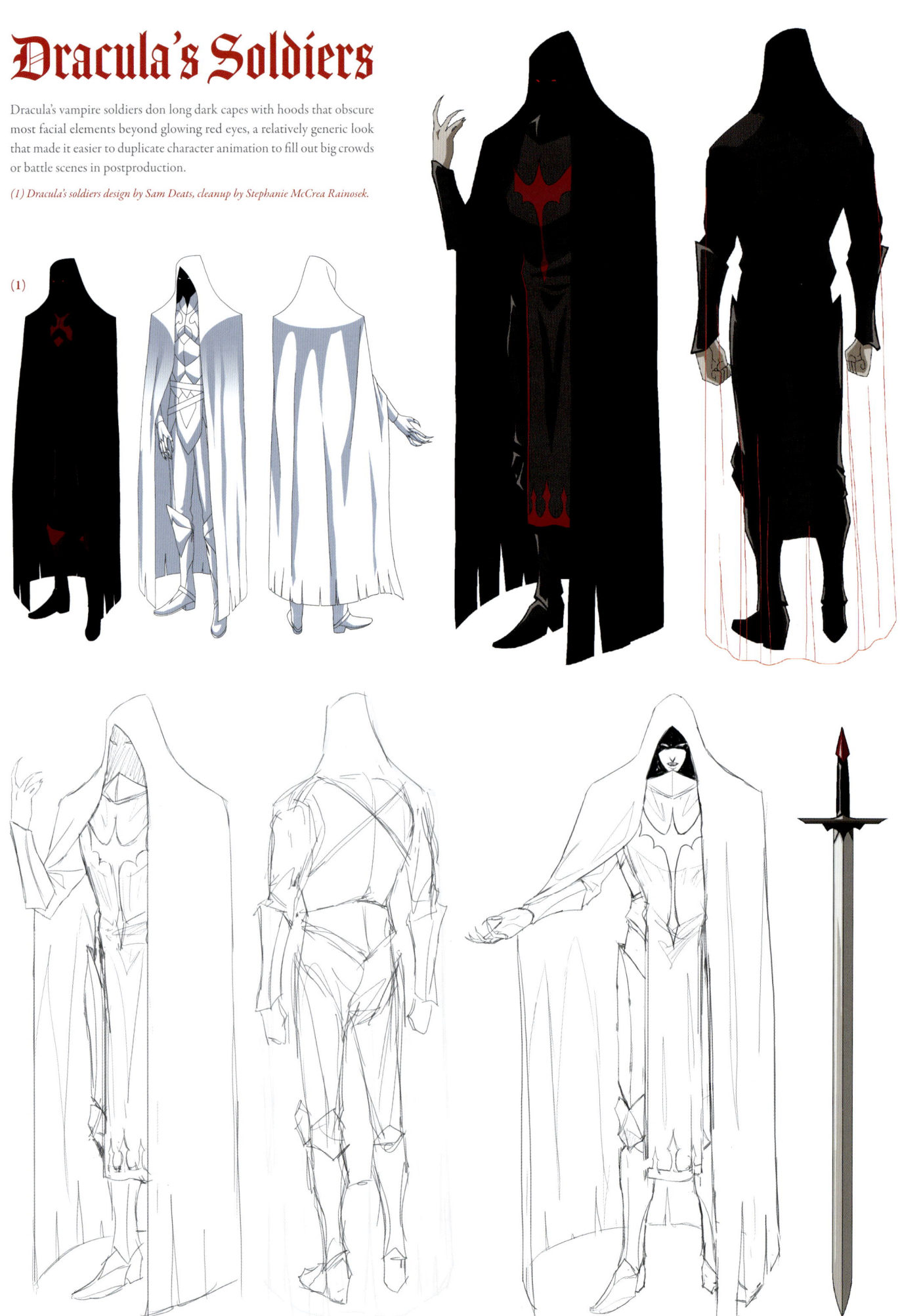

Styrian Soldiers

The Styrian shape language echoes the curved shapes found elsewhere in Carmilla's castle; the metal armor is meant to appear to have a porcelain sheen, and the curves and swoops evoke an almost elven art nouveau flavor.

(2) Styrian soldiers design by Sam Deats, cleanup by Stephanie McCrea Rainosek. (3) Cloaked and casual Styrian soldier designs by Suzanne Sharp.

(2)

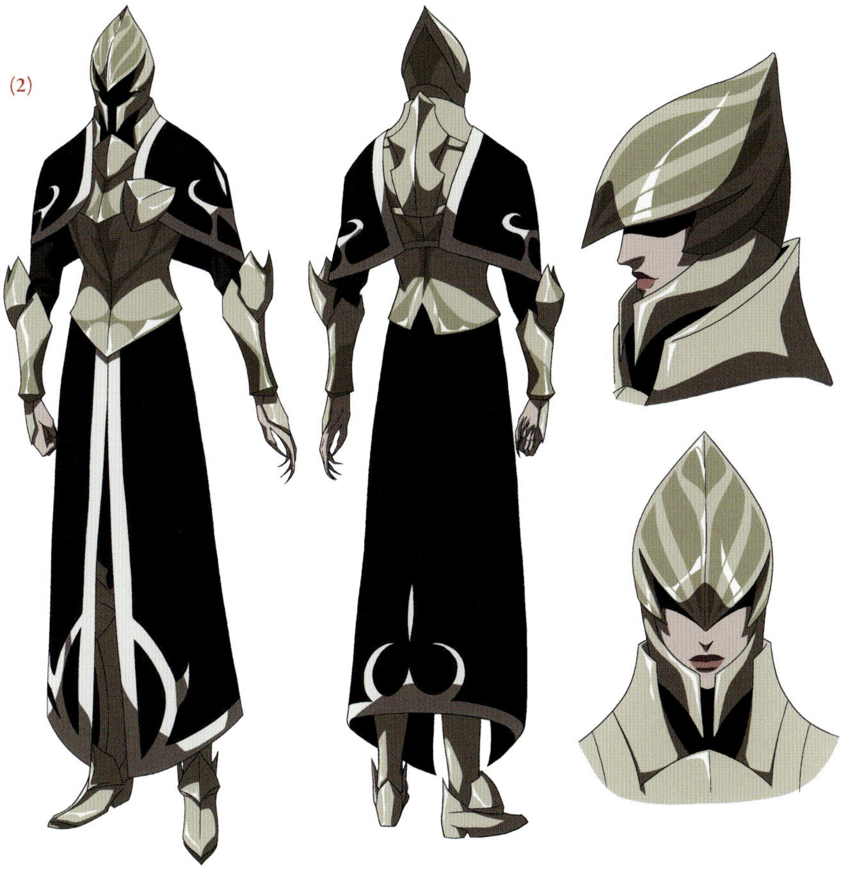

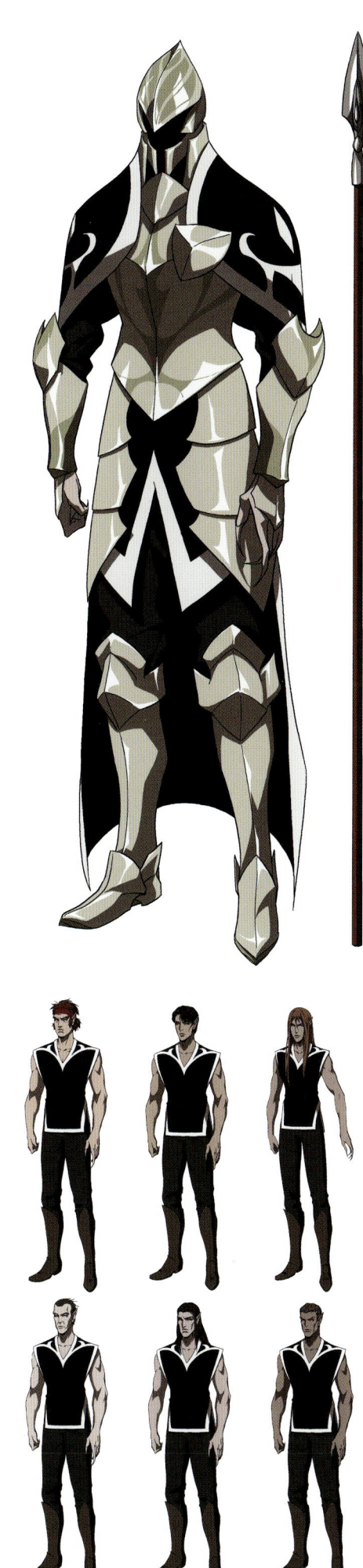

(3)

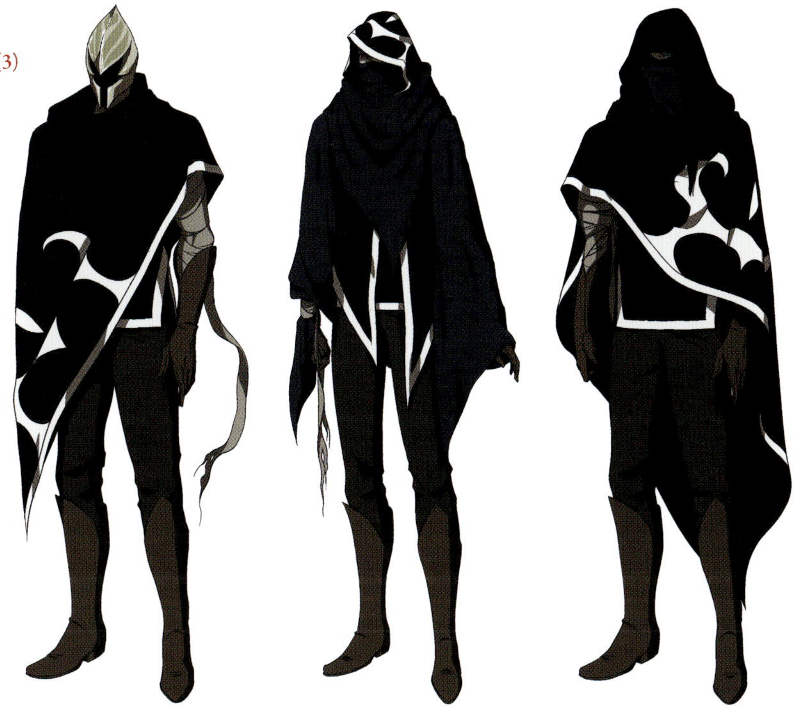

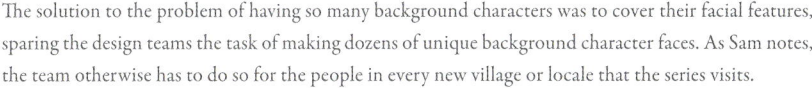

The solution to the problem of having so many background characters was to cover their facial features, sparing the design teams the task of making dozens of unique background character faces. As Sam notes, the team otherwise has to do so for the people in every new village or locale that the series visits.

Vampire Wizards

Having upgraded their abilities and weapons several times over by season 4, our heroes, Trevor and Sypha, required more than physically imposing, brawny vampire opponents, such as Godbrand and Dragoslav. The vampire wizards possess specialized magical abilities and weapons that inform their designs and action in the storyboards, such as the StitchyWitchy, who uses a magic needle and thread for her attacks, or the DusterBuster, who shoots dangerous spikes from their feathered coat.

(1) Vampire wizards designs by Sam Deats, cleanup by Lina Ngo, Suzanne Sharp, and Katie Silva. (2) Designs by Sam Deats, cleanup by Lina Ngo, Suzanne Sharp, and Katie Silva. (3) Vampire magician design by Katie Silva.

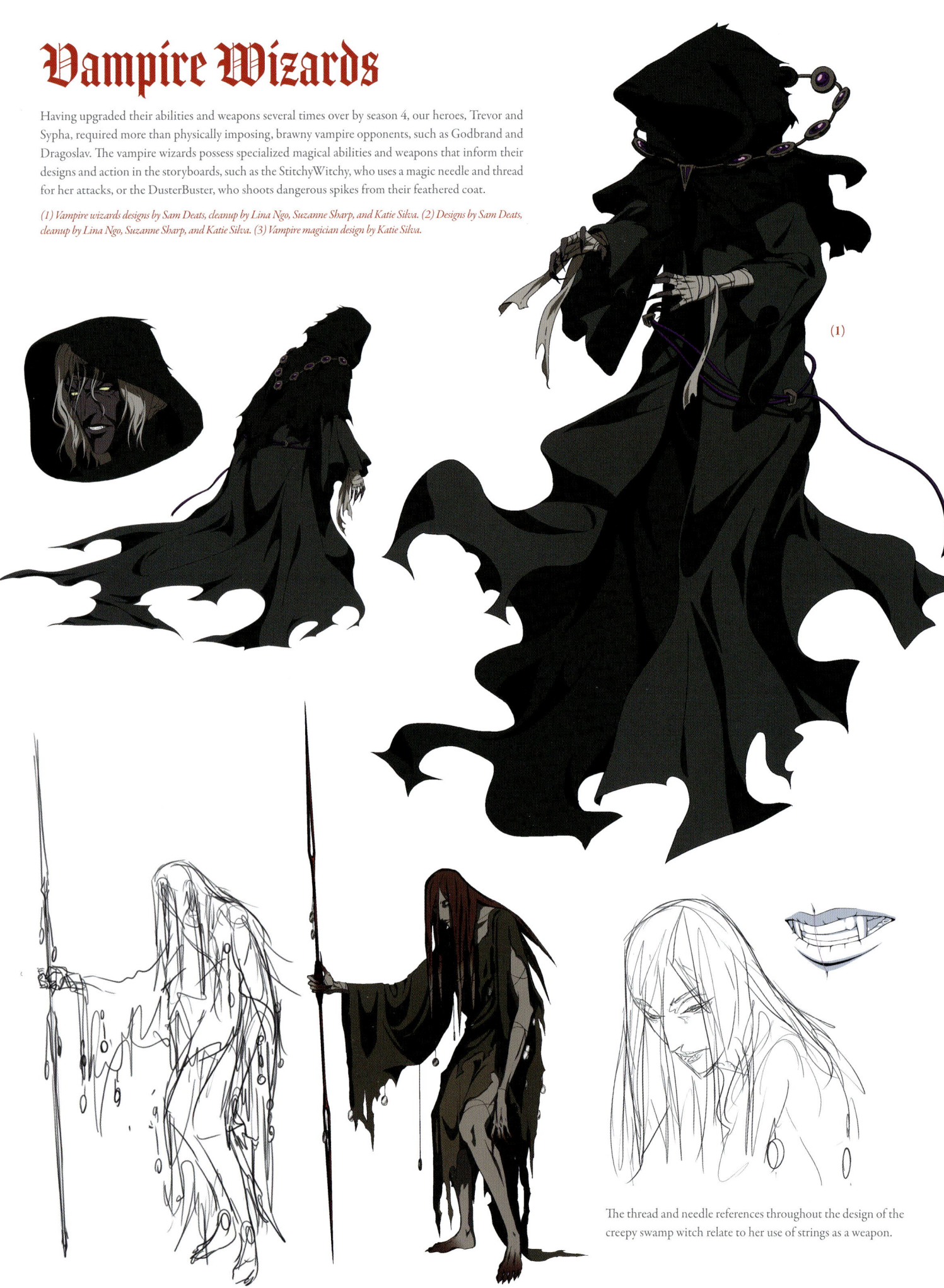

(1)

The thread and needle references throughout the design of the creepy swamp witch relate to her use of strings as a weapon.

CASTLEVANIA : THE ART OF THE ANIMATED SERIES

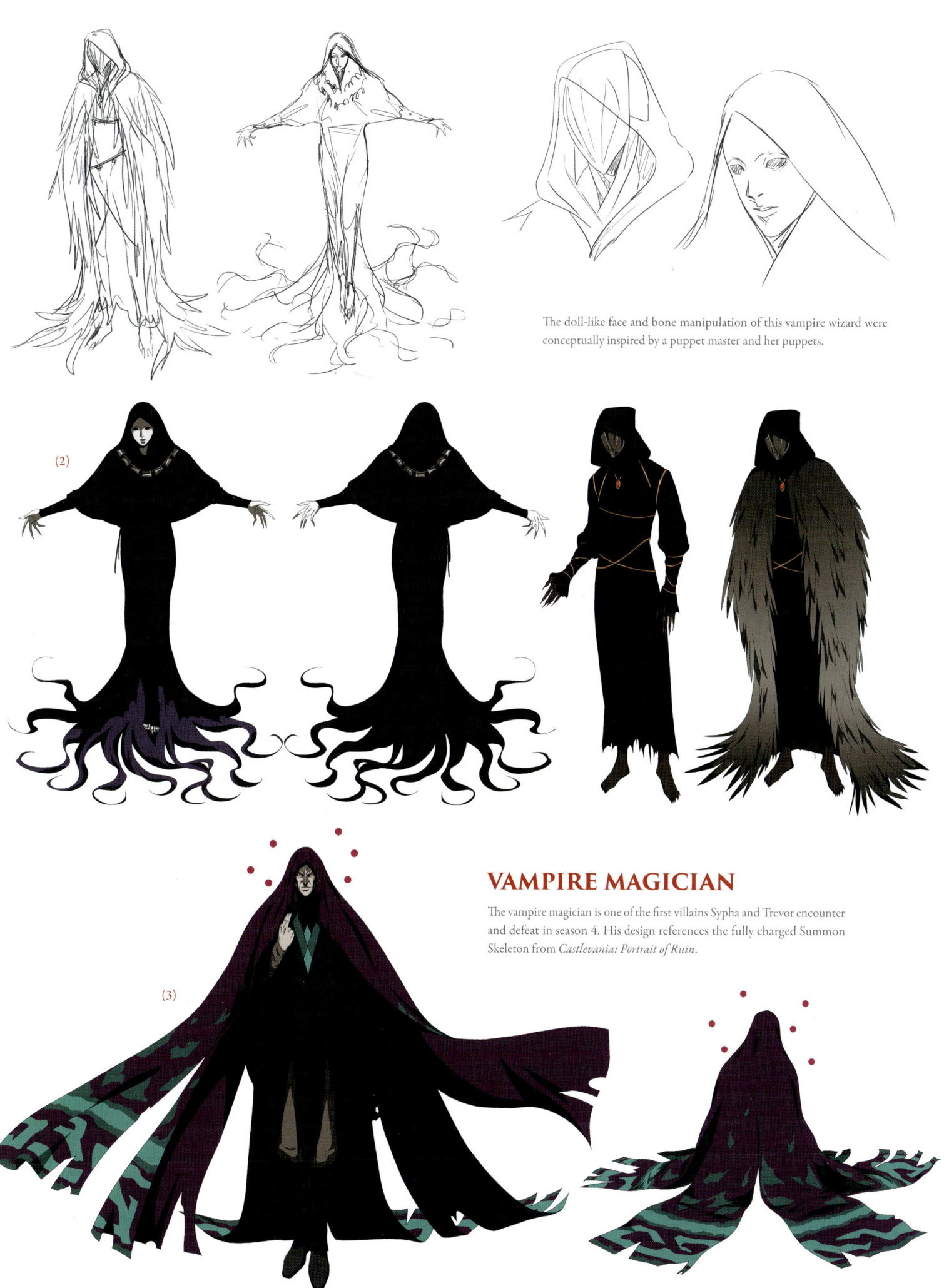

The doll-like face and bone manipulation of this vampire wizard were conceptually inspired by a puppet master and her puppets.

VAMPIRE MAGICIAN

The vampire magician is one of the first villains Sypha and Trevor encounter and defeat in season 4. His design references the fully charged Summon Skeleton from *Castlevania: Portrait of Ruin*.

Beasts of the Night

Mythology and natural forms are mashed up into demon beasts to populate the world of *Castlevania*.

Left page: Designs by Sam Deats, cleanup by Spencer Wan. Right page: (1) Early night creature concepts by Sam Deats. (2) Giant night creature design by Spencer Wan, cleanup by Ed Booth.

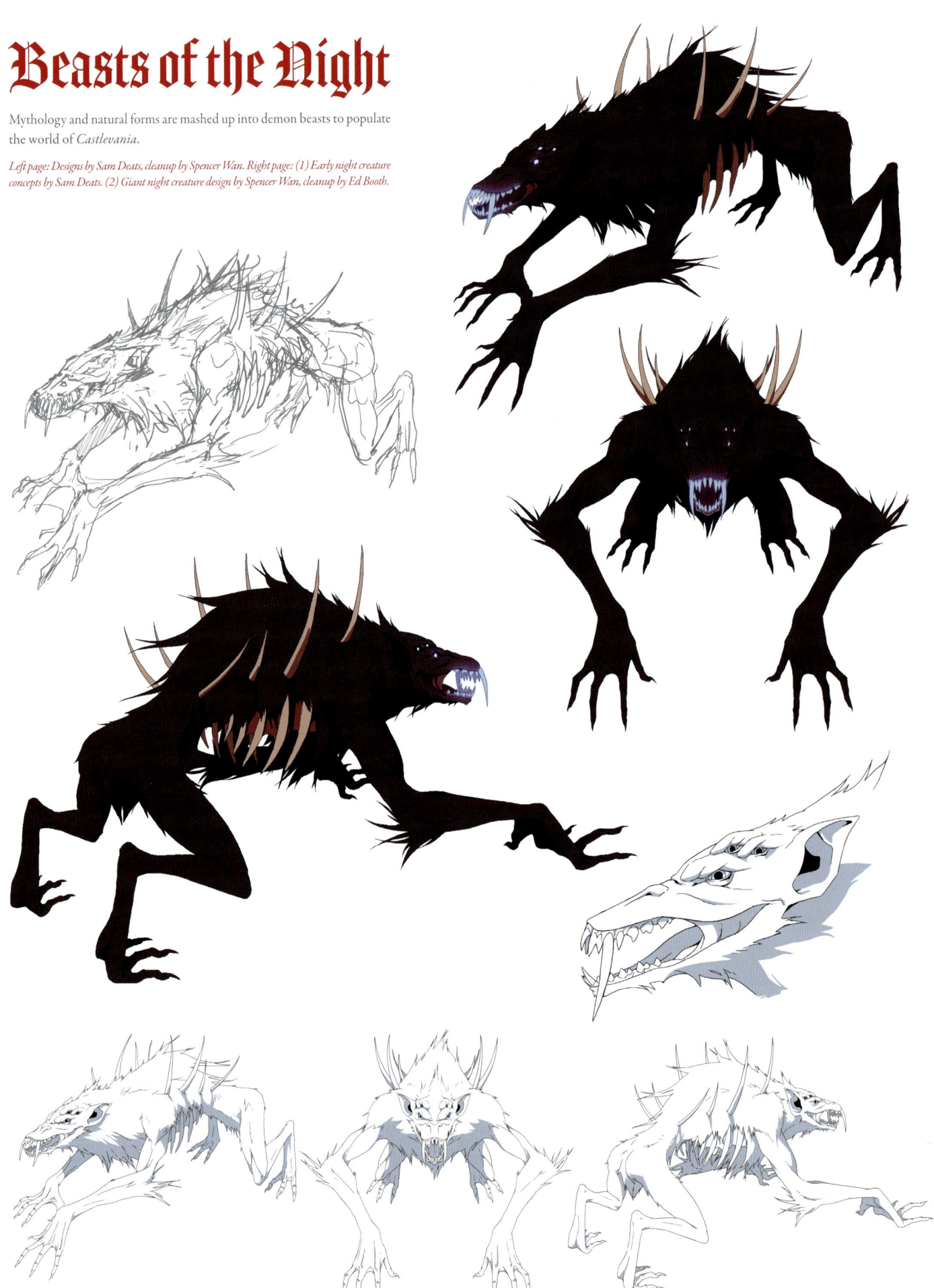

BLUE FANGS

Blue Fangs is a demon of Dracula's horde that leads the attack on Gresit, personally disposing of the bishop along with throngs of villagers doomed by the bishop's unfortunate actions.

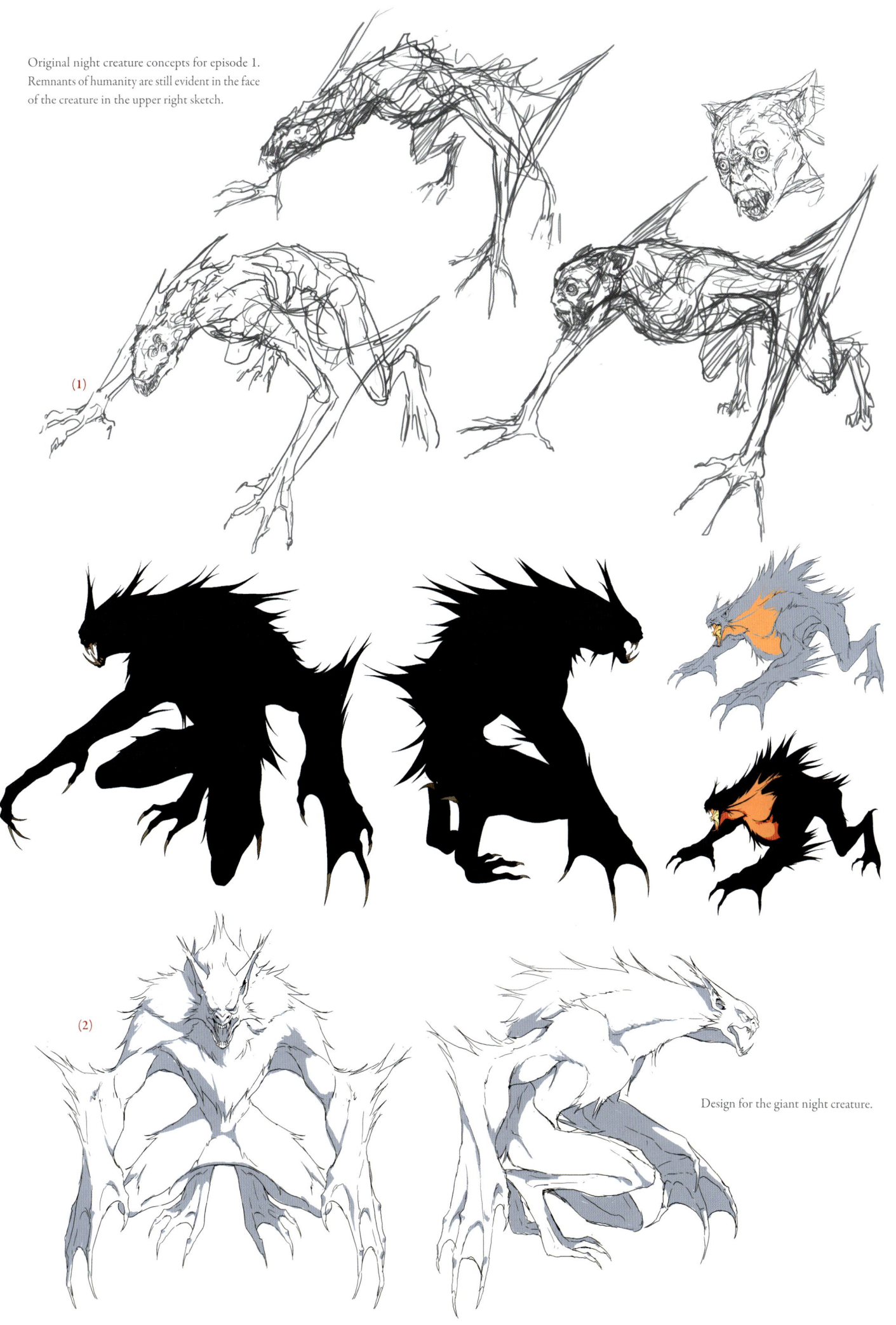

Original night creature concepts for episode 1.
Remnants of humanity are still evident in the face
of the creature in the upper right sketch.

(1)

(2)

Design for the giant night creature.

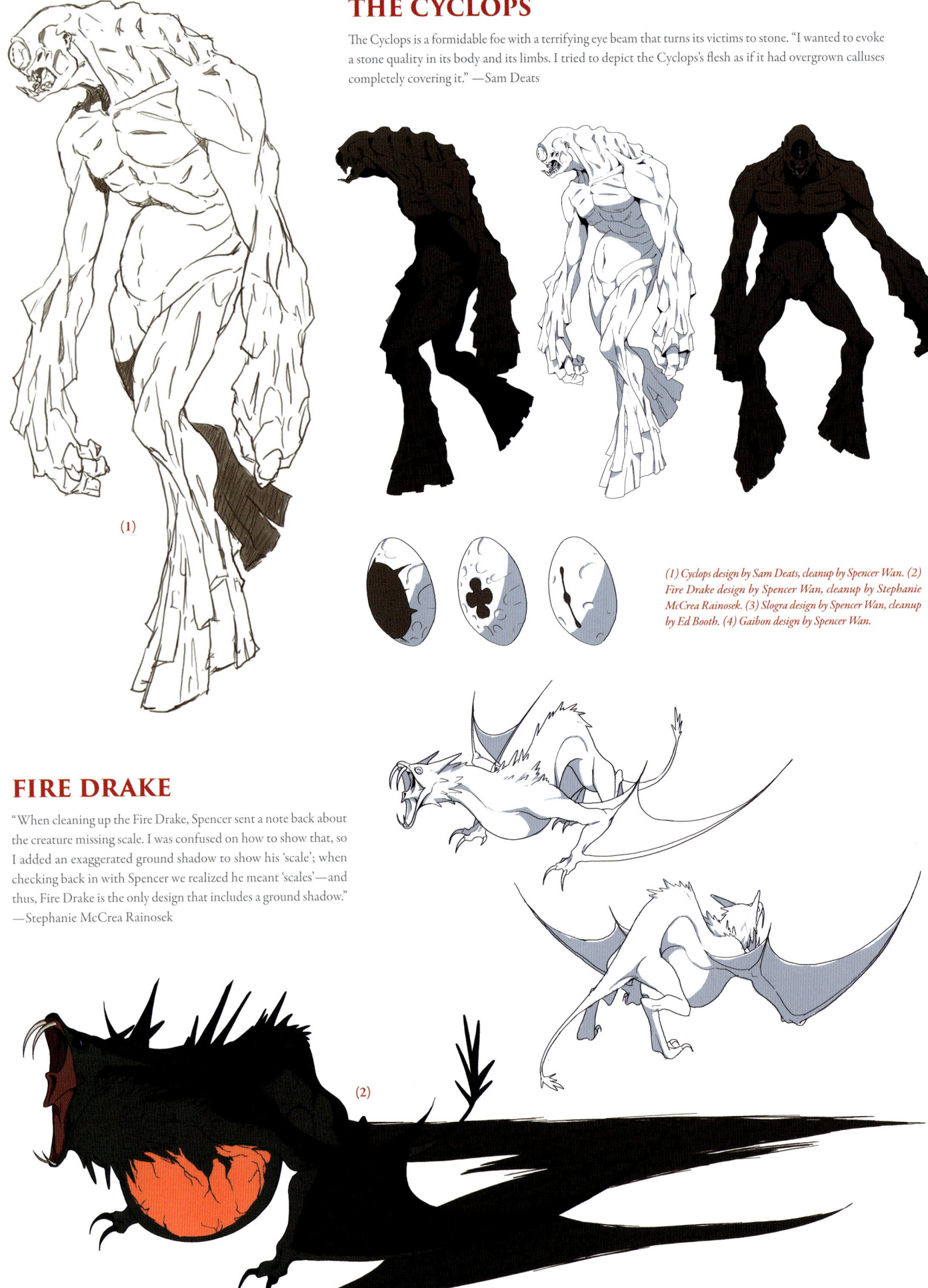

THE CYCLOPS

The Cyclops is a formidable foe with a terrifying eye beam that turns its victims to stone. "I wanted to evoke a stone quality in its body and its limbs. I tried to depict the Cyclops's flesh as if it had overgrown calluses completely covering it." —Sam Deats

(1)

(1) Cyclops design by Sam Deats, cleanup by Spencer Wan. (2) Fire Drake design by Spencer Wan, cleanup by Stephanie McCrea Rainosek. (3) Slogra design by Spencer Wan, cleanup by Ed Booth. (4) Gaibon design by Spencer Wan.

FIRE DRAKE

"When cleaning up the Fire Drake, Spencer sent a note back about the creature missing scale. I was confused on how to show that, so I added an exaggerated ground shadow to show his 'scale'; when checking back in with Spencer we realized he meant 'scales'—and thus, Fire Drake is the only design that includes a ground shadow."
—Stephanie McCrea Rainosek

(2)

SLOGRA

Slogra is a raptor-like demon with a spear weapon. Slogra and Gaibon are both well-known monsters that appear in the *Castlevania* games, and fight together as a duo in *Symphony of the Night*.

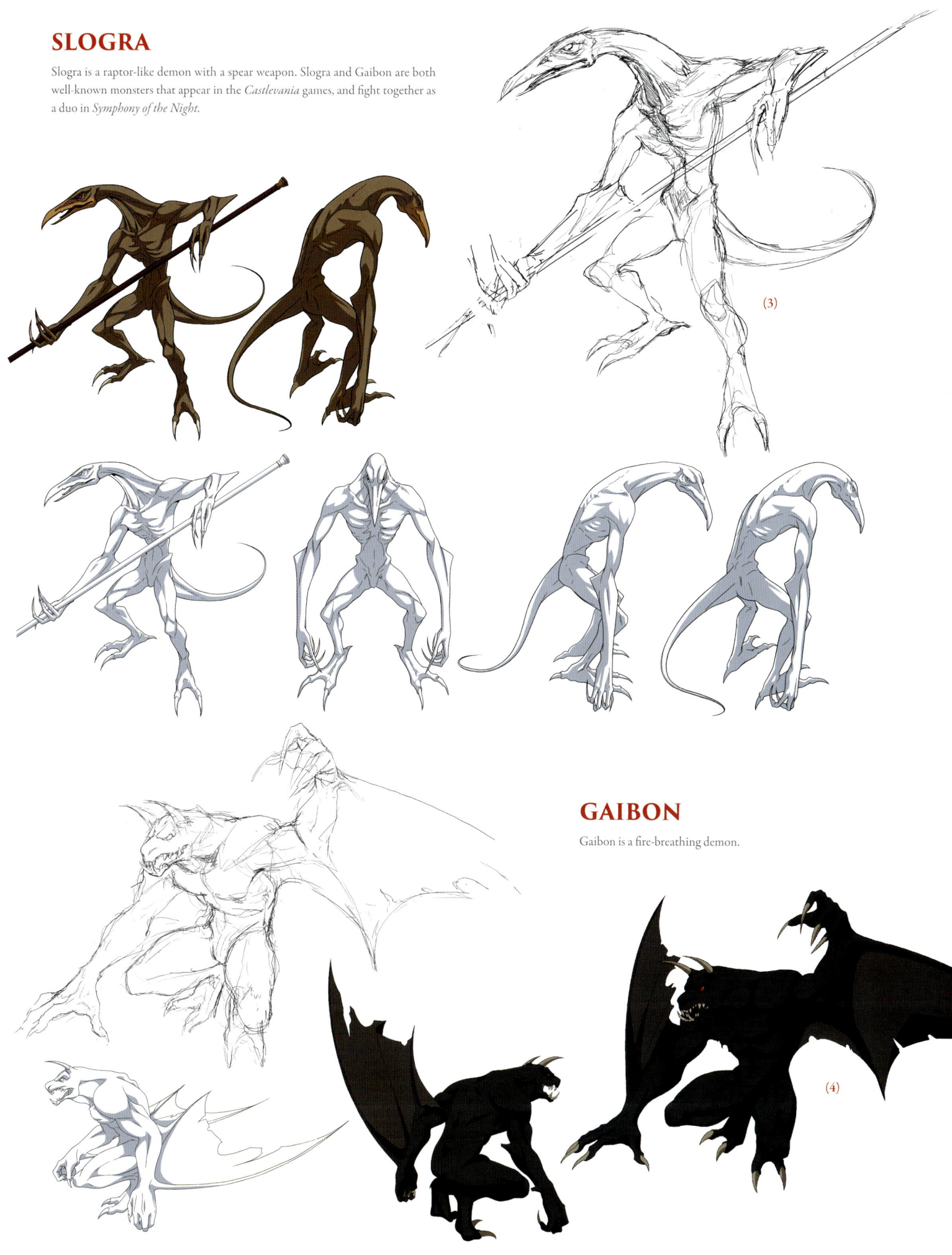

(3)

GAIBON

Gaibon is a fire-breathing demon.

(4)

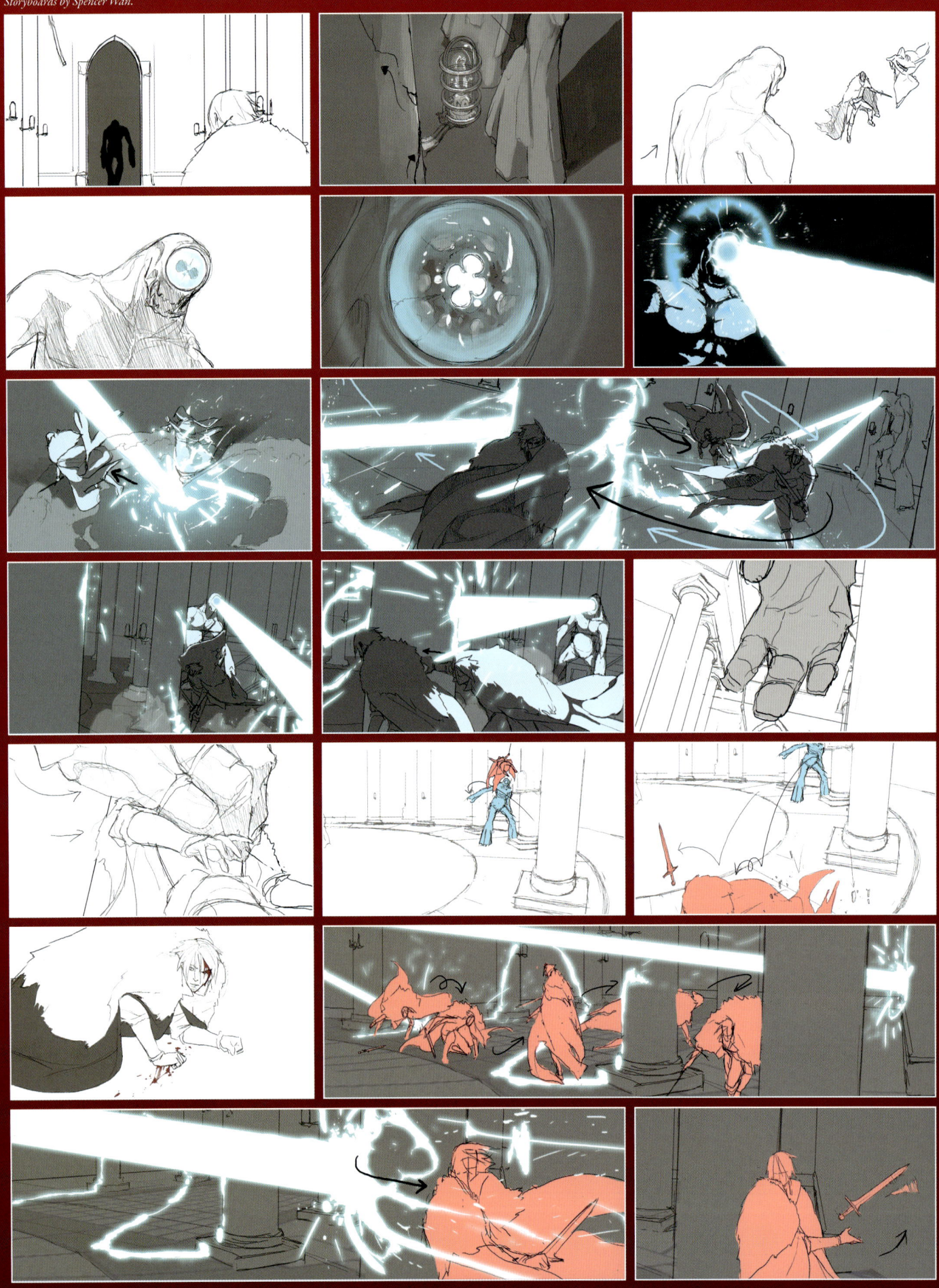

Storyboards for the Cyclops and Trevor fight. Spencer also animated a sizable portion of this sequence.

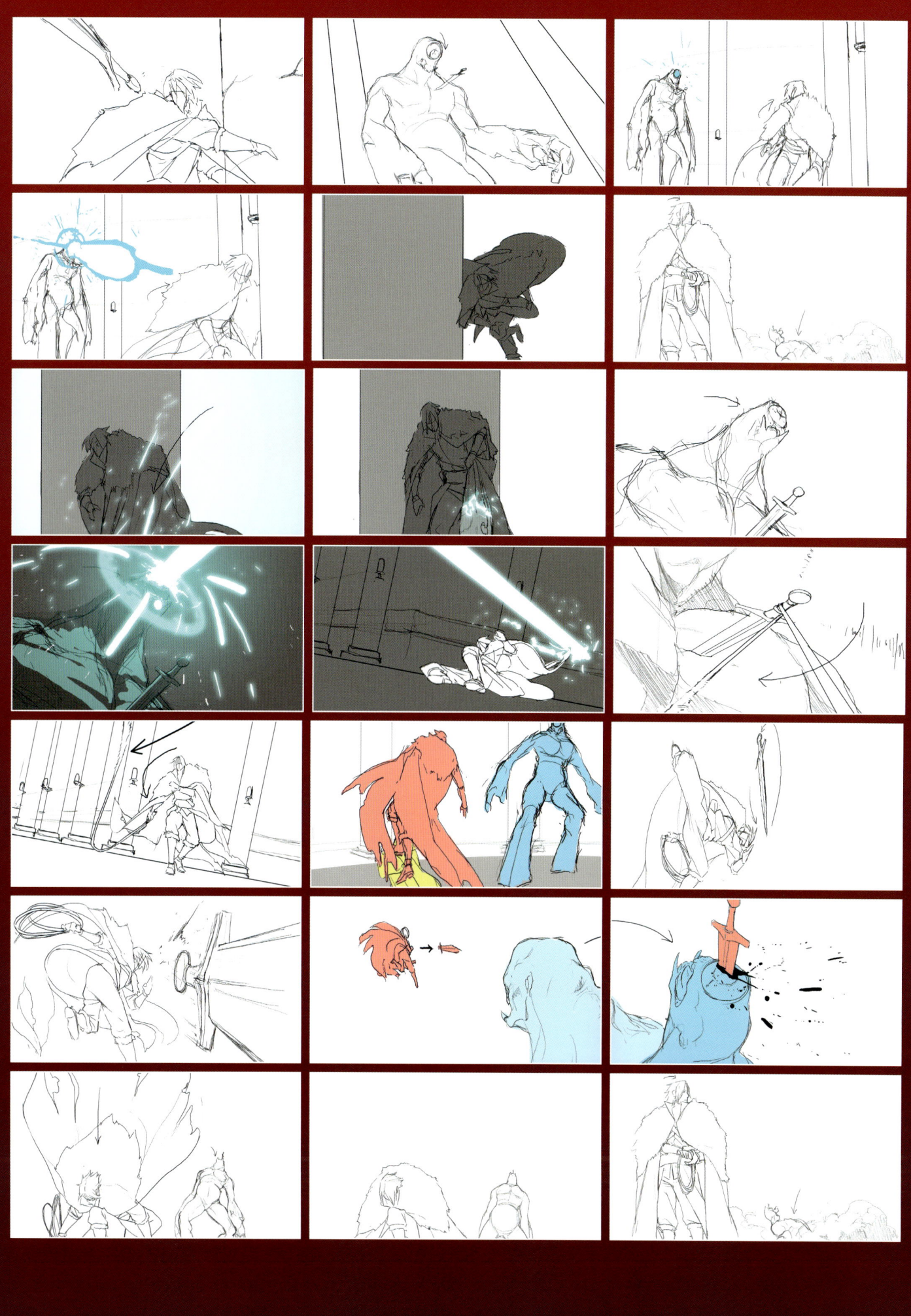

BALD PRIEST

In the season 1 episode "Necropolis," a bald priest gets his eye forcibly removed by Trevor during a street fight. In the following episode, "Labyrinth," the priest is seen in the crowd menacing Trevor with a bandage over one eye socket, ready for revenge. He promptly loses the second eye. As a referential gag, his body is later seen in season 2 on the pile of corpses that were recovered for Hector to reanimate into undead creatures. This night creature is his final form.

(1) Bald priest design by Spencer Wan, cleanup by Evgeny Lubaev. (2) Hammerhands design by Spencer Wan, cleanup by Robby Cook. (3) Velocivampire design by Spencer Wan, cleanup by Ed Booth. (4) Malphas design by Spencer Wan, cleanup by Evgeny Lubaev.

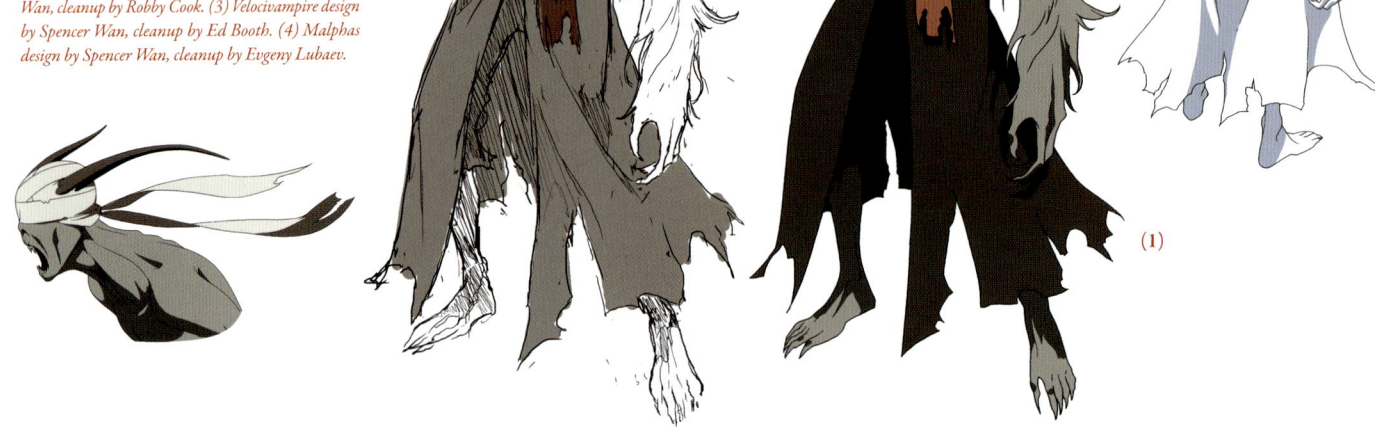

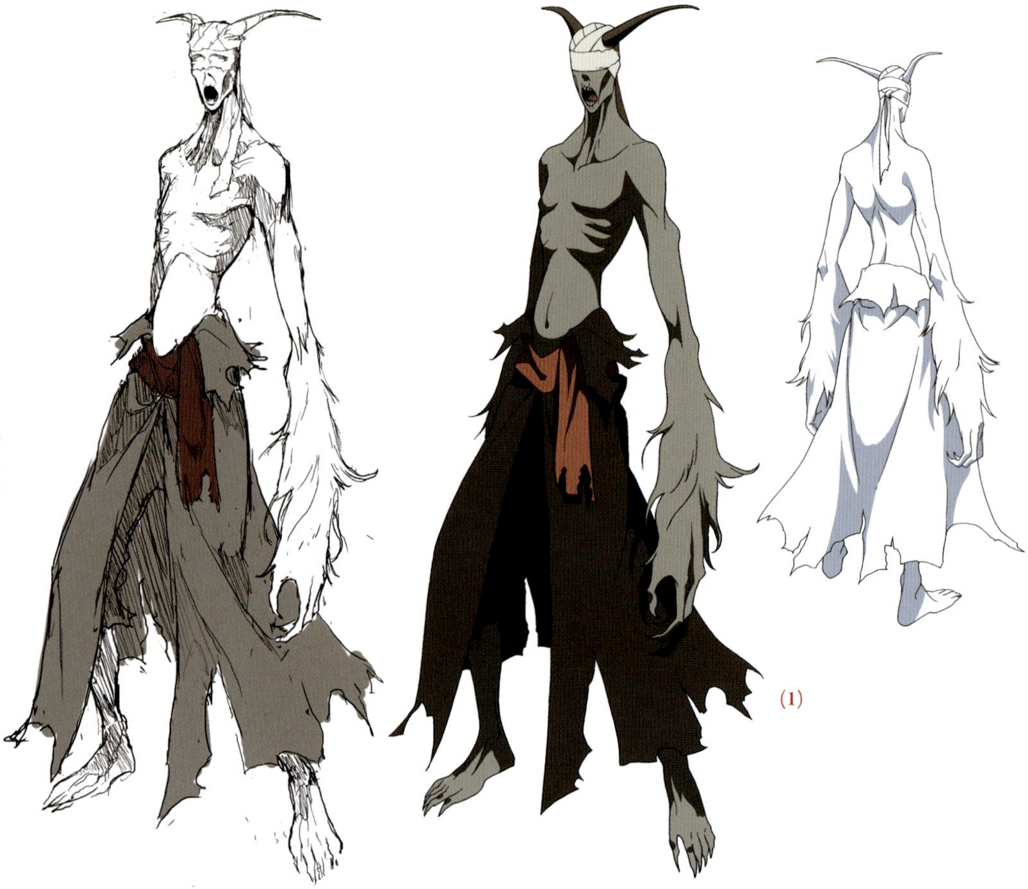

(1)

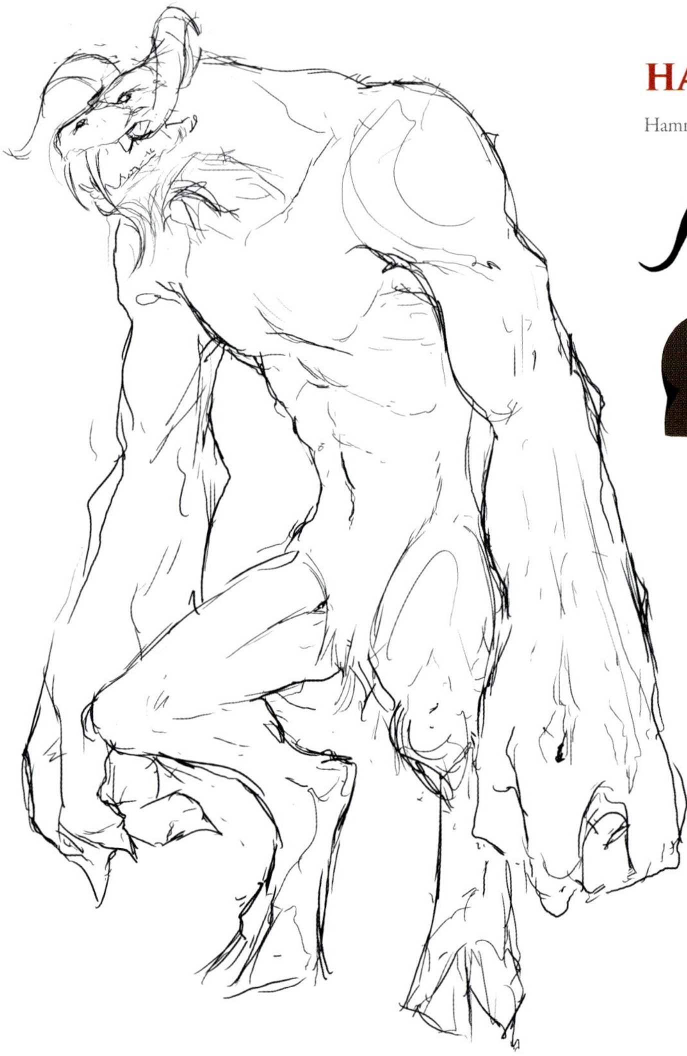

HAMMERHANDS

Hammerhands was designed for practical purposes: to be a massive foe with crushing fists.

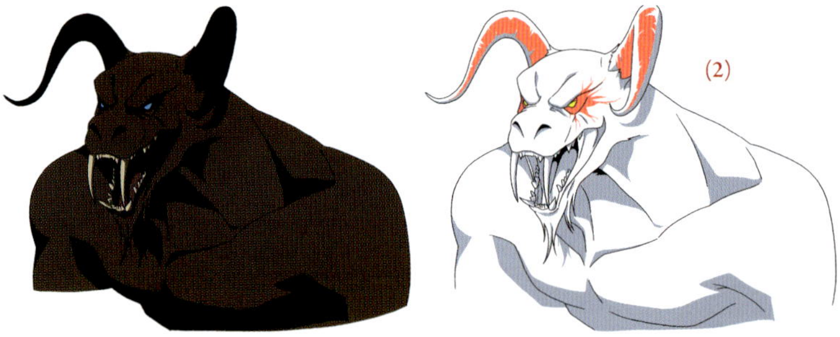

(2)

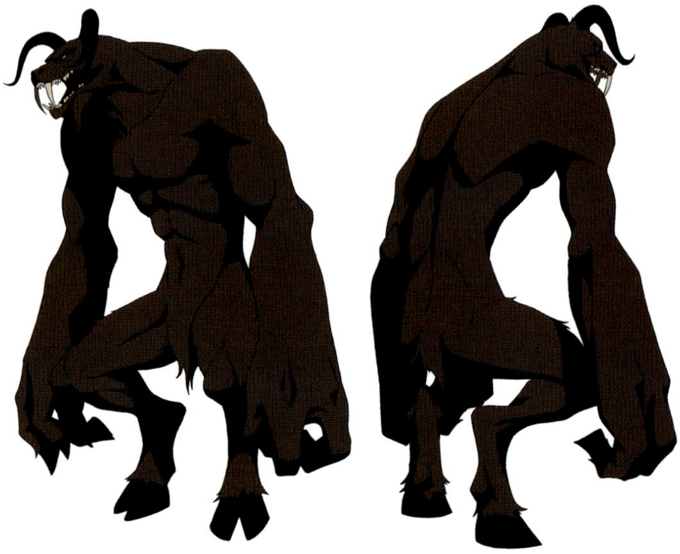

VELOCIVAMPIRE

The Velocivampire was created to be a speedy demon.

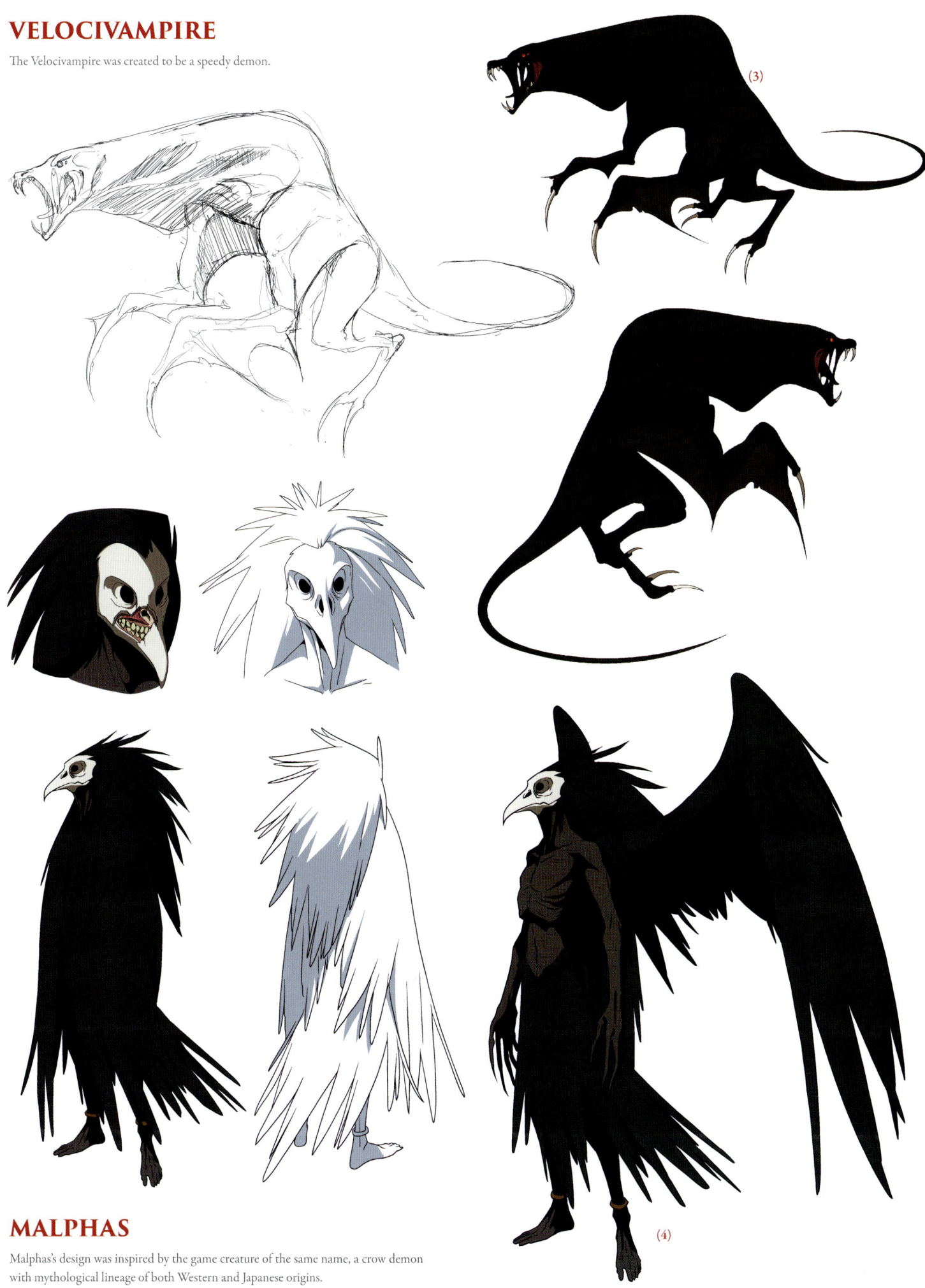

(3)

MALPHAS

Malphas's design was inspired by the game creature of the same name, a crow demon with mythological lineage of both Western and Japanese origins.

(4)

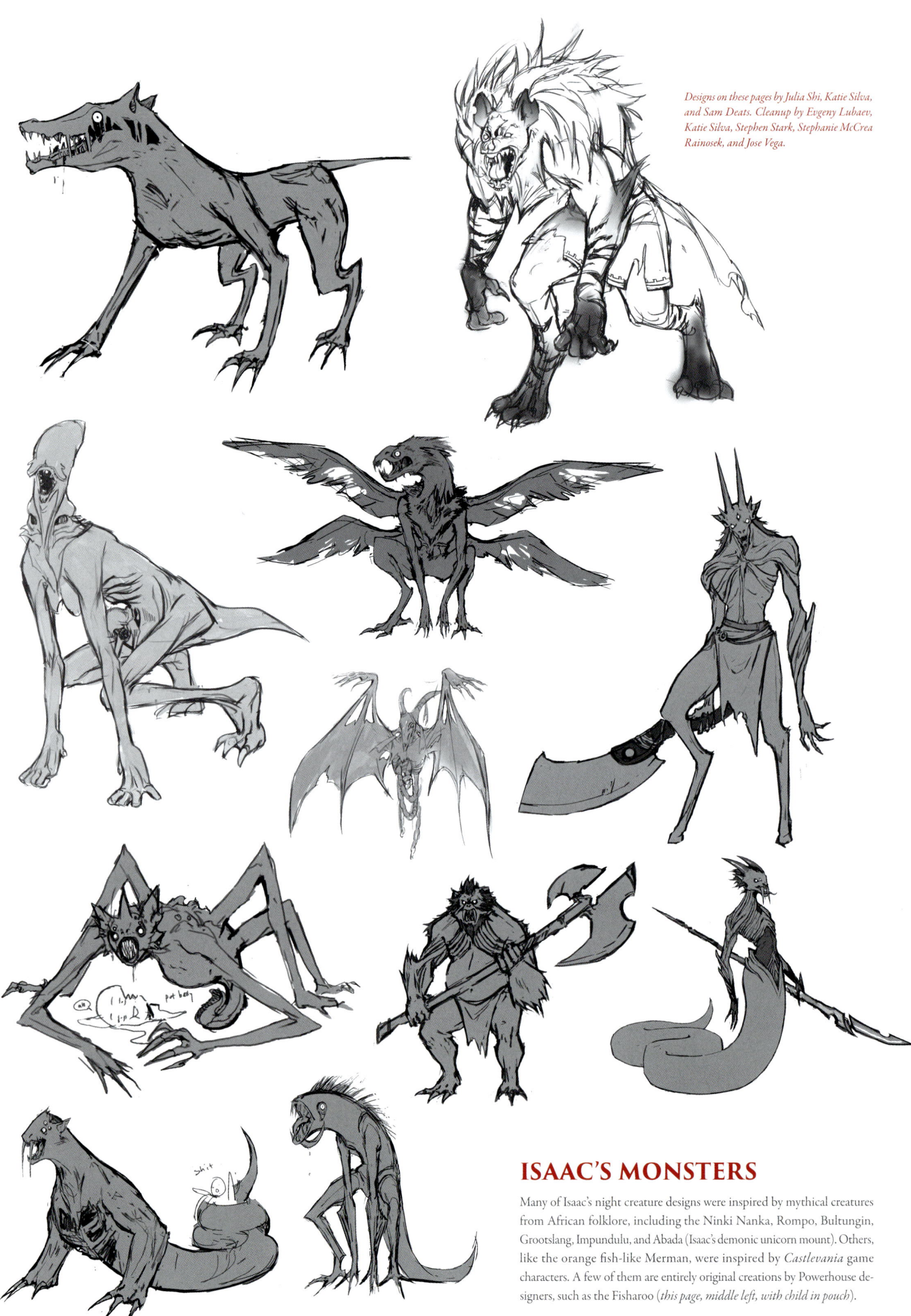

Designs on these pages by Julia Shi, Katie Silva, and Sam Deats. Cleanup by Evgeny Lubaev, Katie Silva, Stephen Stark, Stephanie McCrea Rainosek, and Jose Vega.

ISAAC'S MONSTERS

Many of Isaac's night creature designs were inspired by mythical creatures from African folklore, including the Ninki Nanka, Rompo, Bultungin, Grootslang, Impundulu, and Abada (Isaac's demonic unicorn mount). Others, like the orange fish-like Merman, were inspired by *Castlevania* game characters. A few of them are entirely original creations by Powerhouse designers, such as the Fisharoo (*this page, middle left, with child in pouch*).

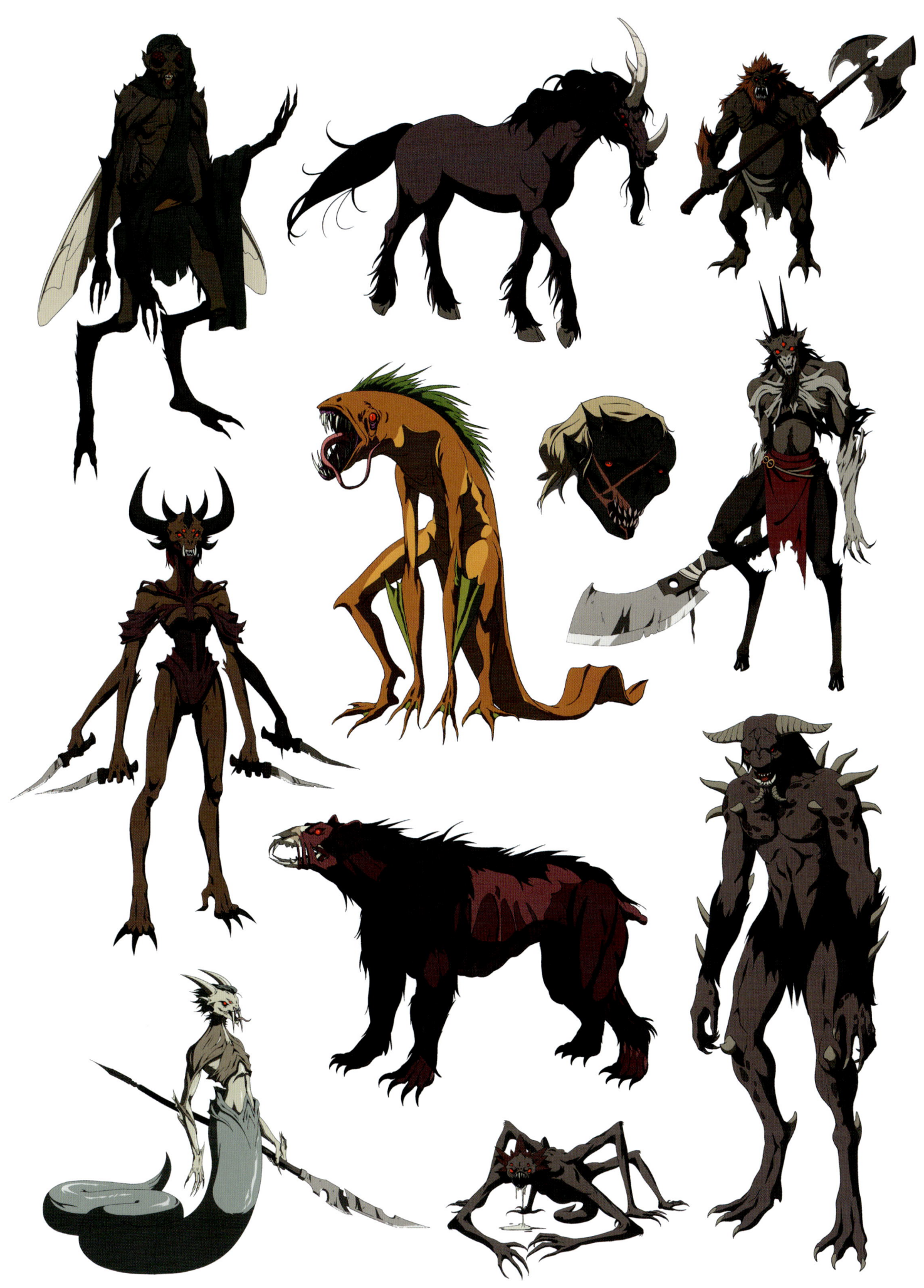

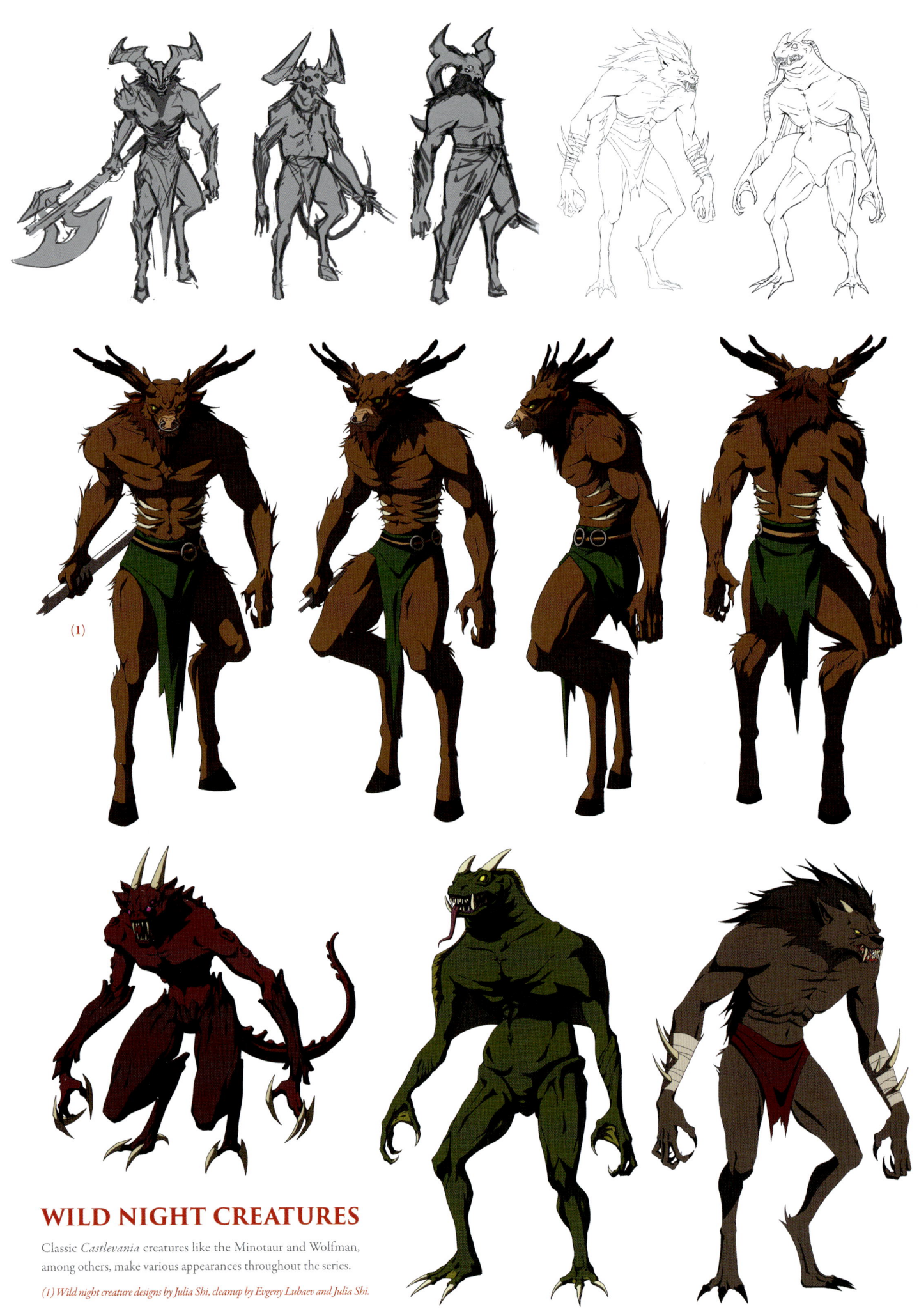

WILD NIGHT CREATURES

Classic *Castlevania* creatures like the Minotaur and Wolfman, among others, make various appearances throughout the series.

(1) Wild night creature designs by Julia Shi, cleanup by Evgeny Lubaev and Julia Shi.

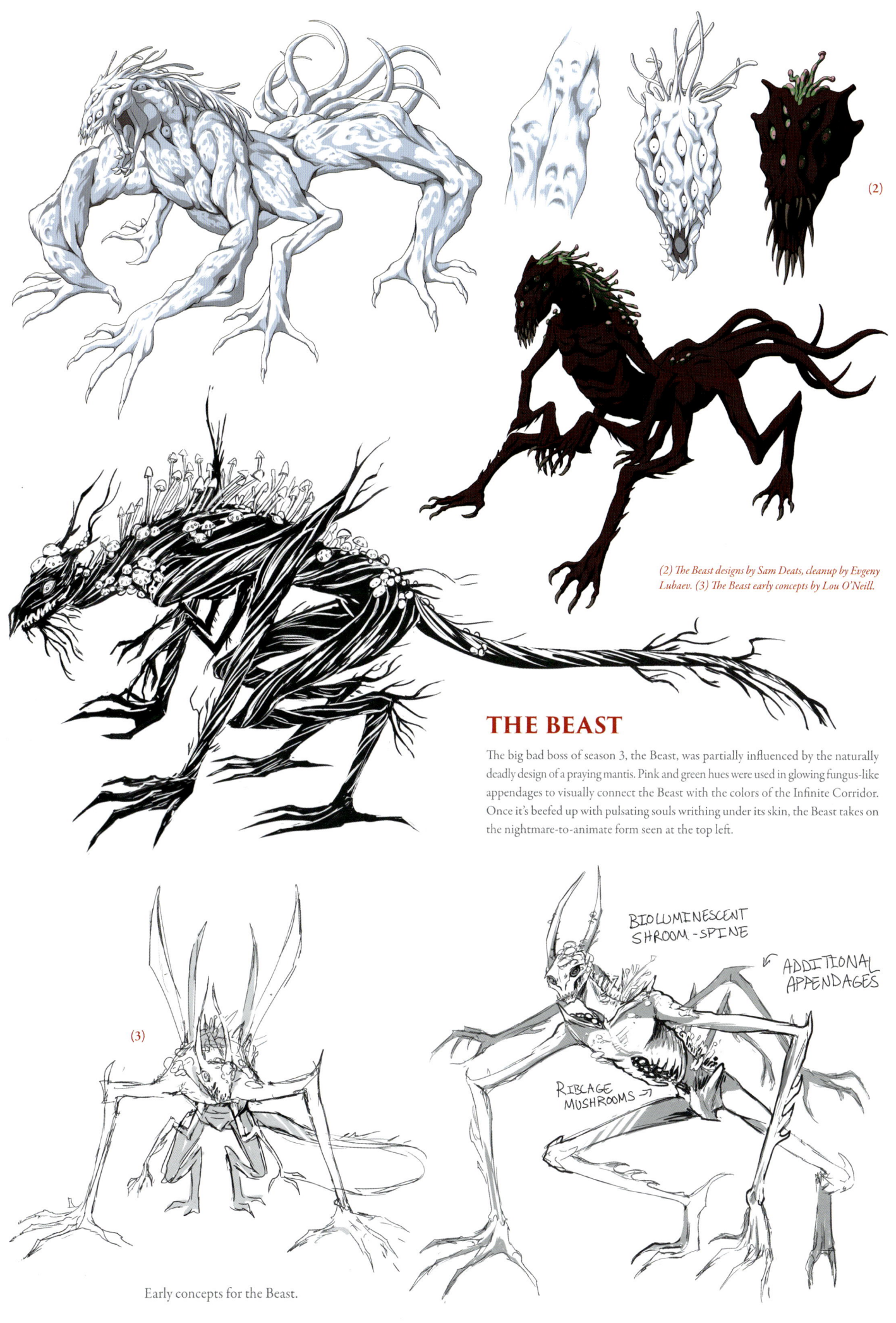

(2)

(2) *The Beast designs by Sam Deats, cleanup by Evgeny Lubaev. (3) The Beast early concepts by Lou O'Neill.*

THE BEAST

The big bad boss of season 3, the Beast, was partially influenced by the naturally deadly design of a praying mantis. Pink and green hues were used in glowing fungus-like appendages to visually connect the Beast with the colors of the Infinite Corridor. Once it's beefed up with pulsating souls writhing under its skin, the Beast takes on the nightmare-to-animate form seen at the top left.

(3)

BIOLUMINESCENT SHROOM-SPINE

ADDITIONAL APPENDAGES

RIBCAGE MUSHROOMS →

Early concepts for the Beast.

SEASON 4 NIGHT CREATURES

Season 4 introduced a slew of new night creatures, both wild and domesticated, including a five-headed, vomiting centipede and Varney's giant pet twin lizards. When Sam Deats saw the script mention the need for two large night creatures in episode 8 with "abnormally large, rocky-looking fists," he saw an opportunity to slip in an Easter egg from the *Castlevania* games by referencing the design of the Golem boss in *Lament of Innocence*.

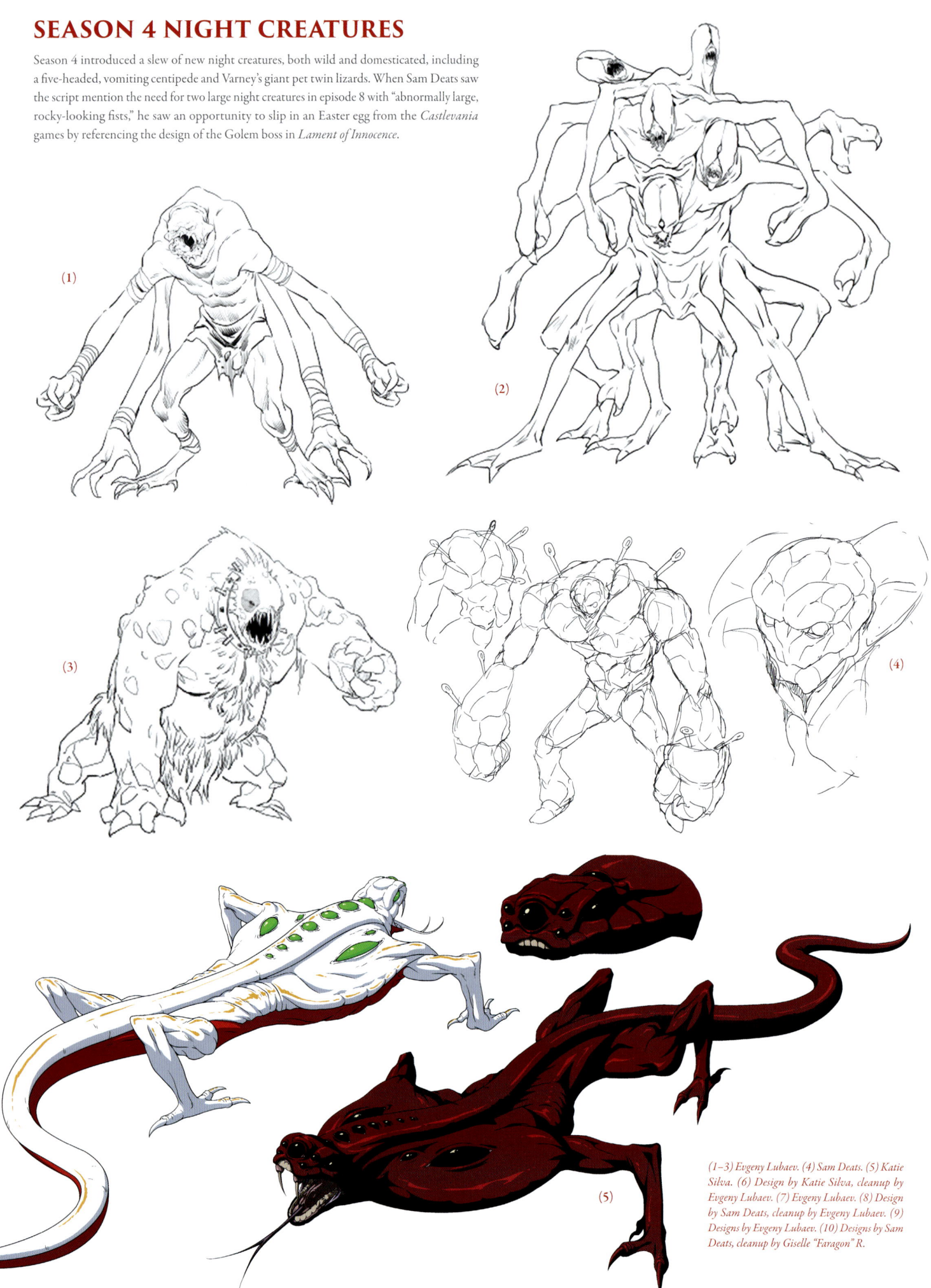

(1)

(2)

(3)

(4)

(5)

(1–3) Evgeny Lubaev. (4) Sam Deats. (5) Katie Silva. (6) Design by Katie Silva, cleanup by Evgeny Lubaev. (7) Evgeny Lubaev. (8) Design by Sam Deats, cleanup by Evgeny Lubaev. (9) Designs by Evgeny Lubaev. (10) Designs by Sam Deats, cleanup by Giselle "Faragon" R.

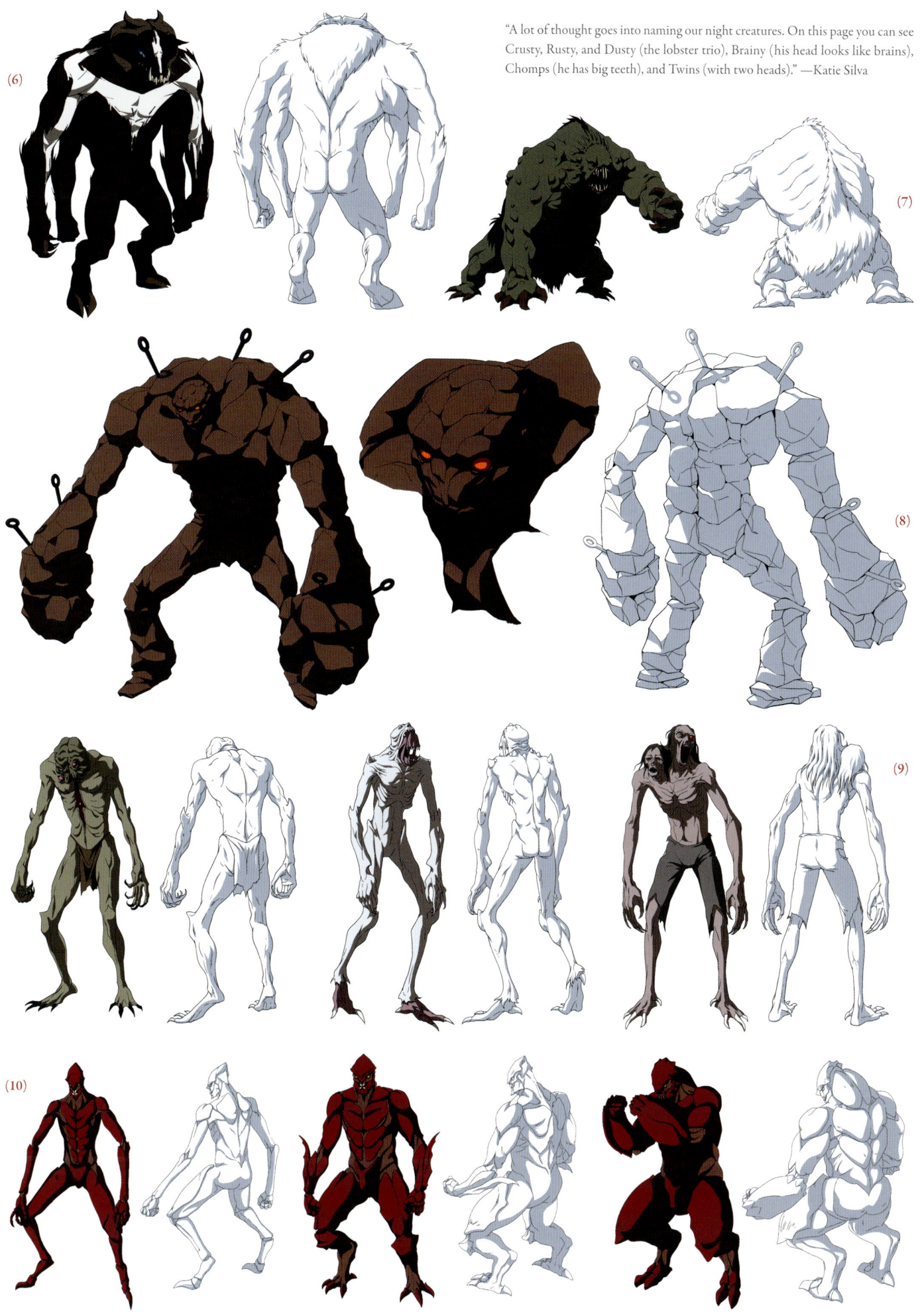

(6)

"A lot of thought goes into naming our night creatures. On this page you can see Crusty, Rusty, and Dusty (the lobster trio), Brainy (his head looks like brains), Chomps (he has big teeth), and Twins (with two heads)." —Katie Silva

(7)

(8)

(9)

(10)

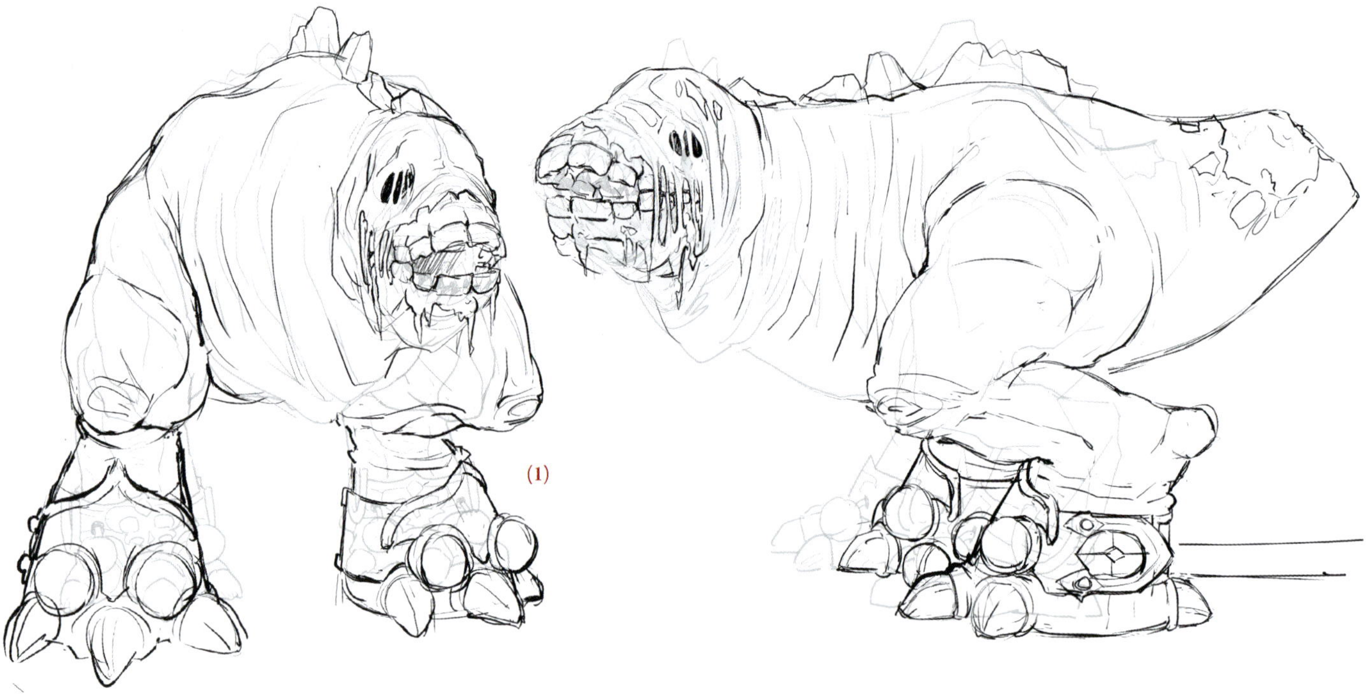

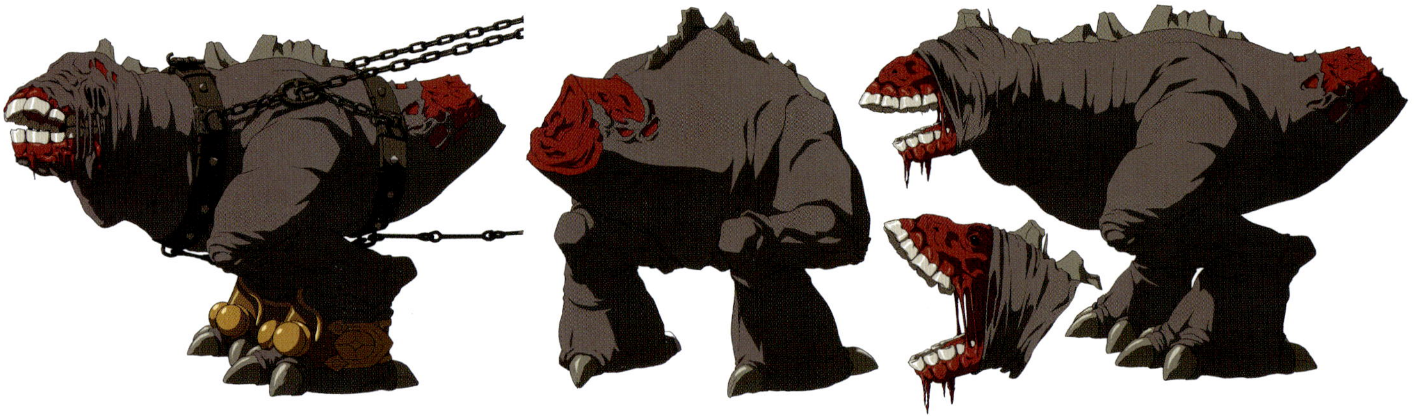

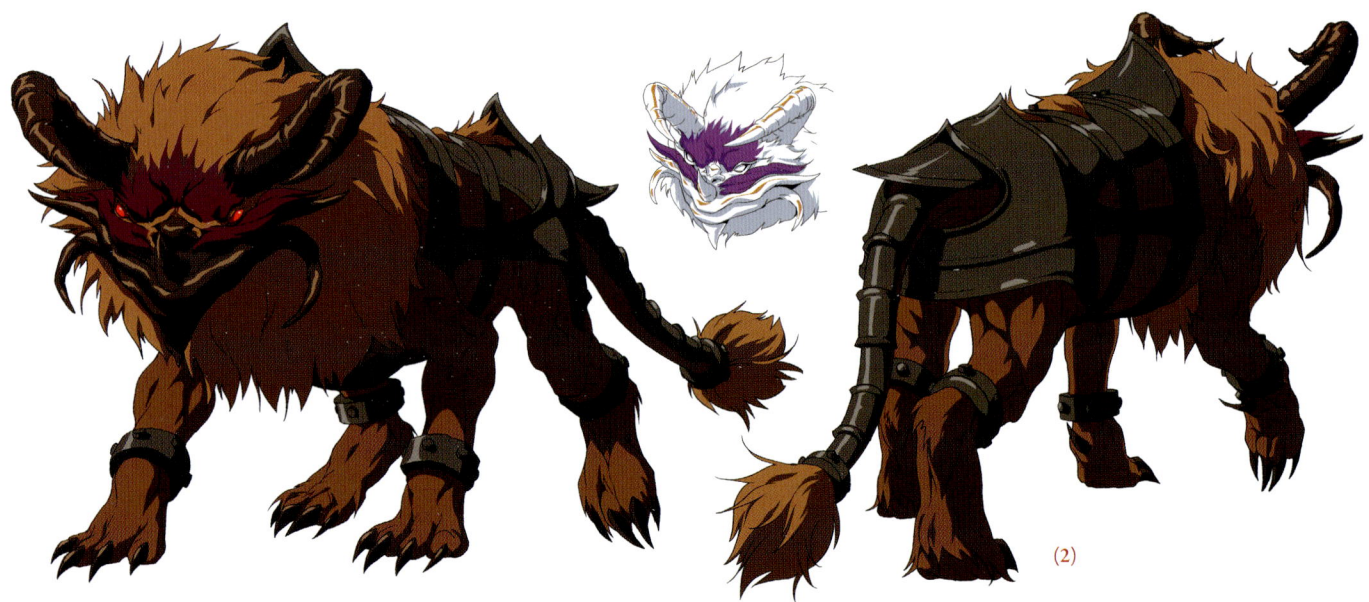

GERGOTH

Gergoth is a creature from the games, with flesh falling from its body and a beam of energy that shoots from its mouth.

ARMORED BEAST

The Armored Beast was also inspired by an in-game creature.

Abel

Abel is an innocent devil who was forged to protect and fight alongside Isaac.

(1) Gergoth designs by Evgeny Lubaev, Katie Silva, and Suzanne Sharp. (2) Armored Beast design by Evgeny Lubaev and Katie Silva. Right page: Abel design by Katie Silva.

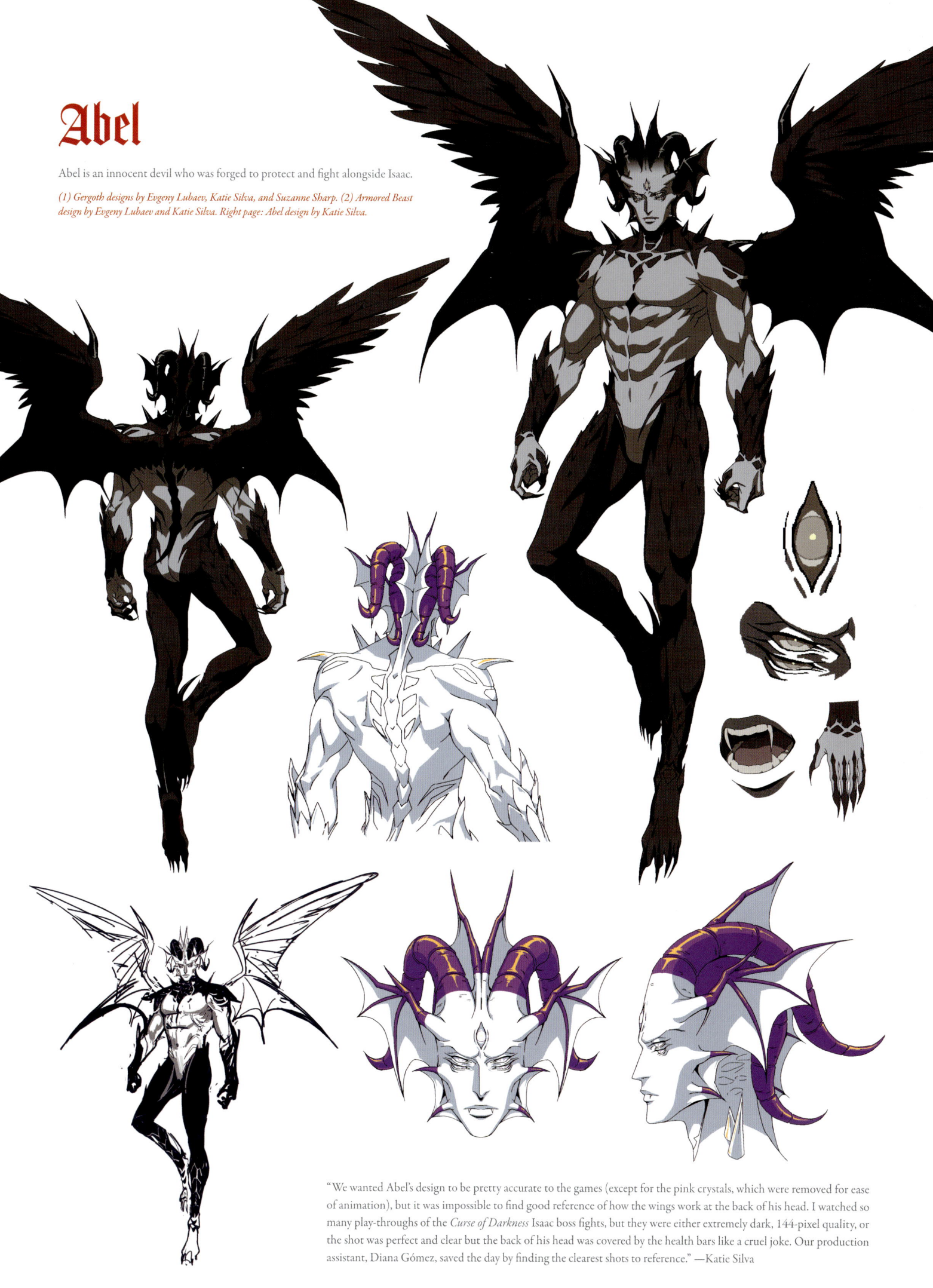

"We wanted Abel's design to be pretty accurate to the games (except for the pink crystals, which were removed for ease of animation), but it was impossible to find good reference of how the wings work at the back of his head. I watched so many play-throughs of the *Curse of Darkness* Isaac boss fights, but they were either extremely dark, 144-pixel quality, or the shot was perfect and clear but the back of his head was covered by the health bars like a cruel joke. Our production assistant, Diana Gómez, saved the day by finding the clearest shots to reference." —Katie Silva

Demons

"The five-legged goat demon is roughly based on the demon Buer, from 'the 16th-century grimoire *Pseudomonarchia Daemonum* and its derivatives, where he is described as a Great President of Hell,' according to Wikipedia."
—Stephanie McCrea Rainosek

Since this creature was also described as something that resembles Sagittarius, Sam Deats used this prompt to mix the lion and archer elements to complete the demon.

Left page: Designs by Sam Deats, cleanup by Stephanie McCrea Rainosek. Right page: (1) Lesser Demon design by Evgeny Lubaev. (2) Malebranche and weapon designs by Sam Deats, cleanup by Evgeny Lubaev and Stephanie McCrea Rainosek.

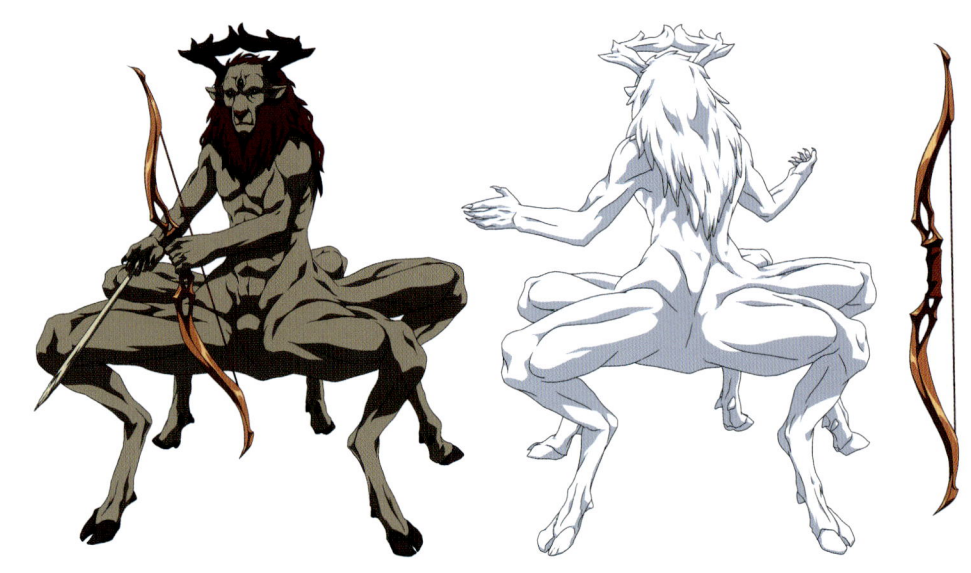

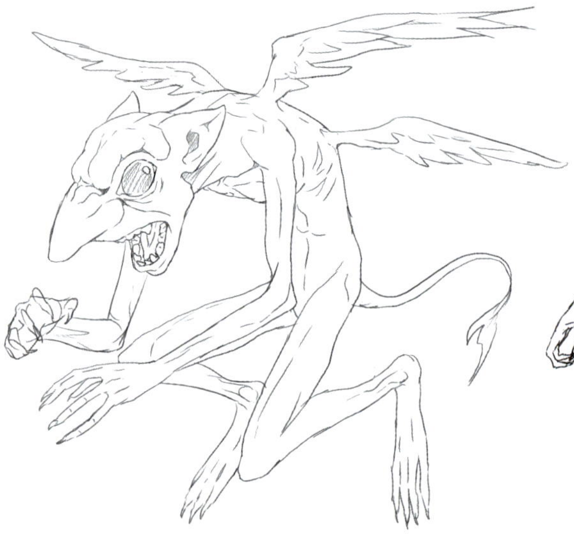

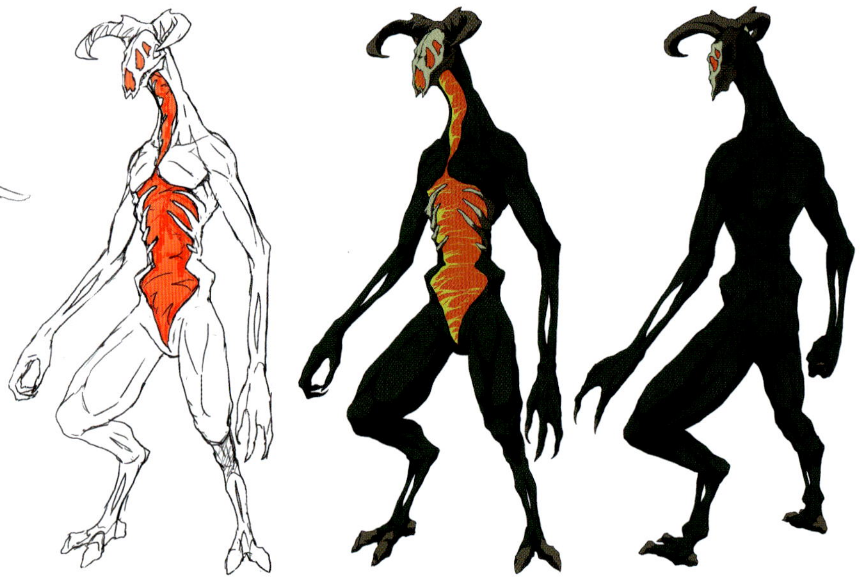

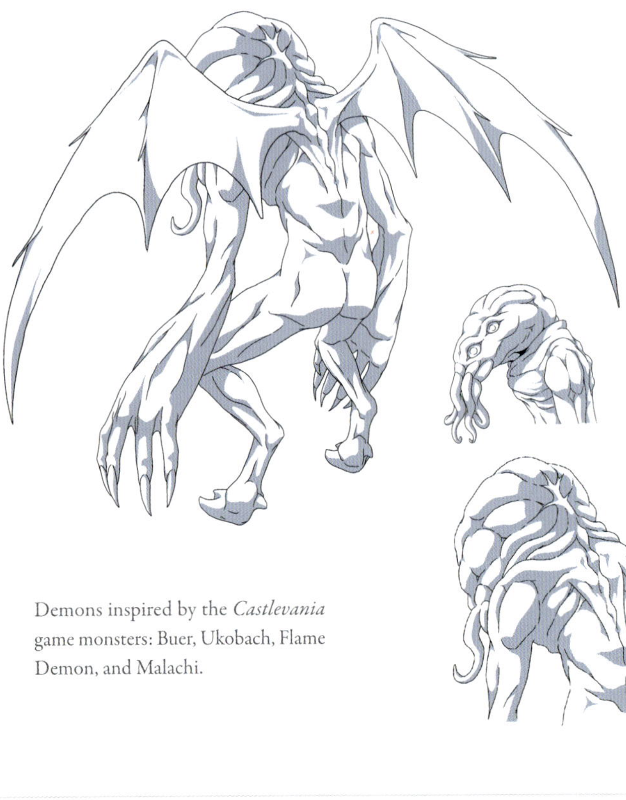

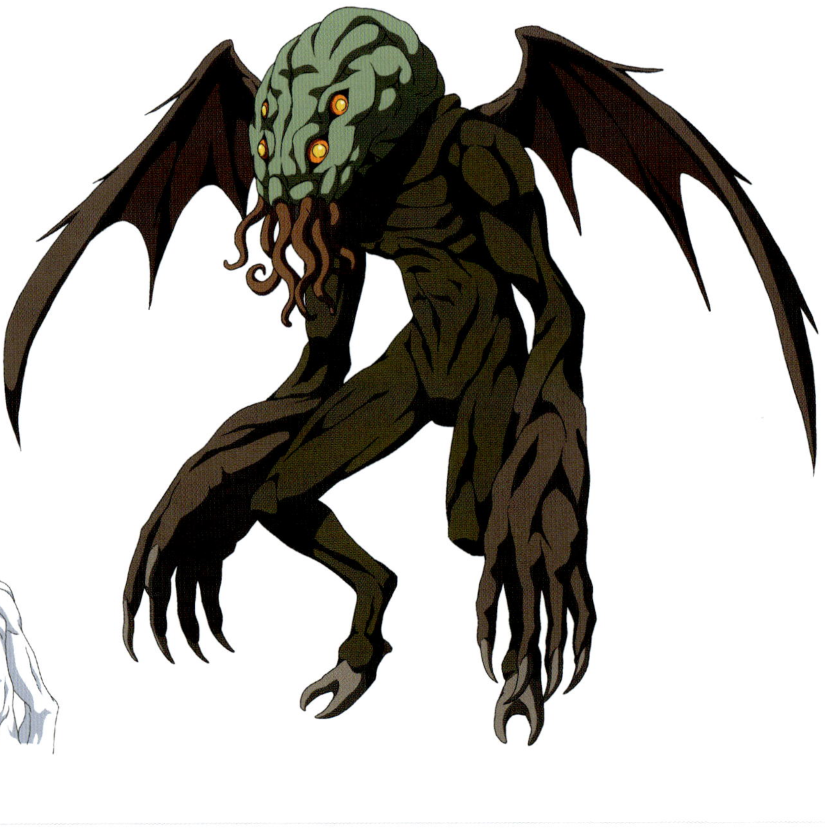

Demons inspired by the *Castlevania* game monsters: Buer, Ukobach, Flame Demon, and Malachi.

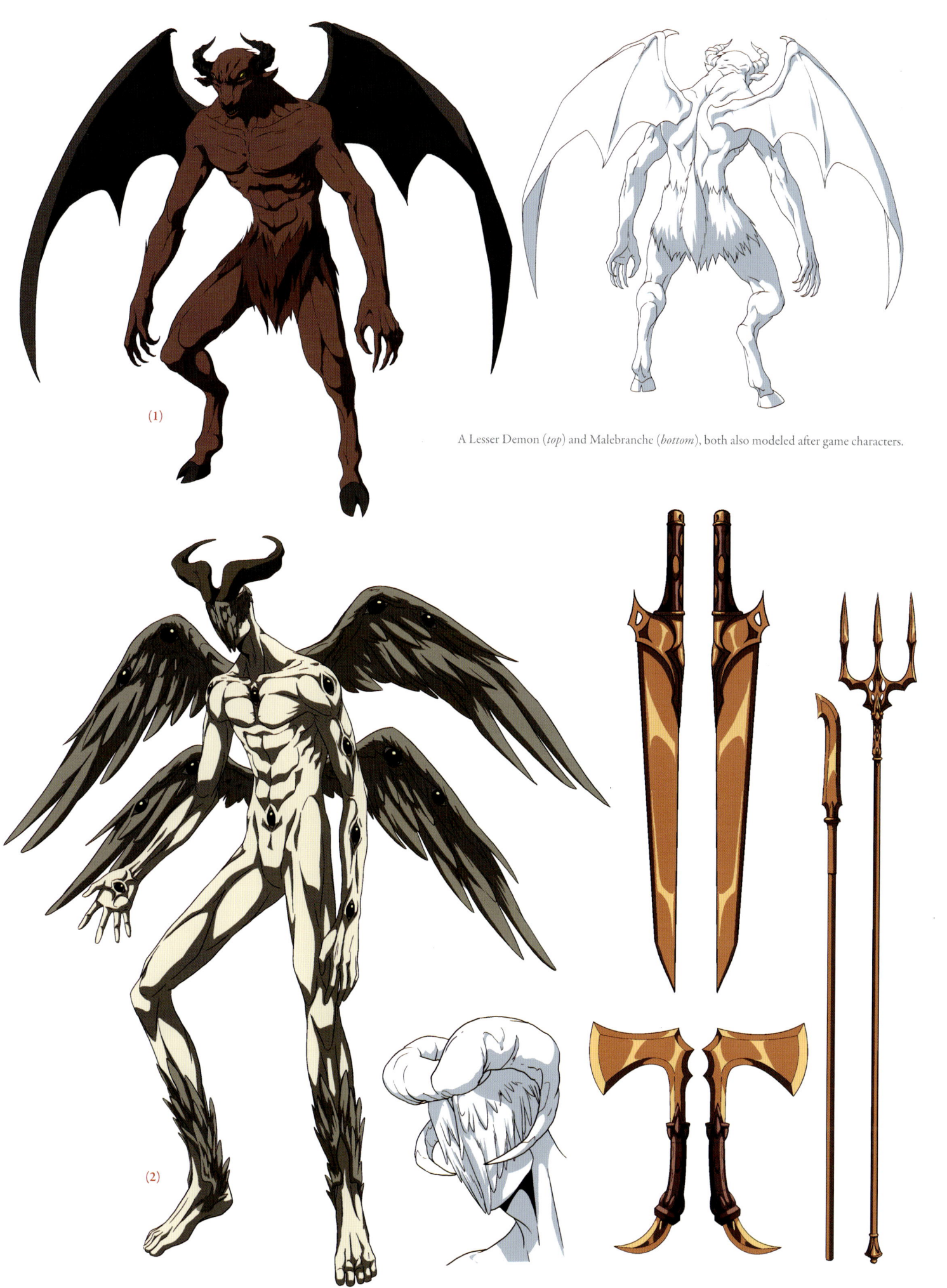

(1)

A Lesser Demon (*top*) and Malebranche (*bottom*), both also modeled after game characters.

(2)

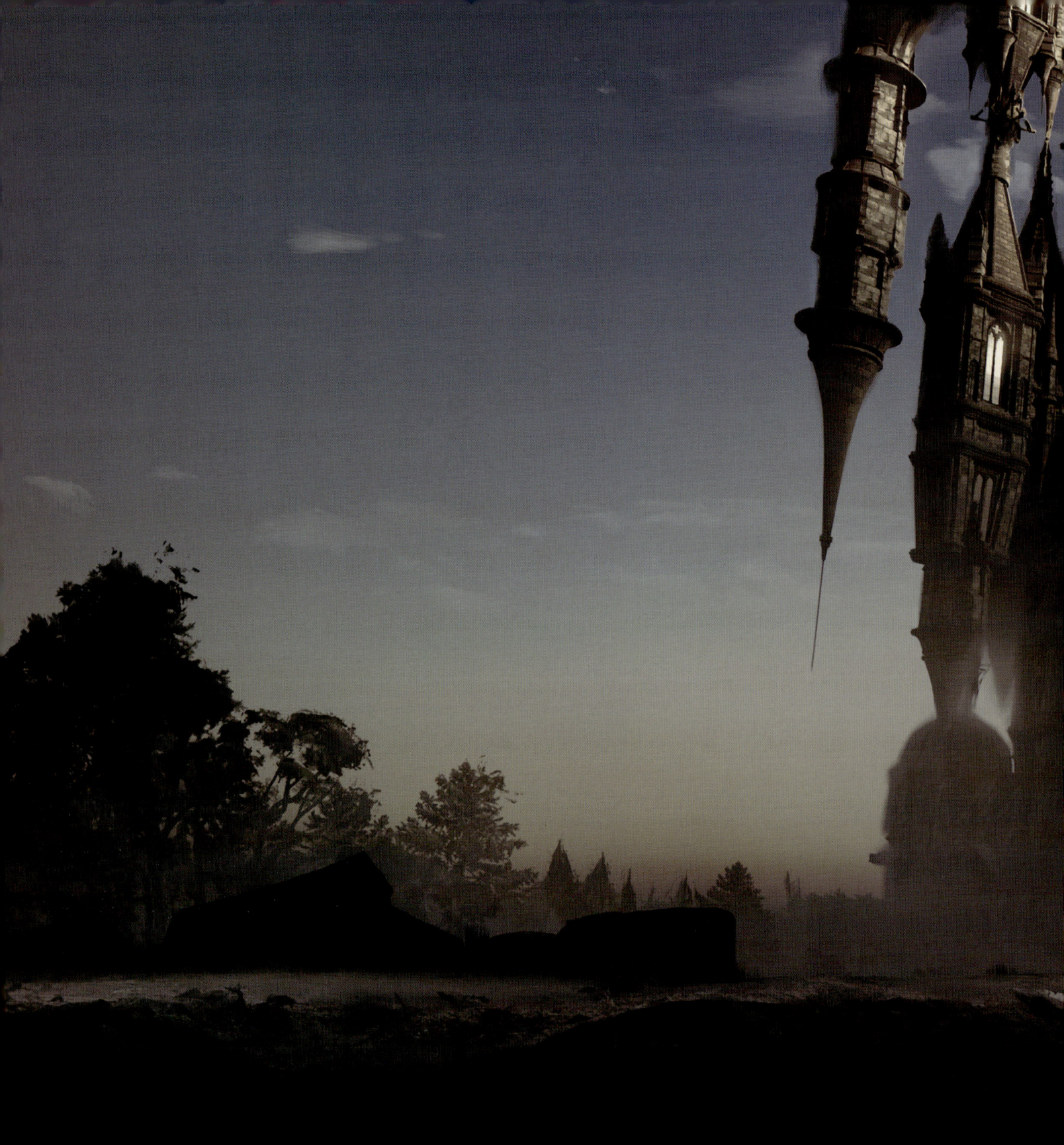

Art by Jose Vega.

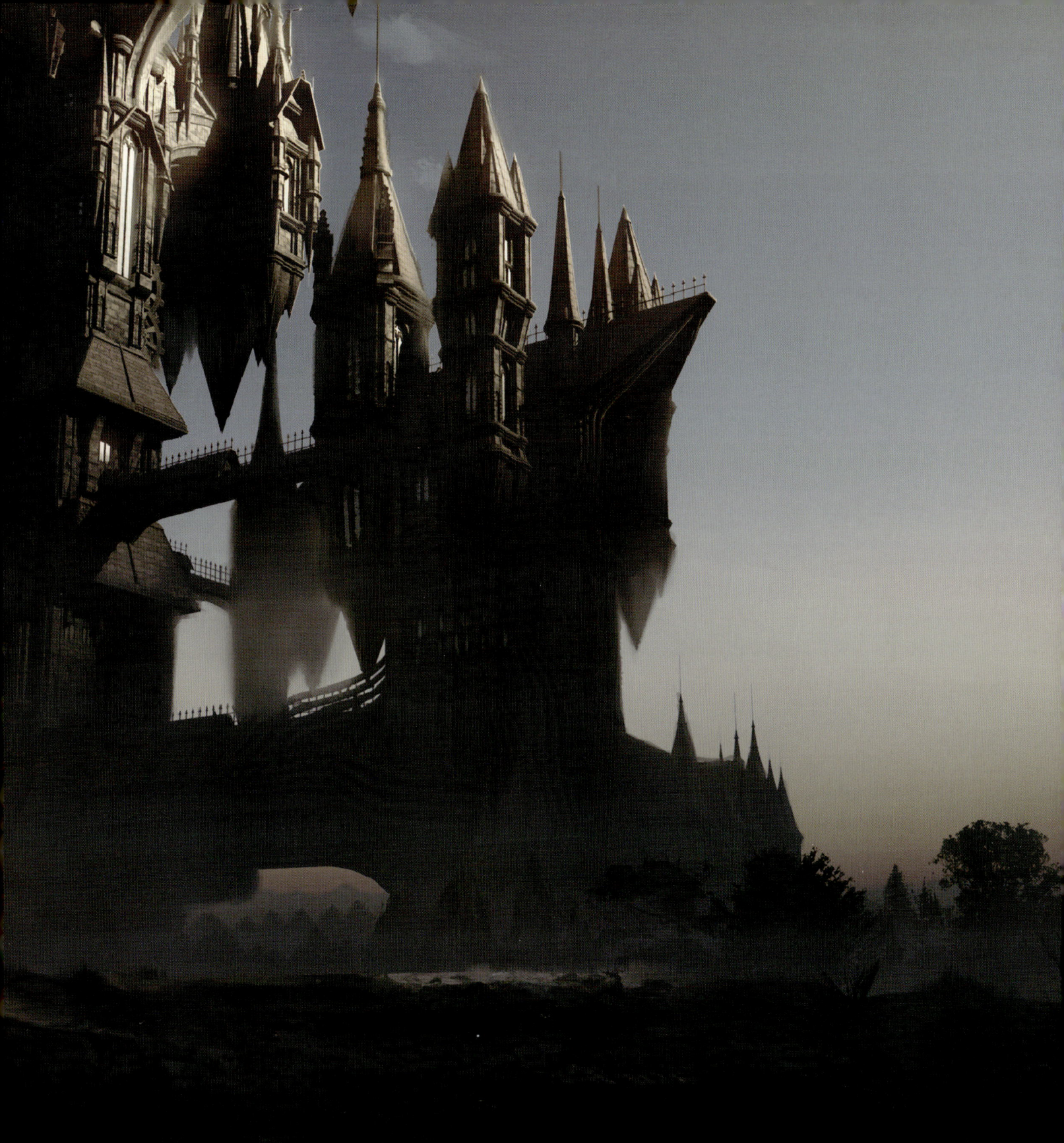

CHAPTER III

Wallachia and the Lands Beyond

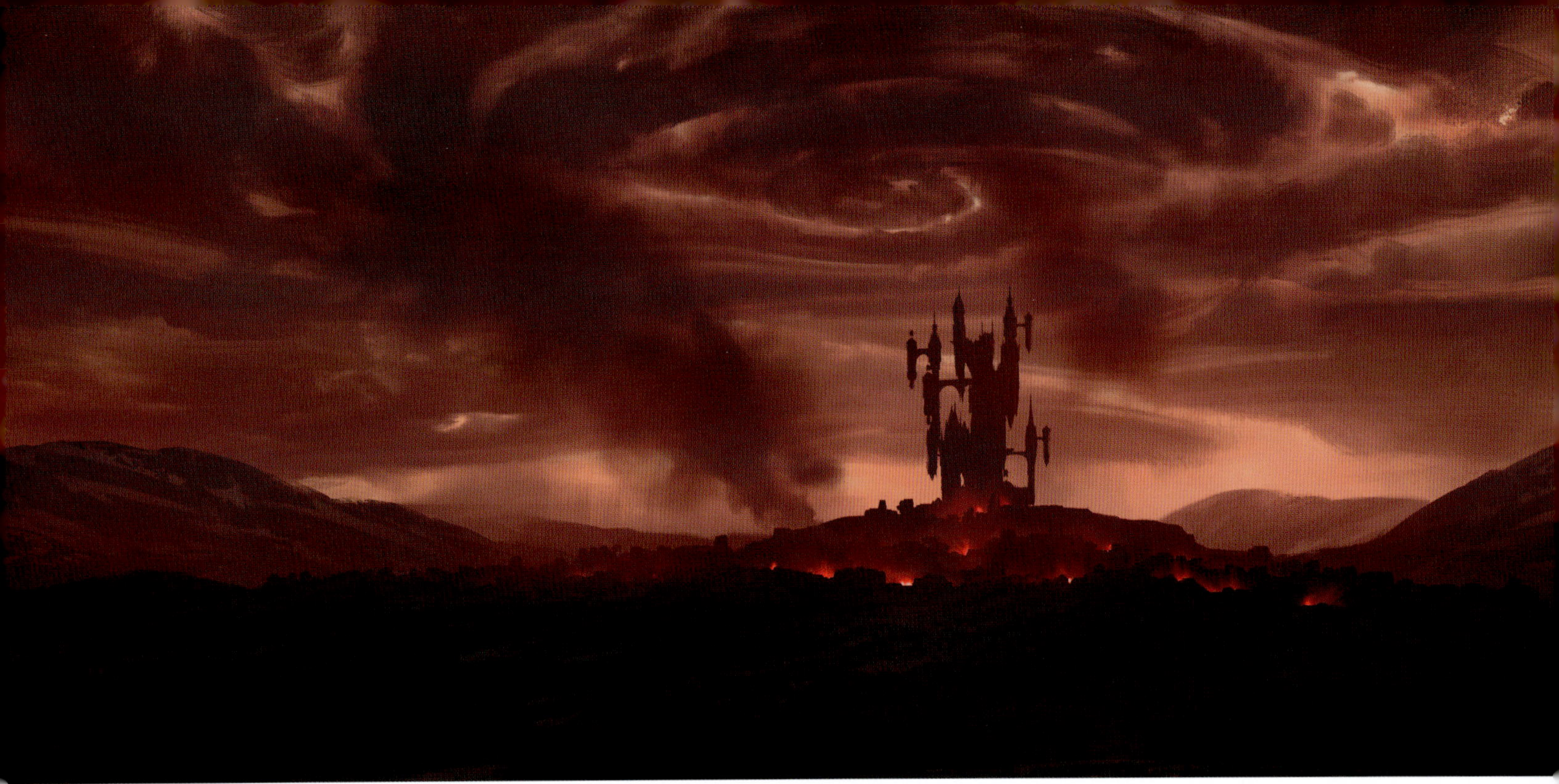

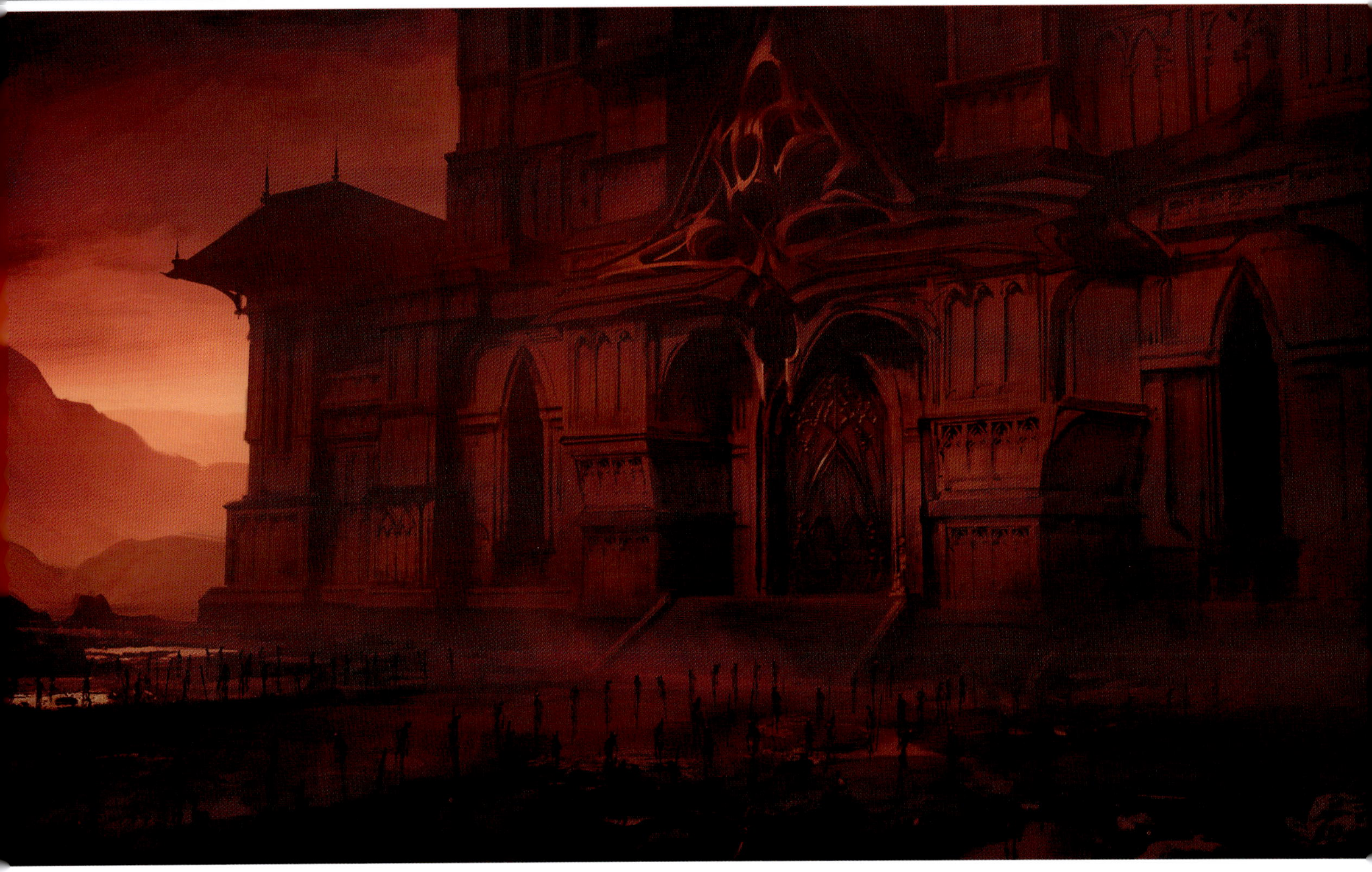

Dracula's Castle

An impossible, intimidating structure, the seat of his power, and the store of centuries of accumulated knowledge, Dracula's castle is an iconic image in the series. "The idea with this castle was to make it this otherworldly, enormous thing that is practically a city in and of itself. It's probably a little too big, it's been a problem. [laughs] We've had to play with its scale at various times. It has a typical Gothic architecture mixed with strange contraptions throughout which might be parts of a scientific research laboratory or might be part of the mechanisms that teleport the structure. There was talk initially of having parts of the building transform and contract in on itself before moving, but this was before we had figured out how it was actually going to move." —Sam Deats

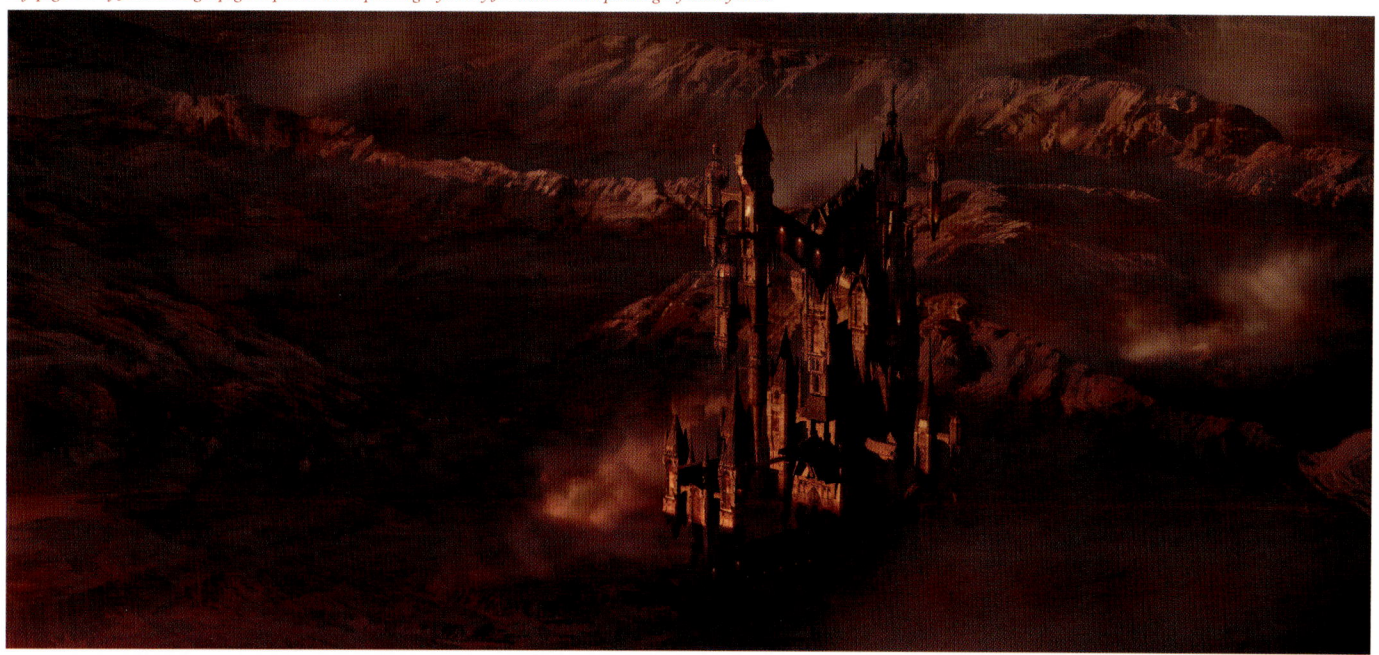

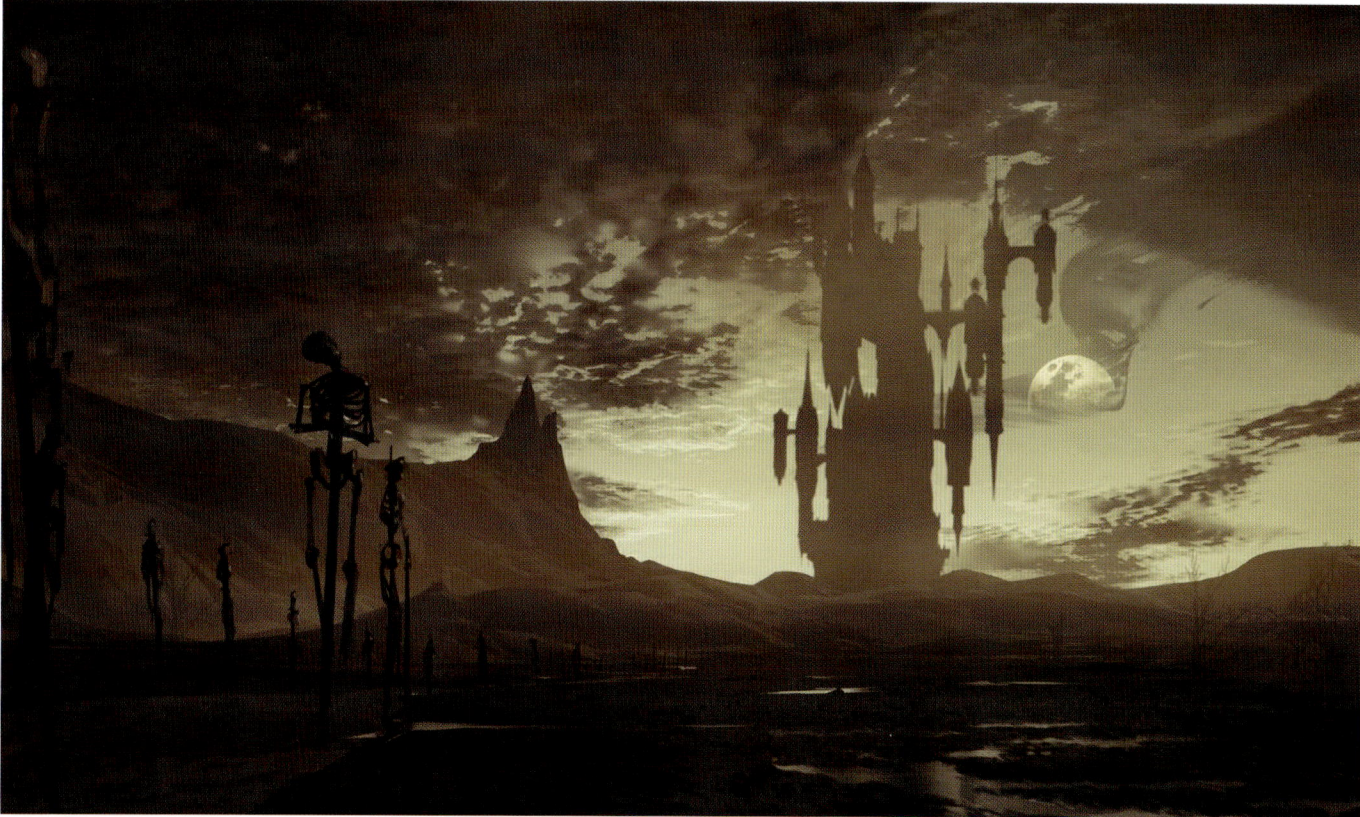

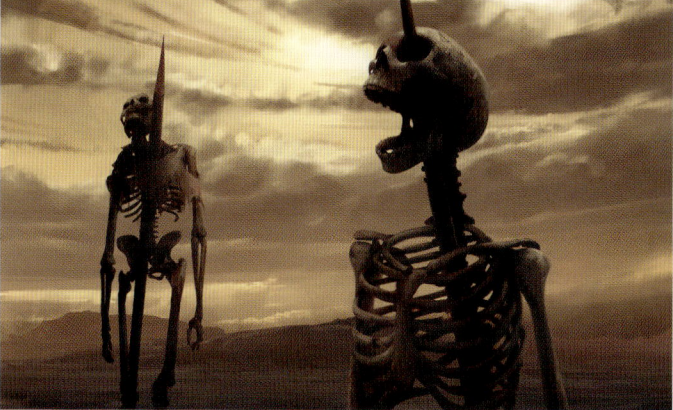 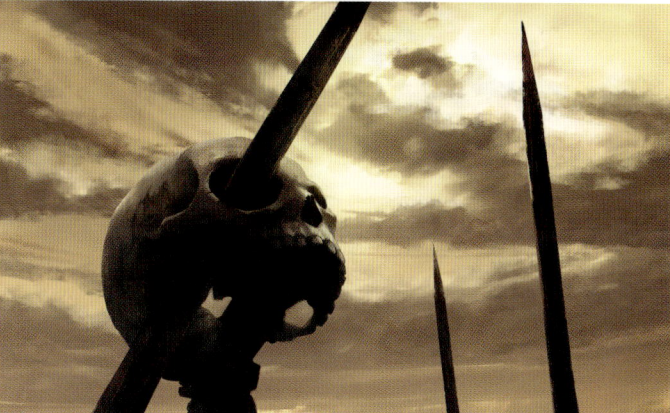

In the opening moments of the series, Lisa is guided along the path to Dracula's castle in Wallachia by impaled corpses that have rotted down to their skeletons.

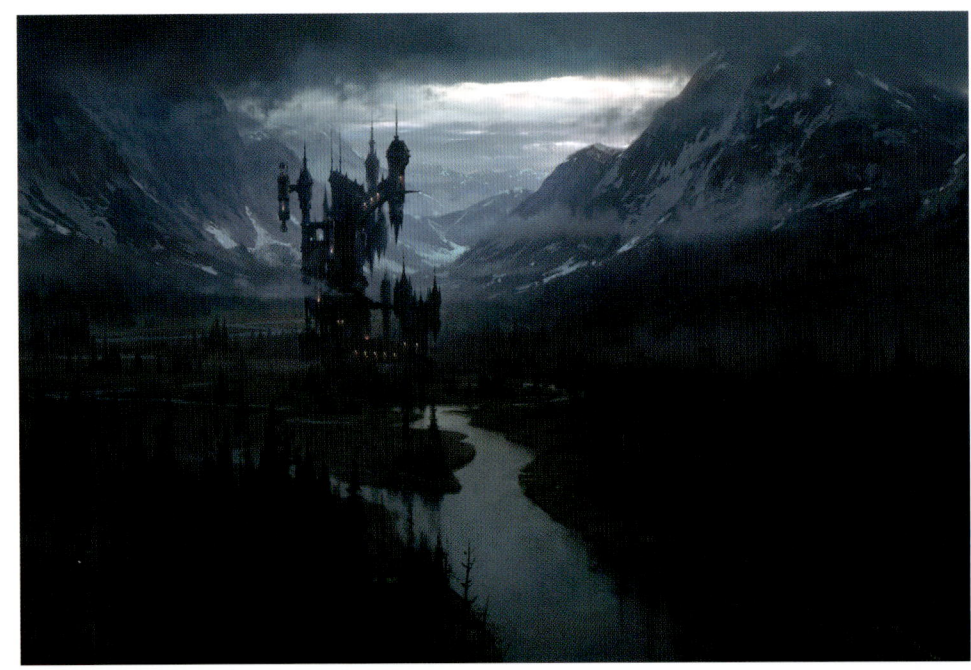

CASTLE VIEWS

"There's technically two 3D models of the castle. In season 1 we used a basic model that was set up in a composition and then painted over. In season 2, when we realized that this thing was going to have to move, we made a fully textured and detailed model that we've used since. We place it in a scene and light it, and then the artists go in and hand paint over it to blend it into a cohesive background painting." —Sam Deats

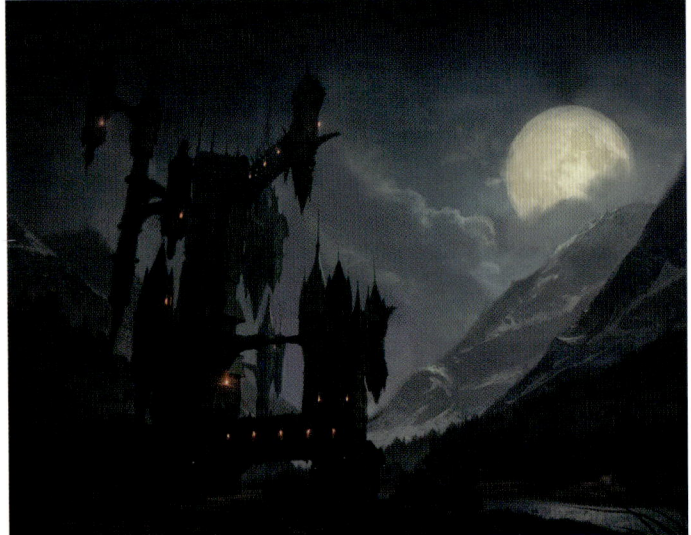

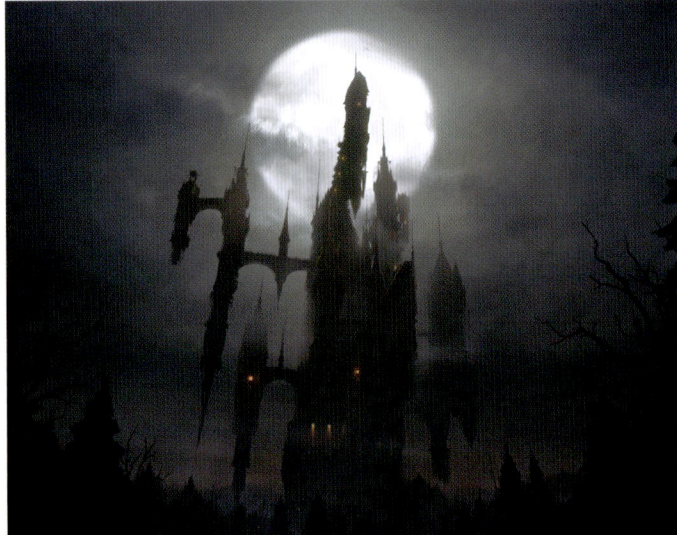

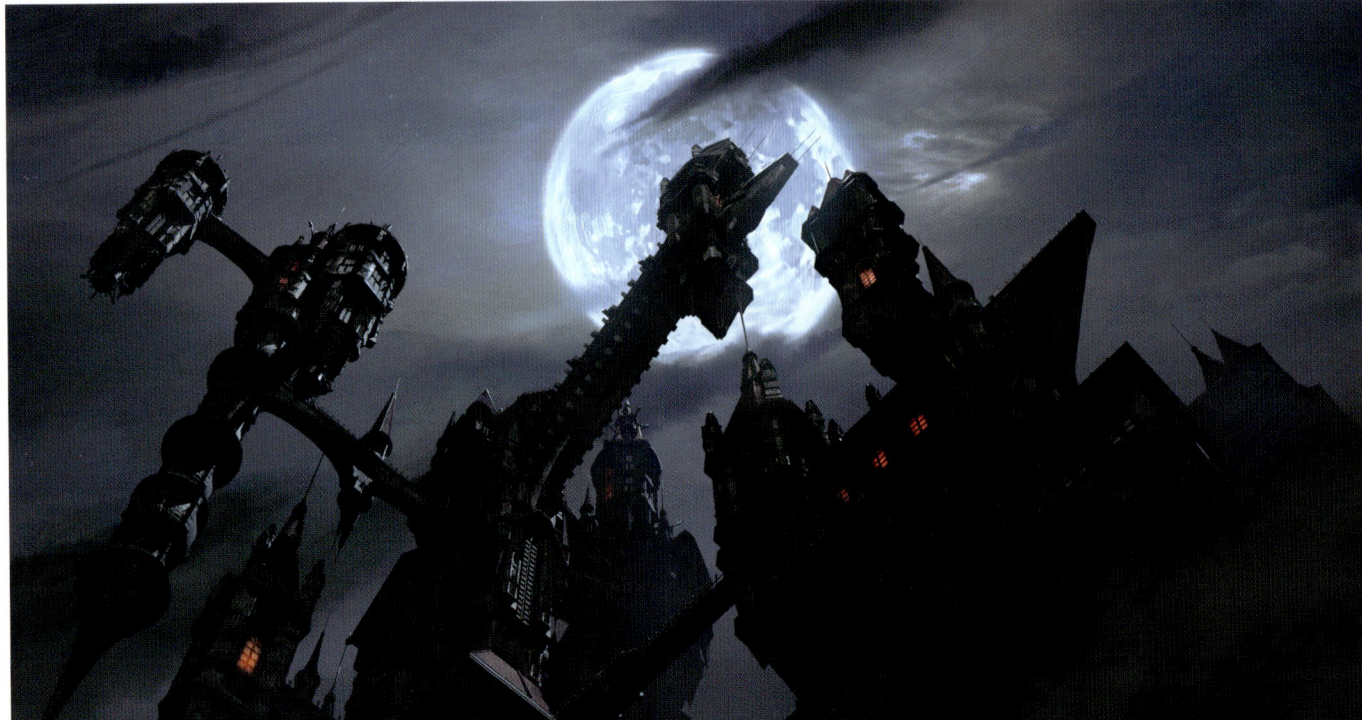

Left page: Top and middle right paintings by Sean Vo. Middle left painting by Alex O'Dowd. Bottom painting by Jose Vega. Right page: Top paintings by Bo Li. Bottom painting by Sean Vo.

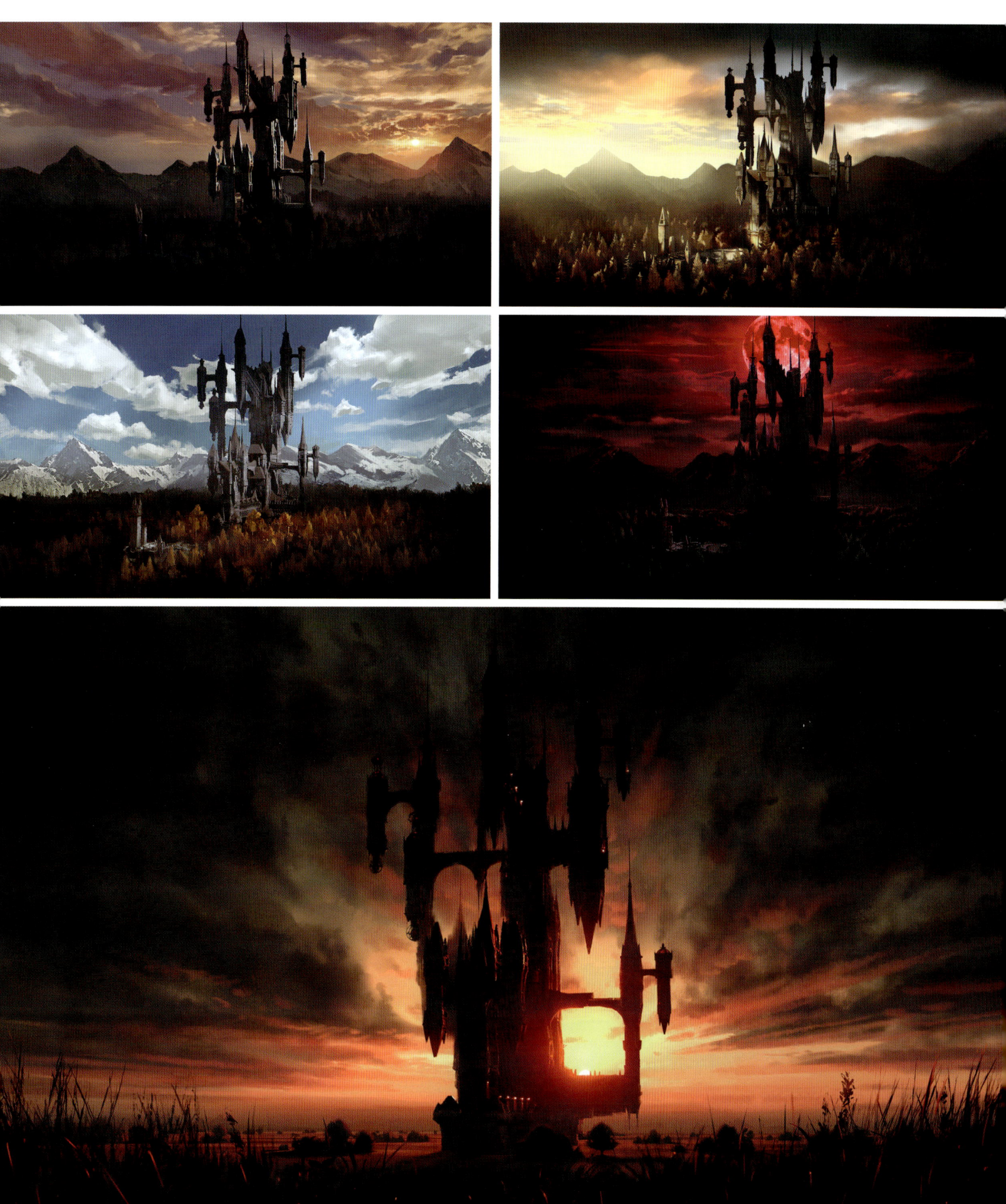

Evening, morning, day, and blood moon lighting concepts cast Dracula's castle in different moods.

Top painting by Bo Li. Bottom left image by Robby Johnson. Bottom right paintings by Jose Vega.

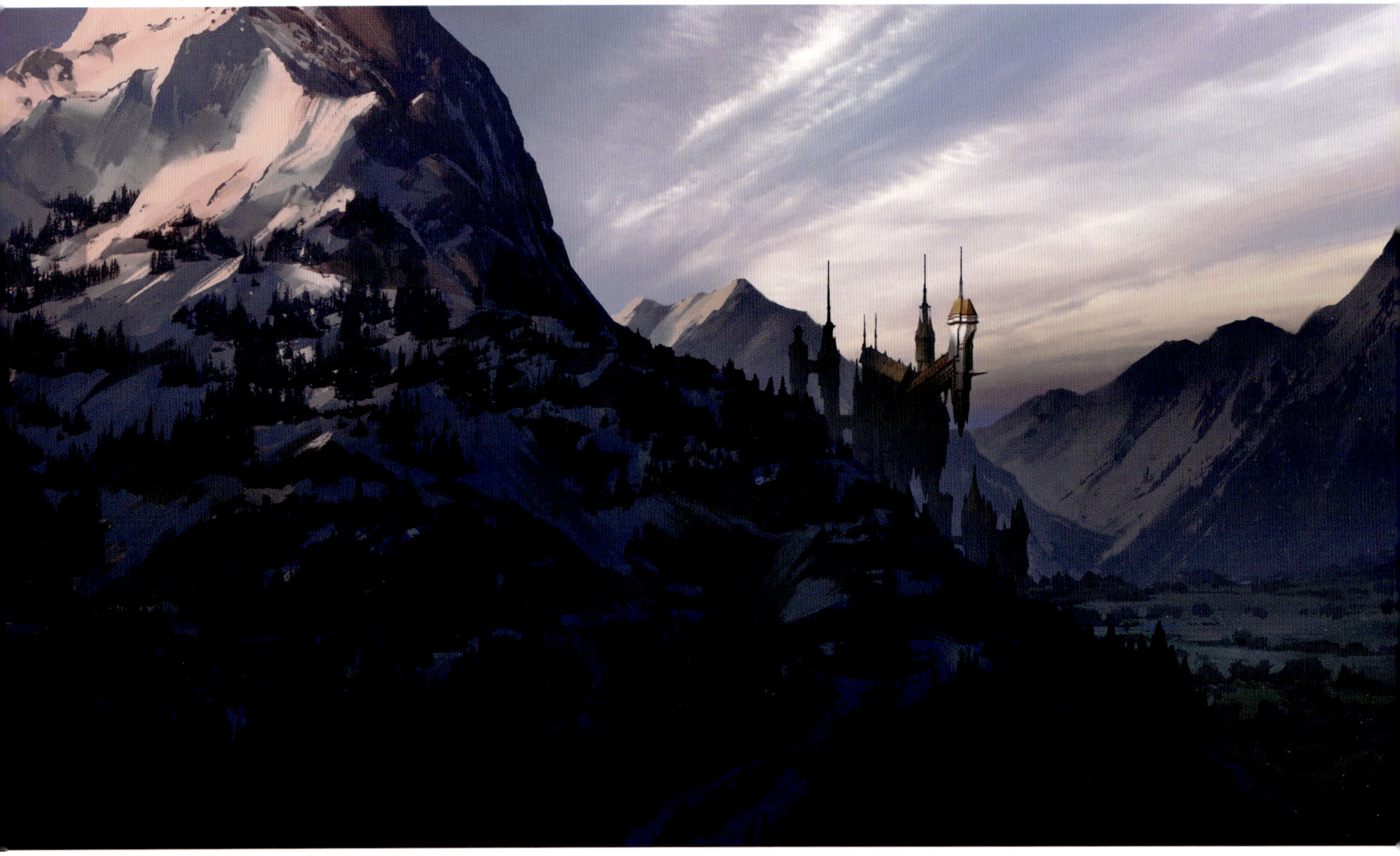

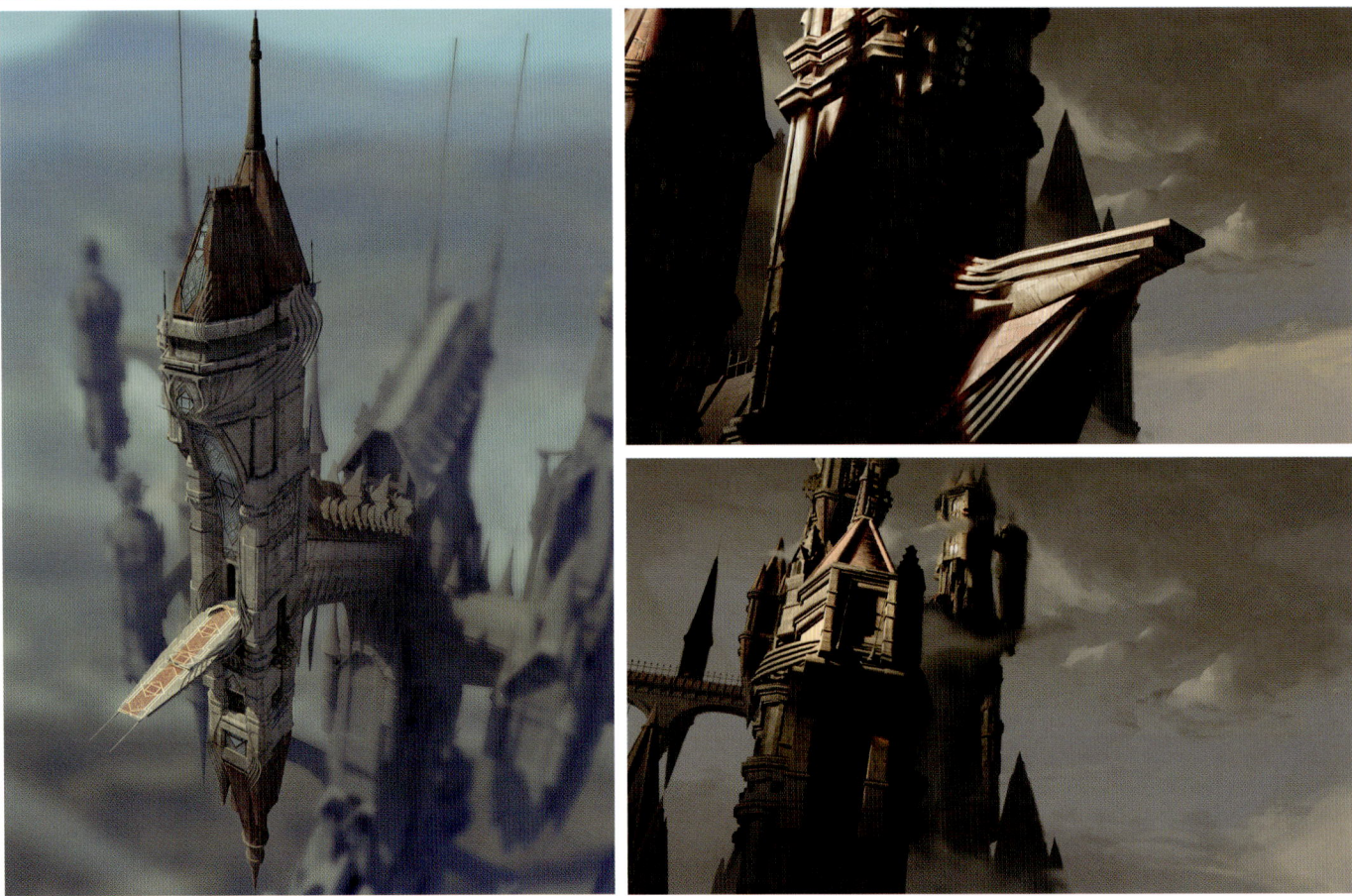

Castle views amid landscapes reveal new details and perspectives.

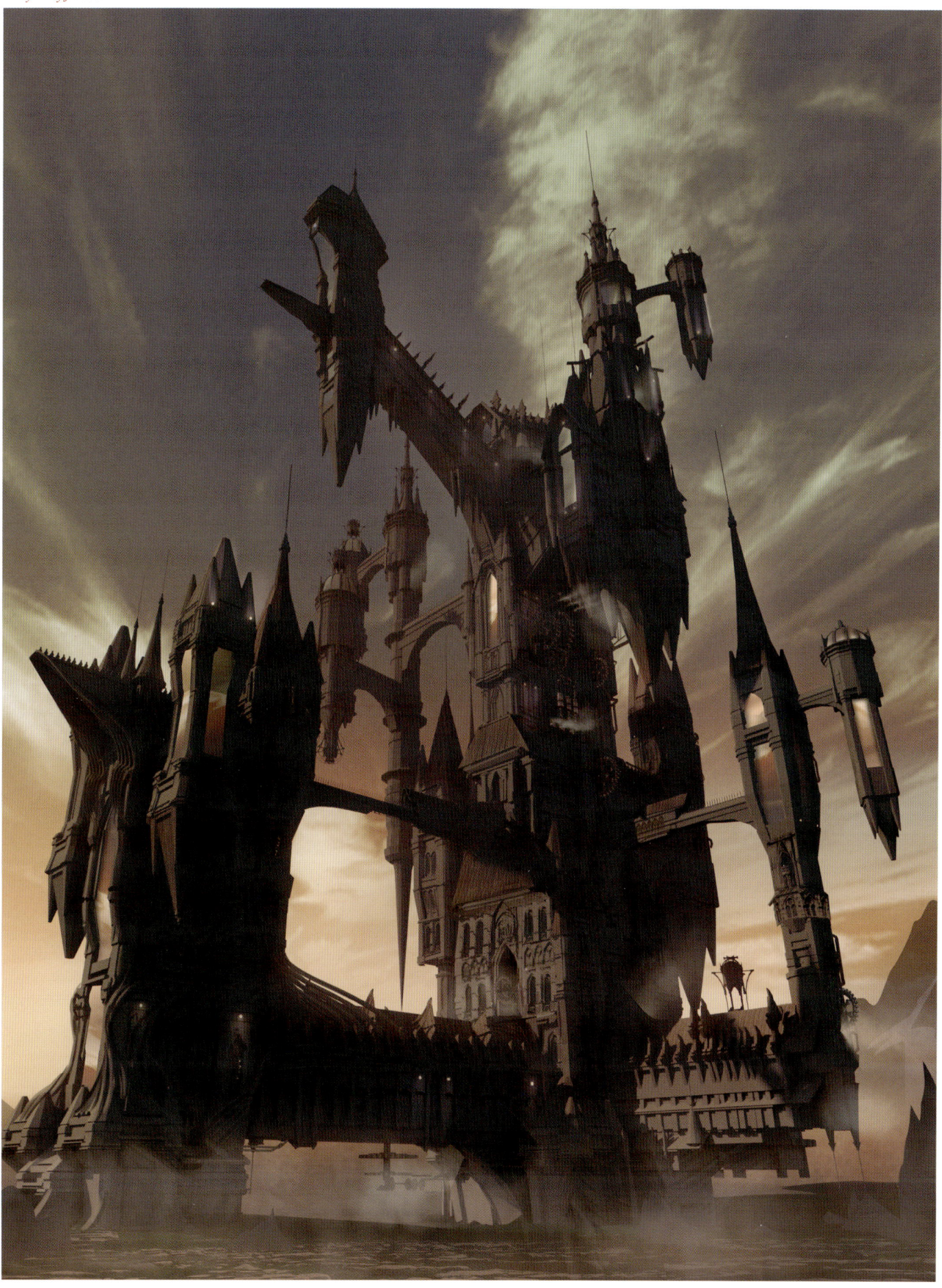

The impossible architecture of Dracula's castle becomes almost believable thanks to the intricate detailing of mysterious machinery embedded throughout, and the knowledge that the entire structure is a teleportation device far beyond even modern technical abilities.

Top painting by Jose Vega. Bottom painting by Stephen Stark.

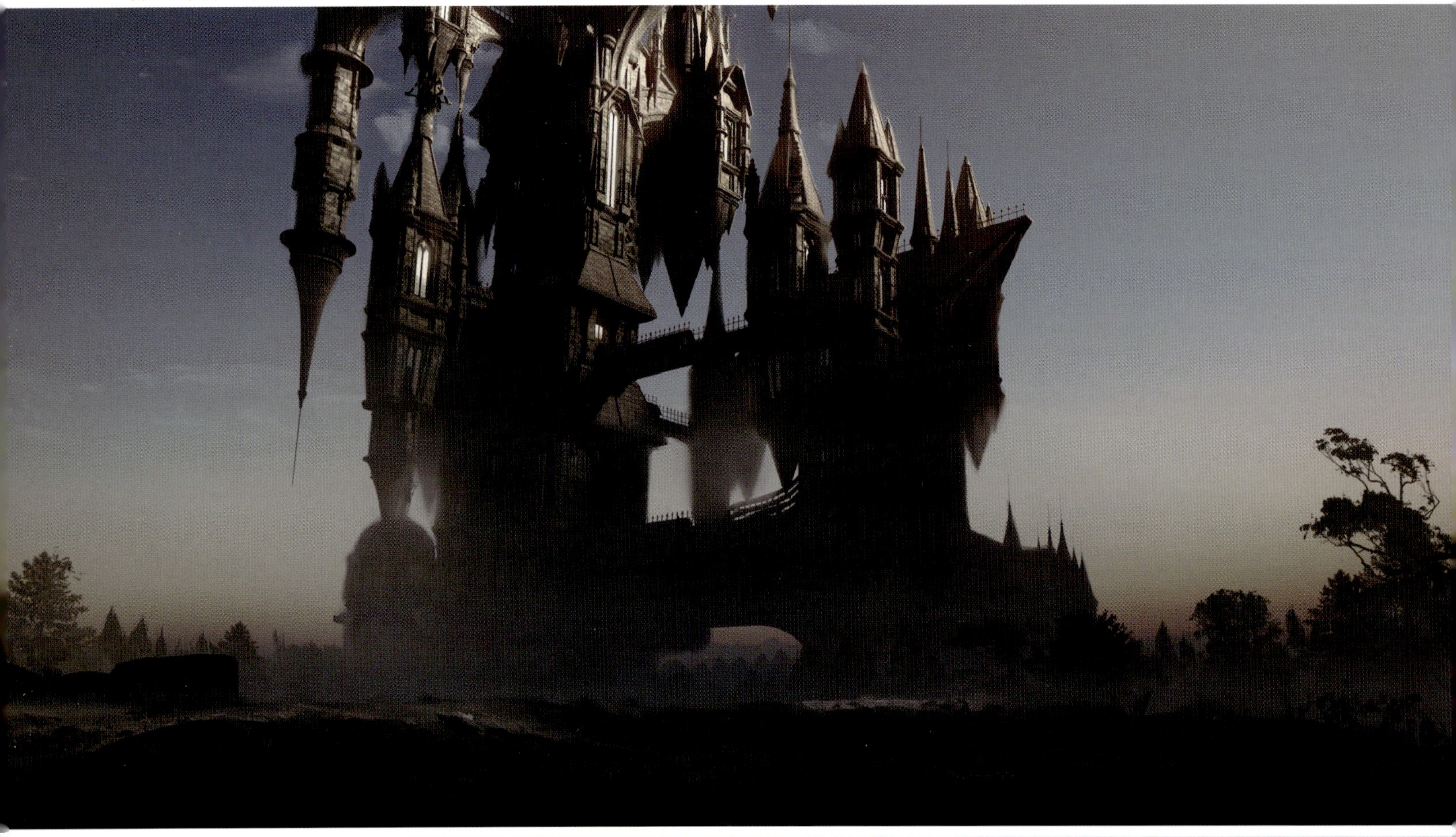

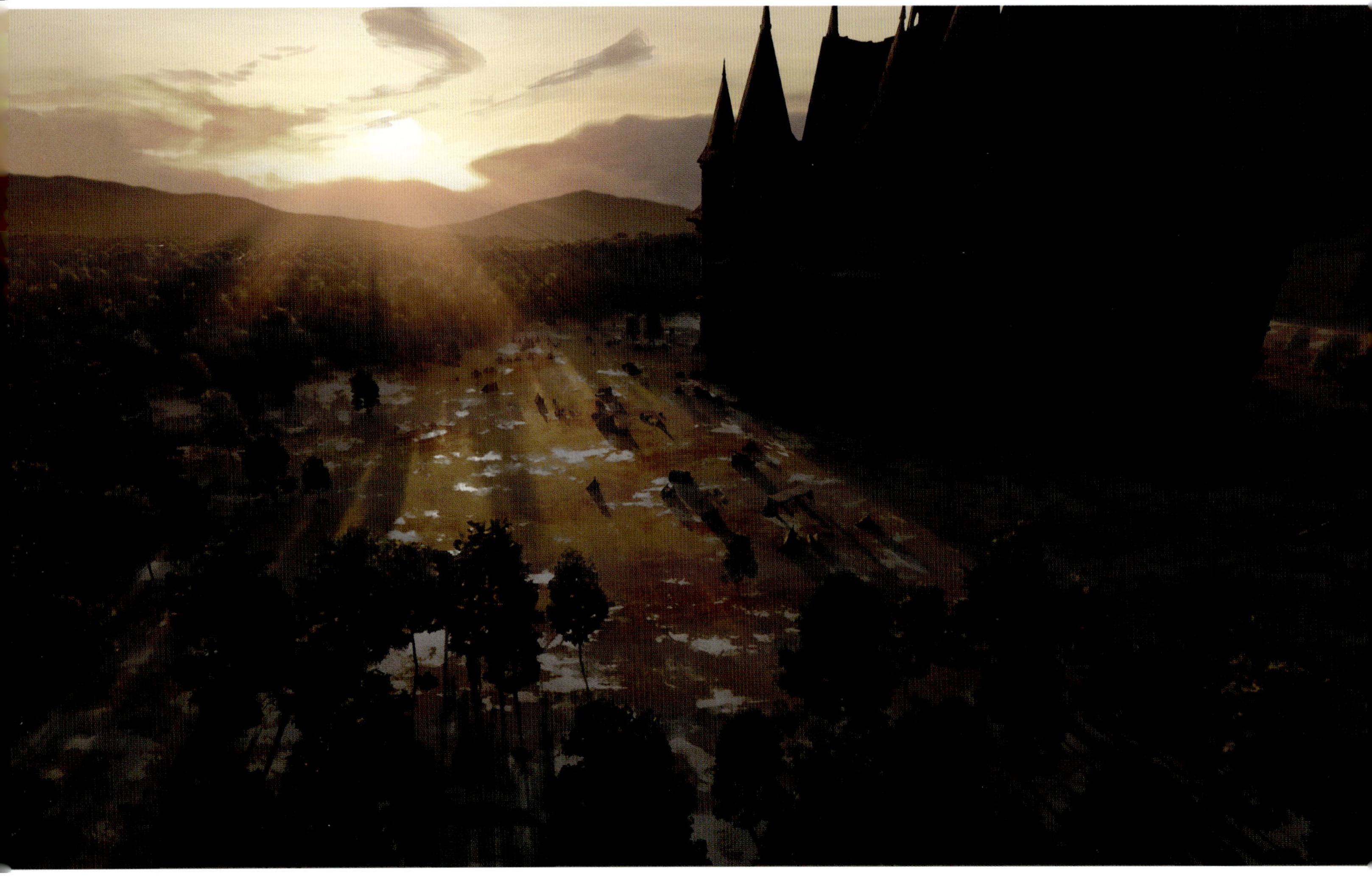

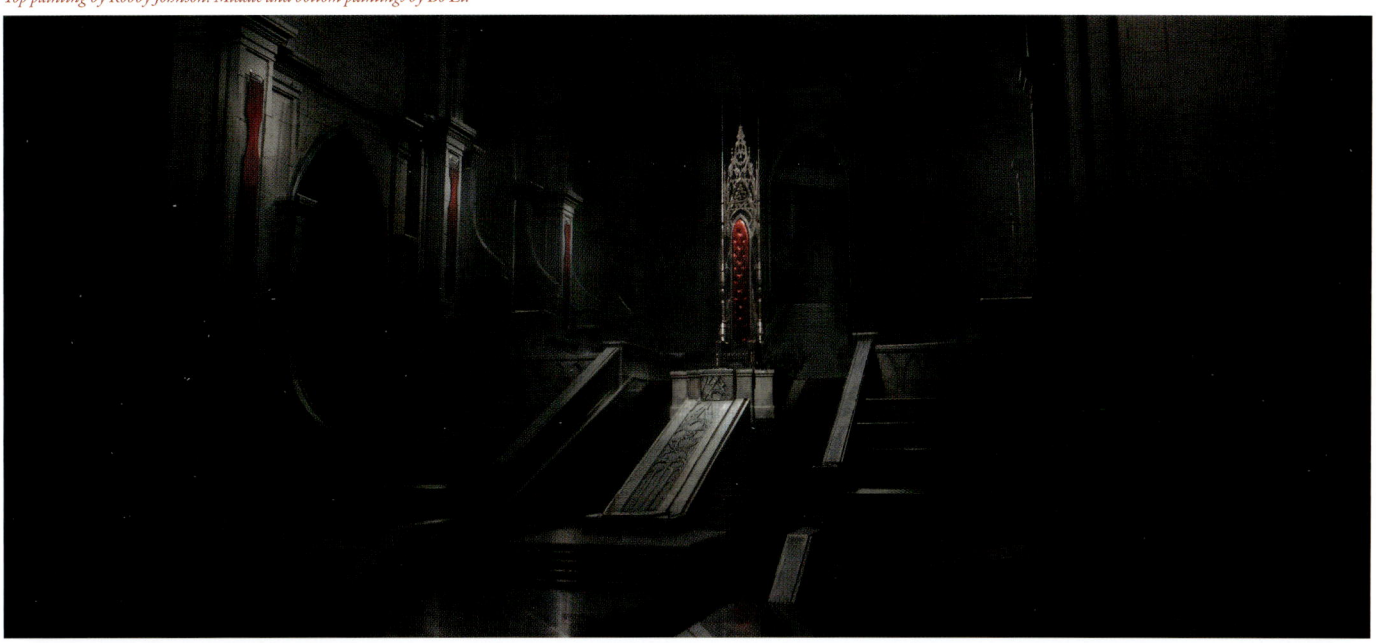

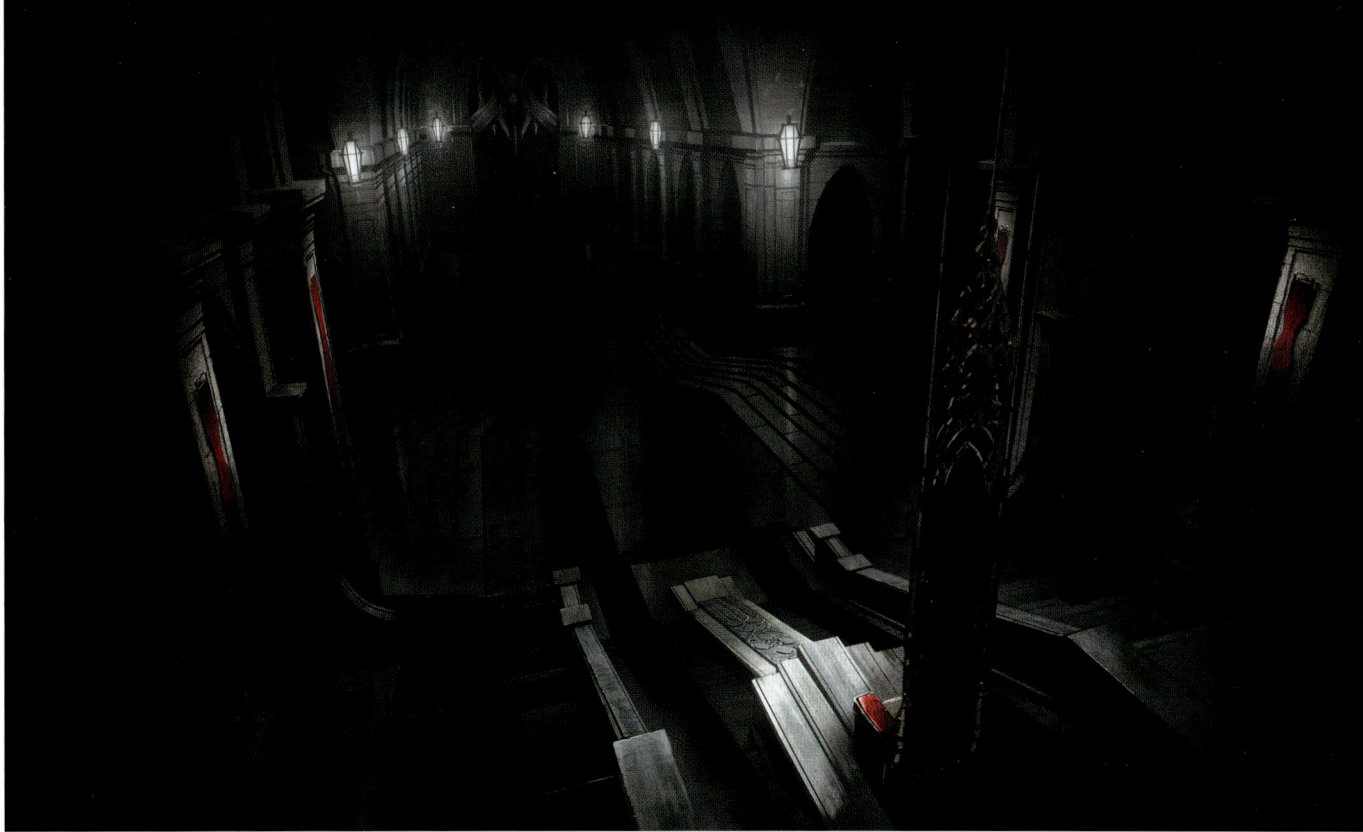

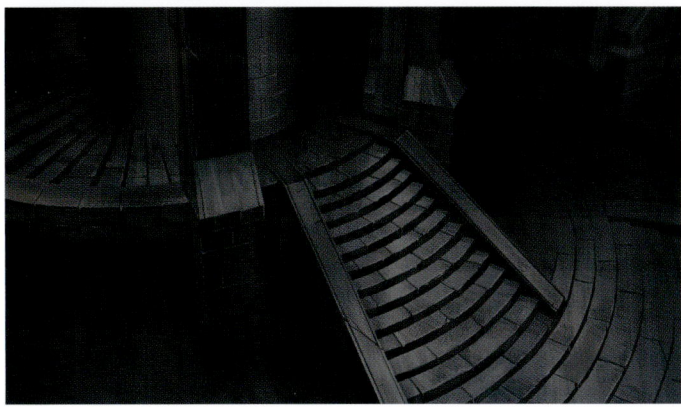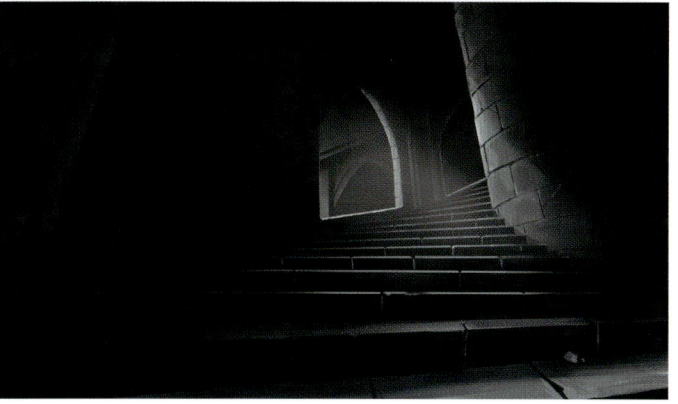

The war hall of Dracula's castle.

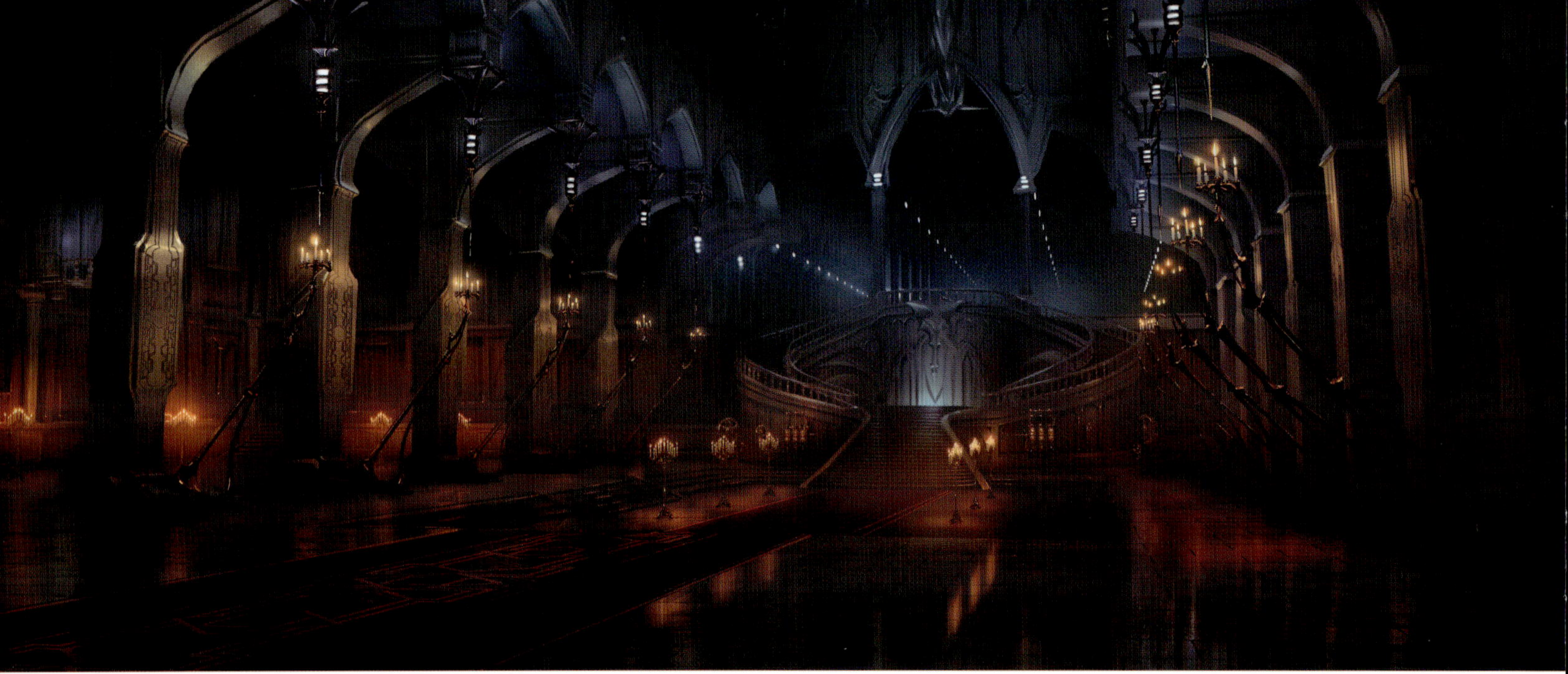

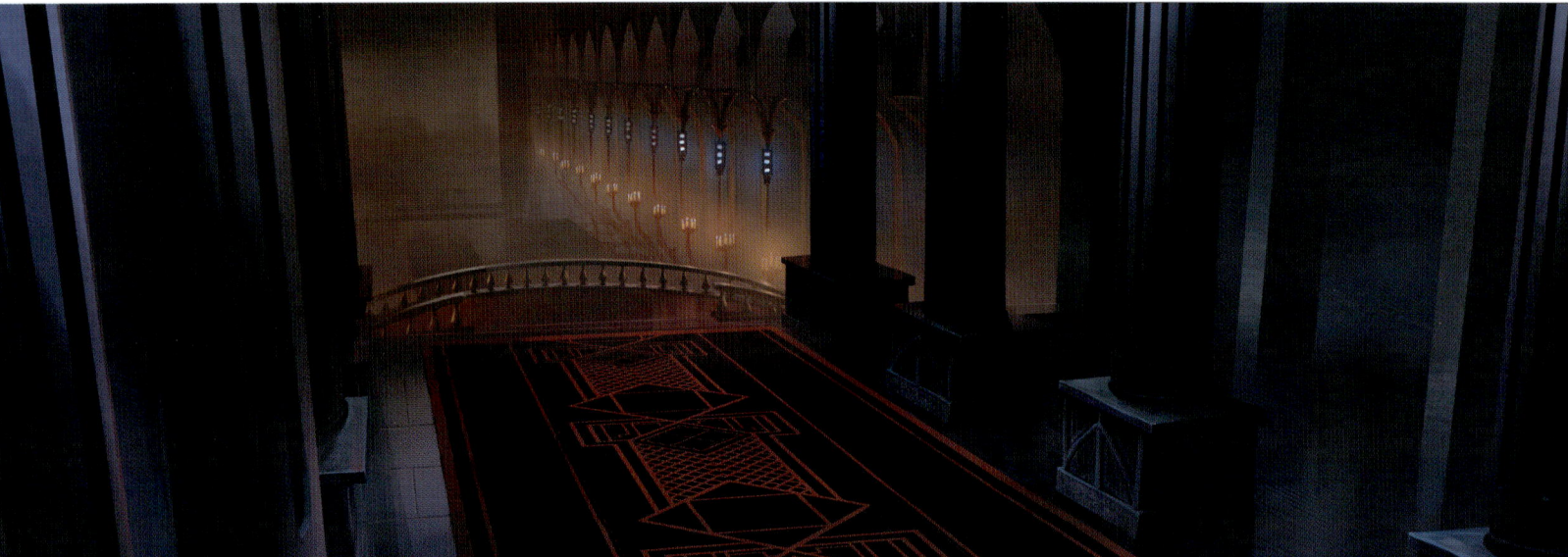

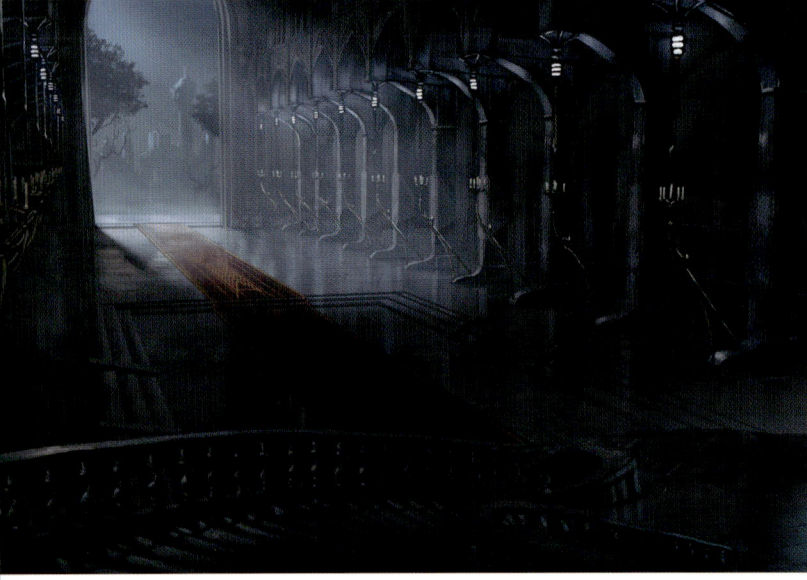
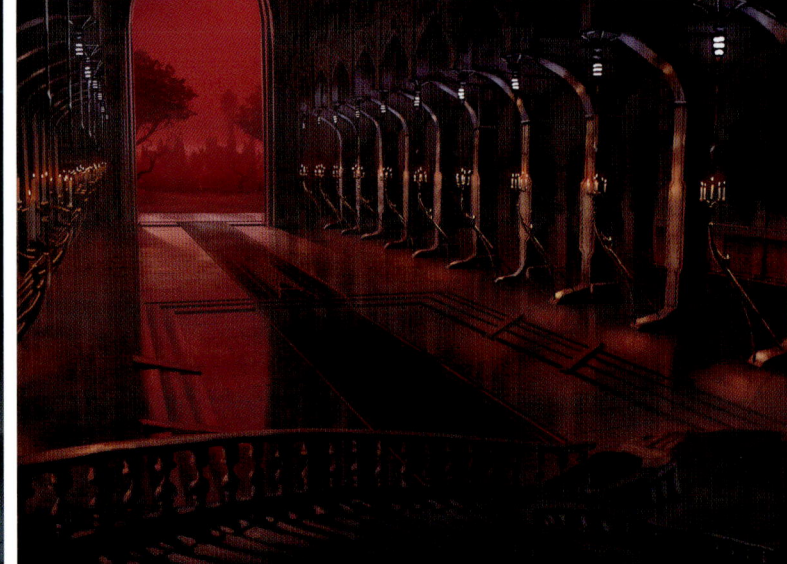

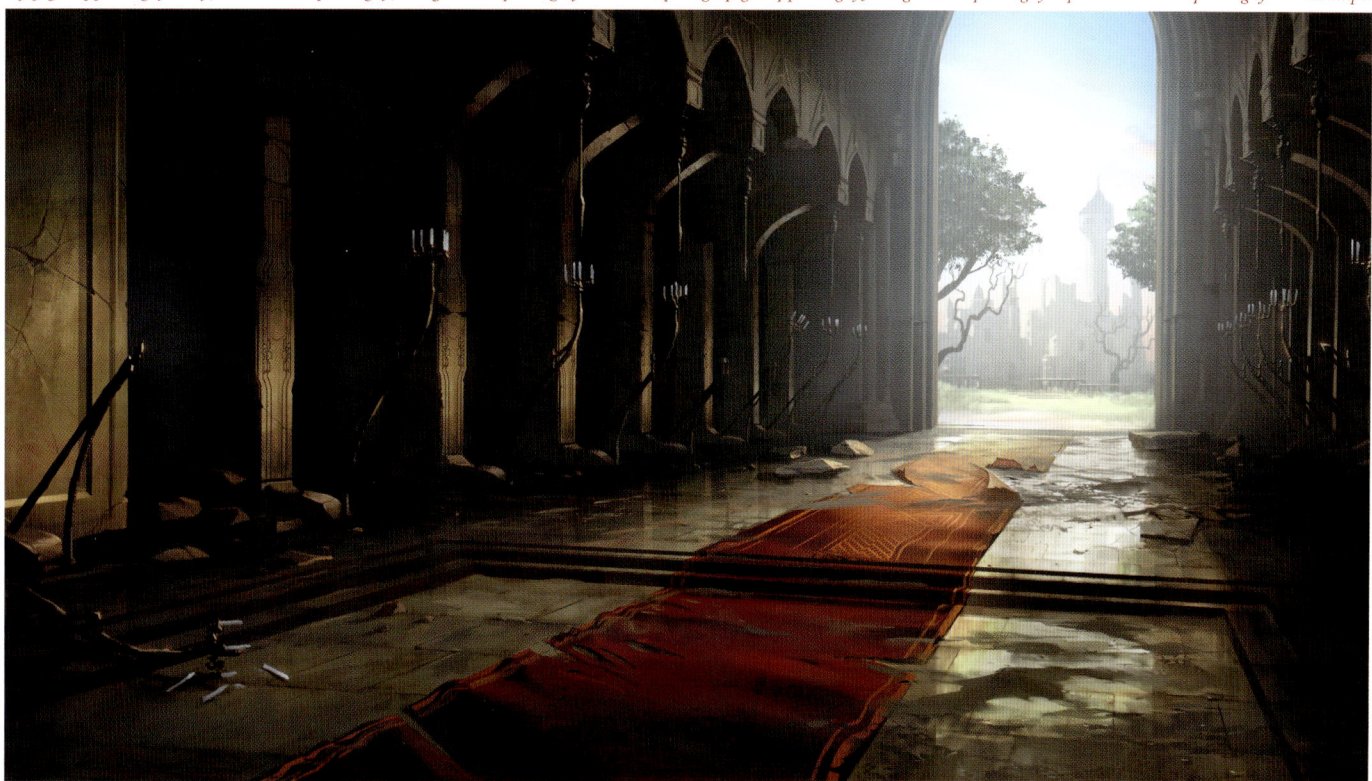

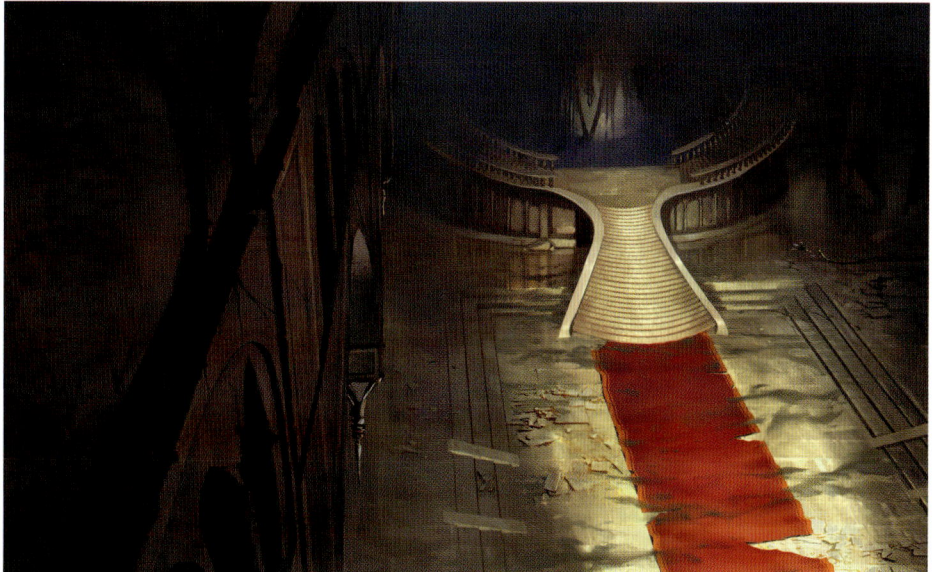

THE CASTLE ENTRANCE

The castle entrance was modeled and textured in finer detail for the season 2 production, which streamlined the process of background art creation for this repeatedly used location. As with the exterior, each computer-generated image is digitally painted over by the background artists to match the series style and add specific details, such as battle damage.

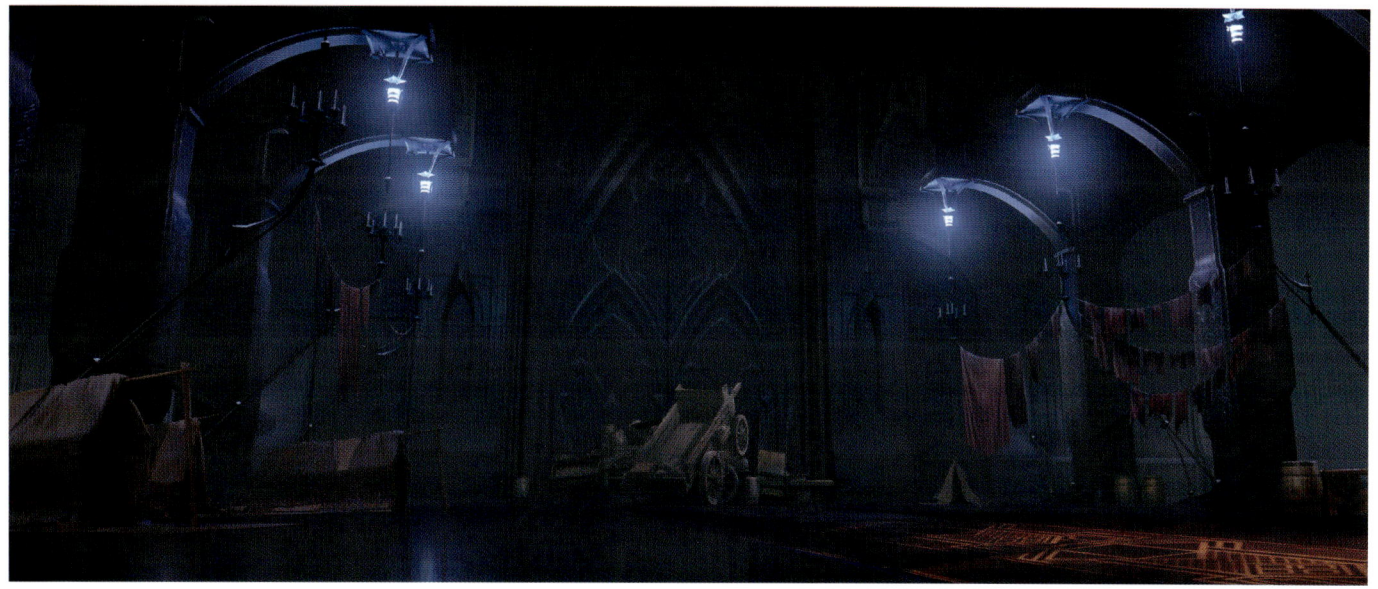

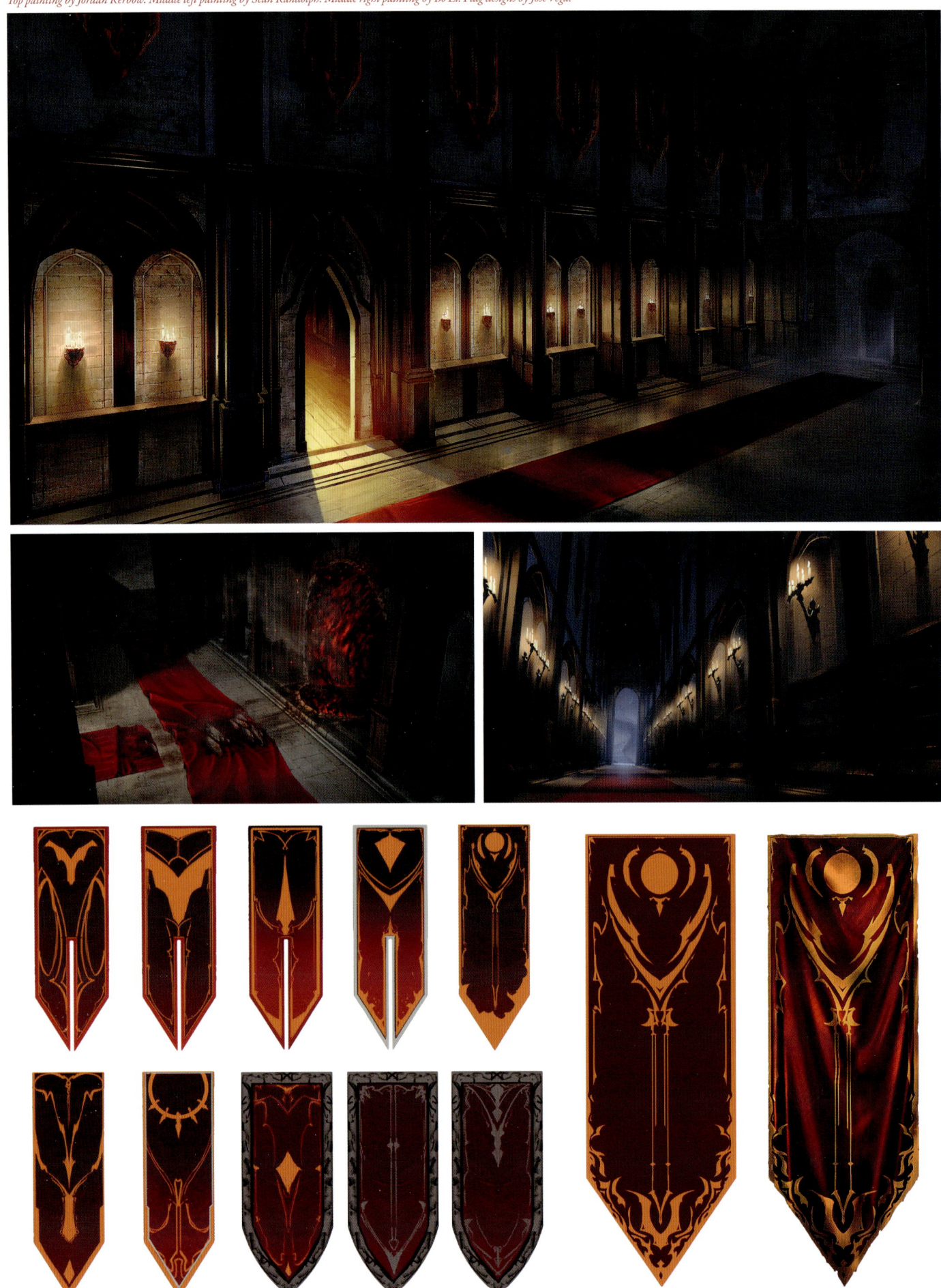

Above: Variations on banners to be hung throughout the castle. The large banner designs are the concepts selected for the series.

THE ENGINE ROOM

Black-and-white layout drawings are completed before painted backgrounds. This is useful for storyboard artists and animators, who work on top of the layouts while background artists complete the paintings. Sam Deats storyboarded the battle that led Dracula and Alucard through the engine room as the gears around them melted to create a heated, hellish set piece. Below are intact and destroyed versions of the space.

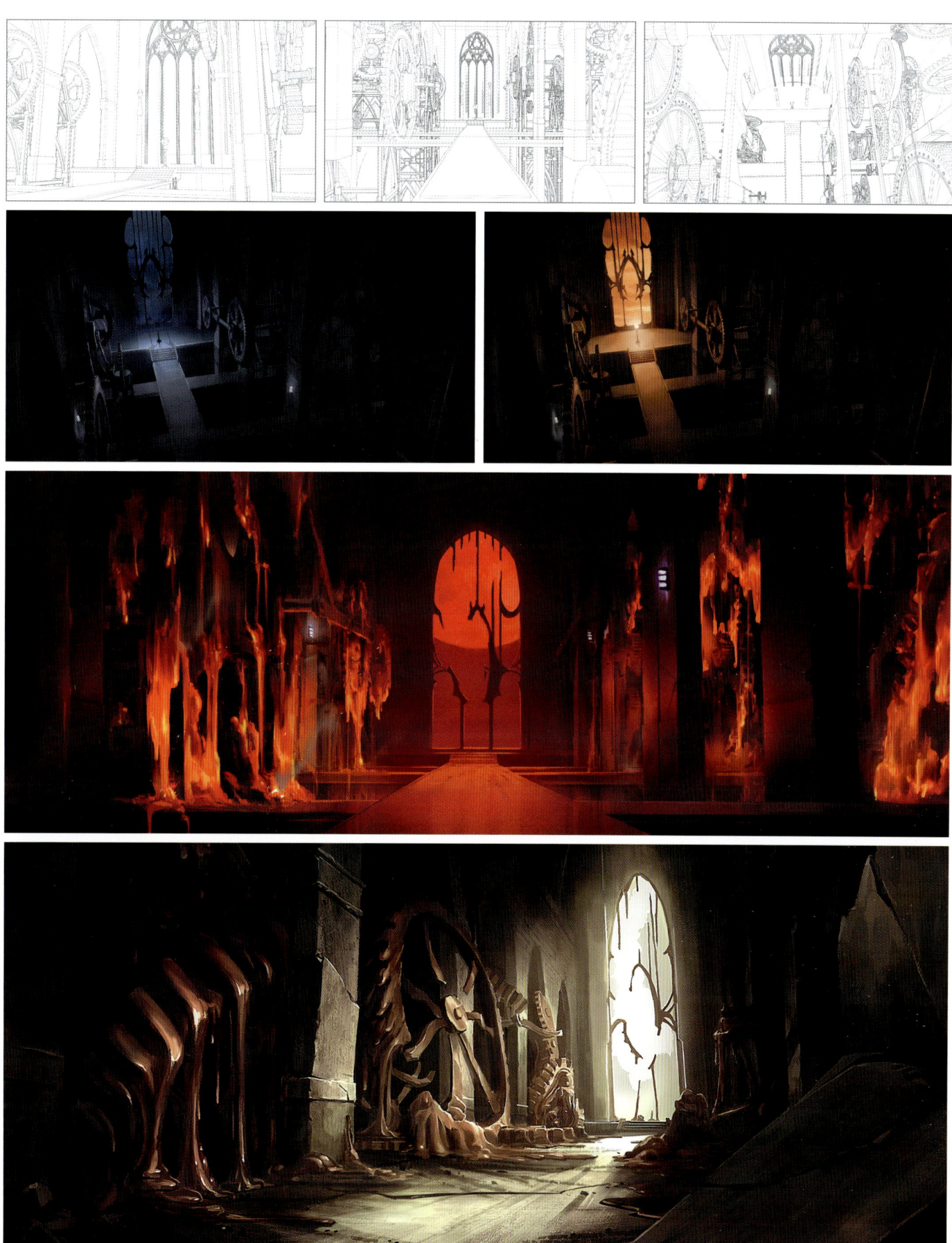

Top layouts by Danny Moll. Top paintings by Danny Moll. Middle painting by Jose Vega. Bottom painting by Bo Li.

Top painting by Stephen Stark. Bottom painting by Bo Li. Mirror design concepts by Robby Johnson and Sean Randolph, 3D model by Adam Conarroe.

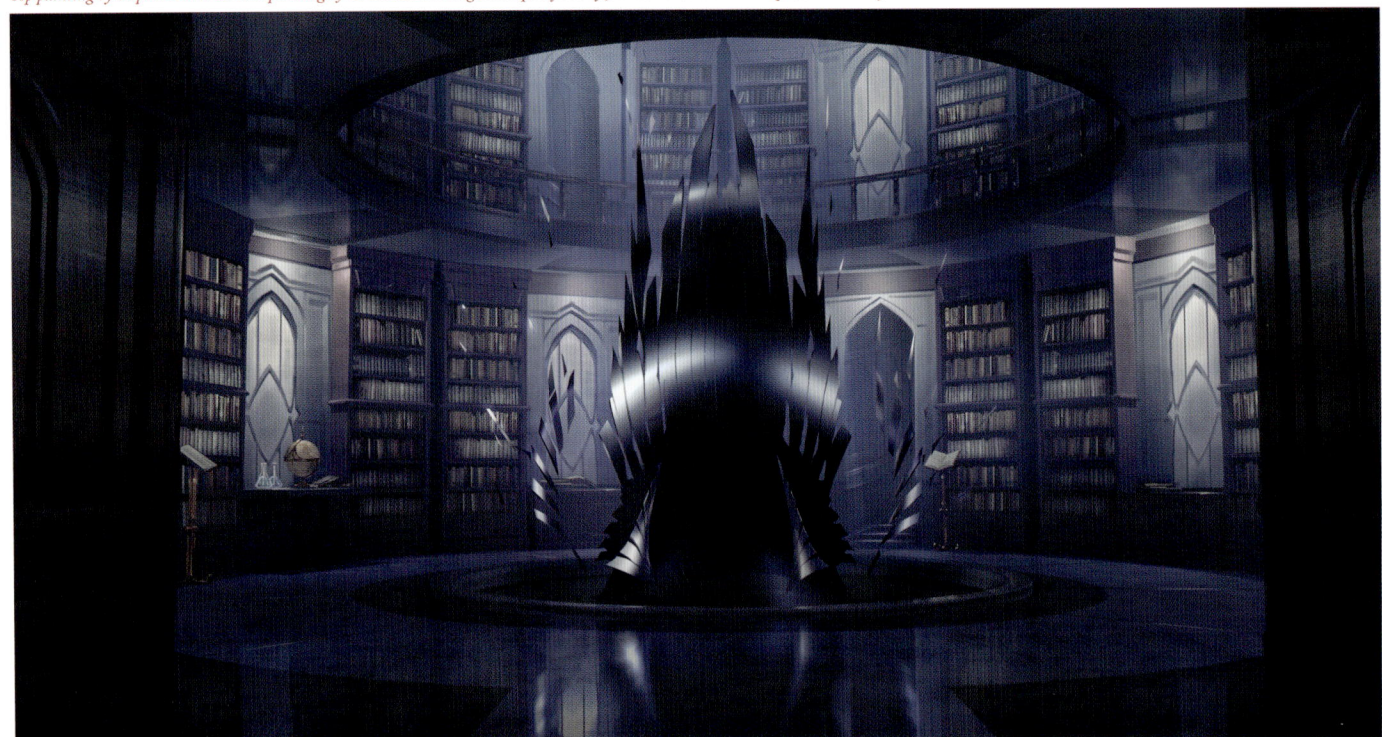

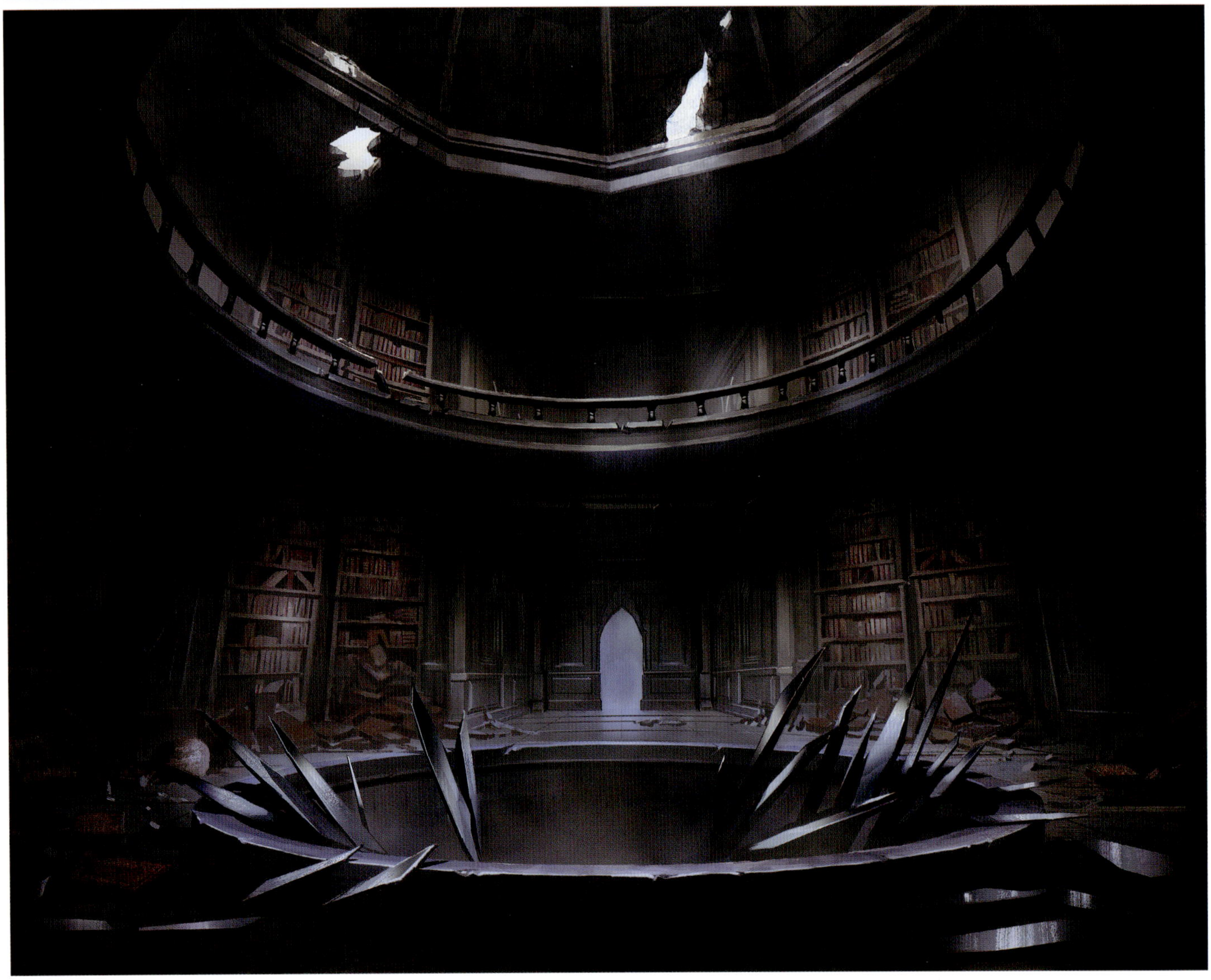

DRACULA'S LIBRARY

Intact and destroyed versions of Dracula's library. The shards of Dracula's mirror are a CGI-animated element in the series.

Top painting by Robby Johnson. Middle painting by Sean Vo, model by Isaak Ramos. Bottom paintings by Sean Randolph.

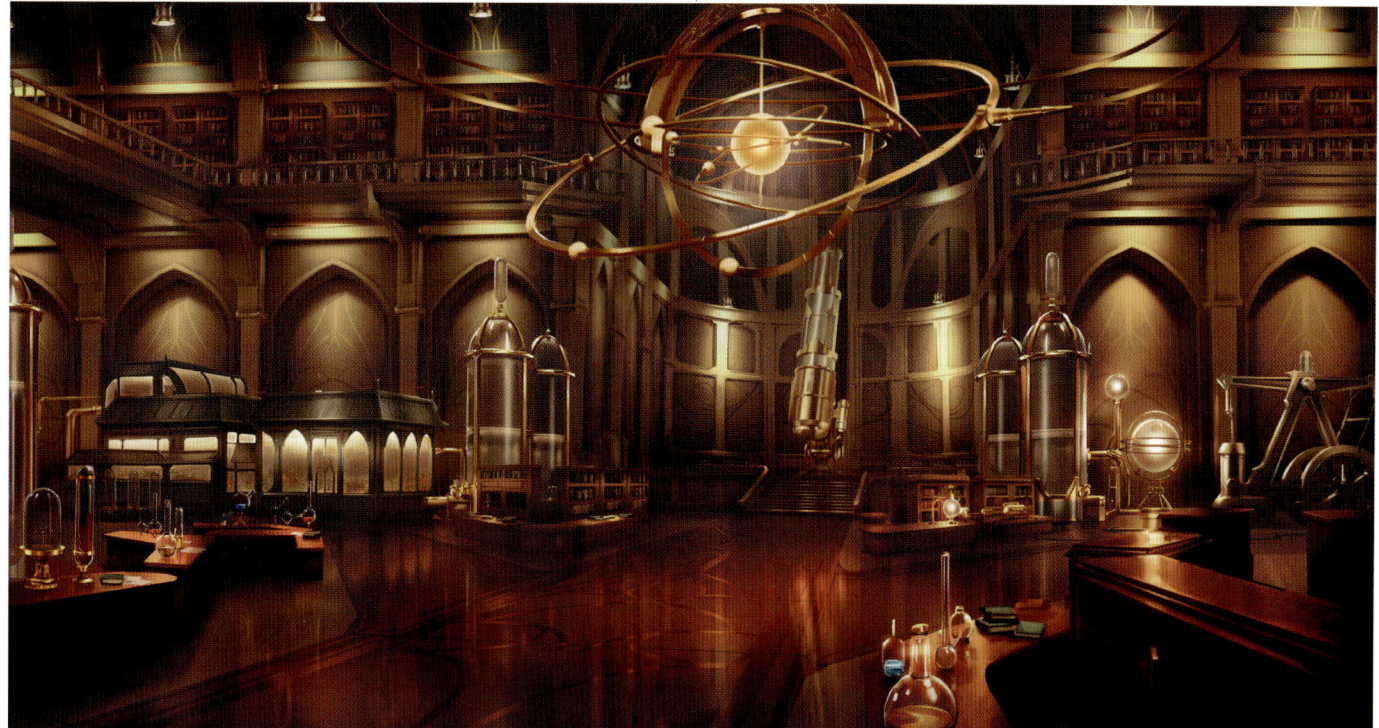

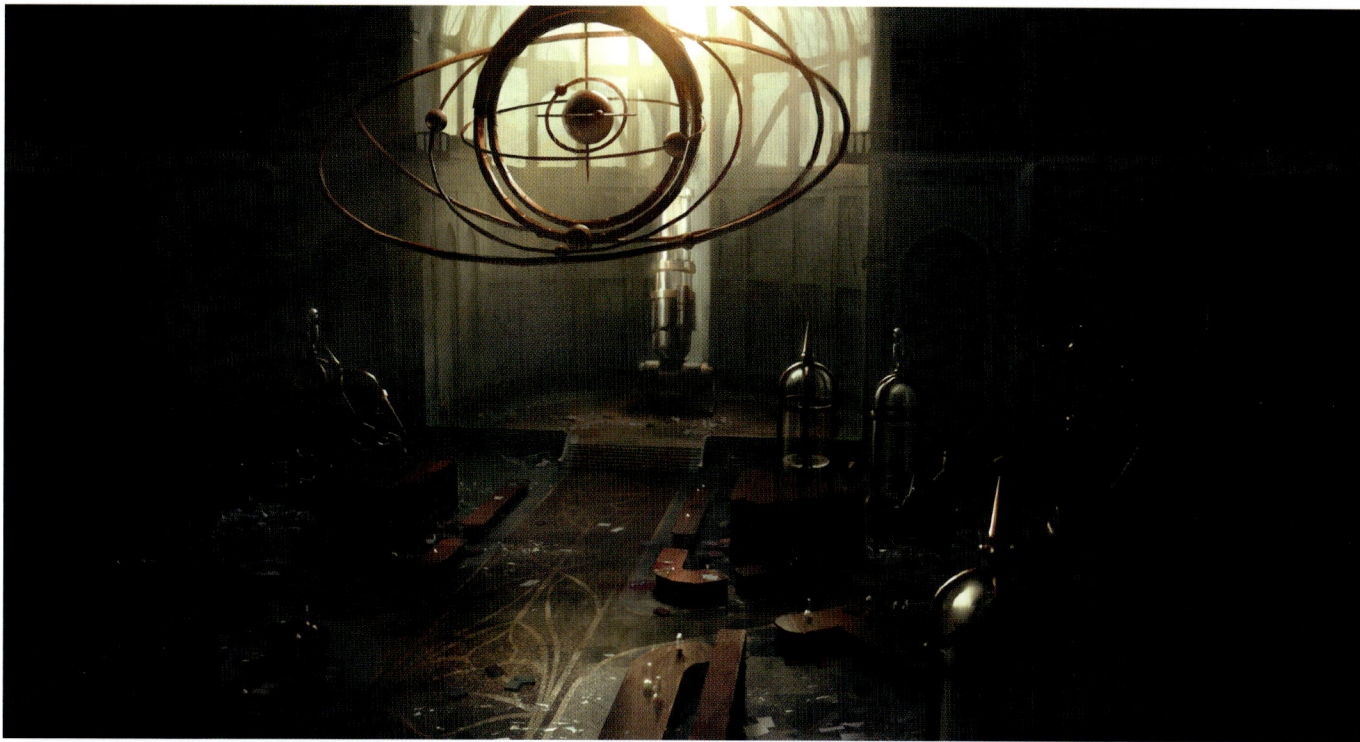

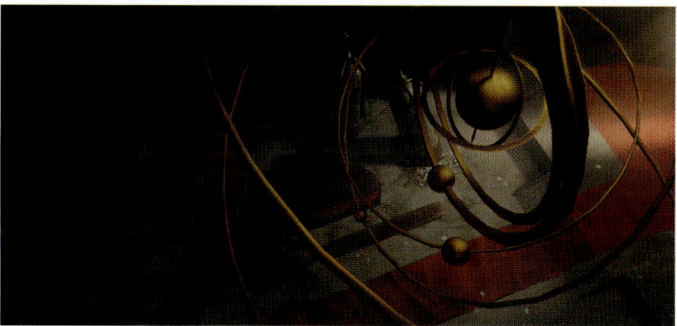
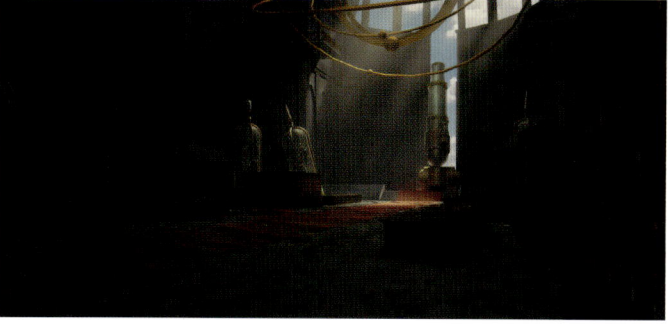

DRACULA'S LABORATORY

Intact and destroyed versions of Dracula's laboratory. The atmospheric, volumetric light is painted on a layer as part of the background for direction and approval from producers, then later re-created in Adobe After Effects as part of the animation and compositing process as needed. This is especially useful if animated figures pass through or interact with it in any fashion.

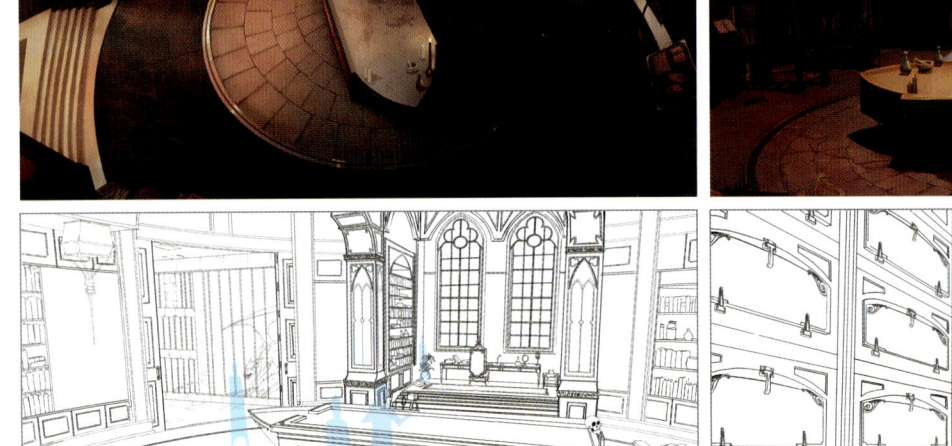

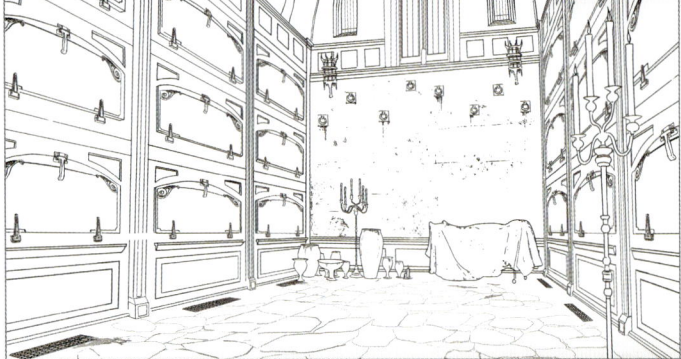

HECTOR'S AND ISAAC'S LABORATORIES

Base 3D models provided structure for Hector's and Isaac's laboratories, among other locations. In addition to being useful for background artists, the models are also used by storyboard artists, who compose their storyboard shots like a cinematographer would and then draw the characters into each panel. The models also provided consistency for the many artists who were simultaneously working on scenes that take place in the same locations.

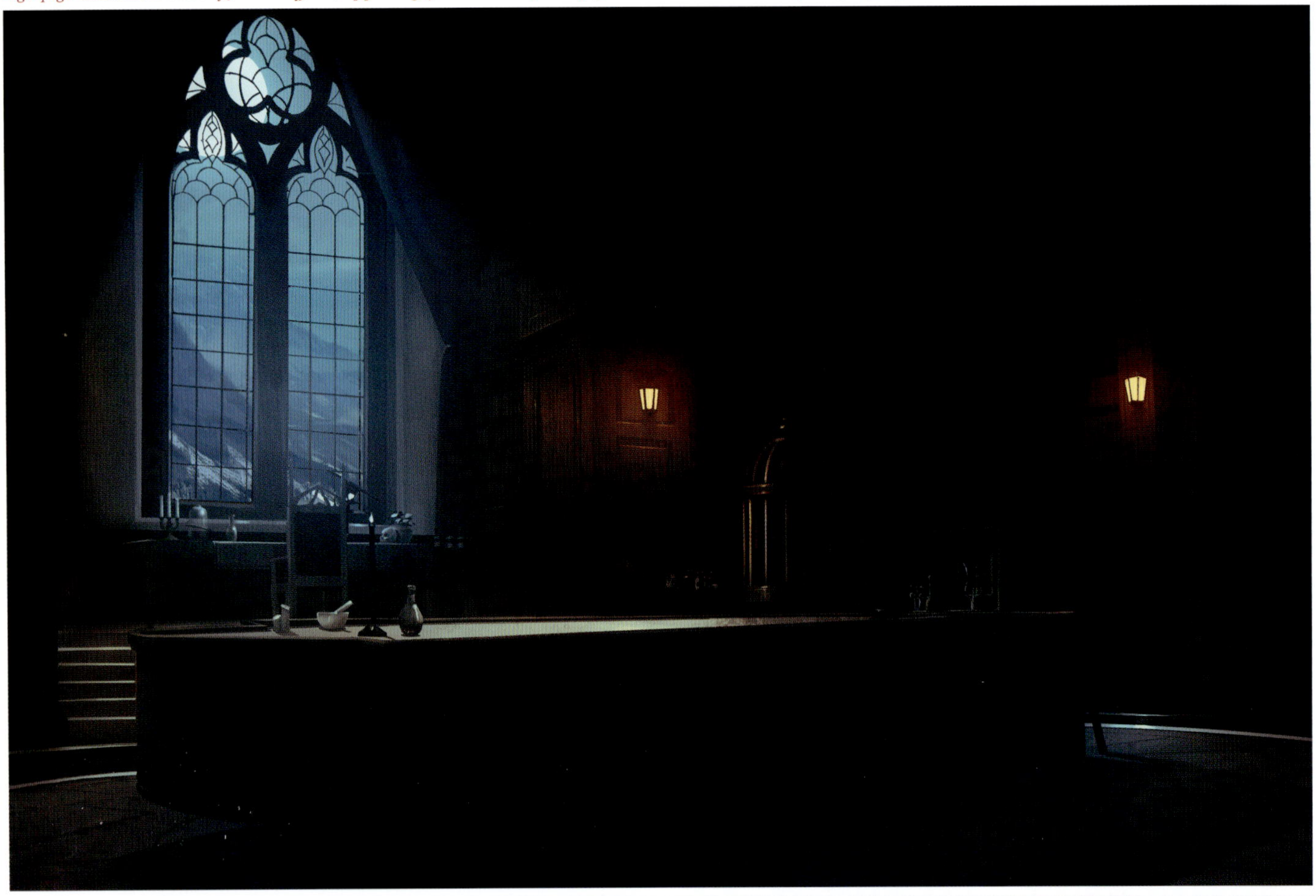

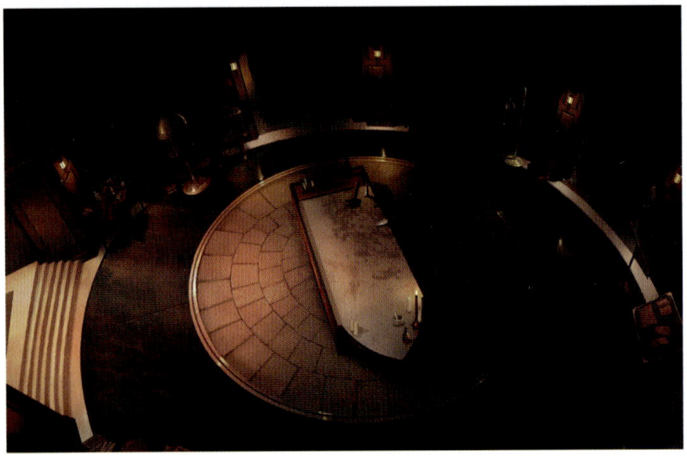

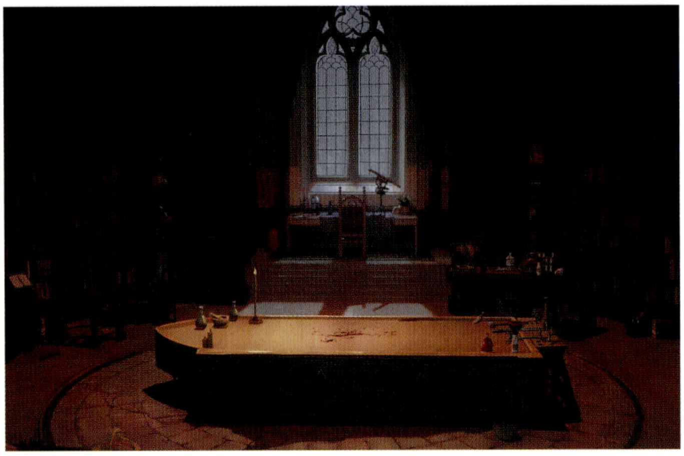

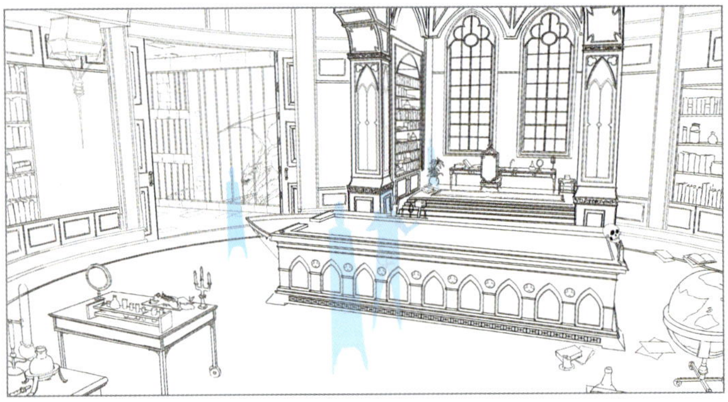

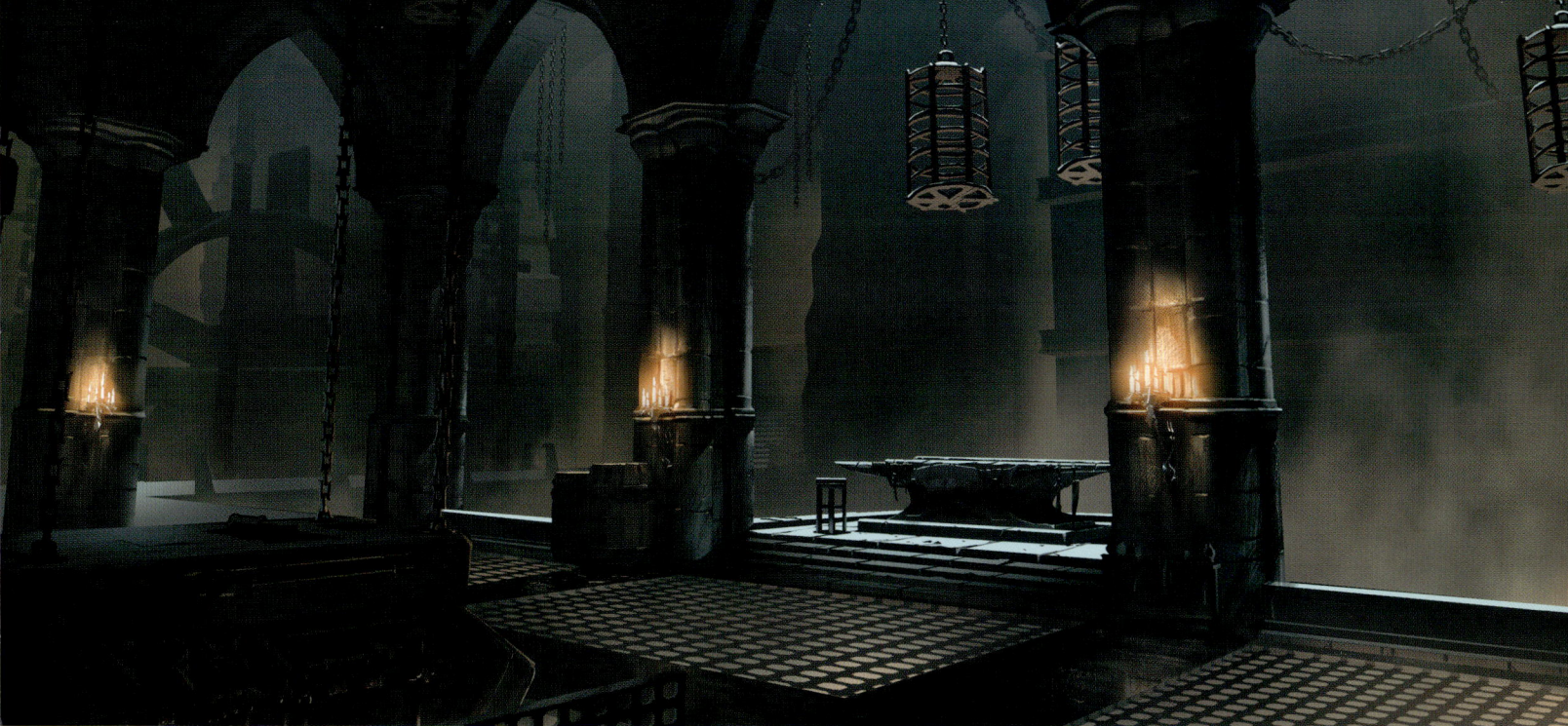

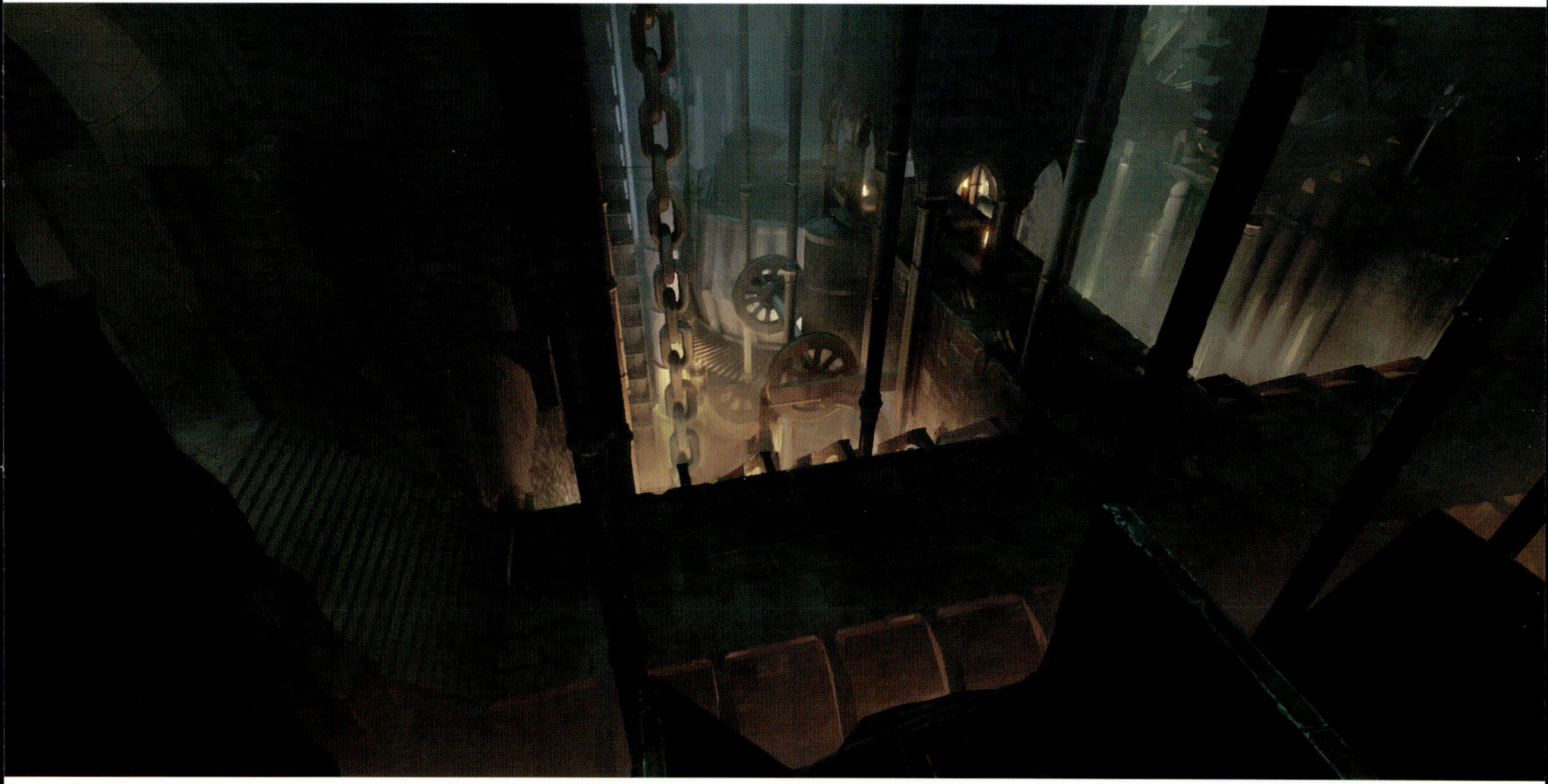

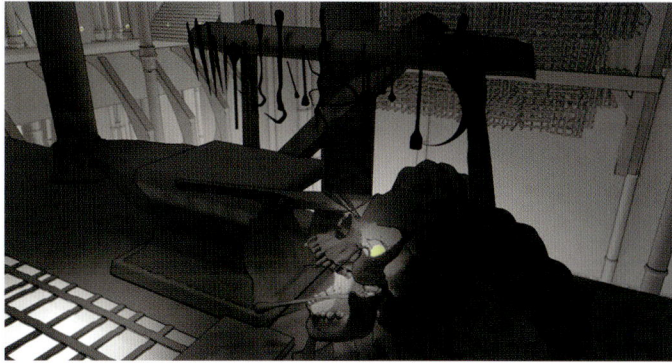

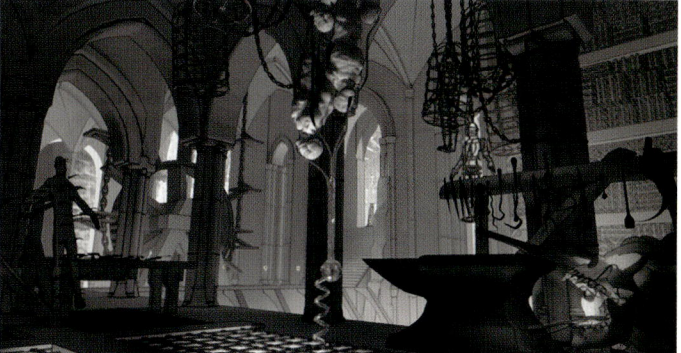

Increasing the detail and fully texturing the 3D background models through season 2 added more flexibility for the team, especially during action sequences, which tend to require many more unique and dynamic camera angles than other sequences. One drawback to having fully textured and detailed models: the temptation to start moving the camera during shots! It would be impossible to hand paint over the detailed and textured backgrounds in motion across multiple frames, so any camera movement in dimensional space lacks the hand-painted finish.

ALUCARD'S CHILDHOOD BEDROOM

Considering his parents' academic prowess, Alucard was fated to be a studious, curious child. These concept sketches depict some areas in his room where he would learn, study, and practice.

Right: Katie Silva's sketches of Baby Alucard were created as preparation for the family portrait seen on page 135. These studies helped determine how old he should be in the final version.

Left page: Baby Alucard sketches by Katie Silva. Alucard's childhood bedroom visual development by Saskia Gutekunst. Right page: Paintings by Jose Vega.

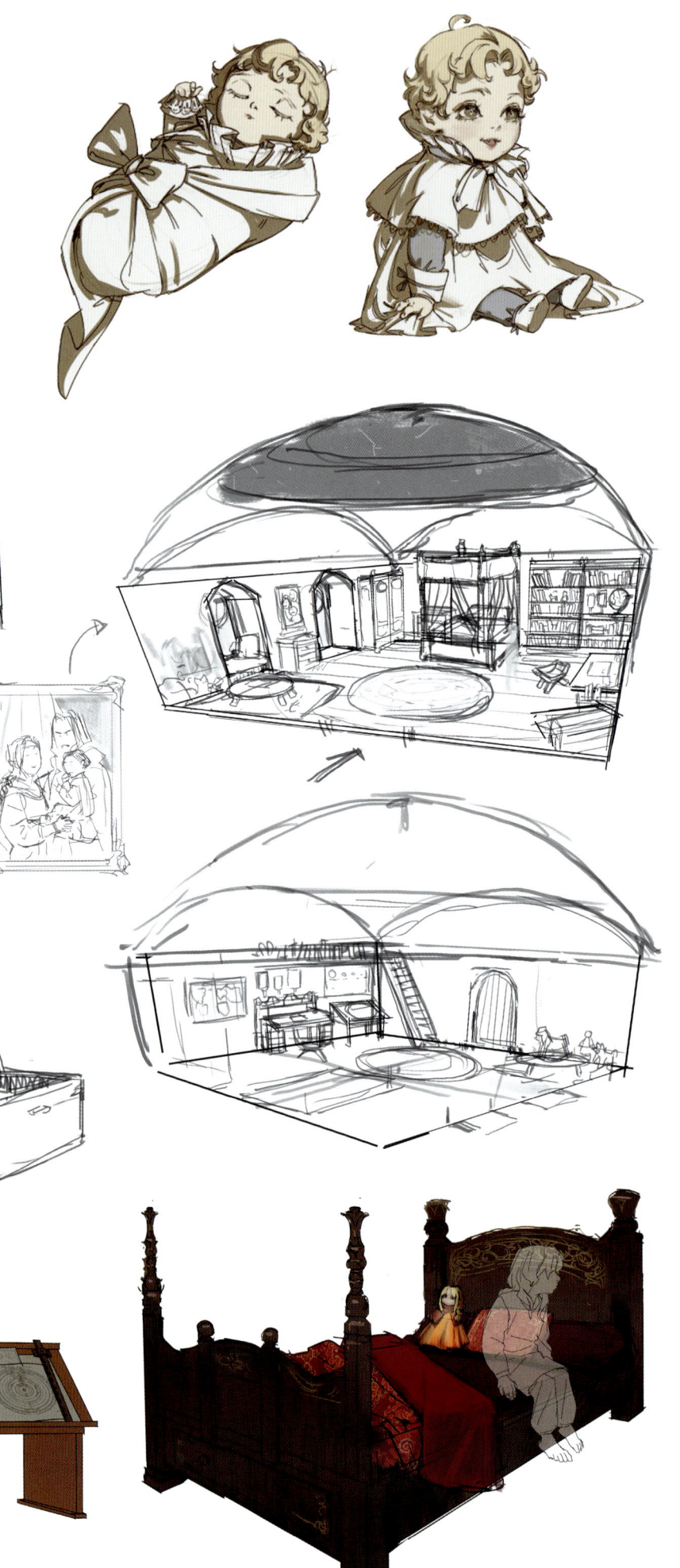

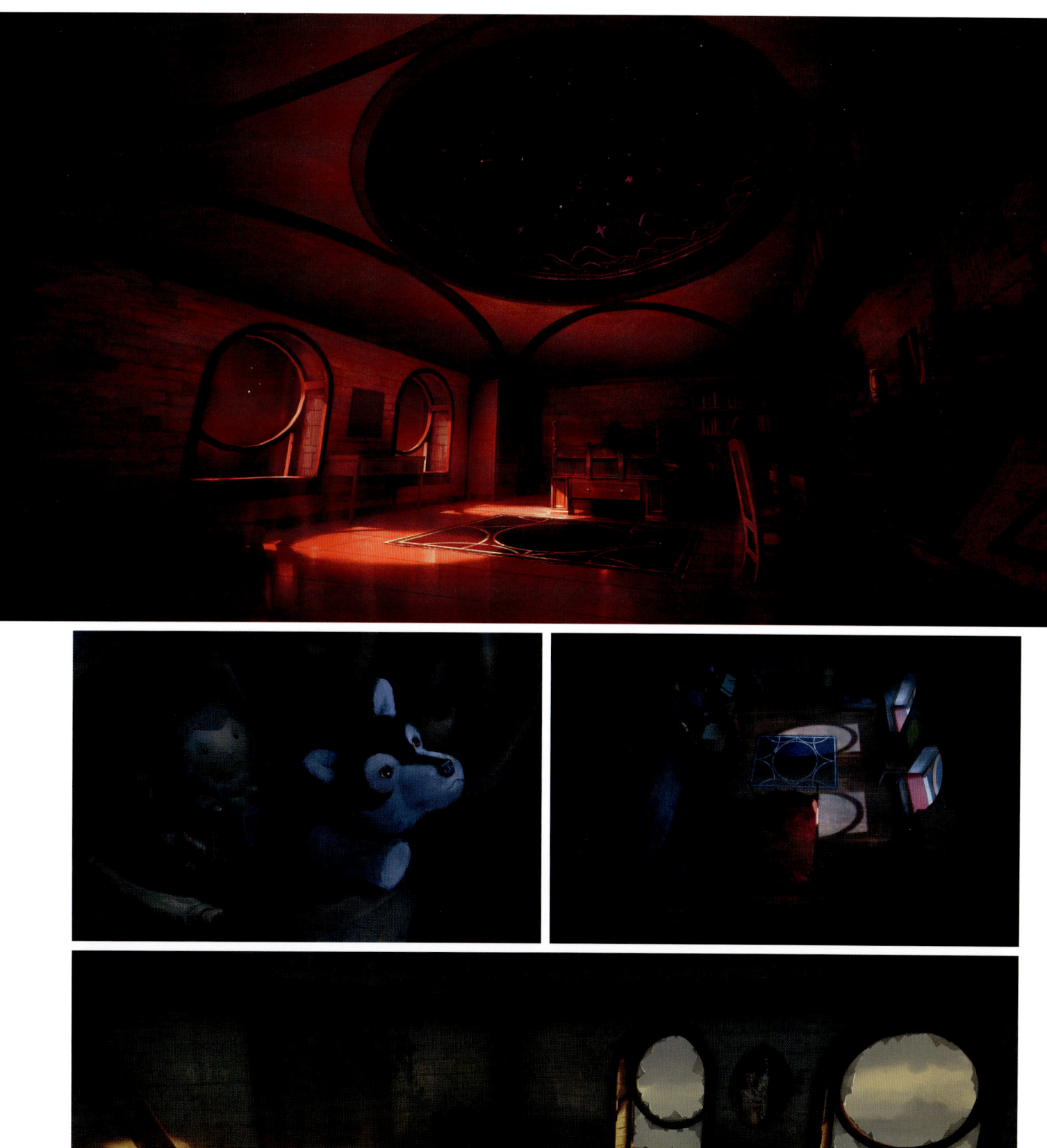

Above: The plush wolf toy was designed to resemble Alucard's wolf form, seen when Dracula recalls the toys that Lisa made for their son.

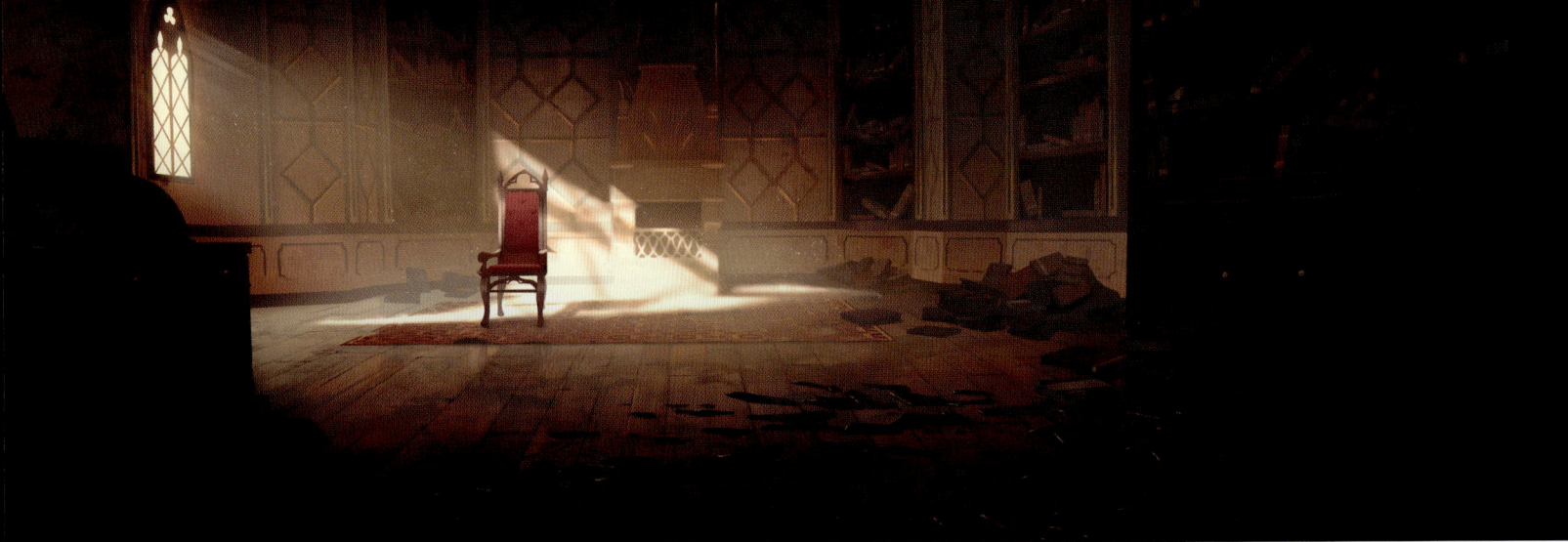

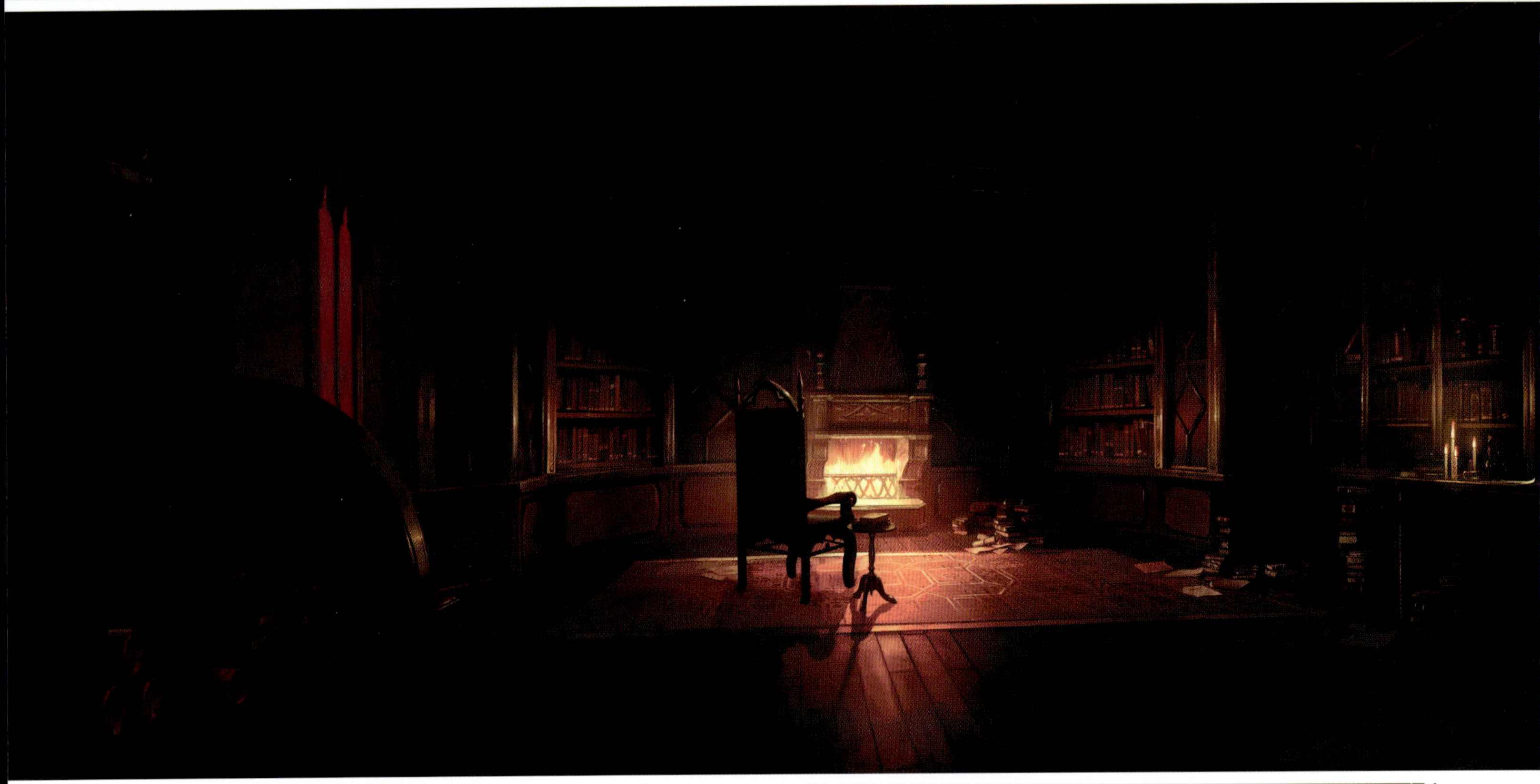

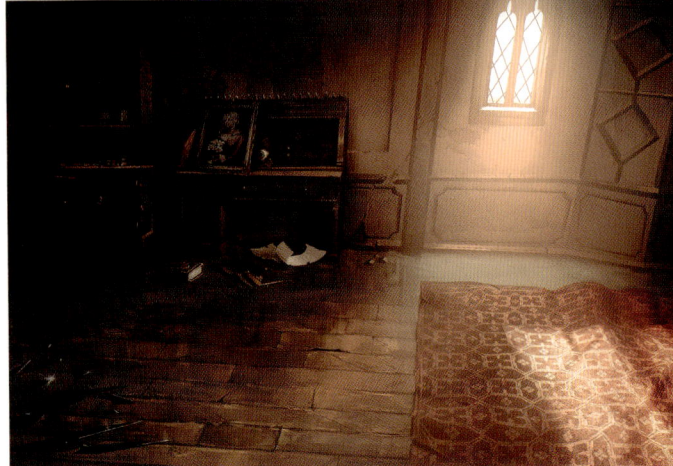

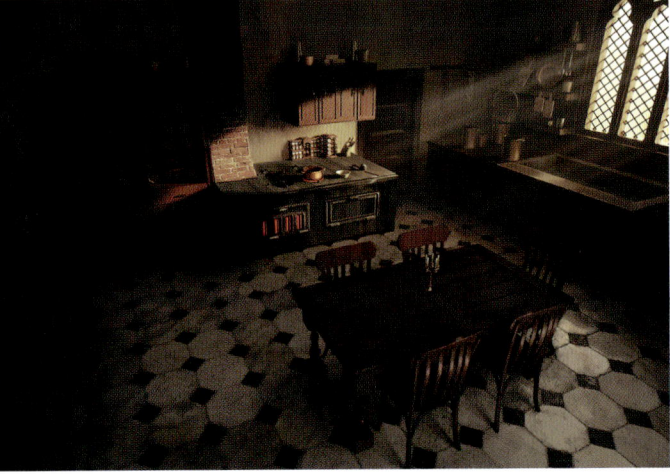

Melancholy locales in Dracula's castle—perfect for a lonely son to haunt listlessly for months after staking his father through the heart. "I wanted the kitchen to feel more like a little kitchen in the castle that a lonely guy would use, as opposed to a more grandiose dining hall." —Sam Deats

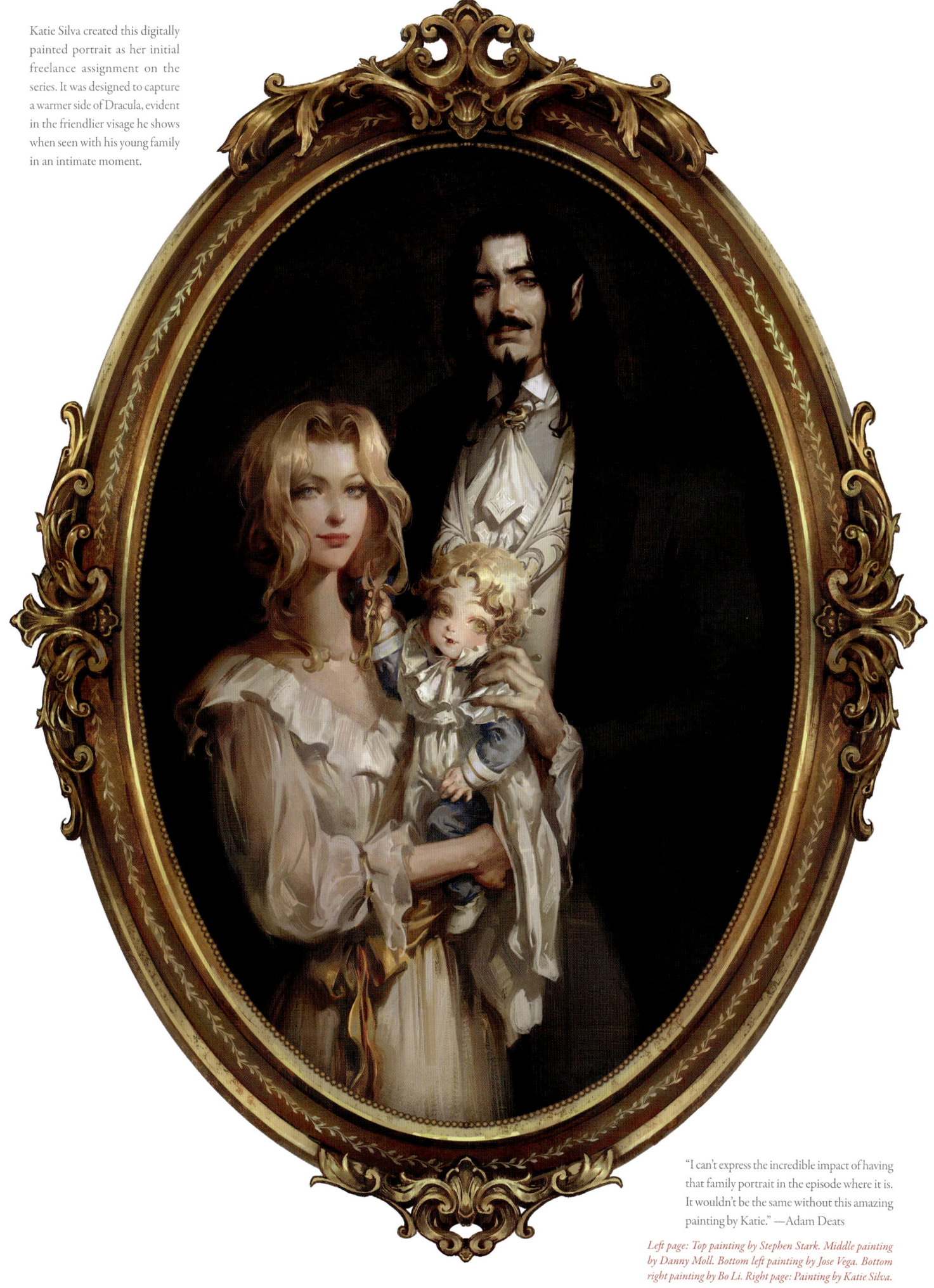

Katie Silva created this digitally painted portrait as her initial freelance assignment on the series. It was designed to capture a warmer side of Dracula, evident in the friendlier visage he shows when seen with his young family in an intimate moment.

"I can't express the incredible impact of having that family portrait in the episode where it is. It wouldn't be the same without this amazing painting by Katie." —Adam Deats

Left page: Top painting by Stephen Stark. Middle painting by Danny Moll. Bottom left painting by Jose Vega. Bottom right painting by Bo Li. Right page: Painting by Katie Silva.

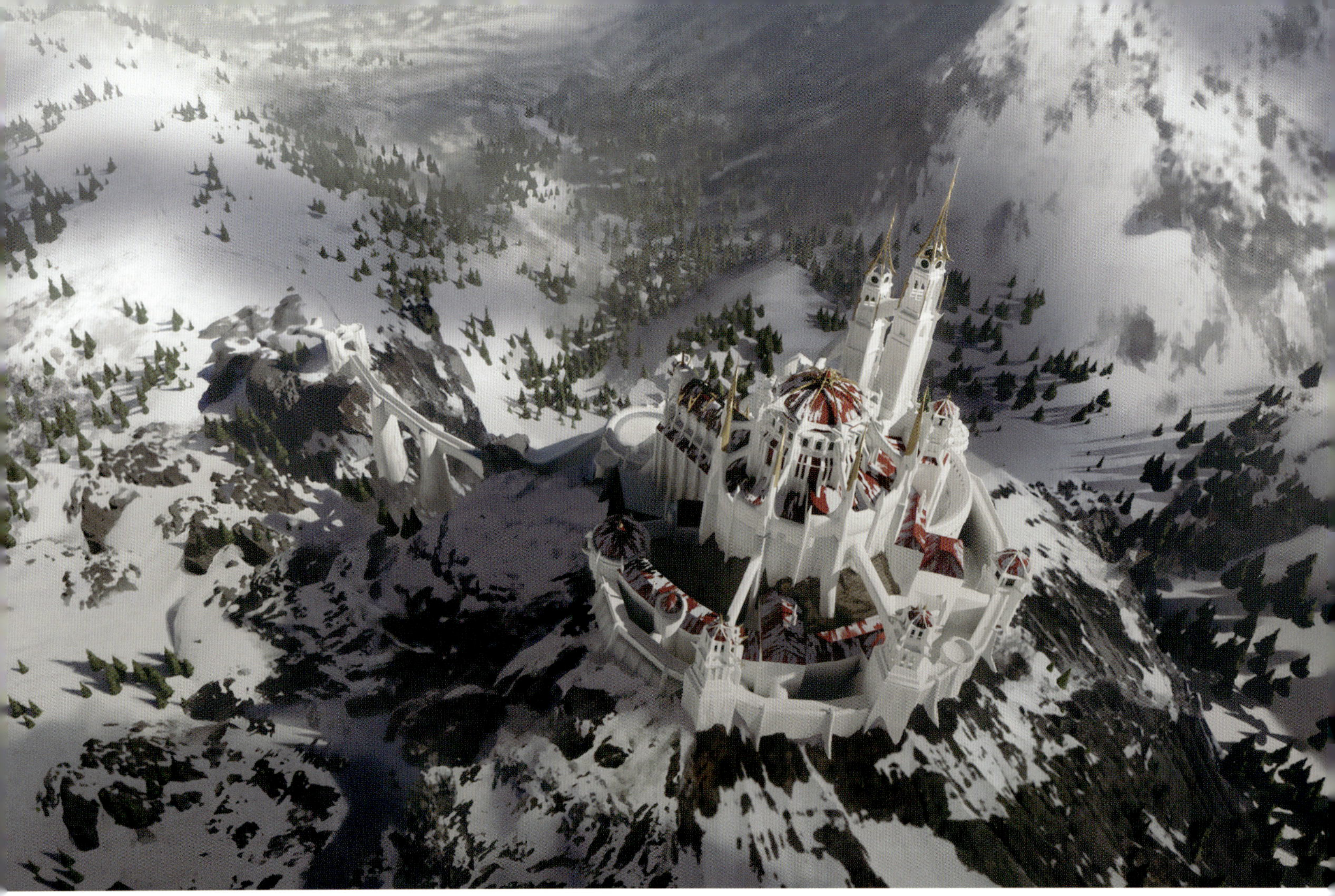

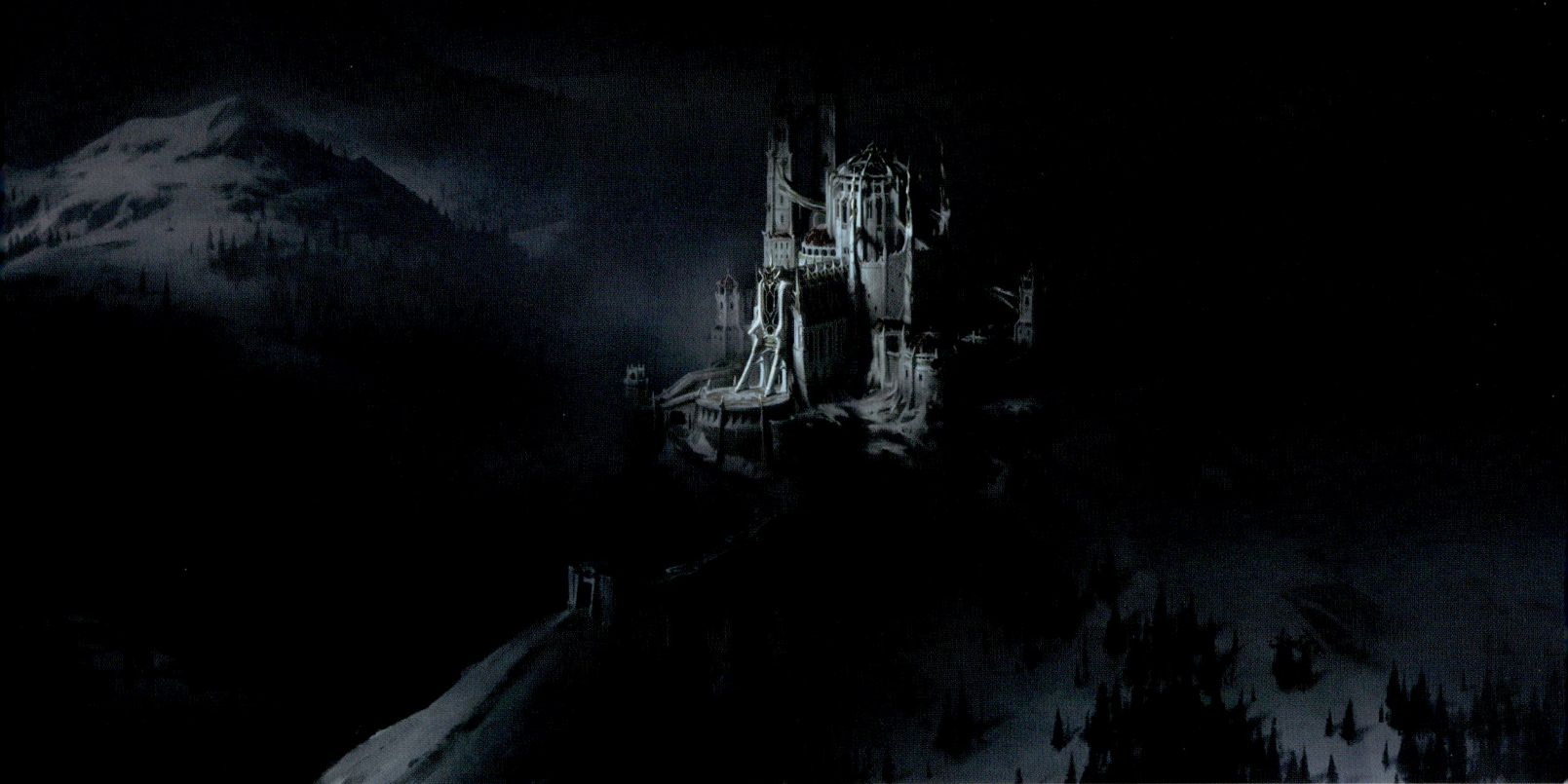

Carmilla's Castle

Opposite: Sean Vo's initial concept designs for Carmilla's Alpine fortress. The art nouveau shape language with bright snowy white and golden highlights provides a marked contrast to Dracula's dark Gothic castle.

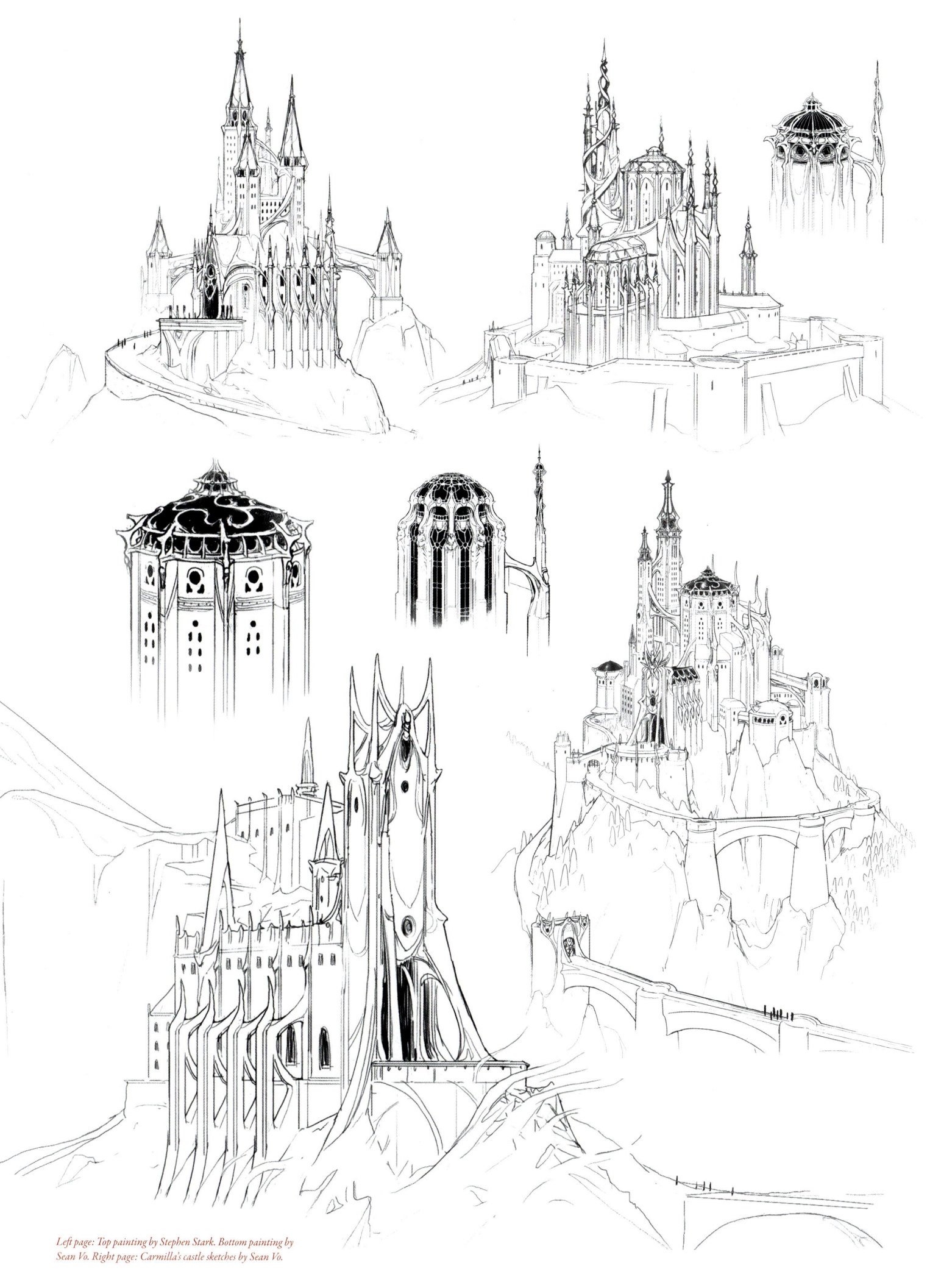

Left page: Top painting by Stephen Stark. Bottom painting by Sean Vo. Right page: Carmilla's castle sketches by Sean Vo.

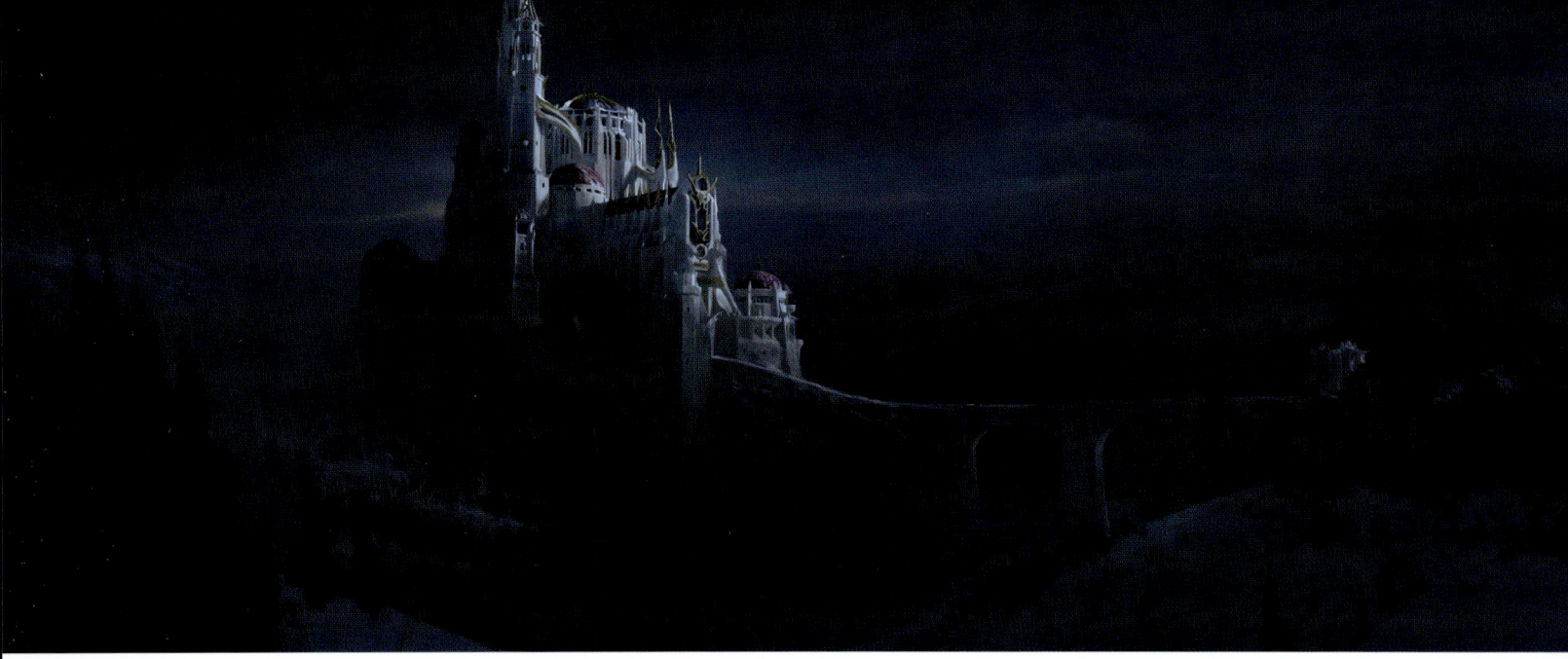

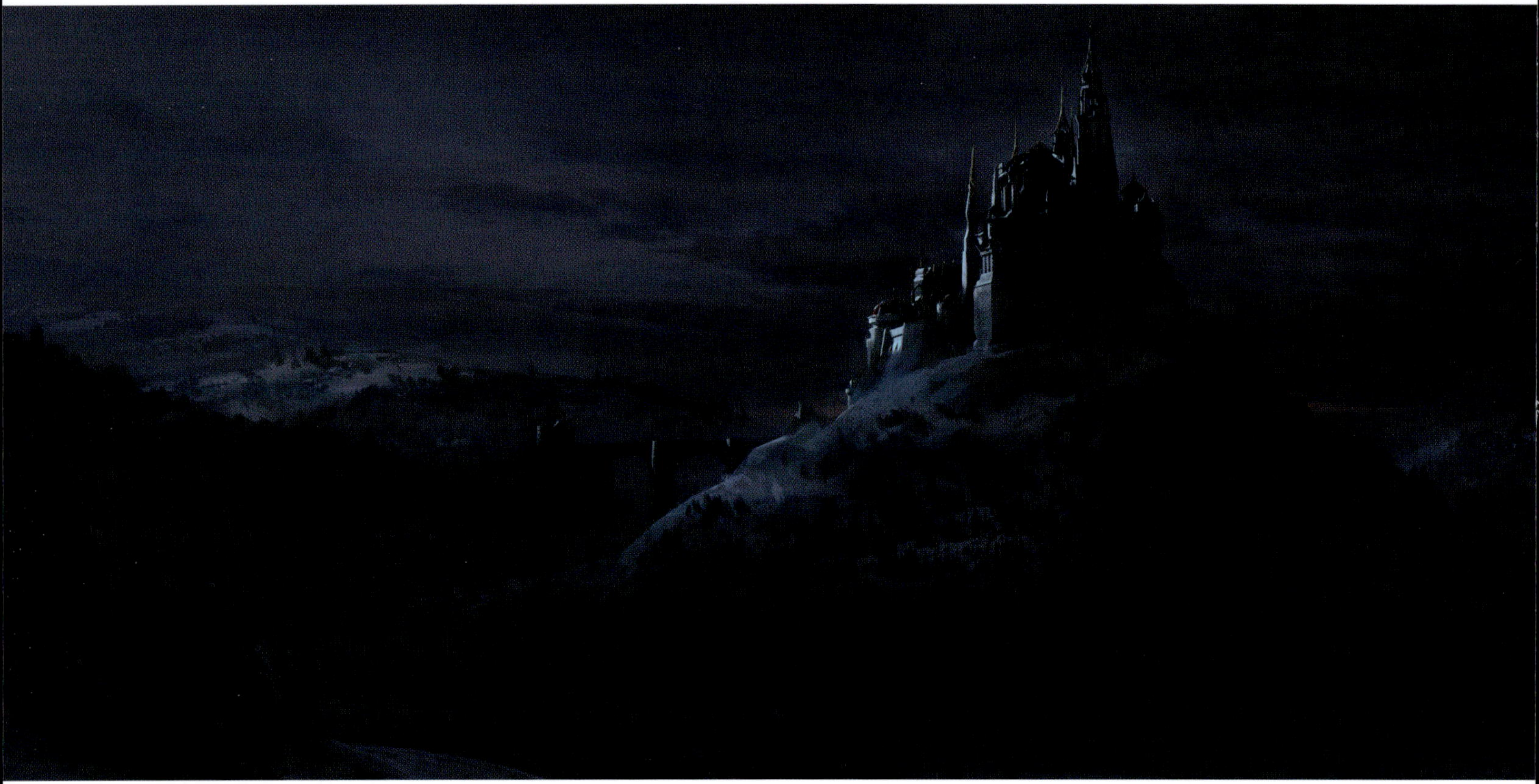

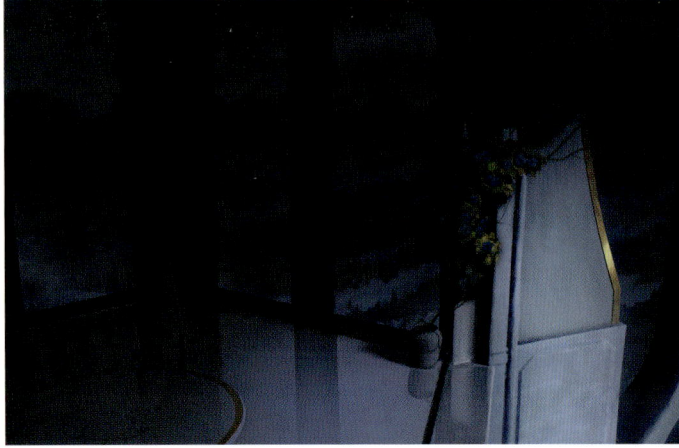

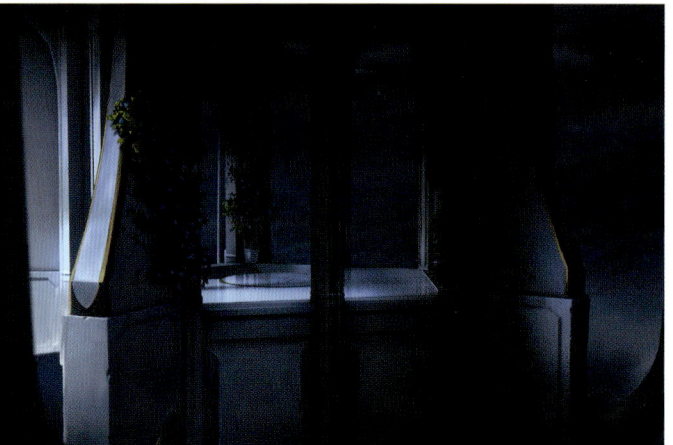

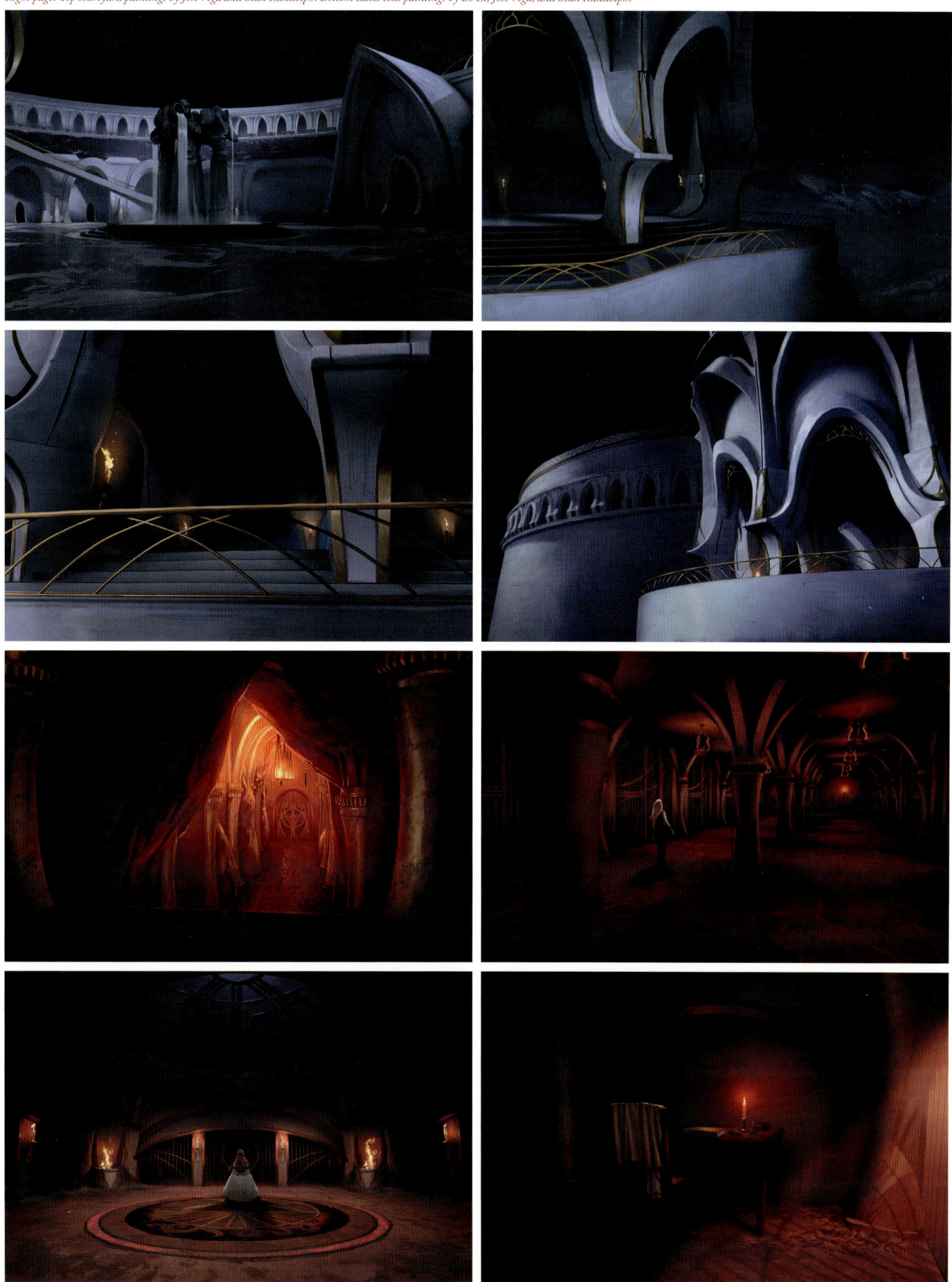

Locations around Carmilla's castle, including the balconies and dungeon where Hector is kept prisoner. As with many vampire structures, this dungeon benefited from the accumulated knowledge of the immortal inhabitants and featured a heating system of warm pipes embedded throughout the floors.

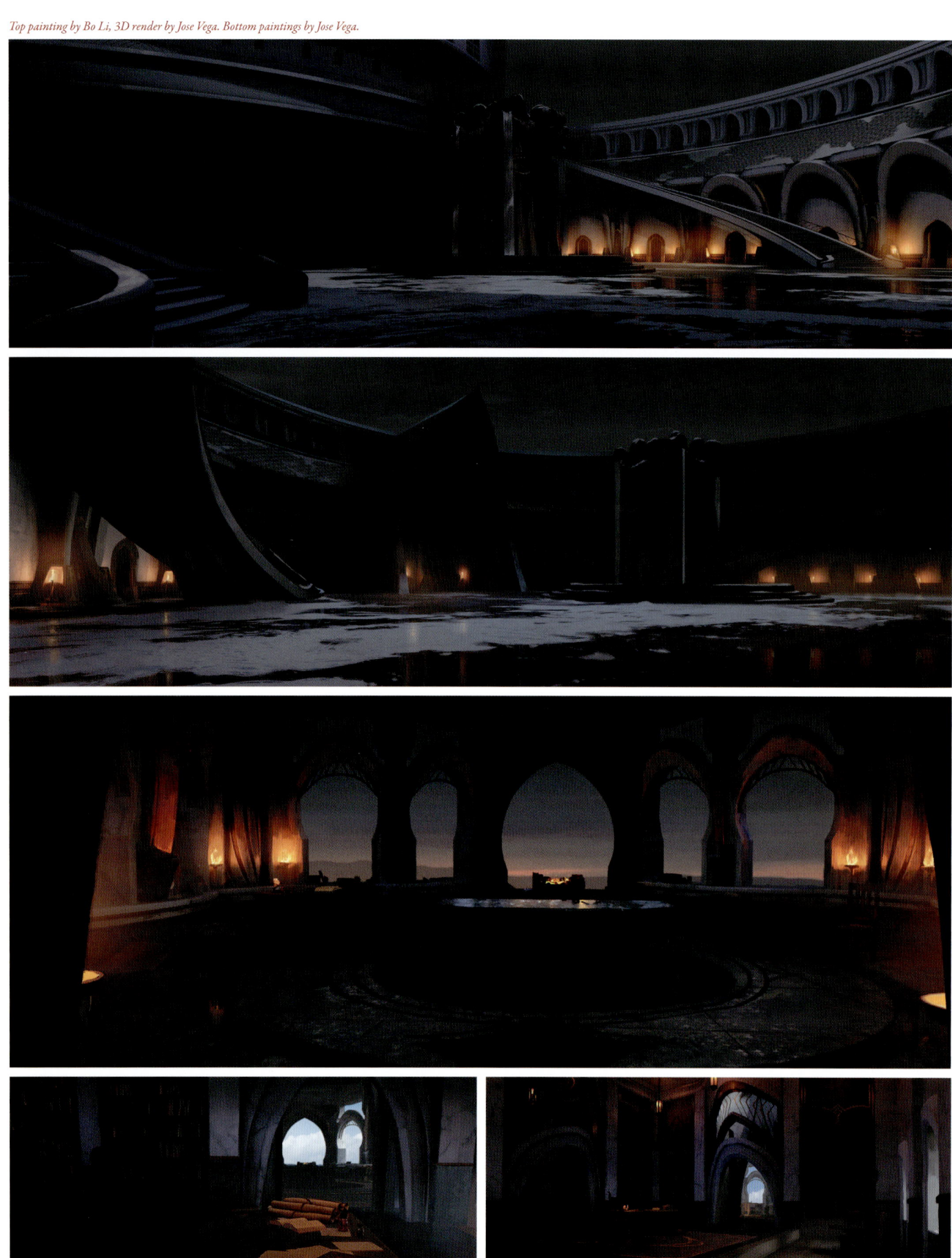

Hector's laboratory and study in Carmilla's castle, where he enjoys the limited autonomy and freedom of a favored prisoner in season 4. As a hidden reference, the circular floor design around Hector's forge recalls the design seen on the bottom of the menu borders in some versions of *Symphony of the Night*.

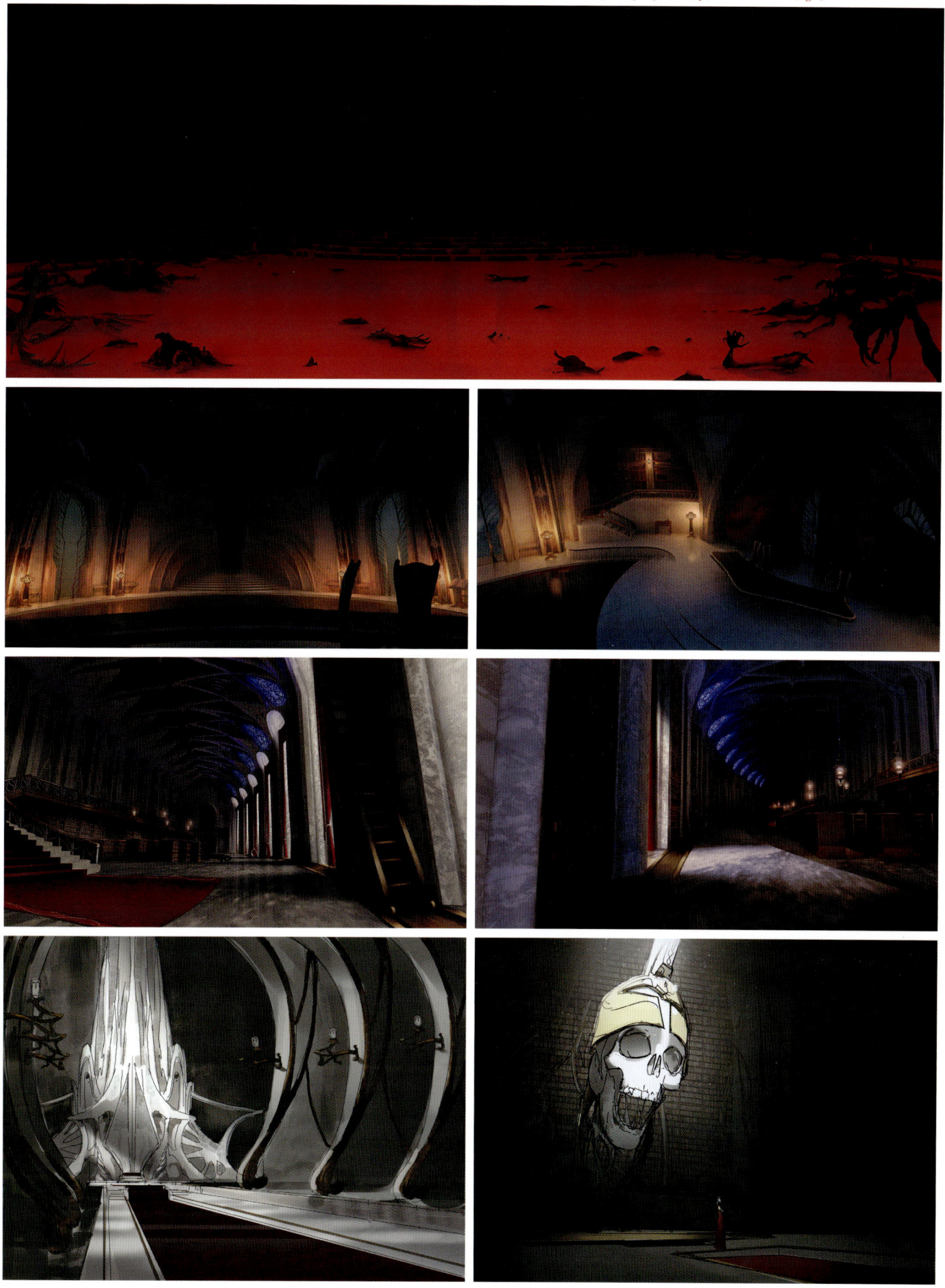

"When designing Carmilla's war room, I really wanted to push the sort of stylistic fusion of art nouveau and art deco we created for the castle. I think the decadent materials and organic shapes help to highlight the regality and cunning of the vampire sisters." —Sean Randolph

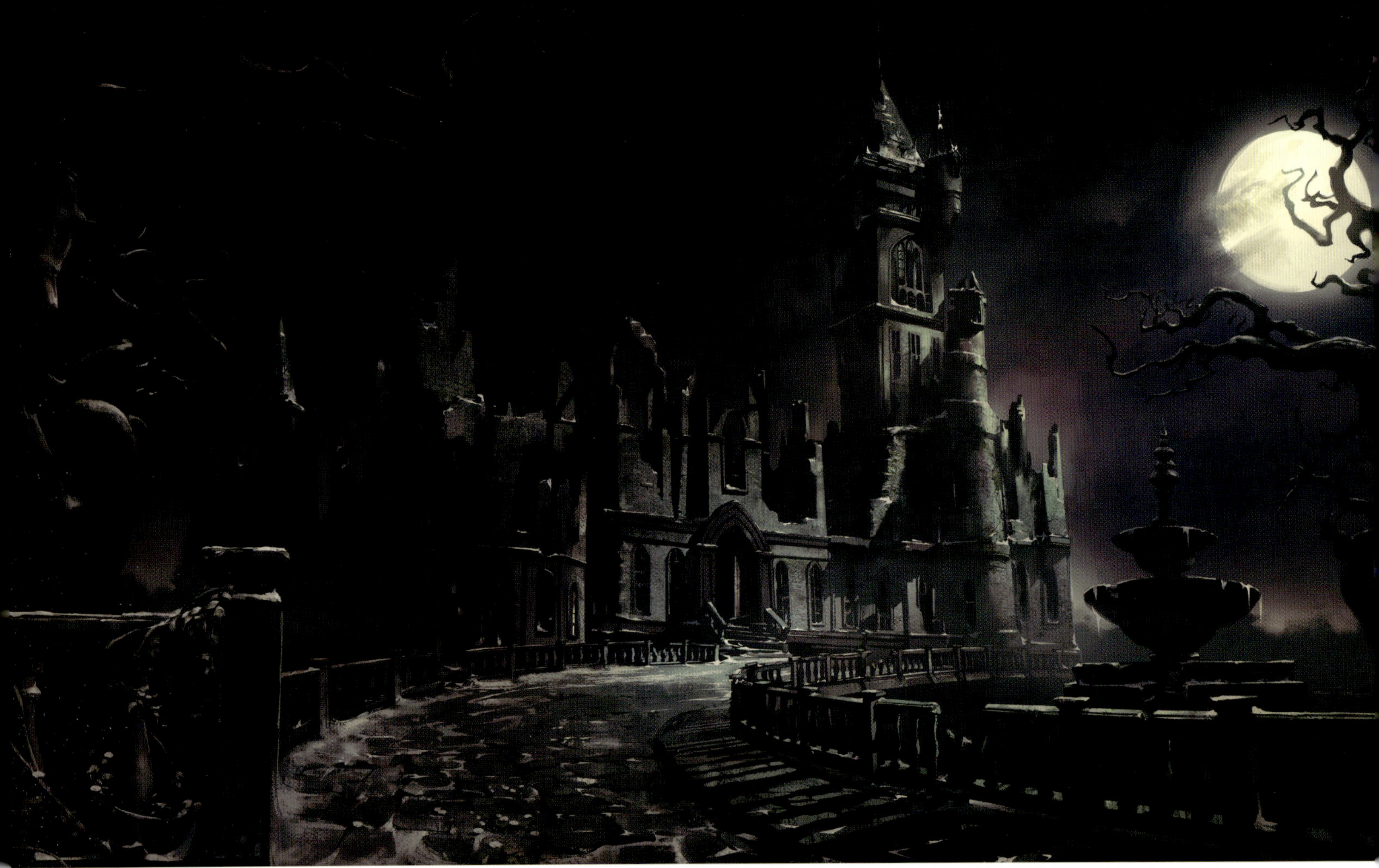

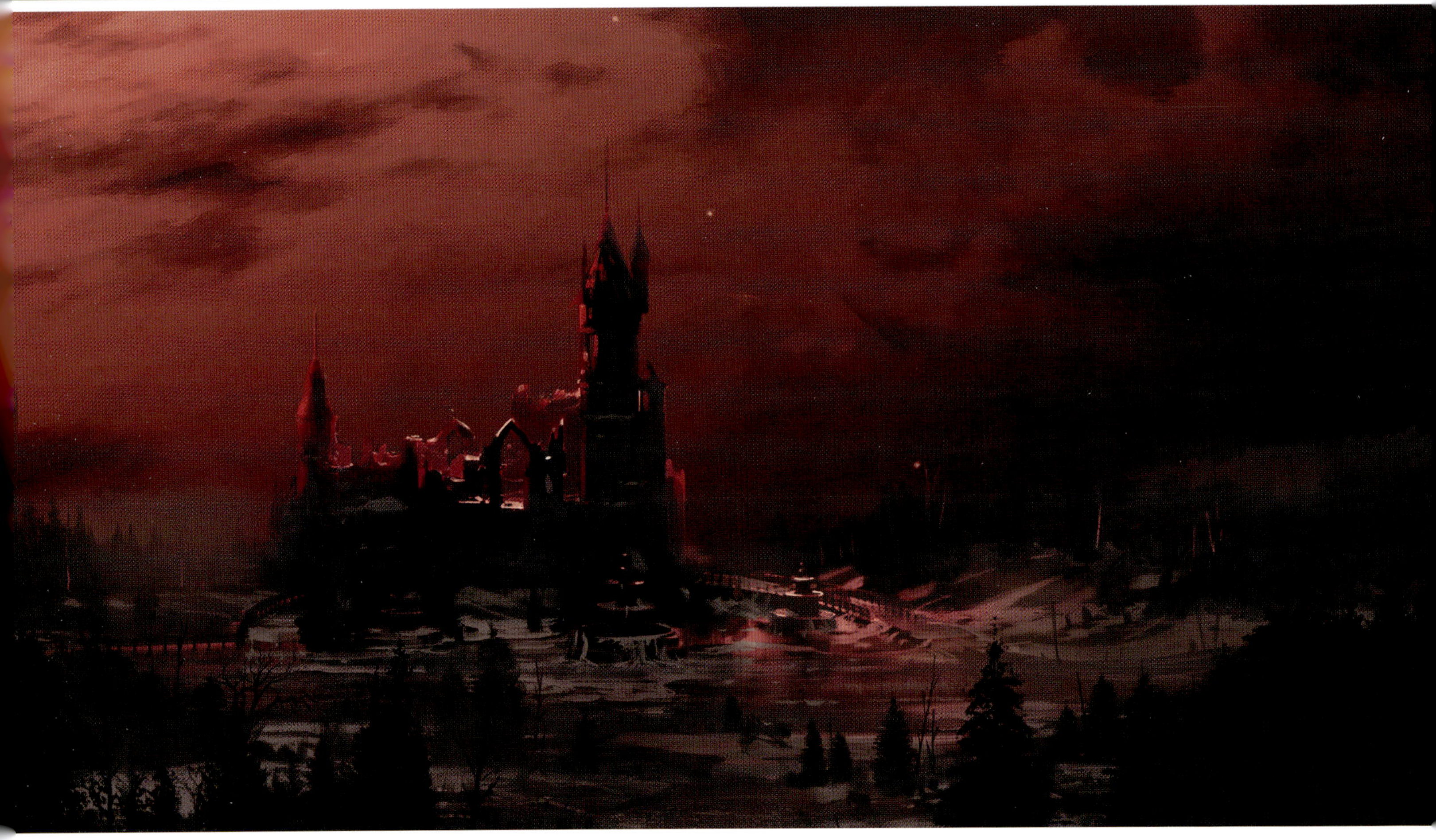

Belmont Estate

The ruins of the Belmont family home stand defiantly atop the Belmont Hold, a priceless store of knowledge, tools, and ephemera from generations of monster slaying.

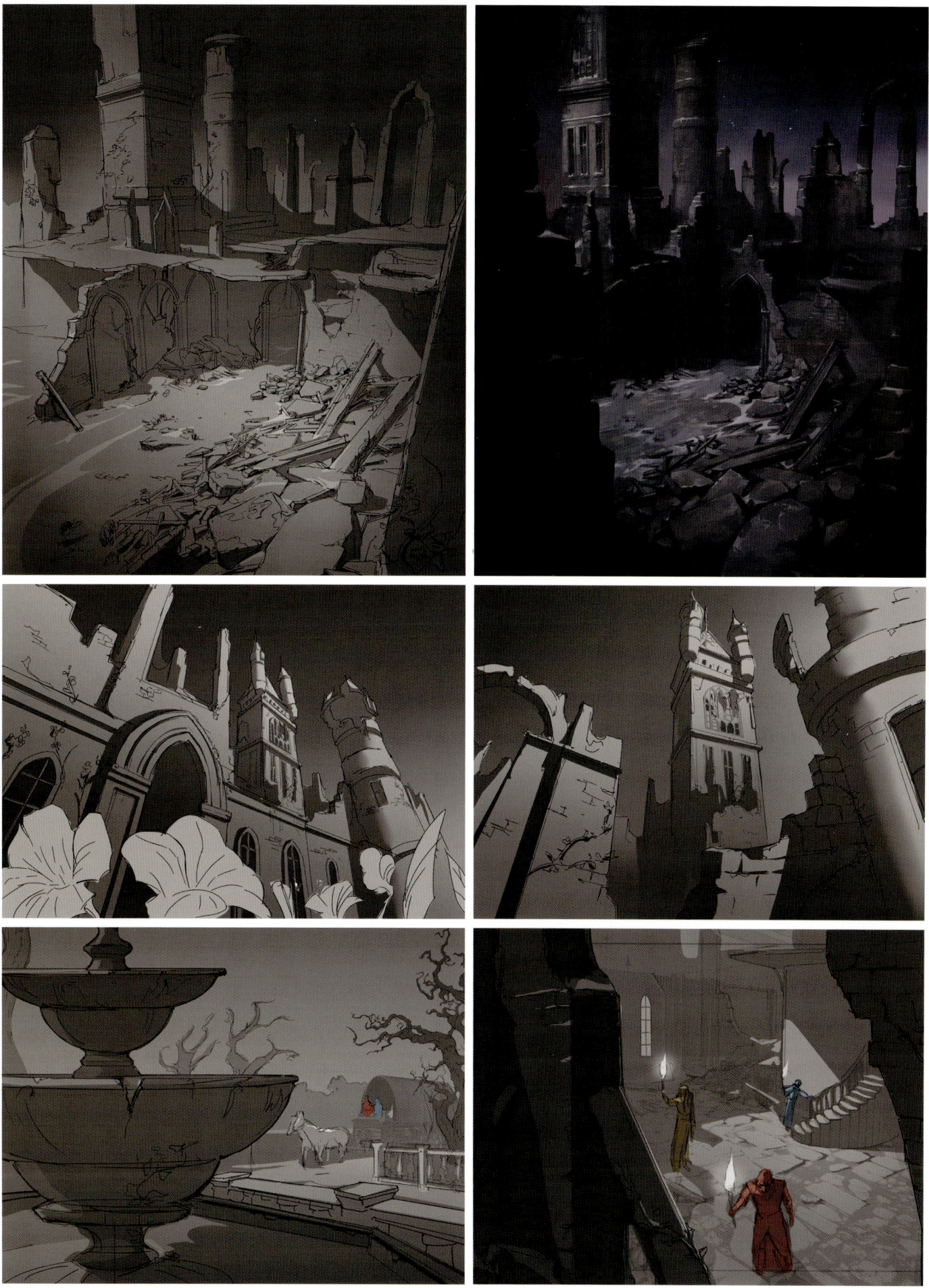

Rough layouts depict various views of the fallen estate.

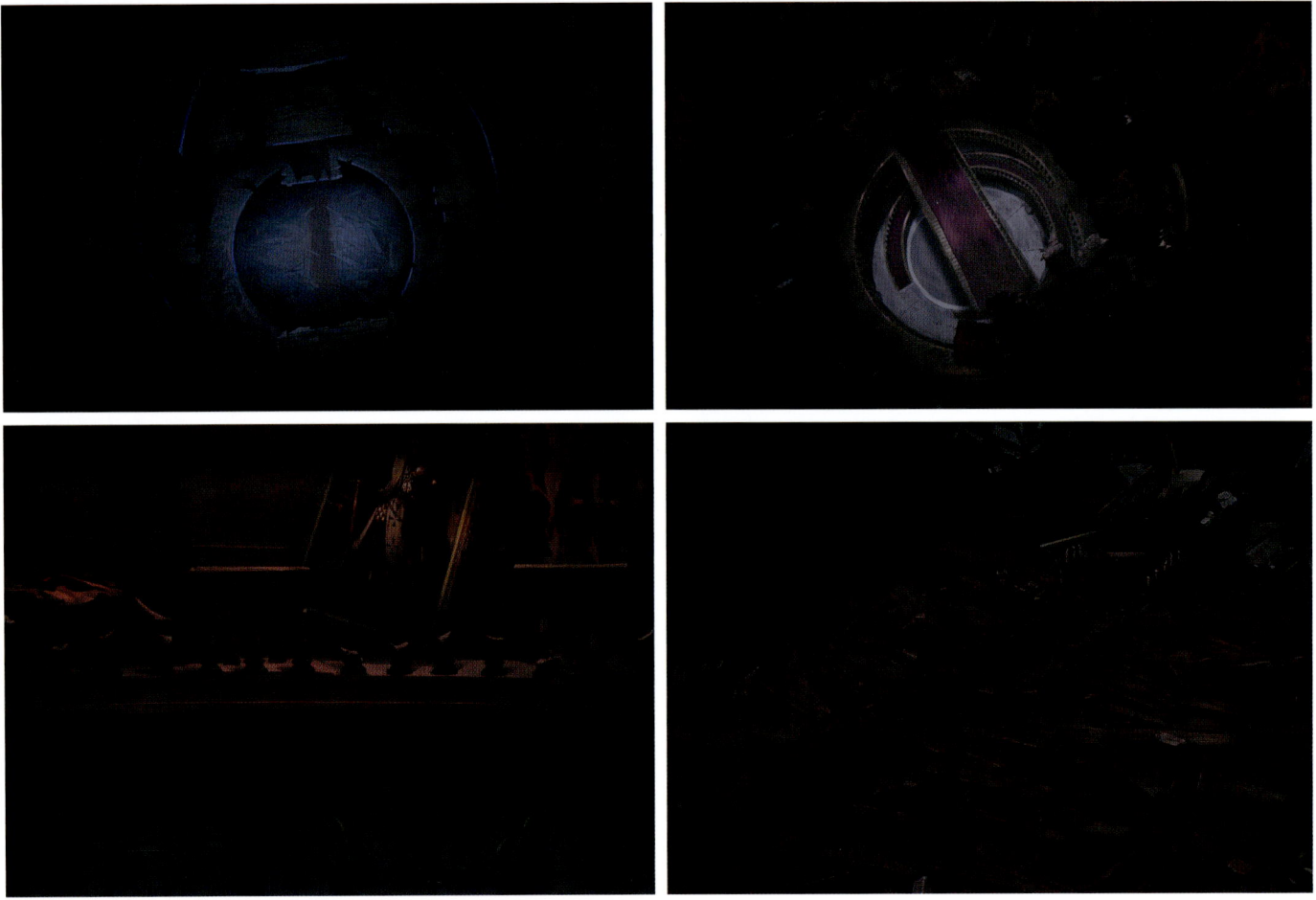

Left page: Top painting by Bo Li. Middle paintings by Stephen Stark. Bottom left painting by Jose Vega. Bottom right painting by Bo Li.
Right page: Top painting by Bo Li. Middle left layout by Bo Li. Middle right layout by Jose Vega. Bottom left painting by Stephen Stark. Bottom right painting by Jose Vega.

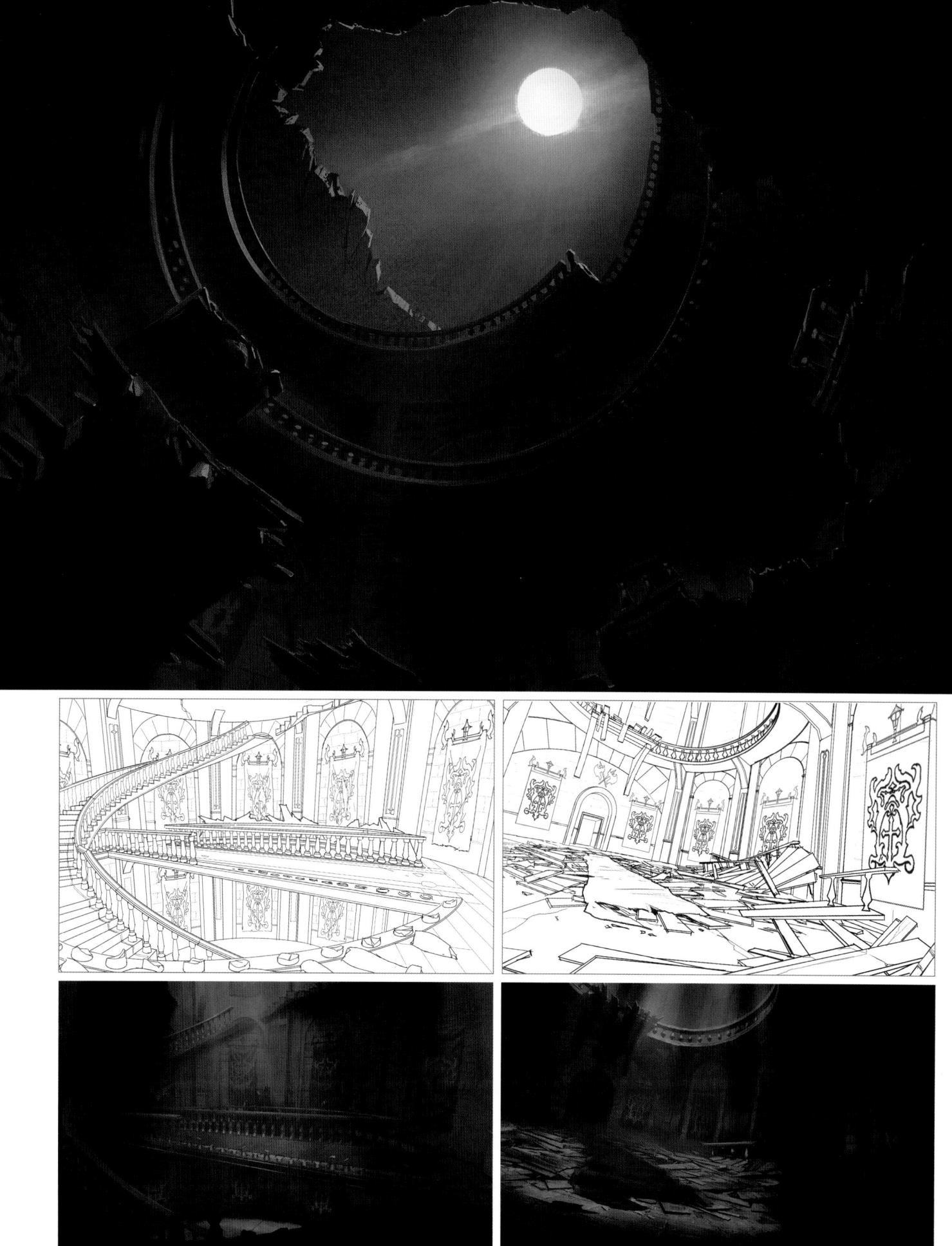

The subterranean hub of Belmont Hold is an impossibly deep silo encircled with spiral staircases and traversed by bridges—perfect for crashing through during an epic night creature boss battle. The hold endures a full-scale night creature attack, fended off by Trevor, followed by the landing of Dracula's castle itself directly above it. Before-and after-battle versions of the space were needed.

BELMONT HOLD

The hold provided the crew with the ultimate opportunity for stocking library shelves with *Castlevania* game–related Easter eggs. "It's a big-ass library of Belmont stuff, with various knowledge that they've gathered over the centuries and magic items and so on. There's lots of little nods to elements of the games. The most obvious here is that big dinosaur-snake skeleton, a monster in the games that, as a skeleton, attacks and shoots fire, and has been around since the first game." —Sam Deats

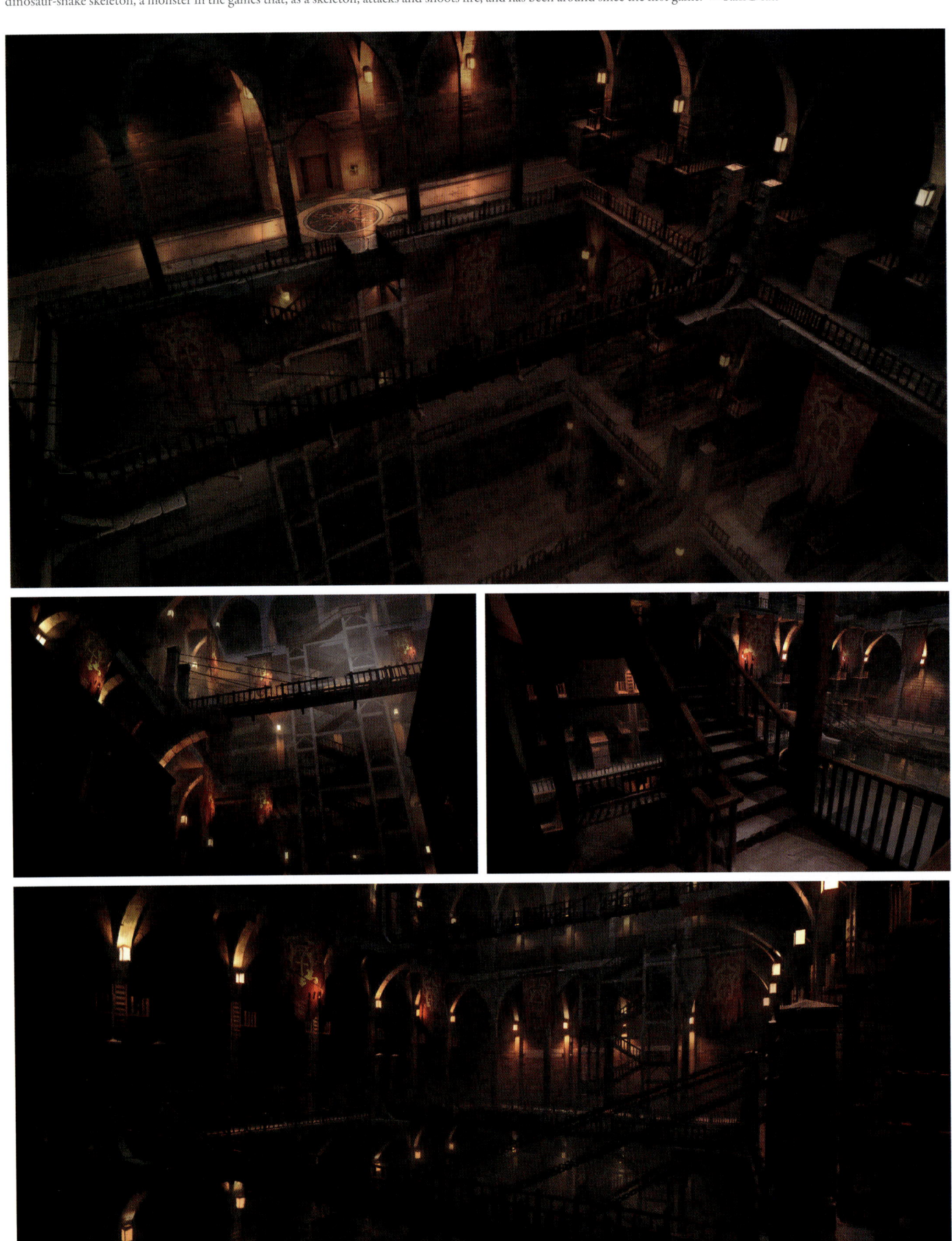

Left page: Belmont Hold design and 3D model by Justin Kauffman. Top painting by Mathias Zamecki. Middle left painting by Danny Moll. Middle right painting by Bo Li. Bottom painting by Sean Vo.
Right page: Top painting by Bo Li. Bottom left Belmont Hold shelf layouts by Sean Randolph. Bottom right paintings by Bo Li (top), Stephen Stark (middle), and Sean Randolph (bottom).

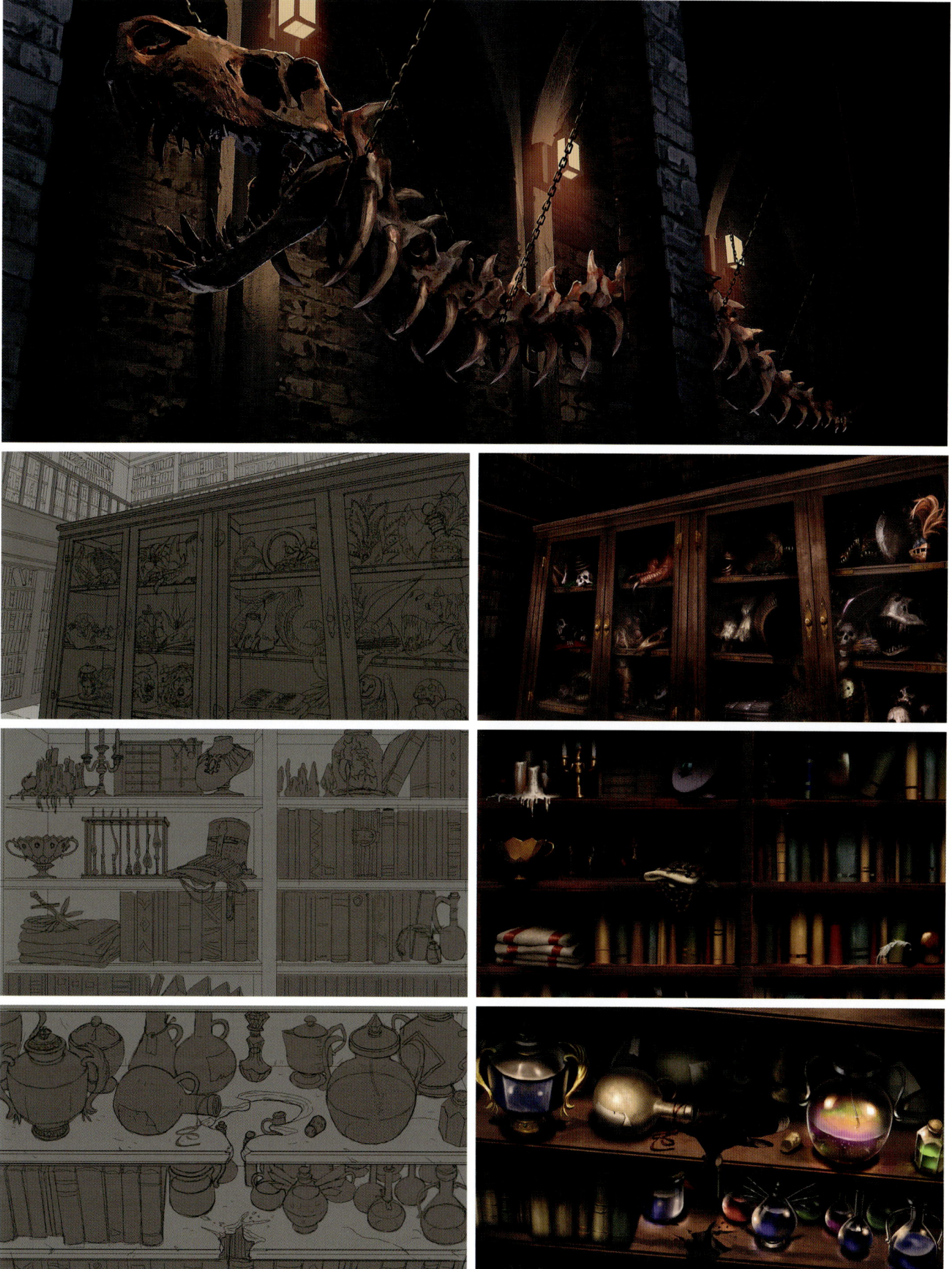

"If you look closely you will find all kinds of game items, from holy water and invisibility potions to boss trophies like the head of Medusa or the boomerang of the Skelerang! There may even be a pork chop somewhere in Dracula's castle . . ." —Sean Randolph

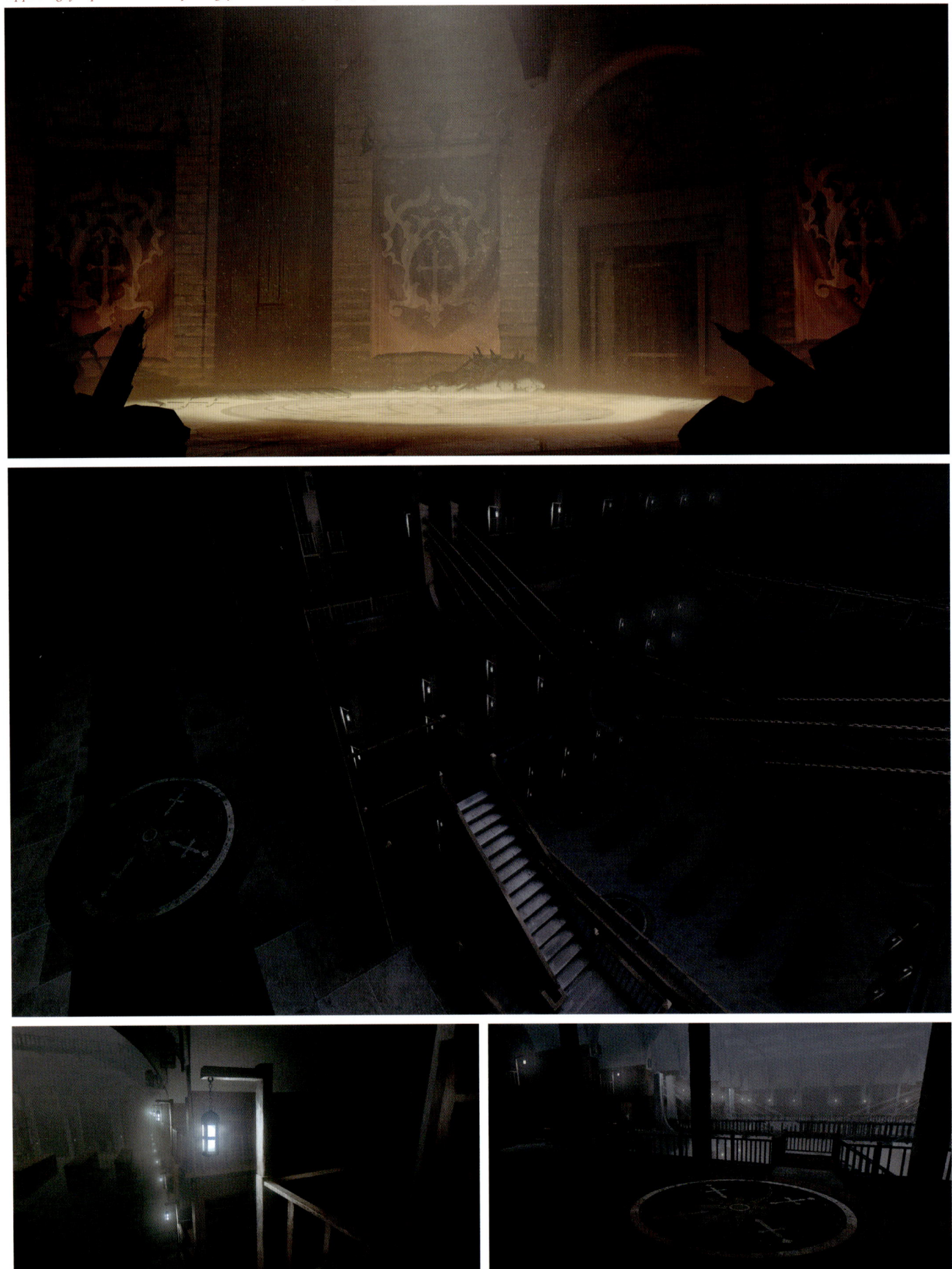

Above: After Alucard installs electric lamps in season 3, the Hold takes on a blue hue after dark. *Opposite:* Katie Silva's digital painting of Leon Belmont in the tradition of Napoleonic portraiture and the work of the Georgian-era English painter Sir Thomas Lawrence.

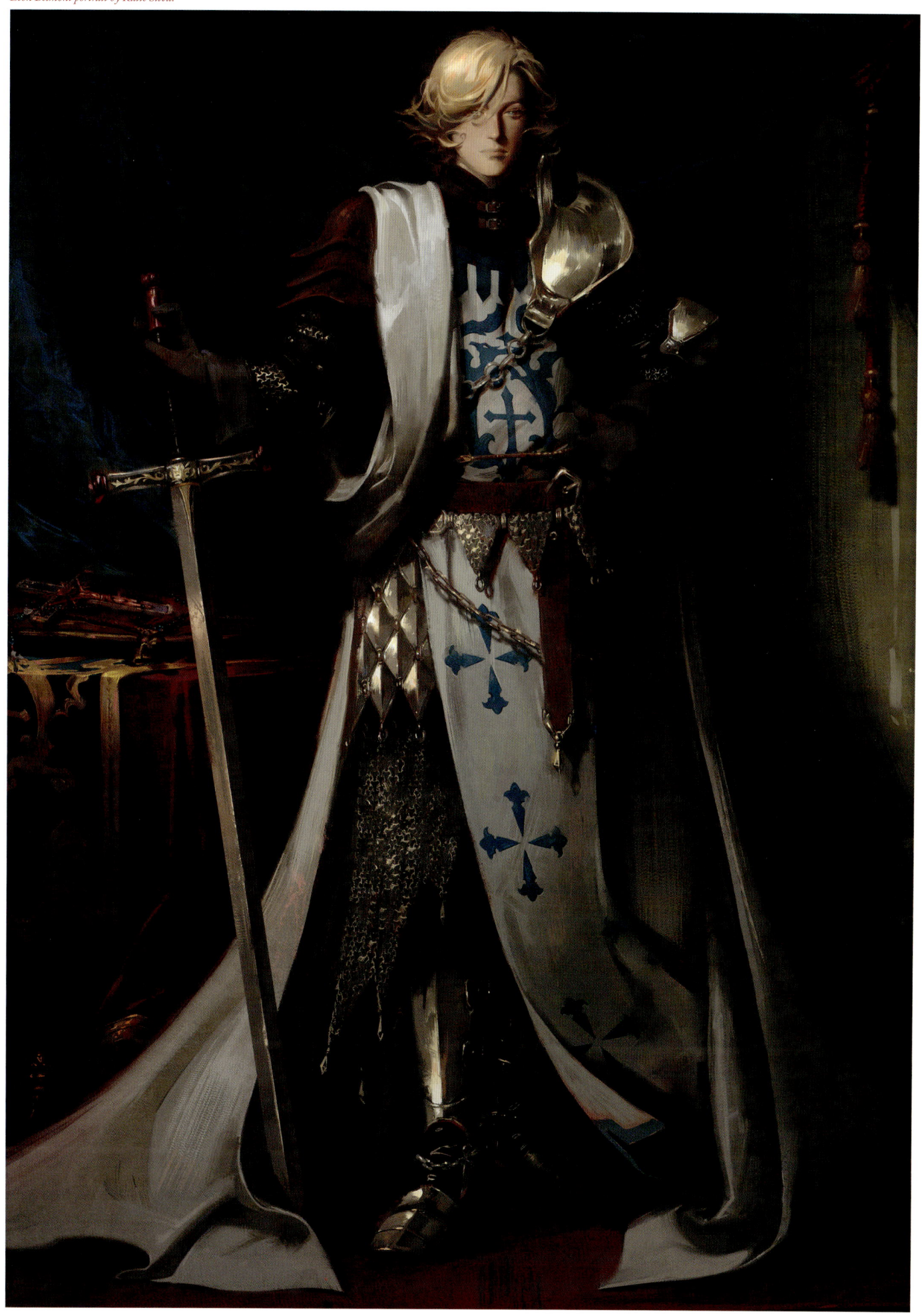

Leon Belmont portrait by Katie Silva.

Lupu Village

Home to Lisa Tepes, the village of Lupu is where she practiced the medicine that she learned from the libraries and teachings of Dracula. Lisa's cottage and laboratory, with all its medicinal healing potential, was no match for the awesome ignorance and suspicion of the bishop and his goon squad.

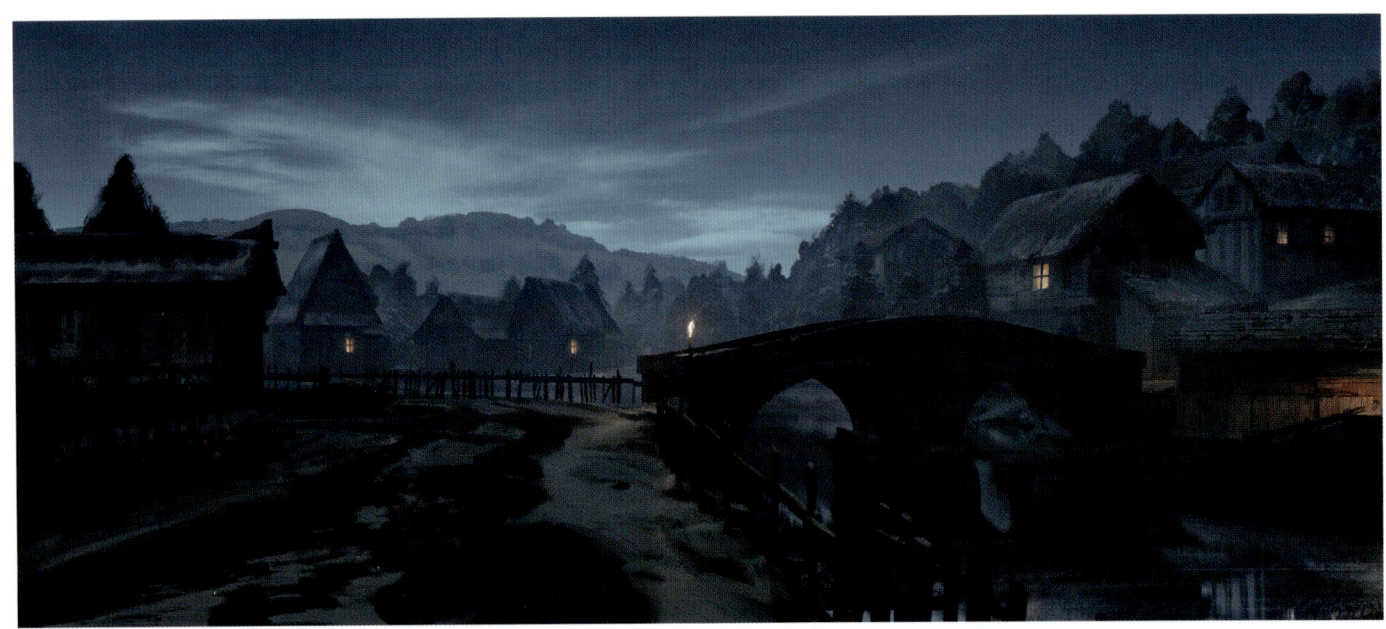

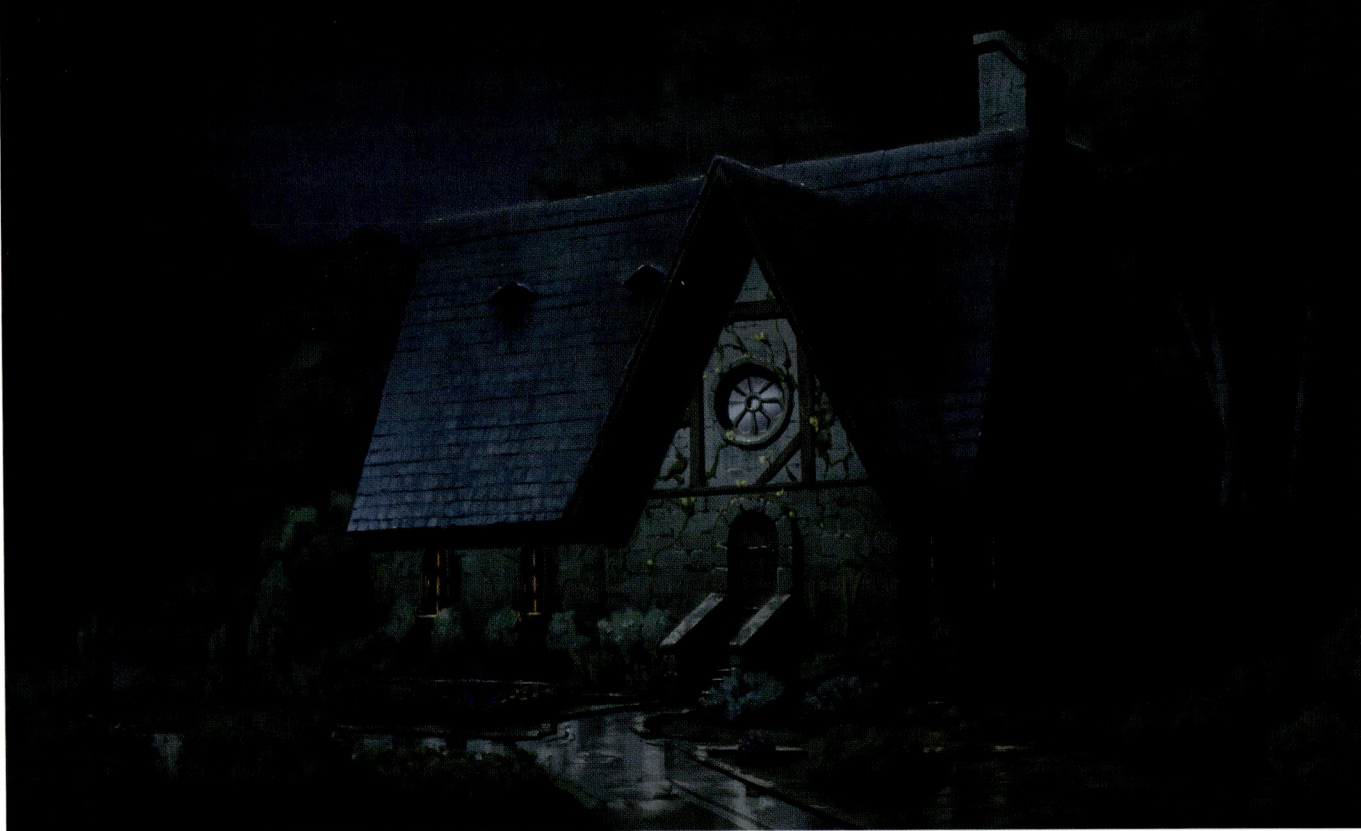

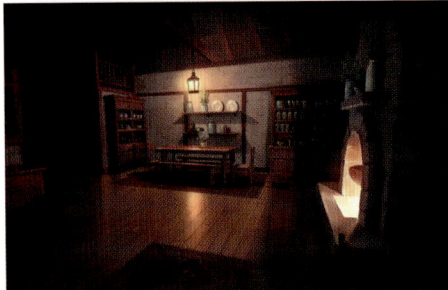 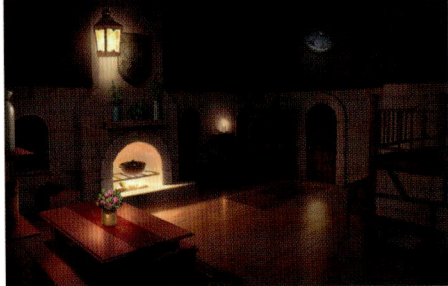 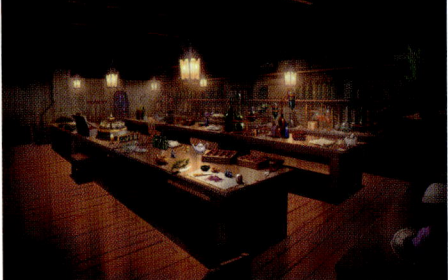

Left page: Top painting by Robby Johnson. Middle painting by Justin Kauffman. Bottom left painting by Bo Li. Bottom middle painting by Justin Kauffman. Bottom right painting by Bo Li. Right page: Sean Vo.

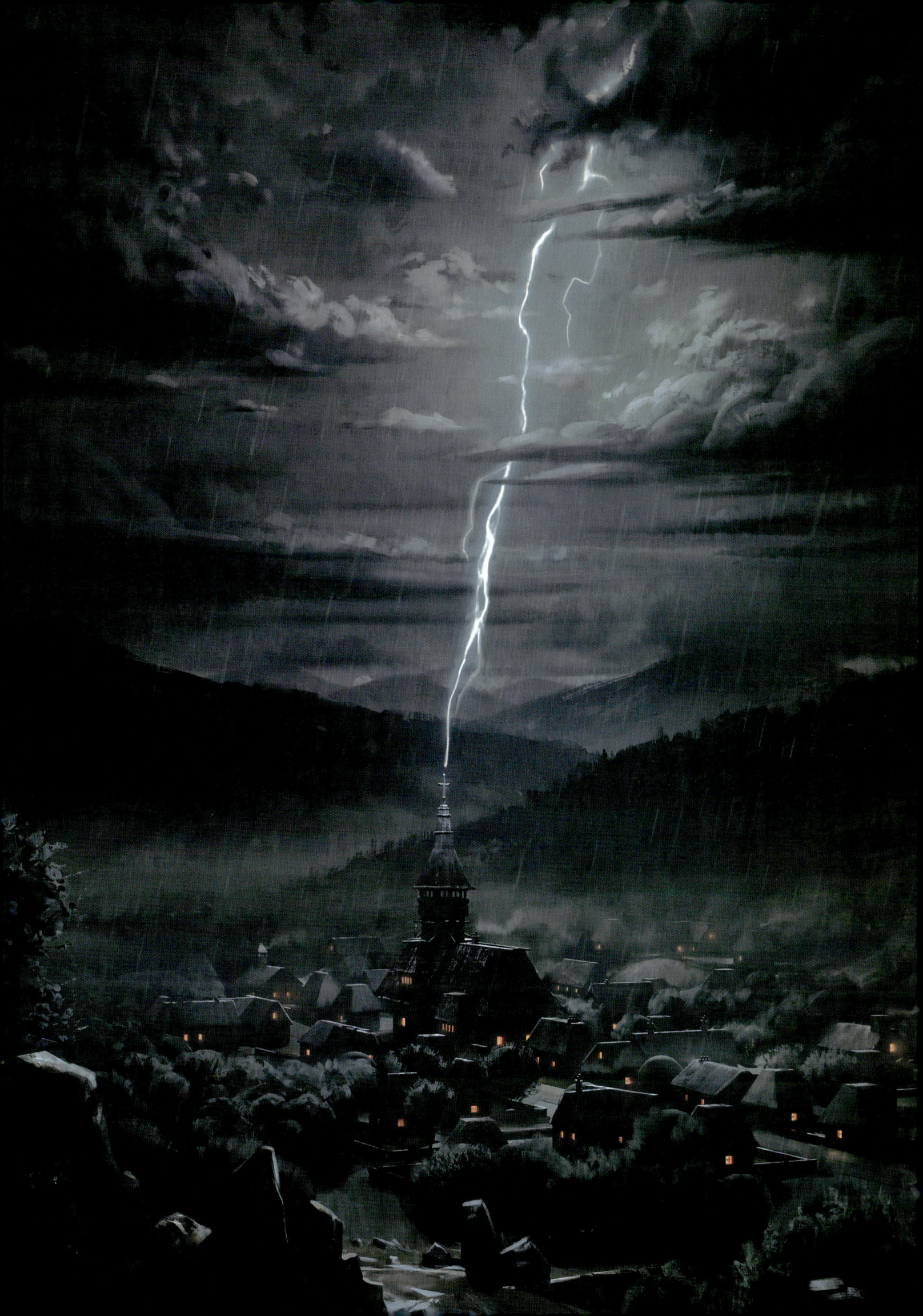

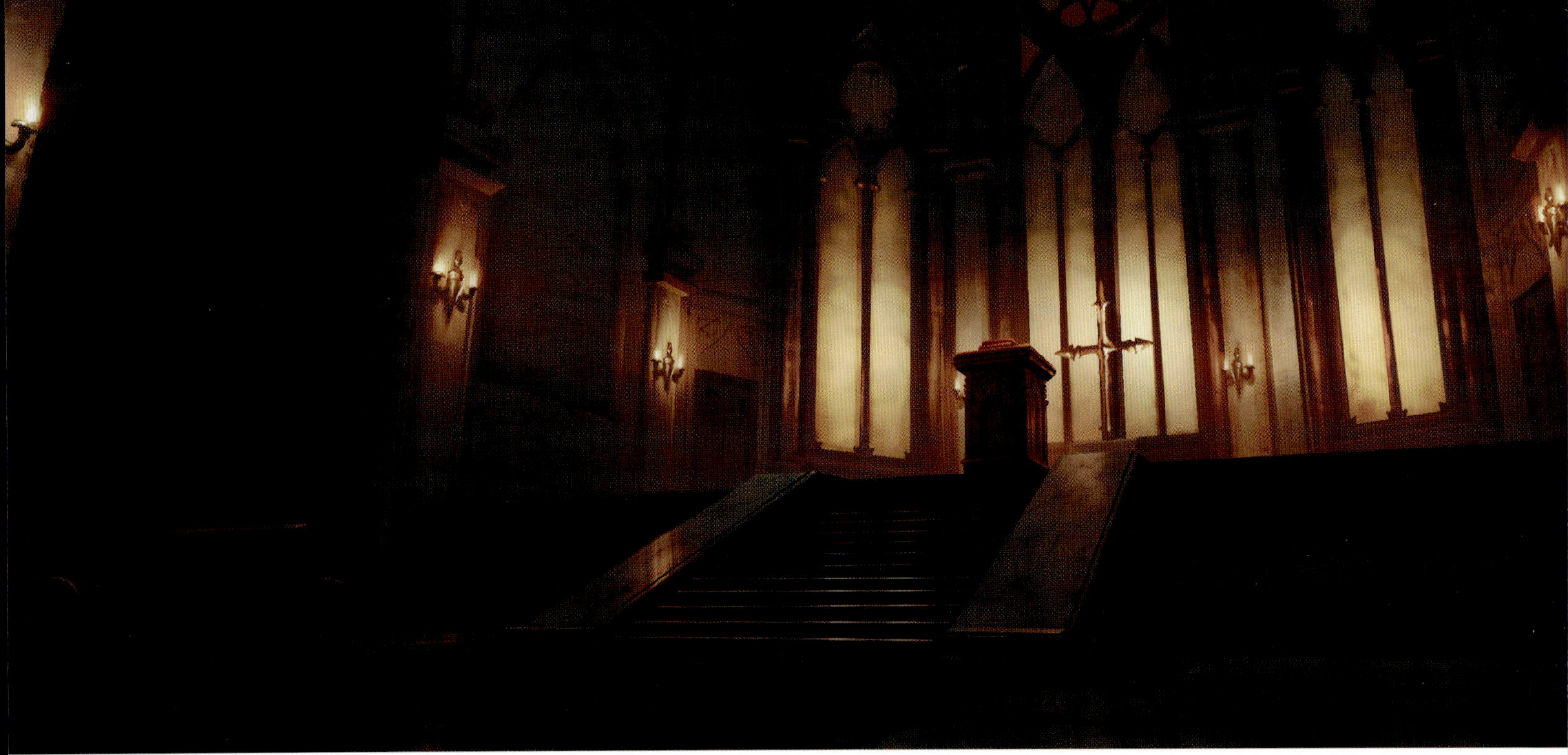

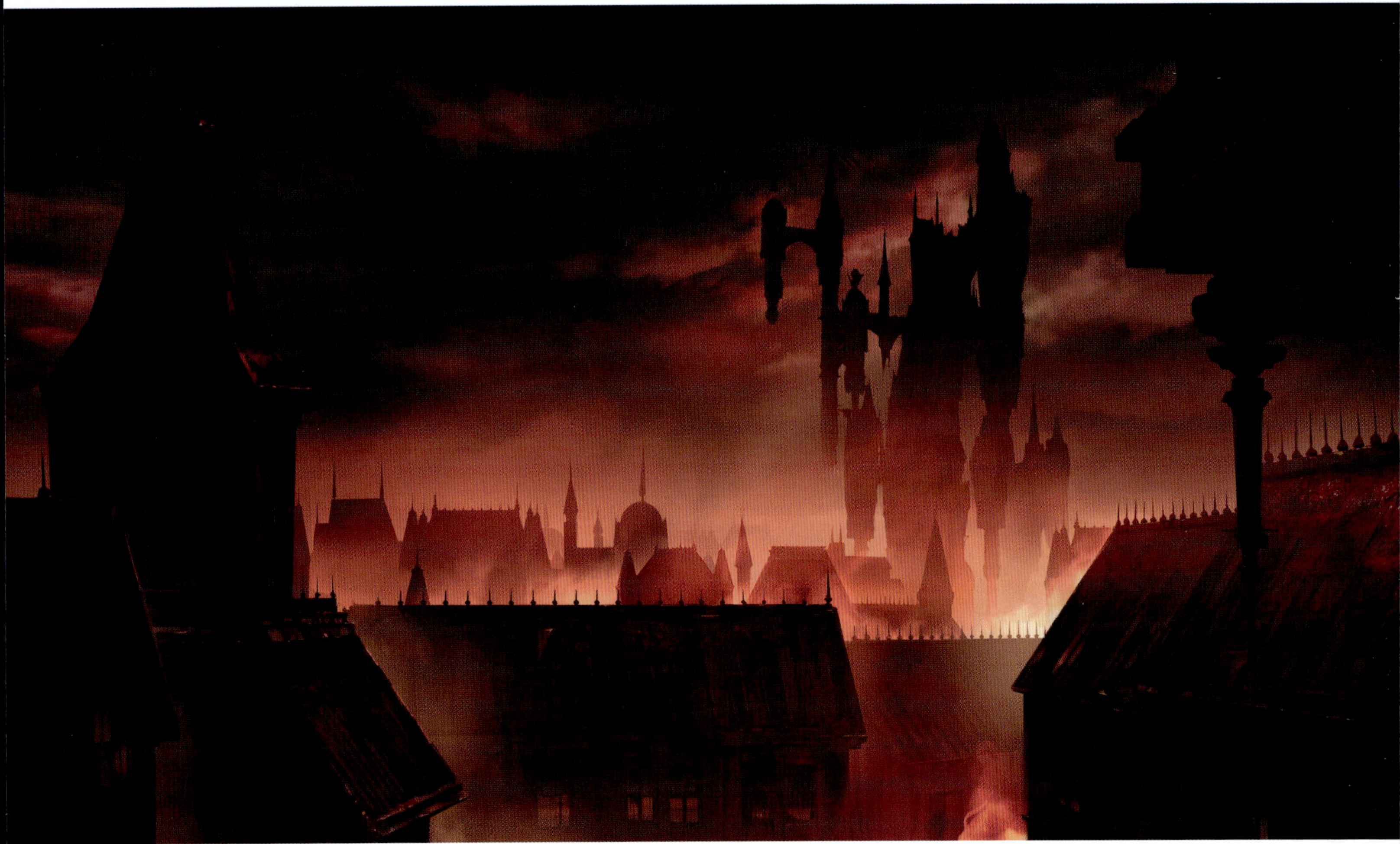

Targoviste

The bishop orders Lisa Tepes burned alive at the stake in the town square of Targoviste for the practice of witchcraft, ensuring the entire populace's doom at the teeth and claws of Dracula's night creature horde. Lording over the people's lives sits the church, locally ruled by the power-hungry bishop, intent on keeping the simple people in obedient ignorance under the threat of death.

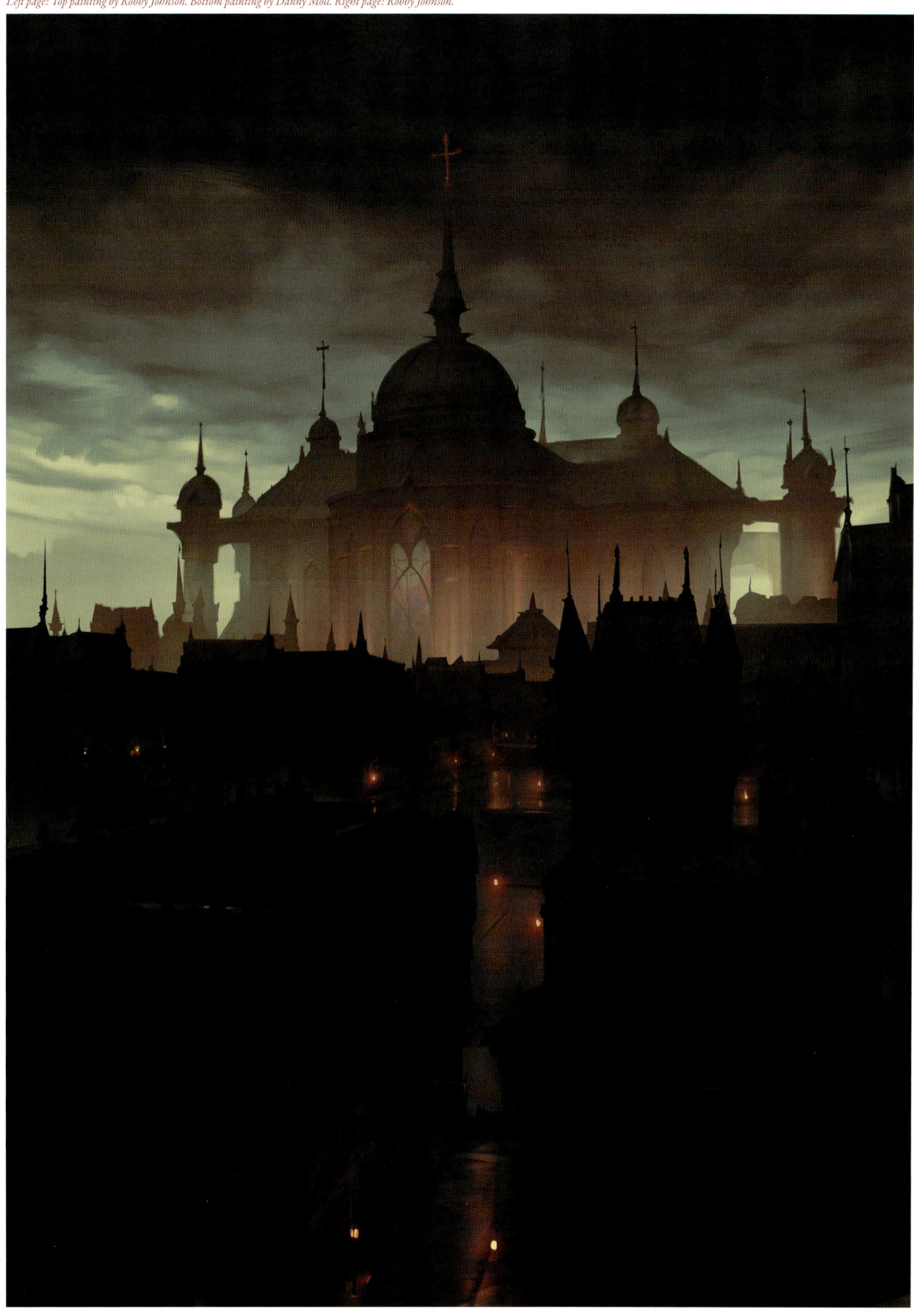

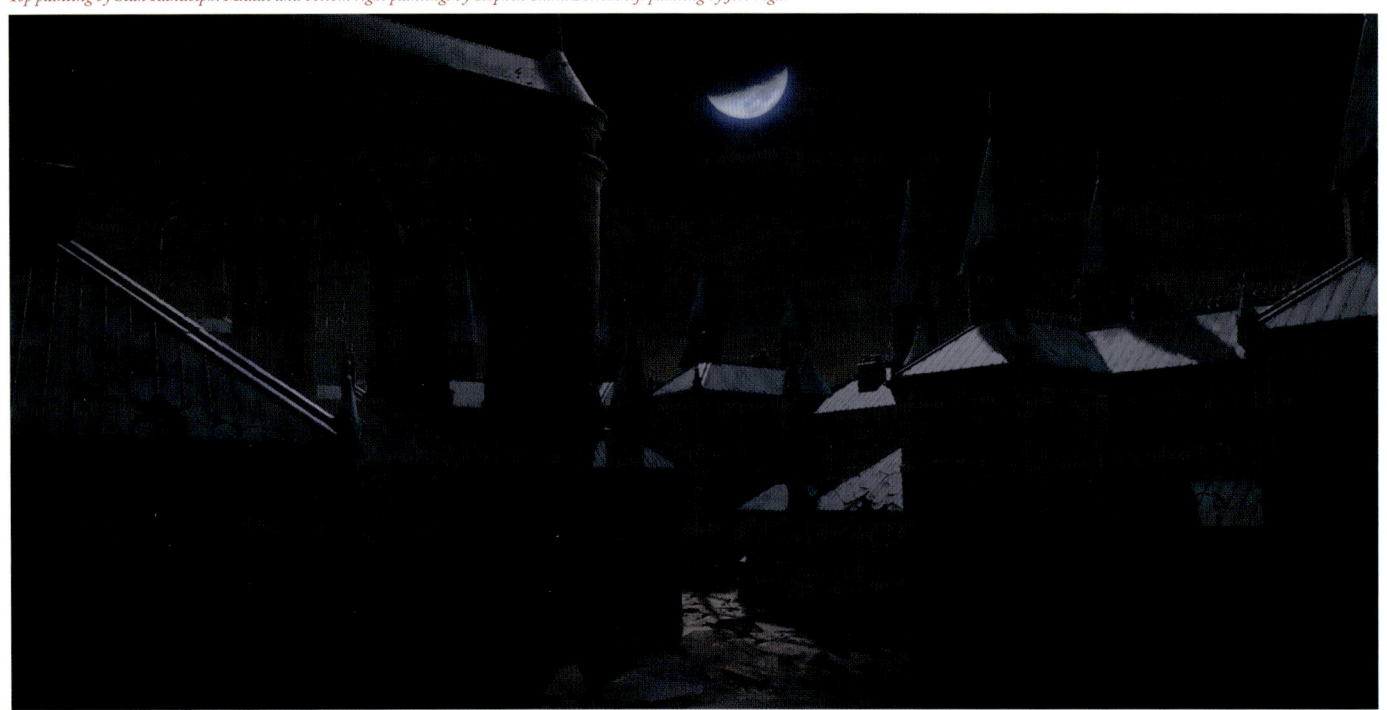

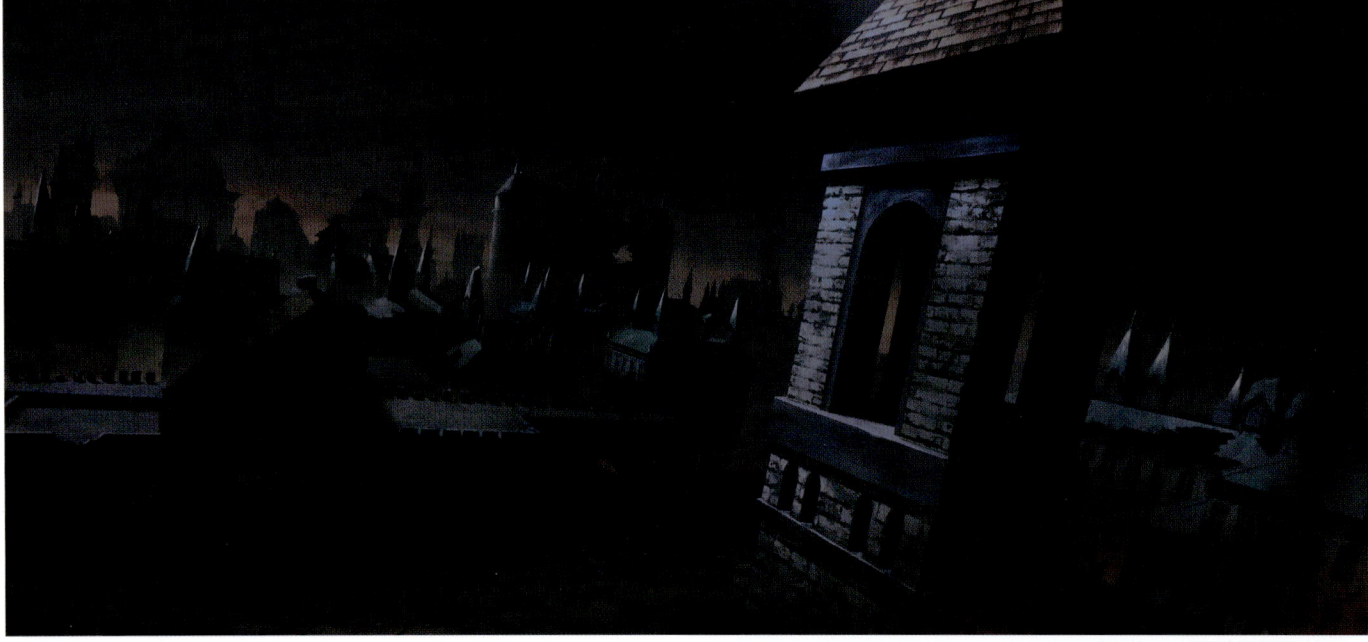

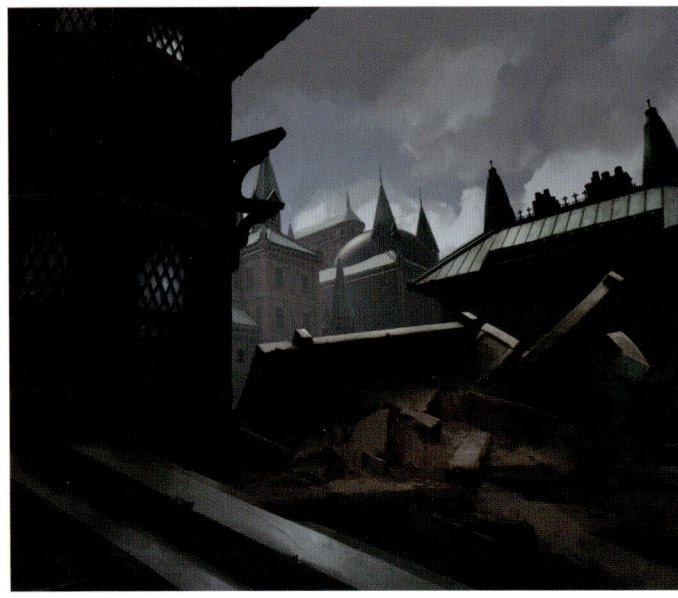

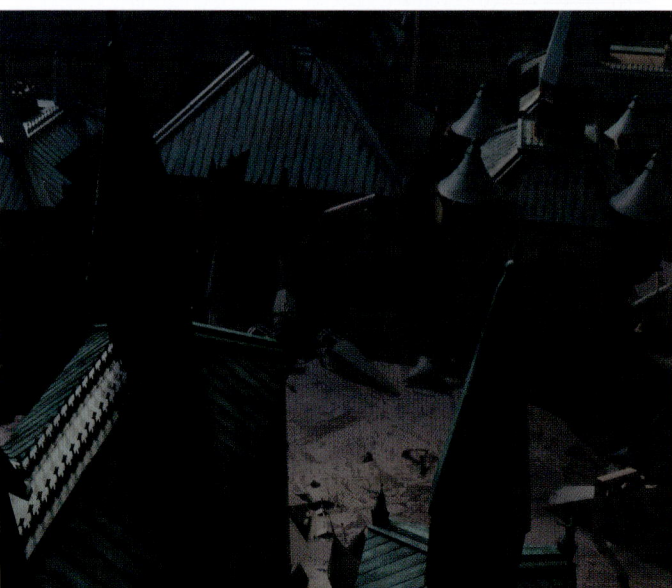

Murdenu

The series introduces Trevor Belmont in a pub in the small town of Murdenu near Gresit. The dismal bleakness of the locale reflects the attitude of the town's inhabitants, a few of whom Trevor must fight off before leaving in search of his next drink.

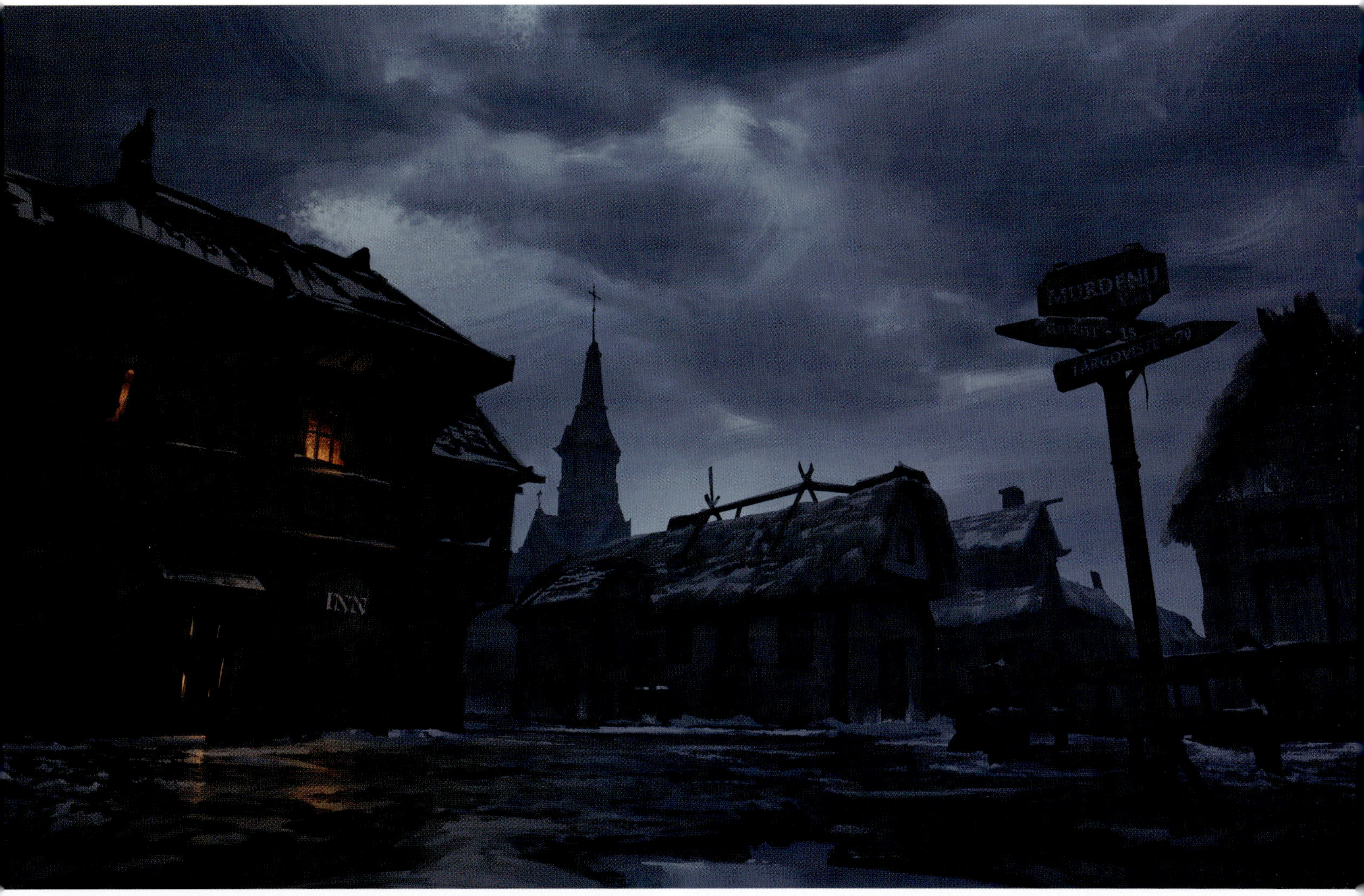

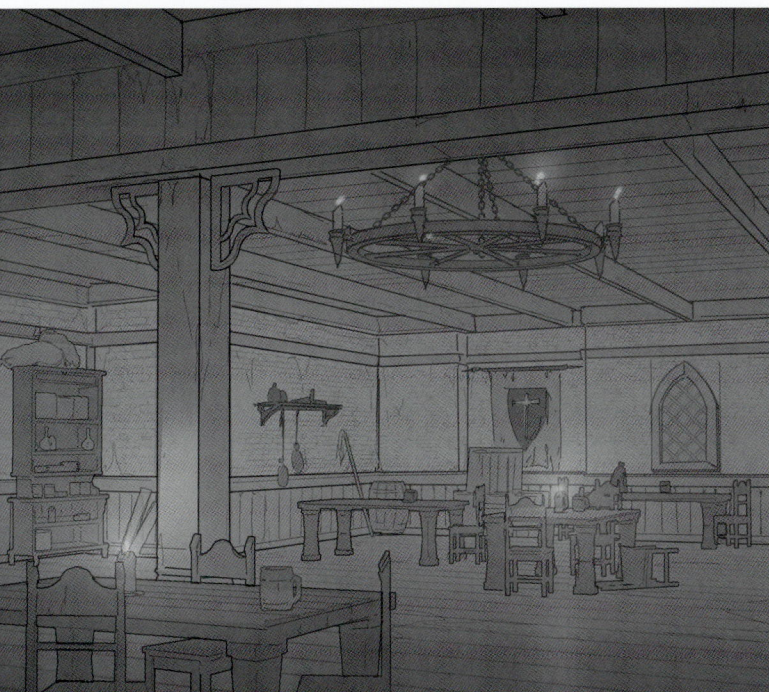

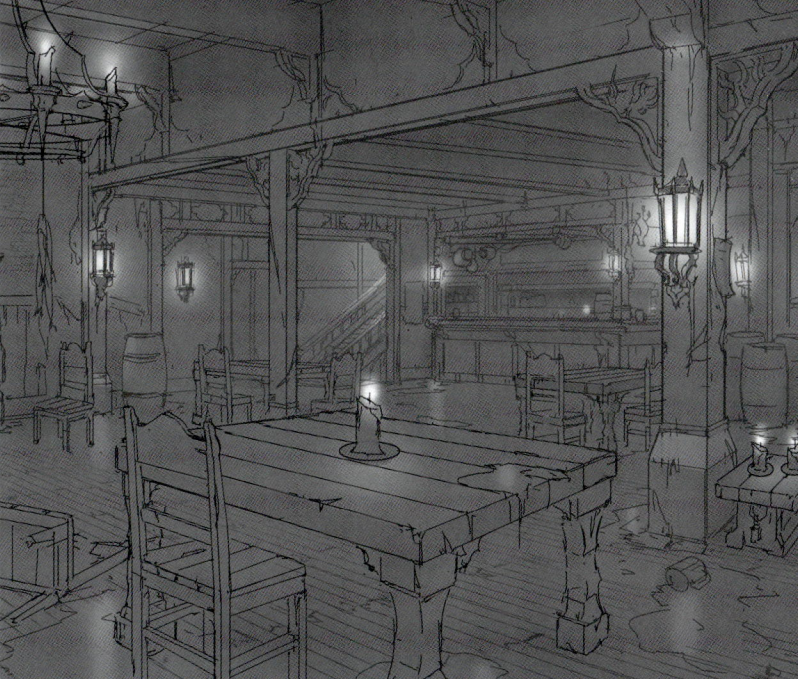

Top painting by Robby Johnson. Bottom layouts by Justin Kauffman.

Gresit

Trevor arrives at the town of Gresit, which is besieged every night by attacks from Dracula's horde. Trevor meets the Speakers here, as well as some unsavory church thugs. He also learns of the legend of the warrior sleeping somewhere beneath in the catacombs.

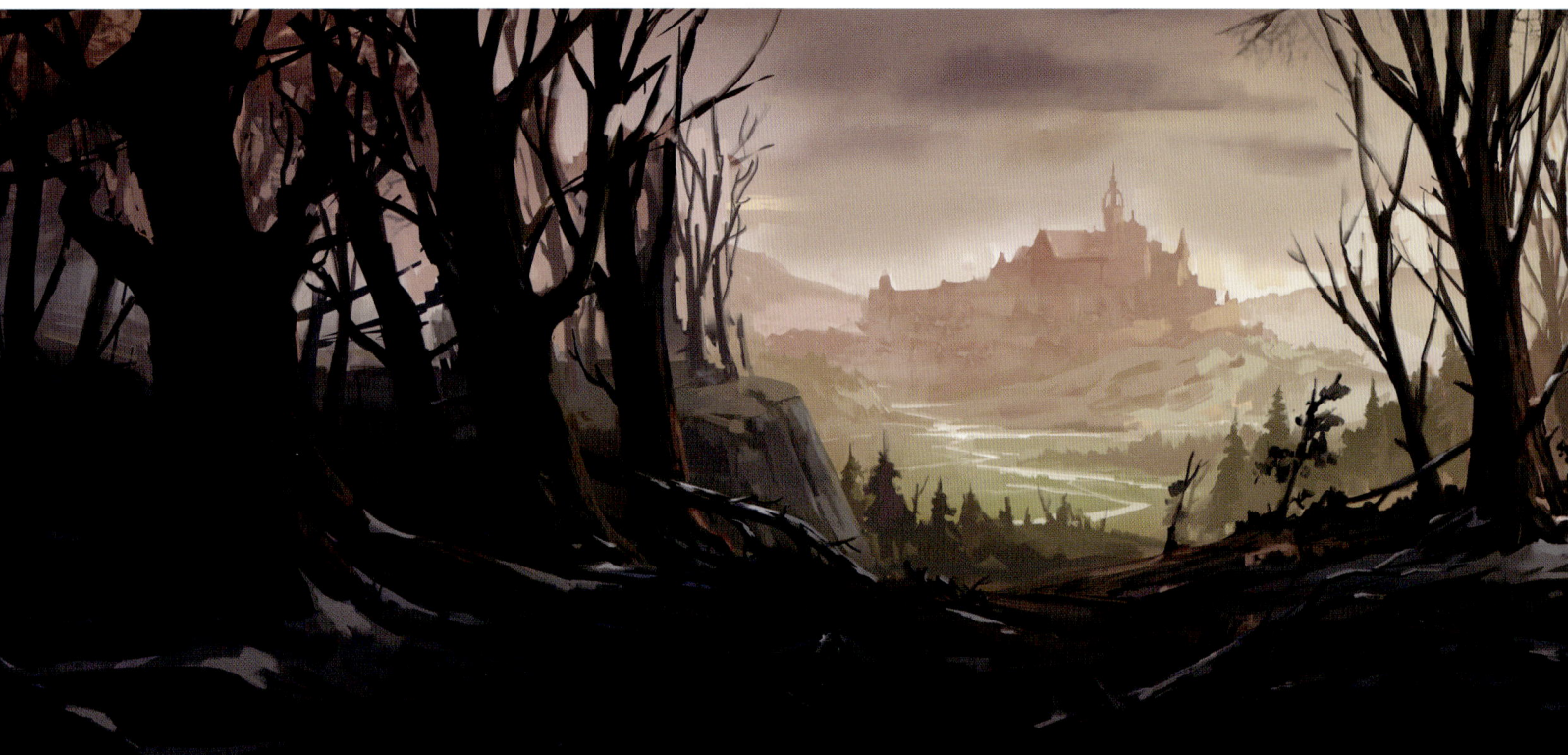

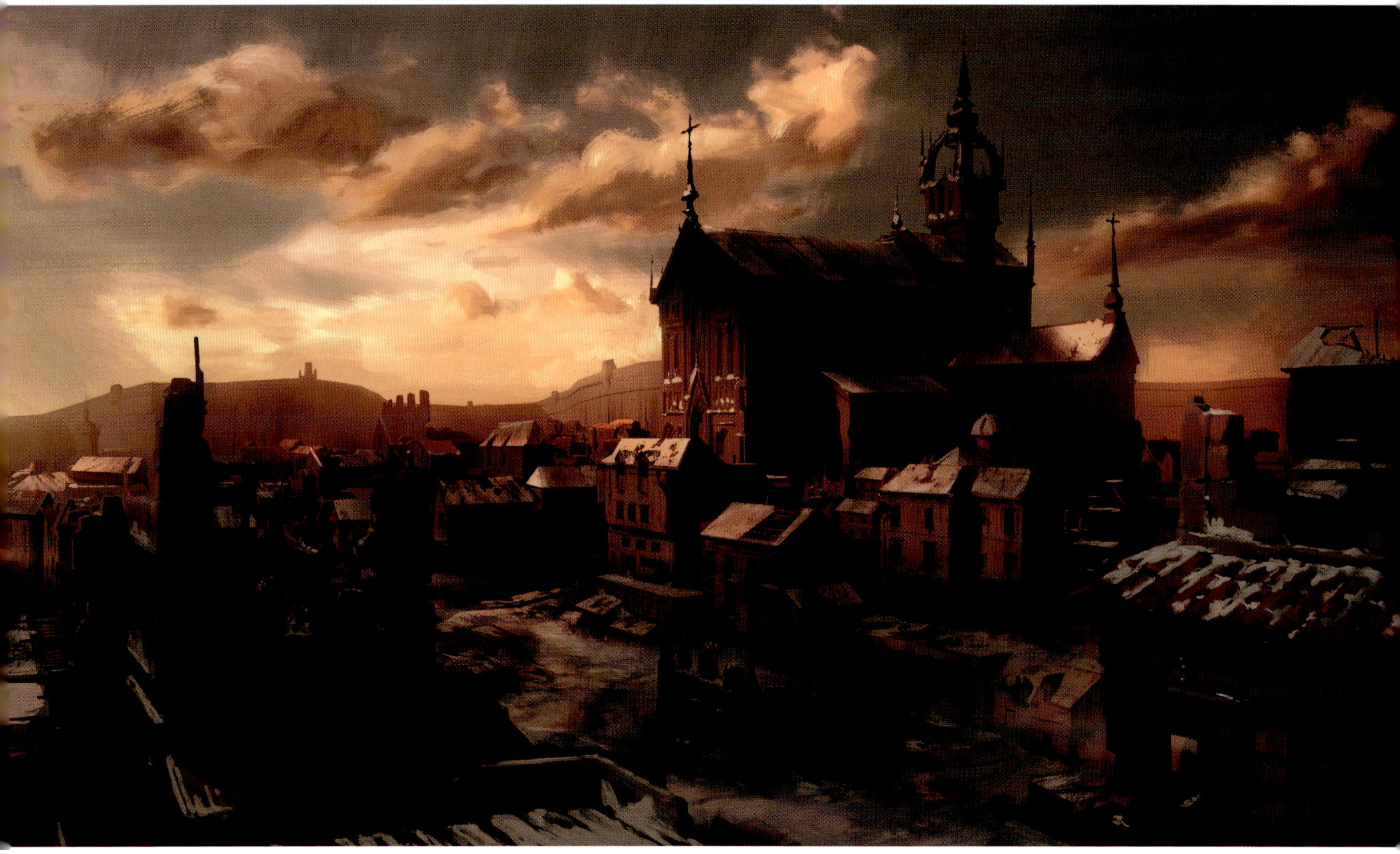

Left page: Top painting by Danny Moll. Bottom painting by Robby Johnson. Right page: Concepts by Danny Moll.

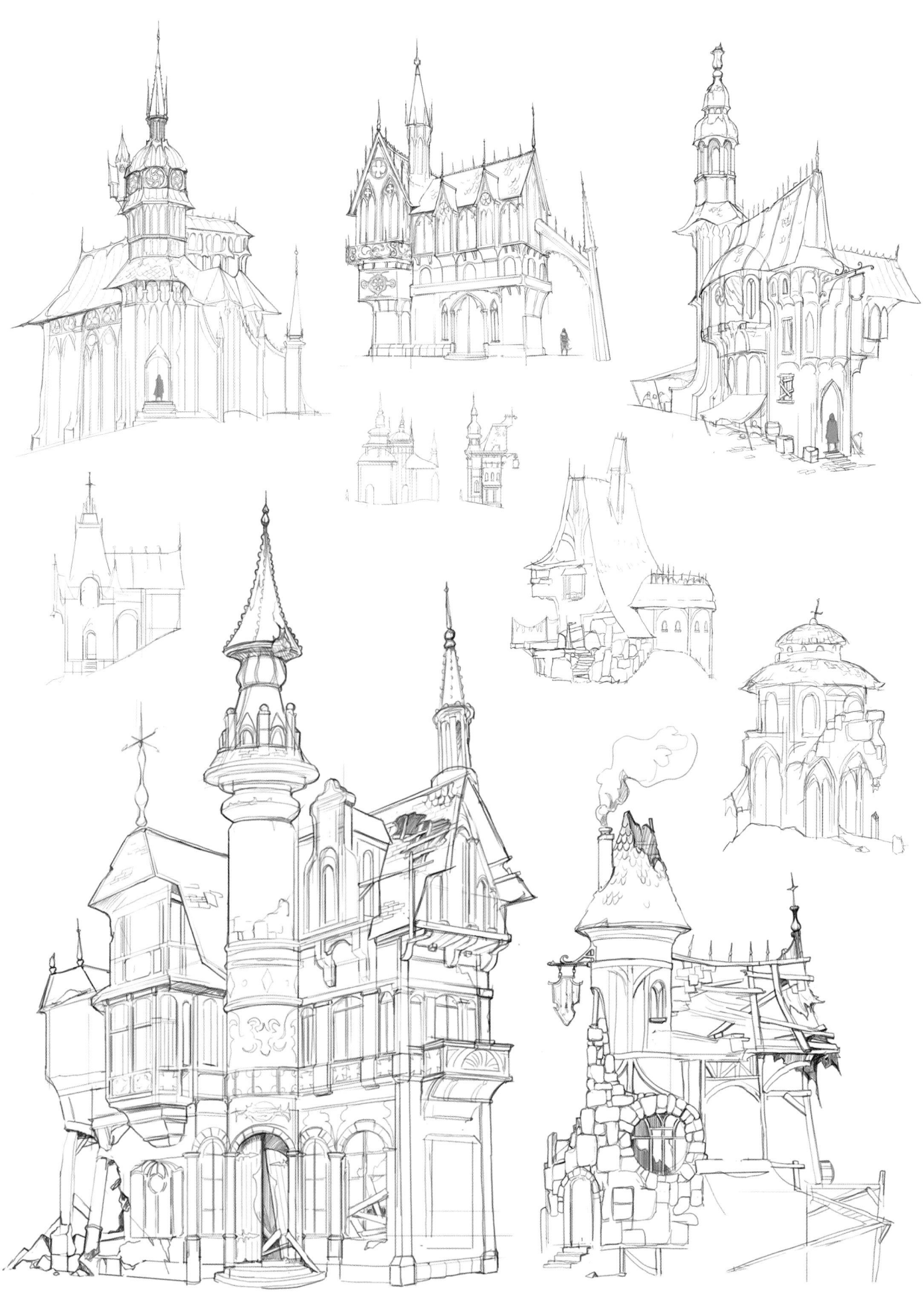

Sketches develop the character and materials of the structures in the medieval village, before and after destruction.

CONCEPT ART

Initial concept work for the series explored a more whimsical direction, stylized coloring, more exaggerated background forms, and a lined background art style, as seen here in these studies of a fictional Gresit.

The exaggerated arch in this Gresit street scene provided a nice verticality, but was deemed too far fetched for what was meant to feel like a dismal medieval burg.

The art direction landed on a more grounded lighting, coloring, and background style that also ended up being helpful from a production standpoint: with the increasing use of 3D models in the background department, this direction made it more straightforward for the team to light and design spaces that leaned toward realism.

Early style tests by Robby Johnson, Danny Moll, and Justin Kauffman.

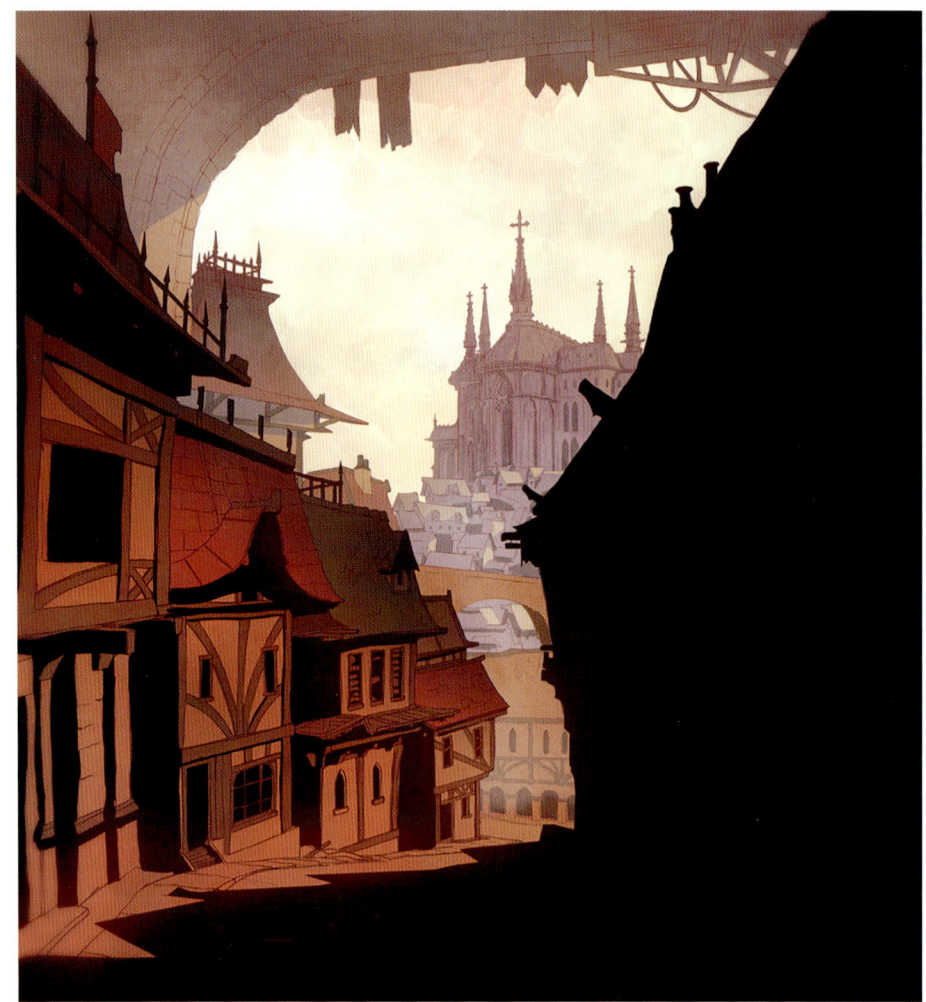

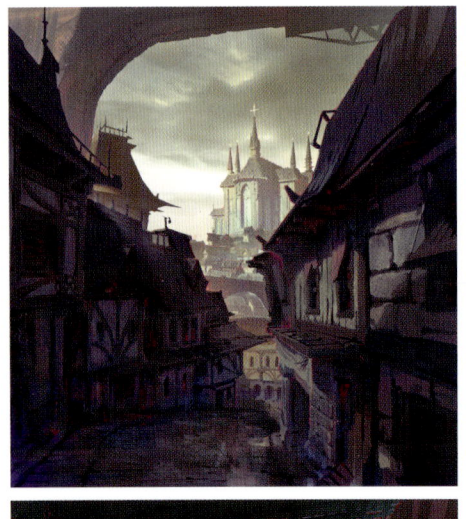
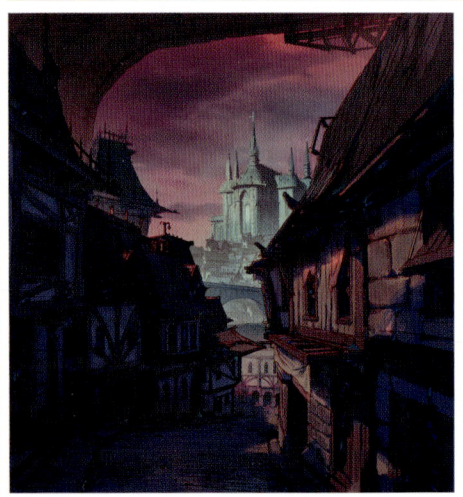
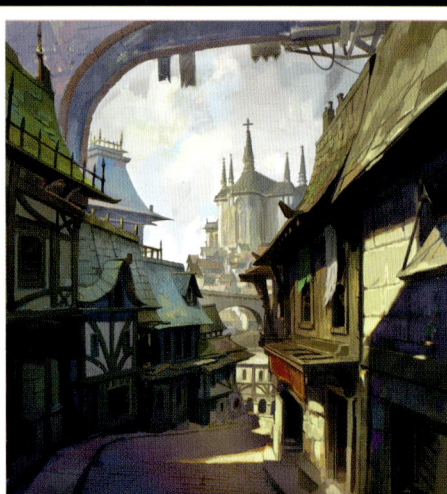
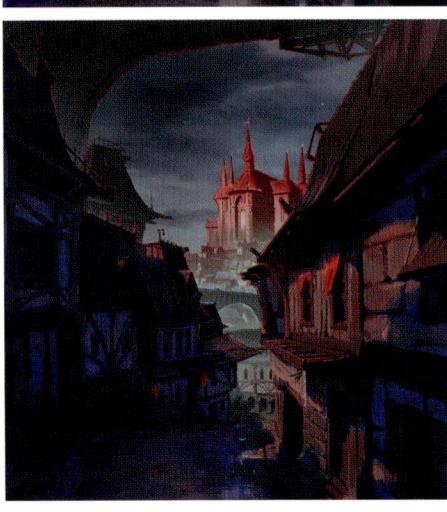
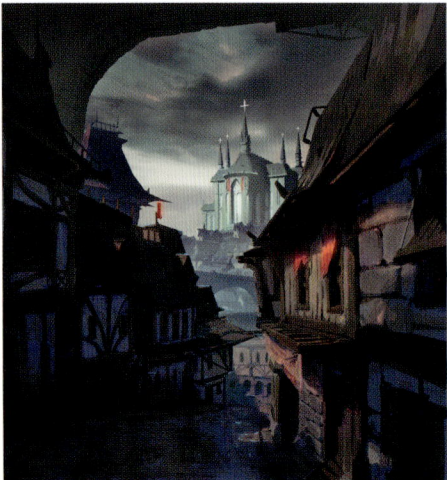
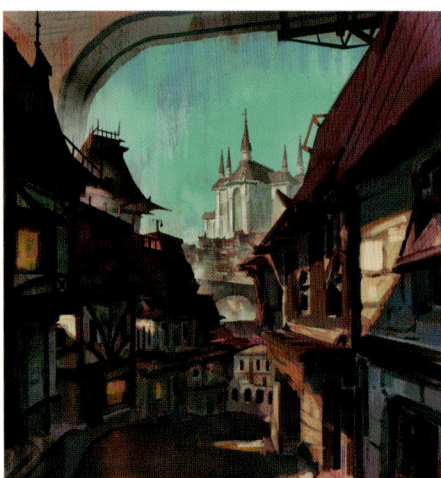

Top painting by Robby Johnson. Middle barn painting by Mauricio Calle. Bottom barn interior paintings by Sylvain Sarrailh.

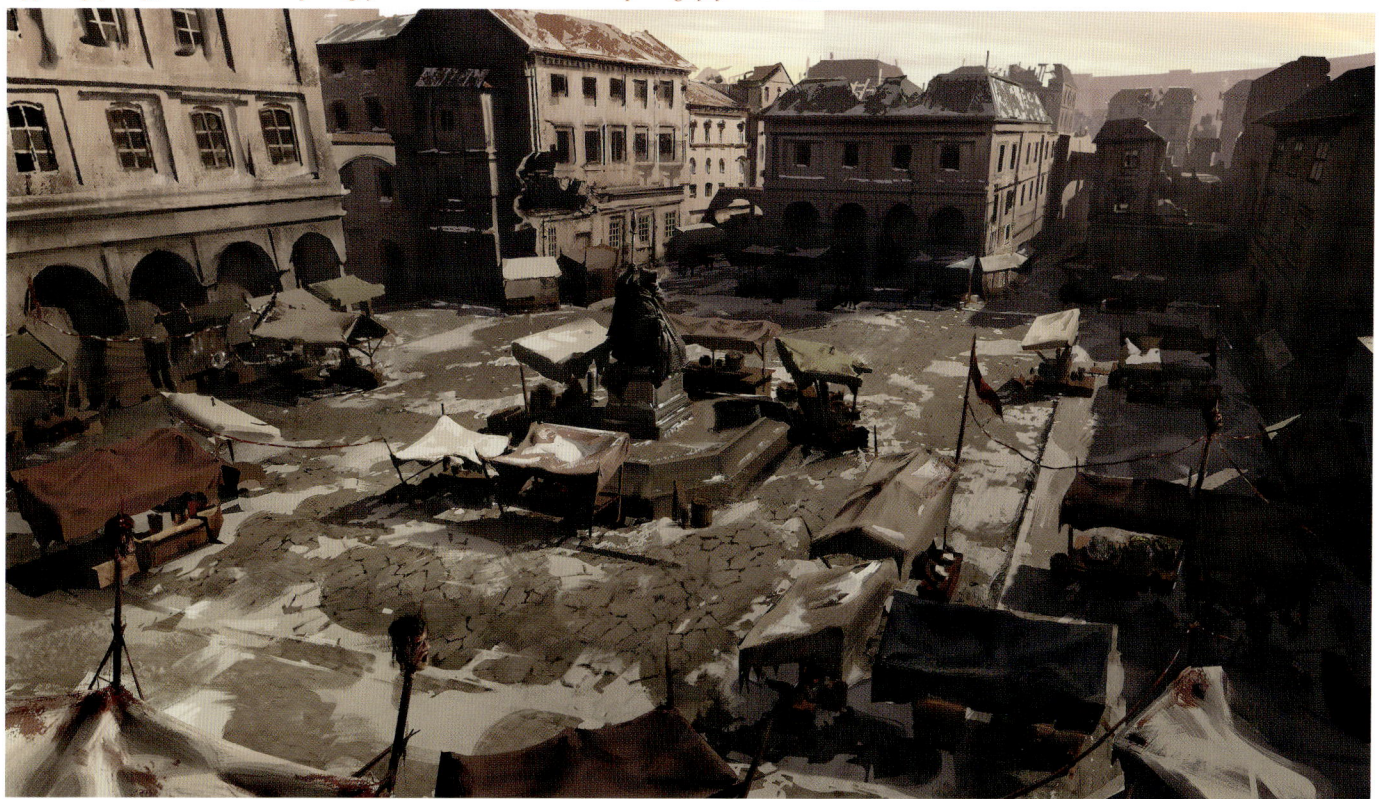

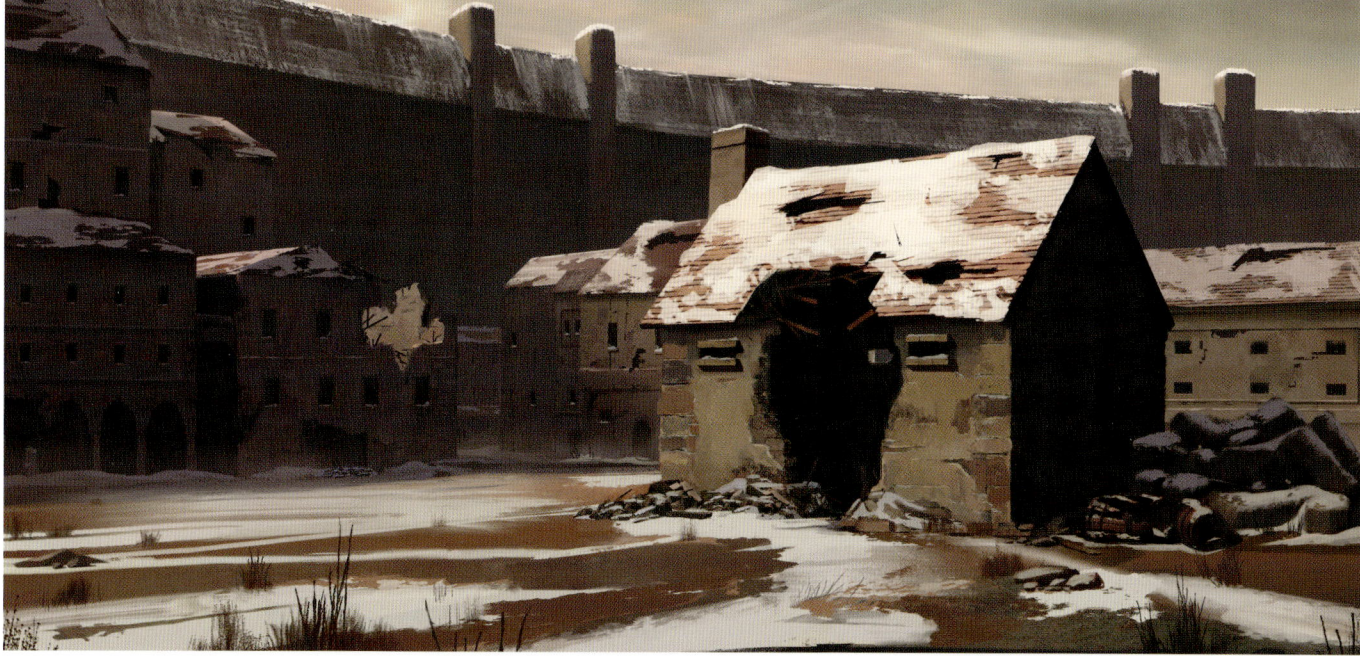

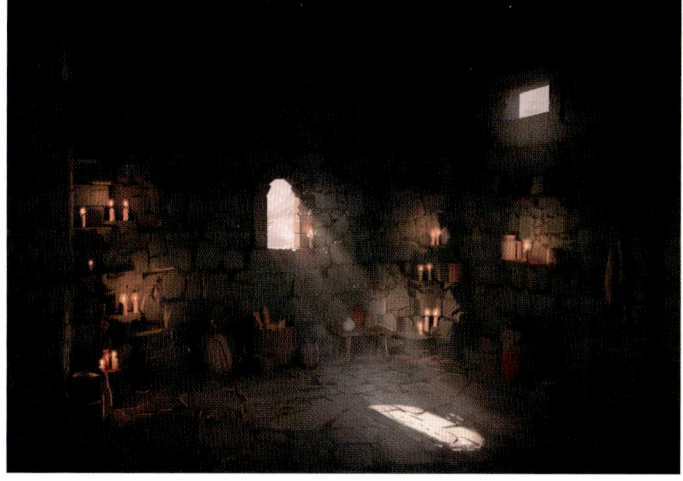
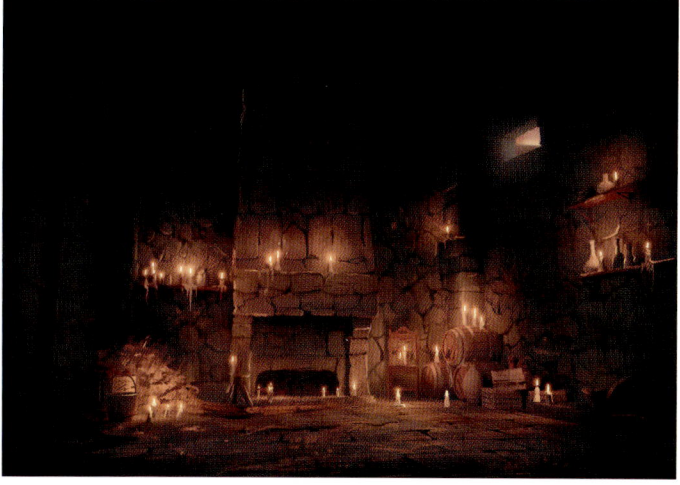

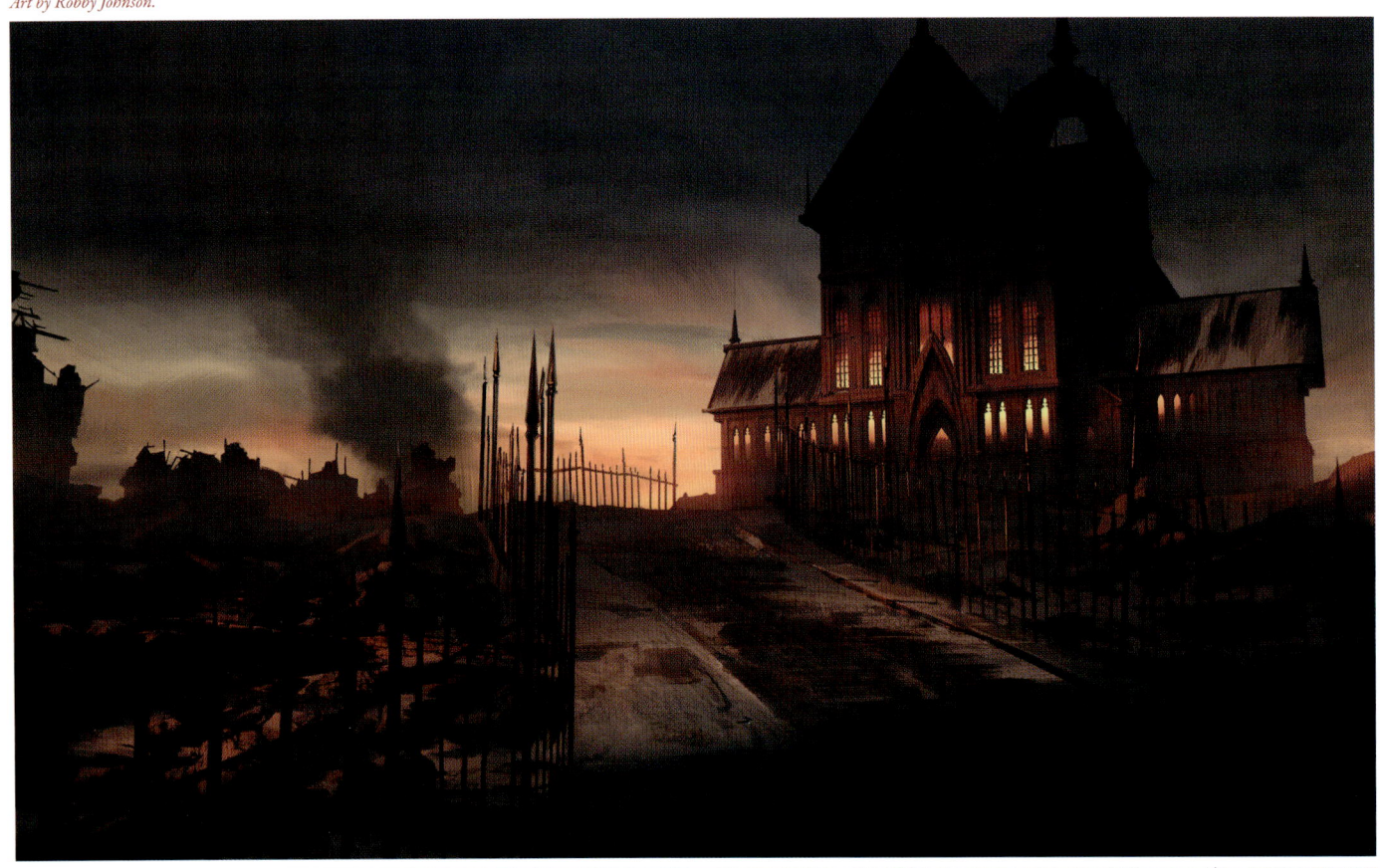

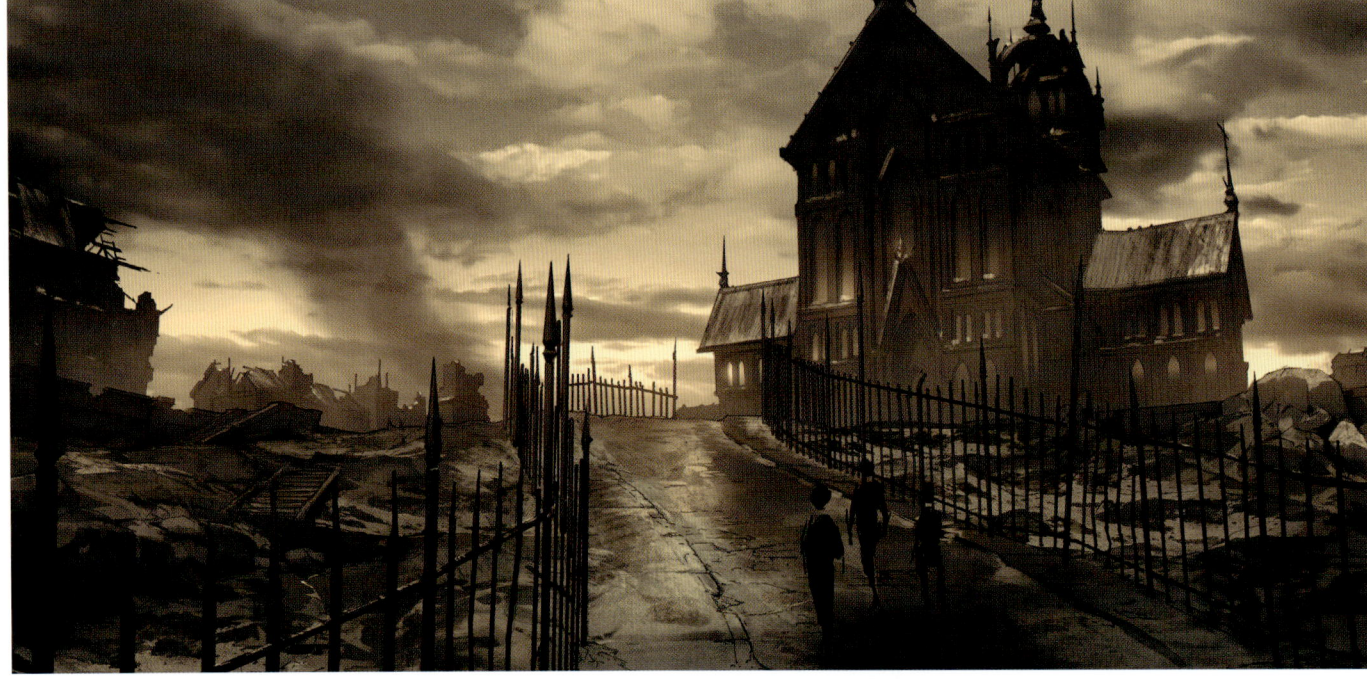

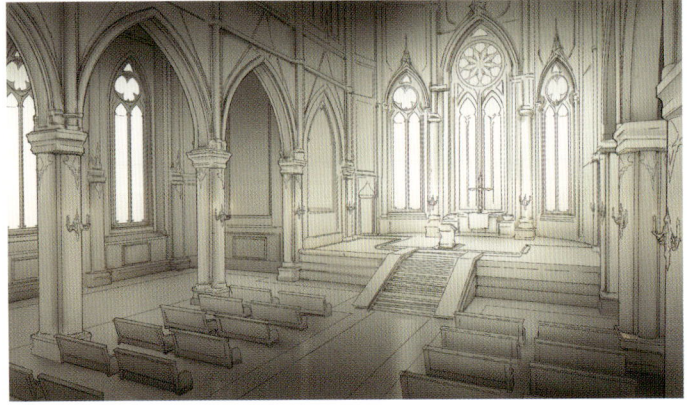

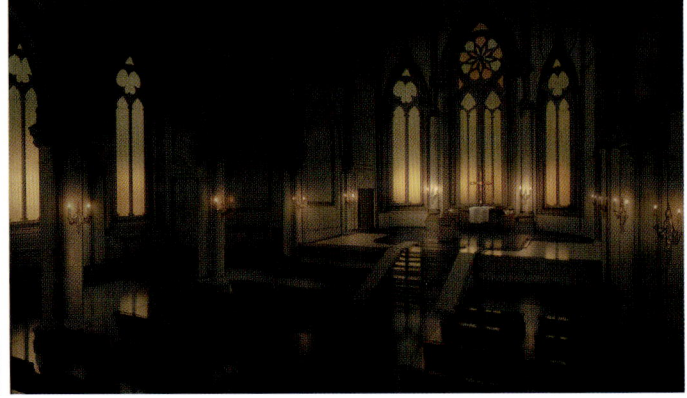

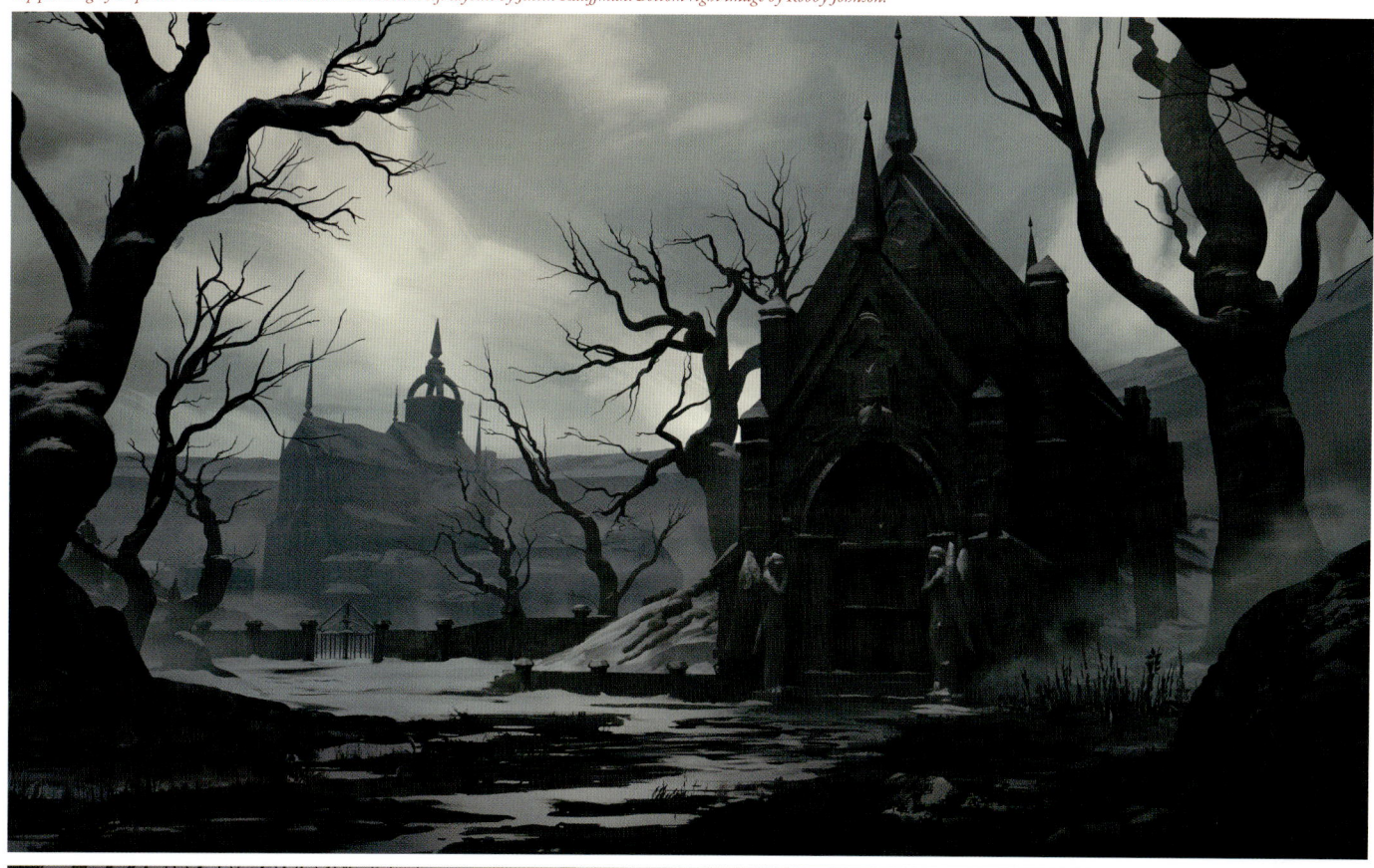

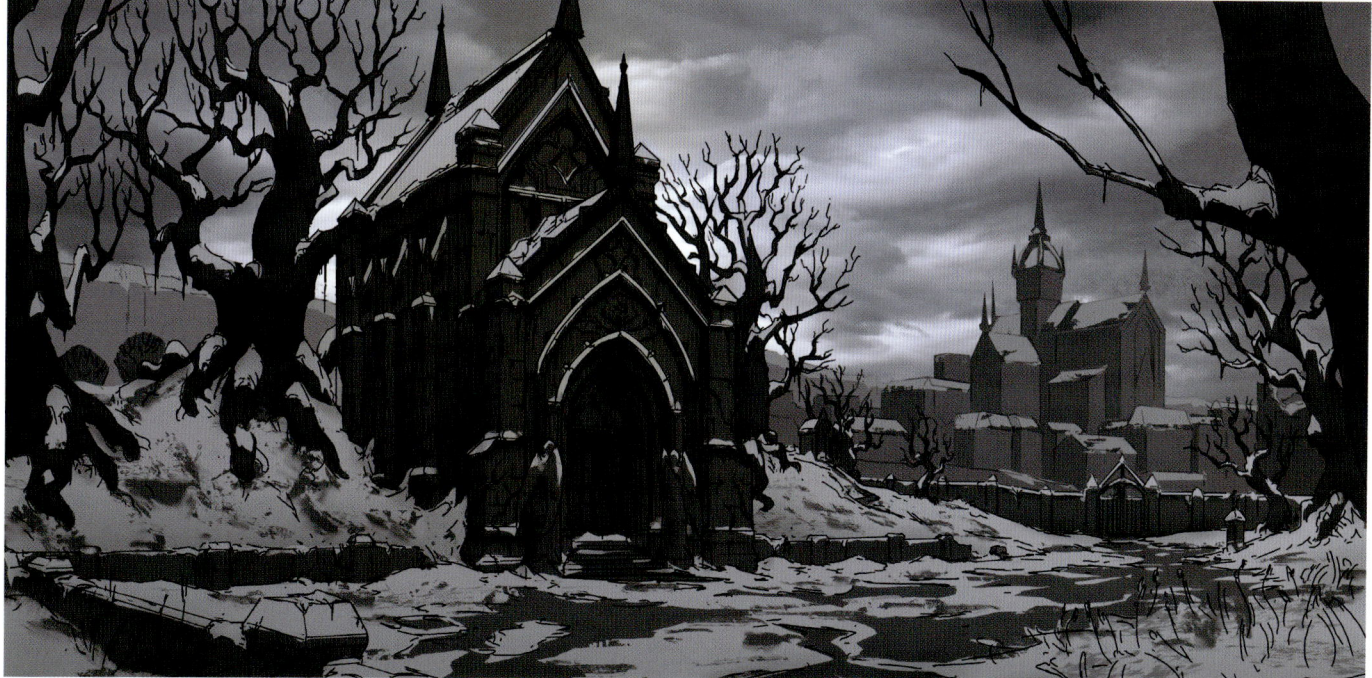

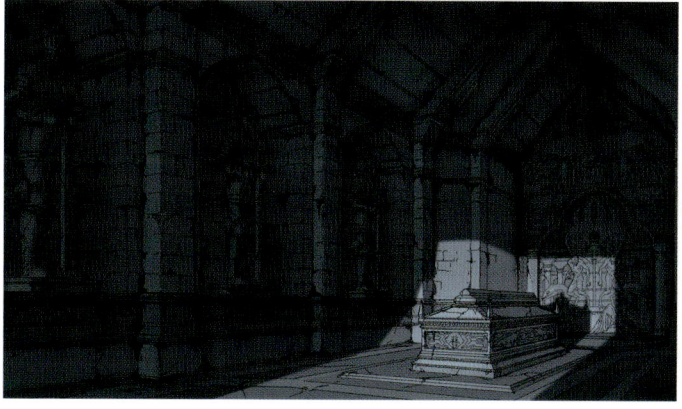
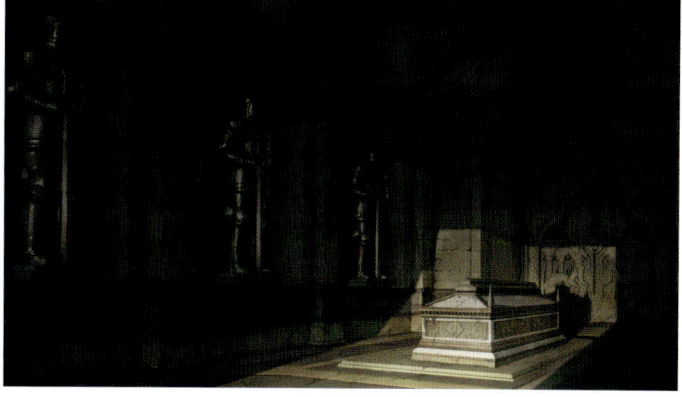

GRESIT UNDERGROUND

Lit by electric light and haunted by a Cyclops, the underground catacombs of Gresit claimed the lives of many who ventured down into them before Trevor.

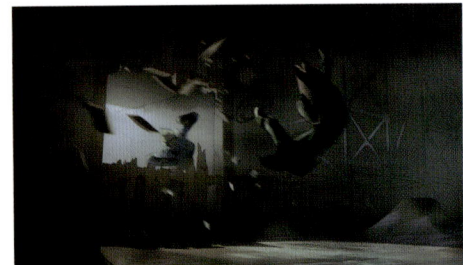
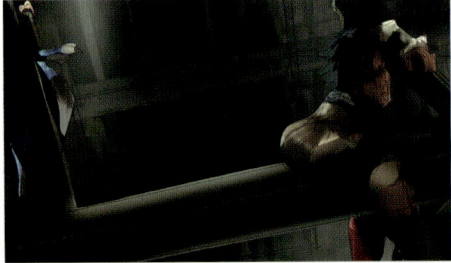
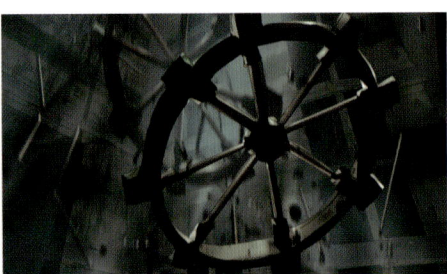

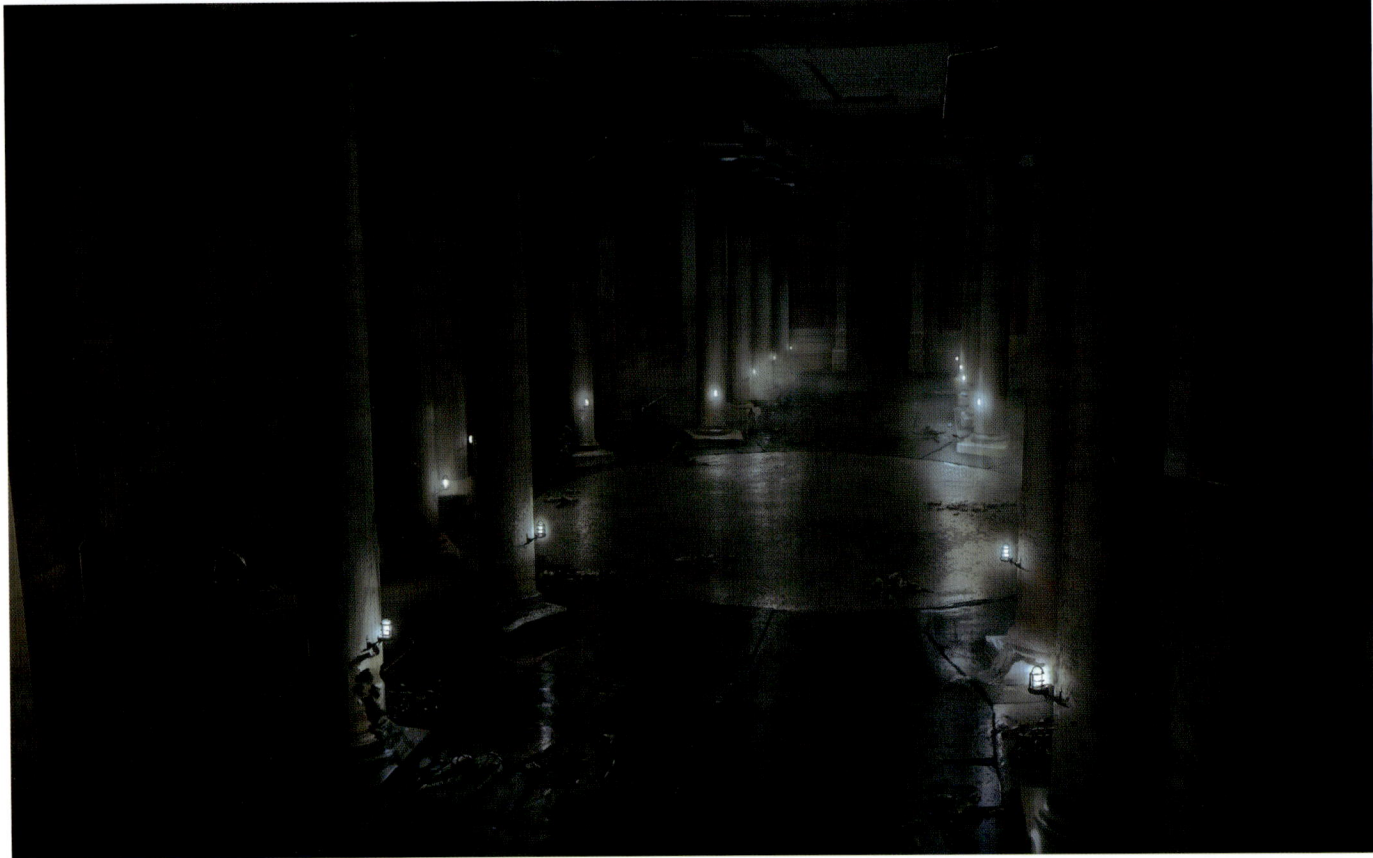

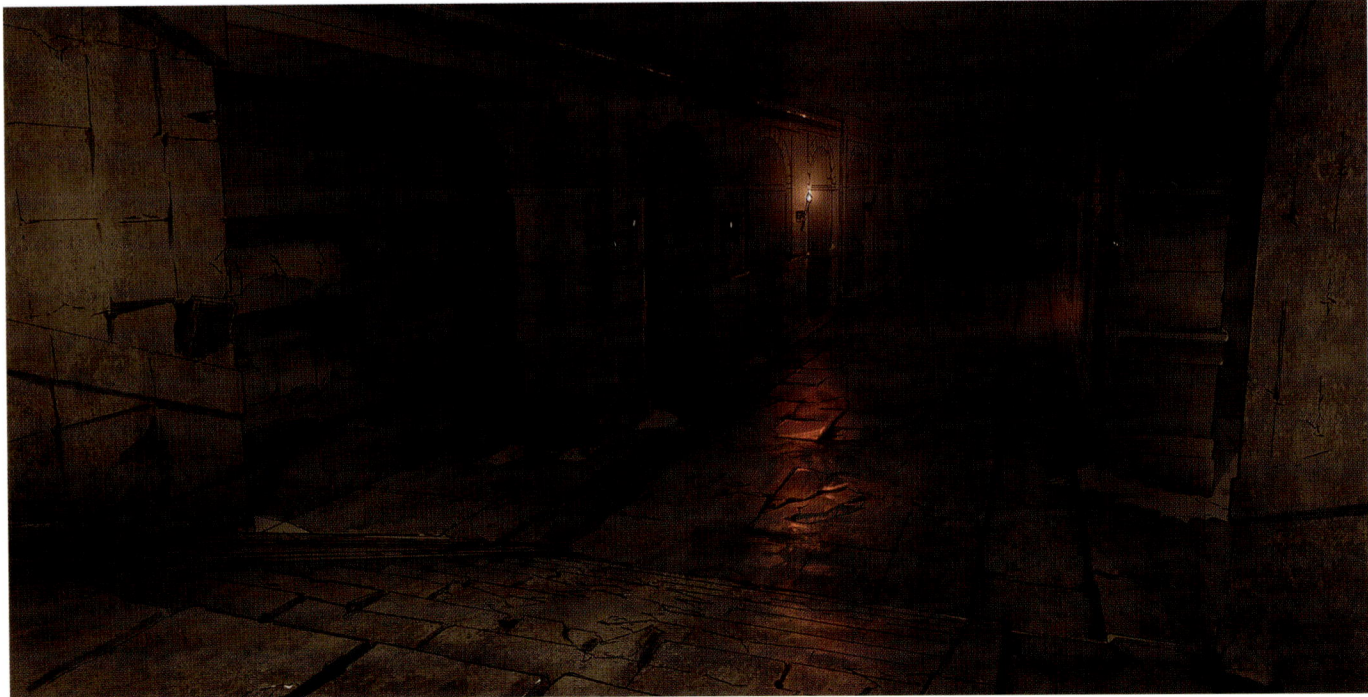

All art on these pages by Robby Johnson.

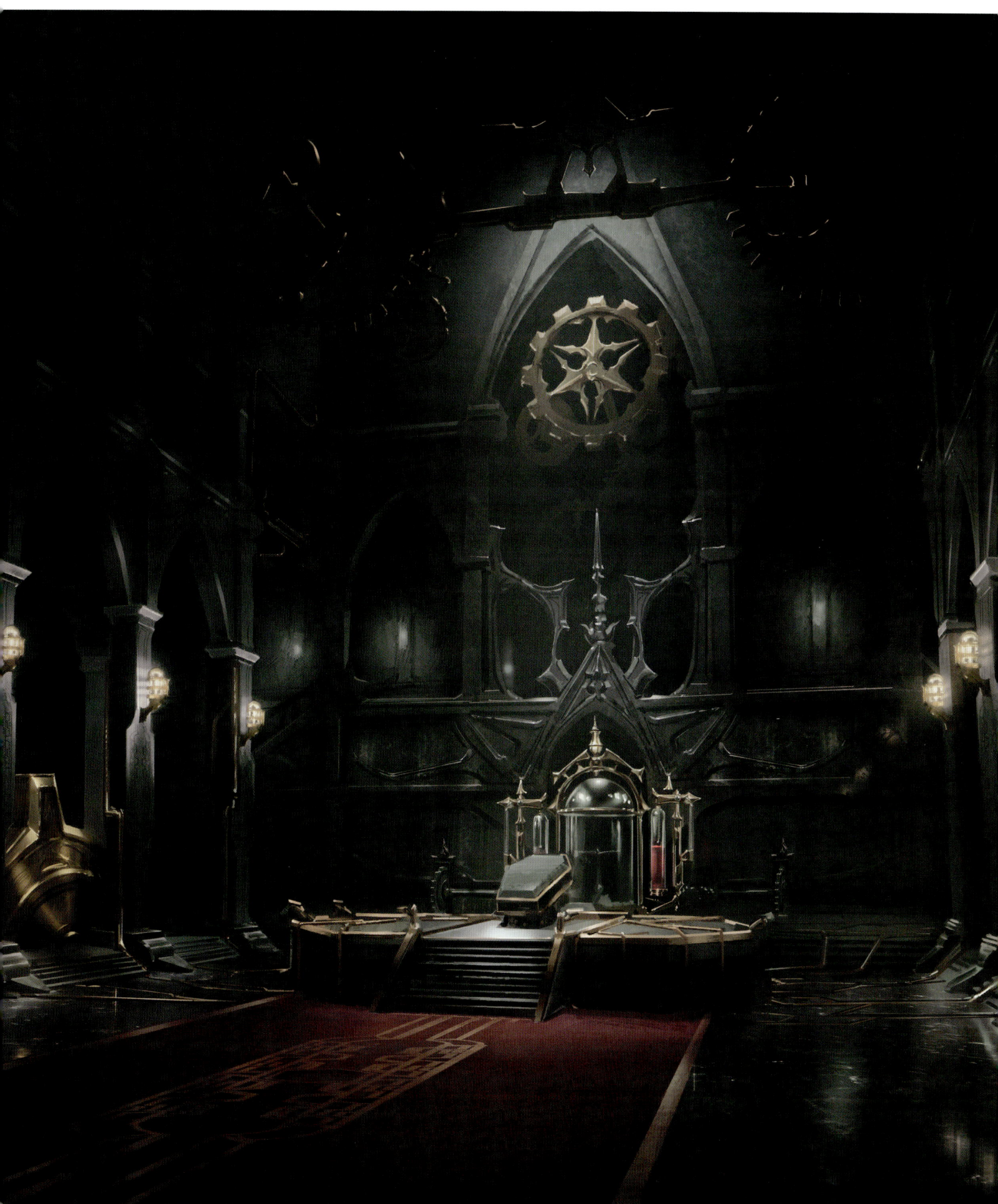

Alucard's subterranean resting chamber under Gresit.

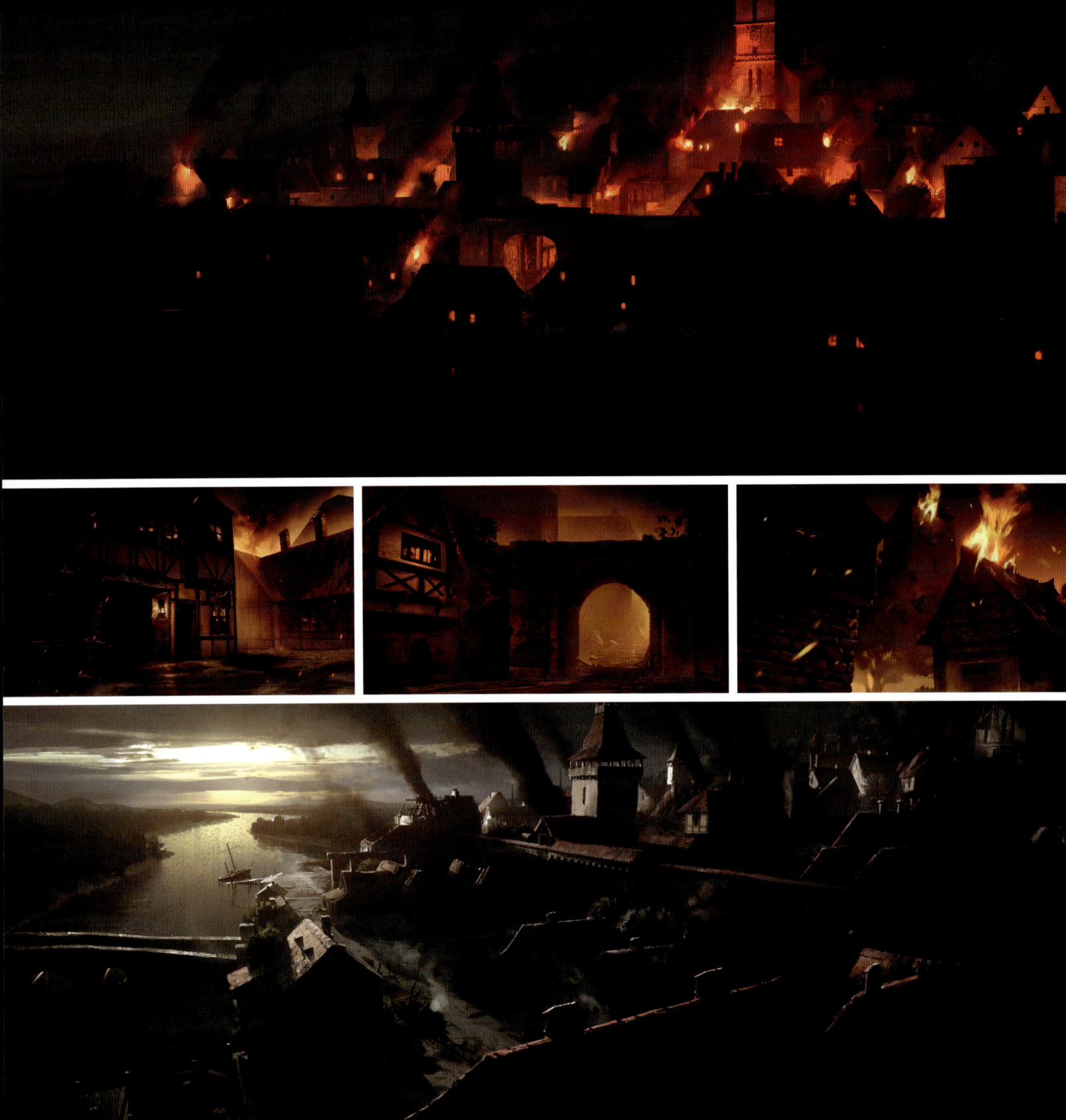

MEDIEVAL TOWN

This unnamed city is seen in a flashback during the season 2 episode "Last Spell," set upon by Dracula and his mysterious robed soldiers. Dracula fondly recalls a time when he relished killing humans, delighting in plotting the details of their grisly torment. Now he admits that he only wishes for the world to be silent.

Cho's Castle

Featured in Taka and Sumi's flashback that detailed Cho's court, these exterior images show a structure steeped in historical Japanese architecture, magnified through a fantasy lens.

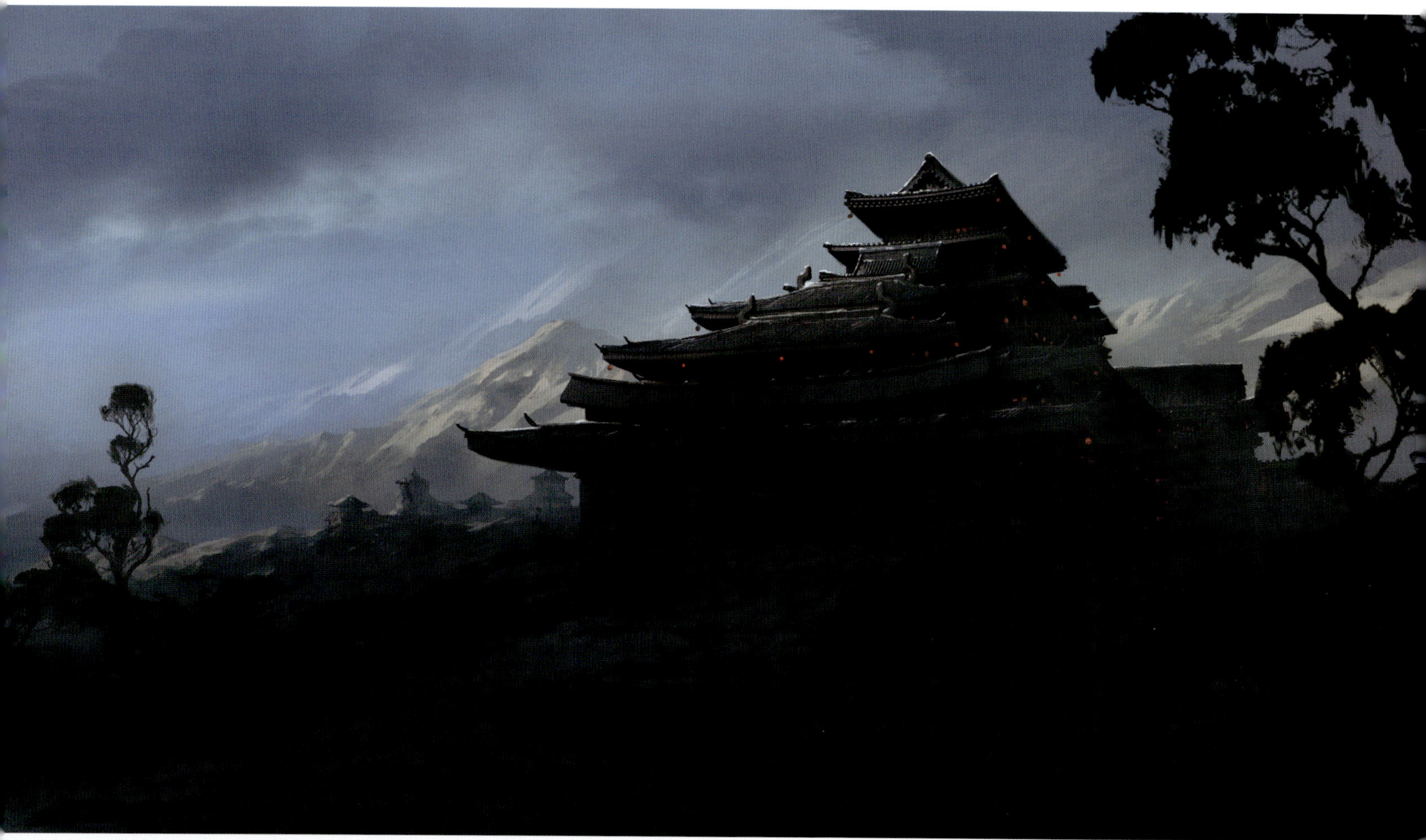

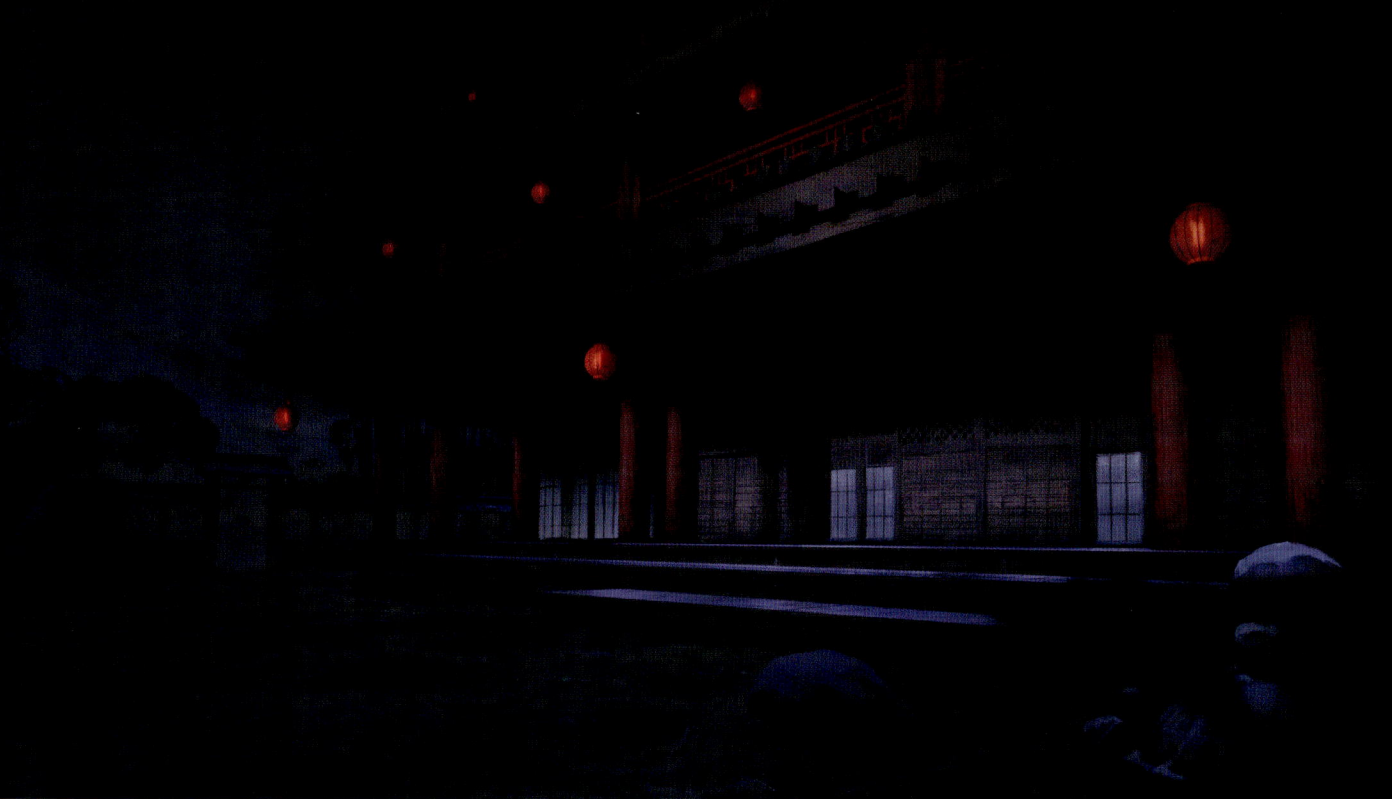

Left page: Top painting by Sean Vo. Middle left painting by Sean Randolph. Middle center painting by Jose Vega. Middle right painting by Stephen Stark. Bottom painting by Sean Vo. Right page: Paintings by Jose Vega.

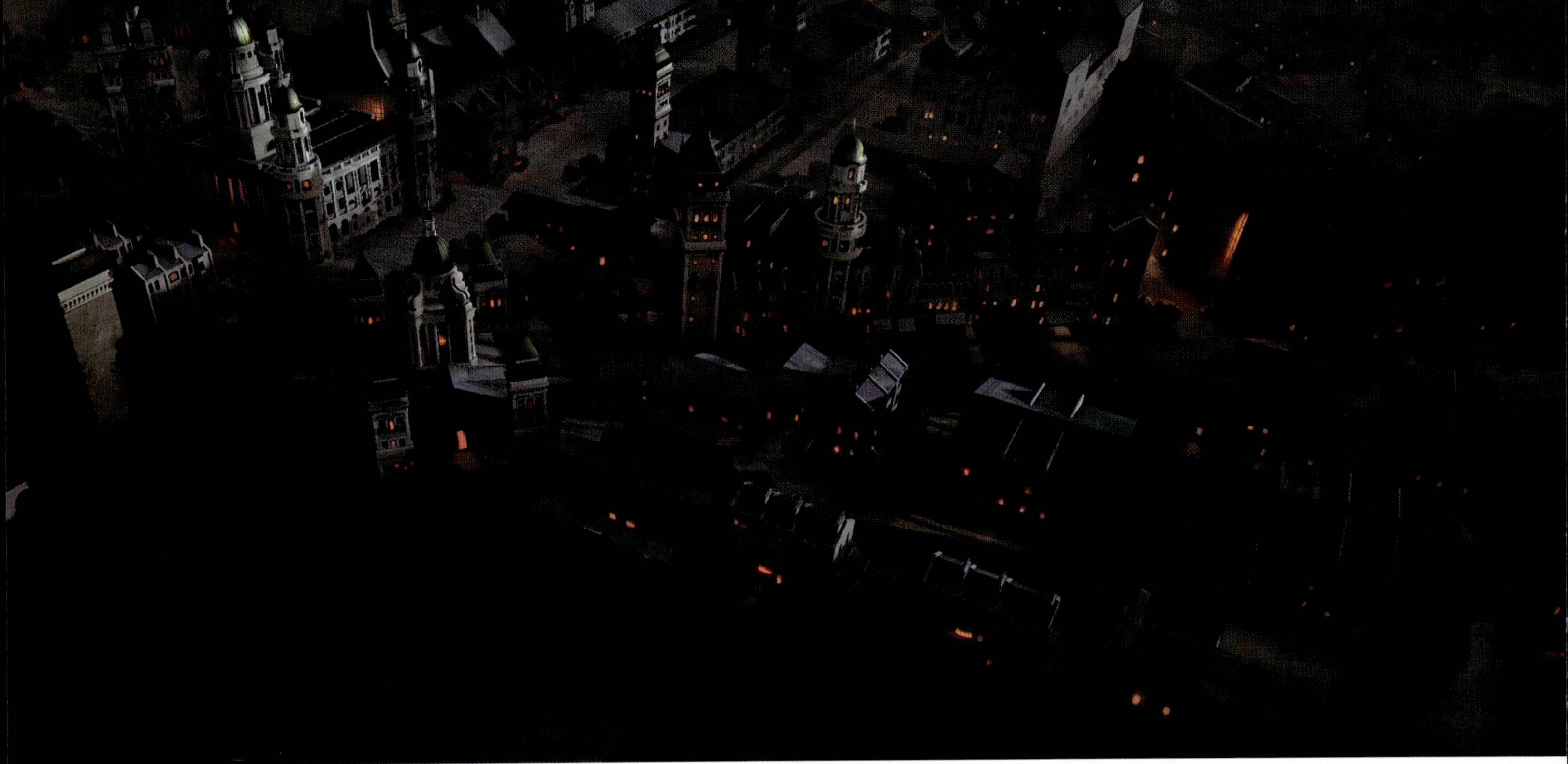

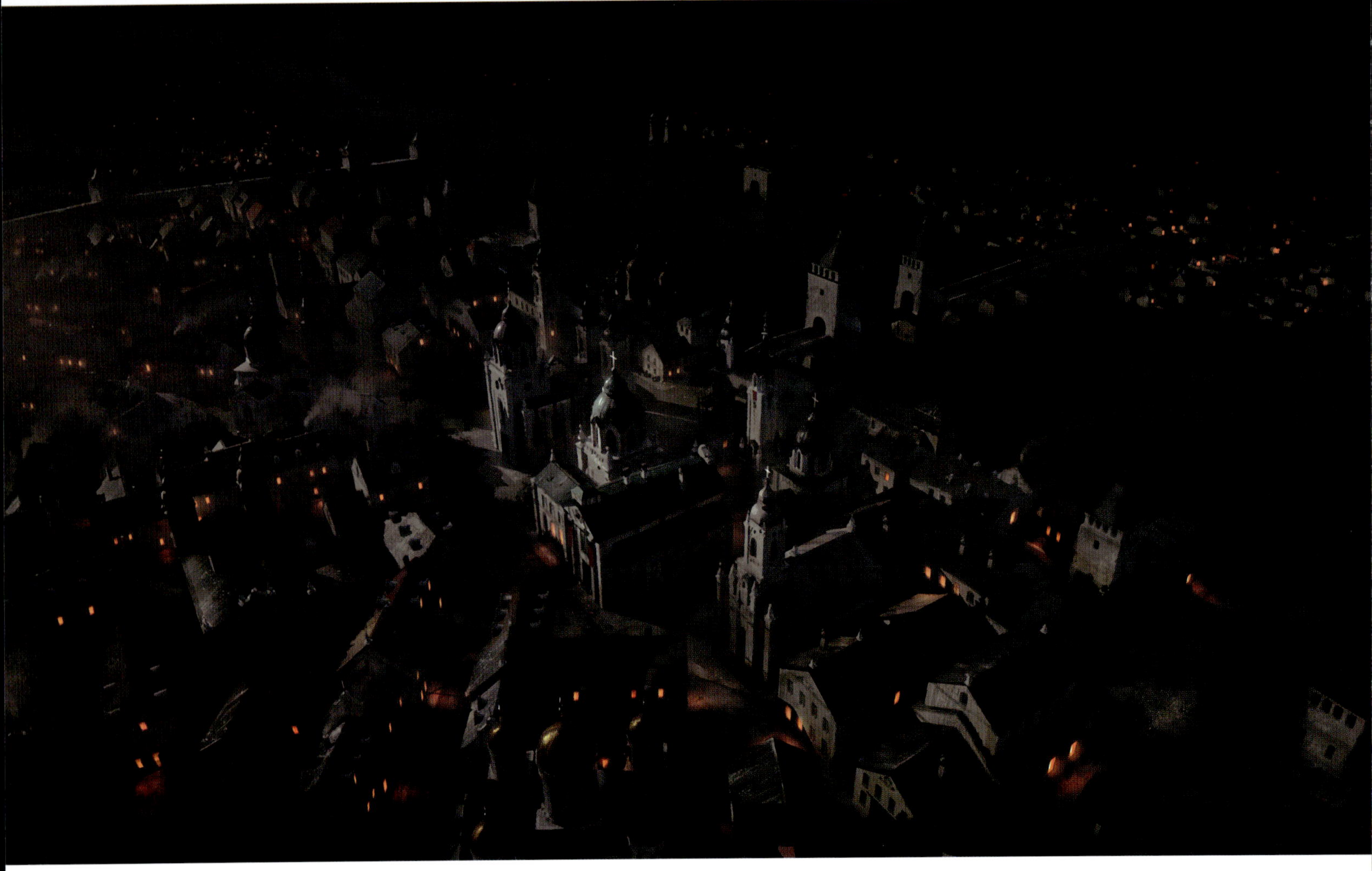

Braila

As a key part of her coup plot, Carmilla convinces Dracula to teleport the castle to Braila, a river town that would allow control over all of Wallachia if captured. Her plan is put into action when the reanimated bishop consecrates the river into holy water, a deadly trap for Dracula's defending army.

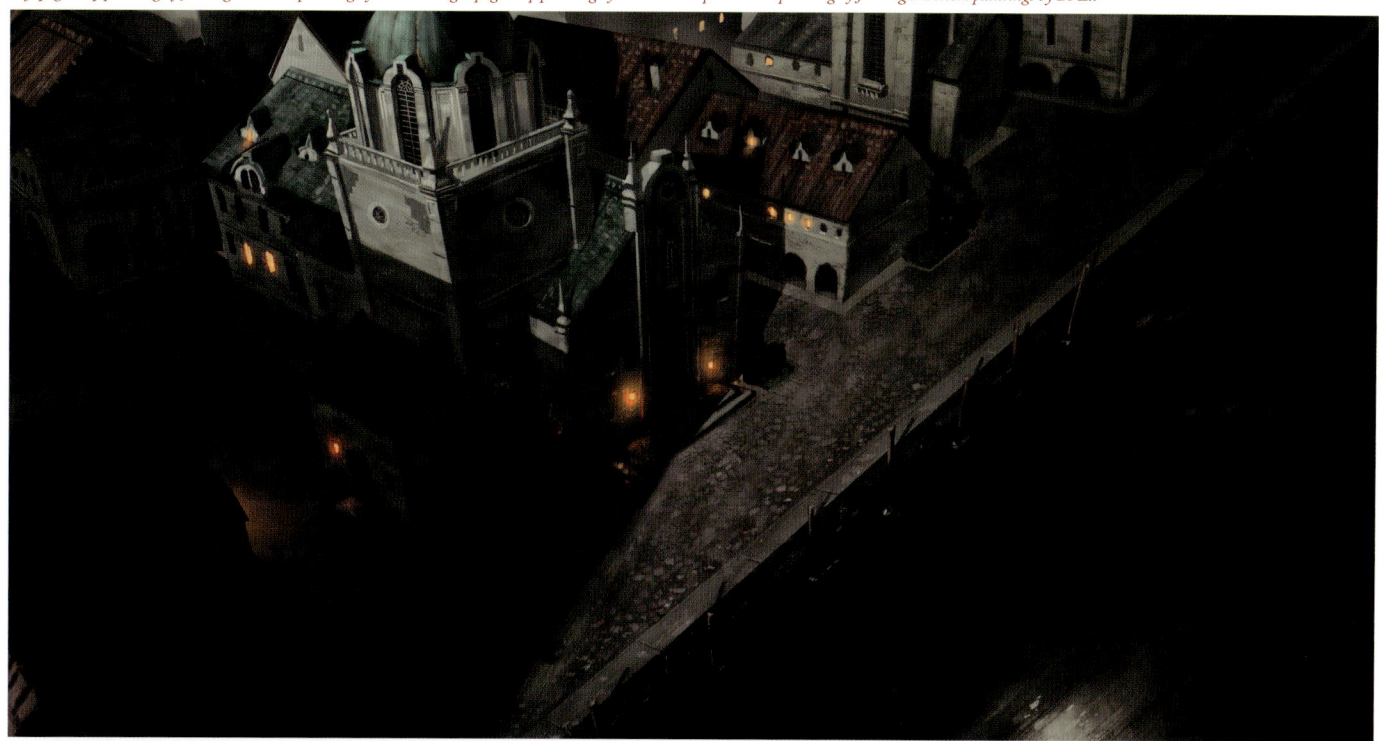

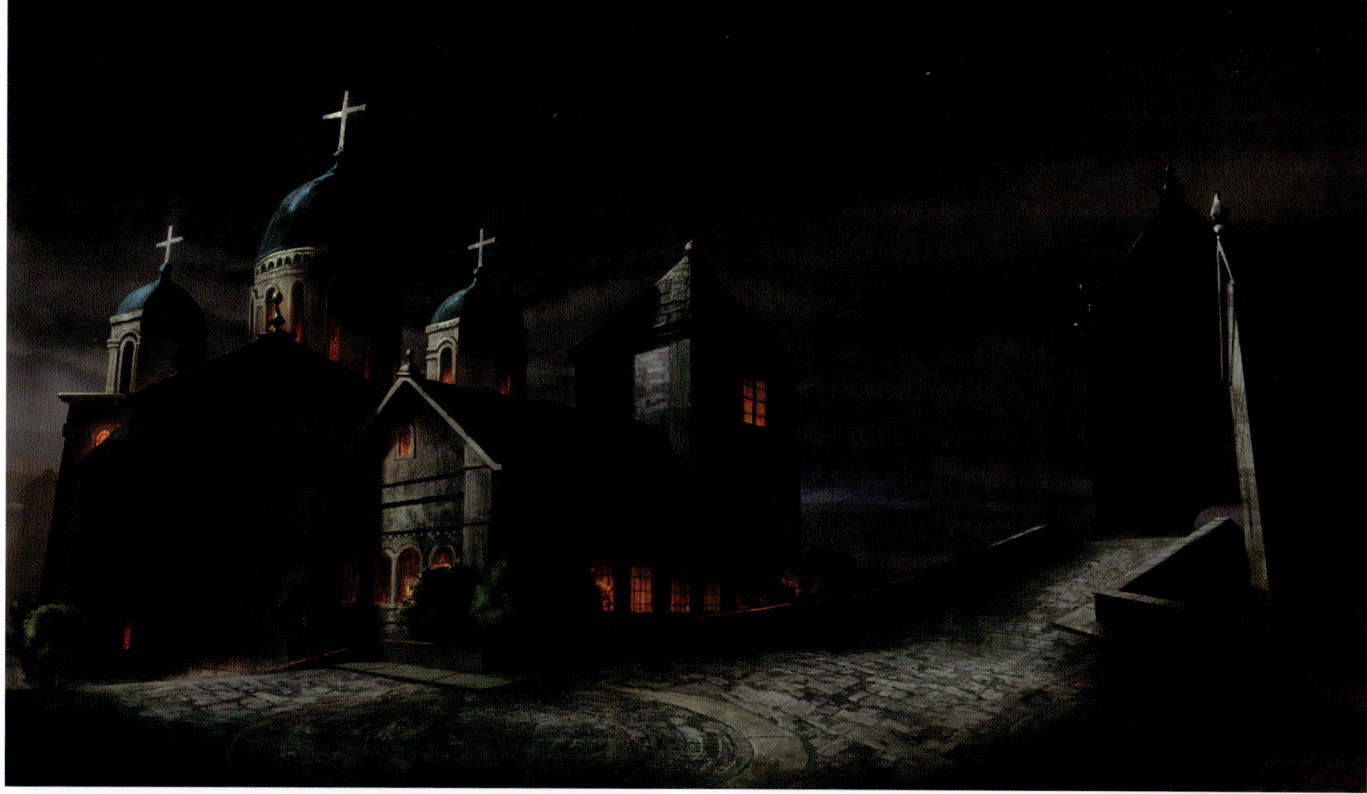

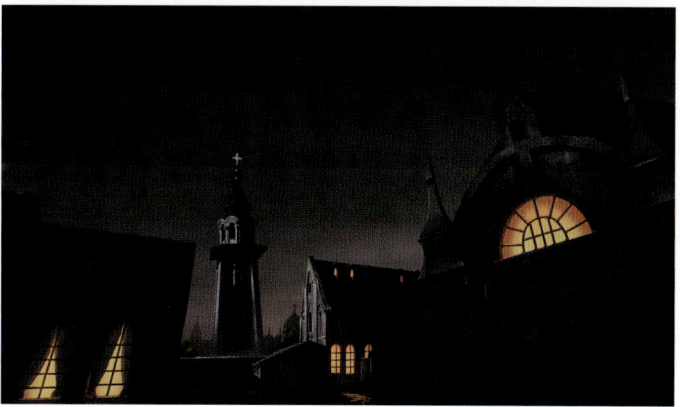

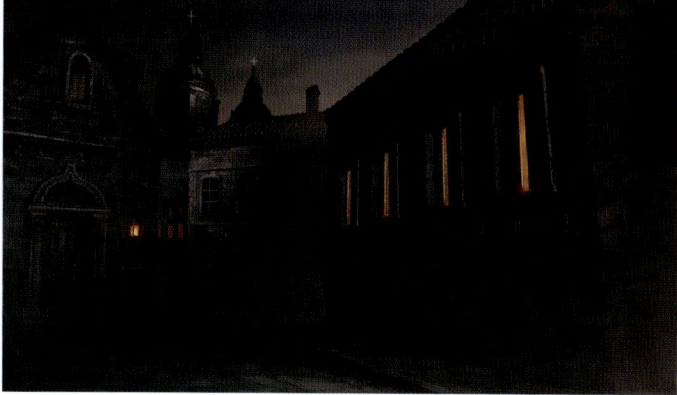

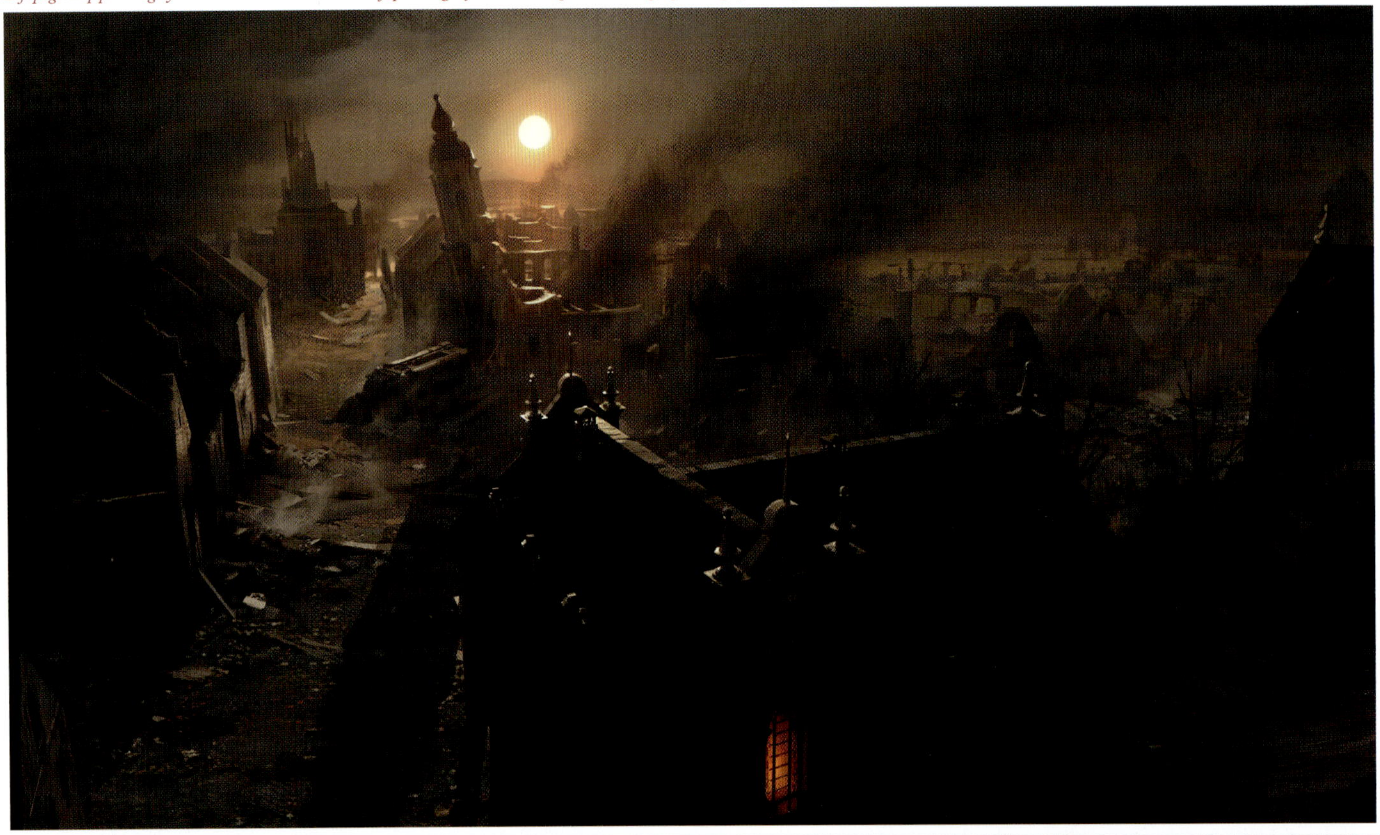

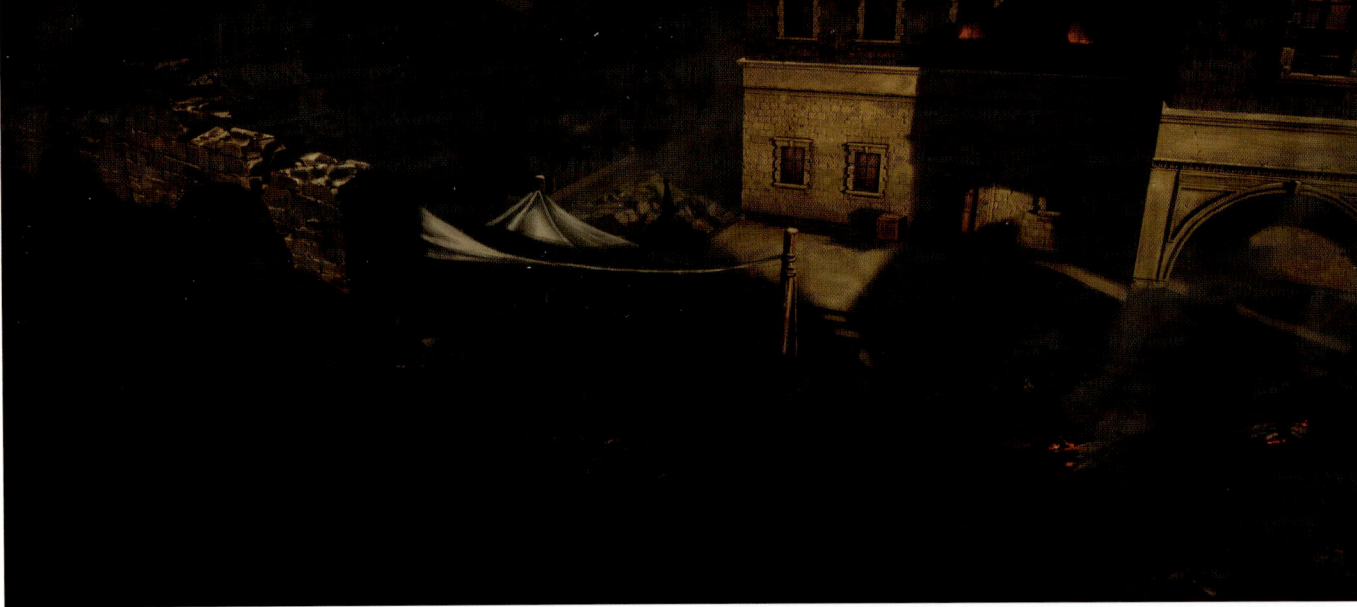

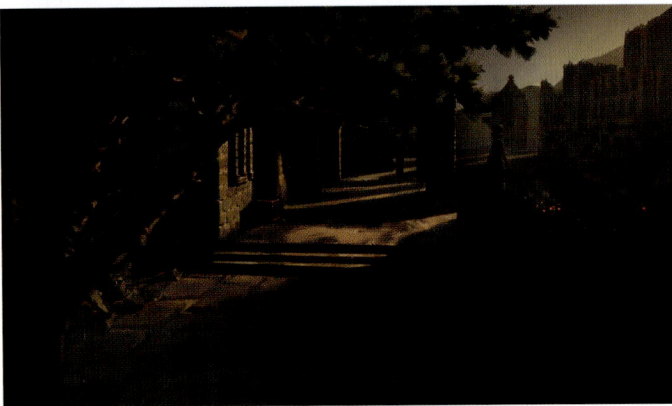

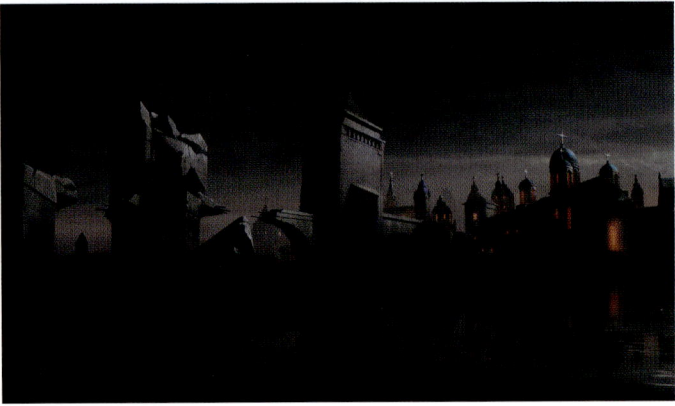

Sypha struggles with the magic needed to take control over the teleportation of Dracula's castle from afar. The castle causes great destruction across Braila as it blinks in and out of existence in various locations through the town.

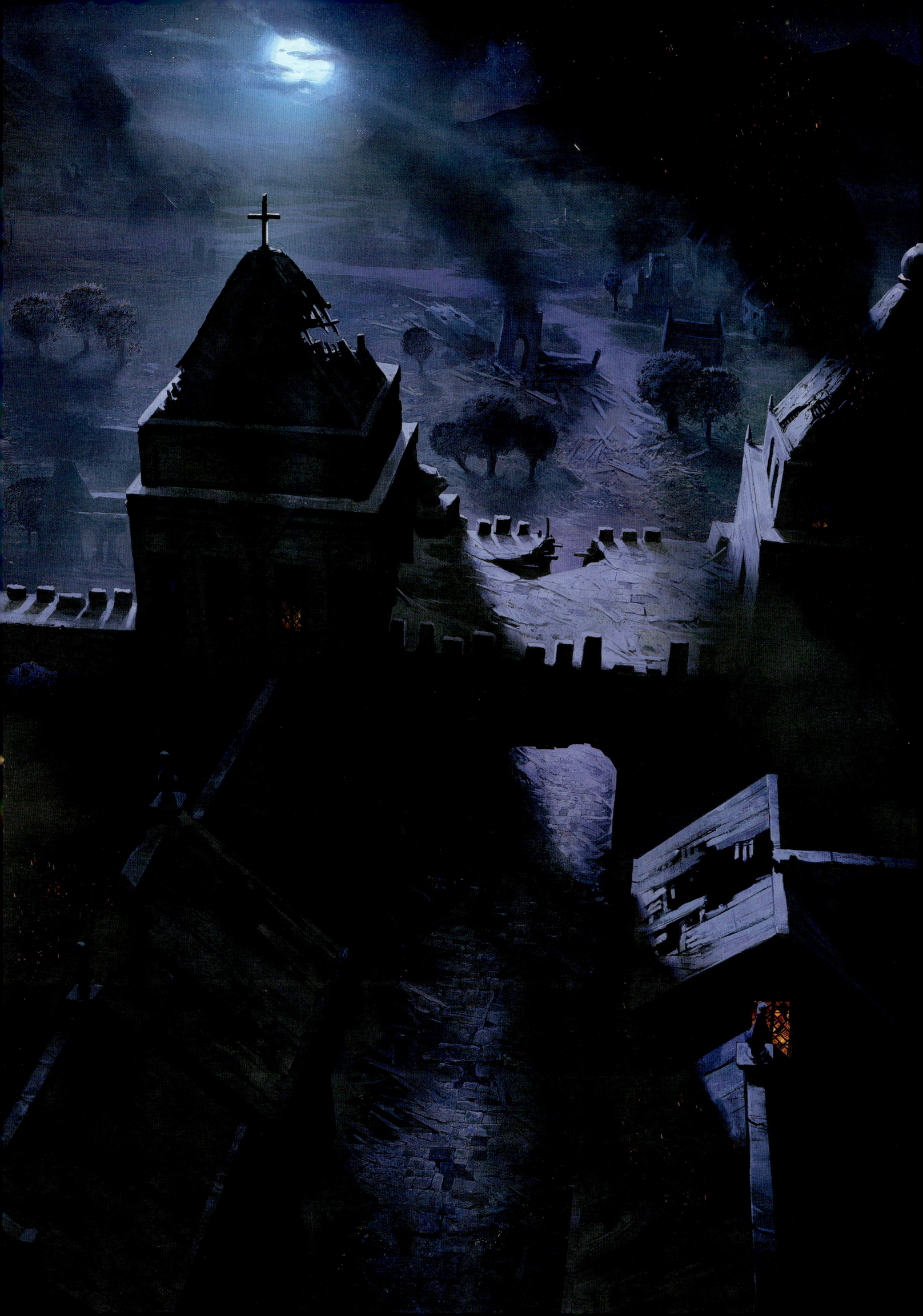

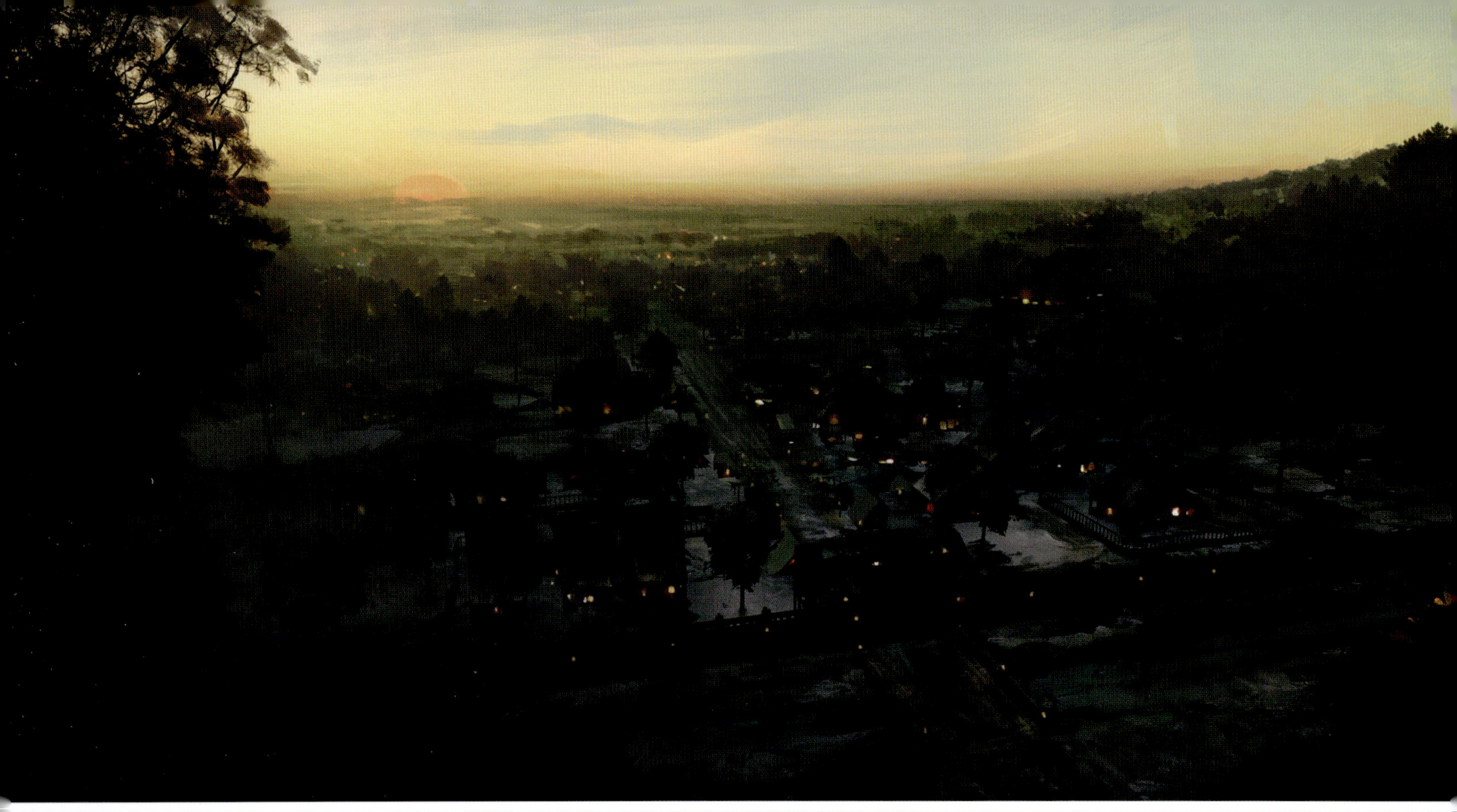

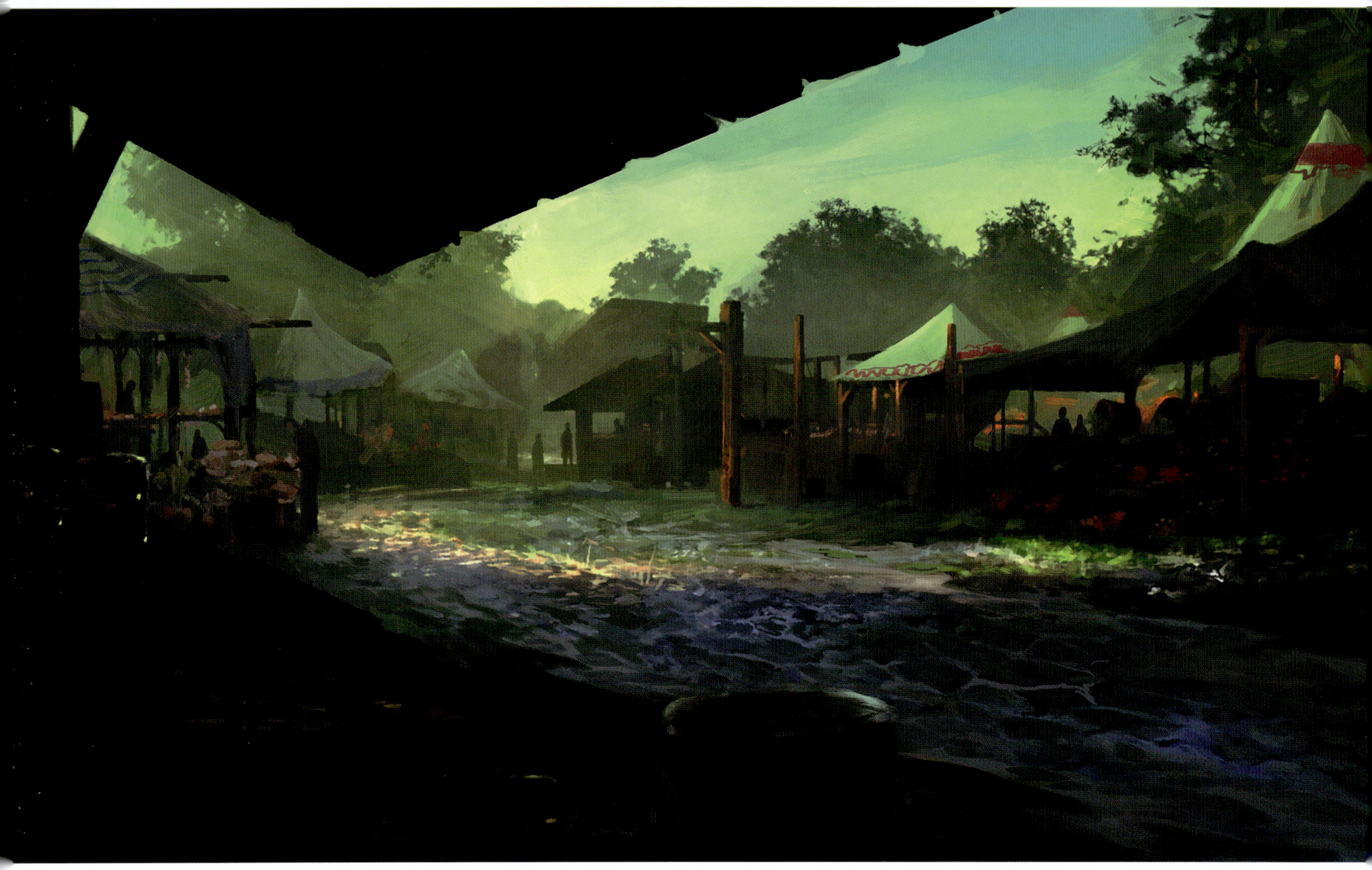

Lindenfeld

After an almost lighthearted romp through the countryside, slaying night creatures with ease as they go, Sypha and Trevor arrive at the small town of Lindenfeld, where they meet Saint Germain, Sala, the cultists, and the judge. Soon this quiet village begins to reveal its secrets.

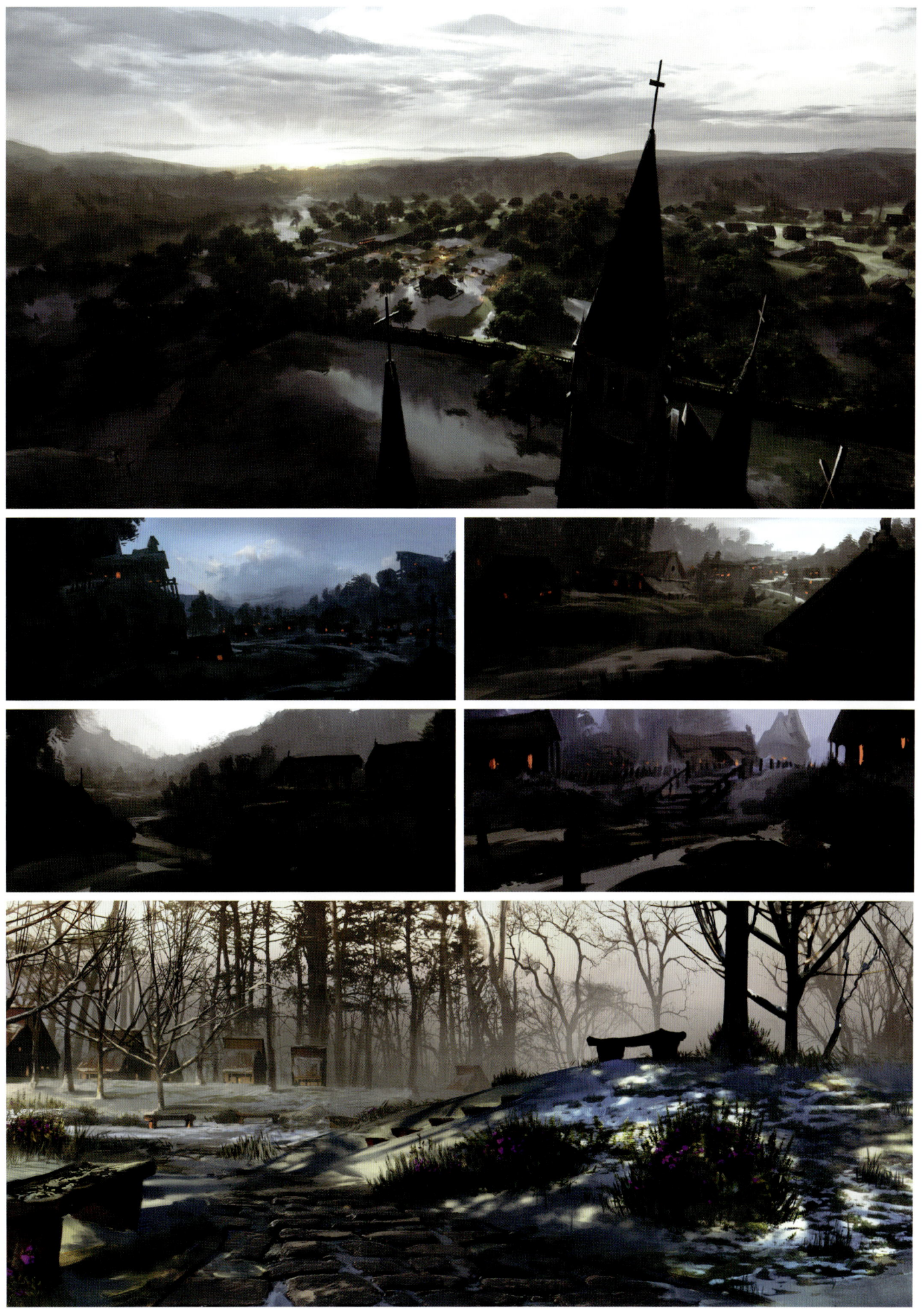

All art on these pages by Jose Vega.

Tranquil scenes around the sleepy Lindenfeld markets, pub, and inns do not outwardly betray the town's murderous judge, demon-worshiping cult, or giant Beast chained over a portal to the Infinite Corridor in the priory basement.

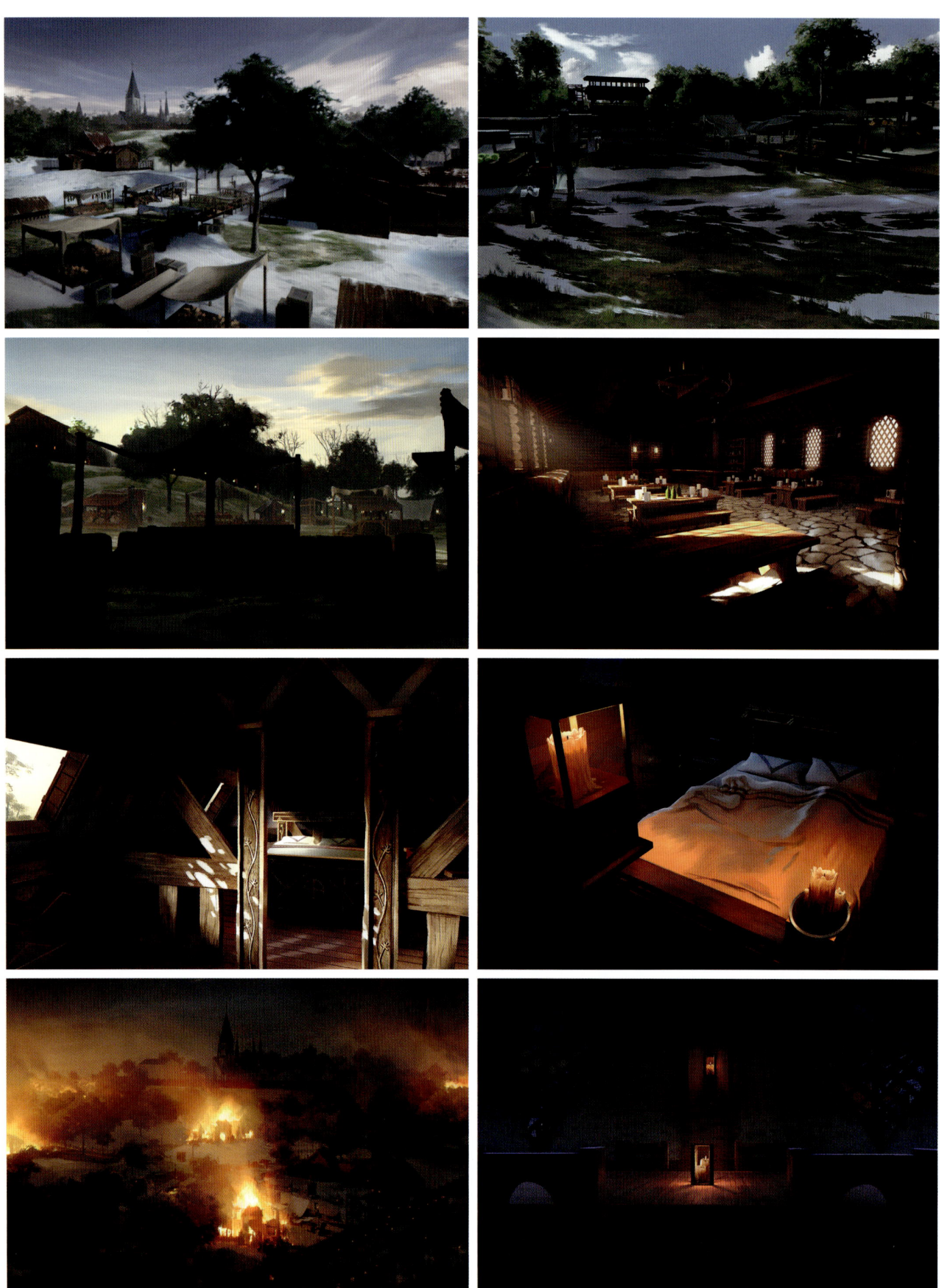

First row paintings by Sean Randolph (left) and Bo Li (right). Second row paintings by Jose Vega (left) and Bo Li (right). Third row paintings by Bo Li. Fourth row paintings by Jose Vega.

THE JUDGE'S HOUSE

Designed as a place of importance and solitude, the judge's house allowed him a space to reminisce about all of the people he sent to fall into his special spiked pit trap just outside of town.

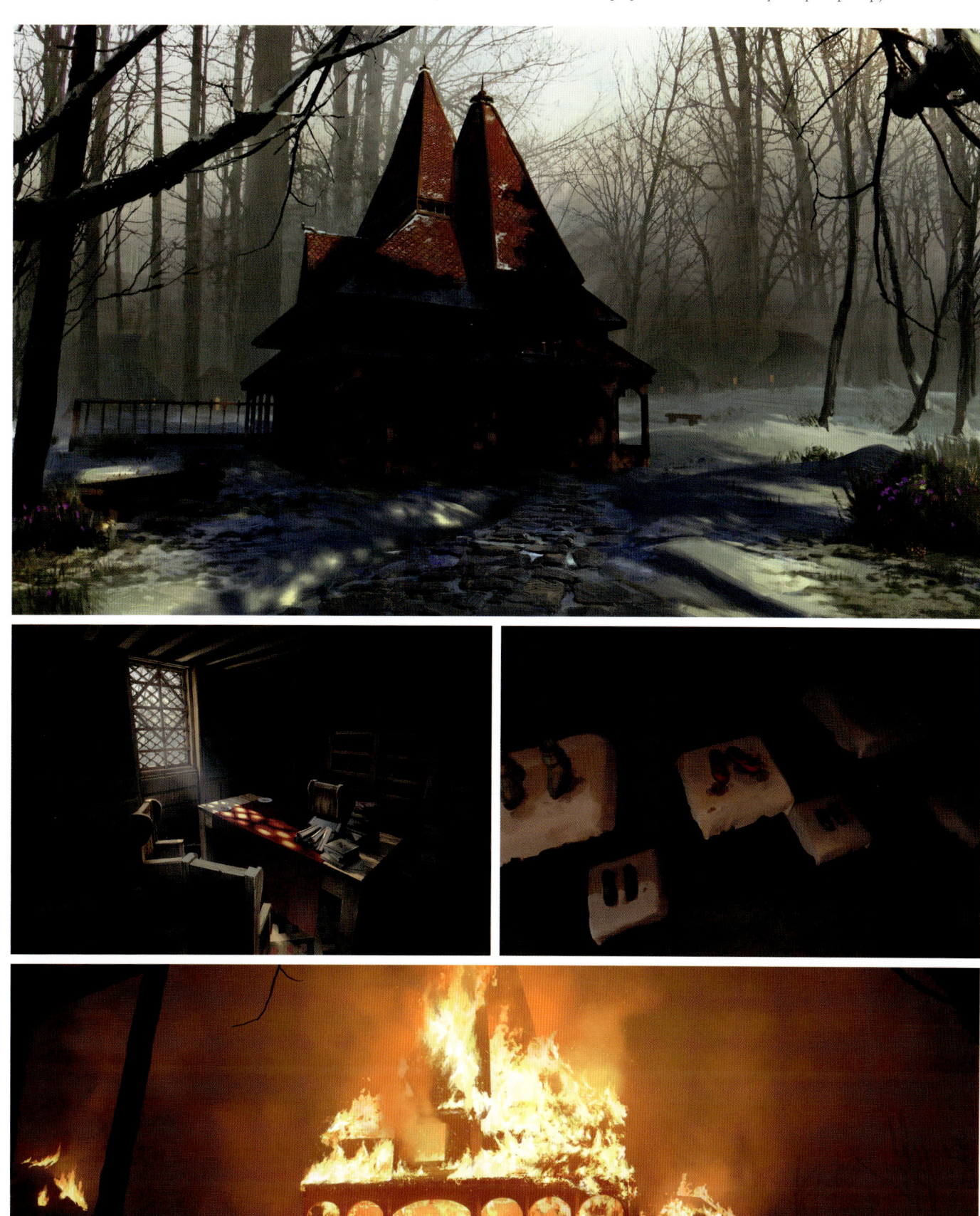

Top painting by Jose Vega. Middle left painting by Bo Li. Middle right painting by Jose Vega. Bottom painting by Stephen Stark.

LINDENFELD PRIORY

The home base of Sala and the cultists, the priory has been defiled with filth and occult markings by the followers of the Beast, who believe they are doing Dracula's will.

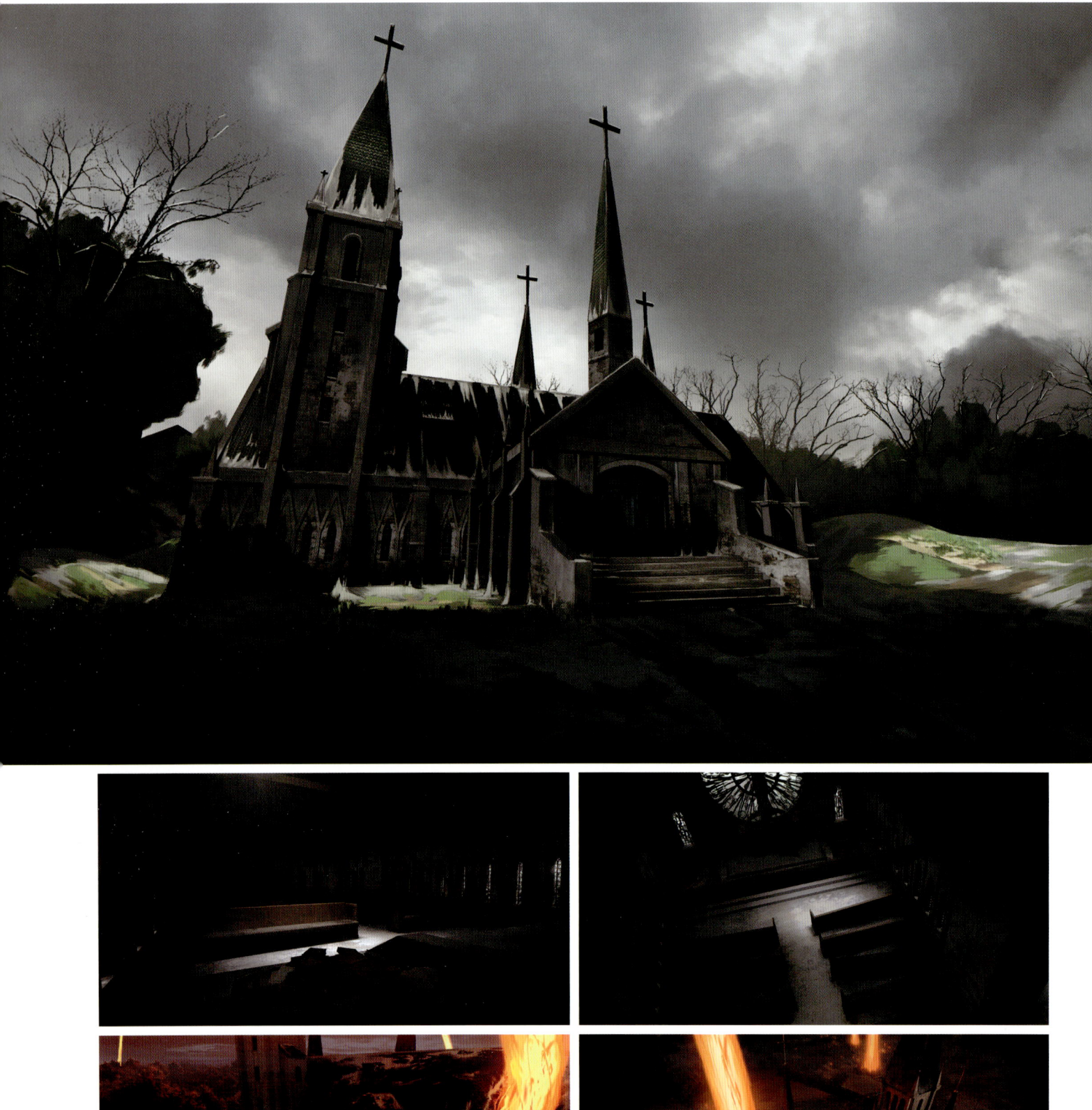

Top painting by Bo Li. Middle and bottom left paintings by Jose Vega. Bottom right painting by Sean Randolph.

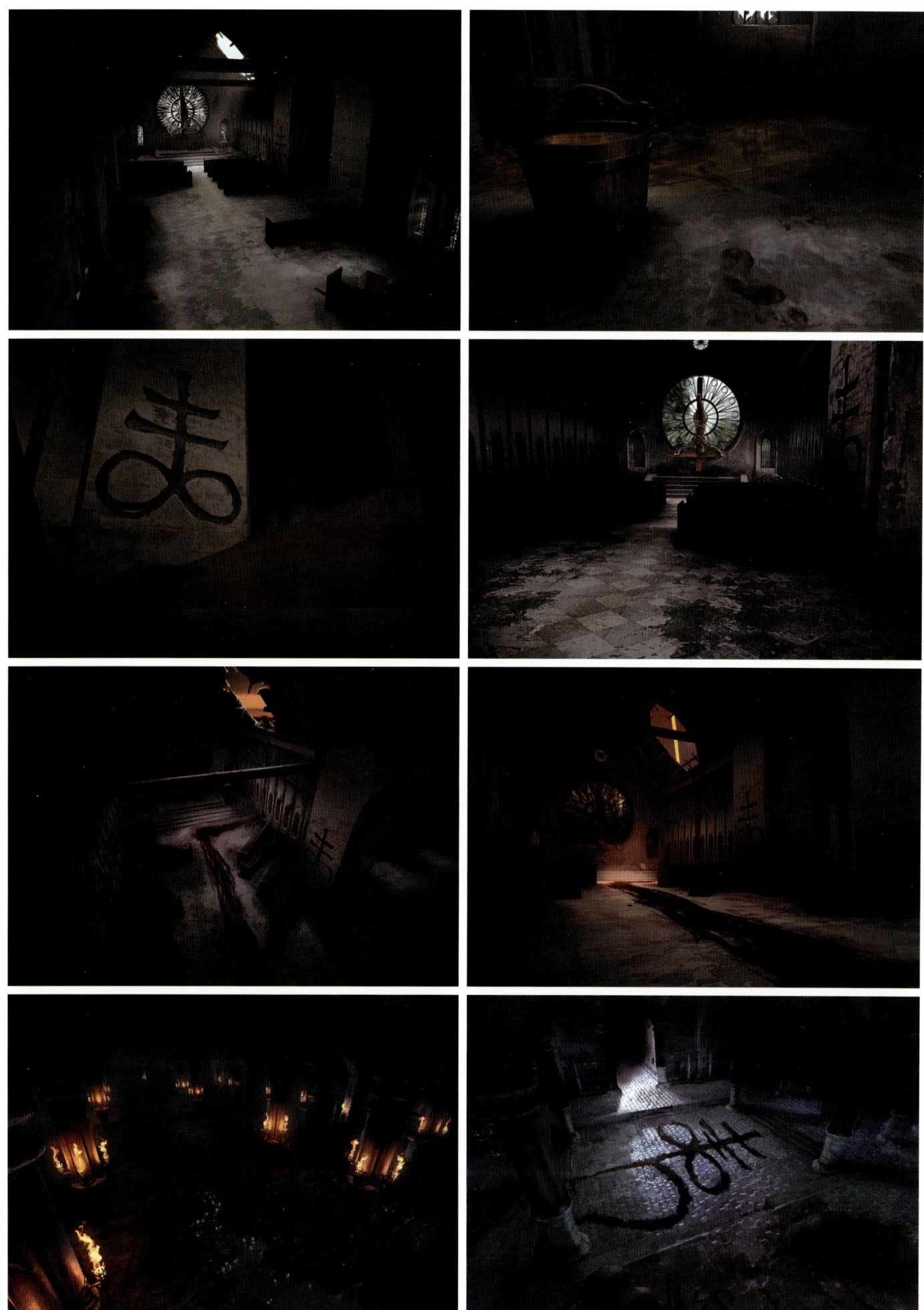

Paintings by Jose Vega.

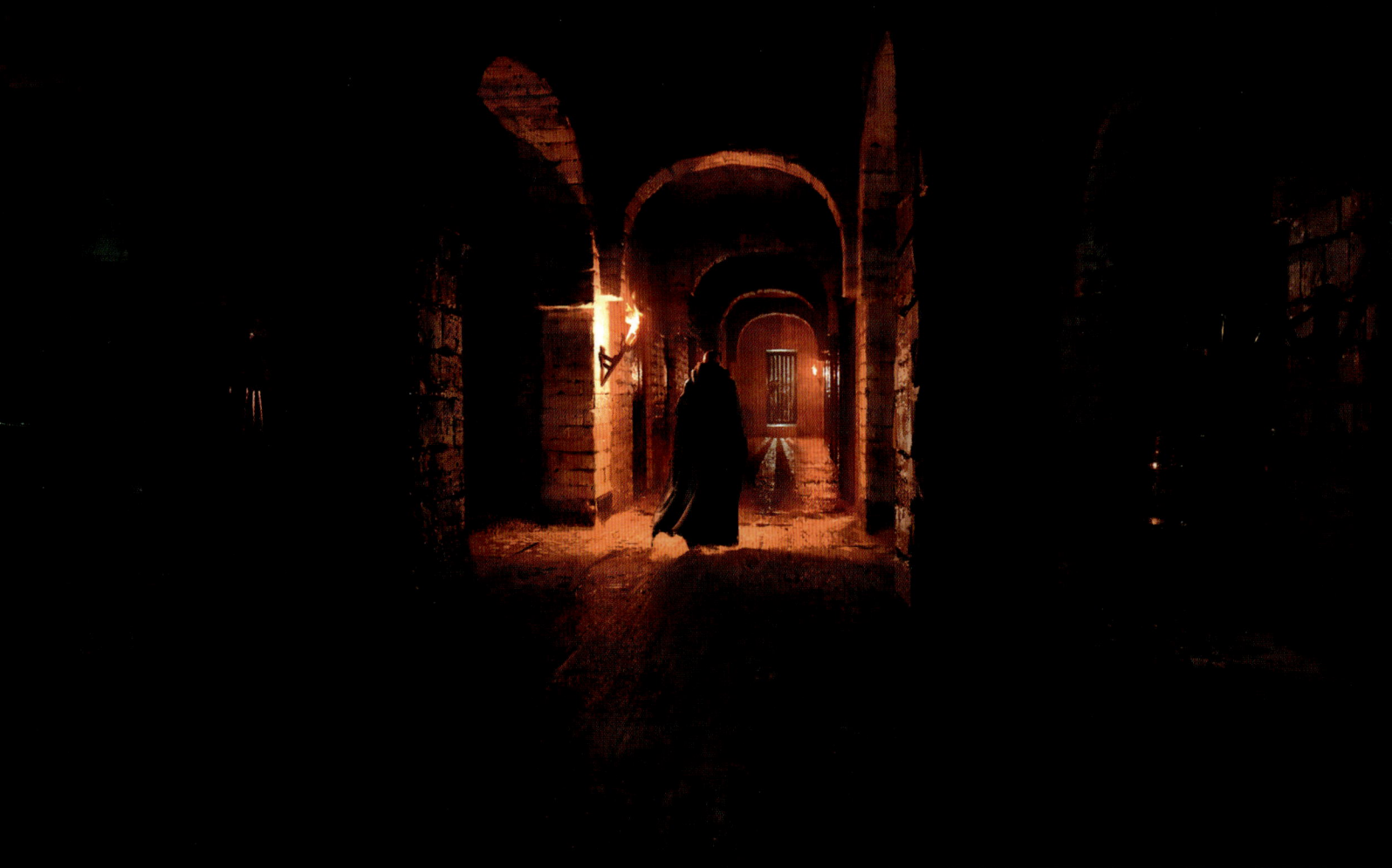

The Desert

Above are depictions of Isaac's Desert Keep, where he lived before Dracula recruited him. Transported to the North African desert by Dracula later, Isaac is saved from inevitably fighting to the death alongside his vampire ruler. Here, at an oasis, Isaac begins to build his own night creature horde from the corpses of all who foolishly get in his way.

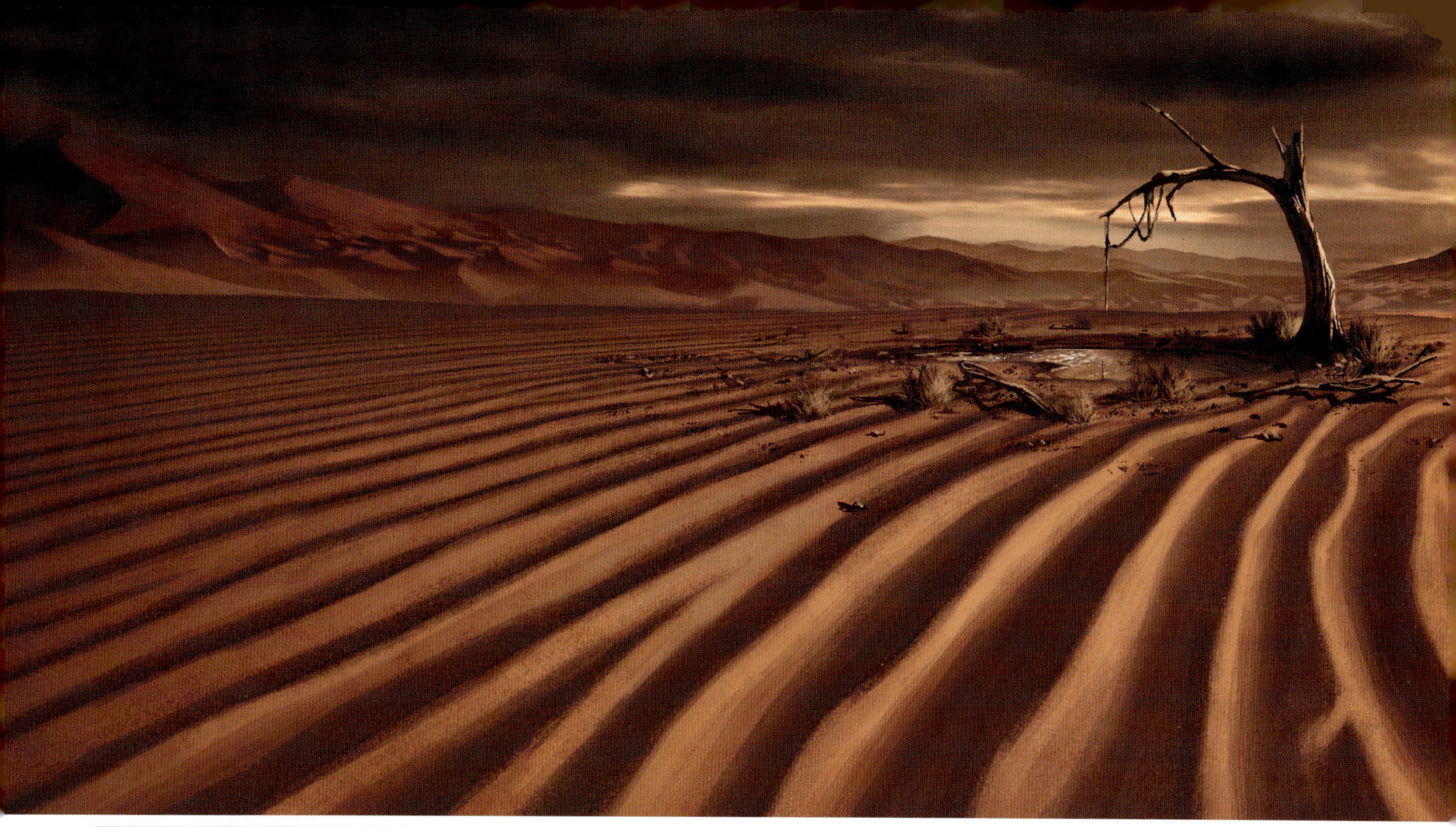

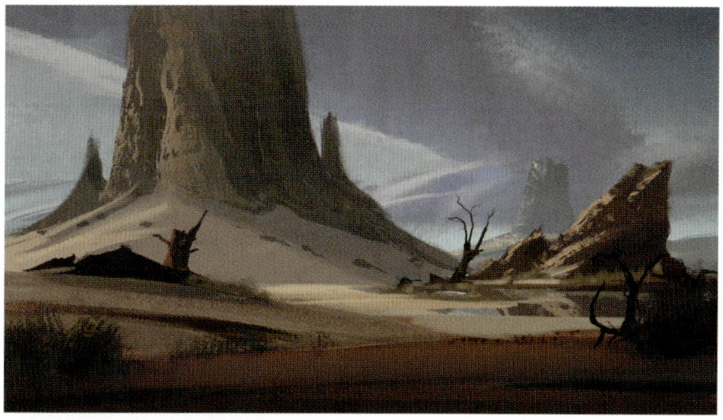

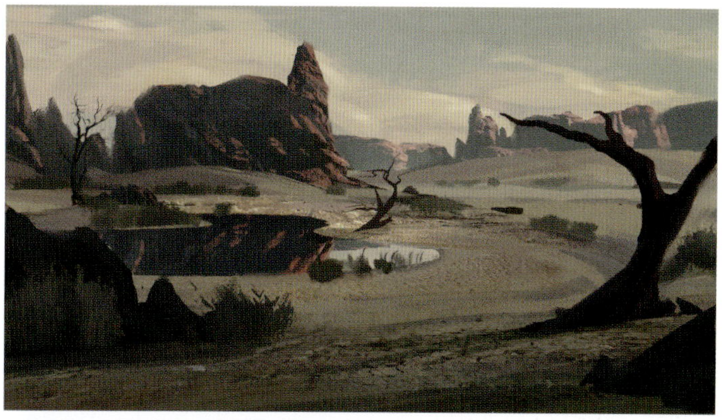

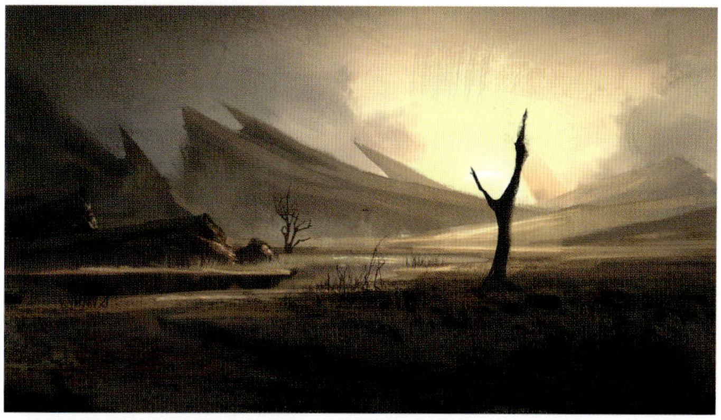

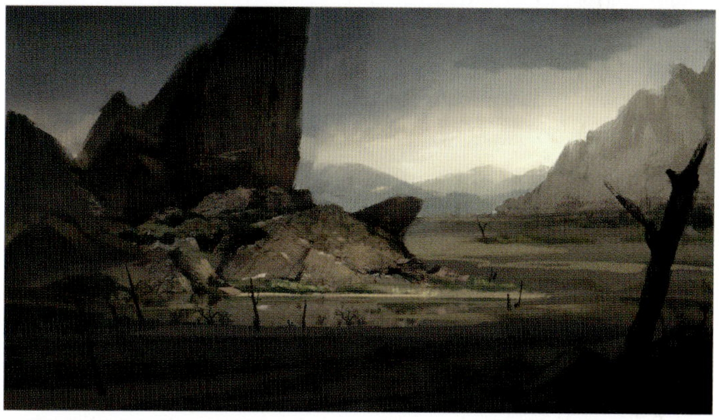

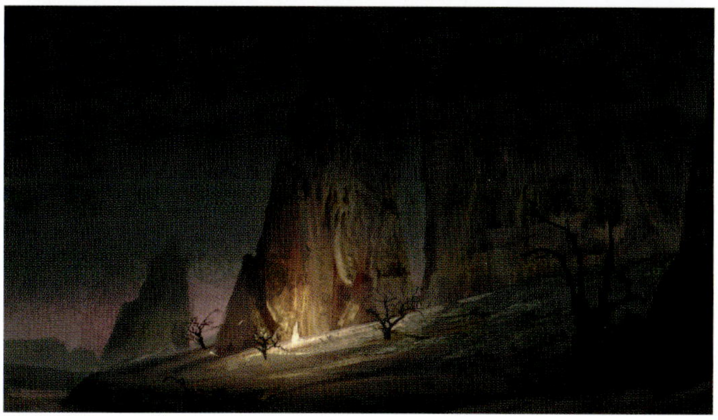

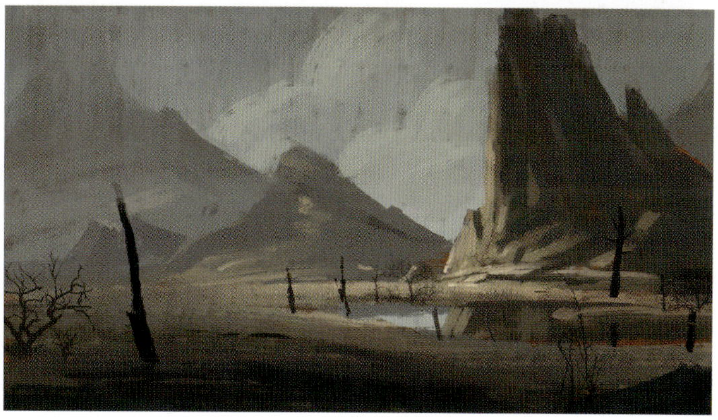

Left page: Desert keep design and paintings by Sean Vo. Right page: Top painting by Sean Randolph. Bottom visual development by Alex O'Dowd.

Tunis

Isaac leads his night creature horde through the market in Tunis, seeking out a shopkeeper who may have an item of value to him. After learning of Hector's location, Isaac leads his horde to the dock, where he falls in with the captain who will transport them across the Mediterranean Sea to Genoa.

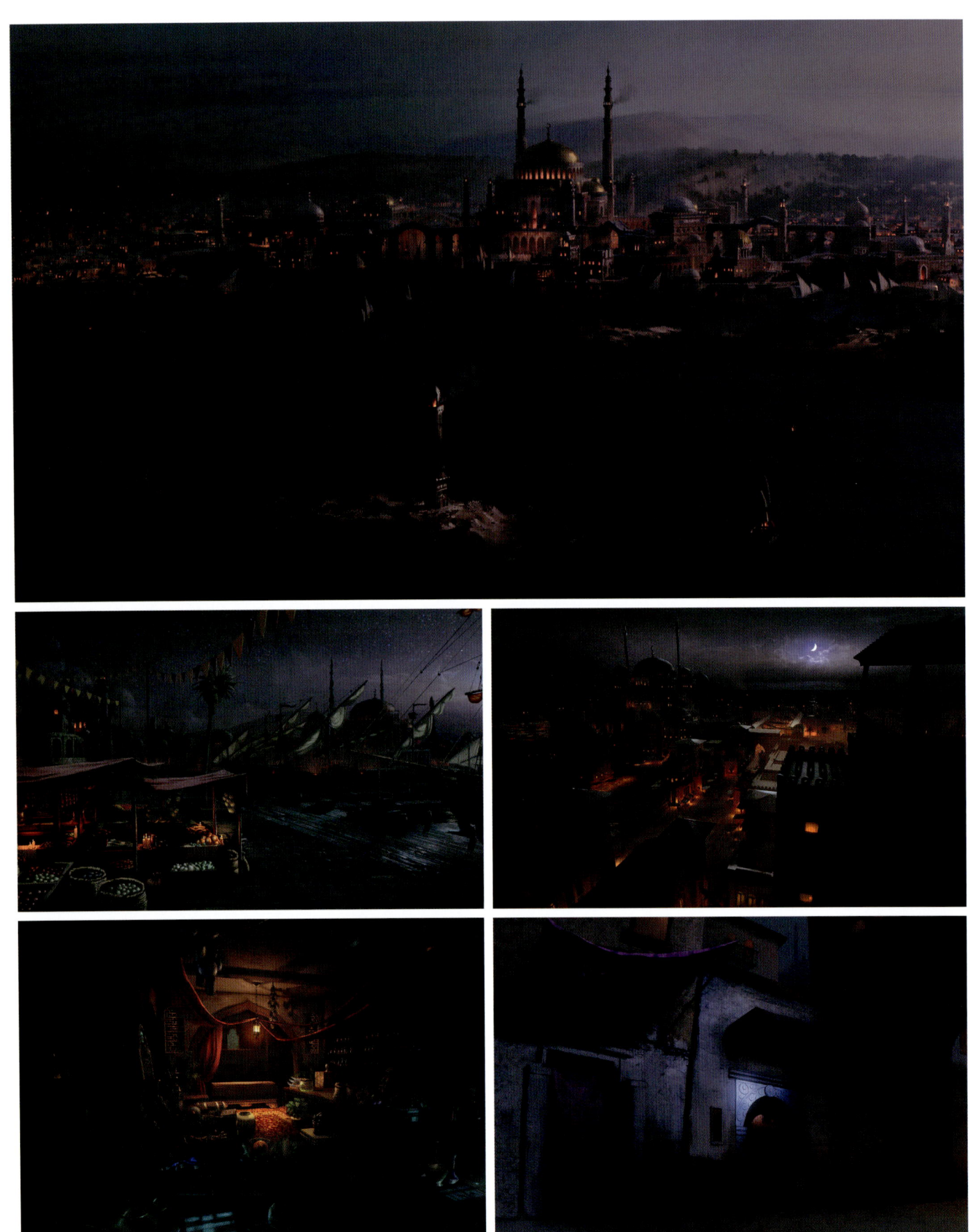

Left page: Top painting by Sean Vo. Middle left painting by Sean Randolph. Middle right painting by Sean Vo. Bottom left painting by Sean Randolph. Bottom right painting by Stephen Stark.

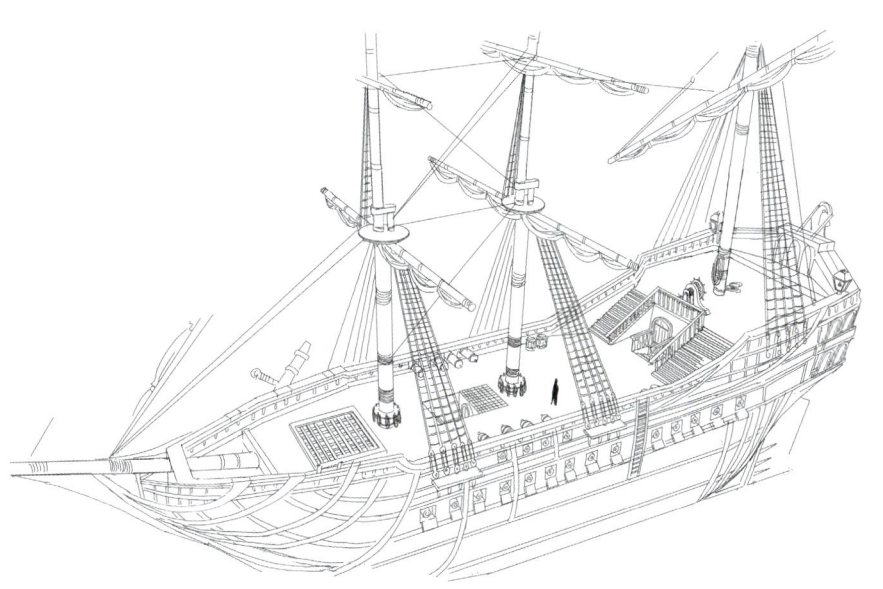

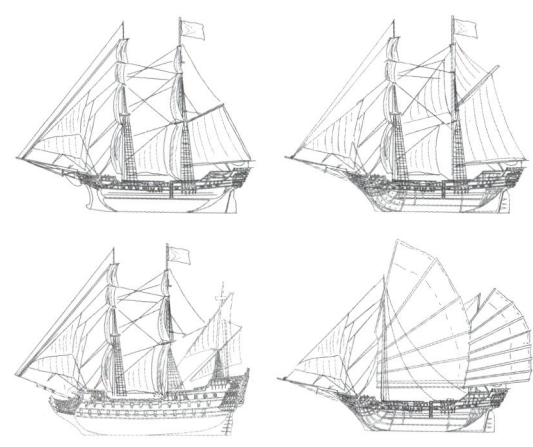

Sketches of the captain's ship, with alternate options for the sail and hull based on contemporary international designs. *Below:* The captain's chamber, where Isaac and the captain debate the merits of a world wherein humans are allowed continued existence.

Top: Captain's ship visual development by Sean Randolph. Middle painting by Stephen Stark. Bottom paintings by Sean Randolph.

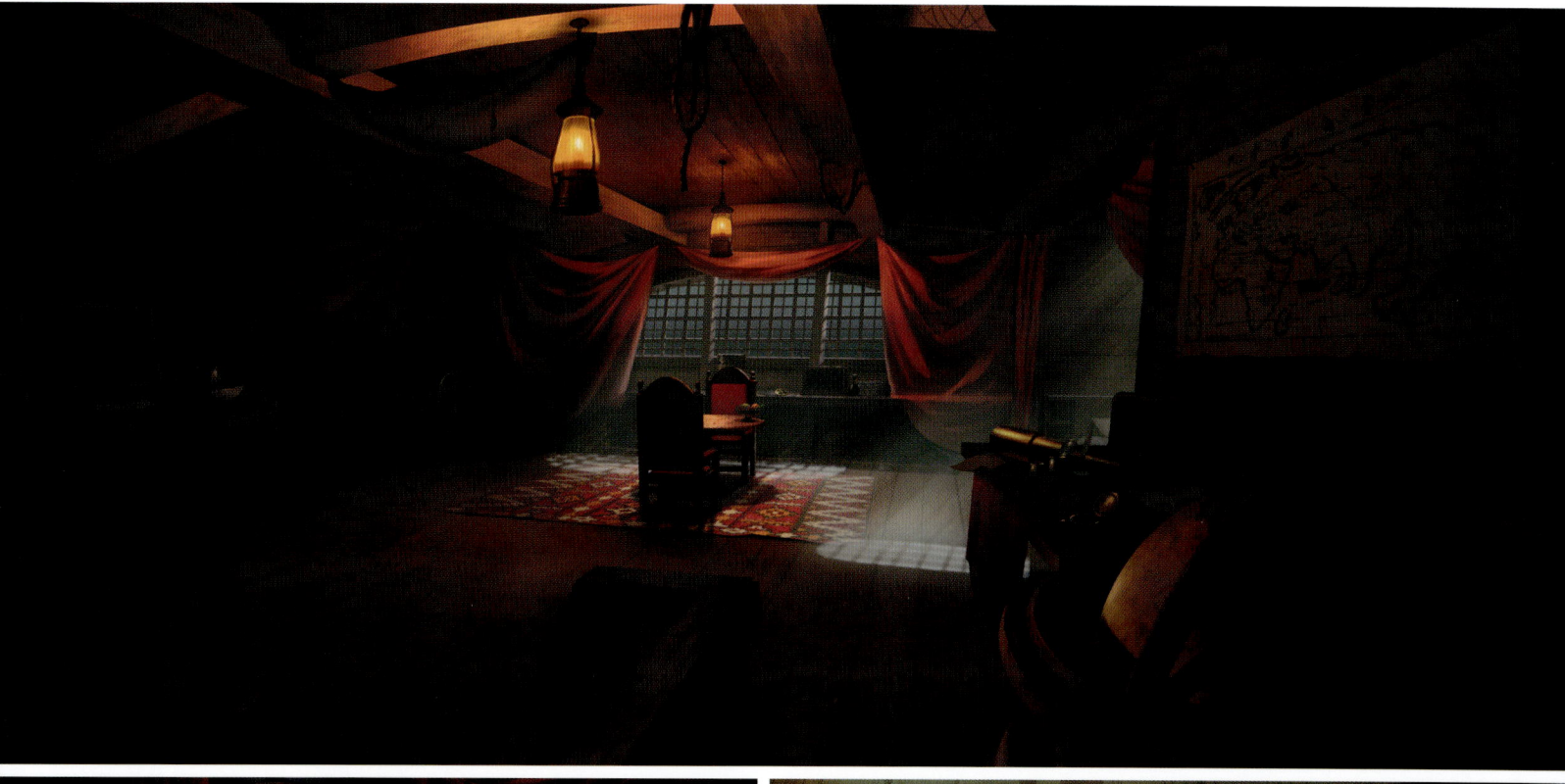

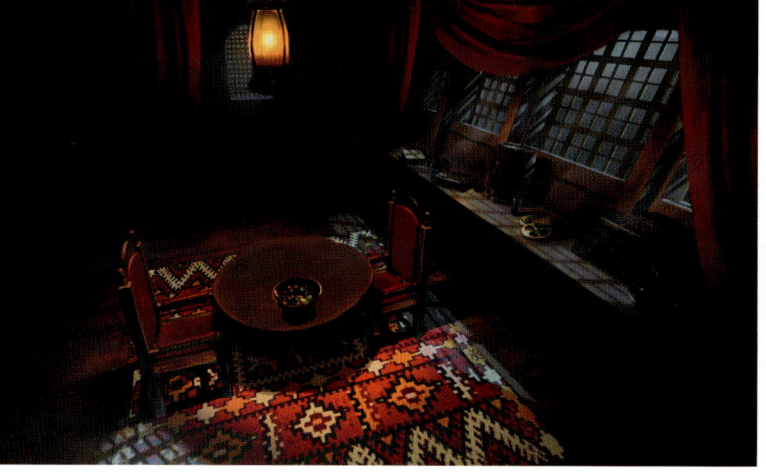

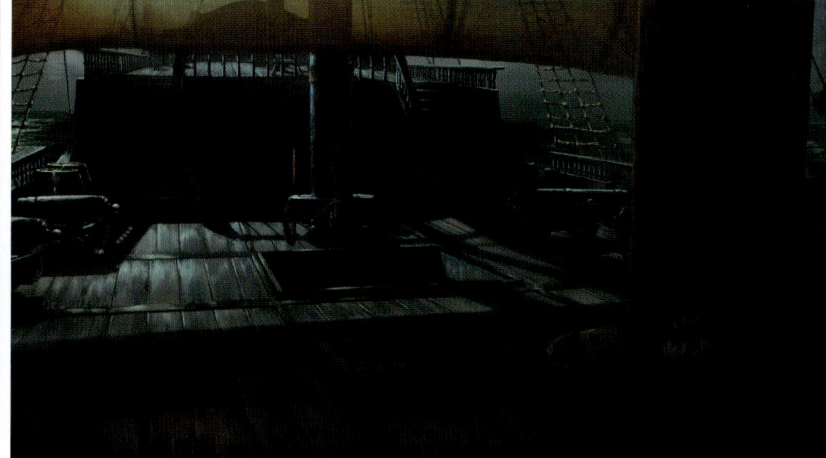

Genoa

Isaac lands at Genoa, but is immediately challenged by the local authorities, who soon also join his horde of corpses when they are reanimated as night creatures.

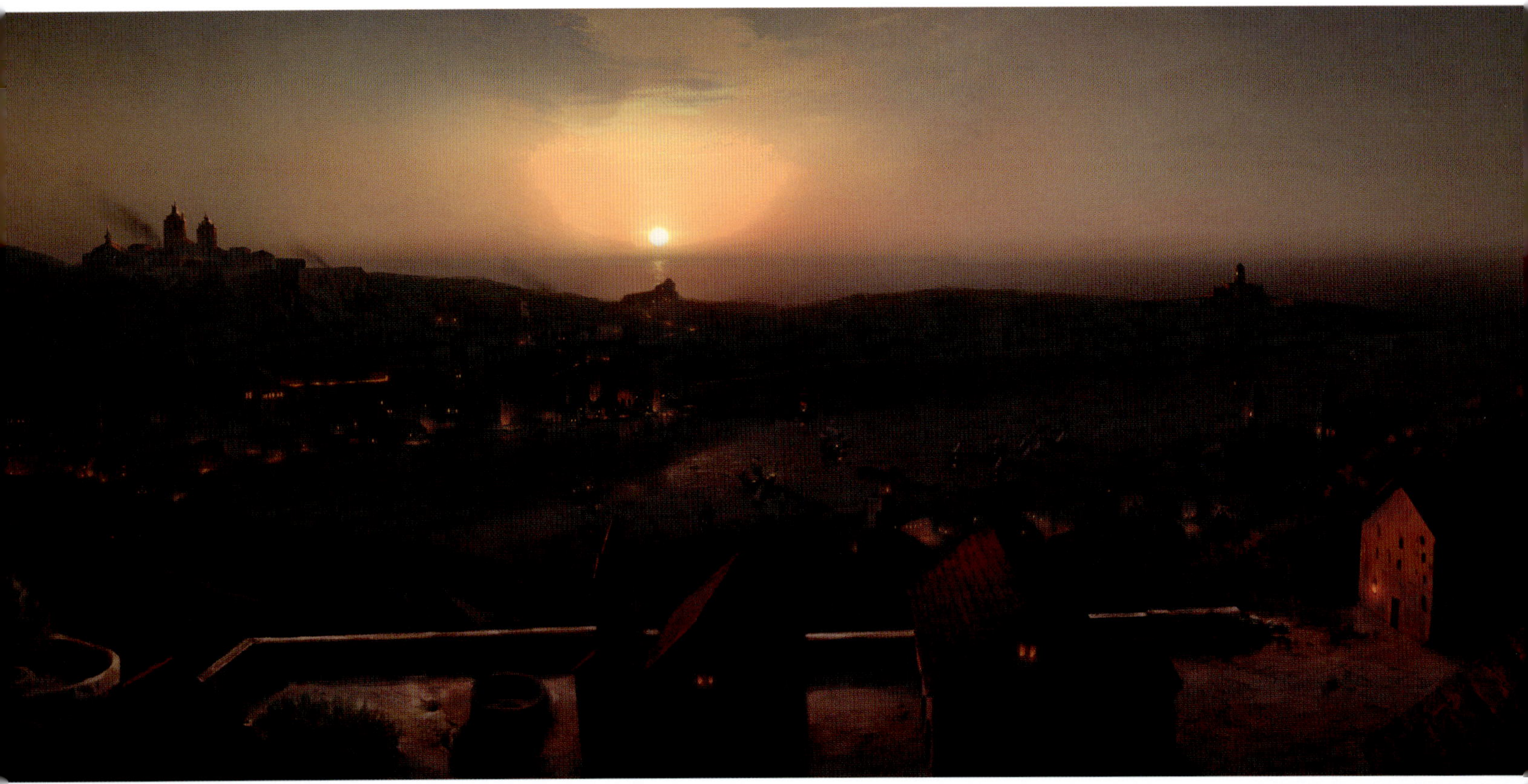

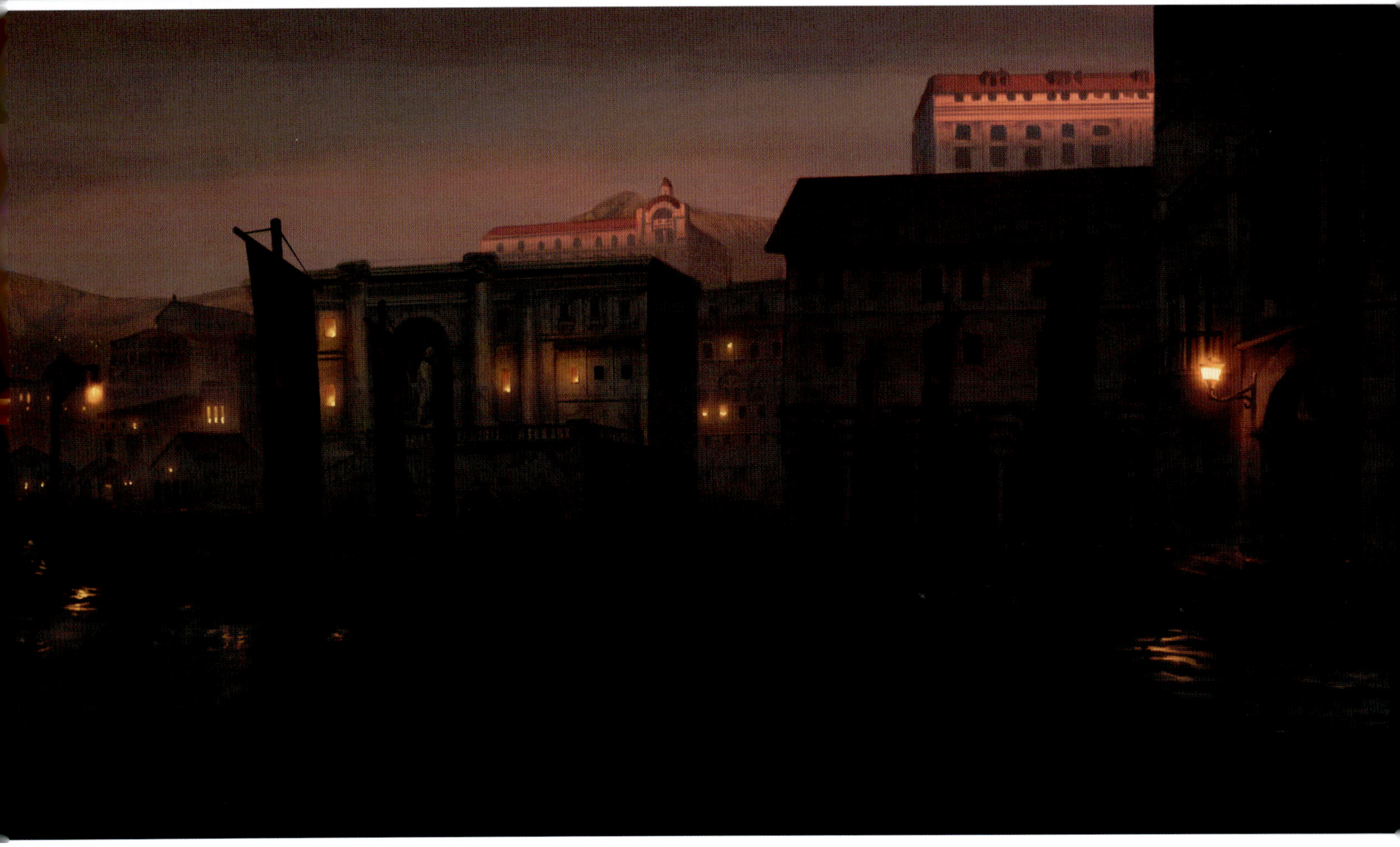

Paintings by Sean Randolph.

 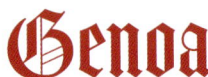

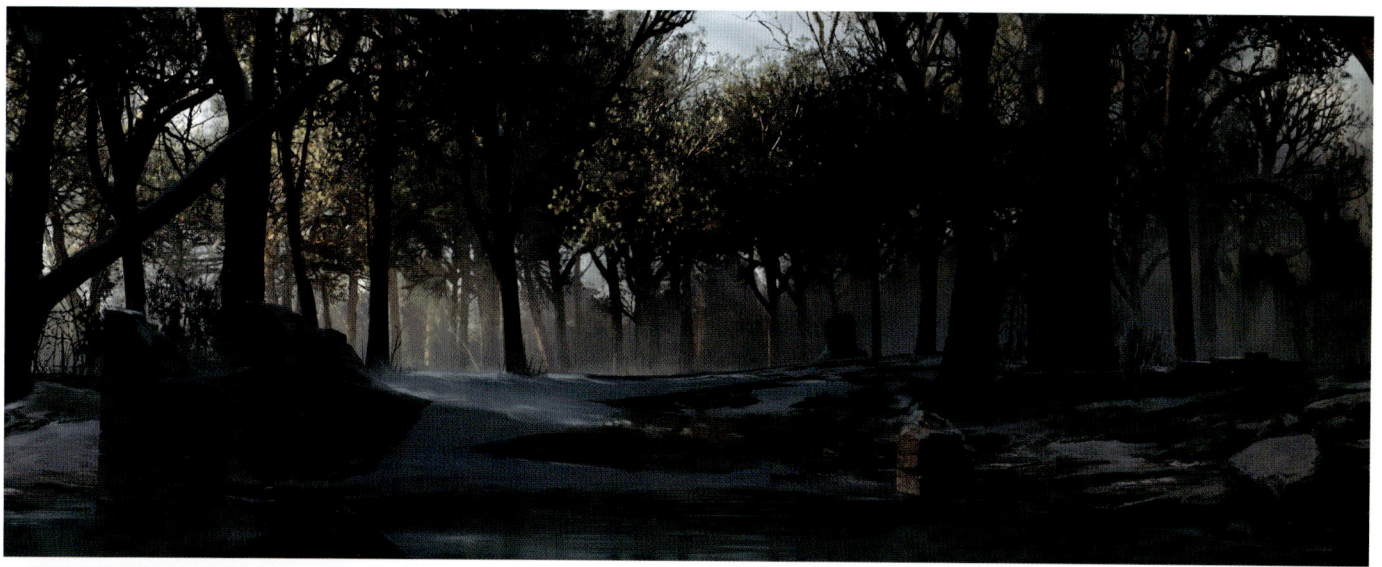

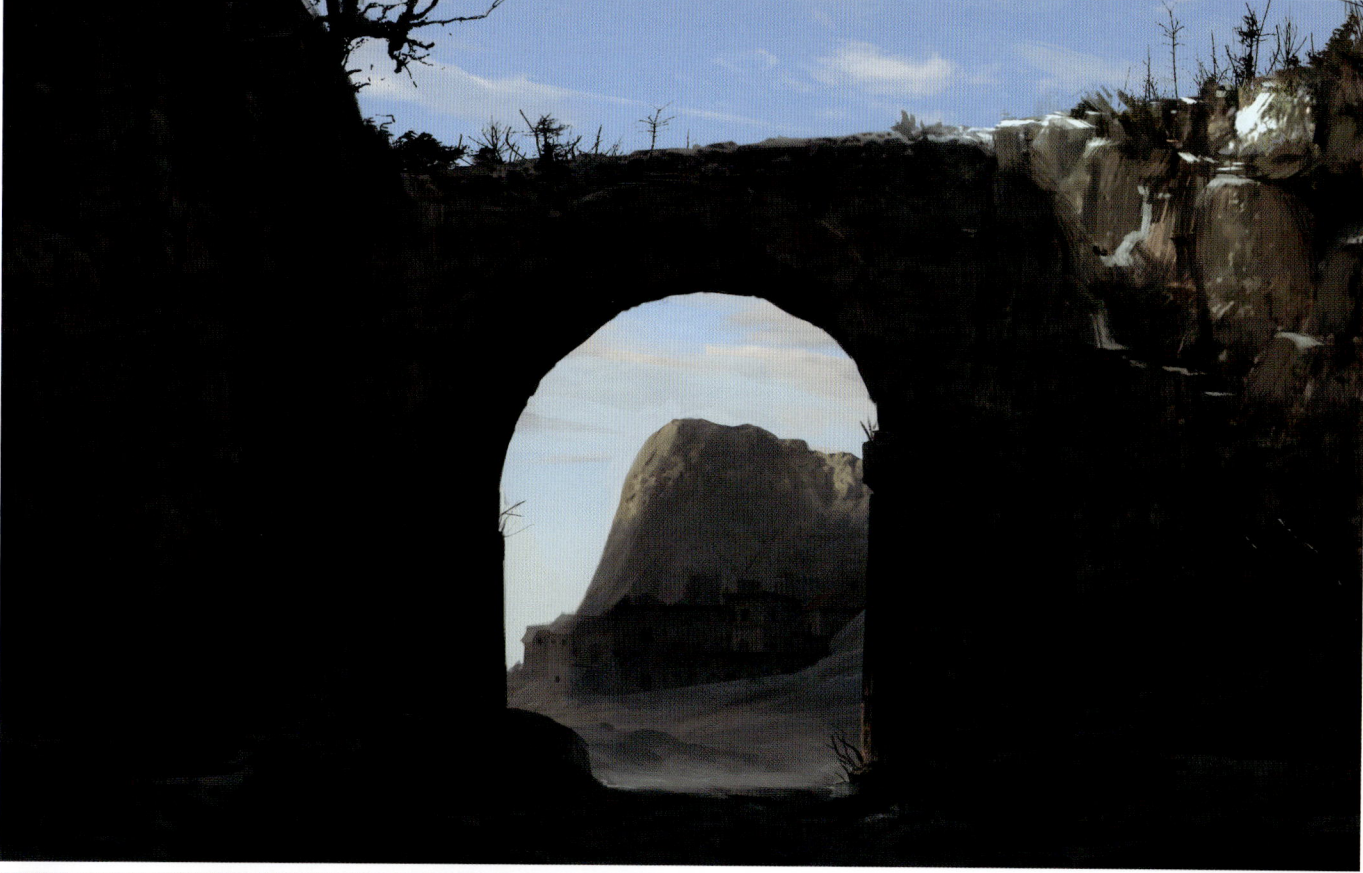

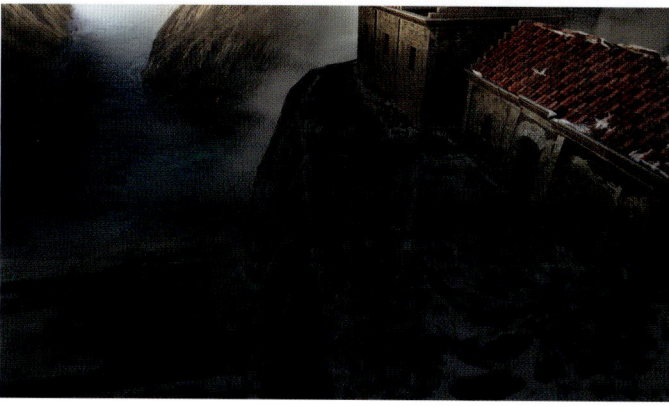
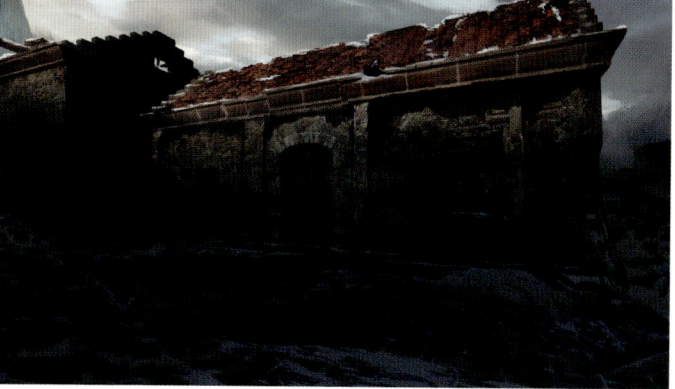

THE STONE VILLAGE

Isaac meets Miranda, a fellow forgemaster, in an abandoned village whose inhabitants have all been enslaved by a nearby magician.

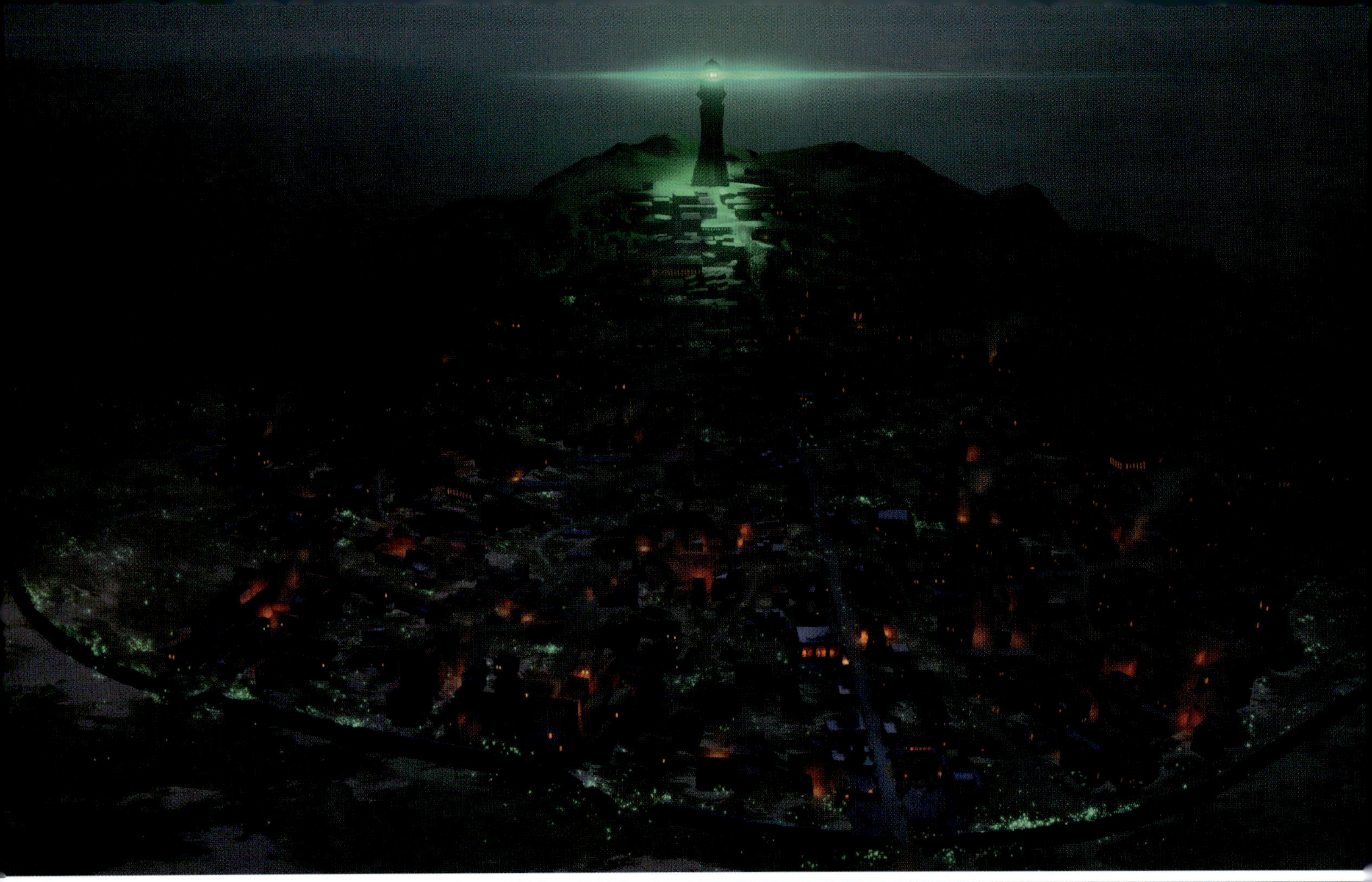

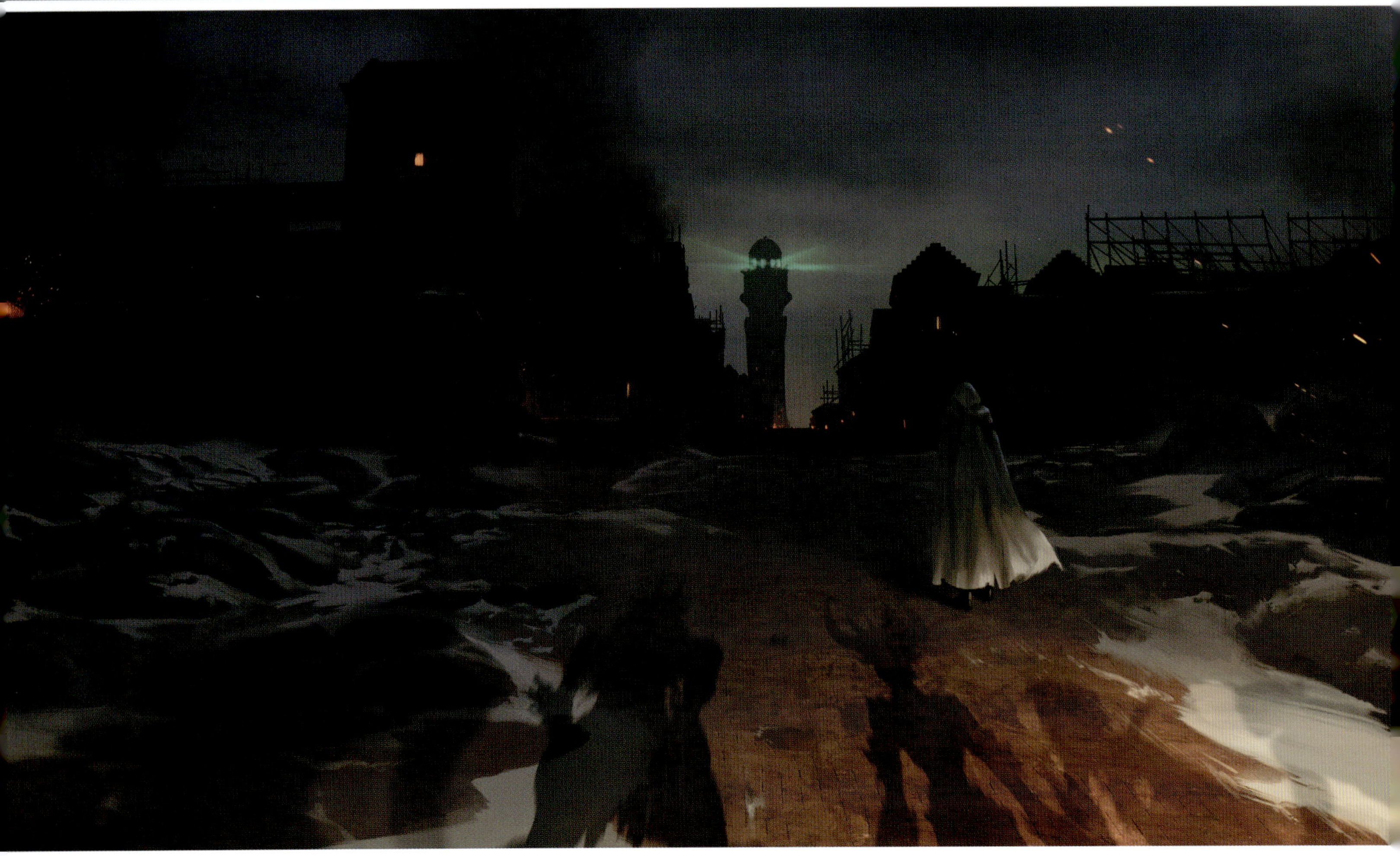

MAGICIAN'S CITY-STATE

The mad magician controls the minds of the entire population from his glowing tower.

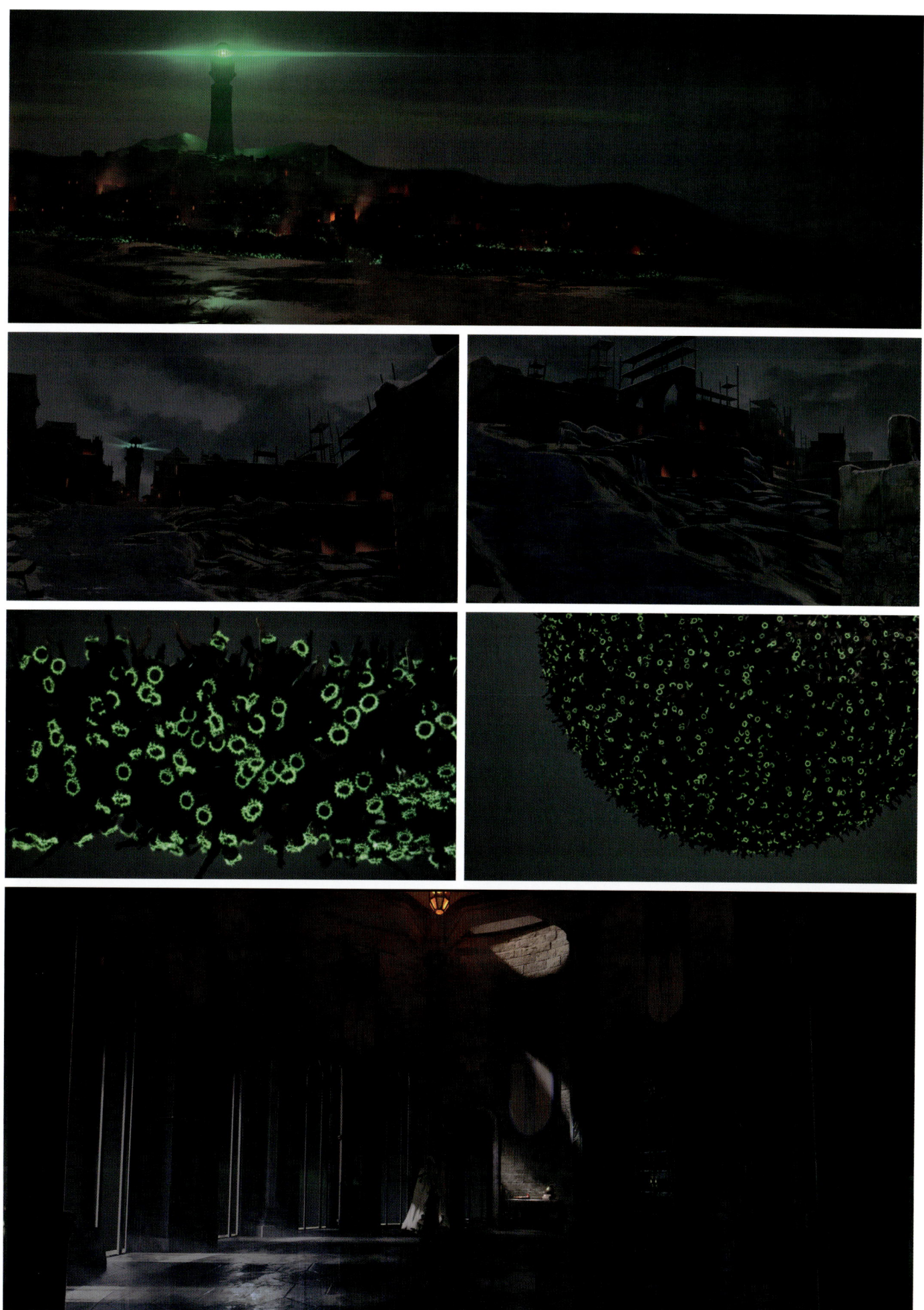

Left page: Top painting by Stephen Stark. Bottom painting by Jose Vega. Right page: Top painting by Stephen Stark. Second row paintings by Bo Li. Third row early 3D model of Legion by Tucker Roche. Bottom painting by Jose Vega.

Styria

"We wanted the conversation between Striga and Morana before the battle to feel very peaceful, almost uneventful. It occurs at nighttime in the tent before the battle in episode 3 of season 4. During dawn, I wanted to portray a beautiful time of day in contrast to the battle and the chaos around the camp." —Jose Vega

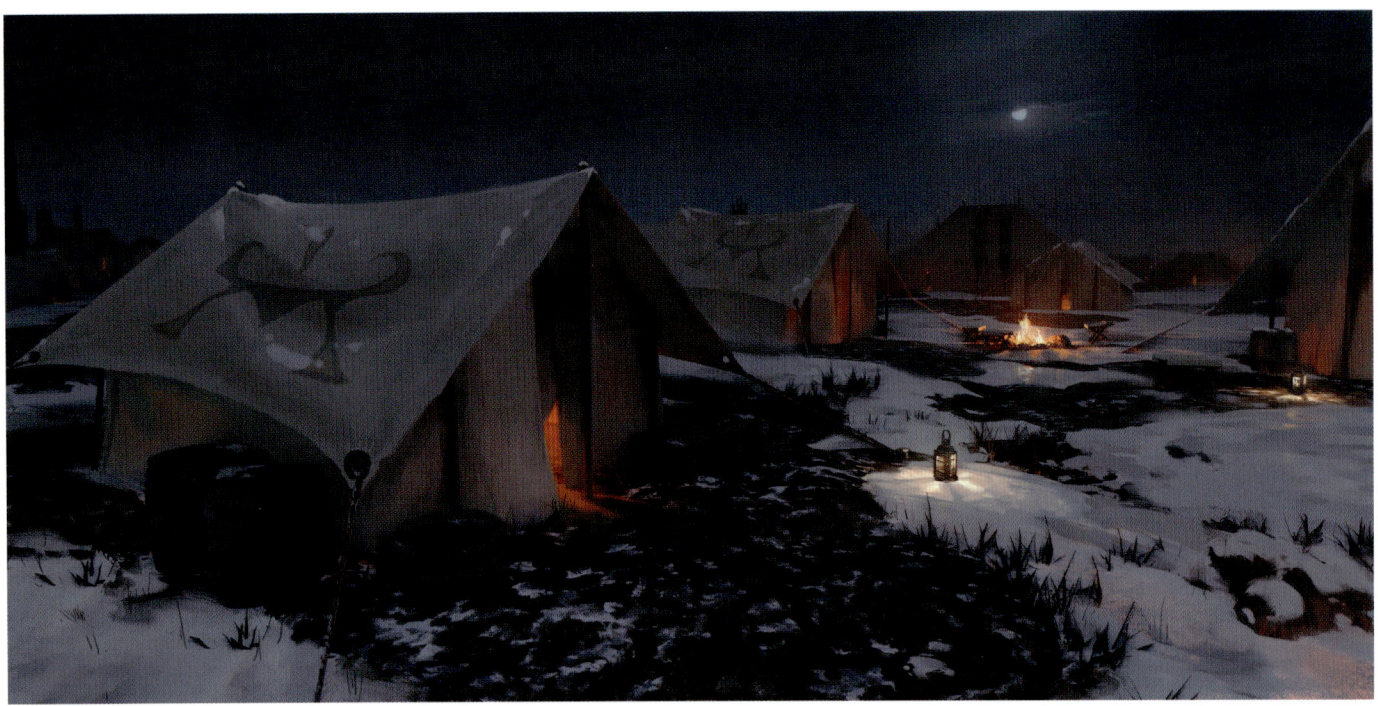

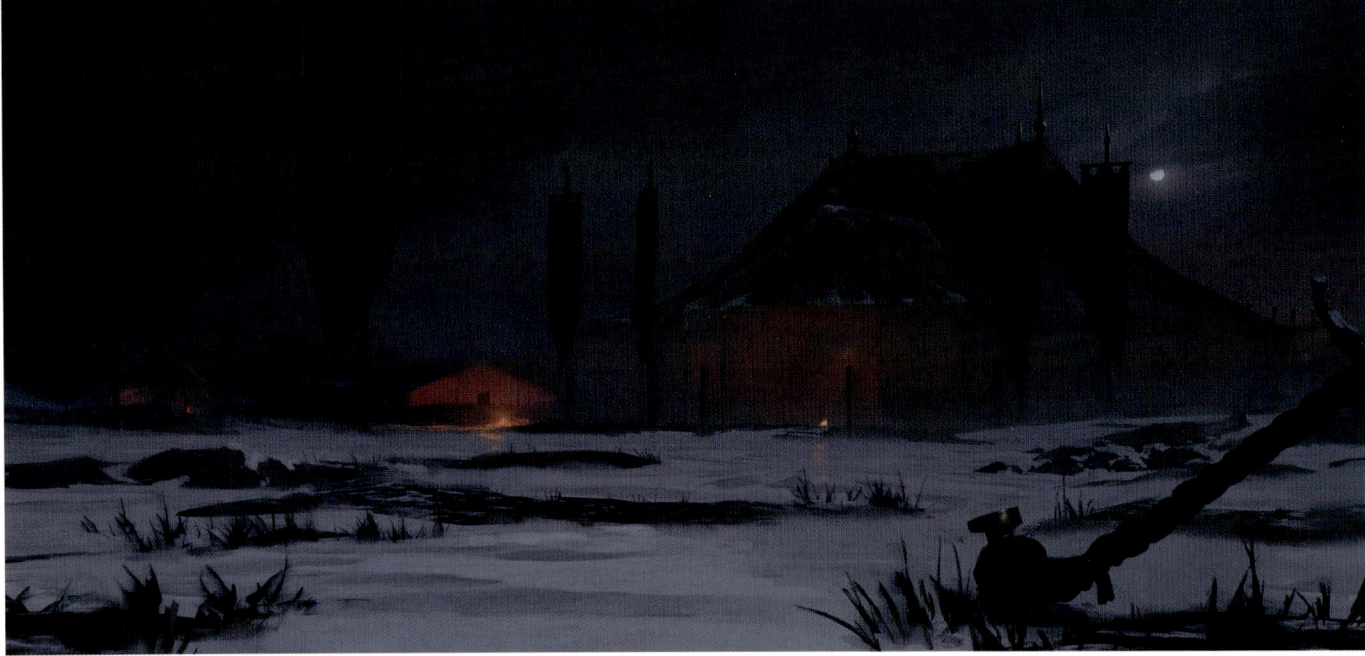

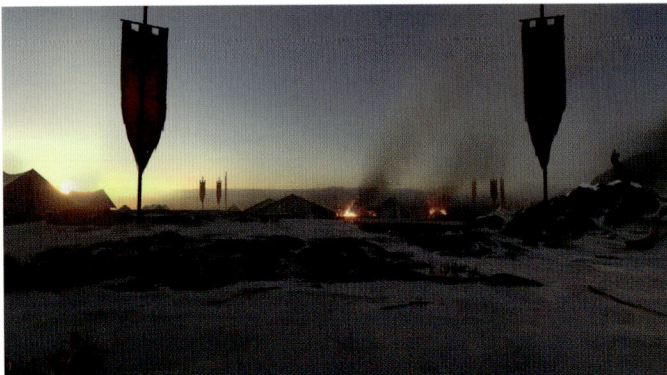

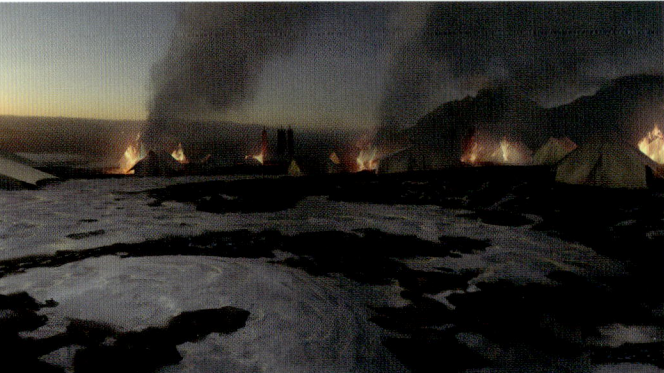

Left page: Paintings by Jose Vega. Right page: Stephen Stark.

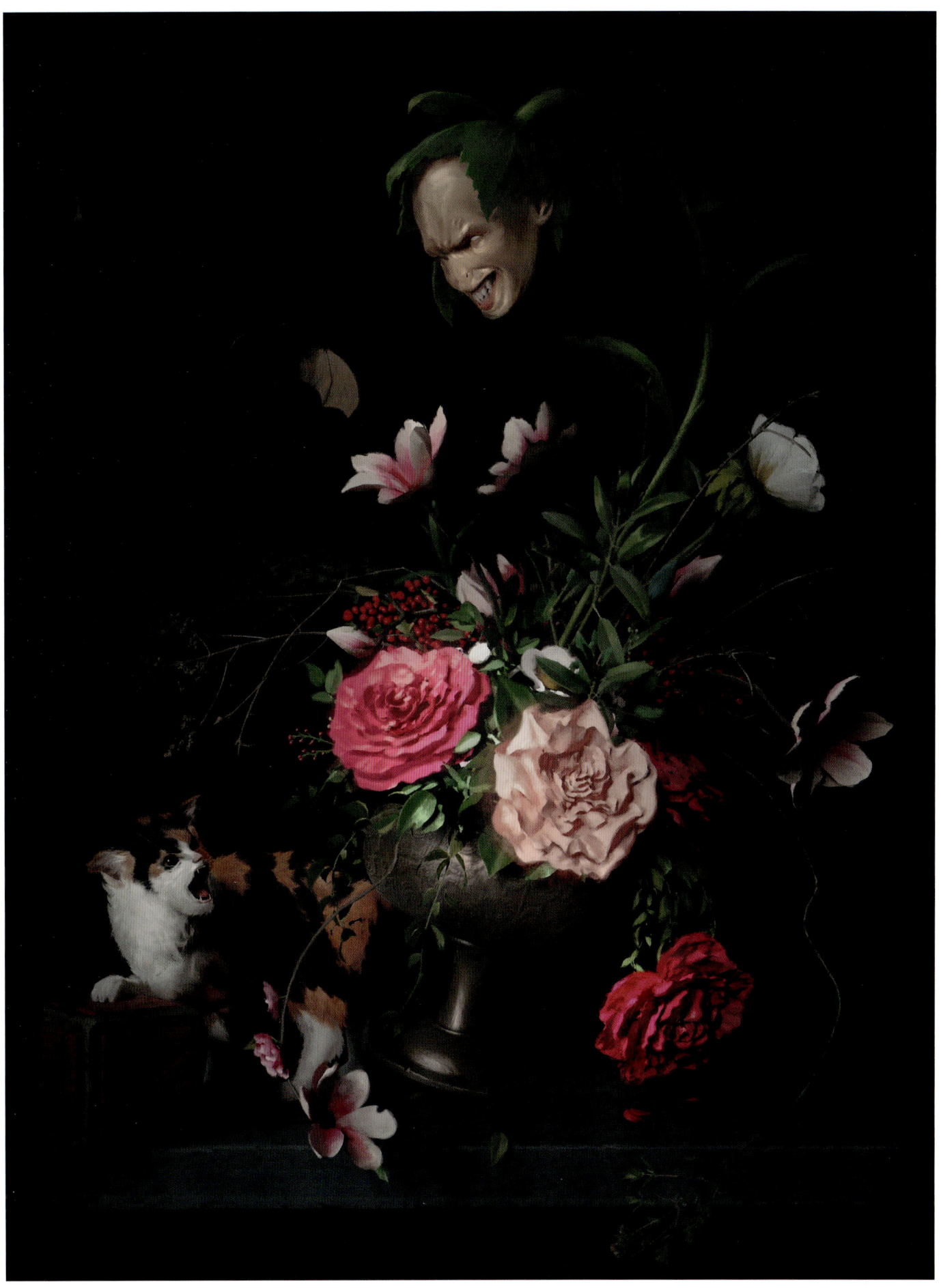

"The idea of this piece originated with Adam Deats's desire to get his cat into the show somehow. Our lead character designer, Katie Silva, suggested we look to one of Abraham Mignon's still lifes for inspiration, and we took off from there. While we did reference specific elements from Mignon's work, we added some *Castlevania* flavor by making the vase home to one of the plant monsters you fight in the games. The cat also has its paw propped up on the Cube of Zoe from *Symphony of the Night*." —Stephen Stark

DANESTI

"We wanted for this location to be placed in the middle of the forest and also to imply that it's temporary. Its impermanence also makes it look a bit vulnerable." —Jose Vega

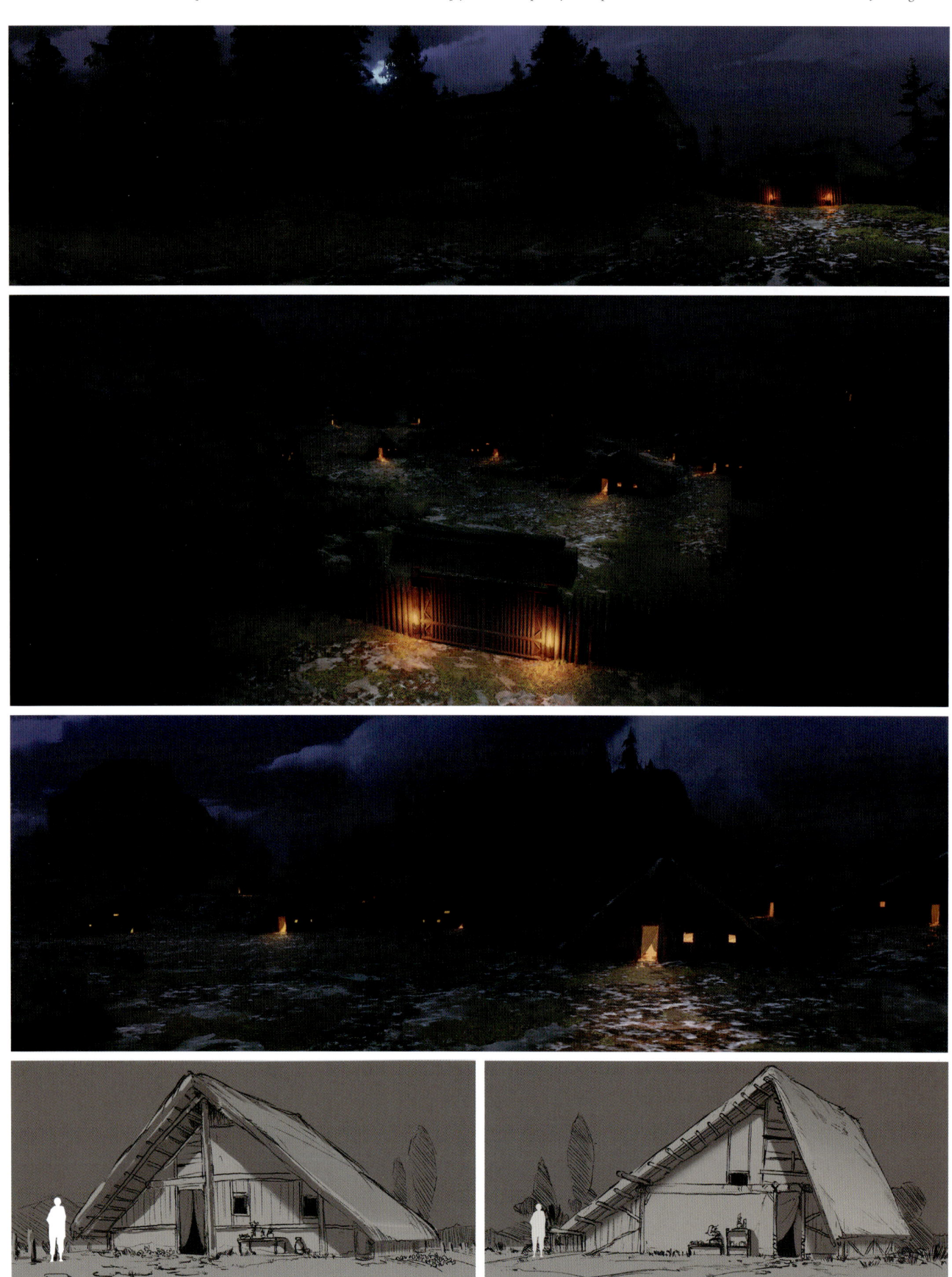

All art on these pages by Jose Vega.

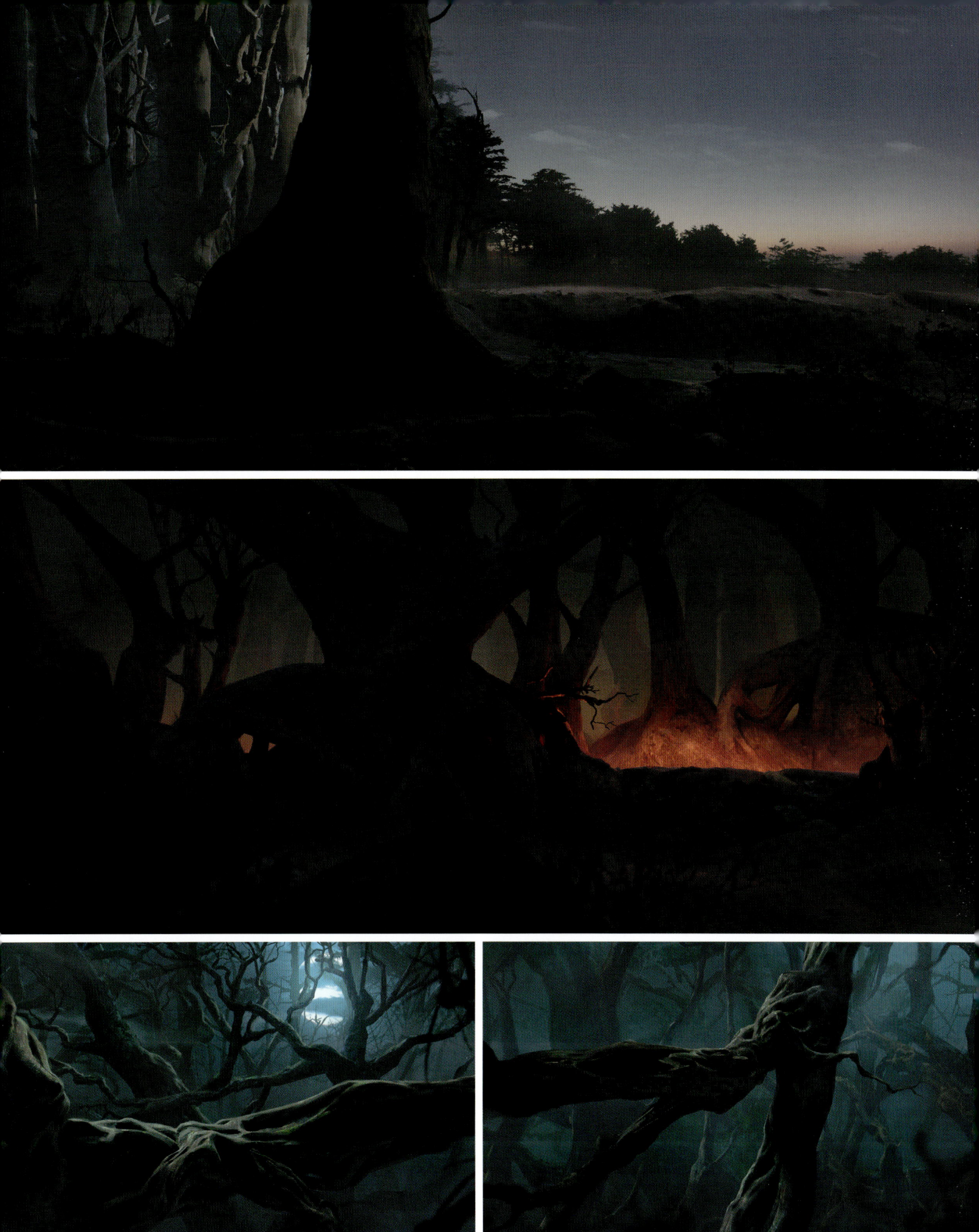

"My goal here was to give this forest a very foreboding and uneasy feel through the trees and lighting. It also generates a nice contrast when the characters reach the more open and inviting environment of the castle." —Jose Vega

The Infinite Corridor

"The visual style of the corridor was loosely based on the visuals present in '70s psychedelic cinema. I built a simple 3D cylinder that I ran animating textures down that was duplicated multiple times to get layered visual effects. This simple approach allowed me to swap out VFX textures very quickly to get immediate, render-efficient results, which was great for iterating when we explored the corridor's look. I eventually landed on the pink-and-green color scheme, which linked up visually with the 'Visitor' creature that's responsible for opening the corridor in season 3, episode 9." —Adam Deats

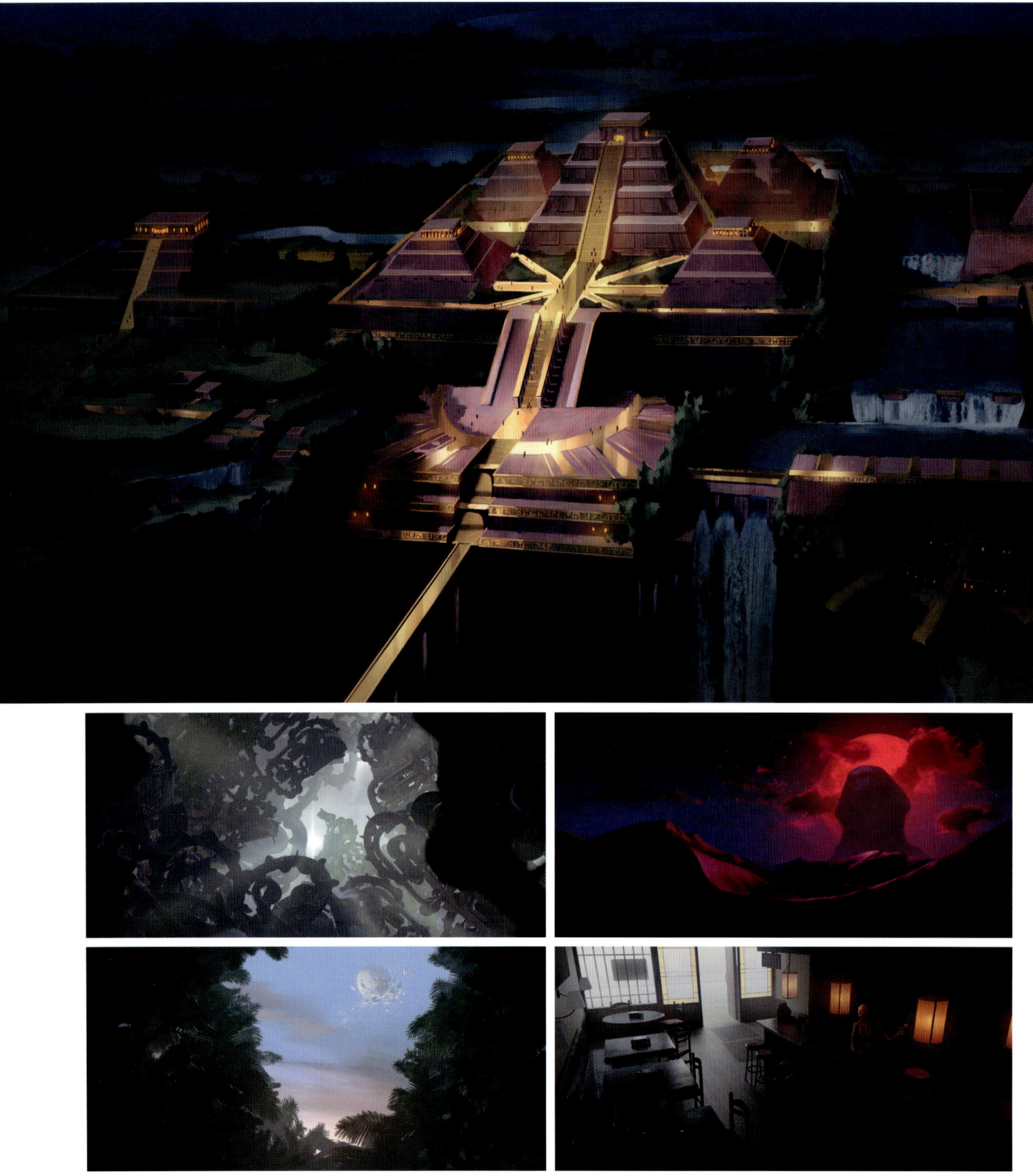

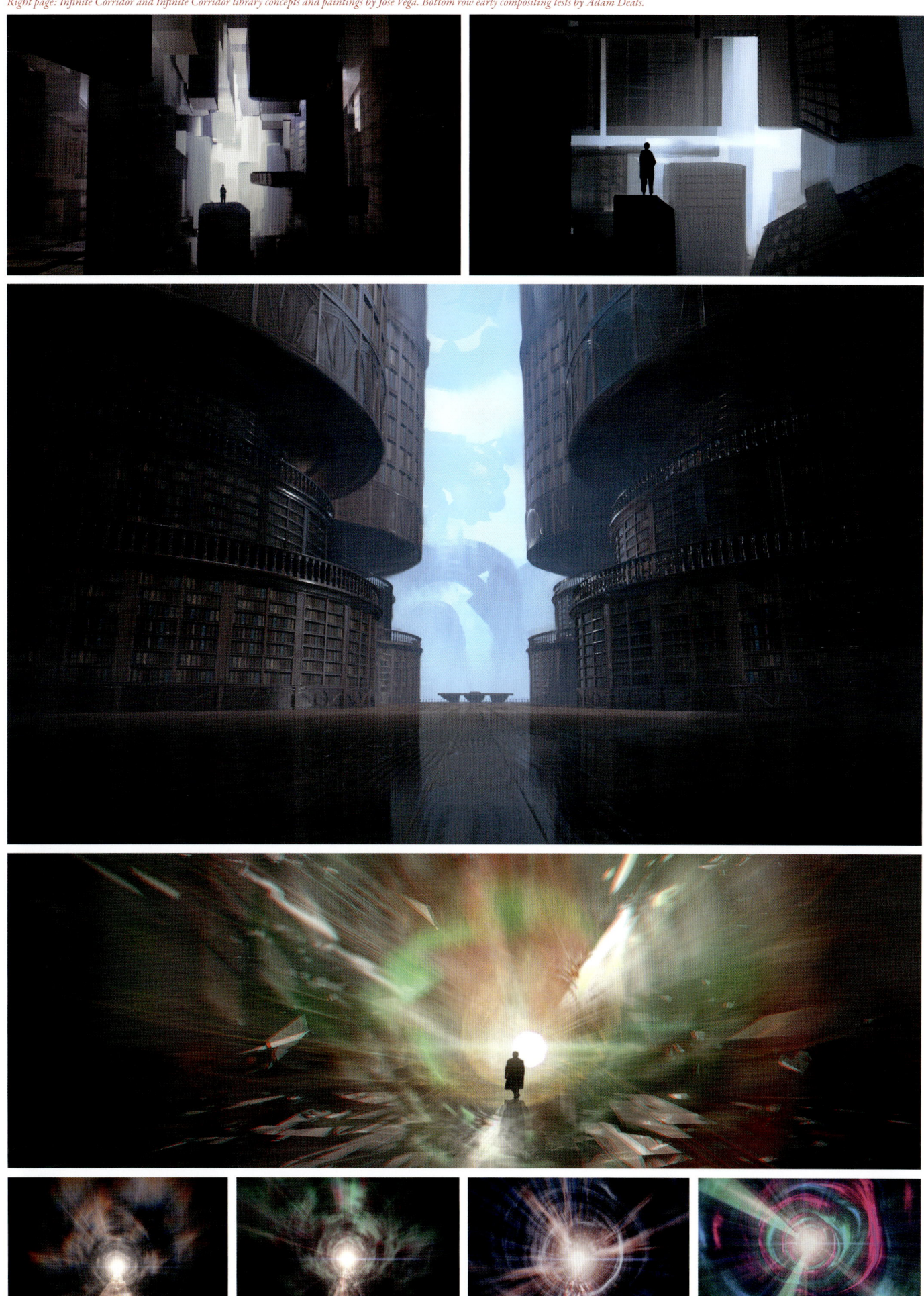

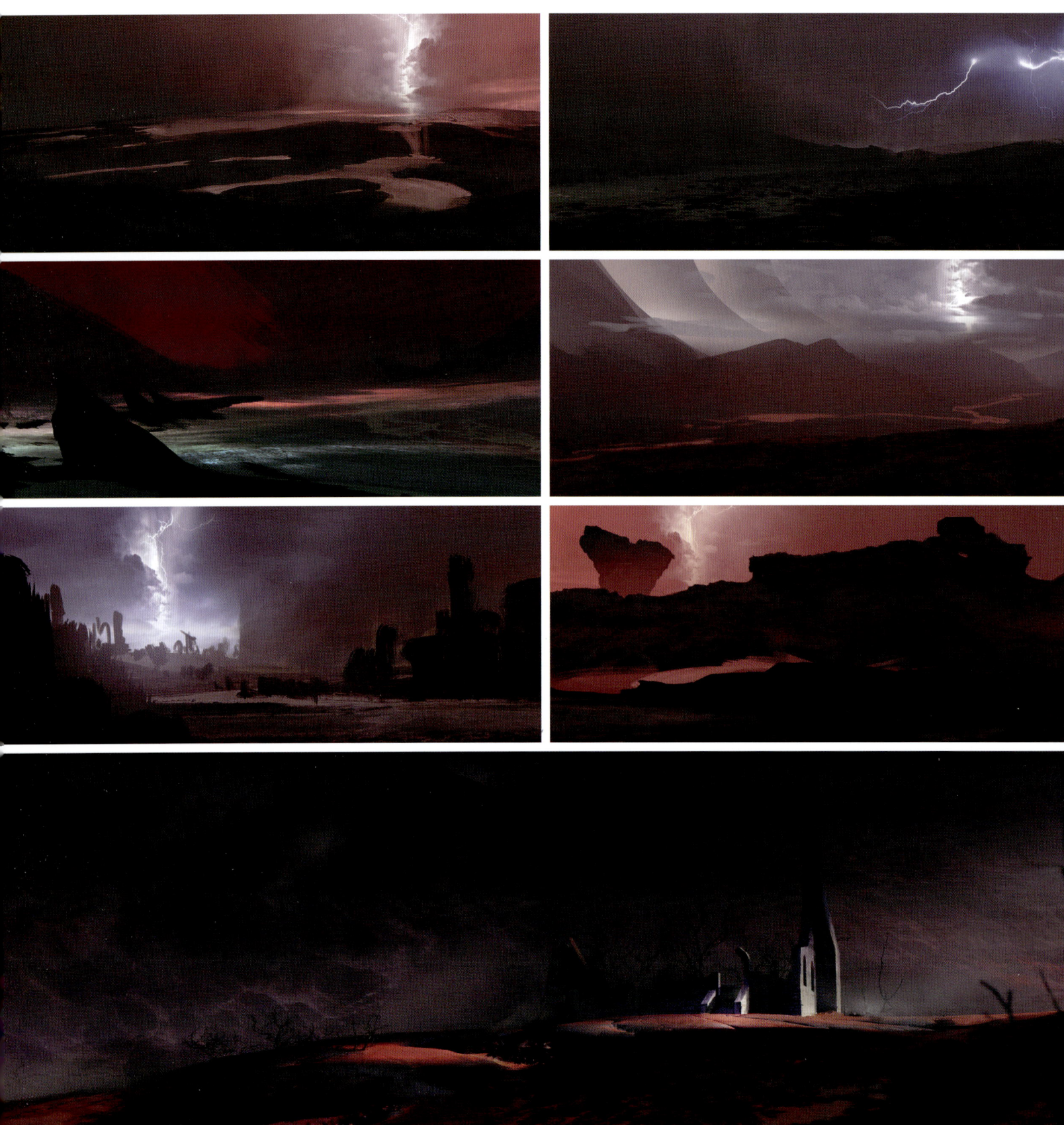

Hell

"Originally, the plan was to fly through all nine circles of hell during this sequence, but we eventually ran into issues with it being too bloated timewise, due to showing too much, or we zoomed through so many locations so fast that nothing read well. In response, we pruned things down to the opening death plain described in the script, then Lust, Violence, Treachery, and Fraud." —Adam Deats

"By creating kits of different objects, such as rocks, buildings, pillars, arches, and statues, I was able to quickly design and piece together large scenes. These scenes were used for the 3D camera fly-through in the hell sequence in season 3. To bring everything together, these scenes were given dark, grungy textures along with dramatic lighting. We wanted each environment to look unique, while still fitting into *Castlevania*'s portrayal of hell." —Tucker Roche

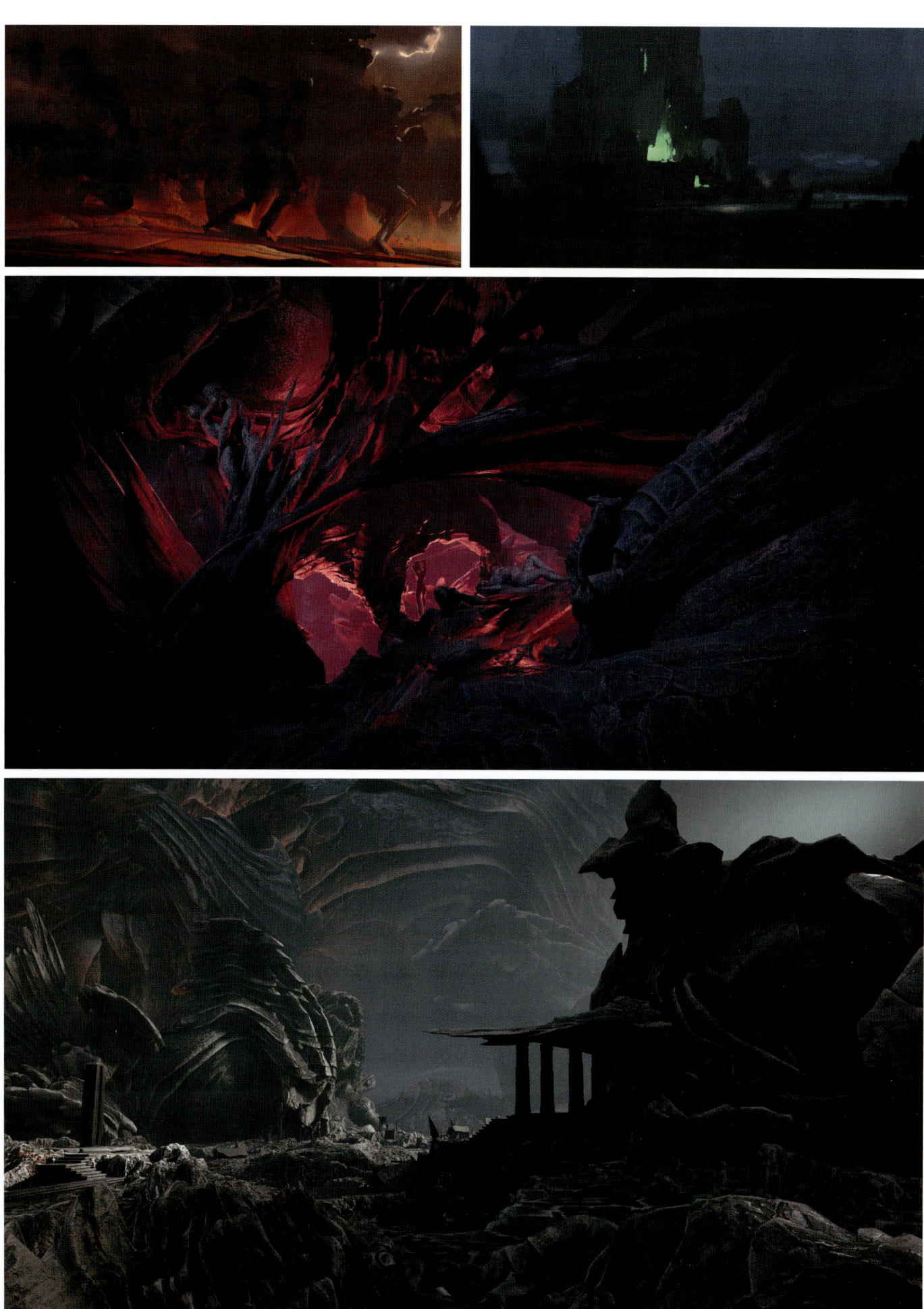

Left page: Jose Vega. Right page: Top two images by Jose Vega. Middle and bottom images by Tucker Roche.

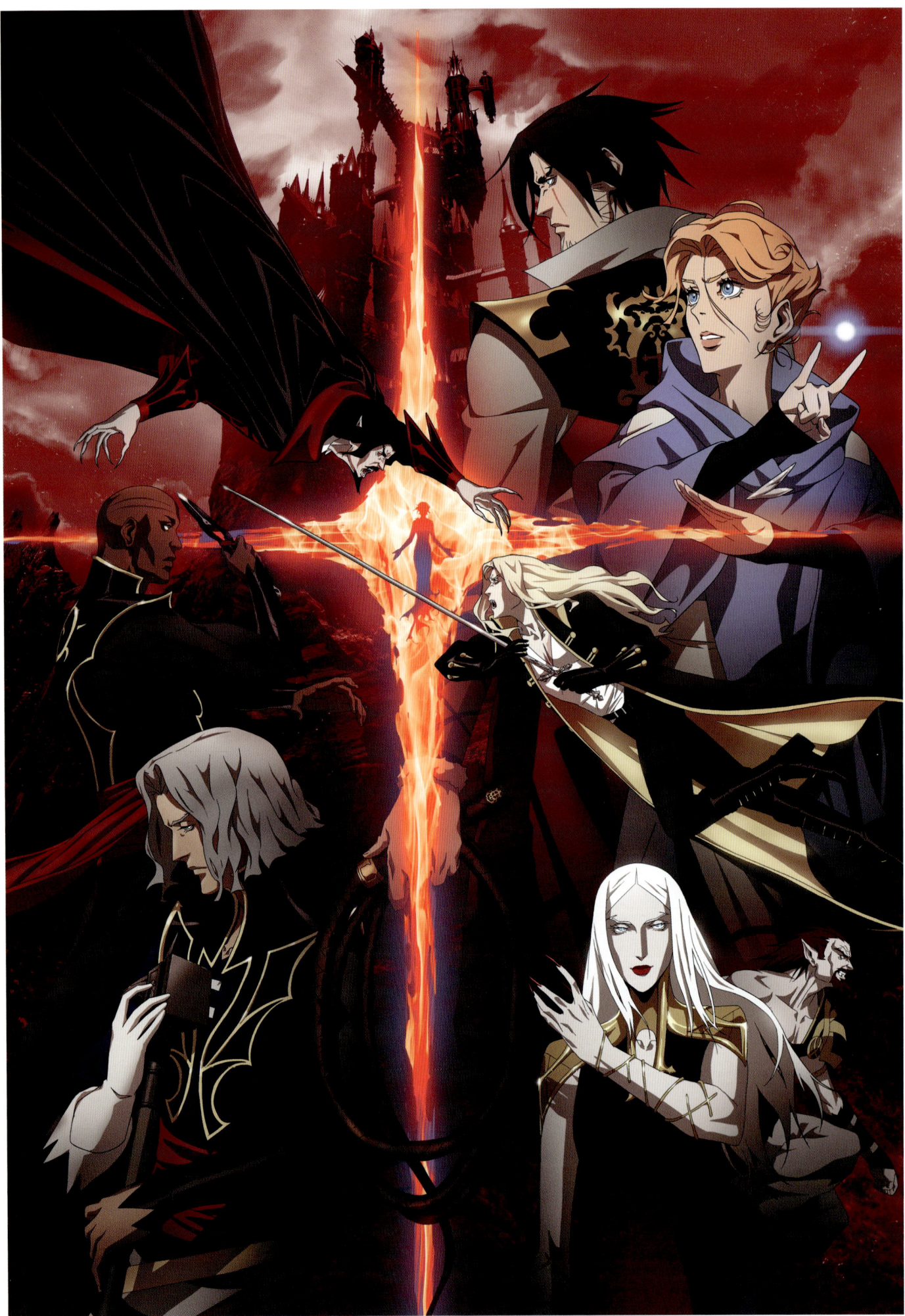

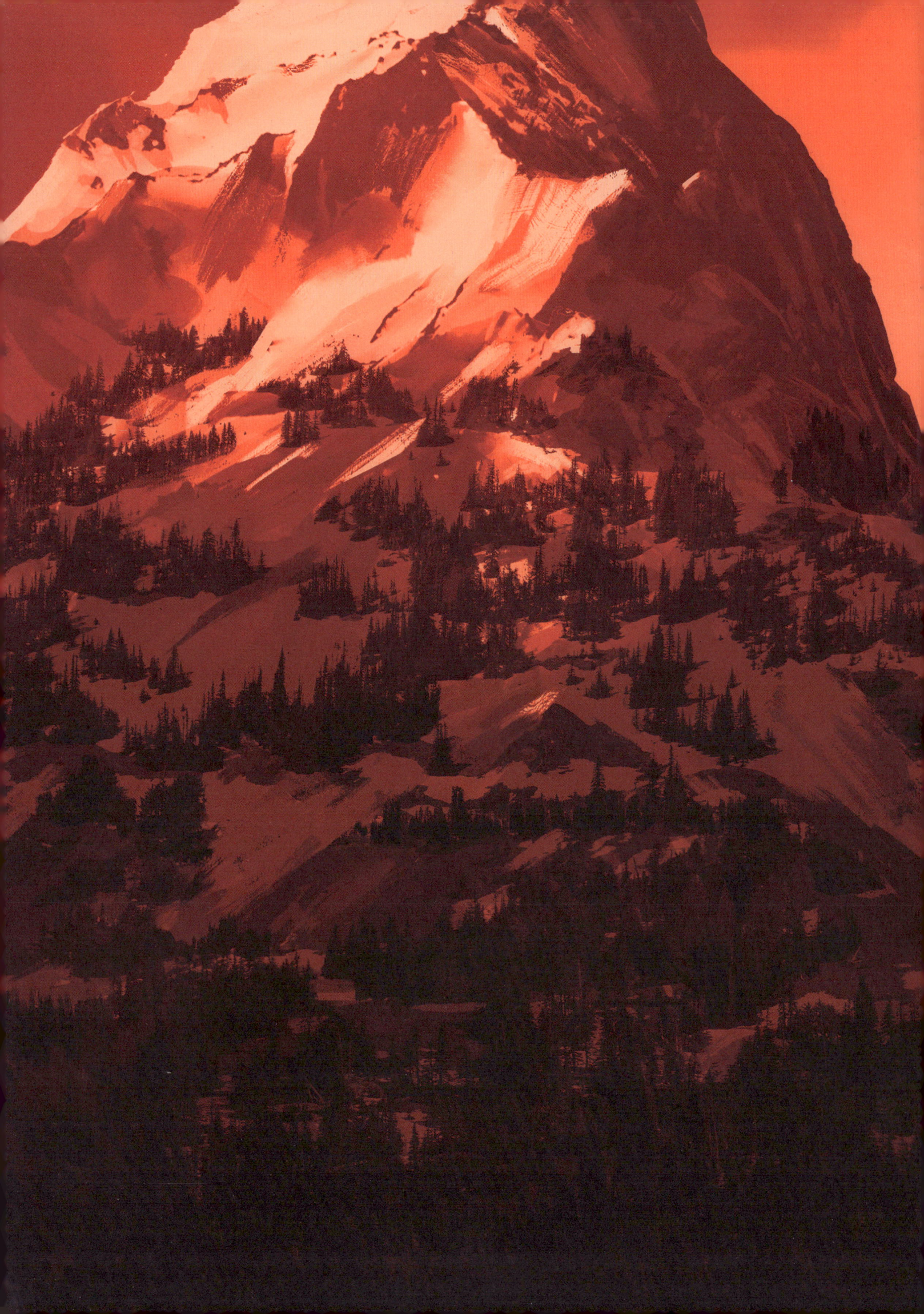